Remembering Kings Past

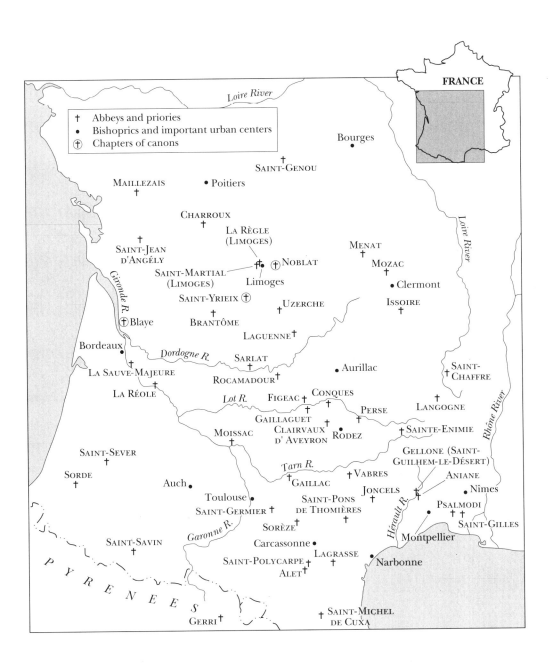

FRANCE

Abbeys and priories †
Bishoprics and important urban centers •
Chapters of canons ⊕

Loire River

• Bourges

SAINT-GENOU †

MAILLEZAIS †   • Poitiers

CHARROUX †

LA RÈGLE (LIMOGES) ⊕   MENAT †

SAINT-JEAN D'ANGÉLY †   MOZAC †

SAINT-MARTIAL (LIMOGES) †⊕ NOBLAT
Limoges •   • Clermont

SAINT-YRIEIX ⊕   UZERCHE †   ISSOIRE †

Gironde R.

⊕ Blaye   BRANTÔME †

Bordeaux •   *Dordogne R.*   LAGUENNE †

LA SAUVE-MAJEURE †   SARLAT †   SAINT-CHAFFRE †

LA RÉOLE †   ROCAMADOUR †   • Aurillac

Lot R.   FIGEAC †   CONQUES †   LANGOGNE †

GAILLAGUET †   PERSE †

SAINT-SEVER †   MOISSAC †   CLAIRVAUX D'AVEYRON †   RODEZ •   SAINTE-ENIMIE †

SORDE †   *Tarn R.*   VABRES †   GELLONE (SAINT-GUILHEM-LE-DÉSERT) †

Auch •   GAILLAC †   ANIANE †   • Nîmes

Toulouse •   SAINT-PONS DE THOMIÈRES †   JONCELS †   PSALMODI †

SAINT-GERMIER †   SOREZE †   SAINT-GILLES †

SAINT-SAVIN †   Carcassonne •   LAGRASSE †   *Hérault R.*   Montpellier •

Garonne R.   SAINT-POLYCARPE †   Narbonne •

ALET †

P Y R E N E E S   *Rhône River*

GERRI †   SAINT-MICHEL DE CUXA †

REMEMBERING KINGS PAST

*Monastic Foundation Legends
in Medieval Southern France*

AMY G. REMENSNYDER

Cornell University Press

ITHACA AND LONDON

First published 1995 by Cornell University Press.

Printed in the United States of America

⊚ The paper in this book meets the minimum requirements of the American National Standard for Information Sciences— Permanence of Paper for Printed Library Materials, ANSI Z39.48-1984.

Library of Congress Cataloging-in-Publication Data

Remensnyder, Amy G. (Amy Goodrich), 1960–
   Remembering kings past : monastic foundation legends in medieval southern France / Amy G. Remensnyder.
       p.   cm.
   Includes bibliographical reference and index.
   ISBN 0-8014-2954-4 (cloth : alk. paper)
       1. Benedictines—France, Southwest—History. 2. Monasticism and religious orders—France, Southwest—History. 3. Legends, Christian—France, Southwest. 4. France—Kings and rulers—Religion—Legends. 5. France, Southwest—Church history.
   I. Title.
BX3032.S66R46   1996
271′.10447—dc20   95-32662

Contents

Illustrations

Acknowledgments

I t is said that writing a book is a long and lonely process. Long it has been, but I have had the good fortune of not finding it lonely. Principal thanks are owed to those who guided this project in its initial stage as a dissertation at the University of California, Berkeley. Thomas N. Bisson patiently encouraged the project from its tentative beginnings and gave generously of his knowledge of the world south of the Loire. In the process he taught me much about being a scholar and a teacher. Robert Brentano made me sensitive to language and nuance, both in my sources and in my own writing. Gerard Caspary's attentive reading and wise comments added depth to my chapters, while Harvey Stahl's constant enthusiasm for the project helped me finish it.

I thank as well Carolyn Dean, Sharon Farmer, and Geoffrey Koziol whose readings of various versions of the manuscript helped me work out certain conceptual issues. The perceptive comments of Barbara Rosenwein and of a second anonymous reader for Cornell University Press greatly aided me in transforming the dissertation into a book. Thomas Head and Richard Landes were unflagging sources of information about eleventh- and twelfth-century monasticism. Lisa Fink, Janelle Greenberg, Margaret Malamud, and Deborah Steiner have patiently listened to me talk about the project and provided much needed moral support. For the latter, I also thank Ellen Reeves. In the course of my research in France, Elisabeth Magnou-Nortier was remarkably kind in discussing with me a number of my sources, even lending me the manuscript of her edition of the charters of Lagrasse. Jean-Claude Schmitt provided me with many references and was particularly helpful in the matter of the Holy Foreskin. Pierre Bonnassie and Dom

Jacques Dubois also took a great interest in the project and pointed me toward a number of new sources.

Several institutions are also owed thanks. The Woodrow Wilson Foundation provided a Mellon Fellowship for Graduate Study in the Humanities which covered three years of my graduate education. The University of California at Berkeley gave me two years of fellowship support. A semester's leave granted by the University of Pittsburgh allowed me to complete the dissertation before taking up my teaching duties there. A final summer of research for the book was funded by Brown University.

Last but not least I would like to thank three people. With his keen intelligence and wit, Philippe Buc accompanied me for much of this meridional odyssey, even during its less sunny moments. His comments and criticism were invaluable. My parents, John and Mary Remensnyder, have supported me in the esoteric pursuit of becoming a medievalist ever since I saw my first cathedral at age eighteen. To their loving encouragement I owe more than I can say.

A. G. R.

Providence, Rhode Island

Author's Note

A list of the ecclesiastical communities considered in this book and the most important texts which compose their legends can be found in Appendix 2. The same appendix also addresses technical matters pertaining to the dating (and manuscripts) of these texts.

I have been unable to refer, except in a most general way, to a recent book that treats certain issues I also consider. This study, Patrick Geary's *Phantoms of Remembrance: Memory and Oblivion at the End of the First Millennium* (Princeton, 1994), was published only after my own project had already been completed.

All translations are my own unless otherwise indicated. The biblical citations refer to the Vulgate.

Bibliographic Abbreviations

AASS	*Acta sanctorum quotquot toto orbe coluntur.* Edited by Jean Bolland et al. Antwerp: 1643–present.
AASSosB	*Acta ordinis sancti Benedict.* Edited by Luc d'Archery and Jean Mabillon. 9 vols. Paris: 1668–1701.
AB	*Analecta Bollandiana*
AD	Archives Départmentales
BM	Bibliothèque Municipale
BN	Bibliothèque Nationale, Paris
GC	*Gallia Christiana.* 2d ed. 16 vols. Paris: 1715–1865.
HL	Claude Devic and J.-J. Vaissète. *Histoire générale de Languedoc avec des notes et les pièces justificatives.* Edition Privat. 16 vols. Toulouse: 1872–1904.
MGH Diplomata Karolinorum, 1	*Monumenta Germaniae Historica inde ab anno christi quingentesimo usque ad annum millesimum et quingentesimum: Diplomata Karolinorum.* Edited by Engelbert Mühlbacher et al. Vol. 1: *Pippini, Carlomanni, Caroli Magni Diplomata.* 2d ed. Berlin: 1956.
MGH SS	*Monumenta Germaniae Historica inde ab anno christi quingentesimo usque ad annum millesimum et quingentesimum. Scriptores in folio.* 32 vols. Hannover and Leipzig: 1826–1934.
MGH SSRM	*Monumenta Germaniae Historica inde ab anno christi quingentesimo usque ad annum millesimum et quingentesimum. Scriptores rerum Merovingicarum.* 7 vols. Hannover: 1885–1916.
MIÖG	*Mitteilungen des Instituts für Österreichische Geschichtsforschung*
PL	*Patrologiae cursus completus, Series Latina.* Edited by J.-P. Migne. 221 vols. Paris: 1844–1864.

Remembering Kings Past

Introduction

On his way to Spain, Charlemagne, accompanied by his knights, stopped off to wrest Narbonne from the Muslims. In a nearby valley he came across seven hermits living in huts surrounding a chapel dedicated to the Virgin. With the counsel of Pope Leo and Archbishop Turpin, the emperor recognized that the valley was a place chosen by God and decided to establish a monastery there. In this legendary version of the abbey of Lagrasse's foundation (a mid-thirteenth-century narrative), Charlemagne moves in the world of the *chansons de geste* and by his very presence consecrates the landscape—a fabulous contrast to the sober eighth-century diploma in which the historical king took the newly founded monastery under his protection.[1]

Lagrasse was only one of numerous western European monasteries that fashioned traditions relating to their origins: foundation legends. Such legends are products of what I have chosen to call "imaginative memory," a certain type of reflection upon the past. This sort of memory as embodied in the legends is certainly also "social" or "collective," but I use "imaginative" in order to evoke the creative flair of the legends and their often fantastic transformations of reality.[2] But why bother with the word "memory" at all, instead of placing these legends in the category of forgery or fiction? Indeed, in the course of my work on this project, I have been often asked: "Who

---

[1] For the diploma of 799, see *MGH Diplomata Karolinorum* 1:253–254, no. 189. The thirteenth-century narrative has been edited by F. E. Schneegans as the *Gesta Karoli Magni ad Carcassonam et Narbonam*, Romanische Bibliothek, 15 (Halle, 1898).

[2] Social memory is used, for example, by Paul Connerton, *How Societies Remember* (Cambridge, 1989); and James Fentress and Chris Wickham, *Social Memory* (Oxford, 1992). For collective memory, see Maurice Halbwachs, *Les cadres sociaux de la mémoire*, 2d ed. (Paris, 1955), and his *La mémoire collective*, 2d ed. (Paris, 1968).

really believed these tales anyway? Weren't they all just deliberate falsification, so much fantasy?" By using the word "memory," I wish to underline that while many of these legends do seem fantastic, the monastic communities constructing these images believed in them at some level. We believe what we remember, even if what we remember is false, even if we have consciously or unconsciously constructed what we remember.[3]

As products of imaginative memory, monastic foundation legends belong in the realm of what was believed to be true, rather than what was seen to be fiction. To be sure, these abbeys' belief in their imaginatively remembered past may not have been cast in the same mold as their belief in the sun's warmth; different modes of belief may coexist simultaneously within one person or social group.[4] But if, for example, the twelfth-century monks of Braunweiler had not believed in some fashion that the site for their abbey had been designated by a miraculous cow with candles burning between her horns, why would they have bothered to commemorate this event—narrated by their legend—with an annual liturgical celebration and a feast at which a cow was the main dish?[5]

Furthermore, if monasteries had not held their constructed images of the past to be true, these legends would not have had the power in the present that they did for these communities.[6] For imaginative memory implies a dialogue between then and now, a dialectic relationship of continuity between the two temporal spaces.[7] The past constructed by imaginative memory, the golden age of heroes, does not merely reflect but also informs the present. It has a power and often an authority that we might call "constitutive"; it creates identity and meaning, whether of the institution, the social group, or even the individual, in the present.[8] Sharing an imagined past can

[3] On how social memory carries what is believed to be true, see Fentress and Wickham, *Social Memory*. On issues of false (and repressed) memory for individuals, see Elizabeth F. Loftus, "The Reality of Repressed Memories," *American Psychologist* 48 (1993): 518–537.

[4] On different modes of belief, see Paul Veyne, *Les Grecs ont-ils cru à leur mythes?* (Paris, 1983), esp. pp. 28–38. Cf. the discussion of simultaneous modes of social cognition in Maurice Bloch, "The Past and the Present in the Present," *Man* 12 (1977): 278–292.

[5] Roman Michalowski makes this argument about belief in his discussion of Braunweiler's extraordinary custom: "Il culto dei santi fondatori nei monasteri tedeschi dei secoli XI e XII: Proposte di ricerca," in *Culto dei santi istituzioni e classi sociali in età preindustriale,* ed. Sofia Boesch Gajano and Lucia Sebastiani (Rome, 1984), pp. 114–115.

[6] Cf. Walter Goffart's argument that the Le Mans forger "honestly believed" in what he made his forgeries say: *The Le Mans Forgeries: A Chapter from the History of Church Property in the Ninth Century* (Cambridge, Mass., 1966), p. 248.

[7] See Claude Lévi-Strauss, "The Structural Study of Myth," *Journal of American Folklore* 28 (1955): 30; Pierre Nora, "Between Memory and History: Les lieux de mémoire," *Representations* 26 (1989): 7–25; and Jean-Pierre Vernant's discussion of anamnèsis, in his *Mythe et pensée chez les Grecs: Etudes de psychologie historique,* rev. ed. (Paris, 1988), pp. 116–117.

[8] See Valerio Valeri (from whom I borrow the term "constitutive"), "Constitutive History: Genealogy and Narrative in the Legitimation of Hawaiian Kingship," in *Culture through Time: Anthropological Approaches,* ed. Emiko Ohnuki-Tierney (Stanford, 1990), pp. 154–192.

establish and reaffirm the cohesion of a group.[9] It provides a common set of symbols that help create the boundaries delineating and containing the community or society. Furthermore, as part of this symbolic set of boundaries, the past creates an identity that is relational, differential, even oppositional. Implicitly or explicitly, this identity situates the group in relation to others and defines it as different.[10]

The constitutive power of the past may be invoked in response to various social needs. In moments of stress, when the community's independence or very existence is in jeopardy, the construction of a common past assures the group of its (threatened) identity.[11] This recourse to the past may also result from a sense of general discontinuity, of alienation from a present characterized by rapid social change, and from a past become too distant. The remedy is found through a rediscovery of the past, the creation of a meaningful continuity between it and the present.[12] Equally, the past may become a means of conceptualizing and understanding present phenomena. Thus, imaginative memory can have aetiological, explanatory, and interpretative functions.[13] Finally, the past may become legitimating, glorifying—even sanctifying—for the present. For example, origins in the past may provide a "charter" justifying extant institutions and customs.[14] Or

[9] See A. P. Cohen, *The Symbolic Construction of Community* (New York, 1985), pp. 98–103; Sharon Farmer, *Communities of Saint Martin: Legend and Ritual in Medieval Tours* (Ithaca, N.Y., 1991), pp. 151–186; Eric Hobsbawm, "Introduction: Inventing Traditions," in *The Invention of Tradition*, ed. Eric Hobsbawm and Terence Ranger (Cambridge, 1983; rpt. 1988), p. 9; Anthony D. Smith, *The Ethnic Origins of Nations* (New York, 1986; rpt. 1988), pp. 174–208, 213; and Valeri, "Constitutive History," pp. 162–163. On the importance of imagination for social cohesion, see Benedict Anderson, *Imagined Communities: Reflections on the Origin and Spread of Nationalism* (New York, 1983).

[10] On symbolic boundaries, see Cohen, *Symbolic Construction*, esp. pp. 12–15; and Peter Sahlins, *Boundaries: The Making of France and Spain in the Pyrenees* (Berkeley, 1990). The very possession of an imaginatively remembered past can function as a principle of social differentiation (usually distinguishing aristocrats from nonaristocrats). See Lila Abu-Lughod, *Veiled Sentiments: Honor and Poetry in a Bedouin Society* (Berkeley, 1986), pp. 45, 87; Marshall Sahlins, *Islands of History* (Chicago, 1985), pp. 25, 49–52; and Valeri, "Constitutive History," p. 165. The same phenomenon may be observed in the proliferation of aristocratic genealogies in medieval Europe (see below at n. 25).

[11] Cohen, *Symbolic Construction*, esp. pp. 44–50, 77–82; Smith, *Ethnic Origins of Nations*, pp. 37–41, 51–56, 74–76, 175–176.

[12] For medieval instances, see Farmer, *Communities of Saint Martin*, pp. 165–186; and Richard Southern, "Aspects of the European Tradition of Historical Writing: 4. The Sense of the Past," *Transactions of the Royal Historical Society*, 5th ser., 23 (1973): 243–263. In general, see Nora, "Between Memory and History"; and Smith, *Ethnic Origins of Nations*, esp. pp. 173–175.

[13] On myth as interpretative, see Lévi-Strauss, "Structural Study." G. S. Kirk focuses on myth as speculative in his *Myth: Its Function and Meaning in Ancient and Other Cultures* (Cambridge, 1970; rpt. 1971). Cf. Louis Marin's brief comments in his "De l'*Utopia* de More à la Scandza de Cassiodore-Jordanès," *Annales E.S.C.* 26 (1971): 308–309. Ovid's *Metamorphoses* provides many vivid examples of the past as aetiology.

[14] Bronislaw Malinowski, "Myth in Primitive Psychology," in his *Magic, Science and Religion and Other Essays* (New York, 1948), pp. 93–148, esp. 107–110, 146.

the past may be a model used (consciously or unconsciously) to structure present action.[15] In defense of threatened rights, institutions, or identities, the past may be appealed to as a bulwark. Similarly, it can serve as the basis for the fashioning of new identities, new traditions, and claims to new rights.[16]

To fulfill these needs, any moment of the imagined past may be invoked. But origins, especially those located in the historicized time of legend rather than in the irrevocable distance characterizing myth, are peculiarly authoritative and paradigmatic for the present;[17] they concentrate the constitutive power of imaginative memory. The authority of origins does not derive merely from their antiquity, from their temporal position. Rather, origins are qualitatively different from other moments of the imagined past. Implying an interplay of being and nonbeing not intrinsic to other portions of the past, origins allow imaginative memory free rein. From nonbeing can come anything that can be imagined. But once it has entered the realm of existence, an entity is subject to strictures, even in the imagination. The remedy, embodied by the motif of decadence and consequent rebirth often found in myth and legend, involves a return to the state of origins, to the moment when all is possible, when all can be constituted.

The foundation legends of medieval monasteries, then, are not mere inert fictions, but texts that illuminate the way in which these communities constructed both their identity and the nexus of social relations in which they were implicated. Nonetheless, despite recent scholarly attention to various aspects of medieval memory, this rich vein of sources has been scarcely tapped.[18] To be sure, a number of historians have considered the legends of individual monastic communities.[19] These studies are extremely

---

[15] A good example of this would be the conscious *imitatio Christi*. For a modern example of the more unconscious use of models from the past, see Sherry Ortner, "Patterns of History: Cultural Schemas in the Foundings of Sherpa Religious Institutions," in *Culture through Time*, pp. 57–93.

[16] See the articles in *The Invention of Tradition*.

[17] Valeri suggests that the imaginatively remembered past can be too distant, too different from the present to be authoritative as a paradigm for action or rules in the present; see his "Constitutive History," p. 164.

[18] For recent studies of various aspects of medieval memory, see Mary Carruthers, *The Book of Memory: A Study of Memory in Medieval Culture* (Cambridge, 1990); and Patrick Geary, *Phantoms of Remembrance: Memory and Oblivion at the End of the First Millennium* (Princeton, 1994).

[19] For example: Farmer, *Communities of Saint Martin*, pp. 151–186; Antonia Gransden, "The Growth of the Glastonbury Traditions and Legends," *Journal of Ecclesiastical History* 27 (1976): 337–358; Thomas Head, "Hrotsvit's Primordia and the Historical Traditions of Monastic Communities," in *Hrotsvit of Gandersheim: Rara Avis in Saxonia?* ed. Katharina M. Wilson, Medieval and Renaissance Monograph Series, 7; (Ann Arbor, 1987), pp. 143–164; Dominique Iogna-Prat (who generously allowed me to read his article before its publication), "La geste des origines dans l'historiographie clunisienne des XIe–XIIe siècles," *Revue Bénédictine* 102 (1992): 135–191; Charles T. Wood, "At the Tomb of King Arthur," *Essays in Medieval Studies: Proceedings of the Illinois Medieval Association* 8 (1991): 1–14.

valuable, often suggesting the interplay between past and present that made such traditions significant for the abbey in question. They whet the appetite, making one wonder what patterns would emerge if these legends were considered not in isolation, but in groupings coherent in time and space.

The few synthetic considerations of monastic foundation legends that do exist do not quite satisfy this curiosity. While insightful in different ways, these studies tend not to take fully into consideration the richness and complexity of the traditions. In a study of the foundation legends of German abbeys, Jörg Kastner poses as his central question one of form (the development and function of the cartulary chronicle).[20] Hans Patze examines a more sharply defined group of German legends with the explicit intention of using such texts as evidence of the crystallization of the nobility's consciousness.[21] In an article comparing the legends of La Trinité Vendôme, Bonport, and Holyrood, Penelope Johnson, like Patze, appears to have a bias toward the abbey's secular patrons. Above all, she is interested in the political motivations of the actual lay founders and how these are translated into legend.[22] Certainly monasteries and secular aristocrats were tightly linked by various sorts of bonds, including those of blood and mutual patronage.[23] But to examine *monastic* legends primarily as so much evidence for the aristocracy is to distort these sources, to lose sight of the significance these traditions had for the monks themselves. Monastic imaginative memory deserves to be treated on its own terms, not on those of the aristocracy.[24]

Perhaps this bias toward the aristocracy in studies of monastic legends reflects one that has prevailed until recently in the study of medieval imaginative memory in general: the traditions of the secular nobility have enjoyed a much larger share of the limelight than those of monasteries. With the renewal of historians' interest in the medieval aristocracy of the post-Carolingian era has come a host of studies of the noble genealogies—certainly products of imaginative memory—composed particularly in the

[20] Jörg Kastner, *Historiae fundationum monasteriorum: Frühformen monastischer Institutionsgeschichtsschreibung im Mittelalter,* Münchener Beiträge zur Mediävistik und Renaissance-Forschung, 18; (Munich, 1974).

[21] Hans Patze, "Adel und Stifterchronik: Frühformen territorialer Geschichtsschreibung im hochmittelalterlichen Reich," *Blätter für deutsche Landesgeschichte* 100 (1964): 8–81; 101 (1965): 67–128.

[22] Penelope Johnson, "Pious Legends and Historical Realities: The Legends of La Trinité Vendôme, Bonport and Holyrood," *Revue Bénédictine* 91 (1981): 184–193.

[23] See below, Chapter 6 at n. 123.

[24] Several studies of such legends, however, do keep the monastic perspective firmly in the foreground, showing that while abbeys might celebrate noble founders in their legends, these communities did so for their own purposes (which did not necessarily converge with the interests of the founders). See Farmer, *Communities of Saint Martin,* pp. 78–116; and Kastner, *Historiae fundationum,* pp. 24–25, 32–36. On such divergence of perspective between abbey and royal patrons, see Gerd Althoff, "Gandersheim und Quedlinburg: Ottonische Frauenklöster als Herrschafts- und Uberlieferungszentrum," *Frühmittelalterliche Studien* 25 (1991): 136–144.

eleventh and twelfth centuries.[25] Through the analysis of these documents we have learned much about how the aristocracy conceived of its identity and its power, and about which layer of the past it used for legitimation.

From a synthetic treatment of monastic imaginative memory, as much can be learned about one of the other dominant groups in medieval society: the regular clergy. Indeed, we can hope to learn even more, for the monastic legends—unlike the noble genealogies—allow us to perceive the creation of a historicized topography that could become part of the consciousness of other social groups. The aristocratic genealogies, although often relating how the lineage acquired the castle that made it a "house," attached an imaginatively remembered past and origin to the family, to this specific group of persons related by blood. Although this type of past could interweave with that of other social groups (for example, religious communities), it was connected primarily to a group of persons that was by definition exclusive.

The monastic foundation legends, on the other hand, while certainly relating to a group, the monastic community, were equally the story of the creation of an institution fixed firmly in space.[26] The sanctification of this community's origins translated into the characterization and definition of topography through a conjunction of divine intervention (miracles) and the action of various persons, larger than life, saintly and often heroic—the founders. The resulting landscape was inclusive rather than exclusive; legends often organized the surrounding territory as the abbey's patrimony, thereby incorporating it into historicized legendary space. Furthermore, because these legends were attached above all to place rather than to a self-limiting group of persons, they could be adopted by or imposed upon nonmonastic inhabitants of the space, such as the denizens of the bourgs that coalesced around many abbeys.[27] Rooted in place, the monastic legends thus fashioned a larger vision of space, one centered on the abbey, to

[25] On the wave of recent studies of the nobility, see Thomas N. Bisson, "Nobility and the Family in Medieval France: A Review Essay," *French Historical Studies* 16 (1990): 597–613. On the genealogies, see for example Gerd Althoff, "Genealogische und andere Fiktionen in mittelalterlicher Historiographie," in *Fälschungen im Mittelalter: Internationaler Kongress der Monumenta Germaniae Historica, München 16.–19. September 1986*, 5 vols., MGH Schriften, 33.1–5 (Hannover, 1988), 1:416–441; Georges Duby, *The Chivalrous Society*, trans. Cynthia Postan (Berkeley, 1980), pp. 59–80, 94–111, 134–148, 149–157; and Karl Hauck, "Haus- und sippengebundene Literatur mittelalterlicher Adelsgeschlechter," *MIÖG* 62 (1954): 121–145. On genealogies produced south of the Loire, see Thomas N. Bisson, "Unheroed Pasts: History and Commemoration in South Frankland before the Albigensian Crusade," *Speculum* 65 (1990): 293–301.

[26] Kastner remarks that unlike most monastic sources in which the monks predominate, in foundation texts the abbey itself is the main character; see his *Historiae fundationum*, p. 83.

[27] Of course, legends relating the foundation of castles could function to characterize and create inclusive topography in a similar way; the noble genealogies, however, are focused not on such foundations but on family.

be sure, but one that at the same time embraced and created a broader landscape.

Monastic legends were not the only locus for the imaginative creation of such landscapes in the Middle Ages. Urban and episcopal foundation legends also offered such possibilities.[28] So too did the developing "national" traditions that have shared the limelight with the aristocracy in the study of medieval imaginative memory.[29] The creation of a "national" past involved the exaltation of a group that we might call "ethnic" (all the while recognizing the constructedness of ethnic identity) and, in most cases, of a royal lineage or race of kings. Nonetheless, although the "national" legends, like the genealogies, focused on a group of persons, they also involved a certain delineation and characterization of space.[30] Let us remember that in Roland's dying reverie figured not only "the men of his lineage" (*des humes de son lign*) and Charlemagne "his lord" (*sun seigneur*) but also "sweet France" (*dulce France*).[31] How did these sets of landscapes—"national" and monastic—relate to each other? Did they intersect, diverge, or run parallel? Were they alternative or similar visions?

Such questions—and others posed by the legends—-can be answered in a meaningful fashion only if these sources are considered in a coherent social, geographical, and temporal context. Only then shall we be able to understand fully the many dimensions of these legends, their constitution of monastic identity and of broader visions of the imaginatively remembered past. I have chosen to focus on the legends elaborated between the very early eleventh and the mid-thirteenth century by traditional Benedictine monasteries in the southwest of France. Let me define each of the elements that render this set of legends a coherent and significant object of study: region; choice of monasteries; period; and finally the sources, that is the legends themselves.

The boundaries of the region are largely those of Aquitaine. By Aquitaine, I mean not the duchy of the central and later Middle Ages that in the twelfth century became part of the Angevin rulers' patrimony, but a much larger area: the old Carolingian subkingdom, that is to say, the territory south of

---

[28] For one study of an episcopal foundation legend, see Goffart, *Le Mans Forgeries*.

[29] On imaginative memory and "national" (admittedly an anachronistic term) traditions, see for example Colette Beaune, *Naissance de la nation France* (Paris, 1985); Joachim Ehlers, "Kontinuität und Tradition als Grundlage mittelalterlicher Nationsbildung in Frankreich," in *Beiträge zur Bildung der französischen Nation im Früh- und Hochmittlalter*, ed. Helmut Beumann (Sigmaringen, 1983), pp. 16–47; Paul Freedman, "Cowardice, Heroism and the Legendary Origins of Catalonia," *Past and Present* 121 (1988): 3–28; and Frantisek Graus, *Lebendige Vergangenheit: Überlieferung im Mittelalter und in den Vorstellungen vom Mittelalter* (Cologne, 1975), pp. 206–239 (73–144 on legends of ethnic origins).

[30] As the studies just cited in n. 29 show.

[31] *La chanson de Roland*, laisse 176, ll. 2379–2380, ed. Cesare Segre, 2 vols. (Geneva, 1989), 1:212.

the Loire and west of the Rhône which extended into the Pyrenees.[32] Given that this area included Septimania, Gascony, and Catalonia, I will refer to it, however, not as Aquitaine but as "the south."[33] To be sure, a term as general as this might be considered to include Provence as well. But the region east of the Rhône followed its own path in this period, and its abbeys are not discussed here.[34]

Within this defining geographical frame, my primary focus will be the legends of approximately forty Benedictine abbeys.[35] I have chosen to consider only the black monks, and not the Cistercians or friars (nor chapters of canons save in exceptional cases), in order to guarantee consistency of the source basis; legends could be quite different according to the type of religious community that fashioned them. For example, Cistercian communities could hardly claim as their founders the Carolingian kings who were so wildly popular in the legends of the black monks; even imaginative memory could not render the white monks contemporaries of these rulers.[36]

With the exception of one abbey, Notre-Dame de la Règle of Limoges, all the Benedictine houses considered here were male communities. This focus on male houses was not a deliberate choice on my part, for I selected monasteries according to the very simple principle of incorporating every abbey for which I could find a legend. Nor does this paucity of legends from women's communities seem to reflect differences between male and female monastic culture; female monasteries in other regions created such legends. Rather, the lack of legends from female abbeys seems to relate to the small number of Benedictine monasteries for women that existed in the south during this period.[37]

[32] For geographical definitions of the kingdom of Aquitaine (whose boundaries fluctuated in the late eighth and the early ninth century but generally comprised the area defined here), see Léonce Auzias, *L'Aquitaine carolingienne (778–987)* (Paris, 1937), pp. 11–16, 71–72, 79–81; and Janet Martindale, "The Kingdom of Aquitaine and the 'Dissolution of the Carolingian Fisc,'" *Francia* 11 (1983): 136–139.

[33] For example, the *Notitia de servitio monasteriorum* of 817 refers to this area as Gascony, Toulouse, Septimania, and Aquitaine (*MGH Capitularia regum Francorum* 1:349–352, no. 171).

[34] Although one of the abbeys considered here, Saint-Gilles, might seem like a Provençal monastery (it was subject to the bishop of Nîmes), the *Notitia de servitio monasteriorum* situates it in Septimania (*MGH Capitularia regum Francorum* 1:351, no. 171).

[35] Other relevant monastic legends will be considered in the notes.

[36] For other differences between legends of the black monks and those of the white monks, see below, Chapter 2 at nn. 12–14.

[37] For example, most female communities in Languedoc were founded only after 1100, and the vast majority only in the thirteenth and fourteenth centuries. Furthermore, Benedictine houses made up only 21 percent of the female communities extant in Languedoc between the eleventh and the fourteenth centuries. Here I draw on Pierre-Roger Gaussin, "Les communautés féminines dans l'espace Languedocien de la fin du XIe à la fin du XIVe s.," in *La femme dans la vie religieuse du Languedoc: XIIIe-XIVe s.*, Cahiers de Fanjeaux, 23 (Toulouse, 1988), pp. 299–332; and Elisabeth Magnou-Nortier, "Formes féminines de vie

I make no pretensions to having recovered every monastic foundation legend from this area. Doubtless more, from female as well as from male communities, await discovery. Nonetheless, since I did not choose between abbeys according to what type of legend they produced, nor eliminate any legend that I unearthed, the legends considered here constitute a random and valid sample—but not for medieval Benedictine monasticism in general. These legends illuminate the monastic culture of the particular region from which they come: the south. This area, vast and variegated though it was geographically, politically, and socially, has a coherence and a particularity that makes it an appropriate frame for this study.[38] This is apparent from this region's history of ambivalent relations with the Frankish and then French kings.

Much more heavily Romanized than the area north of the Loire, the south was wrested from the Visigoths by Clovis (with the collaboration of the Gallo-Roman orthodox episcopate). But while the bishops had welcomed Clovis, many of the region's inhabitants, identifying themselves as Romans, resisted the rule of this Frankish king's descendants. Between the late seventh and the late eighth century, that resistance crystallized in the form of a succession of native leaders (Felix, Lupus, Odo, Hunald, Waïfre and Hunald II) whom northern sources called "dukes," but who styled themselves *principes,* a term that in the south retained the royal connotations it had acquired in classical usage.[39] At the expense of the Merovingians, these princes expanded their realm of influence until it included the region south of the Loire and west of the Rhône. In the eighth century their principal adversary became the family that would be known as the Carolingians. First Charles Martel, then Pippin the Short, and finally Charlemagne led campaigns in the south that successfully whittled away the power of these would-be kings but did not fully extinguish the current of southern anti-Frankishness. Eventually in 778, Charlemagne was able to incorporate this region officially into his realm. But in doing so, he acknowledged its nature as a separate entity. It became the subkingdom of Aquitaine, whose king, crowned at age three, was Charlemagne's son Louis the Pious.[40]

The reintegration of Aquitaine into the Frankish kingdom was permanent—at least in name. Although the subkingdom as a political entity survived only into the second half of the ninth century, this region's difference from the area north of the Loire and west of the Rhône was not

---

consacrée dans les pays du Midi jusqu'au début du XIIe siècle," in the same volume (pp. 193–195).

[38] Michel Rouche calls Aquitaine the oldest Frankish territorial principality and the first regional phenomenon the Franks experienced; see his *L'Aquitaine des Wisigoths aux Arabes 418–781: Naissance d'une région* (Paris, 1979), p. 132.

[39] Rouche, *L'Aquitaine,* pp. 373–385.

[40] For this discussion and interpretation of Aquitaine in the Merovingian and early Carolingian period, I have relied on Rouche, *L'Aquitaine,* pp. 51–132.

erased.[41] This particularism, although no longer incarnated in anti-Carolingian sentiment, was facilitated by the gradual retreat of Frankish royal power. By the later ninth century, the king ventured south of the Loire less and less frequently; his presence and rule were reduced to a waning flow of privileges and confirmations.[42] Under the early Capetians, the south remained, for all intents and purposes, a kingless land. To be sure, Robert the Pious made a pilgrimage to various southern shrines including Saint-Gilles and Sainte-Foy of Conques, but Capetian power, contracted around the Ile-de-France, was no reality in the south.[43] The royal return was heralded by Louis VI's military intervention in Auvergnat affairs (1120s), but this hardly meant that the king was now a presence.[44] Although Louis VII expanded royal influence south of the Loire, it was only under Philip Augustus, and more particularly Louis IX, that much of the south was brought back into the Frankish royal orbit.[45]

In the period of royal absence, the various areas of the south experienced different political and social fates, from the Massif Central with its count-bishops and independent rival petty lineages to the Pyrenean counties dominated by the nascent count-kings of Barcelona (and Aragon). This diversity reflected a general fragmentation and territorialization of power (similar to what occurred north of the Loire) that, having begun in the tenth century, passed through various stages to reach a certain equilibrium by the twelfth century. Numerous aristocratic lineages competed for ecclesiastical and secular preeminence, some, such as the count-kings of Barcelona and the counts of Toulouse, more successful than others at consolidating their control of land, people, and power.[46]

[41] On subsequent Carolingian kings of Aquitaine, see Auzias, *L'Aquitaine;* and Christian Lauranson-Rosaz, *L'Auvergne et ses marges (Vélay, Gévaudan) du VIIIe au XIe siècle: La fin du monde antique?* (Le Puy, 1987), pp. 40–87.

[42] On the disappearance of effective Carolingian power in Aquitaine, see Walther Kienast, "Wirkungsbereich des französischen Königstums von Odo bis Ludwig VI. (888–1137) in Südfrankreich," *Historische Zeitschrift* 209 (1969): 529–565.

[43] On the early Capetians' lack of power in the south, see Jean Dufour, "Obédience respective des Carolingians et des Capétiens (fin Xe siècle–début XIe siècle)," in *Catalunya i França meridional a l'entorn de l'any mil / La Catalogne et la France méridionale autour de l'an mil,* ed. Xavier Barral i Altet et al. (Barcelona, 1991), pp. 21–44; and Kienast, "Wirkungsbereich." On Robert the Pious's pilgrimage, see Lauranson-Rosaz, *L'Auvergne,* pp. 442–454. On the limits of early Capetian power and prestige in general, see Jean-François Lemarignier, *Le gouvernement royal aux premiers temps capétiens (987–1108)* (Paris, 1965).

[44] On these campaigns, see below, Chapter 6 at nn. 124–125.

[45] On Louis VII, see Marcel Pacaut, *Louis VII et son royaume* (Paris, 1964). For Louis IX, see Gérard Sivéry, *Saint Louis et son siècle* (Paris, 1983).

[46] For a convenient sketch of these developments, see the relevant passages in Jean Dunbabin, *France in the Making 843–1180* (Oxford, 1985). There exists no good history of the south in the period from the late eleventh century through the mid-thirteenth century; the relevant regional *thèses* all end with the close of the eleventh century (with the exception of Jean-Pierre Poly's study of Provence which continues to the mid-twelfth century: *La Provence et la société féodale 879–1166: Contribution à l'étude des structures dites féodales dans le Midi* [Paris, 1976]).

Despite such variety, the south during this period retained a certain coherence. The southerners were not yet *Franci* but still *Aquitani*, and were recognized as such by contemporaries, northerners and southerners alike.[47] Modern scholars themselves not only recognize but also underline the differences between north and south in areas as diverse as culture, social structure and social relations, agrarian practices, language, and religious practice and belief.[48] To grasp the particularity of the south, we have only to think of the Cathars, the troubadours and their poetry, the *langue d'oc*, the superb Romanesque architecture which persisted into the thirteenth century, and the flourishing shrines on the pilgrimage routes to Compostela concentrated south of the Loire. The north and the south were separated by more than the absence or presence of the king; the Loire divided the land literally and figuratively. Indeed, by the mid-tenth century lines of common culture and communication ran not so much north–south as east–west, binding the region—and its abbeys—into the broad band that stretched from the alpine valleys of northern Italy into the Pyrenees.[49]

If the south is thus a historically valid object of study, why are this region and the foundation legends of its abbeys an important subject for historical inquiry? These legends open a window onto a world that has suffered from some scholarly neglect, for the history of the south in this period has often been ignored in favor of the north. Southern culture itself has been relegated to irrelevance or, worse yet, judged according to patterns found north of the Loire.[50] Southern imaginative memory has not escaped this fate. Historians try to find in this region the narrative chronicles and other types of historical commemorative texts that proliferated north of the Loire dur-

---

[47] On this consciousness of difference between *Franci* and *Aquitani*, see Walther Kienast, *Deutschland und Frankreich in der Kaiserzeit (900–1270): Weltkaiser und Einzelkönig,* 3 vols., 2d ed., Monographien zur Geschichte des Mittelalters, 9.1–3 (Stuttgart, 1974–1975), 1:15–22, 3:655–657; and Jean-Pierre Poly and Eric Bournazel, *The Feudal Transformation, 900–1200,* trans. Caroline Higgitt (New York: 1991), pp. 231–235.

[48] See in general the articles in *Catalunya i França.* On primarily social and political differences, see for example Pierre Bonnassie, *La Catalogne du milieu du Xe à la fin du XIe: Croissance et mutations d'une société,* 2 vols. (Toulouse, 1975–1976); Archibald R. Lewis, *The Development of Southern French and Catalan Society,* 718–1050 (Austin, 1965); Lauranson-Rosaz, *L'Auvergne;* Elisabeth Magnou-Nortier, *La société laïque et l'église dans la province ecclésiastique de Narbonne (zone cispyrénéenne) de la fin du VIIIe à la fin du XIe siècle* (Toulouse, 1974); Poly, *La Provence;* and Poly and Bournazel, *Feudal Transformation,* pp. 218–240. On particular patterns of agriculture, see Marc Bloch, *French Rural History: An Essay on Its Basic Characteristics,* trans. Janet Sondheimer (Berkeley, 1966), pp. 21–63. On some cultural and religious differences, see Amy G. Remensnyder, "Un problème de cultures ou de culture? La statue-reliquaire et les *joca* de sainte Foy de Conques dans le *Liber miraculorum sancte Fidis* de Bernard d'Angers," *Cahiers de Civilisation Médiévale* 33 (1990): 360–365; and J. W. B. Zaal, *"A lei francesca" (Sainte Foy, v. 20): Etude sur les chansons de saints gallo-romanes du XIe siècle* (Leiden, 1962), pp. 27–60.

[49] On the contacts between Catalonia, Aquitaine, and Provence that were established by the end of the tenth century, see Bonnassie, *La Catalogne,* esp. pp. 331–339.

[50] Exceptions are the Cathars and the troubadours, who have excited much attention, scholarly and otherwise.

ing this period. Using this normative standard, they puzzle over the few instances of the composition of such history in the south.[51] But southern reflection on the past must be defined on its own terms.[52] As the monastic foundation legends reveal, south of the Loire there was a very fertile cultural and imaginative world in which the past was not only remembered but also a living presence.

This book is not intended only to contribute to the reestablishment of historiographic balance in our understanding of the land that would become France.[53] I also chose the south for what seems to be the very reason that its history (at least for this period) has often been neglected in favor of the north: the absence of the king. For is it not an implicit, even unconscious, "royalist" bias that has led to the relative paucity of studies of the southern world in the period before the Capetians descended to make this region part of their realm? But rather than rendering the south an uninteresting backwater, this very lack of a king makes it all the more intriguing. For if this region was part of the outer periphery of the French realm, how did it, or rather its abbeys, relate to the absent political center, the monarch? And upon which sources of authority did monastic imaginative memory draw when the present was characterized by such absence?

I have thus chosen to end my study with the return of the king and the incorporation of much of the south into the Capetian realm in the aftermath of the Albigensian Crusade (the mid-thirteenth century). But the disappearance of the king from the south in the late ninth century does not provide the terminus a quo. In that period there were as yet few monastic foundation legends, although most abbeys were probably not without traditions pertaining to their origins.[54] Only in the late tenth century did such traditions become the object of focused attention, resulting in their translation into tangible forms. The flourishing of the legends themselves thus determines this book's chronological point of departure.

The definitive nascence of the monastic desire to re-create the past, to fix it and thus the community's identity in an accessible form, seems itself to be one of the many changes that marked the years around 1000.[55] But just

[51] Here I think particularly of Bernard Guenée, *Histoire et culture historique dans l'Occident médiéval* (Paris, 1980), pp. 310–311, 312. Southern composers of narrative history were not nonexistent, however, and have found their modern champions; see Richard Landes's study, *Relics, Apocalypse and the Deceits of History: Ademar of Chabannes (989–1034)* (Cambridge, Mass., 1995).

[52] For a nuanced consideration of historical texts (including some monastic foundation legends) produced south of the Loire, see Bisson, "Unheroed Pasts," pp. 281–308.

[53] This process has already been begun by other scholars in their weighty regional studies (which generally, however, cover only the period up to the end of the eleventh century). See the references in n. 48 above.

[54] See, for example, the case of Saint-Gilles below, Chapter 6 at nn. 19–25.

[55] This monastic interest in capturing the past in concrete form dovetails with the transition from "orality" to "literacy and textuality" (to borrow from Brian Stock's terminology in

what was this form? What did a monastic foundation legend look like? There is no one answer to this question. When I use the term "legend," I do not refer to a fixed formal genre, but rather to a type of reflection about a monastery's beginnings. Imaginative memory could crystallize in one discrete narrative text, but it could equally appear in many-layered combinations of saints' lives, miracle collections, forged and narrative charters, cartularies, sculpture, architectural design, and reliquaries. Images of origins did not necessarily emerge all at once, but could be elaborated slowly over time. Legends were mosaics subject to metamorphosis.

I have chosen to consider the entire spectrum of sources through which the legendary impulse could be expressed. Because my subject is not the development of a genre, but rather images of origins, I see little reason to impose artificial barriers between types of sources where none existed. If abbeys invoked and represented their legendary foundations in various types of sources, why should the modern observer reject some of these forms in favor of others? To be sure, the legendary past had a different orientation according to the shape with which it was framed. But these orientations were complementary rather than contradictory or divergent; essentially nonnarrative forms were subjected to a narrative imperative and configured to relate an implicit story. Only by considering the full range of forms can we hope to grasp the intensity and complexity of this reflection on origins and how it translated into the structuring of the abbey's present identity.

I will not, however, treat these sources as one glorious potpourri. Certain concentrations and chronological inflections are evident. Only infrequently did southern abbeys capture their legends in freestanding narrative accounts. The lack of interest in independent narrative accounts remains constant during this period; there seems to be no appreciable increasing predilection for this form. The later narrative sources did differ from the earlier, not so much in length as in content. But this change (which I explore in Chapters 3, 4, and 5) was not particular to these sources. It also inflected the two forms to which the abbeys more often had recourse in their legend building: *vitae* and diplomatic texts such as forged and interpolated charters, privileges, and royal diplomas. Particularly by the twelfth century the southern monasteries favored the latter form. Indeed, the independent narratives dating from this period could be impregnated with diplomatic language and structure.

This mixture of sources reveals the particular flavor of southern reflection upon the past, the lack of interest in narrative per se, the strong notarial

---

his *The Implications of Literacy: Written Language and Models of Interpretation in the Eleventh and Twelfth Centuries* [Princeton, 1983]) or from "memory to written record" (in the words of Michael T. Clanchy, *From Memory to Written Record: England, 1066–1307,* 2d. ed. [London, 1993]).

tradition.[56] Let us not, however, jump to the conclusion that because they often framed the origins of their communities in diplomatic forms, southern monks therefore viewed the past solely in terms of a set of juridical rights. The rights established by authoritative documents such as diplomas were indeed critical to these abbeys. But this proliferation of foundation legends in the guise of charters and diplomas may relate specifically to the change that also affected the content of freestanding narrative texts. Diplomatic forms were particularly appropriate for expressing the types of foundations and founders that the abbeys increasingly sought to claim for themselves by the twelfth century: royal.

Furthermore, to pigeonhole the diplomatic documents as tendentious forgeries and to treat them therefore as fundamentally different from other texts that participate in legend would be to forget the significance of imaginative memory as constitutive of identity and of symbolic boundaries.[57] Forgery and the legendary impulse could be one and the same. Rights and property claimed through these texts, we shall find, were as much a part of identity and boundaries as were other aspects of legendary identity. Even more important, these forgeries were not always mere expressions of such claims. The past they recounted could be explicative, interpretative, and illustrative just as easily as that related by a narrative text could be contentious and polemical.[58]

I shall begin with an examination of diplomatic texts that, while not themselves legendary, demonstrate precisely the narrative and interpretative possibilities of such forms: authentic foundation charters. In these documents we can perceive the actual and historical process of founding a monastery. By starting with the historical as opposed to the legendary, my purpose is not to provide a template of the "real" against which one can then hold up the "fiction" of the process as described in legend. Rather, I intend to show how implicit in the process of historical foundation and its commemoration was already a collapsing of time, a locus of memory, an interplay of past and present.

Indeed, the way in which foundation charters narrated foundation serves to highlight the artificiality of creating stencils of the "real" to be imposed on the "fictional." For the significance of foundation was the same in both charter and legend, although emphasized more strikingly in the latter. Foundation involved the establishment of the abbey's identity as both a sacred space and a human institution implicated in the web of social rela-

---

[56] See Bisson's conclusions in "Unheroed Pasts."

[57] On the vexed question of the significance of medieval forgery, see the five volumes of *Fälschungen im Mittelalter.*

[58] Cf. Nicholas Huyghebaert's argument that the celebrated Donation of Constantine was intended by those who composed it to be not only a polemical piece but also a narrative explaining the origins of the community of clerics at the Lateran: "Une légende de fondation: Le Constitutum Constantini," *Le Moyen Age* 85 (1979): 177–209.

tions. As we shall see in Chapter 2, legends manipulated various motifs to construct this identity—the symbolic boundaries of monastic communities.

The highly charged significance of foundation shaped the figures abbeys chose to associate with their origins: the founders. In Chapters 3, 4, and 5 I explore the identity of the founders favored by the legends, the traits these figures acquired over time as they were integrated into these images of origins, and the resulting symbolic importance for the monasteries themselves. Through the figures of founders, abbeys could locate themselves in relation to various sources of supralocal authority. Furthermore, these founders situated the monasteries in relation to their actual neighbors who wielded power, both secular and religious. This very local context, the subject of Chapter 6, helps us understand even more clearly the relational nature of monastic identity as established by legend. For legends most often crystallized in the course of conflicts that posed a threat to the community's identity.

These legends are multifaceted objects that catch the light from different directions, reflecting and refracting it to create one image which is really many. I shall turn them in every direction, in order to show each facet and how it relates to the others. Such an approach is thus structured more according to the legends' multivalence than according to chronology, internal or external. Nonetheless, time can hardly be absent in a study of the dynamic interaction between past and present. Throughout this book I shall be concerned with those changes in the present which stimulated imaginative memory as well as with those in the imaginatively remembered past which in their turn affected the present. Only by fixing the legends in time and space, only by observing their changing shapes, can we hope to understand the full implications these products of monastic imaginative memory had for the present.

THE DIMENSIONS

OF FOUNDATION

1

The Historical Process

"Foundation"—the term conjures up a specific act at a specific moment by a specific person or persons. This seemingly compact and precise historical event was often recorded in documents known as foundation charters. The nature of these charters, however, raises questions about the discreteness of foundation. Such charters record, among other things, lands granted to the church. These donations could be considered as the actual foundation, and hence the donors as the founders.[1] But such a characterization of foundation is not necessarily helpful; the dating of the foundation charters that describe the donations presents knotty problems. The witness lists and names of donors often contain anachronisms and impossibilities that provoke not merely historians' puzzlement but also suspicion about the authenticity of the charters. In the year invoked, the status ascribed to certain donors or subscribers may be inaccurate, or indeed the person may have already died. For example, the foundation charter of Gaillac, dated 972, not only mentions the donations made in that year by Raymond Pons III of Toulouse, one of the monastery's founders, but at times even takes his voice ("I Raymond . . .").[2] Yet Raymond was dead by at least 960. Such apparent anomalies are resolved when we realize that foundation charters often commemorate donations that had been made orally several years earlier. All the endowments are thus subsumed under one date, that of the charter—which is typically the date of the

---

[1] See the eleventh- and twelfth-century English monastic chronicles cited by V. H. Galbraith, "Monastic Foundation Charters of the Eleventh and Twelfth Centuries," *Cambridge Historical Journal* 4 (1934): 215.

[2] Interestingly, his subscription does not appear on the document, but that of his wife, Countess Garsindis, does. *HL* 5:269–270, no. 123.

first or last donation and/or of the new or rebuilt church's consecration.[3] The Gaillac foundation charter, for example, takes as its date that of the abbey's consecration.

Like the other chronological inconsistencies that riddle foundation charters, Raymond Pons's "presence" at this ritual occurring some twelve years after his death reveals a certain textual dynamic. These charters manipulated time to make one significant moment contain and represent the various constitutive elements and actors in the process of foundation. As such temporal compression indicates, foundation was a process—a number of acts extended in time and space involving a number of people, all of whom contemporaries considered to be founders.[4] It is the charters themselves that rendered this process discrete and compact, collapsing a series of events into one moment and invoking as witnesses the names of all the founders (dead or alive). According to this logic, Raymond Pons's textual appearance at Gaillac's consecration was natural: he was after all the abbey's principal founder.

Such temporal conflation and compression can hardly be considered unusual for this period, an era in which typological interpretations habitually collapsed time in a similar fashion. Nor can it be considered unconscious or naive; in 1003 William V of Aquitaine, importuned by the abbot of Maillezais, drew up a charter of *libertas* for this monastery which his mother and father had established several decades earlier. The duke and his *nobiles* subscribed, and then, according to the author of Maillezais's legend of foundation (ca. 1070), William "had the name of his mother written with those of the witnesses just as if she were alive, because it was the anniversary day of her death."[5] William's mother, Emma of Blois, thus was commemorated intentionally and appropriately on the day of her death not only with

---

[3] On the dating method used in foundation charters, see *Les actes de consagracions d'esglésies de l'antic bisbat d'Urgell (Segles IX–XII)*, ed. Cebrià Baraut (La Seu d'Urgell, 1986), pp. 25–26; Marjorie Chibnall, "Charter and Chronicle: The Use of Archive Sources by Norman Historians," in *Church and Government in the Middle Ages: Essays presented to C. R. Cheney . . .* , ed. C.N.L. Brooke et al. (Cambridge, 1976), pp. 11–12, 14; Galbraith, "Monastic Foundation Charters," pp. 214–217, 220–222; and Giles Constable, "Monasticism, Lordship and Society in the Twelfth-Century Hesbaye: Five Documents on the Foundation of the Cluniac Priory of Bertrée," *Traditio* 33 (1977): 161–173 (reprinted in his *Cluniac Studies* [London, 1980]).

[4] Although charters often reserve the technical term of *funditor* or *conditor* for those who endowed the monastery with the necessary property, other types of texts use the same terminology for people active otherwise in the foundation; see, for example, *Vita S. Geraldi Silvae-majoris primi abbatis et fundatoris (AASSosB.* 6.2:866–892).

[5] Peter of Maillezais, *De antiquitate et commutatione in melius Malleacense insulae sive qualiter fuit constructum Malleacense monasterium et corpus sancti Rigomeri translatum (PL* 146:1264). In the sole extant manuscript of this text (twelfth-century Paris, BN Latin 4829, ff. 246ra–255vb), the title reads, rather, *Qualiter fuit constructum Malliacense monasterium et corpus sancti Rigomeri translatum.* Accordingly, this text will be referred to henceforth as *Qualiter fuit constructum Malliacense.* A new edition of this text is being prepared by Georges Pon.

the monks' prayers but also with her subscription on the privilege establishing the liberty of her foundation.[6]

The presence of Emma's name reveals neither interpolation nor "forgery." Rather, like Raymond Pons's posthumous presence at Gaillac's consecration, it demonstrates that foundation charters were the memory, commemoration, and interpretation of the process of foundation, not the phenomenon itself. As memorial texts, these charters intersect with foundation legends, for the latter also represented the memory of foundation. Furthermore, although foundation charters and legends possessed their own distinct commemorative vocabularies, both proposed a reading of foundation's significance defined by the same central ambiguity. A monastery was an institution that existed in the world, and whose relationship with the larger community of humans (as well as its internal constitution) had to be negotiated. In medieval terms, though, a monastery was also a community populated by humans who lived like angels in a physical space that recuperated the earthly Paradise and presaged the heavenly Jerusalem.[7] The monastery was thus different from human topography, yet part of it. The origins of such a community had to make manifest its sacred nature while at the same time guaranteeing its position in the web of terrestrial relations (indeed, this guarantee was often the monastery's status as sacred space). Hence, all texts, legendary or not, that narrated these origins constructed them along these lines.

The foundation charters typically related the process of foundation by distilling it into these elements. As we have seen, the date usually assigned to foundation charters was either that of the abbey church's consecration as sacred space or that of the first or last of the foundation donations establishing it as an earthly institution. These temporal points could become the explicit theme of the charter, as they do in that relating to yet another of Raymond Pons III's foundations: Saint-Pons-de-Thomières. According to this text (ca. 937), Raymond and his wife Garsindis gave one of their estates to God, the Virgin, and Saint Pons with the express purpose of founding a Benedictine abbey. After mentioning briefly the importation of monks from Aurillac and the election of the abbot, the charter describes in detail the abbey's privileges as a community that enjoyed papal protection, and the establishment and sanctification of its property boundaries by the bishops present at the church's consecration (and a subsequent council). Then, invoking Psalm 82 and the wrath of God which would fall upon those who

---

[6] According to the register of acts pertinent to Maillezais compiled by L. Delhommeau, *Notes et documents pour servir à l'histoire de l'abbaye de Saint-Pierre de Maillezais* (Paris, 1961), this privilege is extant only as it is presented in Peter of Maillaezais, *Qualiter fuit constructum Malliacense.*

[7] See Farmer's formulation, *Communities of Saint Martin*, p. 185.

dared to disturb the *sanctuarium Dei*, the charter declares in no uncertain terms that the abbey was sacred and inviolable.[8]

In no aspect other than its eloquence does this text distinguish itself from other foundation charters. Such charters typically related the endowment of the abbey with privileges and property, and concluded with thunderous clauses of anathema hedging the abbey with the sanctions of the divine. The organizing and overlapping themes that articulate foundation became the regulation of the abbey's position in human society with respect to property, rights, and privileges, and the demonstration that the monastery was sacred space, established by the ritual of consecration and protected by God and the relics of patron saints. In their foundation charters, then, monastic communities remembered selectively; the play of memory and "reality" marked the nonlegendary as well as the legendary representation of foundation.

But beneath the charters' commemorative depiction and temporal compression of foundation lay the iceberg of a process that could well embrace several generations of one family, and shifting configurations of religious and lay people, princes, and prelates. This process was part of the historical context in which foundation legends were produced, part of the reality by which these imaginative images of origins were shaped and which they helped to shape. Hence, focusing particularly but not exclusively on those moments which structure the textual commemoration of foundation, I shall explore the actual process by which historical actors established a monastery. My discussion includes the late eighth and ninth as well as the tenth through the thirteenth centuries, since the legends often look back to the Carolingian period, sometimes because the monastery was founded then, sometimes for less obvious and more intriguing reasons. Furthermore, between the early Carolingian era and the late tenth century, changes specific to the south—in particular, certain shifts in balance between the role of the king and that of the aristocracy in foundation—occurred that influence how we can read the legends.

Implicit and primary in foundation was an impulse on the part of one or several persons to create a religious community. The desire to found a monastery might arise among individuals who wished to embrace the religious life and who would later form the core of the monastic community. Or a person not intending to become a monk or nun might decide to establish a monastery.[9] Whether the community was self-constituting or cre-

---

[8] *HL* 5:176–179, no. 69.

[9] See Emile Lesne's distinction of these two types in his discussion of Merovingian foundations: *Histoire de la propriété ecclésiastique en France*, 6 vols. (Paris, 1910–1945), 1:79–80, 112. Other historians categorize foundations as either lay or ecclesiastical; see, for example, J. Dereine's comments on Jean-François Lemarignier, "Aspects politiques des fondations de

ated, the factors prompting the choice of a site were most often left unexplained in the documents describing foundation.[10] Sometimes, in laudatory passages laden with rhetorical flourishes, monastic chroniclers praised either the natural lushness of the site or its barreness and desolation. The one—the *locus amoenus*—was as much a topos as the other—the *eremum*. These reveal more about monastic ideals than about the founders' selection of a site, although isolated and less accessible locations were perhaps more popular among founders of an ascetic bent who intended themselves to live religiously.

This latter type of founder included individuals seeking solitude in which to live as hermits. Intentionally or not, they might attract disciples who would settle nearby and adopt a similar life-style. Equally, a charismatic person, lay or religious, accompanied by a group of followers, might choose a site (or sites) upon which to settle and form a religious community. Such was the case for Benedict of Aniane and his coterie of Anianus, Nibridius, and Attilo. They came to Septimania in the late eighth century and founded a cluster of monasteries: Aniane, Lagrasse, Caunes-en-Minervois, Saint-Hilaire, and Montolieu.[11] So, too, sometime in the 840s (before 854 in any case), a group of priests, deacons, and monks, whose leader was a certain Protasius, retreated to Eixalada on the River Tet and bought a site on which to build a monastery for themselves. After a disastrous flood in the 870s, the members of this community moved to a more protected site nearby at Cuxa. There they transformed the church of Saint-Germain, founded by Protasius on land that was his own, into the monastery that would later be famous as Saint-Michel-de-Cuxa.[12]

Some three centuries later (ca. 1078), a certain Gerald fled from the abbey of Saint-Vincent of Laon and his oppressive duties as abbot of its recalcitrant monks. He and a group of like-minded men (who were knights

---

collégiales dans le royaume de France au XIe siècle," in *La vita comune del clero nei secoli XI e XII*, Miscellanea del Centro di Studi Medioevali, 3.1 (Milan, 1962), p. 47. The utility of this latter kind of categorization is highly questionable, for it ignores those many instances in which lay aristocrats *and* prelates participated in foundation (e.g., the tenth-century foundation of Saint-Michel of Gaillac: *HL* 5:269–270, no. 223).

[10] On some geographical factors determining the choice of a site, see Romain Plané, "Géographie et monachisme: Sites et importance géographique de quelques abbayes de la région de l'Aude," in *Mélanges Albert Dufourcq: Etudes d'histoire religieuse* (Paris, 1932), pp. 21–35.

[11] On these foundations see Theodulf, *Carmina* 30, ll. 67–70, in *MGH Poetae Latini Aevi Carolini*, 1:522; E. Griffe, *Histoire religieuse des anciens pays de l'Aude* (Paris, 1933); Wilhelm Pückert, *Aniane und Gellone: Diplomatisch-kritische Untersuchungen zur Geschichte der Reformen des Benedictinerordens im IX. und X. Jahrhundert* (Leipzig, 1899), pp. 209–210.

[12] On Eixalada-Cuxa's foundation, see the privilege of Charles the Bald in *Catalunya carolíngia*, ed. Ramon d'Abadal y de Vinyals, 3 vols. (Barcelona, 1926–1955), 2.1:88–90; and a late ninth-century charter edited by Ramon d'Abadal in his "Com neix i com creix un gran monestir pirinec abans de l'an mil: Eixalada-Cuixa," *Analecta Montserratensia* 8 (1954/55): 278–280.

not clerics) arrived in Aquitaine. There the group acquired land from Duke William VIII (Guy-Geoffrey) and a certain Autgerius of Rions and settled as the community that would become the abbey of La Sauve-Majeure.[13] The same dynamic was at work in the constitution of the monastic community of La Trinité du Tor in the marshy wastes of the Camargue (1161–1175).[14] Such communities could exist for some time as an agglomeration of individuals without becoming a monastery. Necessary for the transition was the adoption of a rule, the formal monastic *disciplina,* which from 816/817 on was normally the Benedictine Rule.[15]

Two changes in the nature of these self-constituting communities bespeak the increasing importance of the aristocracy in foundation.[16] In the eighth and ninth centuries, groups seeking the religious life—for example, Benedict of Aniane and his companions—settled on land that belonged to one of the members, or that they bought, or that was fiscal. By the eleventh century, however, such incipient communities overtly petitioned land for their foundation from the local aristocracy, lay or ecclesiastical, as did Gerald of La Sauve-Majeure. This change is suggestive of the effective disappearance of the king from the south and the increasing power of the aristocratic lineages.[17] The composition of these self-constituting communities varied over time as well. It seems that in the earlier period such (male) groups were composed typically of men already belonging to the clergy, whether secular or regular. In the eleventh and twelfth centuries, the original members of the community seem at least as often (if not more often) to have been converts from the secular life. This development (hardly unique to southern France) reveals how the secular aristocracy was increasingly incorporated into monastic life in a different and more intimate fashion.[18]

Certainly not all foundations in which the aristocracy was active in this later period involved conversion. Aristocrats, then as earlier, were agents in

[13] See the charters edited in *AASSosB* 6.2:867–869.

[14] *Bullaire de l'abbaye de Saint-Gilles,* ed. Abbé Goiffon (Nîmes, 1882), pp. 87–88 (here 87) no. 65.

[15] See the decision to adopt the Rule by the group of men who had been living communally at La Trinité du Tor: *Bullaire de l'abbaye de Saint-Gilles,* pp. 87–88, no. 65.

[16] Given the limited number of sources under consideration here, my discussion can hardly be regarded as conclusive.

[17] See above, Introduction at nn. 42–45.

[18] These types of foundations relate to the general shift from oblates to adult converts, a development institutionalized by the Cistercians. For an example of a southern French Cistercian foundation involving such conversion, see that of Silvanès (ca. 1136) in *Cartulaire de Silvanès,* ed. P.-A. Verlaguet, Archives Historiques de Rouergue, 1 (Rodez, 1910), pp. 371–390. On aristocratic conversions in general, see Herbert Grundmann, "Adelsbekehrungen im Hochmittelalter: *Conversi* und *nutriti* im Kloster," in *Adel und Kirche: Gerd Tellenbach zum 65. Geburtstag dargebracht von Freunden und Schülern,* ed. Josef Fleckenstein and Karl Schmid (Freiburg, 1968), pp. 325–345; and Joachim Wollasch, "Parenté noble et monachisme réformateur: Observations sur les 'conversions' à la vie monastique aux XIe et XIIe siècles," *Revue Historique* 264 (1980): 3–24.

the second general type of foundation: a person not intending to embrace the monastic life him- or herself decided to found (or restore) a monastery.[19] Such founders in the eighth and ninth centuries were typically the king, a member of the secular aristocracy, a bishop, or an abbot.[20] By the tenth century in the south the king had disappeared from this constellation.[21] From this point on, the impulse to found a monastery typically came from an aristocratic family, often in tandem with the abbot of a nearby monastery (or, less often, a bishop) who might be a member of the same family.[22]

This change in the social identity of founders is yet another indication of the gradual retreat of the king from southern France. It also illustrates a phenomenon familiar to historians of this period: the devolution of power from king to count (or duke) to the lesser nobility.[23] By establishing or reforming a monastery, aristocrats were in certain ways claiming regalian privileges and powers.[24] Furthermore, given that such privileges were grounded in a grant of authority from God, lay aristocrats could find in their association with monasteries a source of sacrality that legitimized and further elevated their own power.[25] Perhaps Raymond Pons III's foundation charter for Saint-Pons-de-Thomières should be read in this fashion.[26] Raymond not only proclaimed a nominal and affinitive identity between himself and the patron saint but also styled himself *primarchio et dux Aquitanorum* ("*primarchio* and duke of the Aquitainians")—a princely title that he seems to have used only in documents pertaining to monasteries he founded.[27]

---

[19] These foundations were often refoundations or restorations of the abbey in question. See Lauranson-Rosaz, *L'Auvergne*, pp. 228–229. The situation was similar in Burgundy: Constance Brittain Bouchard, *Sword, Miter, and Cloister: Nobility and the Church in Burgundy, 980–1198* (Ithaca, N.Y., 1987), pp. 92–93, 102–103.

[20] See the types of foundations in the Narbonnais listed by Magnou-Nortier, *La société laïque*, pp. 102–106.

[21] Cf. above, Introduction at nn. 42–45.

[22] On this type of foundation in the Auvergne, see Lauranson-Rosaz, *L'Auvergne*, pp. 229–230.

[23] The clearest statement of the devolution of power is the work of Jean-François Lemarignier. See, for example, his "La dislocation du 'pagus' et le problème des 'consuetudines' (x–xie siècles)," in *Mélanges d'histoire du Moyen Age dédiés à la mémoire de Louis Halphen*, ed. Charles-Edmond Perrin (Paris, 1951), pp. 401–410. But see the general reevaluation of this theory in Geoffrey Koziol, *Begging Pardon and Favor: Ritual and Political Order in Early Medieval France* (Ithaca, N.Y., 1992).

[24] Koziol, *Begging Pardon*, pp. 90–93. For other discussions of links between extension of aristocratic power and foundation, see Lemarignier, "Aspects politiques," pp. 19–40; and Penelope Johnson, *Prayer, Patronage, and Power: The Abbey of La Trinité, Vendôme* (New York, 1981), pp. 13–14, 16.

[25] Koziol, *Begging Pardon*, pp. 90–93.

[26] *HL* 5:176–179, no. 69.

[27] *Primarchio* has no equivalent in English; it is a superlative form of *marchio* (margrave). On Raymond's selective use of the title, see Auzias, *L'Aquitaine*, pp. 486–487. Karl Brunner accepts as authentic the texts in which the title appears; see his "Die fränkischen Fürstentitel im neunten und zehnten Jahrhundert," in Herwig Wolfram et al., *Intitulatio*, II: *Lateinische*

An intriguing statement in one version (ca. 1154) of the chronicle of the abbey of Alaó makes another sort of link between foundation and the amplification of aristocratic power. The text describes first how the childless Guifred, count of Ribagorça (964–ca. 979) and his wife Sancia were buried at Alaó. It then declares that "from the time of Louis, son of Charles, it was the custom of kings and counts that each one build a monastery in which he would be buried after death."[28] Here the motivation for foundation is the creation of a tomb, certainly a memorial, for the founder.

Interestingly, however, the most conclusive evidence for such memorial foundations in the south comes from the region under the control of the count-kings of Barcelona. For example, it does not seem that the dukes of Gascony were buried at Saint-Sever, a monastery they founded.[29] Only some of the dukes of Aquitaine (William V, William VI, and Eudes) were buried at Maillezais, founded by Duchess Emma and her son William V—and Emma herself was not interred there.[30] Nor did the counts of Toulouse/Saint-Gilles have a consistent burial practice. Four eleventh-century members of this family are buried in early Christian sarcophagi in an *enfeu* near the door of the south transept of Saint-Sernin of Toulouse; Raymond IV of Saint-Gilles received a privilege from Urban II permitting him to establish a family burial ground at La Daurade.[31] Although the history of the origins of both these churches remains rather obscure, neither was a comital foundation.[32] The southern families thus seem not to have had burial policies associating them exclusively with monasteries they had founded. These abbeys did not necessarily guard the physical remains of their noble founders' families, nor, as we shall see, did they celebrate their memory textually.[33]

But even if southern aristocrats of this period did not establish these monasteries in order to provide for their bodies after death, evident in their foundations could be a concern for the future health of the soul. Charters of foundation typically described how the founders wished the monks to pray

---

Herrscher- und Fürstentitel im neunten und zehnten Jahrhundert, MIÖG suppl. 24 (Graz, 1973), pp. 233–234. Cf. Koziol's remarks about the conjunction of supplication (recognition of the divine basis of princely authority) and the use of a prince's title as lay abbot: *Begging Pardon*, pp. 38–39.

[28] *Chronica d'Alaó renovada*, in *Catalyuna carolíngia*, 3.1:22.

[29] Robert-André Sénac commenting on Charles Higounet and Jean-Bernard Marquette, "Les origines de l'abbaye de Saint-Sever: Révision critique," in *Saint-Sever: Millénaire de l'abbaye. Colloque international 25, 26 et 27 mai 1985* (Mont-de-Marsan, 1986), pp. 35–37.

[30] On Emma and William V: Peter of Maillezais, *Qualiter fuit constructum Malliacense* (*PL* 146:1258, 1271). On William VI and Eudes and on other burial sites used by this family, see Michel Dillange, *Eglises et abbayes romanes en Vendée* (Marseille, 1983), pp. 115–116, 123.

[31] Marcel Durliat, *Saint-Sernin de Toulouse* (Toulouse, 1986), pp. 77–79.

[32] Magnou-Nortier, *La société laïque*, p. 91, n. 67.

[33] See below, Chapters 3–5. This lack of family necropolises is not necessarily surprising. Georges Duby (looking at northern French lineages) points out that it is not until after 1100 that the practice emerges: "Le lignage: Xe–XIIIe siècle," in *Les lieux de mémoire*, ed. Pierre Nora, 3 vols. to date (Paris, 1984–), 1:46–47.

for them, and thus obtain forgiveness for their sins and for those of their family. Furthermore, beginning in the late tenth century, foundations often accompanied or were the fruit of aristocratic penitential pilgrimages.[34] By the eleventh century, aristocratic foundations might also incarnate devotion to the Holy Land. The founder of Villeneuve of Aveyron (ca. 1053) specified and emphasized that the monastery be built on the plan of the Holy Sepulcher.[35] The passion roused by crusade might also express itself in the form of foundation; circa 1098, Bishop Isarn of Toulouse persuaded a certain noblewoman, Emerias of *Alteias,* "who had raised (*levaverat*) a cross on to her right shoulder to go to Jerusalem," to establish a monastery instead.[36] The result was the refoundation of Saint-Orens, some ten kilometers southeast of Toulouse. Pious and penitential impulses could thus motivate aristocratic founders.

Whatever their motivations, founders not only had to provide the site, and to build or rebuild the abbey church and claustral buildings, but also to supply the monastery's inhabitants. Often founders would import monks from another monastery, most particularly from one whose abbot participated in the foundation. Aurillac provided monks for newly reformed Saint-Chaffre and the new comital foundation of Saint-Pons de Thomières (937), and Saint-Chaffre in turn sent monks to the refounded Sainte-Enimie (951); in approximately 1129 Gellone provided monks for Saint-Pierre of Sauve.[37] In many such instances, this kind of peopling of the monastery implied ties of dependency; the new foundation might join the ranks of the priories of the abbey providing the monks.[38]

The community, however, was not yet formally a monastery. Several more stages of foundation had to occur, some of which are nicely articulated by a late twelfth-century chronicle from Saint-Martin-du-Canigou. Describing

[34] See Lauranson-Rosaz, *L'Auvergne,* p. 291. Also see the penitential foundation (although not associated with pilgrimage) of Sainte-Foy of Morlaas in 1083 by Centullus, viscount of Béarn: *GC* 1, instr. 161.

[35] The foundation charter is edited by Jacques Bousquet, in his "La fondation de Villeneuve d'Aveyron (1053) et l'expansion de l'abbaye de Moissac en Rouergue," in *Moissac et l'Occident au XIe siècle: Actes du colloque international de Moissac, 3–5 mai 1963* (Toulouse, 1964), pp. 195–215.

[36] *HL* 5:756–758, no. 401.

[37] Saint-Chaffre: *Cartulaire de l'abbaye de St-Chaffre du Monastier, suivi de la Chronique de St-Pierre-du-Puy,* ed. Ulysse Chevalier (Paris, 1884), pp. 47–49, no. 53. Saint-Pons: *HL* 5:176–179, no. 69. Sainte-Enimie: *Cartulaire de l'abbaye de St-Chaffre,* pp. 127–130, no. 375 (also *HL* 5:211–213, no. 91). Sauve: *Cartulaires des abbayes d'Aniane et de Gellone publiés d'après les manuscrits originaux,* ed. A. Cassan and E. Meynial, 2 vols. (Montpellier, 1898–1900), 1:311–320, nos. 381–384. Acquiring monks for a new foundation could be problematic, as Gerald of Aurillac's difficulties in creating a community for his abbey show: Odo of Cluny, *De vita sancti Geraldi Auriliacensis comitis* (*PL* 133:674).

[38] For evidence of the establishment of priories in this way in the eleventh-century Ile-de-France, see Lemarignier, "Aspects politiques." In fact, an abbot might refuse to participate in the foundation and to send monks unless he were granted *potestas* over the new foundation; see the case of Sainte-Enimie (*HL* 5:211–213, no. 91).

the community's origins, this chronicle states: "in 1001, Count Guifred began to build the monastery of Saint-Martin-du-Canigou. In 1014, Selva, a monk of Saint-Michel-de-Cuxa, was elected as the first abbot. In the same year relics of the confessor Saint Gauderic were brought from the region of Toulouse. In 1026, the abbey church was consecrated."[39] Election of an abbot (whether chosen from inside the community or outside its ranks), the construction of a church and claustral buildings, the endowment of the community with property and relics, the consecration of the church—these completed foundation. While often skimming over or omitting the first two elements, foundation charters tended to highlight the latter two, thus underlining their importance in the constitution of the monastery's identity.[40] Endowment and consecration did not always seem to follow a fixed order, and frequently the texts present them as simultaneous. Given, however, that the ritual of consecration was predicated upon endowment with both material property and spiritual patrons, I shall begin with these latter elements.

According to the widely used pontifical (dubbed by its editors the "Romano-Germanic Pontifical"), which circulated in various versions from the tenth century on, no church was to be built, never mind consecrated, until the founder had established sources of sustenance for the church and its priest, and had settled the matter of the general endowment.[41] A monastery needed land—not only the site on which it was built, but properties that would provide the revenues (whether in kind or in cash) necessary to sustain the community. The majority of Carolingian foundations in the south, at least those in the Narbonnais, benefited from royal grants of fiscal land as well as from private donations.[42] As we have seen, from the tenth century on, foundation endowments by kings vanished from the south, leaving noble families and prelates to provide property for the new monastery.[43] Whatever the identity of the donors, foundation charters typically contain detailed inventories of the properties granted to the new community. These lands established the abbey as a physical entity and also delineated it from other communities, a concern reflected in the charters' evident attention to estates' exact boundaries.[44]

But an abbey's identity was not merely its estates; the charters often include precise lists of other elements of the foundation endowment. These

---

[39] *HL* 5:54–55.

[40] In certain charters, though, the election of the abbot was critical. See the charter for La Trinité du Tor (*Bullaire de l'abbaye de Saint-Gilles*, p. 88, no. 65); and that for Sant Feliu and Sant Martí de Ciutat (*Actes de consagracions*, pp. 98–99, no. 34).

[41] *Pontifical romano-germanique du dixième siècle*, ed. Cyrille Vogel and Reinhard Elze, 3 vols., Studi e Testi, 226, 227, 269 (Vatican, 1963–1972), 1:122–123, no. 36.

[42] Magnou-Nortier, *La société laïque*, p. 93.

[43] Much noble land in this period, of course, was land that had been fiscal.

[44] This concern was not unique to charters of foundation but appears in many other types of charters.

objects—candelabra, *coronae*, vestments, altar cloths, chalices, patens, pyxes, and so forth—express the monastery's nature as a religious institution. Furthermore, despite Benedict of Aniane's apparent protests and those most celebrated ones of Bernard of Clairvaux, such objects were traditionally fashioned from precious metals and stones.[45] As the disapproval of Benedict and Bernard indicates, in addition to a distinctly religious meaning, these materials possessed secular value, proclaiming wealth and power. Hence liturgical objects could be public statements of the abbey's status in the human world. They also reflected upon the founders; the same nobles or kings or bishops who had granted the land for the foundation might bestow upon the monastery liturgical vessels, books, and vestments in intentional displays of equal munificence.[46]

These donations were necessary for the liturgical life of the religious community, but they did not constitute the monastery as sacred space. The acquisition of more ambiguous and sacrally charged objects, saints' relics, began this process. Socially necessary, attracting pilgrims and donations, relics formed such an integral part of a monastic community's identity that no foundation was effectively complete without them—any more than it was without estates.[47] Indeed, the exhaustive lists of relics typical of foundation charters represent a counterpart to the equally but differently detailed inventories of the estates representing the foundation endowment.[48] For example, in an anonymous eleventh-century text describing Lavoûte-Chilhac's foundation, lists of relics and of property balance each other almost exactly in length and detail.[49] The correlation is not coincidental. Relics and property had analogous significance. Relics established the monastery as a sacred

[45] Ardo, *Vita Benedicti abbatis Anianensis et Indensis* (*MGH SS* 15.1:204); Bernard of Clairvaux, *Apologia*, in *S. Bernardi Opera*, ed. Jean Leclercq and Henri M. Rochais, 8 vols. (Rome, 1957–1977), 3:53–108.

[46] For examples, see *Actes de consagracions*, pp. 75–76, 84–85, 91–101, 124–129, 154–158, nos. 16, 24, 30–35, 51, 71. Alternatively, if the foundation was only a priory, the mother abbey might furnish these necessities. Thus Gellone for Sauve: *Cartulaires des abbayes d'Aniane et de Gellone*, 1:311–320, nos. 381–384.

[47] On relics and their necessity according to canon law, see Nicole Hermann-Mascard, *Les reliques des saints: Formation coutumière d'un droit* (Paris, 1975), pp. 166–167. On the relation between patron saints and their monastic communities from the late tenth through the twelfth century, see most recently Farmer, *Communities of Saint Martin;* and Thomas Head, *Hagiography and the Cult of Saints: The Diocese of Orléans, 800–1200* (Cambridge, 1990). For an exhaustive bibliography on relics and saints' cults, see *Saints and Their Cults: Studies in Religious Sociology, Folklore and History*, ed. Stephen Wilson (Cambridge, 1983).

[48] See, for example, the lists of relics in the consecration charters for Sainte-Marie de Roudeille (1119), in *Cartulaire de l'abbaye de Lézat*, ed. Paul Ourliac and Anne-Marie Magnou, 2 vols. (Paris, 1984–1987), 1:29–30, no. 38; and that for Cassan (1115), in *HL* 5:850–851, no. 455.

[49] "Histoire anonyme de la fondation du prieuré de Lavoûte-Chilhac par Odilon, abbé de Cluny," ed. Pierre-François Fournier, in *Bulletin Philologique et Historique (jusqu'à 1715) du Comité des Travaux Historiques et Scientifiques, 1958* (1959): 108–115.

community, and estates gave it a physical existence. Relics situated the community in relation to other monastic communities that possessed the same or different saintly patrons, just as the estates situated the abbey in relation to other human groups. Furthermore, the two could coincide in meaning: property was not only secular, nor were relics only sacred. The community's property was its patron's possession as well, and as such could take on sacred significance, while relics could function in secular disputes over property and other "worldly" matters.[50]

Foundation documents do not always specify the provenance of relics. Sometimes the monastery was founded, as it were, on relics; it was built over the tomb of a holy man or woman who might or might not have been one of the founders of the community. If a saint's body was not already present, it was necessary to obtain one, or at least part of one. Foundations and refoundations thus often occasioned the discovery of relics hidden somewhere in the fabric of the church or translations of relics from elsewhere.[51] Equally, founders might complement their donations of lands and liturgical objects with gifts of relics; with what appears to have been great diligence and diplomacy, Odilo of Cluny amassed relics from Agaune, Auxerre, Saint-Denis, Sens, and Trier for his foundation (ca. 1024/25) of Lavoûte-Chilhac.[52]

Such donations might have a commemorative function; according to the anonymous monk who wrote of Lavoûte-Chilhac's foundation, Empress Cunegunde sent to the new community a fragment of the True Cross "for her remembrance and that of her lord husband" (*ob sui memoriam et sui senioris*).[53] The implication is perhaps liturgical: that she and Henry should be remembered in the monks' prayers. Nonetheless, here the relic of the Cross appears as a locus for memory, hardly surprising since a relic could be called a *memoria,* as could a saint's shrine or an altar dedicated to a saint.[54]

This commemorative quality, we shall see, suffused the ritual during which the relics were incorporated into the fabric of the monastery: the consecration of the abbey church (or at least its main altar if the construction was still under way).[55] This ritual represented a central moment, if not

---

[50] On the special significance of property, see Barbara Rosenwein, *To Be the Neighbor of Saint Peter: The Social Meaning of Cluny's Property, 909–1049* (Ithaca, N.Y., 1989). On relics functioning in secular disputes, see Patrick Geary, "Humiliation of Saints," in *Saints and Their Cults,* pp. 123–140.

[51] For a general discussion of translations, see Martin Heinzelmann, *Translationsberichte und andere Quellen des Reliquienkultes* (Turnhout, 1979).

[52] "Histoire anonyme," pp. 108–110. Cf. Odo of Cluny's statement that Gerald provided for Aurillac all that was necessary: relics, liturgical vessels and vestments, and income from estates (*De vita sancti Geraldi; PL* 133:690).

[53] "Histoire anonyme," p. 108.

[54] "Memoria," in J. F. Niermeyer, *Mediae Latinitatis lexicon minus* (Leiden, 1984), p. 669.

[55] By the eighth century the originally separate rites of the relics' deposition and the altar's dedication had blended together to create the ritual of the church's consecration. See

the culmination, of the process of foundation. Remember that foundation charters often took as their date the year of the abbey church's consecration; so frequent was this practice that it has been recently proposed that such texts be called "consecration charters" instead.[56] Indeed, in some texts, consecration is literally defined as the "beginning" of the monastery. The anonymous author who narrated the foundation of Lavoûte-Chilhac stated that he wished to write an account "from that very beginning of the monastery's inception and consecration" (*ab ipso initio incoeptionis vel consecrationis monasterii*).[57]

This ritual "beginning" of the monastery announced the community's status as a sanctified space fortified with human and celestial patronage—announced quite literally, for this ritual was a public event, a festive occasion, a social event.[58] The founders themselves and the officiating clerics came; quite often, too, various local *potentes* as well as the crowd of the *populus* attended. They assisted as witnesses at a ritual that not only defined the abbey's special nature but also marked, and might already commemorate, its origins. Because of the centrality of consecration for foundation in all these ways, I shall follow in some detail this ritual as it would have been conducted between the tenth and the thirteenth centuries in the south.[59]

Suitbert Benz, "Zur Geschichte der römischen Kirchweihe nach den Texten des 6. bis 7. Jahrhunderts," in *Enkainia: Gesammelte Arbeiten zum 800 jährigen Weihegedächtnis der Abteikirche Maria Laach am 24. August 1956*, ed. Hilarius Emonds (Düsseldorf, 1956), pp. 62–109.

[56] For this suggestion see *Actes de consagracions*.

[57] "Histoire anonyme," p. 106. Equally striking are certain consecration charters which repeat the Ten Commandments and the opening verses of each Gospel (*initium sancti evangelii secundum . . .*), thus framing the consecration with the foundations or cornerstones of the Christian faith from both Testaments: *Actes de consagracions*, pp. 123–124, 141, 143–144, 150, 179, 187, 190–191, 194, nos. 49, 50, 56, 59, 65, 83–84, 89, 94, 97. For another example, see the relic list in the reliquary of Saint Germier recording the consecration (1156) of Saint-Germier at Muret (near Toulouse), edited by C. Douais in his "Saint Germier, évêque de Toulouse au VIe siècle: Examen critique de la vie," *Mémoires de la Société Nationale des Antiquaires de France* 50 (1889): 101.

[58] Here I paraphrase the editor's remarks in *Actes de consagracions*, pp. 16–17.

[59] Unless otherwise noted, the sources I use here are the following: the tenth-century *Pontifical romano-germanique*, 1:124–173, no. 40; Guillaume Durand of Mende's thirteenth-century *Pontifical*, in *Le pontifical romain au Moyen-Age*, ed. Michel Andrieu, 3 vols., Studi e Testi, 86–88 (Vatican, 1938–1940), 3:455–478; and a sermon (ca. 1028) of Ademar de Chabannes, Paris, BN Latin 2469, ff. 94r–95r (this sermon has been partially edited in Charles de Lasteyrie, *L'abbaye de Saint-Martial de Limoges . . .* [Paris, 1901], pp. 422–426). The ceremony described in the *Pontifical romano-germanique* is representative of the ritual as it would have been performed in this period; not only did this pontifical enjoy wide contemporaneous diffusion, but it was also the basis for later pontificals. Furthermore, at least one of the abbeys used a version of this pontifical's consecration ritual. Inserted into an eleventh-century liturgical manuscript from Lagrasse was a quire written in a twelfth-century hand containing an *Ordo ad consecrandam ecclesiam* very similar to the published text of the *Pontifical romano-germanique*: Paris, BN Latin 933, ff. 155r–162v. For other examples of consecration rituals, see Edmond Martène, *De antiquis ecclesiae ritibus libri tres . . . editio novissima* (Venice, 1783), 2.13, pp. 240–283. On the manuscripts Martène used, see Aimé-Georges Martimort, *La documentation liturgique de Dom Edmond Martène: Etude codicologique*, Studi e Testi,

The ceremony was inaugurated by a period of purificatory fasting for the local clergy, the populace, and the presiding bishop. Then, on the eve of the dedication, the bishop would proceed to the new church. There he would enshrine the relics to be enclosed in the altar(s) in an appropriate container. In a tent pitched near the church, he and his clerics would perform vigils before the relics. The next morning the bishop would clear the church of everyone save his deacon, whom he would then shut inside the church. The enclosed deacon would light twelve candles disposed about the church.

Outside, meanwhile, the bishop and his other clerics would circumambulate the church, sprinkling it with holy water. Each time the procession came to the closed doors, the bishop would rap upon them with his staff, the symbol of his authority, intoning: "Princes, raise up your gates and, gates of glory, be lifted up." From the other side of the door the deacon would respond, "Who is·that king of glory?" and the bishop would answer, "The steadfast Lord, the Lord powerful in battle" (Psalm 23.7–10).[60] At the end of the third sequence, the deacon would open the doors to the bishop, who entered with a final verse from Psalm 23: "Peace to this house." After a prayer at the altar, the bishop would inscribe two alphabets with his staff along the diagonals (previously scattered with ashes) of the church floor, thus forming a cross.[61]

Next the bishop would proceed to a preliminary blessing of the altar, making one cross upon its surface in the center and four in its corners with a mixture of salt, water, and ashes. Then he would circumambulate the altar seven times, sprinkling it with an infusion of the herb typically used in exorcism: hyssop. Using the same liquid, he would exorcise the body of the church, walking around the walls three times, and would then create yet another cross by walking from one long wall to the other and from one short to the other. Returning to the main altar, he would mix a cement with prepared materials and pour out the remaining holy water at the base of the altar. With incense and holy oil he would once again make the five crosses on the altar. Meanwhile the verses from Genesis 28.18 recounting the anointing of a biblical type of the Christian altar, the stone at Bethel, were sung. Reiterating Jacob's actions, the bishop would then spread oil on the altar's surface. With chrism, he next marked twelve crosses on the church walls. After yet another anointing of the altar, the bishop would bless the vestments, ornaments, and sacred vessels.

Exiting the church and making a cross with chrism on the threshold, the bishop would retrieve the relics from the pavilion. In a solemn procession of

---

279 (Vatican, 1978).

[60] On the Byzantine origins of this part of the ceremony and its development into dialogue form, see Benz, "Kirchweihe," pp. 96, 102–103.

[61] On the origins of this ritual, see Herbert Thurston, "The Alphabet and the Consecration of Churches," *The Month* 115 (1910): 621–631; and Benz, "Kirchweihe," pp. 97–98.

clerics bearing cross, thuribles, and candles (*lumina*), the bishop carrying the relics would circumambulate the church once again. He and the crowd of attendant clergy would stop before the doors. In this liminal space, the bishop would then turn to the people and proclaim the identity of the church as such, materially and spiritually. Among the things he was to mention were the tithes and offerings to the church, the anniversary of its dedication, and the name of the saints in whose honor it was dedicated or who were enshrined there. Finally, he would admonish the "lord (*dominus*) and builder of this church . . . about its endowment and what type of honor and care he ought to show for the church and its priest." This lord (presumably the founder) was to respond that he would act accordingly.[62]

Only after thus publicly regulating the interaction of the church with its earthly patrons would the bishop proceed inside to enshrine the celestial patrons in the altar(s). He would approach the main altar, veil it, and then place inside it the relics as well as chrism, three pieces of the host, and three grains of incense. After having anointed the underside of the altar's top slab (*tabula*), he would set it in place and seal the edges with the mortar prepared earlier. The incorporation of the saints into the church fabric seems in some senses to be the climax of the ceremony, the moment of the greatest proximity of the sacred, so near that it had to be hidden from the eyes of all but the bishop. Indeed, in a ninth-century commentary upon the dedication ceremony (which was much borrowed from), it was at this moment that the apocalyptic imagery of the heavenly Jerusalem with which the whole text is impregnated becomes almost tangible.[63]

After again making the five crosses on the altar's surface with chrism, the bishop would retreat to the sacristy to change his vestments. When he reemerged, the church, previously lit only by the glimmer of twelve candles, would be filled with the light of many. The introitus would be sung and then he would celebrate mass. The festivities were prolonged for eight days during which public mass was performed in the church. Among these masses, at least one would be said for the founders (*conditores*).[64] Thus the material founders were admonished *and* commemorated in the ceremony as well as in the charter that might be drawn up on the occasion of the consecration.

This ritual had a complex set of symbolic meanings, one of which perhaps

---

[62] *Pontifical romano-germanique*, 1:169 (cf. Paris, BN Latin 933, f. 159v). The use of the word *dominus*, which in this era implied lordship and domination, is interesting. For other examples of admonishments concerning endowment at consecration, see Martène, *De ritibus* 2.13, p. 244.

[63] *Pontifical romano-germanique*, 1:90–121, here 117–120. This text is reproduced also by Martène, *De ritibus* 2.13, pp. 276–282. In manuscripts this text is usually found together with the pontifical. On its date and author, see Benz, "Kirchweihe," pp. 104–105; and Martimort, *La documentation liturgique*, pp. 398–399, no. 804.

[64] "In dedicatione novae ecclesiae ad missam pro conditoribus," *Pontifical romano-germanique*, 1:176–177.

is paramount.[65] The essence of consecration was the separation and delineation of sacred space from undifferentiated secular space. The many crosses inscribed in various ways by the bishop's motions made the church into Christ's body.[66] Furthermore, the repeated circumambulations demarcated this area from its profane surroundings and, like the twelve crosses upon the wall and the cross marked upon the threshold, enclosed the church protectively, warding off demons.[67]

The repeated exorcisms with hyssop and holy water mediated as well as effected this transformation from profane to sacred. The space had to be purged of demons if it was to become holy. As the more or less extended tropological parallels many medieval writers made between the consecration of the physical temple and the baptism of the spiritual temple (the individual Christian) show, the entire ritual of consecration was itself an exorcism. It expelled demons and protected the church against them.[68] Ademar of Chabannes even writes that the bishops who consecrate churches have as types the apostles who "purified" (*purificare*) the Gentiles with baptism, "cleansed" (*mundare*) them from their idolatry, and drove the demons from the believers in Christ.[69] The apotropaic qualities of this exorcism of space are proclaimed in one of the hymns for the anniversary of consecration: "here" [in the church] the demons must release their prey and flee.[70]

---

[65] For various contemporaneous reflections on the meaning of consecration (which tend toward the tropological), see for example the following: Peter Damian, *Sermo* 72; in *Sermones*, ed. J. Lucchesi, Corus Christianorum Continuatio Medievalis, 57 (Turnhout, 1983), pp. 420–430; Bruno of Segni, *De sacramentis ecclesiae . . . (PL* 165:1089–1136); ?Ivo of Chartres, *PL* 162:527–535 (cf. Benz, "Kirchweihe," pp. 105–106); Jacobus of Voragine, *Legenda aurea vulgo Historia Lombardica dicta*, ed. Th. Graesse (Warsaw, 1890), pp. 845–857; the apocryphal sermon attributed to Peter Damian (*PL* 144:897–902); and the *Sermones in dedicatione ecclesie* in a mid-eleventh-century manuscript from Moissac (Paris, BN Latin 3783.2, ff. 331va–332vb). Most of these betray the influence of the ninth-century text on dedication (see n. 63, above).

[66] See Ademar's interpretation of the alphabets written on the floor as a multivalent Christological symbol (Paris, BN Latin 2469, f. 94v); and de Lasteyrie, *L'abbaye*, p. 425.

[67] On circumambulations as delineation of sacred space and as protection against demons, see Geoffrey Koziol, "Monks, Feuds, and the Making of Peace in Eleventh-Century Flanders," in *The Peace of God: Social Violence and Religious Response in France around the Year 1000*, ed. Thomas Head and Richard Landes (Ithaca, N.Y., 1992), pp. 253–254.

[68] For consecration as baptism, see the texts cited in n. 65 above. Consecration's nature as exorcism also appears in the ninth-century author's glosses on the "Tollite portas principes" dialogue: *Pontifical romano-germanique*, 1:94, no. 35 (this passage is repeated almost verbatim in ?Ivo of Chartres, *Sermo* 4, *PL* 162:530). It is doubtless no accident that in the *Gospel of Nicodemus*, this same dialogue is used for the Harrowing of Hell. The demons literally lift the gates and Christ enters: *The Gospel of Nicodemus: Gesta Salvatoris*, ed. H. C. Kim (Toronto, 1973), pp. 40–41.

[69] Paris, BN Latin 2469, f. 94r–v; de Lasteyrie, *L'abbaye*, p. 423.

[70] "In dedicatione ecclesie," in *Thesauri hymnologici hymnarium: Die Hymnen des Thesaurus Hymnologicus H.A. Daniels . . .* , ed. Clemens Blume, Analecta Hymnica Medii Aevi, 51 (Leipzig, 1908), pp. 112–114, no. 103. According to Blume, this hymn appears in many tenth- and eleventh-century manuscripts, including one from Moissac.

The next verse of this hymn articulates yet another way in which consecration sacralized space—or, rather, how consecration revealed the monastery's nature as a representation of Paradise: "this place . . . is called . . . the snowy-white gate of heaven (*caeli porta*) which receives all those seeking the country of life." Indeed, the ritual of consecration insistently and repeatedly invoked the biblical type of Jacob's anointment of the stone at Bethel.[71] It thus implied that the church, like Bethel, was a place where the heavens open and meet the earth, the *porta caeli* of Genesis 28.17 recalled in the hymn. Furthermore, consecration was the moment of revelation not only of this *porta caeli*, but also of the church's nature as a prefiguration of the heavenly Jerusalem (a common trope by no means limited to interpretations of consecration). Consecration rendered the celestial city almost tangible. Elements of the ritual deliberately echo the Apocalypse. And among the prayers for the anniversary of consecration in an eleventh-century text from Lagrasse was one reading: "I saw the holy city of the new Jerusalem descending from the sky just like a bride splendidly adorned for her husband" (Apoc. 21.2).[72] In similar words, a hymn composed for the same liturgical occasion captured this vision of the heavenly city's descent.[73]

The revelation of the celestial Jerusalem and the establishment of a space where demons quaked before the power of God and his saints—these were the ways in which the abbey remembered its consecration. For the feast of the church's consecration was integrated into the monastery's liturgical year, into its memory. Not only was the feast of consecration celebrated annually, creating cyclical time through commemoration, but the ritual itself could be repeated and become a linear framework for the monastery's memory. Circa 1147 a monk composed a sober history of Ripoll, concluding his text with these words:

> moreover there were forty-seven years from the first dedication of this monastery to its second, from the second to the third forty-two, from the third to the fourth fifty-six, and from that one to the present year of the Incarnation of the Lord 1147 one hundred and sixteen. Indeed from the first dedication of this

[71] Not only would the bishop repeat Genesis 28.18 during one of the anointments of the altar, but according to the ninth-century commentary, when the bishop reemerged into the now brilliantly lit church, the cantor sang: "Terribilis est locus iste" (Genesis 28.17). *Pontifical romano-germanique*, 1:121. A mid-eleventh-century manuscript from Moissac stipulates the readings for dedication: Genesis 28.10–22 (as well as 3 Kings 7.48–8.9 and 2 Paralipomenon 5.11–6.16—the dedication of Solomon's temple). See Paris, BN Latin 3783.2, ff. 329vb–331va. On this manuscript, see Jean Dufour, *La bibliothèque et le scriptorium de Moissac* (Paris, 1972).

[72] Paris, BN Latin 933, f. 87r. This prayer does not appear in the *Pontifical romano-germanique*.

[73] *Thesauri hymnologici hymnarium*, p. 110, no. 102 (cited and briefly discussed by Ernst H. Kantorowicz, *The King's Two Bodies: A Study in Medieval Political Theology* [Princeton, 1957], p. 83, n. 103). According to Blume, this hymn also appears in many tenth- and eleventh-century manuscripts, including one from Moissac.

place to this year of the Incarnation of the Lord there are two hundred and sixty one years.[74]

Although the author had not divided his text in this fashion, when he did reflect explicitly on time, the successive consecrations created the epochs. Each of these moments represented a temporal point from which he could count—and a refoundation, a new beginning for the abbey.

The very fabric of the abbey church might also participate in this commemoration. Inscriptions on the main altar or on a slab set into a wall would often record and memorialize the consecration and the names of those *potentes,* lay and ecclesiastical, who had been present.[75] Alternatively, inscriptions could be interpreted as memorials of consecration; Ademar of Chabannes reads incised crosses on the altar at Saint-Cybard of Angoulême as proof and result of its sixth-century consecration.[76] Here the miracle implicit in consecration impresses itself onto physical reality. In an opposite but equal movement, the consecration inscriptions fixed in stone the highly charged moment, renewed annually in liturgical celebrations, when the heavenly Jerusalem had descended to earth and the church had become sacred space.[77]

Continuously recalled within the monastery in these ways, the memory of consecration also had a public dimension. It might come to punctuate the monastery's relationship with its dependents: certain *census* were due the abbey of Aniane "on the feast of . . . [its] consecration."[78] Furthermore, the carved letters of the consecration inscriptions would be seen not only by the monks but by visitors. These inscriptions embody the public nature of the ritual itself: besides the consecration, they commemorated those representatives of the hierarchy of human authority who had been witnesses. Indeed, consecration was the occasion for the establishment of the monastery's position in relationship to that hierarchy.

Implicit in the ritual itself was a statement about the relationship of the abbey to the outside world. Only a bishop—not an abbot—could consecrate the church. Typically this was to be the bishop ordinary, unless the monastery had been granted either the right to select the bishop it wished for this

[74] *Brevis historia monasterii Rivipullensis,* in Pierre de Marca, *Marca Hispanica sive Limes Hispanicus . . .* (Paris, 1688), col. 1301.

[75] For some examples of dedication inscriptions of this period, see *HL* 5:2*–3*, 5*–7*, 10*, 21*–22*, nos. 3, 5, 6, 13, 16, 19, 34, 73, 78.

[76] Ademar of Chabannes, *Chronicon* 1.29 (*Chronique d'Ademar de Chabannes,* ed. Jules Chavannon [Paris, 1897], p. 32).

[77] Perhaps the enigmatic capital in the east gallery of the cloister of Moissac is such a memorial. It is inscribed with three somewhat jumbled alphabets (as well as with Psalm 53.3) perhaps intended to recall the consecration alphabets; cf. Ernst Rupin, *L'abbaye et les cloîtres de Moissac* (Paris, 1897), pp. 250–252.

[78] *Cartulaires des abbayes d'Aniane et de Gellone,* 2:299–300, 426–427, 440–441, nos. 161, 306, 322. These documents range from the ninth to the twelfth centuries.

function or exemption from the authority of the local bishop. Such coveted privileges were increasingly common by the later eleventh century, and by the later twelfth century abbots had begun to receive regularly the right to wear the episcopal insignia and thus to perform episcopal functions.[79]

These latter privileges were much sought after because consecration was an emblem of the episcopal exercise of power over monasteries.[80] Not only the right but also the rite expressed the power and authority of the agent of consecration; as we have seen, the bishop's staff was in constant play during the ceremony. The formula used in Catalan consecration charters reveals just how closely consecration was associated with episcopal dominion: "just as the canons prescribe, we [the founders] deliver these churches for consecration into the power (*potestate*) of our lord and bishop."[81]

Hence the monastery's choice of a certain bishop to perform the consecration could be a political statement. In 1098, for example, the abbot of Saint-Pierre of Uzerche asked the bishops of Limoges and Périgueux and the archbishop of Lyon to consecrate altars in the abbey church. The abbot had evidently been involved in some conflict with the two local prelates, for, according to the cartulary of Uzerche, his request represented a reconciliation with them—apparently his predecessor had severely snubbed the bishop of Limoges by asking Urban II to consecrate the abbey church.[82] Indeed, monastic communities often appealed to papal legates or to the pope himself to consecrate their church, making clear that they were (or wished to be) subject only to the bishop of Rome.[83] Certainly Urban II's tour through southern France in 1095–1096, when he consecrated an impressive number of churches and altars, traced out just such a network of alliances.[84] Furthermore, Urban granted privileges of exemption to many of

---

[79] On grants of the *pontificalia* to abbots, see Georg Schreiber, *Kurie und Kloster im 12. Jahrhundert*, 2 vols., Kirchenrechtliche Abhandlungen, 65–66, 67–68; (Amsterdam, 1965; reprint of 1910 ed.), 1:153–158.

[80] This is true also of the episcopal right to consecrate or bless the new abbot; see below, Chapter 6 at nn. 37–45, 164–167, 192–195. Abbots and bishops were aware of the power implied in the right of consecration. In 1008, for example, Fulbert of Chartres wrote a letter of protest to Richard, abbot of Saint-Médard of Soissons, who had presumed to reconsecrate a church. The crux of the matter for Fulbert was the way in which the abbot's action reversed the right hierarchy of ecclesiastical authority. *The Letters and Poems of Fulbert of Chartres*, ed. Frederick Behrends (Oxford, 1976), pp. 28–30, no. 14.

[81] *Actes de consagracions*, pp. 69, 70, 96 (et passim), nos. 10, 11, 33. This formula is also used by abbots in their requests that a bishop come and consecrate the abbey church.

[82] *Ex historia monasterii Usercensis*, in *Cartulaire de l'abbaye d'Uzerche (Corrèze) du Xe au XIVe siècle avec tables, identifications, notes historiques*, ed. J.-B. Champeval (Paris, 1901), pp. 35, 37. See below, Chapter 6 at nn. 164–167.

[83] See Schreiber's remarks, *Kurie und Kloster*, 1:184–185. Volkert Pfaff sees papal consecrations as definitively making an abbey exempt from episcopal jurisdiction but does not explain why: "Sankt Peters Abteien im 12. Jahrhundert," *Zeitschrift der Savigny Stiftung für Rechtsgeschichte: Kanonistische Abteilung* 57 (1971): 158–159, 172.

[84] See René Crozet, "Le voyage d'Urbain II en France (1095–1096) et son importance au point de vue archéologique," *Annales du Midi* 49 (1937): 42–69.

these churches, or confirmed privileges they had already received. The link between these papal privileges and the consecration was an intimate one. Often the texts state that because Urban had consecrated the church with his own hand, he endowed it with privileges.[85]

Consecration seems often to have been the moment when, by the later tenth century, privileges were accorded or at least formalized. As we have seen, during this ceremony in the presence of the populace, the bishop admonished the founders about the endowment and their duties. Did these latter include the privileges? In any case, foundation charters typically mention the grant of such privileges made by the lay founders, by the bishop presiding at the consecration, and/or by the king and perhaps the pope at the request of the founders.[86]

These privileges, which were of varying nature depending on the authority that guaranteed them and on the time period in which they were issued, delineated the new abbey's position in a network of relations, rights, and powers. Through them, king and pope particularly, alternately as well as in combination, assured varying degrees of monastic liberty in relation to the lesser and local agents of secular and ecclesiastical powers.[87] Through the early tenth century, abbeys or their founders most frequently turned to the king for the establishment or confirmation of their privileges. In these diplomas, the Frankish kings granted immunity that included both fiscal and judicial exemption from royal and secular agents and the establishment of a certain territorial inviolability.[88] Under Louis the Pious and his immediate successors, royal protection (*tuitio* or *mundeburdium*) as well as the right of electing the abbot without outside interference were almost invariably associated with grants of immunity.[89] Royal protection involved various military and financial obligations to the king, but it also clothed the abbey with

---

[85] Crozet, "Le voyage," pp. 60–63. Cf. the case of Charroux, below: Chapter 6 at n. 194.

[86] See, for example, the foundation of a monastery near Cahors which was given to Cluny via Moissac, (*GC* 1, instr. 39) and that of the church of Sant Llorenç near Bagà (*Actes de consagracions*, pp. 109–112, no. 40). On grants of protection by the pope at the request of founders in the twelfth century, see Schreiber, *Kurie und Kloster*, 1:181–188.

[87] For a thorough discussion of the shifting juridical meanings of the word *libertas*, see Brigitte Szabó-Bechstein, *"Libertas Ecclesiae": Ein Schlüsselbegriff des Investiturstreits und seine Vorgeschichte, 4.–11. Jahrhundert*, Studi Gregoriani, 12 (Rome, 1985), esp. pp. 29–47, 78–101, 118–123, 176–192 for its use in monastic privileges.

[88] For the development of Merovingian and Carolingian immunity, see Elisabeth Magnou-Nortier, "Etude sur le privilège d'immunité du IVe au IXe siècle," *Revue Mabillon* 60 (1984): 465–512; and Barbara Rosenwein, "Property, Peace, and Privacy: The Medieval Immunity," paper presented at the December 1990 meeting of the American Historical Association. Cf. Jean-François Lemarignier, *Etude sur les privilèges d'exemption et de juridiction ecclésiastique des abbayes normandes depuis les origines jusqu'en 1140* (Paris, 1937).

[89] On the nature of royal privileges and how they changed under the Carolingians, see the differing interpretations of Goffart, *Le Mans Forgeries*, pp. 10–22; and Josef Semmler, "Traditio und Königsschutz: Studien zur Geschichte der königlichen monasteria," *Zeitschrift der Savigny-Stiftung für Rechtsgeschichte: Kanonistische Abteilung* 45 (1959): 1–33.

immunity from secular jurisdiction.[90] If the founders had delivered the monastery to the king in what was known as a *traditio,* royal protection had a further significance. It emblazoned the abbey as property that was royal and inalienable from the king's possession.[91]

By the later ninth century, however, such *traditiones* became less common and were increasingly accompanied by restrictive clauses guaranteeing certain rights of the episcopal and/or aristocratic founder(s).[92] Even diplomas reconfirming the abbey's rights vanished from the south by the later tenth century, as did royal donations (and indeed the royal presence and power).[93] With rare exceptions, only in the mid-twelfth century would kings again begin to issue diplomas of privileges for southern monasteries.

From the tenth century until Louis VII's appearance in the south, southern abbeys looked for privileges to their local founders and patrons—and to the pope. Earlier, papal protection had been a mere complement to that granted by the king.[94] Between the seventh and the late tenth centuries, privileges granted by the pope could place the abbey in question under papal protection, free it from the temporal though not the spiritual jurisdiction of the bishop ordinary, and give it secular immunity.[95] Only in the last decade of the tenth century were abbeys granted the right to be free from the spiritual jurisdiction of the ordinary ("exemption," an anachronistic term). This privilege was much coveted by the late eleventh century as the

[90] Semmler, "Traditio und Königsschutz," pp. 27–33. Semmler lists as well the necessity to appoint an *advocatus,* but the existence of such agents for southern monasteries has been disputed by Elisabeth Magnou-Nortier, "Abbés seculiers ou avoués à Moissac au XIe siècle," in *Moissac et l'Occident,* pp. 123–132.

[91] Besides those which the founders had delivered to him through the judicial act of the *traditio,* Carolingian royal abbeys included those the king had founded or confiscated as well as those established on fiscal land. Semmler, "Traditio und Königsschutz," p. 3. On the Carolingian policy of placing all monasteries under royal protection in order to make them into royal abbeys, see Josef Semmler, "Episcopi potestas und karolingische Klosterpolitik," in *Mönchtum, Episkopat und Adel zur Gründungzeit des Klosters Reichenau,* ed. Arno Borst, Vorträge und Forschungen, 20 (Sigmaringen, 1974), pp. 305–395.

[92] Semmler, "Traditio und Königsschutz," pp. 15–16; cf. H. E. J. Cowdrey, *The Cluniacs and the Gregorian Reform* (Oxford, 1970), p. 11.

[93] See Lesne, *Histoire de la propriété ecclésiastique,* 2.3:2–4; the detailed tables in Kienast, "Wirkungsbereich," pp. 546–547, 552; and the maps and charts that conclude Lemarignier's *Le gouvernement royal.*

[94] Under Louis the Pious, papal protection became paired with royal *tuitio.* Semmler, "Traditio und Königsschutz," p. 14.

[95] H. Appelt, "Die Anfänge des päpstlichen Schutzes," *MIÖG* 62 (1954): 101-111; Hans Hirsch, "Untersuchungen zur Geschichte des päpstlichen Schutzes," *MIÖG* 54 (1942): 363–433; Jean-François Lemarignier, "L'exemption monastique et les origines de la réforme grégorienne," in *A Cluny: Congrès scientifique: Fêtes et cérémonies liturgiques en l'honneur des saints abbés Odon et Odilon, 9–11 juillet 1949* (Dijon, 1950), pp. 288–340; Lesne, *Histoire de la propriété ecclésiastique,* 1:128–130; and, perhaps most incisively, Wilhelm Schwarz, "*Jurisdicio* und *Condicio.* Eine Untersuchung zu den *Privilegia libertatis* der Klöster," *Zeitschrift der Savigny-Stiftung für Rechtsgeschichte: Kanonistische Abteilung* 45 (1959): 34–98.

greatest possible liberty an abbey might possess.[96] But even in this later period, papal protection remained distinct from exemption, and many abbeys enjoying the former (and hence at least nominal status as papal abbeys) were obliged to submit to the authority of the local bishop for consecration of church and abbot.[97] As we shall find, those who did not enjoy this greatest liberty guaranteed by the pope often tried to acquire it.

This shift from king to pope as the guarantor of monastic rights and immunity shows once again how the balance among the actors in the process of foundation changed over the centuries. The king as an active presence gradually disappeared, leaving the local aristocracy (lay and ecclesiastical) predominant, seconded by the pope in distant Rome. More and more frequently nobles themselves became monks after a secular career; they were also, along with bishops and abbots of other monasteries, the material founders and protectors. But as we shall see, beginning in the late eleventh century, the desire of the monasteries for liberty, for independence from just these powers—the lay aristocracy, bishops, and other abbeys—was expressed unmistakably in both action and text.[98]

Nonetheless, although the actors in the process of foundation may have changed over time, the meaning of the process itself remained constant. Foundation represented the monastery's introduction into space, human and sacred, at least according to the texts that commemorate foundation. As the monks remembered and narrated their community's foundation, they played with time in order to compress the extended process of establishing a monastery into its most significant elements: the delineation of the abbey's status vis-à-vis its terrestrial neighbors and the assertion that the monastery was sacred space watched over by God and the saints.

Accordingly, it is not surprising that the author of the early twelfth-century *Vita S. Geraldi Silvae-majoris* could write of La Sauve-Majeure's foundation: "in the year 1079 . . . lord Gerald came with his companions to La Sauve-Majeure on, as it is said, the feast of Simon and Jude. In the second year the monastery was begun (*incoeptum est monasterium*), namely on the eleventh of May, in the honor of the blessed virgin Mary and the holy apostles Simon

---

[96] On the nonexistence of "exemption" before the close of the tenth century, I follow the analysis of Schwarz, "*Jurisdicio* und *Condicio*," and of Cowdrey, *The Cluniacs*, pp. 22–36. For a recent consideration of the earliest explicit privilege of "exemption," that of Gregory V for Fleury (997), see Marco Mostert, "Die Urkundenfälschungen Abbos von Fleury," in *Fälschungen im Mittelalter*, 4:287–318. On the difficulties of satisfactorily delineating "exemption," see Pfaff's problems in arriving at a definition in "Sankt Peters Abteien," pp. 150–195.

[97] On the difference between protection and exemption, see Lemarignier, "L'exemption monastique," pp. 288–340, esp. 296–298; and Schreiber, *Kurie und Kloster*, 1:27–63. On abbeys under papal protection as papal property, see Cowdrey, *The Cluniacs*, p. 14; Schreiber, *Kurie und Kloster*, 1:6–26; and Hans Hirsch, *Die Klosterimmunität seit dem Investiturstreit: Untersuchungen zur Verfassungsgeschichte des deutschen Reiches und der deutschen Kirche* (Cologne, 1967; reprint of 1913 ed.), pp. 26–65.

[98] See below, Chapters 3–6.

and Jude."[99] This description implies a process extended over two years. It began with the moment when Gerald, seeking peace and quiet after his turbulent years governing the monks of Saint-Vincent of Laon, came to the site of the future monastery. It culminated in one formal act: the abbey church's consecration. The author designated the latter not only as the monastery's technical inception, but also as a commemoration of Gerald's arrival; the monastery was dedicated to the two apostles on whose feast day Gerald had first come to La Sauve-Majeure. The consecration, the formal beginning of the monastery's existence, recalled and contained the foundation's anterior history, as would the feast of dedication celebrated annually by the monastery. *Incoeptum est monasterium* thus referred to one moment—the ceremony of consecration. But, like the foundation charters frequently composed on the occasion, that ritual compressed an extended process which had already passed into the realm of memory.

[99] *Vita S. Geraldi Silvae-majoris* (*AASSosB* 6.2:888).

2

The Legendary Process

Monastic communities could commemorate the constitutive moments of their origins by allowing free rein to the imaginative construction of the past hinted at in foundation charters. The products of this imaginative remembering were foundation legends, colorful images of origins often suffused with the miraculous. In these tales, frequently populated by miraculous animals and epic kings, elements of the historical process of foundation can be discerned. But an etymological approach to the legends, an effort to peel back their layers to reveal the skeleton of the historical process would not only be unilluminating; it would also do violence to the legends themselves.[1] The transposition into the legendary mode results in more than a playful version of the actual process. The legends weave their own interpretation of foundation—but one that coincides with what we have already encountered in the foundation charters. In legend, foundation becomes the process of the symbolic constitution of the boundaries, exclusive and inclusive, delineating the abbey's identity as a sacred space. No indelible line can be drawn between the image of foundation created by legends and that which is implicit in foundation charters. Legends do not represent fiction any more than the foundation charters represent reality. Rather, the truth, the socially significant belief

---

[1] For cautions against trying to peel away the layers of legends to try to find their elusive (and often nonexistent) "historical kernel," see Frantisek Graus, *Lebendige Vergangenheit*, pp. 1–28; and Friedrich Prinz, *Gründungsmythen und Sagenchronologie*, Zetemata. Monographien zur klassischen Altertumswissenschaft, 72 (Munich, 1979). Also see the more general remarks of Steven Knapp, "Collective Memory and the Actual Past," *Representations* 26 (1989): 123–149.

conveyed and commemorated in each, is the same: the highly charged nature of foundation as a site of significance.[2]

The legends fashion this meaning through a particular language: motifs and topoi juxtaposed to create various messages. This is not a vocabulary restricted to southern legends, or even to medieval texts; many of these motifs belong to the general stock employed in the Indo-European tradition (and beyond) to describe origins. Nonetheless, just as the legends are localized in time and space, so too are the motifs they employ grounded in specificity: the combination of cultural context, imaginative memory, and the desires of the monasteries themselves.

Five stages of legendary foundation will provide the framework for my discussion of how communities used such motifs in their legends to create the significance of foundation: the revelation of the site, the abbey's construction, endowment, consecration, and acquisition of privileges. I could parse the legends in another fashion but, significantly, this structure is implicit in the texts themselves. It highlights the meaning that, we shall find, the monks' imaginative memory imparted to foundation.

Revelations

Space, in religious and social terms, is not homogeneous.[3] Certain sites are charged with a value that renders them significant and different. The legends make monasteries into such places, distinguished and demarcated from their secular surroundings. Indeed, the monastery's nature as a sacred place is perhaps the paramount concern in legends. But if the monastery is a sacred site, it can hardly be chosen by human beings. No mere human being can designate space as part of sacred topography, as a "gate of heaven" (Gen. 28.17). Theophany, an irruption of the divine, is necessary.

In the historical process of foundation, the ritual of consecration provokes such theophany. Although this ritual may appear in the legends, it is almost invariably overshadowed by a preceding spectacular revelation of the site as sacred. Indeed, revelation tends to be the most important and usually the first stage of legendary foundation. It, not consecration, is the theophany that suffuses the legends. Consecration and revelation are on a

---

[2] See the argument that memory carries what is accepted to be the "truth" in Fentress and Wickham, *Social Memory*.

[3] Emile Durkheim deals with this concept in social terms: *The Elementary Forms of the Religious Life*, trans. Joseph Ward Swain (New York, 1965), pp. 23–25. Mircea Eliade places it in a religious context: *Le sacré et le profane* (Paris, 1965), pp. 30–31. For specific examples of how space is constructed in a differential fashion, see Hilda Kuper, "The Language of Sites in the Politics of Space," *American Anthropologist* 74 (1972): 411–425; and Emiko Ohnuki-Tierney, "Spatial Concepts of the Ainu of the Northwest Coast of Southern Sakhalin," *American Anthropologist* 74 (1972): 426–457.

continuum, each making manifest the site's sacredness. Consecration can be seen as the formalized, ritualized revelation channeled by human beings, and the revelation of the site as a consecration not framed by human ritual. In her account of her community's origins, Hrotsvit of Gandersheim (ca. 932–ca. 1000) (admittedly geographically distant from the texts under consideration here) rendered the continuum between the two moments tangible; she wrote that Gandersheim's church was consecrated on the anniversary of the site's miraculous revelation.[4]

Nonetheless, the emphasis in legend on revelation rather than on consecration is significant. In the legends, revelation most often occurs through the medium of the place itself, human beings guided by God, or animals— or some combination of them.[5] Hinted at by each of these types of revelation is a temporality of the sacred site different from the one we have already encountered in the ritual of consecration. In the nonlegendary texts, the abbey becomes sacred space at the moment when the celestial Jerusalem descends: during the ritual of consecration. The legends, on the other hand, by using the trope of revelation, assure that the space which will become the monastery, the earthly incarnation of the celestial Jerusalem, is already, intrinsically and essentially, sacred. Through revelation, the abbey's identity is rooted in preextant sacred space and given an implicit prehistory.

Place: Continuity and Discontinuity

The creation of such continuity is clearest in those legends in which the site itself functions as the medium of revelation. In such instances, the inherent sanctity of the place is made not only explicit but also timeless. I do not mean to imply that the legends shape revelation as the unveiling of naturally (pagan) sacred sites. Instead, even in those few legends that feature springs, high places, or caves—places considered in many religious traditions as in and of themselves sacred—the texts create the revelation of the site as an unveiling of inherently Christian space. For example, the early twelfth-century *Vita sanctae Enimiae* recounts how Enimia, a Merovingian princess, was afflicted by leprosy on her wedding night.[6] She spends years pursuing futile cures until finally, in a vision, an angel tells her to go the Gévaudan, where she will find a spring whose waters will cure her. After several false leads, she discovers the spring which, in an episode the text

---

[4] Hrotsvit of Gandersheim, *Primordia coenobii Gandeshemensis*, ll. 375–382, in *Opera*, ed. H. Homeyer (Munich, 1970), p. 464. Interestingly, a ceremony for the designation and blessing of a chosen site before its actual full consecration existed: *Pontifical romano-germanique*, 1:122–123, no. 36, (excerpted in Durand, *Pontifical; Le pontifical romain au Moyen-Age*, 3:451–452). Do the legendary revelations echo and replace this episcopally controlled ceremony?

[5] Kastner also considers some of the motifs that can be used to make a place sacred in monastic legends: *Historiae fundationum*, pp. 90–130.

[6] "Vita, inventio et miracula sanctae Enimiae," edited by Clovis Brunel in *AB* 57 (1939): 257.

describes with baptismal overtones, restores her skin to its former aristocratic whiteness. Enimia remains there, living as a recluse, and eventually decides to establish a monastery for women (which would be known as Sainte-Enimie and eventually become a male community).

The centrality and the sacrality of the spring in this legend cannot be denied. But the spring is presented as an already Christian conduit for God's virtue; Enimia's cure is framed as one typical of those operated by pilgrimage saints. First she tries several springs (shrines) which do not have any effect; after her cure, she is unable to leave the spring/shrine without being reafflicted by her disfiguring disease. Furthermore, the spring may explain the choice of site, but the Christian presence of Enimia is equally a necessity for the site's revelation as a holy place.

To be sure, one could argue that the spring was intrinsically sacred and was probably considered so in pagan tradition, and that this foundation (probably Merovingian) therefore was an intentional Christianization of a pagan site, like some of those recounted by Gregory of Tours. Nonetheless, the twelfth-century legend does not recall this process; the *vita* presents the foundation not as Christianization but as the revelation of a site that is already firmly Christian.[7]

Indeed, as the motif most often used in the legends for the revelation of inherently sacred sites makes clear, the landscape, at least as remembered, was safely Christian. Foundations were no longer commemorated as instances of bishops destroying pagan temples or building churches near lakes that were worshipped.[8] Instead, legends associated foundations with the discovery of an old altar or the crumbling walls of an ancient church.[9] The mid-eleventh-century legend of Maillezais, for example, relates how William IV Fierabras and his hunters came across the ruins of an old church hidden in the midst of a thicket of brambles. Its three altars, although eroded by frost and rain, still stood, signifying that this was a consecrated place. When a huntsman inadvertently clutched at one of them for support, he was struck by blindness, a punitive miracle underlining the ruins' sacredness. Then, at the urging of his wife, Emma, William decided to refound and rebuild the church in the form of a monastery.[10] In other legends, too, the discovery of

[7] On the probability that Sainte-Enimie was a Merovingian foundation, see Rouche, *L'Aquitaine*, p. 244.

[8] On churches built near sacred lakes, see Gregory of Tours's celebrated account in *Liber in gloria confessorum* (*MGH SSRM* 1.2:299–300). For other examples of Merovingian transformations of pagan sacred places, see Graus, *Volk, Herrscher und Heiliger im Reich der Merowinger: Studien zur Hagiographie der Merowingerzeit* (Prague, 1965), pp. 184–188.

[9] To be sure, already in the seventh century Gregory of Tours described the miraculous revelation of the neglected tombs of holy men and holy women and how oratories would be built over the tombs: *Liber in gloria confessorum* (*MGH SSRM* 1.2:307–308, 328–331, 335, 340, 363–364, nos. 17, 18, 50, 51, 52, 57, 63, 71, 103). This, however, represents the assimilation of space into an orthodox framework; conversion, not restoration, was the leitmotiv.

[10] Peter of Maillezais, *Qualiter fuit constructum Malliacense* (*PL* 146:1250–1252).

an abandoned or deserted small church occasions refoundation and thus the reestablishment of the proper boundaries between sacred and profane space.[11]

Such insistence on foundation as refoundation distinguishes these legends sharply from contemporaneous ones associated with Cistercian foundations. Cistercian legends, such as those of Cîteaux, Clairvaux, and the more local Silvanès, stress to the contrary how the founders sought a "desert" that was not only uninhabited and uncultivated but also virgin of prior religious foundations.[12] These Cistercians thus presented themselves as heirs to the desert fathers and as religious pioneers. In reality, though, at least in the south, they implanted themselves in regions that were not only centers of population but also had been under cultivation long before they established their granges. Furthermore, in spite of their legends, they typically utilized preextant churches and monasteries for their foundations.[13]

In contrast to the white monks, the traditional Benedictines in the south typically remembered themselves as restorers, as refounders. As we have seen, they often were just that; many foundations in the tenth and eleventh centuries were refoundations. Furthermore, in the eleventh and twelfth centuries, the churches and buildings of these monasteries underwent important architectural changes; often, older structures with wooden roofs were replaced with more ample stone-vaulted churches. These changes may be partially expressed in the motif of refoundation on the site of the abandoned church.

Memory and legend, however, as the case of the Cistercians shows, cannot be reduced to direct reflections of reality. The black monks associated their foundations with refoundation as consciously and deliberately as the Cistercians linked theirs with the "desert."[14] In doing so, they emphasized the permanence of sacred place summed up in a canon of the council of Chalcedon (451) and repeated by Charlemagne's *Admonitio generalis* (789)

[11] For example: Clairvaux-d'Aveyron, Issoire, La Sauve-Majeure, Saint-Sever, San Juan de la Peña, San Martín de Cercito. This motif appears as well in the short version of the *Moniage Guillaume*, ll. 828–879, in *Les deux rédactions en vers du Moniage Guillaume, chanson de geste du XIIe siècle* . . . , ed. Wilhelm Cloetta, 2 vols. (Paris, 1906–1911), 1:35–37.

[12] Cîteaux: *Exordium parvum* translated in Louis J. Lekai, *The Cistercians: Ideal and Reality* (Kent State, 1977), pp. 451–461; Clairvaux: William of Saint-Thierry, *Vita prima sancti Bernardi* (*PL* 185:226–268); Silvanès: *Cartulaire de Silvanès*, pp. 371–390. Later Cistercian legends, however, do use the topos of the ruined church; see those cited (unfortunately without any indication whatsoever of the date of the texts) by Anselm Dimier, "Quelques légendes de fondation chez les Cisterciens," *Studia Monastica* 12 (1970): 97–107.

[13] In this paragraph, I draw on Constance H. Berman, *Medieval Agriculture, the Southern French Countryside and the Early Cistercians: A Study of Forty-Three Monasteries*, Transactions of the American Philosophical Society . . . , 76 (Philadelphia, 1986).

[14] In a striking episode, Robert of La Chaise-Dieu deliberately seeks as his hermitage "ecclesiam . . . aliquam in eremo, desertam licet ac dirutam, tamen parochialem . . . parochialem ut credo, ne si novum in alieno collacarent oratorium, veteribus locis inferre viderentur injuriam." Marbod of Rennes, *Vita S. Rotberti abbatis Casae-Dei* (*AASS* April 3:321).

as well as by Burchard of Worms in his eleventh-century collection of canons: "places that have once been dedicated to God as monasteries shall remain monasteries perpetually, lest they later become secular dwelling places."[15] The principle is self-evident; the sanctification of space was considered irreversible, as the monks were well aware. When in the mid-eleventh century Abbot William III of Saint-Chaffre wished to rebuild the abbey church on a different site, he wrote to Hugh of Cluny for advice. "Because of its ancient sanctification (*antiqua sanctificatio*), if in any way it is feasible to retain the site, it should not be permitted that [the monastery] rashly be transferred to another place. Diligent care . . . should be taken that service be paid to the Lord always in that same place," replied Hugh.[16] A consecrated space could (or should) never blend back into the surrounding secular landscape.

In the legends, the trope of the refounding of abandoned churches expressed this permanence emphasized by Hugh. Furthermore, it established a framework of continuity—temporal and spatial—for the foundation, making concrete the anteriority of the site's sacredness implied by the general motif of revelation. A striking example of the desire for such continuity appears in a charter describing the refoundation of the cathedral of Elne (1042–1057). This text relates that the church had twice been destroyed by Muslim raids. The bishop, Berengar (1031–1053), decided that a new cathedral should be built in the upper and more protected part of the city. Berengar then "took up parchment and described and drew (*descripsit, pinxit*) or had described and drawn the shape (*formam*) of the said church [the old church] in the dimension of its width as well as of its length. And he built or had built and founded (*fundari*) in just this same form the cathedral church in the upper city (*villa*) of Elne."[17] The new cathedral was then as exactly as possible the old; the disjunction implied in the shifting of the site was remedied. Here, as in legends using the motif of refoundation, the relationship becomes one of genealogy; the new church is heir to the ancient and is thus endowed with an implicit (pre)history.

This establishment of lineage and claim to a more ancient Christian past informs another topos of refoundation: the monastery that has been either neglected or destroyed, and then refounded. In this case, revelation is only

[15] "Loca que semel deo dedicata sunt ut monasteria sint, maneant perpetuo monasteria, ne possint ultra fieri saecularia habitacula" (*MGH Capitularia regum Francorum* 1:56, no. 22). Cited by Burchard of Worms, *Decretorum libri XX* 3.19 (cf. 3.15–16) (*PL* 140:676). This canon may very well reflect Roman law relating to the permanence of temple sites; see John E. Stambaugh, "The Functions of Roman Temples," *Aufstieg und Niedergang der Römischen Welt: Geschichte und Kultur Roms im Spiegel der Neueren Forschung*, 2.16.1 (1978):567–568.

[16] *Cartulaire de l'abbaye de St-Chaffre*, p. 46, no. 52 (for a less explicit example of the same principle, see p. 45, no. 50).

[17] See de Marca, *Marca Hispanica*, no. 172, cols. 1148–1149, here 1148. On the cathedral's reconstruction, see Marcel Durliat, *Roussillon roman*, 4th ed. (La Pierre-Qui-Vire, 1986), pp. 180–181.

implied. The leitmotiv is rather the reestablishment of the abbey, the rehabilitation of the sacred site—a process that may involve its purging from the filth of the secular world which had contaminated it.[18] Myths and legends of origins in general often describe such periods of decadence and decline, followed by periods of rebirth.[19] By this return to the moment of origins when all is possible, the community can refashion itself in whatever way it likes.[20]

The abbeys used these creative possibilities of discontinuity and refoundation in various ways. Most often, the rupture was attributed to external rather than internal forces—a guarantee that the discontinuity would not reflect badly on the monks.[21] Invasions or persecutions were a favorite metaphor, allowing the monastery to explain and claim a number of things. Invasions and resulting displacements and returns of communities could provide the locus for property claims. According to an eleventh- or twelfth-century diploma of Charlemagne, for example, the monks of Psalmodi fled from the Muslims (which they actually did, but in approximately 909). In this diploma, supposedly delivered upon their return (which actually occurred in the early eleventh century), Charlemagne grants the monks some estates.[22] Furthermore, such invasions can justify relocations of communities or churches which, as we have seen, were not supposed to be moved from one site to another; hence, the charter describing the refoundation of Elne invokes destruction by the Muslims, whereas the actual motivation seems to have been quite different.[23] Equally, invasions could explain why saints' bodies needed to be moved from one church to another, as in the case of the translation of the relics of Saint Austremonius first from Issoire to Volvic and then from Volvic to Mozac recorded in various versions of a *translatio*.[24]

[18] A play between the impurity of decadence (implying the pollution of sinking back into the secular landscape) and the purity of refoundation (reintegration into sacred topography) occurs in the twelfth-century prologue to Uzerche's cartulary. In this legend, a nobleman decides to restore an abbey, partly because in a vision he saw twelve men dressed in white appear and carry the accumulated dirt out of the neglected church: *Ex historia monasterii Usercensis*, in *Cartulaire de l'abbaye d'Uzerche*, p. 19. Cf. Gerald's literal cleansing of an abandoned church which had been used as a barn. *Vita S. Geraldi Silvae-majoris* (*AASSosB* 6.2:882).

[19] Smith, *Ethnic Origins of Nations*, p. 192.

[20] See above, Introduction at n. 17.

[21] See Farmer, *Communities of Saint Martin*, pp. 160–165, 173–177.

[22] *MGH Diplomata Karolinorum* 1:455–456, no. 303. On the reestablishment of the monastery at Psalmodi and its architecture, see Pierre A. Clément, *Eglises romanes oubliées du Bas-Languedoc* (Montpellier, 1989), pp. 65–67. On the trope of invasions used in property claims, see Albert D'Haenens, *Les invasions normandes en Belgique au IXe siècle: Le phénomène et sa répercussion dans l'historiographie médiévale*, Université de Louvain. Recueil de Travaux d'Histoire et de Philologie, 4th ser., 38 (Louvain, 1967), pp. 162–168; and Farmer, *Communities of Saint Martin*, pp. 160–165, 173–177.

[23] Durliat argues that the problem was revenue lost as a result of property alienations: *Roussillon roman*, pp. 180–81.

[24] *Vita prima S. Austremonii* (*AASS* November 1:53–54); *Vita secunda S. Austremonii* (*AASS*

The topos of invasions and resulting refoundation also allowed the monastery to acquire new founders and patrons, and thus a longer history as a sacred site. Each time the abbey presented itself as having been destroyed or abandoned, it could lay claim to a new layer of people: those who participated in its reestablishment. Thus Psalmodi acquired Charlemagne, and Mozac the king who was instrumental in Austremonius's translation there, Pippin the Short. The discontinuity obviates the necessity for proof of a connection between these figures and the foundation, because, as inhabitants of monastic communities knew only too well, disasters often caused documents to disappear.[25]

This loss of the *monumenta* of the past could even be transposed in legend to explain how a monastery could be "refounded" on a site where there was no evidence of former buildings.[26] The mid-eleventh-century narrative opening the cartulary of Saint-Savin of Bigorre claims Charlemagne as the monastery's original founder. It next relates how the monastery suffered for so many years from "slothful negligence" that eventually all physical evidence of the abbey was completely erased: "in no way could any trace of the original buildings be discerned."[27] It was then "refounded" in approximately 947 by Raymond I, count of Bigorre. Here the fiction of oblivion (*his . . . oblivionis multum nebulis diuque deditis . . . ;* "when these things had been very much given over to the clouds of oblivion for a long time . . .") endows the monastery with a more ancient past and a more prestigious founder. It

---

November 1:58–61); *Vita tertia S. Austremonii* (*AASS* November 1:75–77); *Revelatio corporis S. Austremonii et ejusdem duplex translatio* (*AASS* November 1:77–80) (the earlier texts emphasize general neglect and decline rather than invasion as the cause of the translations). On the dating of these texts, see Pierre-François Fournier, "Saint Austremoine, premier évêque de Clermont," *Bulletin Historique et Scientifique de l'Auvergne* 89 (1979): 417–471.

[25] See the very late tenth-century description of the destruction by fire and invasion of the charters and library of Sant Pere de les Puelles and the nuns' attempts to reconstitute the lost documents: *Les marches méridionales du royaume aux alentours de l'an mil: Inventaire typologiques des sources documentaires,* ed. Michel Zimmermann (Nancy, 1987), pp. 153–155.

[26] Legend could also prop up a monastery's claims to its priories. For example, according to a series of charters and privileges probably fabricated by approximately 1080, Charlemagne founded the monastery of La Réole and gave it to Fleury. Then the Normans invaded and destroyed the monastery, necessitating its "refoundation" (by 977) by Bishop Gumbald and his brother Guillaume-Sanche, duke of Gascony. The copy of the "refoundation" charter inserted in the cartulary of Fleury contained an interpolation that related how the Normans had also destroyed all the charters—hence there were no records of Fleury's previous possession of La Réole. The invasions thus allow La Réole to claim Charlemagne, and Fleury to claim La Réole. See the texts and remarks in *Recueil des chartes de l'abbaye de Saint-Benoît-sur-Loire,* ed. Maurice Prou and Alexandre Vidier, 2 vols. (Paris, 1907–1912), 1:39–43, 114–119, 154–165, 170–173, 185–188, 215–219, 236–238, nos. 18, 40, 62, 65, 71, 83, 90; and "Cartulaire du prieuré de Saint-Pierre de La Réole," ed. Charles Grellet-Balguerie, *Archives Historiques de la Gironde* 5 (1863): 144–145, no. 99.

[27] *Cartulaire de l'abbaye des Bénédictins de Saint-Savin en Lavedan (945–1175),* ed. Charles Durier (Paris, 1880), p. 2, no. 2. On the (twelfth-century) church of Saint-Savin, see Marcel Durliat and Victor Allère, *Pyrénées romanes* (La Pierre-Qui-Vire, 1969), pp. 295–308 and pls. 118–131.

creates a memory of more distant origins, just as the topos of the discovery of the ruined church does.

In the prologue to the chronicle of Conques, this extension of the past by appeal to successive external disruptions and refoundations that destroy documents is taken to its logical extreme.[28] The refoundations by Clovis, Pippin the Short, and Charlemagne are occasioned by the destruction wrought upon successive monastic communities at Conques by invasions first of generic "worshippers of idols," then of Theudebert, and finally of the Muslims after the Battle of Poitiers in which latter "all . . . records and things pertaining to it [the monastery] were ruined." This loss of the documents preceding the mid-eighth century is the device with which Conques, probably a Carolingian foundation, could make its beginnings coterminous with those of monasticism; according to the prologue, the site was first inhabited in the fourth century by a group of Egyptian-style hermits. Discontinuity and rupture thus become the tropes for continuity and antiquity—indeed, for the permanence of the sacred site.

In all these cases, the site is revealed as the "gate of heaven" (*porta caeli*) of Genesis 28.17; once consecrated, it is always sacred. But how are the ruined churches to be brought to the attention of those humans who will restore them? Furthermore, what of those sites where no church existed before? How are they to be recognized as specially charged places? A different sort of theophany is necessary, one in which the agent of revelation is directed by God, often by being itself in some way sacred or "other." Such theophany is captured in the succinct image of foundation that appears on two twelfth-century capitals, one from the Auvergnat church of Bulhon, and the other from its neighbor, Trizac (see Figure 1).[29] A man and a woman kneel, holding between them a freestanding column topped with a sculpted capital, a synecdoche for the church they have established. Above, the hand of God emerges from a cuff of cloud, indicating that what might seem like purely human initiative had been divinely directed.

---

[28] This prologue has been edited as the "Chronique du monastère de Conques . . ." in Marc Antoine François de Gaujal, *Etudes historiques sur le Rouergue*, 4 vols. (Paris, 1858–1859), 4:391–394. This text represents the final stage of the legend of the Saracen invasion of Conques. Cf. the possibly forged diploma of Pippin I of Aquitaine (838), in *Cartulaire de l'abbaye de Conques en Rouergue*, ed. Gustave Desjardins (Paris, 1879), pp. 411–414, no. 581, and the better edition in *Recueil des actes de Pépin Ier et Pépin II rois d'Aquitaine (814–848)*, ed. Léon Levillain (Paris, 1926), pp. 133–151, no. 32; the verse account (late eleventh century) of the translation of Saint Foy's relics from Agen to Conques, *Translation metrica S. Fidis virginis et martyris* (*AASS* October 3:290); and the probably slightly later prose version of this text; *Translatio altera* (*AASS* October 3:295–96). On the dating of the *translatio* texts, see Patrick Geary, *Furta Sacra: Thefts of Relics in the Central Middle Ages*, 2d ed. (Princeton, 1990), pp. 58–63, 138–141.

[29] On these capitals, see Zygmut Swiechowski, *Sculpture romane d'Auvergne* (Clermont-Ferrand, 1973), p. 253 and figs. 248–249. In several other Auvergnat capitals depicting foundation, some sort of divine intervention seems to be implied; see Swiechowski, *Sculpture romane*, pp. 149–152, 228, 253, figs. 117, 244–247.

FIGURE 1. Twelfth-century capital from Trizac representing a scene of foundation. The founders hold between them a column with a sculpted capital, a metaphor for the church they found. The hand of God hovers above. Photo Zodiaque.

Divine Guidance: Revelation through People

Divine guidance is often made explicit in visions or other signs sent to individuals, commonplaces of texts describing foundation.[30] At its simplest, this motif may appear in a laconic statement such as that in the mid-twelfth-century version of the legend of Figeac. Pippin the Short, "warned by a divine messenger," decided to restore the ancient abbey of Jonant by moving it to a new site, Figeac.[31] Here the vision prompts the foundation; it could also reveal the specific place where the monastery should be built. A charter describing the foundation of Langogne, a priory of Saint-Chaffre, relates how Stephen, viscount of Gévaudan, was divinely instructed one night that he should "build a church in honor of Saints Gervasius and Protasius in the diocese of Millau." His wife, Almodis, then told him she had had a similar vision. Accordingly, they journeyed to Rome. There, while they performed the typical pilgrim vigils in Saint Peter's, the vision repeated itself. They told the pope about the divine admonishments. In response, he exhorted them to build "the church which the Lord showed . . . [them] in their dreams (*in somnis*)."[32]

Divine designation of place through vision is even more striking in the foundation legend of Menat. The *Vita Menelei* and the *Vita S. Theofredi* (both probably composed in the twelfth century) relate how Meneleus, a man of imperial descent, fled from marriage and by chance met Theofredus, abbot of Saint-Chaffre.[33] After spending seven years in training with the abbot, Meneleus received an angelic warning to quit the monastery and return to the exact spot in the river valley where he had first encountered Theofredus. There, according to the *Vita Menelei*, Meneleus fell asleep beneath a leafy oak, a type of tree associated with visions and the foundation of altars ever since Abraham arrived in the valley of Mambre (Gen. 12.4–9, 18.1–8).[34]

[30] Such visions may even appear in visual representations of foundation (although I have found no southern French examples). See the twelfth-century capital at Saint-Lazare of Autun (Burgundy): Denis Grivot and George Zarnecki, *Gislebertus: Sculpteur d'Autun*, 2d ed. (Paris, 1965), pp. 20 and 70 and pl. 13. Cf. the roundel of the late twelfth-century shrine of Heribert relating to the abbey of Deutz (Germany): Hermann Schnitzler, *Der Schrein des heilgen Heribert* (Mönchnengladbach, 1962), fig. 33.

[31] This version appears in an apparently authentic twelfth-century interpolation (post 1163) of Ademar of Chabannes' *Chronicon*, Paris, BN Latin 5926, f. 36r (*Chronique*, p. 58, n. s*). I would like to thank Professor Richard Landes for information about the dating of Latin 5926. On this (re)foundation, see below, Chapter 4 at nn. 117–123. Cf. also the twelfth-century legend in which Pippin has a vision of the Virgin causing him to refound Sorèze: *Recueil des actes de Pépin*, pp. 269–275, no. 62.

[32] For the charter, see Paris, BN Latin 12767, ff. 61r–64r (partial editions in *HL* 5:331–333, no. 156, and in *Papsturkunden 896–1046*, ed. Harald Zimmermann, 3 vols. [Vienna, 1984–1989], 2:731–732, no. 378).

[33] *Vita Menelei abbatis Menatensis* (*MGH SSRM* 5:129–157); *Vita S. Theofredi abbatis Calmeliacensis, martyris in Gallia* (*AASSosB*, 3.1:476–485).

[34] On oak trees and visions, see Hugh of Saint-Victor, *De bestiis et aliis rebus* (*PL* 177:114); Jonas of Bobbio, *Vita Columbani abbatis* (*MGH SSRM* 4:105); and Peter Comestor, *Historia scholastica* (*PL* 198:1093).

The angel of the first vision appeared again to Meneleus and commanded him to build a monastery on the spot "so that there the frequent sublimity of angelic visitation will open the gates of eternal consolation for those who pray."[35] Menat, twice indicated by an angel and graced by an oak tree recalling Abraham's dedication of the altar at Mambre, was thus indubitably revealed as a sacred place.

Also operative in this revelation was the conjunction of sacred person and site, for Menat was founded on the meeting place of two saints, Meneleus and Theofredus. Indeed, the medium of revelation was often the presence of people endowed with special characteristics (such as sanctity) which showed that they were close to God. In a sense, their specialness served as a conduit for revelation and transferred itself to the site.[36] Perhaps a stranger, typically a pilgrim who appears and then vanishes (a figure beloved of hagiographers), might help to designate the site, as in the earliest version (sometime just after 1047) of the legend of Charroux.[37] This narrative text opens by describing how Charlemagne, passing through the territory of Count Roger of Limoges, encountered a pilgrim, Fredelandus, returning from Jerusalem. Charlemagne asked him for details of his pilgrimage. Fredelandus's confession that he had acquired a piece of the True Cross for a church he had built piqued Charlemagne's piety. After much urging and promises of munificence, the king persuaded Fredelandus to accept a royal offer: the relic would be enshrined not in Fredelandus's church but in one Charlemagne would build on an appropriate nearby site. The next morning, the forested spot where they had met had been miraculously cleared of trees, offering a flat space of just the right size for the church. The pilgrim vanished without comment by the text. Not only had he endowed the monastery with a fragment of the True Cross, which was until the later eleventh century its most important relic, but through his presence he had also designated the site for the foundation.

In the foundation legend of Saint-Pierre of Clairvaux-d'Aveyron (a priory of the abbey of Conques), the stranger is even more liminal and thus powerful. According to this legend (two narrative charters included in the twelfth-century cartulary of Conques), a stranger making a pilgrimage "throughout the whole world" came to the Rouergue. He is assigned a completely fictive identity as an English prince named Alboynus/Albodenus, son of "King

---

[35] *Vita Menelei* (*MGH SSRM* 5:141). Earlier the text compared Meneleus fleeing from his marriage feast to Abraham leaving his homeland (p. 138). This same *vita* (p. 142) recounts another vision designating a site where a *cella* is to be founded for Meneleus's female relatives.

[36] See Graus's argument that in Merovingian hagiography places were not charged with any particular magical or sacred value until the presence of a saint endowed them with such a quality: *Volk, Herrscher und Heiliger*, p. 50.

[37] *Chartes et documents pour servir à l'histoire de l'abbaye de Charroux*, ed. Pierre de Monsabert, Archives Historiques de Poitou, 93 (Poitiers, 1910), p. 2.

Harold" and "Alvena."[38] In the course of his penitential pilgrimage, this prince came across the ruins of a *monasterium* formerly dedicated to Peter in a valley called Clairvaux. After praying there, he decided the church should be restored to its former state. Alboynus thus approached the *seniores* of the two castles perched on the opposing heights of Panat and Cassagnes above Clairvaux, and persuaded them and all their followers to help him refound the monastery.[39] In this case, the stranger—Alboynus—was the mediator between the two *castra,* as was the monastery between them whose refoundation he prompted. One charter implies that conflict between the two *castra* and their *milites* had caused the church's ruin;[40] the refoundation obviously created peace between them, as indicated by the conditions recorded in the charters to which both sets of *seniores* agreed.[41] An outsider, a pilgrim with an aura of liminality that could shade into the saintly, wondrous and authoritative because of his royal blood and his improbable and foreign descent, Alboynus thus could reveal the sacred ruins and establish a point of consensus between the two castles.

More often than the pilgrim stranger, an even more liminal and saintly figure appears in the legends as the agent of such revelation: a hermit who consecrates the site by his or her very presence. According to the mid-thirteenth-century *Gesta Karoli Magni ad Carcassonnam et Narbonam,* for example, seven pious hermits were living in the valley of the Orbieu near a humble oratory dedicated to the Virgin when Charlemagne and his entourage stumbled on them. The text states the connection between the holiness of the site and the hermits; Charlemagne decided to found the monastery of Lagrasse there "because he well knew that the Lord loved those good men and that the place was good and holy."[42] The dynamic made explicit here is

---

[38] Alboynus: *Cartulaire de l'abbaye de Conques,* p. 19, no. 15, (the other charter gives him instead the name Albodenus, and does not specify his parentage, merely describing him as from English royal stock: p. 16, no. 14). No son of Harold II had a name that at all suggests Alboynus. This name is derived from the toponymic Albion, making the princely pilgrim into a timeless embodiment of the misty isle. On Harold II's sons, see Edward A. Freeman, *The History of the Norman Conquest of England,* 6 vols. (Oxford, 1877–1879), 4:791–793, 725–755. Neither Freeman nor Frank M. Stenton (*Anglo-Saxon England,* 3d ed. [Oxford, 1989]) mentions Harold I's offspring.

[39] *Cartulaire de l'abbaye de Conques,* p. 16, no. 14.

[40] *Cartulaire de l'abbaye de Conques,* p. 19, no. 15.

[41] Not only do both sets of *seniores* endow the monastery, but they agree that it will be the common burial place for the inhabitants. Furthermore, they agree, no violence will be perpetrated on the abbey's territory. The establishment of such sanctuaries related in part to attempts during this period to regulate violence and establish peace. On this latter phenomenon, see most recently the articles in *The Peace of God.* For an even more explicit example of a monastic foundation creating peace between two *castra* in legend, see the eleventh-century (?) charter describing the ninth-century foundation of San Martín de Cercito in *Cartulario de San Juan de la Peña,* ed. Antonio Ubieto Arteta, Textos Medievales, 6 (Valencia, 1962), no. 9, pp. 37–39.

[42] *Gesta Karoli Magni,* p. 22.

at work in other foundation legends that attach a hermit to the site of the monastery. In 1166, according to Robert of Torigny's *Chronica* (ca. 1184), the body of a holy hermit, Amator, a servant of the Virgin, was found in a chapel in Quercy. The *inventio* stimulated pilgrimage to this shrine of the Virgin which was known as Rocamadour.[43] The pilgrims' devotional focus was a statue of the Virgin, not the relics of the hermit; Amator probably represented only so much aetiological icing on the cake. But a legend of origin was necessary, and in the later twelfth century, the choice of a hermit was only too natural. Sainte-Enimie and Saint-Gilles also have legends in which a hermit comes to live in the place where the monastery will be, and lends his or her name to the future community.[44]

Other legends show even more clearly the desire for the eremitic origins that might delineate and reveal the site as a "good and holy" place. In these instances, the original version of the legend was altered (sometimes awkwardly) so as to include or amplify the hermit motif. For example, in the narrative introduction to the cartulary of Saint-Chaffre, a pious prince, Calminius, founds Mozac and Saint-Chaffre.[45] In the later (twelfth-century) *Vita S. Theofredi,* however, Calminius has acquired new characteristics; he now withdraws from the world to lead a quasi-eremitic life before establishing the two abbeys.[46] In a parallel development, Laguenne (near Tulle), another church that claimed Calminius as its founder, shaped him as a man who had lived an ascetic life; on an early thirteenth-century enamel reliquary, he appears next to Saint Martin as a figure in a monk's cowl and with bare feet.[47] A most famous founder, Guillaume of Gellone, was undergoing a similar transformation—but in the vernacular tradition. The Guillaume *chanson* cycle concludes with the *Moniage Guillaume,* in which the hero becomes a hermit in the "wilderness" of the valley of Gellone (after a spec-

---

[43] Robert of Torigny, *Chronica* (*MGH SS* 6:519).

[44] Sainte-Enimie: "Vita, inventio et miracula sanctae Enimiae," pp. 237–298. Saint-Gilles: see the three versions of the *Vita S. Aegidii* in *AB* 8 (1889): 102–120; in *AASS* September 1:299–304; and in E. C. Jones, *Saint Gilles: Essai d'histoire littéraire* (Paris, 1914), pp. 98–111.

[45] *Cartulaire de l'abbaye de St-Chaffre,* p. 5.

[46] *Vita S. Theofredi* (*AASSosB* 3.1:476–477).

[47] Ernst Rupin, "La chasse de saint Calmine à Laguenne," *Bulletin de la Société Scientifique, Historique et Archéologique de la Corrèze* 13 (1891): 353–362. The reliquary is conserved today at the Musée Dobrée of Nantes; see Dominique Costa, *Catalogue du Musée Dobrée* (Nantes, 1961), 1:32–35, no. 35, and pl. 35. Perhaps this image has its roots in earlier traditions at Laguenne. Unfortunately the only narrative texts dealing with this Limousin version of Calminius date from at least several centuries later. I have not been able to identify these vernacular-narrative texts, which, at least in the seventeenth century, were at Limoges where they were seen by I. Collins, who provided summaries (to be used with care) in his *Histoire sacrée de la vie des saints principaux et autres personnes plus vertueuses . . . en divers lieux du diocèse de Limoges* (Limoges, 1672), pp. 339–349. On the legend of Saint Calminius, see below: Chapter 3 at nn. 1–7, 64–72.

tacularly unsuccessful stint with the mean-spirited monks of Aniane).[48] In the twelfth and thirteenth centuries, other epic heroes became hermits; the ascetic struggle was the fitting spiritual culmination and equivalent of the secular battles in which the hero was previously glorious.[49]

The *ermitage* was the last stage of these heroes' lives; in the foundation legends, it represented the primordial phase of the monastery's existence. Even in cases where successive versions of one monastery's legend made the foundation more and more ancient, the eremitic and sanctifying stage was always made to come first. This process was at work in the case of Conques. This abbey seems genuinely to have owed its foundation and location to an early ninth-century hermit, Dado. In his *Carmen* (ca. 826–828), Ermoldus Nigellus relates such an odd tale of this man's conversion to the eremitic life that it almost rings true. The Muslims captured Dado's mother during one of their raids and would not surrender her despite his threats. When Dado indignantly refused to give up his horse in exchange for his mother's life, the Muslims cut off first her breasts and then her head. Crazed with grief, Dado became a hermit. The poet then tells us that eventually Louis the Pious heard of Dado's piety and with his aid founded a monastery upon the site of his retreat.[50] Indeed, Louis's diploma of immunity and protection (819) described how Dado had come to live as a hermit at Conques.[51] This tradition appears without embroidery in the late eleventh- or early twelfth-century chronicle of Conques.[52]

The elaborate and perhaps later (late twelfth- or thirteenth-century) "prologue" to this chronicle fabulously aggrandizes this tale of eremitic origins. Not one lone Carolingian hermit, but a whole colony of desert fathers consecrates Conques's foundation. In 371, this text relates, an eremitic community sprang up in the valley of Conques in imitation of the Thebaid. One day the pagans of the area murdered all one thousand of them. Successive communities, this time cenobitic, settled there, only to suffer the same fate at the hands of first Theudebert in 564 and next the Muslims in the

---

[48] Cf. *Moniage Guillaume* (long version), ll. 2472–2535, in *Les deux rédactions en vers*, 1:158–161. Guillaume's nature as a hermit is even more full-fledged in the later *Miracles de Nostre Dame par personnages d'après le manuscrit de la Bibliothèque nationale*, ed. Gaston Paris and Ulysse Robert, 8 vols. (Paris, 1876–1893), 2:1–53.

[49] See Micheline de Combarieu, "'Ermitages' épiques (De Guillaume et de quelques autres)," and Jean-Charles Payen, "L'érémitisme dans le 'Moniage Guillaume': Une solution aristocratique à la conversion chevaleresque," both in *Les Moniages. Guiborc. Hommages à Jean Frappier*, ed. Philippe Menard and Jean-Charles Payen (the third volume of Jean Frappier's, *Les chansons de geste du cycle de Guillaume d'Orange*, 3 vols. [Paris, 1955–1983]), pp. 143–180, 181–207.

[50] Ermoldus Nigellus, *Poème sur Louis le Pieux et épitres au roi Pépin*, ed. Edmond Faral (Paris, 1964), ll. 224–301, pp. 22, 24, 26.

[51] *Cartulaire de l'abbaye de Conques*, pp. 409–410, no. 580.

[52] This text has been edited without its fantastic and later prologue as *Chronicon monasterii Conchensis*, in *Thesaurus novus anecdotorum . . .* , ed. Edmond Martène and Ursin Durand, 5 vols. (Paris, 1717), 3:1387–1388.

730s. Dado then appears—but as a holy man whom Pippin the Short appointed to assemble other such men in service of the monastic rule.[53]

This legendary transformation of Conques's origins into an Egyptian-style eremitic community, as well as the reshapings of Calminius and Guillaume, certainly reflect the increasing importance of the eremitic ideal in monastic life from the late eleventh century on. In the general vogue for hermits, even these traditional Benedictine monasteries, exemplary of collective life in a stable community, felt the need to endow themselves with founders of an eremitic aura.[54] Significantly, most legends that fashion such a founder manage in some way to integrate the hermit into the cenobitic community. Dado became a cenobitic figure, Gilles became the monastery's abbot; Enimia decided to found a monastery; the hermits of Lagrasse were buried there, as was Amator at Rocamadour, and so on. In other words, the all too possible contrast and conflict between eremitic and cenobitic life were deflected and defused; continuity between the hermit and the monastery was assured.[55] These manipulations of eremitic founders, like the transformations of Calminius and Guillaume into hermits, do not relate only to trends in monastic spirituality; they also betray the abbeys' desire to hallow origins, to create the site of the monastery as a place of revealed sanctity. Fashioned or refashioned as hermits, as holy men and women close to God, the founders gain the qualities rendering them the suitable medium for such a revelation; their sanctity translates itself to the site.

Animals and the Sacred Site

Special human beings, then, or human beings inspired by a vision, could designate the sacred site. But sometimes in the legends' depiction of theophany, human beings were aided—or even replaced—by a different sort of agent: an animal. Gilles, for example, had as his bosom companion a hind who plays a critical role in the revelation leading to the foundation of Saint-Gilles.[56] In many other instances, animals alone defined, delineated, and demarcated the location for the future monastery.[57] Sometimes they even

---

[53] "Chronique du monastère de Conques," p. 393.

[54] These abbeys also created institutional space for the eremitic impulse; see the documents relating to the monk of Maillezais who wished to live as a hermit, in *AASSosB* 6.2:867–868. See also Giles Constable, "Eremitical Forms of Monastic Life," in his *Monks, Hermits and Crusaders in Medieval Europe* (London, 1988), pp. 255–263.

[55] See the brief remarks of Joachim Wollasch, *Mönchtum des Mittelalters zwischen Kirche und Welt*, Münstersche Mittelalter-Schriften, 7 (Munich, 1973), pp. 138–139.

[56] See below at nn. 84–92.

[57] Perhaps the most celebrated medieval legend describing revelation by animals is that of Saint Michael of Monte Gargano (Italy), recounted in the late sixth-century *Liber de apparitione sancti Michaelis in Monte Gargano* (*MGH Scriptores rerum Langobardicorum et Italicarum saec. VI-IX* [Hannover, 1878], pp. 540–543). This text was much copied and disseminated and appeared in several manuscripts from southern France under the rubric "Dedicacio sancti

established its perimeter in a fashion that recalls (and replaces) the sanctifying circumambulations of bishop and clergy in the ceremony of dedication.[58]

These legends form a continuum with rituals from other cultures in which animals serve as markers and designators of sacred sites.[59] The Romans, for example, established urban boundaries by driving a bull and a cow yoked to a plow around the edge of a city. The city wall was built on the inner edge of the furrow, and the space immediately inside and outside the wall was considered sacred and inviolable—the *pomerium*. It demarcated the space of the city as different and sacred.[60] Certainly this rite, mentioned by Livy and other classical authors much copied and read in the Middle Ages, would have been remembered. But I do not want to suggest a determinative relationship between this or any other ritual and the instances of revelations by animals in the legends. Rather, like these rituals, the legends recognize and create the symbolic and imaginative possibilities of animals as designators of sacred space. If no ordinary human being can provoke theophany, someone or something out of the ordinary must do so. Animals, often associated with the sacred, can function as such agents.[61]

Not surprisingly, the legends play upon this quality of animals in order to make them into agents of God's will; the episodes in which animals delineate sacred sites tend to be framed as visions, a form that makes the animals' nature as celestial messengers indubitable.[62] Mythic beasts seen in a vision actually construct the walls of the church at Moissac, according to the foundation legend contained in the admittedly late *Chronicon* written by this

---

Micaeli archangeli." See, for example, the eleventh-century Saint-Martial manuscript, Paris, BN Latin 5365, ff. 86r–87r; and the mid-tenth-century calendar from Ripoll described by H. Moreu-Rey, "La dévotion à Saint Michel dans les pays catalans," in *Millénaire monastique du Mont Saint-Michel*, 4 vols. (Paris, 1966–1967) 3:373.

[58] For a striking northern French example involving a bull marking the exact outline of the site, see the legend from Mont-Saint-Michel known as the *Revelatio ecclesiae sancti Michaelis* (ca. 850), edited by Thomas Le Roy in his *Les curieuses recherches du Mont-Sainct-Michel*, 2 vols. (Caen, 1878), 1:407–419, esp. 412. This legend is based on that of Monte Gargano.

[59] See the examples cited in Eliade, *Le sacré et le profane*, pp. 30–31 and Alexander H. Krappe, "Guiding Animals," *Journal of American Folklore* 55 (1942): 228–246.

[60] On the *pomerium*, see Livy, *Ab urbe condita libri*, 1.44, ed. W. Weissenborn, 6 vols. (Leipzig, 1874–1897), 1:46, and *Paulys Real-Encyclopädie der classischen Altertumswissenschaft*, ed. Georg Wissowa et al., 2d ed., 49 vols. to date (Stuttgart, 1894-), 42:1867–1876.

[61] Eliade, *Le sacré et le profane*, pp. 30–31. For concrete examples of animals associated with the sacred (in late antiquity), see Bernhard Kötting, "Tier und Heiligtum," in his *Ecclesia Peregrinans: Das Gottesvolk Unterwegs: Gesammelte Aufsätze*, 2 vols. (Münster, 1988), 1:336–344.

[62] Constantine's *sanctio* of Constantinople (drawing the line of the walls with his lance) was transposed in such a fashion in medieval legend to involve both an animal and a vision; see William of Malmesbury, *Gesta regum Anglorum atque historia novella* 4.354, ed. Thomas D. Hardy, 2 vols. (London, 1840), 2:545–547. On the circumstances of the actual *sanctio*, see Richard Krautheimer, *Three Christian Capitals: Topography and Politics* (Berkeley, 1983), p. 43; and L. Voelkl, *Die Kirchenstiftungen des Kaisers Konstantin im Lichte des römischen Sakralrechts*, Arbeitsgemeinschaft des Landes Nordrhein-Westfalen, 11 (Cologne, 1964), pp. 19–21.

monastery's abbot, Aymeric de Peyrat (1377–1406).[63] On his way to attack Toulouse, Clovis had a vision of two griffins who transported stones with their beaks to a certain valley where they constructed a church. The next day, the king and his host traversed just this valley. There the king seems to have glimpsed the griffins again. He announced to his army what he had seen and his resulting intention to found a monastery. Here, assimilated into the foundation legend, are the animals that, rampant on the imposts of the capitals in Moissac's cloister and gamboling on a mosaic near the abbey's main altar, were seen daily by the monks.[64] Perhaps these images were the source of the legend's griffins; these animals do not seem to have carried a symbolic charge that would otherwise explain their part in the abbey's origins.[65] In any case, as fabulous animals witnessed in a vision, they assured Moisac a theophanic foundation.

More typically, the animals of foundation legends possessed a symbolic meaning that rendered their actions a Christian epiphany. For example, a tumble of animals in a vision informed Gerald where to build the church for the monastery of La Sauve-Majeure. According to his early twelfth-century *vita*, Gerald had begun to build a dwelling for his disciples but could not decide on an appropriate site for the church. He voiced his dilemma in prayer and in response had a vision. He saw a plow or cart (*currus*) drawn by two oxen coming from the east—the direction of the rising sun, a typical image used for the advent of Christ (Yves of Chartres even compared the ox and his plow to Christ and his cross).[66] The oxen, animals often depicted in

---

[63] Aymeric de Peyrat, *Chronicon* (Paris, BN Latin 4991A, ff. 103vb–104va).

[64] Meyer Schapiro reproduces a few of these capitals in "The Romanesque Sculpture of Moissac I and II" in his *Romanesque Art* (New York, 1977), figs. 79 and 83. The mosaic with griffins is mentioned by Aymeric, who reads it as a symbol of Clovis's vision (Paris BN Latin 4991A, f. 103vb). This mosaic, no longer extant, probably dates from the mid-eleventh century. Marcel Durliat, "L'église abbatiale de Moissac des origines à la fin du XIe siècle," *Cahiers Archéologiques* 15 (1965): 164–166, 174–177. Although the choice of griffins as the subject of the mosaic may have been influenced by the legend, I have found no evidence that the legend in this form was extant in the eleventh century; furthermore, mythic animals were a common theme of eleventh-century mosaics in churches of this region.

[65] Griffins do not seem to have been subject to allegorical treatment in the bestiaries; see, for example, Hugh of Saint-Victor, *De bestiis et aliis rebus* (*PL* 177:84). Perhaps they appeared in the Moissac legend not only because of their depiction on capitals and mosaics, but because of their possible associations with royal power. The best textually known griffins in this period are the ones Alexander was supposed to have hitched to his chariot for his journey to the heavens. *Der Alexanderroman des Archipresbyters Leo*, ed. Friedrich Pfister, Sammlung mittellateinischer Texte, 6 (Heidelberg, 1913), p. 126. This motif appeared in Romanesque sculpture. V.-H. Debidour, *Le bestiaire sculpté du Moyen Age en France* (Grenoble, 1961), p. 391; R. S. Loomis, "Alexander the Great's Celestial Journey," *Burlington Magazine* 32 (1918): 136–140, 177–185. Indeed, a cloister capital at Moissac itself has been traditionally considered to bear the same motif; see Schapiro, "The Romanesque Sculpture of Moissac I and II," p. 135, and the tentative identification in François Avril, Xavier Barral i Altet, and Danielle Gaborit-Chopin, *Les royaumes d'Occident* (Paris, 1983), p. 71, fig. 53.

[66] On Yves's interpretation, see Debidour, *Le bestiaire sculpté*, p. 336 (who gives no precise reference).

legend as leading humans to a sacred site, then metamorphosed into a horse, an animal just as frequently assigned a similar role.[67] Continuing toward the west, the horse was then transformed into the crucified Christ. The cross upon which he rested joined heaven and earth: "the lower part of the cross was touching the ground, and indeed the upper [part] was raised up to the sky . . . in the same place where the sign (*signum*) of the cross was fixed, there he [Gerald] was supposed to found (*fundare*) the church."[68] This last sentence provides the obvious exegesis of the vision: the animals revealed the site as a place of union between heaven and earth, like the stone at Bethel upon which Jacob rested his head and which is invoked in the actual ritual of dedication, like the Cross itself.[69] This visionary sequence of animals with the Christological crescendo thus designated the site of Sauve-Majeure's church as sacred.

The Christian epiphany created by animals is underlined even more strongly in a twelfth-century text from Mozac. In a set of interlocking visions recounting this abbey's "refoundation" by Pippin the Short, the agent of revelation is a deer.[70] The purported author of the text, Abbot Lamfred,[71] relates that one Christmas Eve

> a deer, shining white as snow, seemed to me to enter my monastery . . . and in the cemetery, which was next to the sacred church of the lord apostle Peter and Saint Caprasius, a certain division [made] by the deer's horns and hooves could be seen . . . It was in the measure of the church which was to be built. And the trace of its horns and hooves appeared in the earth beneath the snow in the same manner as they did on the snow itself.

Seven days later, the abbot had another vision in which he was brought before King Pippin in his palace at Orléans. The abbot recounted his vision, and the king responded by relating one he had had on the same night. Mozac's patron saint, Austremonius, had led Pippin to the monastery and pointed at the tracks in the snow. When the king wondered what they

[67] On the role of oxen and horses as guiding animals in Merovingian legends, see Graus, *Volk, Herrscher und Heiliger,* pp. 233–235. On horses in legends (and on their role in Germanic myth and ritual as guides between this world and the world beyond), see the brief comments by Karl Hauck, "Tiergärten im Pfalzbereich," in *Deutsche Königspfalzen,* 3 vols., Veröffentlichungen des Max-Plancks-Instituts, 11.1–2 (Göttingen, 1963–1965), 1:72–73, and the more general ones in Vladimir Propp, *Les racines historiques du conte merveilleux,* trans. Lise Gruel-Apert (Paris, 1983), pp. 222–236, 274.

[68] The description of the vision is in *Vita S. Geraldi* (AASSosB 6.2:886–887, here 887).

[69] Cf. above, Chapter 1 at n. 71.

[70] See the edition by Bruno Krusch in his "Reise nach Frankreich im Frühjahr und Sommer 1892. Fortsetzung und Schluss. 3. Aufzeichnung des Abtes Lamfred von Mozac über König Pippins Beziehungen zu seinem Kloster," *Neues Archiv der Gesellschaft für ältere deutsche Geschichtskunde* 19 (1894): 24–25.

[71] Lamfred appears otherwise only in a charter of approximately 864: *Cartulaire de Brioude: Liber de honoribus sancto Juliano collatis,* ed. Henry Doniol (Paris, 1863), pp. 187–189, no. 176.

meant, his saintly guide informed him that the tracks were those of a "holy angel" and that the king should restore the abbey to its former glory. Some time later, continues the text, when Pippin was campaigning against Waïfre, he came to Mozac and traded stories with Lamfred. In order to convince the king of the truth of their visions, the abbot led the king to the cemetery, where the deer's tracks still could be seen. Presented with this tangible proof, the king ordered that a church be built on the exact spot (*in eodem loco*).

This short text is rich in theophanic references. The deer that delineates the monastery from the surrounding space with his antlers and hooves is not just any animal. His color, as white and pure as the snow on which he traces the monastery's physical foundations, guarantees his identity as a heaven-sent messenger. Indeed, he represents an "angel"—perhaps even more. The timing of the two visions, Christmas Eve, makes the monastery's rebirth parallel to Christ's incarnation and suggests a further symbolic reading of the deer: as Christ himself.

From the late second century onward, exegetical and hagiographic traditions interpreted the deer as an allegory of Christ. This interpretation was based on traditions of classical natural history filtered through the second-century *Physiologus*, the grandfather of the medieval bestiary tradition. The classical authors, including Pliny, described the deer as the mortal enemy of the snake. The deer killed the serpent in one of two ways (depending on which author or bestiary one consults). Either he drank a vast amount of water and spit it into the snake's hole, effectively drowning his adversary, or he snuffled up the snake from his lair with his strong breath and swallowed him, rejuvenated by the poison.[72] The deer conquering and exterminating the snake was translated into Christ triumphing over the devil (who, of course, had been represented as the snake ever since Eden).[73]

The Christological value of the deer which may underlie the Mozac vision is made concrete in several legends (admittedly none of those under consideration here) in which a crucifix appears between or replaces the deer's antlers. A church is then founded on the spot of this unmistakable epiph-

---

[72] On origins of this belief see Herbert Kolb, "Der Hirsch, der Schlangen frisst: Bermerkungen zum Verhältnis von Naturkunde und Theologie in der mittelalterlichen Literatur," in *Mediaevalia litteraria: Festschrift für Helmut de Boor zum 80. Geburtstag*, ed. Ursula Hennig and Herbert Kolb (Munich, 1971), p. 589.

[73] For example, see the facsimile of the lovely ninth-century "Bern Physiologus": *Physiologus Bernensis*, ed. Otto Homburger (Basel, 1964), ff. 17r–v. Isidore provides no exegesis of the deer's nature, but Origen, Ambrose, Jerome, and Bede all reproduce the allegory of the *Physiologus* (see Carl Pschmadt, *Die Sage von der verfolgten Hinde: Ihre Heimat und Wanderung, Bedeutung und Entwicklung mit besonderer Berücksichtigung ihrer Verwendung in der Literatur des Mittelalters* [Greifswald, 1911], pp. 53–63) as does Hugh of Saint-Victor, *De bestiis et aliis rebus* (*PL* 177:64). The rejuvenation of the deer through the serpent's flesh could symbolize the resurrection of Christ; see Kastner, *Historiae fundationum*, pp. 114–115, n. 545.

any.[74] Alternatively, the deer has candles instead of antlers, or it meta-morphoses into an angel.[75] In either case, the deer's nature as a heavenly messenger manifests the sacredness of the site it designates.

Often the deer or another animal does not actually delineate the sacred site but leads human beings to it.[76] A twelfth-century relief on the façade of the Pyrenean church of Saint-Aventin depicts a steer finding the body of the saint on the site of the future church; an angel hovering above is proof of the revelation.[77] In these instances, the animal functions as a guide, accord-ing to a general folklore motif.[78] Animals as revealers of safe passages, new lands, and sacred sites were part of the medieval imaginative stock, inherited partly from classical texts such as the *Metamorphoses*. Examples of this general motif abound in medieval texts, Latin and vernacular, ranging from the histories of Procopius and Gregory of Tours to the marvelous beasts of the *chansons* and romances.[79]

In the southern French legends, this motif most commonly takes a partic-ular shape which adds another layer of significance: a hunted animal reveals the sacred site, typically a hermitage or ruined church.[80] Especially given that in legends thickets almost invariably surround, conceal, and protect the hermit or crumbling church, some mechanism of discovery is necessary.[81]

[74] The most famous instance of this (although associated with conversion and not founda-tion) is the legend of Saint Eustace. For examples of such epiphanies in the context of foundations, see Pschmadt, *Die Sage von der verfolgten Hinde*, pp. 51–58.

[75] A deer with burning candles among his antlers: Joannis de Thcurocz, *Chronica Hun-garorum ab origine gentis* in *Scriptores rerum Hungaric. veteres ac genuini . . .* , ed. Joannis Sch-wandneri, 3 vols. (Vienna, 1766), 1:155–156.

[76] This motif is often associated with shepherds and their animals; see "Vita, inventio et miracula sanctae Enimiae," pp. 259–260. See in general L. Schmidt, "Hirtenmotive in Wall-fahrtsgründungslegenden," in *Festschrift Niklaus Grass: Zum 60. Geburtstag*, ed. Louis Carlen and Fritz Steinegger, 2 vols. (Innsbruck, 1974–1975), 2:199–218.

[77] The relief is reproduced in Debidour, *Le bestiaire sculpté*, fig. 390; and in Durliat and Allègre, *Pyrénées romanes*, pl. 22. On the saint's legend (of which I have been unable to find any medieval text), see Bénédictins de Paris, *Vies des saints et bienheureux . . .* , 13 vols. (Paris, 1935–1959), 6:223.

[78] For general discussions of this motif, see Krappe, "Guiding Animals"; and M. B. Ogle, "The Stag-Messenger Episode," *American Journal of Philology* 37 (1916): 387–416.

[79] See the inventory in Pschmadt, *Die Sage von der verfolgten Hinde*, pp. 38–44; and Krappe, "Guiding Animals." For a typical example, see Gregory of Tours, *Historia Francorum* 2.37 (*MGH SSRM* 1.1:99–102).

[80] Lagrasse: *Gesta Karoli Magni*, pp. 12, 20, 22, 26, 28. Maillezais: Peter of Maillezais, *Qualiter fuit constructum Malliacense* (*PL* 146:1250–52). In the eleventh-century legend of San Juan de la Peña, an ancient church is found. *Cartulario de San Juan de la Peña*, pp. 37–39, no. 9.

[81] For thickets, see the legends of: La Sauve-Majeure, *Vita S. Geraldi Silvae-majoris* (*AASSosB* 6.2:886). Maillezais: Peter of Maillezais, *Qualiter fuit constructum Malliacense* (*PL* 146:1251). Saint Gilles: *Vita S. Aegidii* (in *AB* 8 [1889], p. 113; *AASS* September 1:301; and Jones, *Saint Gilles*, p. 105). Saint-Jean of Sorde: *MGH Diplomata Karolinorum* 1:567–586. The church of Venayrols (one of Conques's properties): *Cartulaire de l'abbaye de Conques*, pp. 53–54, no. 53. For a Spanish example, see that of San Martín de Cercito: *Cartulario de San Juan de la Peña*, pp. 37–39, no. 9.

The hunted animals bring these hidden sacred places to people's attention by leading their pursuers to the spot. The general shape of the story can be sketched as follows. A king or prince pursues a deer (or, less frequently, a boar or a wild sow) that is exceptional in some way: very large or very beautiful or very white. This animal finds sanctuary with the hermit or at the altar of the crumbling church. The hunters and their horses and dogs are struck with paralysis, and their prey, rendered docile by the hermit (as wild animals typically are by saints) goes scot-free. If he is wise, the prince realizes that he has stumbled on a sacred place and decides to found a church or monastery there.

These legends certainly have no monopoly on this motif. Already, in the context of foundation, Gregory of Tours used various versions of it in his immensely popular hagiographic works, as did the *Gesta Dagoberti* for the refoundation of Saint-Denis.[82] It also became part of the stock of *exempla* in the thirteenth and fourteenth centuries.[83] Nonetheless, in the southern French legends, it is more than a mere literary device of discovery. Not only does it speak of theophany, it also transmits messages about lordship, monastic boundaries, and identity. The *vita* of Saint Gilles perhaps best illustrates these levels of meaning.[84]

Gilles lives as a hermit in a cave along the banks of the River Rhône. His sanctity is highlighted by his diet—not just the roots and herbs of the ordinary hermit, but the milk of a hind that has become his friend. One day Flavius, "king of the Goths," comes to hunt in the forest surrounding Gilles's refuge. The king and his hunters start the saint's deer, losing her trail when she escapes to the sanctuary of Gilles's cave, which the dogs cannot penetrate. The next day, the sequence repeats itself. Flavius suspects that the mystery may hinge upon something miraculous (one version of the *vita* even explains that the king wonders whether there might be a pious hermit living in the forest).[85] Accordingly, he asks the bishop of Nîmes to accompany him on the third day's hunt. This time a hunter manages to track the deer to the thicket that encircles Gilles's cave. He shoots an arrow blindly into the bushes, missing the hind but striking the saint. Bleeding, Gilles stands patiently and heroically outside the cave. King and bishop and their retinue break through the thicket with their swords and fall horrified at the hermit's

---

[82] Gregory of Tours, *Vitae patrum* (*MGH SSRM* 1.2:711–715). *Gesta Dagoberti I. regis francorum* (*MGH SSRM* 2:396–425). See also the later texts cited in Johnson, "Pious Legends and Historical Realities," pp. 184–193; Pschmadt, *Die Sage von der verfolgten Hinde,* pp. 51–58.

[83] *Erzählungen des Mittelalters in deutscher Übersetzung und lateinischen Urtext,* ed. Joseph Klapper, Wort und Brauch. Volkskundliche Arbeite . . . , 12 (Breslau, 1914), pp. 320–321, no. 109.

[84] See the various versions of the *Vita S. Aegidii: AB* 8 (1889): 111–117; *AASS* September 1:301; Jones, *Saint Gilles,* pp. 104–108.

[85] For Flavius's conjecture that the mystery relates to a hermit's presence, see *Vita S. Aegidii,* in *AB* 8 (1889): 112.

feet.[86] They beg him for forgiveness, which he grants; he in turn requests clemency for the deer which they accord.

This episode is certainly about theophany. The site of the future monastery is consecrated not only by Gilles's presence but by its designation by an animal allegorical of Christ. Furthermore, the saintly hermit is himself assimilated to Christ through both his wounds (and implied martyrdom) and his source of sustenance, the hind's milk (in an implicit reversal of Christ's gender).[87] Here the hero is nourished by the milk of an animal whose characteristics he then acquires—much like Romulus and Remus, other famous founders with an animal wet nurse. Christlike, Gilles and his deer mark the site as other, as sacred. Gilles is also characterized as such by the hunters' actions. When the bishop and the king humble themselves before his bleeding body, they perform a ritual action that implies not only submission but also recognition that Gilles has God-given power and authority.[88]

But the gesture of bishop and king must also be read in terms of another message implicit in the motif of the hunt. Theophany is complemented by a statement about the abbey's boundaries and its relations with the representatives of human power. Hunting was a royal or noble pursuit conducted in forests that, as *saltus,* were public domains and hence under princely control.[89] Medieval texts usually invoked the hunt as a demonstration of princely power not only over animals but also over humans, that is, subjects.[90] In the legends, however, the meaning of the motif is inverted. The prince is thwarted. His dogs and horses are rendered impotent. The hermit tames the wild animals the prince cannot catch. The prince's power is abruptly terminated in the middle of his own forest. In other words, although the motif of the hunt serves to associate the prince with the foundation, it also shows that the sacred site of the future monastery is exempt from human *dominatio.*

That this is one level of the meaning of the hunt is made explicit by two nuances that the Saint-Gilles legend introduces in the generic pattern. No other legend that I have found mentions a bishop's presence during the hunt and at the revelation of the sacred site, never mind underlines it as in this text. Here episcopal power, too, is shown that it cannot penetrate the

[86] The detail about the swords does not appear in one version of the *Vita S. Aegidii* (*AB* 8 [1889]: 113).

[87] For other examples of saints nourished and protected by deer, see Pschmadt, *Die Sage von der verfolgten Hinde,* pp. 58–63.

[88] On the complex meanings of the ritual of prostration and request for pardon and how they imply theophany, see Koziol, *Begging Pardon.*

[89] Kings from the Carolingians onward even hunted in enclosed parks or preserves that belonged to them; see Hauck, "Tiergärten."

[90] See, for example, the interpretations of biblical commentators: Philippe Buc, "Pouvoir royal et commentaires de la Bible (1150–1350)," *Annales E.S.C.* 44 (1989): 696–699, developed further in his *L'ambiguïté du livre: Prince, pouvoir, et peuple dans les commentaires de la Bible* (Paris, 1994), pp. 112–122.

site of the monastery. Just as unusual, the revealed hermit is wounded by the hunters; typically, the deer or boar escapes without the hermit receiving the hunter's arrow. Not only is Gilles thus made into a martyr, but King Flavius and the bishop of Nîmes must prostrate themselves to beg the saint's forgiveness. The representatives of princely and episcopal power humble themselves in the ritual gesture of penance before the saint whose body they have wounded—the body that is a metaphor for the monastery itself.[91] In the later eleventh century, we shall see, this monastery was involved in acrimonious and often violent conflicts with princes (the counts of Toulouse/Saint-Gilles) and with prelates (the bishops of Nîmes).[92] The hunt and its startling climactic image function specifically in the context of this debate about the boundaries of power and monastic identity.

The hunt, then, not only revealed the sacred site but could become a trope for expressing the abbey's (desired) relations with the larger social world, particularly with representatives of human authority. Might not the other motifs used for theophany—pious hermits, deer drawing architectural plans in the snow with their antlers, mysterious strangers who vanish into thin air, visions of angels and griffins, ruined church foundations—also imply the tracing of boundaries around the future monastery? For, by framing the constitutive moments of origins as the revelation of sacred space, do the legends not hint that the site intrinsically possesses immunity from human power? After all, the sacred is inviolable, even untouchable (except by those who are themselves saintly or have taken the appropriate ritual and purificatory precautions); remember the huntsman who was struck blind when he grasped the altar of the ruined church that would be refounded as Maillezais.[93] Revealed as sacred from its inception, the abbey passed into the class of that which could not be touched or violated without retribution.

Relations

Once revealed as a "gate of heaven," the sacred space needed to be embodied as an abbey. In the ways in which the legends depict this process, the play of inclusion and exclusion inherent in the construction of monastic identity becomes even more explicit; the process resolves itself into both the constitution of the abbey's physical identity and the ordering of its relations with the external world. Furthermore, although the legends center on the abbey, these products of monastic imaginative memory implicitly create visions of that larger world. The building of the abbey, its endowment with

[91] The wound may not be necessary. In the northern *Vita Carileffi abbatis Anisolensis*, the hermit is not wounded but the king still prostrates himself (*MGH SSRM* 3:392).
[92] See below: Chapter 6, under "Saint-Gilles and the Three Enemies."
[93] See above at nn. 9–10.

land and relics, its consecration, and the acquisition of the final concrete element of its identity—privileges—these particularly are the loci for such expressions of order.

Construction

The construction of the monastery could be elided as self-evident. In some cases, however, legends exploit the imaginative possibilities offered by this stage of foundation. The creation of the monastery's physical fabric was intrinsically an expression of the abbey's identity, and of the imposition of order upon the landscape. In some instances, it involved the structuring of relations between the natural world and the human world; natural forces incarnated in fabulous creatures such as dragons and giants had to be tamed, or defeated, or killed. According to the *vita* of Saint Enimia, for example, the princess decided to build a monastery at the miraculous spring where she had been cured. There, on the banks of the Tarn River, construction began. But each week, a dragon that lived in the river methodically destroyed the masons' work. One day Enimia was conversing with her friend, Hilarus, bishop of Gévaudan, when the denizen of the river suddenly came thundering by. Enimia beseeched Hilarus for aid. Brandishing his weapon—a cross hastily made from two branches—the bishop chased the monster through the rugged river gorges. The chase ended when Hilarus, by the force of his prayer, caused the dragon to fall to a rocky death.[94]

This story, recounted with obvious relish by the author of the *vita*, may be aetiological, explaining the great rockslide at the Pas-de-Souci (some twenty-five kilometers to the west) as the shower of boulders that buried the dragon.[95] But matters other than interpreting the surrounding landscape also informed the legend. The struggle between the protagonists recalls myths of origin in which a primordial monster's death or sacrifice occasions creation. Furthermore, the conquest of the dragon is a typical motif of medieval foundation legends, urban and ecclesiastical, in which autochthonous forces must be mastered so that humans can establish themselves in the space.[96] In the case of Sainte-Enimie, the dragon attempting to im-

[94] "Vita, inventio et miracula sanctae Enimiae," pp. 270–272. On Hilarus, see Clovis Brunel, "Saint-Chély: Etude de toponymie," in *Mélanges d'histoire du Moyen Age offerts à M. Ferdinand Lot par ses amis et ses élèves* (Paris, 1976; reprint of 1925 ed.), pp. 83–101. For an interesting modern version of this motif, see Xavier Ravier, *Le récit mythologique en Haute-Bigorre* (Aix-en-Provence, 1986), pp. 85–89.

[95] Here I follow Brunel's suggestion (and the statement by the *vita*'s author that the dragon's place of death could still be seen today; see "Vita, inventio et miracula sanctae Enimiae," p. 240).

[96] Here I follow Jacques Le Goff, "Culture ecclésiastique et culture folkorique: Saint Marcel de Paris et le dragon," in his *Pour un autre Moyen Age: Temps, travail et culture en Occident: 18 essais* (Paris, 1977), pp. 236–279.

pede the construction of the monastery, that is the imposition of human meaning upon the landscape, must be eliminated. Like other foundation texts, the *vita* transposed this battle into explicitly Christian terms;[97] the dragon was the devil. Its defeat thus represented an exorcism, a drawing of boundaries between sacred and profane space.

More often, however, the building of the abbey becomes a metaphor for monastic relations with human neighbors and powers. The construction of the abbey can either include or exclude. Inclusive relations are implied by the most extended and elaborate description of construction among the legends: that of Lagrasse in the mid-thirteenth-century *Gesta Karoli Magni*. In this flamboyant text, Charlemagne and his heroes design the abbey's architectural plan down to the last detail. Charlemagne tells Turpin to indicate where the monastery should be placed, and Aymo of Bavaria and the abbot of Saint-Denis lay out the foundations accordingly.[98] Turpin next instructs the architect precisely, telling him exactly how many bays, how many windows, how many pillars, and how many chapels the church is to have. Lagrasse's material fabric accordingly expresses the will of these legendary figures and commemorates their presence.[99] The heroes physically complete the monastery; when they return from their first battle for Narbonne, Roland and the other knights raise the beams while the clerics sing the *Te Deum*.[100] In all these ways, the monastery claims the imprint of the heroes upon its physical self. The buildings they designed and completed recall them. Through its construction, Lagrasse integrates itself into the epic world and makes its physical fabric a statement of its relation to the king and his epic companions.

The twelfth-century *vita* of Guillaume of Gellone depicts this abbey's building in terms of identification with the founder. But in this case, the inclusion is also an implicit exclusion. The *vita* describes in careful detail how the saintly founder has the monastery built by master craftsmen, how he oversees their work, and how he himself measures the space for the church

---

[97] A devil (autochthonous river monster) is twice defeated by Guillaume at Gellone in the *Moniage Guillaume* (long version), ll. 2536–2742, 6547–6614 (*Les deux rédactions en vers*, 1:161–172, 363–368). The Latin *vita* makes no mention of this tradition, but the opening episode of the *miracula* hints at it obliquely: *Historia miraculorum [S. Willelmi ducis]* (*AASS* May 6:822). In one episode, this monster-devil attempted to prevent Guillaume from building a bridge across the River Hérault—probably the still extant Pont du Diable, actually constructed jointly in the first half of the eleventh century by Aniane and Gellone: *Cartulaires des abbayes d'Aniane et de Gellone* 1:23, no. 20. Cf. Honorat's exorcism of the site of Lérins which was infested with snakes: *Vita sancti Honorati . . .* , ed. Bernhard Munke et al. (Halle, 1911), pp. 56–57.

[98] *Gesta Karoli Magni*, p. 34.

[99] When Charlemagne orders the architect to record in writing Turpin's instructions about various architectural details, the architect answers: "Vestri et eorum voluntatem in omnibus faciemus" (*Gesta Karoli Magni*, p. 44).

[100] *Gesta Karoli Magni*, p. 78.

and the claustral buildings.[101] Furthermore, he lays the cornerstone of the church, an honor reserved in Guillaume Durand's pontifical for bishops.[102] The legend thus invests Guillaume with the power of measuring and consecrating sacred space, heightening his saintly nature. Perhaps more important, Guillaume's direction of the construction also excludes the participation of anyone else—specifically any representative of Aniane, Gellone's neighbor and rival—in the monastery's establishment.[103] Other legends indicate that construction could be configured to convey exactly the sort of claims Aniane was making in relation to Gellone in the eleventh and twelfth centuries: ones to lordship over another monastery.[104] Here Gellone uses construction to do the opposite, to ward off any such pretensions on Aniane's part.

Equally, foundation involving construction could signify a transfer of lordship resulting from exclusion and then co-optation of that which was excluded. A *castrum*, a castle or military emplacement, could be transformed, in what could be a metaphor for religious conversion, into a *claustrum*, a differently fortified and powerful site.[105] A late twelfth-century legend from the abbey of Issoire using this topos highlights the continuum and the conflict between the two architectural forms.[106] According to this text, Issoire was refounded by monks who, fleeing the abbey of Charroux during the Norman incursions, had taken refuge at a *castrum* in their possession, Petra-Incisa, the present-day Saint-Yvoine. Later, rebelling against the domination of the Poitevin mother abbey, these monks decided to destroy the *castrum* and refound the venerable abbey of Issoire.[107] They did so, using the stones of the *castrum* to rebuild Issoire. The *castrum* was thus eliminated—or,

---

101 *Vita [S. Willelmi ducis]* (*AASS* May 6:813).

102 Guillaume Durand, *Pontifical* 2.1, in *Le pontifical romain au Moyen-Age*, 3:451–454.

103 On the rivalry between these two abbeys, see below, Chapter 6 at nn. 268–307.

104 For example, in the *Vita Menelei*, Meneleus summons workers from one of the priories the abbey had just been given so that they might help in the rebuilding of the mother abbey. *MGH SSRM* 5:148–149.

105 This legendary motif seems to correspond to a historically real process. See the examples (diocese of Liège) in Constable, "Monasticism, Lordship and Society," p. 213. Peter the Venerable hints at the idea of conversion as he defends Cluny's possession of *castra:* "si castrum aliquod monachis detur, iam castrum esse desinit, et esse oratorium incipit" (*Epistolae* 28, in *The Letters of Peter the Venerable*, ed. Giles Constable, 2 vols. [Cambridge, Mass., 1967], 1:86). For some later legendary examples (not from southern France) of castles transformed into monasteries, see Hermann the Jew, *Opusculum de conversione sua*, ed. Gerlinde Niemeyer, MGH Quellen zur Geistesgeschichte des Mittelalters, 4 (Weimar, 1963), p. 89 and *Erzählungen*, pp. 347–48, no. 150. I thank Jean-Claude Schmitt for these latter two references.

106 *Additamentum de reliquiis S. Austremonii* (*AASS*, November 1:80–82).

107 For further discussion of this text in the context of acrimonious relations between abbeys, see below, Chapter 6 at nn. 240–243. One can still see today the remains of a tower and fortifications at Saint-Yvoine, a tiny village perched on a steep height overlooking the plain where Issoire is located.

rather, reformed and reconfigured as the monastery.[108] Its bitterly resented power passed literally and figuratively to the abbey. In this legend, as in others, the lordship represented by the castle was excluded, eradicated, resolved into its elements, and appropriated by the monastery, which replaced castle as the architectural expression of order and authority.[109]

Endowment

Subtle (and not so subtle) statements of the abbey's identity in relation to its founders and its neighbors appear as well in the legends' depiction of another aspect of the material abbey's establishment: its endowment. As we saw in Chapter 1, endowment with the necessary land and dependencies, church furnishings, relics, and privileges not only made the monastery into an institution, but also most ostensibly established its position vis-à-vis its founders and neighbors, lay and ecclesiastical. Hence, the depiction of endowment could be simultaneously the most transparent part of legend and the most difficult, the locus of the most exact intersection with events occurring at the time of the legend's production and of the most wishful thinking on the part of the monks. Nonetheless, we should not yield to the temptation to find in the legends' often detailed descriptions of endowment only tendentious efforts to claim property or rights that the abbey did not have but wished to possess. Such material interests did shape the legends, but these interests coincided and converged with the process of the symbolic construction of the abbey's identity.

This convergence is particularly clear in legendary depictions of the abbey's endowment with lands.[110] For if origins were constitutive, then property acquired at those origins constituted the community.[111] Legends could shape the way in which the abbey received its lands as symbolic statements of

[108] The monastery itself may have borrowed the appearance of the *castrum;* there are traces of tenth- and eleventh-century fortifications of the refounded monastery. Gabriel Fournier, *Le peuplement rural en Basse Auvergne durant le haut Moyen Age* (Paris, 1962), pp. 145–154.

[109] See also the twelfth-century layer of Mozac's legend in which the stones of a fortification are used to build the monastery (discussed below: Chapter 4 at nn. 145–146 and Chapter 6 at nn. 140–141). In the legend of Maillezais, the abbot insists that William V destroy a fortification near the abbey and rebuild it as the monastery: Peter of Maillezais, *Qualiter fuit constructum Malliacense* (*PL* 146:1262–65). Actual fortified churches became part of the landscape (especially in southern France) beginning in the twelfth century; see Sheila Bonde, *Fortress-Churches of Languedoc: Architecture, Religion and Conflict in the High Middle Ages* (Cambridge, 1994).

[110] Legends could also present endowment in topical and generic language. See, for example, the brief description of Guillaume's endowment of Gellone: *Vita [S. Willelmi ducis]* (*AASS* May 6:813).

[111] The symbolic value of such property places it into the category of what Rosenwein so nicely calls "special property." She argues that such land possesses what anthropologists call "hau" and surmises that it was ascribed this quality because of its special location or because of the donors' identity. Rosenwein, *To Be the Neighbor of Saint Peter,* pp. 109–143, 162–196.

such identity between community and foundation patrimony, as the striking legend of one of Figeac's priories, Saint-Quintin of Gaillaguet (*Gaillacus*) shows.[112] In a diploma fabricated late in the eleventh or early in the twelfth century, Pippin the Short, in the role of founder, ordains that twenty-two monks should live at Gaillaguet and endows the priory with the same number of dependent churches. This unusual and precise figure was chosen, the text relates, because Quintin himself had been affixed (to a cross? the manner of his martyrdom is not exactly clear) with twenty-two nails.[113] Thus the legend highlights the equivalence between various aspects of the abbey's identity: the monastic community itself, the patron saint, and the foundation endowment (and founder).

The correspondence between monastery and the patrimony acquired at the moment of origins even characterizes those legends which seem above all to be vehicles for property claims.[114] In two instances, rival monasteries proclaimed as their legendary endowment the same set of estates— seemingly clear cases of conflict over property. But in these disputes, conducted through a tangle of legendary texts, the estates per se were not at stake. Rather, these claims emerged in the course of acrimonious debates about the original (and hence proper) hierarchy between the two abbeys. Aniane claimed that Gellone was its priory, and Conques had similar pretensions in relation to Figeac.[115] In these instances, the foundation endowment functioned above all as an emblem and incarnation of one of the monasteries. This is perhaps clearest in the case of Figeac and Conques, for the estates that each claimed encircled Figeac, literally defining this abbey.[116] For Conques to claim them was thus to claim Figeac. Similarly, Aniane's appropriation in various legendary texts of Gellone's original patrimony represented its attempt to incorporate Gellone into its own sphere of lordship as a priory, while Gellone's simultaneous legendary proclamations that the patrimony was its own underlined its status as no one's dependent.

---

[112] This document, a late eleventh- or early twelfth-century piece (Paris, BN Latin 5219, no. 2), is edited in *MGH Diplomata Karolinorum* 1:48–49, no. 34. Scholars have traditionally identified *Gaillacus* as Gaillac, but Philippe Wolff has recently and convincingly argued that it is instead Gaillaguet, a site close to Figeac: "Note sur le faux diplôme de 755 pour le monastère de Figeac," in his *Regards sur le Midi médiéval* (Toulouse, 1978), pp. 313–314.

[113] Traditionally, if founders specified how many monks were to live in the monastery, they chose the apostolic number: twelve.

[114] Rosenwein points out that "special property" (see n. 111 above) tends to appear again and again in charters as the subject of gifts, negotiations, settlements, and countergifts. Cf. James W. Fernandez's remarks about the way in which contested parts of the whole can symbolize the whole in his "Enclosures: Boundary Maintenance and Its Representations over Time in Asturian Mountain Villages (Spain)," in *Culture through Time*, p. 124.

[115] For a full consideration of the conflict between Gellone and Aniane, that between Figeac and Conques, and the various legendary documents relating to foundation endowment, see below, Chapter 6 at nn. 247–307.

[116] See the map in Wolff, "Note sur le faux diplôme," p. 331.

As these cases show, not only was the foundation endowment charged with special significance, but it could also adumbrate relations of exclusion and inclusion. In their legends, Figeac and Gellone excluded; Conques and Aniane attempted to include. Often in legends the very demarcation of the space that will become the abbey's property makes such statements. Typically a saint would literally trace out the abbey's property, creating a bounded physical space as meaningfully charged as his or her body. The correspondence, as in the case of Saint-Quintin of Gaillaguet, is once again between saint, property, and community. For example, in a rather humorously recounted episode of an eleventh-century version of the *vita* of Saint Gilles, King Flavius, ruler of the Goths, decided to endow the monastery he had just founded on the site of the saintly hermit's retreat.[117] To determine the amount of property he would grant, the king proposed the following to Gilles. He, Flavius, would return to Nîmes. Gilles meanwhile should get up early the next morning and set out to meet the king. The king would then endow the monastery with as much land as Gilles had traversed. But the next morning, Gilles performed what seems to have been the full office of matins before setting out. As a result, he met the king a mere two miles from his cave. The king realized that this distance would hardly translate into sufficient land for the monastery and admonished Gilles to wake up earlier the next morning. Gilles did so and covered five miles. Flavius accordingly allotted to the monastery the territory with this radius around Gilles's cave. The repetition of the process would have provoked some smiles among listeners or readers of the *vita*. It also would have impressed upon them the extent of the territory embraced by the monastery's jurisdiction.

Although the donation was thus royal, Flavius himself did not have the crucial role of delineating the property. Rather, in this case as in others, the patron saint's movements created the territory that became the abbey (and the abbey's).[118] Furthermore, while royal patronage was claimed for the abbey, royal power over it was implicitly limited; Gilles's actions carve out an area of immunity in the midst of the royal domain.[119] In other cases, though, the significant body which becomes the basis of the correspondence between abbey and property is instead that of a king. In the *Gesta Karoli Magni*, for example, Lagrasse's patrimony comes into being through the actions of Charlemagne and his epic peers.[120] Charlemagne's step, much like that of Gilles, demarcates the sacred space that centers on the

---

[117] *Vita S. Aegidii*, in *AB* 8 (1889): 116–117, here 116. The episode is recounted in less dramatic terms in the versions of this *vita* in *AASS* September 1:301–302 and in Jones, *Saint Gilles*, p. 107.

[118] Cf. the case of Saint-Germier (see below, Chapter 4 at nn. 48–56) and that of Noblat (*Vita sancti Leonardi confessoris*, in *AASS* November 3:153).

[119] Here I am influenced by Walter Goffart's reading of a similar incident in the *Vita Carileffi; Le Mans Forgeries*, pp. 75–76.

[120] For details see below, Chapter 5 at nn. 197–200.

abbey and becomes its own; the bodies of the king's fallen peers, enshrined in chapels that he donates to Lagrasse, become metaphors for the abbey's royally defined identity.[121] Here the king is definitively included, just as he was implicitly excluded in Saint-Gilles's legend.

In these two legends, relations are ordered not just between the monastery, patron saint, and/or founder, but also between the monastery and the surrounding landscape. Indeed, in legend, endowment often becomes the locus for the expression of a more general construction of the larger physical world. Already established as a sacred site by its revelation, the monastery, through its endowment, now becomes the inclusive center of the landscape. As in the case of Saint-Gilles, the legendary delineation of monastic patrimony often organizes territory in a concentric fashion, making of the abbey in question the symbolic focal point. Legendary endowment, moreover, might cause a web of lines to emanate from the monastery, connecting this center with other topographical points. In the process, generic, undefined space is named and organized—a world is created and ordered. The motif is that of the founder's further foundations, the creation of ecclesiastical communities subordinate to the first established.

For example, in the third version of the *vita* of Austremonius, a text from the second half of the eleventh century composed at Issoire, the saint founds not only this monastery but also a series of churches and chapels in its vicinity.[122] Although Austremonius does not explicitly grant them to Issoire, his actions trace connections between his foundations, primary and secondary. Furthermore, other sources reveal that at least some of these churches were actually Issoire's priories.[123] In an interesting twist on this motif, churches might be built for family members of a saintly founder. Here kinship becomes the trope for inclusion of these churches in the circle of dependencies of the monastery. The *vita* of Meneleus recounts how this saint's female relatives (including his rejected wife), unable to live without him, searched desperately for him. When they finally discovered him at Menat, Savinianus, one of Meneleus's companions, suggested that a *cella* be built for them (the site is then indicated by an angel).[124] The resulting church, Sainte-Marie of Lisseuil, located some six kilometers south of Menat, was one of this abbey's priories, although the *vita* does not say so.[125] But is this not implied in the episode? After all, the church that housed the saint's family surely belonged to the family of the saint's monastery. More-

---

[121] On the extremely important parallel between king and saint adumbrated here, see below, Chapters 3–5.

[122] *Vita tertia S. Austremonii* (*AASS* November 1:61–77, esp. 69, 70, 73).

[123] See Fournier's identifications in "Saint Austremoine," pp. 458–459.

[124] *Vita Menelei,* (*MGH SSRM* 5:142).

[125] On Lisseuil's status as a priory, see the editor's remark in *Vita Menelei* (*MGH SSRM* 5:142, n. 6).

over, does not the gender of Meneleus's relatives indicate, underline, and reinforce the subordinate status of their church?[126]

This process of organizing patrimonial space through further foundations can become the morphological principle of the entire legend, as it is in Lagrasse's *Gesta Karoli Magni*. This text illustrates very vividly how the abbey's own origins become a means of creating specific space from generic space. The legend is replete with place names—and with descriptions of how those places came into being through Charlemagne's actions as he founded the abbey. For example, on the "plain" of Mirailles (about one and a half kilometers to the southwest of Lagrasse, now a large open patchwork of fields), Charlemagne dubs three thousand of his knights and erects a large stone, declaring that this place should be known as Petrafixa.[127] Also, Charlemagne fights one of his first battles on a promontory very near Lagrasse; Turpin declares it should be called henceforth Mons Bressorum, since among the thousands of Muslims captured there were seven hundred infants *in bressibus* (diapers? breeches?) whom he baptized.[128] Charlemagne accepts Turpin's proposal and constructs there a chapel dedicated to Saint Vincent. The king, his prelates, and his princes found additional chapels that form a ring around Lagrasse.[129] As burial places for various fallen peers, they found two more monasteries, one very local (Sainte-Marie des Palais; modern Les Palais on the River Nielle, ten kilometers east of Lagrasse) and one distant (Saint-André of Sorède, fifteen kilometers south of Perpignan)—but each made explicitly Lagrasse's dependent.[130]

Charlemagne grants to the abbey several of the other places thus defined and named by the legend. Even in those cases where he does not, other sources show us that many of these were Lagrasse's properties. By the tenth century, for example, Lagrasse had acquired estates at Mons Bressorum (modern-day Ville Bresses, a gentle hill some one and a half kilometers to the south of the abbey), and by at least the thirteenth century it had a priory at Mirailles.[131] In any case, the legend implicitly endows Lagrasse with all the space it defines. This world is constructed through the abbey's origins and

---

[126] Cf. the case of Guillaume of Gellone's sisters, who plead with their brother to allow them to enter the religious life with him: *Vita [S. Willelmi ducis]* (*AASS* May 6:813). Does this episode serve as the trope for the foundation of the community of nuns (over which the abbot held certain rights) at Gellone? See G. Henschius's remarks in *AASS* May 6:814, note q, and those of Jean Mabillon in *AASSosB* 4.1:72.

[127] *Gesta Karoli Magni*, p. 78.

[128] *Gesta Karoli Magni*, p. 32. This site is probably also the one referred to in the text as Ville Bercianis. Both Mons Bressorum and Ville Bercianis appear in connection with Rupe Gileria, a place near Lagrasse that I have been unable to identify (pp. 54, 90). Furthermore, the text locates both Mons Bressorum and Ville Bercianis in the same place in relation to Lagrasse.

[129] *Gesta Karoli Magni*, pp. 28, 30, 32.

[130] *Gesta Karoli Magni*, pp. 48, 72, 92.

[131] In 959 the archbishop of Narbonne sold to Lagrasse the church he and his canons held at *Villa Berciano*. *GC* 6, instr. 19–20.

hence relates back to Lagrasse. As in other legendary forms of endowment, a map is created, and the abbey is at its center.

Through its legendary endowment with land, then, the monastery acquired yet another layer of identity, physical and symbolic, that might communicate a message about relations between the abbey and its patrons, and between the abbey and its surroundings. Equally symbolic loci were the gifts—books, liturgical furnishings, reliquaries, and so on—that were part of the endowment. Legends might not mention these at all. Or they might describe these objects as a glorious, generic conglomeration embodying the abbey's wealth.[132] More strikingly, these objects could be fashioned as individual and specific statements about the abbey's status.[133]

For example, among Charlemagne's lavish gifts to Lagrasse detailed in the *Gesta Karoli Magni* were a chalice and paten made of precious stones. Of the latter the king says: "there are none its equal . . . in this world except for three others: namely, one at Saint-Denis and one at Saint Sophia of Constantinople [the text omits the third]." Thus the paten proclaims Lagrasse as the equal of one of the greatest churches of Christendom, the Hagia Sophia, and of the royal monastery par excellence, Saint-Denis. Moreover, this was to be a public statement; both chalice and paten were placed on the main altar so that they "might be seen by everyone," and Charlemagne ordered that they remain in view there "forever." These gifts embodied Lagrasse's status relative not only to other churches, but also to its founder; Lagrasse was the apple of the royal eye. The king places his gloves on the altar as a "sign of his affection for the monastery" (and a pledge of future donations)—a meaning that must extend to all his generous gifts.[134]

In the so-called *Chronicle* of Aniane (around 1100), Charlemagne, made Benedict's partner in this abbey's foundation, presents gifts that form a complex of such symbols.[135] The *Chronicle* insists in lavish detail on the king's sumptuous offerings, which included not only "innumerable" lands, thirteen dependent monasteries, various gold and silver vessels, and a fabulous stone (*abeston*), but also a magnificent manuscript containing the Gospels copied by, the *Chronicle* underlines, Alcuin himself. Here the text trumpets the Carolingian connection represented by Charlemagne's munificence and the transmission of the words from the hand of the prestigious Alcuin (who in fact had been Benedict's personal friend). The *Chronicle* describes another even more charged gift from the emperor: an

---

132 See the description of Clovis's gifts to Saint-Germier below (Chapter 4 at n. 52).

133 For examples of such gifts functioning as statements in conflicts between two abbeys, see the case of Aniane and Gellone below (Chapter 6 at nn. 268–307).

134 For all these gifts, see *Gesta Karoli Magni*, pp. 236–238.

135 Paris, BN Latin 5941, f. 40. The list of gifts in the *Chronicle* bears no resemblance to Charlemagne's donations described by Ardo, *Vita Benedicti* (*MGH SS* 15.1:208).

ebony scepter topped with the image of a lion's head. The more typical abbot's crozier bore a deer's head, a lamb, or a biblical scene; the lion scepter recalls rather the armrests of thrones common in Romanesque and Gothic imagery.[136] The *Chronicle* makes no bones about it; the ebony scepter endows the monastery with a quasi-regal power: "this is considered to have had the power of judgment because just as the lion is the most powerful of the animals, thus his image is a sign of threats. Through the image of the lion also, they should know fury's force because it is written: 'the anger of the king is the messenger of death' [Proverbs 16.14]."[137] The evocation of the lion as a symbol of royal anger (an association not explicit in Proverbs 16 but in neighboring Proverbs 19.12 and 20.2) resonates at two levels. The monastery's anger is to be feared as that of the king's; and any affront to the monastery would incur the anger of the king, the towering Charlemagne.[138]

This cluster of gifts thus embodied Aniane's status and privilege. Furthermore, as we shall see, it probably represented a challenge to Gellone, the abbey that Aniane was trying to claim as a *cella* at the time of the *Chronicle*'s composition.[139] Charlemagne's gifts to Aniane form a counterweight to the most important legendary offering Guillaume made to his foundation of Gellone: the piece of the True Cross that the patriarch of Jerusalem had sent Charlemagne. In a developed and purposeful episode, the *vita* of Guillaume presents the legendary founder as the provider of this relic for which Gellone was famous.[140]

This relic was certainly special, as was its source: Charlemagne.[141] But Guillaume's provision of the relic for Gellone was not necessarily so; he was accomplishing what in legend and often in reality was considered part of the founder's duty. Spiritual patrons, like material property, were critical elements of monastic identity.[142] An abbey was incomplete without them, as Maillezais's foundation legend underlined. The monastery had been estab-

---

[136] Such lion imagery recalls the biblical type of Solomon's throne (3 Kings 10.18–20). For actual examples of lion armrests on thrones and bishops' *cathedrae*, see Percy Ernst Schramm, *Herrschaftszeichen und Staatssymbolik: Beiträge zu ihrer Geschichte vom dritten bis zum sechzehnten Jahrhundert*, Schriften der MGH, 13.1–3 (Stuttgart, 1954–1956), 1:326, 339, 3:709.

[137] Paris, BN Latin 5941, f. 40r.

[138] In another passage, the *Chronicle* makes the scepter explicitly royal: among Charlemagne's other gifts was a "sceptrum regale ex ebore valde mirificum" (Paris, BN Latin 5941, f. 33v).

[139] See below, Chapter 6 at nn. 268–307.

[140] For a detailed discussion, see below, Chapter 5 at nn. 73–75. The fame of Gellone's Cross is underlined in the late twelfth-century foundation legend of Silvanès. This text relates that crowds congregated at Gellone on Good Friday "ad adorandum crucem" (*Cartulaire de Silvanès*, p. 379).

[141] On the significance of the association between Charlemagne and the True Cross, see below, Chapter 5 at nn. 82–88.

[142] See above, Chapter 1 at nn. 47–54.

lished and richly endowed by the stormy couple Emma of Blois and William IV of Aquitaine. But according to the legend, Maillezais's abbot, Theodelinus, was tormented (*angebatur*) because, although the monastery enjoyed abundant material possessions, it lacked "saints' relics, by which it would be honored and defended."[143]

Theodelinus's complaint both underlines the necessity of relics and hints at one of their many valences. Relics could "defend" the monastery, that is encircle it with a protective power. Hence as a passage from the late eleventh-century cartulary *Chronicle* of Saint-Chaffre stated, relics could assure a monastery's position in the larger social world. This latter text proudly proclaimed that the relics of the patron saint guaranteed and were the source of the monastery's freedom from subjection to any king, prince, or bishop (save that of Rome) and of its right to elect its own abbot.[144] Like the saint's steps, the saint's relics could demarcate the sacrosanct boundaries of monastic identity.

In legend, the acquisition of relics traced a circle around the abbey; it could also draw lines that radiated out from the abbey to connect it with other sources of power and authority. For unless the abbey was literally founded on a saint's body, relics had to be brought from elsewhere. Foundation and translations of relics were so interrelated that the association might transpose itself to the textual level; foundation legends might not merely mention translations but could explicitly take the form of a *translatio* narrative.[145] In either case, the legendary translations metaphorically mapped a web of relations linking the abbey, the source of the relics, and the agent of the translation. Unless the source of the relic was unwilling, making the legendary acquisition of relics a "sacred theft" (*furtum sacrum*), these relations were those of association and friendship.[146]

In the *Vita Menelei*, for example, Barontus, whose daughter was spurned by Meneleus, wages war upon the saint and his companions. Finally Barontus desists and becomes their ally and patron, granting to Menat (Meneleus's foundation) various properties, including the monastery of Tres-

---

143 Peter of Maillezais, *Qualiter fuit constructum Malliacense* (*PL* 146:1265–1266).

144 "Nulli enim regi vel principi aut alicui potestati terrenae nec etiam episcopo . . . novimus esse subjectum; sed habet libertatem propriam . . . eligendi sibimet . . . abbatem . . . hanc vero nostri vel ecclesiae libertatem, non incolarum religiosa probitas aut excellentis ingenii prudentia contulit, sed meritum praecipue beati martyris Theofredi," (*Cartulaire de l'abbaye de St-Chaffre*, p. 8, no. 9).

145 For example, Peter, the author of Maillezais's legend, gave it the title *Qualiter fuit constructum Malliacense monasterium et corpus sancti Rigomeri translatum* (Paris, BN Latin 4829, f. 246ra). The importance of the second half of the rubric is made visual: "Rigomeri" is capitalized. The foundation of Saint-Jean-d'Angély appears in a text called *Angeriacensium de translatione capitis [s. joannis baptistae] ad suum monasterium* (*AASS* June 5:650–652).

146 On *furta sacra*, see Geary, *Furta Sacra*. On gifts of relics establishing friendship, see Roman Michalowski, "Le don d'amitié dans la société carolingienne et les *translationes sanctorum*," in *Hagiographie, cultures et sociétés, IVe–XIIe s.: Actes du colloque organisé à Nanterre et à Paris, 2–5 mai, 1979* (Paris, 1979), pp. 399–416.

fagium.[147] Later, Barontus is petitioned by one of Meneleus's followers to provide relics for this priory, and does so. The passage describing his gift of relics is studded with words deriving from *amicitia*, and qualifies Barontus as "that man of known friendship (*amicitia*)."[148] The donation of relics was thus a pledge of goodwill and friendship toward Meneleus and his disciples.[149]

The donor of relics thus becomes the friend of the monastery, a mutual association that implies obligations on both sides and is not without a hint of power; the giver of patron saints becomes him- or herself the abbey's patron. Who, then, do the legends choose as the sources of these powerful distillations of the sacred, as the donors whose role becomes assimilated to that of the relics as patrons and protectors of boundaries? Sometimes, as in the case of Menat, legends assign this part to aristocratic founders. Emma of Blois and Hugh of Le Mans provide relics for Maillezais.[150] Guillaume does the same for his foundation of Gellone;[151] Calminius, founder of Mozac, travels to Agen where he obtains relics of Caprasius.[152] And a late twelfth-century text describes how Roger, "duke of Aquitaine," had acquired from Pippin the Short the head of Saint Austremonius on the occasion of the translation of his relics from Volvic to Mozac. Roger later transmitted this precious relic to the abbey he founded at Charroux.[153]

In many of these instances, the aristocratic founders provide relics that were in their own possession.[154] Often the legends do not mention the

[147] *Vita Menelei* (*MGH SSRM* 5:147–148). I have been unable to identify Tresfagium; the *vita* locates it in the territory of Issandon.

[148] "[A]micitie . . . amicabiles . . . amicabilis" (*Vita Menelei*, in *MGH SSRM* 5:155).

[149] The episode also appears (although cast differently) in Pseudo-Hermenbertus's *Vita Vincentiani confessoris Avolcensis* (probably composed in the eleventh century and probably the text that served as a basis for the *Vita Menelei*); see *MGH SSRM* 5:119–120. Yet another version is contained in the *Vita sancti Saviniani abbatis* (Clermont-Ferrand, BM 150, f. 51v).

[150] In the very late tenth century, Countess Emma gathered relics for the abbey; see Peter of Maillezais, *Qualiter fuit constructum Malliacense* (*PL* 146:1254). In the mid-eleventh century, the abbot asked Hugh III, count of Maine (992–1015/16), about available relics; Hugh granted to Maillezais those of a Saint Rigomer. See Peter of Maillezais, *Qualiter fuit constructum Malliacense* (*PL* 146: 1266–1269). These latter relics were those Peter of Maillezais identifies with the foundation. The monks' appeal to Hugh of Le Mans probably related to the complex political rivalries between the dukes of Aquitaine, the counts of Le Mans, and the counts of Anjou. Through the legendary translation, Hugh becomes a patron who counterbalances the dukes of Aquitaine (the abbey's founders), and Angevin power is strictly limited. On the political situation, see Robert Latouche, *Histoire du comté du Maine pendant le Xe et le XIe siècle* (Paris, 1910), pp. 54–56; and Olivier Guillot, *Le comte d'Anjou et son entourage au XIe siècle*, 2 vols. (Paris, 1972), 1:65–68, 86–87, 119–123.

[151] *Vita [S. Willelmi ducis]* (*AASS* May 6:815–816).

[152] *Vita S. Calminii confessoris* (*AASS* August 3:761).

[153] *Additamentum de reliquiis S. Austremonii* (*AASS* November 1:80–82) (this text relates that eventually Issoire, Austremonius's own monastery, was refounded as the relic's shrine). For another example of a noble providing relics, see the refoundation of Sainte-Eulalie of Elne: de Marca, *Marca Hispanica*, no. 172, cols. 1148–1149.

[154] Such is the case with Barontus for Menat's priory, and with Emma and Hugh of Le Mans for Maillezais.

source of these relics. When they do, it is almost invariably a king. Charlemagne grants relics for Gellone to Guillaume, and Roger acquires those for Charroux from King Pippin. In many legends, no aristocrat functions as a conduit through which relics pass from king to monastery; a king, typically Charlemagne, grants the relics directly to the abbey. The attribution of this role to Charlemagne has striking consequences for that monarch's legendary image, but here let me emphasize rather the consequences for the abbey.[155] Such translations tacitly assert that the abbey was a royal foundation; through the gift of relics, the abbey claims the king, who, like the saint, becomes its patron.

Equally, using the same trope, monasteries could render themselves papal. For if founders had no relics, they could obtain them by making a pilgrimage to some important source of relics, typically Rome which from the ninth century on engaged in a flourishing relic trade. In that century, Einhard related how he sent representatives to Rome to acquire relics for the monastery he wished to found, the future Seligenstadt. There they suffered from the chicanery of the relic dealers and finally, in desperation, furtively dug up relics.[156] In the southern legends, the founders have an easier time obtaining the objects of their desire; they receive relics from the hands of the pope himself. Calminius, for example, only goes to Agen on his way back from Rome, where he had successfully petitioned the pope for relics of Saint Peter.[157] These apostolic relics surely link the monastery they grace, Mozac, with their source, Peter's successor, as do those relics of Christ which Alet's legendary founder, Bera, receives from Pope Leo III—and as do all acquisitions, legendary or not, of relics from the pope.[158]

Legends might make this absolutely explicit; a papal grant of privileges sometimes accompanies the relics. A legendary charter relates that Stephen, viscount of the Gévaudan, and his wife, Almodis, went to Rome and gave their foundation of Langogne to Pope Sylvester. The pope recognized the *traditio* in two forms: he "gave us some of the wood of the holy cross and some relics. . . . He also gave us a privilege written . . . on parchment."[159] Both types of objects received from the hands of the pope served as proof of the monastery's special status and enjoyment of papal protection, as reminders of the new community's symbolic and sacred boundaries.

---

[155] On Charlemagne as provider of relics, see below: Chapter 5, under "King, Christ, and Relics."

[156] *Translatio et miracula sanctorum Marcellini et Petri* (*MGH SS* 15.1:238–264). For a discussion of this text and of the foundation's significance for Einhard, see Josef Fleckenstein, "Einhard, seine Gründung und sein Vermächtnis in Seligenstadt," in his *Ordnungen und formende Kräfte des Mittelalters: Ausgewählte Beiträge* (Göttingen, 1989), pp. 84–111.

[157] *Vita S. Calminii confessoris* (*AASS* August 3:761).

[158] For Alet's legend, see *HL* 2:79–80, no. 23. On the political meaning of translations of Roman relics, see for example Friedrich Prinz, "Stadtrömisch-italienische Märtyrerreliquien und fränkischer Reichsadel," *Historisches Jahrbuch* 87 (1967): 9–25.

[159] Paris, BN Latin 12767, ff. 61r–64r.

Consecration

The legendary description of the incorporation of the relics into the fabric of the abbey church—the ritual of consecration—could sometimes be the locus for even more flamboyant statements about the monastery's position in the social hierarchy. Generally this ritual, at least in legend, simply represented a formalization of the antecedent revelation of the site as sacred space. Thus, especially in those legends which embroider the theme of revelation elaborately, the consecration might not be mentioned; after all, the site was already manifestly a "gate of heaven." Or the legend might provide merely the date of the consecration, and a sober list of the names of the officiating bishops and attending *potentes*. In other cases, however, the legends play with consecration, heightening its meaning, even at moments rendering concrete the descent of the heavenly Jerusalem implied in the ritual. As they do so, the legends make assertions, subtle and not so subtle, about the abbey's relations with external authorities, most particularly but not exclusively about those who conduct the ritual: bishops.

Such statements were made in one or both of two ways. A legendary figure could perform the consecration. According to the legend of Charroux and the charter describing Urban II's dedication of that church in 1096, Leo III had consecrated the original abbey.[160] This latter pope was also associated with the dedication of Alet in the charter (composed in the twelfth century?) describing this monastery's foundation; the text specifies that the founder, "count Bera" wished "that the dedication of this place which is about to occur should be done most properly and with you, lord pope Leo, being favorable to it." No other bishop figures as being involved in the consecration.[161] Finally, Leo and/or Archbishop Turpin (depending on which version of the abbey's legend one consults) officiate at the consecration of Saint-Jean of Sorde; and in the "Pseudo-Turpin," Turpin conducts that of Compostela.[162]

In these cases, the legends focus on the identity of specific representatives of the Charlemagne myth; the ritual becomes a means of intimately associating these figures with the abbey's origins. Furthermore, the legends symbolically exclude local representatives of episcopal power from the role assigned to the gilded figures. As we have seen, the right of consecration was a part of episcopal jurisdiction over monasteries. Here the legends—just like the authentic privileges many of the abbeys received—divest the local

---

[160] *Chartes et documents pour servir à l'histoire de l'abbaye de Charroux*, pp. 6–7, 25–26.

[161] *HL* 2:79–80 (here 80), no. 23.

[162] Sorde: *MGH Diplomata Karolinorum* 1:567–68 and *Cartulaire de l'abbaye de Saint-Jean de Sorde . . .*, ed. Paul Raymond (Paris, 1872), p. 158, no. 184 (this garbled text attributes the consecration to Turpin and to the "apostolicus Miloleo," a combination of the name of the pope who accompanies Charlemagne in Latin legend [Leo] and that of the pontiff who is at his side in the *chansons* [Milo]). Compostela: *Historia Karoli Magni et Rotholandi, ou Chronique du Pseudo-Turpin*, ed. Cyril Meredith-Jones (Paris, 1936), pp. 169, 171, 173.

bishops of that power. Leo represents papal power; local bishops could not claim to be his heirs. Nor could southern bishops present themselves as the successors of the epic archbishop of Reims, Turpin.

In even more extreme statements of the abbey's independence, legendary figures were not the agents of the consecration, although they might be present as witnesses. Rather, the ritual was accomplished through a miracle in which the celestial Jerusalem descends to earth, and the angels—or Christ himself—climb down Jacob's ladder.[163] Typically, such legends recount how a bishop was intending to consecrate the church and had made the necessary preparations. On the eve of the appointed day, however, Christ and/or (arch)angels perform the entire ceremony, witnessed in a vision or by a person inadvertently shut into the church. Alternatively, the legend could be structured according to a most powerful biblical type of miraculous consecration: that of Solomon's temple (3 Kings 8.10–12, 2 Paralipomenon 5.13–14, 6.1–2). A cloud (*nebula*) would fill the church and prevent the bishop and clerics from entering. When the cloud dissipated, they would find the altars and walls of the church already anointed.[164] Pippin the Short and Pope Stephen were the awed witnesses of Figeac's consecration by such a cloud, as were Charlemagne and the bishop of Cologne in the case of Aniane.[165] Sometimes, too, brilliant light flooding the church could help signify the miraculous consecration.[166]

These instances in which consecration became a revelation as spectacular as that which designated the site insinuated that the abbey was free not only from episcopal but from all human authority. Popes and bishops may have been present, but it was Christ or one of his celestial representatives who

---

[163] For an explicit (although certainly not southern French) example of a miraculous consecration in which angels are seen descending "as if" on Jacob's ladder, see Ailred of Rievaulx, *Vita S. Edwardi regis et confessoris* (*PL* 195:756). Less strikingly, the consecration could be accompanied by miracles, rather than performed by them. Aymeric de Peyrat recounts that "sub tempore vero consecracione ultime ecclesie moyssiacensi . . . nonem qui fuerant incarcerati et fortissime inchatenati precibus principis apostolorum petri gloriossime fuerunt liberati" (*Chronicon;* Paris, BN Latin 4991A, f. 8ra).

[164] See Gregory the Great, *Dialogi* 2.30, in *Dialogues*, ed, and trans. Aldebert de Vogüé, 3 vols., Sources Chrétiennes, 251, 260, 265 (Paris, 1978–1980), 2:382. See above, Chapter 1, n. 71.

[165] Figeac: Wolff, "Note sur le faux diplôme," pp. 298–311; Paris, BN Doat 126, ff. 15r-17r, 18v-20v, edited in GC 1, instr. 43. See also the post-1163 interpolation of Ademar's *Chronicon* (Paris, BN Latin 5926, f. 36r; *Chronique*, p. 58, note s*), and the first lines of a list of Figeac's relics in an early twelfth-century hand in Paris, BN Latin 5219 ("sacrosancta dei ecclesia que fundata est a domno pipino rege francorum in honore domni nostri iesu christi . . . quam ipse domnus per semedipsum cum multitudine angelorum consecrare dignatus est"). Aniane: *Vita Karoli Magni* 3.10, in Gerhard Rauschen, *Die Legende Karls des Grossen in 11. und 12. Jahrhundert*, Publikationen der Gesellschaft für Rheinische Geschichtskunde, 7 (Leipzig, 1890), pp. 77–78. See also the probably twelfth-century sermon of Pseudo-Ardo Smaragdus, *Sermo sancti Ardonis, cognomento Smaragdi . . .* (*AASSosB* 4.1:225–226).

[166] Pseudo-Aurelianus, *Vita eiusdem B. Martialis episcopi Lemovicensis et galliarum apostoli*, in *De probatis sanctorum vitis . . .* , ed. Laurentius Surius, 4 vols. (Cologne, 1618), 2:372.

consecrated the church. In the hierarchy of authority, hint the legends, the monastery belonged under the dominion of Christ alone. Consecrated not by human hands but by a miracle, the abbey became a space upon which no external power could infringe.

Like nonlegendary consecrations, these miraculous ones could be recalled and their meaning thus made continuously present. Some sort of physical proof of the miracle might be left behind that could function as a relic or a memorial.[167] At Lagrasse, according to the *Gesta Karoli Magni,* Christ performed the dedication, accompanied by a host of angels and witnessed in a vision by Leo III. He left behind an abundant quantity of consecrated water. As indubitable proof of its miraculous provenance, the water cured three blind men. Turpin then enclosed what remained of it in an ampulla and placed it in the altar "so that the water might always be kept in memory (*in memoria*)"; the abbey's fabric incorporated the physical proof of the miraculous consecration and its meaning.[168]

To be sure, we remain here within the legend and its logic. We do not know if there was actually a relic to which the monks pointed and said, "That is the ampulla with the water Christ used." Other cases, however, indicate more clearly how the legendary consecration might permeate the monastery's consciousness of itself in the present. The charter of Alet links the consecration approved by Leo III with the monastery's acquisition from that same pope of its most famous relic, a piece of the True Cross.[169] Here an object actually present in the monastery is interpeted as a sign of the legendary consecration.[170] Even more strikingly, Leo III's consecration of Charroux was recalled and invoked by the charter describing Urban II's dedication of the same church in 1096. Not only did Leo function as a type for Urban's actions, but the altar that Urban consecrated had been built over the one dedicated by Leo, relates this charter.[171] Urban's actions implicitly mirror those of Leo III in yet another way; or, rather, Urban's actions reveal the meaning of Leo's. At the consecration, Urban takes Charroux under papal protection, effectively designating it as independent; Leo's legendary consecration is a trope representing the same privilege, rooting it in the past and creating it in the present.

---

[167] For striking examples beyond the south of France, see Charles J. Liebman, "La consécration légendaire de la basilique de Saint-Denis," *Le Moyen Age,* 45 (1935): 252–264; *Liber de apparitione sancti Michaelis,* pp. 540–543; and *Chronica monasterii sancti Michaelis Clusini* (*MGH SS* 30:963).

[168] *Gesta Karoli Magni,* pp. 230, 232, 234, 236 (here 236).

[169] Alet was known to have this relic by the mid-eleventh century; the *querimonia* (ca. 1059) of Berengar, viscount of Narbonne, mentions "ecclesiam sancte Mariae coenobium loci Electi, ubi mirificum habetur lignum dominicum" (*HL* 5:499–500, no. 251).

[170] Cf. Ademar of Chabannes's interpretation of inscribed crosses as proof of consecration; see above, Chapter 1 at n. 76.

[171] *Chartes et documents pour servir à l'histoire de l'abbaye de Charroux,* pp. 25–26.

Privileges

The message implied in legendary consecration—the abbey's independence—is made crystal clear in the acquisition of privileges, often the culminating stage of legendary foundation. More explicitly than the other elements of monastic identity, the charter of privileges, whether accorded by pope, bishop, king, or prince, delineated the monastery's relations with these external powers and their agents. Not surprisingly, then, legends often take the form of such texts. Privileges, the explicitly structured relations between the abbey and the outside world, become the image of origins and of the abbey's identity.[172] Here the thirst for liberty that informs the legends is at its most evident.

In those legends which appear in narrative rather than diplomatic texts, the claim to various liberties can be just as transparent. Such legends may describe the acquisition of privileges with little imaginative embroidery; the pope or king, perhaps at the request of one of the immediate founders, grants various rights (secular immunity, papal protection, exemption, and so on) to the new monastery.[173] In other instances, though, legends exploit the symbolic possibilities of the according of liberties and make a metaphoric statement about the monastery's power.

In the *Gesta Karoli Magni,* for example, Leo III admonishes the monks and the newly elected abbot of Lagrasse: "you should always love the king of France and answer to him and the Roman bishop and you should have no other lord. . . . I give this privilege to you and all your successors so that you should not be subject to any bishop or archbishop nor should you answer in any matter to anyone except the Roman bishop." To these sweeping privileges, which bind the monastery in no uncertain way with the mythic king and his pope, Leo adds a more startling one. The abbot is to make the journey *ad limina* not annually but once every five to seven years.[174] There, "so that the whole world may know with what great affection the Roman *curia* loves the monastery of Lagrasse," the pope would present the abbot with the papal steed, a white horse. The abbot would have the horse for a year and could grant it to the bishop of Carcassonne when he came to Lagrasse (at the abbot's invitation only) to celebrate mass on Assumption Day.[175]

The *Gesta Karoli Magni* reiterates that the gift of the white horse symbol-

---

[172] The majority of the southern legends involve at least one such document.

[173] See, for example, Guillaume's acquisition of a royal privilege for Gellone: *Vita [S. Willelmi ducis]* (*AASS,* May 6:813).

[174] Exemptions from the (financially onerous) annual visit to Rome were granted by the late twelfth century. See, for example, *Bullaire de l'abbaye de Saint-Gilles,* p. 82, no. 60.

[175] *Gesta Karoli Magni,* pp. 96 and 98.

izes the friendship and affection linking each pair of prelates. Certainly we can interpret it in this way. To this explicit meaning, however, we can add a further implicit one. By at least the eleventh century, white horses or horses adorned with white clothes belonged to the papal repertoire of insignia borrowed from the imperial tradition.[176] On such horses, the pope and cardinals rode in processions designed as expressions of sovereignty and lordship. The cascading grants of the white horse in the *Gesta Karoli Magni* thus set up a hierarchy of authority and power. The abbot who receives the horse is constituted as the pope's proxy and as a member of the upper echelons of the Roman clergy. He in turn can transmit the emblem of power to the bishop of Carcassonne. This latter grant, however, depends on the abbot's judgment of the bishop's character: "if [the bishop] be virtuous," reads the text (an inverted and oblique reference to the bishop's right to decide whether an abbot-elect is fit for office?). Thus Leo III's privilege not only grants Lagrasse exemption, but also symbolically establishes the abbot as the bishop's superior—and as the immediate representative of apostolic authority.

Concrete symbols of liberty can accompany the privilege as well as being implied in it. The *vita* of Saint Gilles climaxes and culminates when the saint journeys to Rome to obtain papal protection.[177] He offers his monastery to the pope expressly so that it will never be subjected to any layman. Gilles receives a physical pledge complementing the written privilege: a pair of cypress doors sculpted with the figures of Peter and Paul. To everyone's amazement, the saint heaves the doors into the Tiber. Some time after his return to the monastery, the doors wash up on the shores of the Rhône. Their miraculous trajectory represents a conduit between Rome and the monastery, a direct link reminiscent of the one implied in translations of Roman relics. The doors themselves, of course, embody papal protection. Peter and Paul guard and control the entrance to the monastery.[178] Their

---

[176] Schramm, *Herrschaftszeichen*, 3:714–715, who also mentions that by the twelfth century certain abbeys owed as their *census* to the pope just such white horses. See also Ernst H. Kantorowicz, "The 'King's Advent' and the Enigmatic Panels in the Doors of Sancta Sabina," *The Art Bulletin* 26 (1944): 217, n. 66; and Hans-Walter Klewitz, "Die Krönung des Papstes," *Zeitschrift der Savigny-Stiftung für Rechtsgeschichte: Kanonistische Abteilung* 30 (1941): 117–118. The Lagrasse text nicely reverses the direction of the payment. For an example of the papal use of such horses, see Suger, *Vita Ludovici. Vie de Louis VI le Gros*, ed. and trans. Henri Waquet (Paris, 1929), p. 62.

[177] *Vita S. Aegidii: AB* 8 (1889): 119; *AASS* September 1:303; Jones, *Saint Gilles*, p. 110.

[178] It is possible that in the eleventh century Saint-Gilles actually flaunted such doors; for examples of church doors from this period with narrative and symbolic programs (a revival of an Italian, particularly Roman, tradition), see Walter Cahn, *The Romanesque Wooden Doors of Auvergne* (New York, 1974); and Robert G. Calkins, *Monuments of Medieval Art* (New York, 1979), pp. 103–106. Are the doors of the Saint-Gilles legend a reminiscence of those famous fifth-century Roman doors—those of Santa Sabina, carved from cypress wood? If so, they carry a double formal Roman reference.

images guarantee and proclaim in figural terms the immunity recorded in the written privilege of the legend and, even more strikingly, the liberty that, as we shall see, Saint-Gilles claimed in a stunning series of papal forgeries.[179] Here, as in the legends recounted in the shape of charters of privileges, the abbey becomes its liberty.

With bold sharp strokes, the legends draw the dimensions of monastic identity. Using slightly different legendary syntax and emphasizing different topoi, each monastery fashions an image of itself as a place (*locus*) of inherent sacrality. This place, revealed by agents who themselves are necessarily as special as the site, incarnates the verse of Genesis that formed the refrain of the consecration ritual: "How terrible is this place!" (Gen. 28.17). In this process of revelation, the monastery traces around itself lines over which external powers may not cross. Implicitly or explicitly, the legendary motifs rendered the abbey immune to human authority, hedging it with the sanctions of the sacred.[180] Through its legend, the abbey might organize the surrounding landscape as its patrimony and make statements about its relationship with the representatives of human power. An image of social order, of the world, both local and larger, is adumbrated—and the abbey is placed at its symbolic center.

The most magnificent manuscript containing a southern French legend renders these dimensions of the creation of monastic identity concrete both in its structure and in an actual image. In the eleventh century, the Gascon abbey of Saint-Sever had made for itself a richly illustrated *Beatus* commentary on the Book of Apocalypse. Late in that same century, the legendary charter describing the abbey's foundation was copied onto the first of the folios left blank at the end of the manuscript.[181] Thus, as one read the manuscript, the description of the celestial Jerusalem's revelation (Apocalypse) introduced and framed the account of the monastery's beginnings, announcing and guaranteeing Saint-Sever's nature as the earthly incarnation of the heavenly city. Even before the reader arrived at the foundation legend, he or she would have been presented with the abbey's image of itself as a sacred center. A map of the world occupies two facing folios of the *Beatus* commentary (see Figure 2). On it, three structures are immediately distinguishable from the plethora of tiny schematic buildings: Rome, Jerusalem, and Saint-Sever.[182] Of these three sacred places, the last is particularly

[179] See below; Chapter 6, under "Saint-Gilles and the Three Enemies."

[180] See also Kastner's conclusion that the German foundation legends he studied were "spiritual swords" intended to defend the abbey's liberty: *Historiae fundationum*, esp. pp. 83–90.

[181] For an edition of the fabulous foundation charter copied in the *Beatus* (Paris, BN Latin 8878), see "Documents transcrits à la fin du *Beatus*," in *Saint-Sever*, pp. 114–116.

[182] Paris BN Latin 8878, ff. 45bis v–45ter.

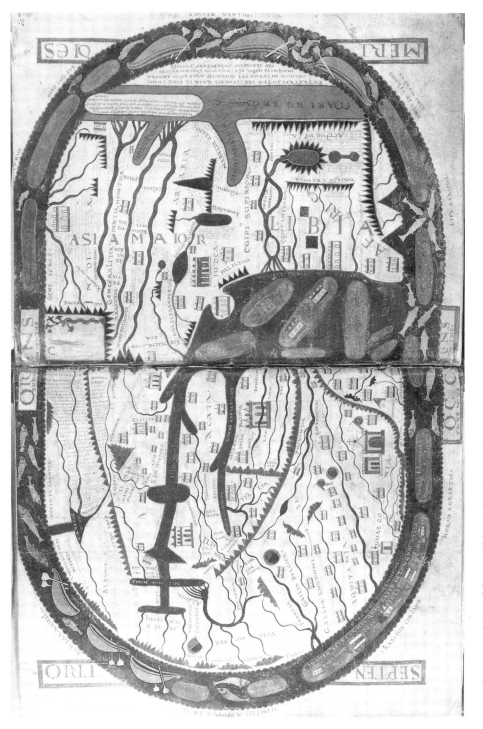

FIGURE 2. Map of the world from the *Beatus* of Saint-Sever (Paris, BN Latin 8878), late eleventh century. Saint-Sever is the large and distinct structure in the lower-left quarter. © cliché Bibliothèque Nationale de France, Paris.

highlighted, painted with more vivid shades of color, and given an architectural design different from any other on the map. According to the visual homology, Saint-Sever is the most significant of these centers of Christendom—and the abbey imagines itself not in isolation but on a map of the world.

A POETIC HISTORY:

THE FOUNDERS

3

Of Halos and Crowns

I n their creation of meaning through legend, monastic communities did not only manipulate motifs. They also carefully wrought images of those figures to whom they chose to attribute their origins: the founders. The characteristics that caused the abbeys to select certain figures rather than others for this highly significant role have much to reveal about the communities' conceptions of themselves. Monasteries did not choose their founders at random any more than they did their patron saints. Indeed, the affinity between monastery and founder was akin to that between monastery and patron saint: the traits of the founder or saint transmitted themselves to the abbey. In each instance, these characteristics could be either intrinsic to the figure selected to play the part or acquired after the fact. Just as a monastery might tailor a patron saint to suit itself—such that the Saint Michael of Mont-Saint-Michel was not a carbon copy of the archangel venerated at Monte Gargano—so too an abbey might reshape the figure it chose to associate with its origins. Reflected in founders' acquired and desired characteristics, then, are monasteries' images of themselves.

Acquired Characteristics: Sanctity

Foundation's significance embraced not only the abbey but also those people identified as founders. While legends created the abbey as a sacred space, in many cases they also invested founders who were not originally saints with the authority and aura of saintliness (sometimes the founders even assumed the role of patron saint). Such unofficial sanctifications may betray monasteries' hardly surprising desire to hallow their founders and thus themselves as much as possible. But evidence hints that these transformations could also spring from an intimate connection between the role of founder and the quality of saintliness.

Sometime in the last years of the twelfth century, Peter, abbot of Mozac, commissioned for his community a large enamel reliquary in the style of Limoges (see Figure 3).[1] This reliquary, like so many others of the Limoges school, recounts on one long side in rich blues and greens the salient episodes of the saint's life; on the other long face are scenes from the life of the saint's model, Christ.[2] On the lower register of the saint's side are three panels with inscriptions identifying the personages and narrating the action. In each of these panels, a certain Calminius and his wife, Namadia, preside over the construction of a monastery: from left to right are Saint-Chaffre, Tulle, and Mozac. Above these foundation scenes are three more panels, again with inscriptions. In the first two are Calminius and then Namadia lying on their tombs at Mozac while their souls are led heavenward, as the inscriptions relate, by angels (the last panel represents the patron of the shrine: Abbot Peter).[3] Calminius and Namadia thus reign in heaven with their model, Christ. And it is not just the final panels of this narrative sequence that urge this message upon the viewer. Not only are both figures depicted with halos from start to finish, but the inscriptions throughout the narrative identify Calminius as "saint" (*sanctus*); Namadia is called *beata*, though only in the panel depicting her death. The reliquary's narrative and visual structure proposes the reason for their status: founders of monasteries on earth (in the panels) below, they are therefore saints in heaven (in the panels) above.

This reliquary represents the end point of a process: the metamorphosis of Mozac's founders into saints. Calminius and Namadia (also called Numadia) first appear at Mozac in a late eleventh-century forged diploma of Pippin the Short and in the probably contemporaneous section of the third version of Saint Austremonius's *vita*.[4] In these texts, husband and wife were proclaimed the abbey's founders, but neither was called "saint." By 1160, however, among Mozac's dependencies was a church dedicated to "Saint

[1] The dating of the reliquary is problematic; see Marie-Madeleine Gauthier (who argues that the reliquary was begun under Peter III, abbot ca. 1168–1181, and completed ca. 1197), *Emaux du Moyen Age occidental* (Fribourg, 1972), pp. 333–335, no. 58.

[2] On these reliquaries, see the work of Marie-Madeleine Gauthier, particularly *Emaux méridionaux: Catalogue international de l'œuvre de Limoges*, 1 vol. to date (Paris 1987-), but also her *Emaux du Moyen Age occidental,* and "La légende de sainte Valérie et les émaux champlevés de Limoges," *Bulletin de la Société Archéologique du Limousin* 85 (1955): 35–80.

[3] See the transcription of the inscriptions in Gauthier, *Emaux du Moyen Age occidental,* p. 334.

[4] *Recueil des actes de Pépin,* pp. 227–242 (here 239), no. 58 (for a more detailed discussion of this charter, see below, Chapter 4 at nn. 140–141); *Vita tertia S. Austremonii* (*AASS* November 1:79). Neither Calminius nor Namadia appears in the relevant passages of the earlier *Vita prima S. Austremonii* or the *Vita secunda S. Austremonii* (*AASS* November 1:53, 59).

FIGURE 3. The late twelfth-century shrine of Saint Calminius from Mozac. In each of the lower panels, Calminius and Namadia found a monastery. In the left two upper panels, their souls are led to heaven at their death; the third panel depicts Abbot Peter, the reliquary's patron. Photo Zodiaque.

Calminius."[5] In roughly this same era, a fulsome *vita* celebrating this new saint was composed at Mozac.[6] The reliquary provides a visual explanation for the metamorphosis: Calminius and Namadia became saints because they were founders.[7]

[5] This church was mentioned in a bull of Alexander III (1165) (*GC* 2, instr. col. 112) and in a diploma of Louis VII (1169) (*GC* 2, instr. col. 114). See Fournier, "Saint Austremoine," p. 442.

[6] *Vita S. Calminii confessoris* (*AASS* August 3:760–761).

[7] There is evidence of Calminius's sanctity preceding the *vita*, although not from Mozac but from a church distant from that abbey: Laguenne (near Tulle). Several ninth-century documents mention a church at Laguenne dedicated to a "Saint Calminius"; see Etienne Baluze, *Historiae Tutelensis libri tres* (Paris, 1717), app., pp. 351, 364. By the early tenth century and through the eleventh, however, this church no longer appears under Calminius's name. *Cartulaire des abbayes de Tulle et de Rocamadour,* ed. J.-B. Champeval (Brive, 1903), pp. 23, 96–97, 317, 335, nos. 12, 165, 594, 602. It is unlikely that Mozac borrowed Calminius from Laguenne, taking him instead, perhaps, from the legendary tradition at Saint-Chaffre (see

An intriguing incident in the *Vita Vincentiani* suggests as well that the role of founder and the attribute of saintliness have a structural connection. Donatus, a nondescript pilgrim from Gothia, obtained a relic of Saint Vincentianus and took it back home. There, he and other inhabitants of the area built a church in which to enshrine the precious object. In its conclusion to this episode, the *vita* characterizes the founder as a saint ("sanctus ipse Donatus").[8] But why was Donatus a saint? The *vita* may have elided information about his life, borrowing bits and pieces from another hagiographic source which depicted him in a more conventional fashion as a saint.[9] Nonetheless, this text makes no reference to any such tradition. It leaves the audience with only two reasons for understanding why or how Donatus was saintly: his acquisition of the relic and his resulting establishment of the church, that is to say, his role as a founder.

Donatus, Calminius, and Namadia were not alone; other founders too were elevated over time to become saintly. Founders participated in the revelation and consecration of the site of the future monastery, a sacred place. Hence, they had to be in some way sanctifying themselves. The saints, hermits, and animals of Chapter 2 intrinsically possessed this quality; their very presence could consecrate the site. And if sacredness was contagious, the process of transmission might work in the other direction. Founders who were not saintly to begin with could become tinged with the very sacredness they had helped reveal. Thus, in imaginative memory, founders might acquire the traits implicit in their role as agents who delineated and established sacred space.[10]

Desired Characteristics: Authority

The vertical, elevating dimension of the founders' identity was balanced by a horizontal one. For foundation signified more than the sanctification of

---

below at nn. 64–69). Calminius seems to have reappeared at Laguenne only in reaction to the development of the Mozac/Saint-Chaffre legends; see the text describing his *inventio* (1172) at Laguenne in Thomas d'Aquin de Saint-Joseph, *Histoire de la vie de sainct Calmine Duc d'Aquitaine*. . . (Tulle, 1646), pp. 293–294. On the relationship between the three legends, see Fournier, "Saint Austremoine," pp. 446–450.

[8] Pseudo-Hermenbertus, *Vita Vincentiani confessoris Avolcensis* (*MGH SSRM* 5:120).

[9] The only Saint Donatus I have been able to identify who was venerated in Provence is a hermit of Sisteron. See the brief description in Ado of Vienne's martyrology: *Martyrologe d'Adon: Ses deux familles, ses trois recensions*, ed. Jacques Dubois (Paris, 1984), p. 278 (also *AASS* August 3:735). But this saint does not resemble at all the Donatus of the *Vita Vincentiani*.

[10] This phenomenon was perhaps not confined to southern France. Cf. the foundation legends from the diocese of Cologne discussed in Michalowski, "Il culto dei santi fondatori." By the twelfth century, legend ascribed sanctity to Eilbert of Florennes, founder of Waulsort. Daniel Misonne, *Eilbert de Florennes: Histoire et légende, la geste de Raoul de Cambrai* (Louvain, 1967), pp. 37–38, 44.

space and persons. As we have seen, inextricably interwoven with this aspect was another: the relational nature of monastic identity as constituted at origins. This aspect too shaped abbeys' construction of their founders. For, given the affinity between founder and foundation, exploring the founders' identity is the metaphoric equivalent to entering the world of social relations as conceived by the abbey in question. The selection of a legendary founder reveals the monastery's conception of its identity and shows where it sought to situate itself on the current as well as the past political and cultural map.

In general, the founders favored by these monasteries did not incarnate the south as a separate region, nor did they represent a vision of power narrowed down to the local level alone. Rather, these figures embodied sources of authority that eclipsed the local. Through the medium of such founders, however, monastic communities also brought this authority into the local sphere of relations—and hence into their own world. A local figure might be transformed into an embodiment of the larger authority, or a personage who originally represented this authority could be shaped to become part of the local landscape. In either case, through their founders the abbeys come to participate in and enjoy the qualities of the larger authority.

Hence, legends invoking aristocratic founders were relatively rare in the south.[11] Only with difficulty could the persons of local aristocrats, male or female, incarnate the supralocal authority southern abbeys desired to claim for their origins. The few legends that did celebrate aristocratic founders were thus unusual—and in more ways than one. For it is in these legends that most of the very few women to be ascribed the role of founder by southern monastic imaginative memory appeared. Even these legends, however, shape the presence of women in a way that echoes their absence in the vast majority of southern legends, Although in this period aristocratic women in southern France wielded considerable (if diminishing) power, and could and did found monasteries, the legends rarely depicted them functioning as independent agents.[12]

[11] Exceptions to this general rule among the abbeys studied here are the legends of Langogne and Maillezais. Maillezais may be different because it was located in the northernmost part of the region and at times fell within the orbit of Angevin power. To these legends celebrating nobles we might add the eleventh-century *vita* of Vincentianus, in which "Duke" Barontus is depicted in a favorable light as the lay partner in foundation. See Pseudo-Hermenbertus, *Vita Vincentiani (MGH SSRM* 5:112–128). In the *Vita Menelei*, however, Barontus has become a villain (*MGH SSRM* 5:129–157). There is evidence of the commemoration of aristocratic dynasties as founders in some texts which seem to be sober histories rather than legends, but I have found very few examples of this kind of text from the south. See *Initia Madirensis monasterii in diocesi Tarbiensi scripta ab anonymo, qui tempore Urbani papae II vixit,* in *Thesaurus novus anecdotorum . . . ,* 3:1203–1210; and the *Brevis historia monasterii Rivipullensis.* Also see Bisson, "Unheroed Pasts."

[12] For nonlegendary instances of southern female aristocrats founding abbeys, see Lauranson-Rosaz, *L'Auvergne,* p. 229; and Magnou-Nortier, *La société laïque,* pp. 411–412. On female patronage of southern abbeys (Cistercian), see Constance H. Berman, "Women as

Instead, in legends, aristocratic women are typically wives whose husbands are just as active in the foundation; it is only as half a couple that Almodis (wife of Stephen, viscount of Gévaudan), participates in Langogne's legendary foundation.[13] Almodis's part is at least equal to that of her husband. Such is not the case for Namadia, wife of Calminius, founder of Mozac, Saint-Chaffre, and Laguenne/Tulle. After all, there is a *vita* of Calminius, but none (extant) for Namadia. On the reliquary at Mozac, even though Namadia sports a halo, the inscriptions title her merely *beata* while honoring Calminius as *sanctus*—a gendered hierarchy of sanctity that diminishes her importance in relation to him.[14] Moreover, he enjoys his title from the beginning of the visual narrative, but she acquires hers only in the panel depicting her death.

Even a married woman who is more central to the legend than her husband exists textually in the shadow of a similarly gendered hierarchy. Maillezais's legend clearly ascribes to Countess Emma, wife of William IV of Aquitaine, the role as motivator of this abbey's foundation. It is Emma who knows what to do when hunters discover a ruined church in her husband's forest, and who consequently persuades William to restore the church in the shape of an abbey.[15] Furthermore, she provides the new monastery with its relics, a function typically associated with the role of founder, and endows it with property received from her husband upon their marriage.[16] Later, Emma appears again as the abbey's patron. As before, though, she acts through persuasion: she encourages her son, the new duke of Aquitaine, to maintain Maillezais in his affections.[17] In these ways, then, the legend does shape Emma as founder and patron of Maillezais, although as one who most often acts through influencing her husband or son. Nonetheless, the text opens with a prologue that trumpets as the abbey's founder not Emma, but her son, Duke William ("with whose aid and support the walls of the monastery of Maillezais were founded"). The prologue mentions Emma—but not as (co)founder of Maillezais, or even as William's mother, but rather as the bride of William's father.[18] Maillezais originated with men, not with Emma,

---

Donors and Patrons to Southern French Monasteries in the Twelfth and Thirteenth Centuries," in *The Worlds of Medieval Women: Creativity, Influence, Imagination,* ed. Constance H. Berman et al. (Morgantown, W. Va., 1985), pp. 53–68. On women's power in southern France in this period, see David Herlihy, "Land, Women and Family in Continental Europe, 710–1200," in *Women in Medieval Society,* ed. Susan Mosher Stuard (Philadelphia, 1976), pp. 13–45.

[13] See above, Chapter 2 at n. 32.

[14] See above at n. 3.

[15] For an analysis of women and their role as persuaders, see Sharon Farmer, "Persuasive Voices: Clerical Images of Medieval Wives," *Speculum* 61 (1986): 517–543; and Farmer, *Communities of Saint Martin,* pp. 96–116.

[16] Peter of Maillezais, *Qualiter fuit constructum Malliacense* (PL 146:1254).

[17] Peter of Maillezais, *Qualiter fuit constructum Malliacense* (PL 146:1257).

[18] Peter of Maillezais, *Qualiter fuit constructum Malliacense* (PL 146:1250).

the prologue seems to urge. The tension created between text and prologue problematizes Emma's role.

Nonetheless, in those instances in which southern abbeys chose to associate their imaginatively remembered origins with a local aristocratic family, women might appear. Most southern abbeys, though, ignored or diminished aristocrats, female and male alike, seeking instead to endow themselves with founders of the greatest possible authority. This desired supralocal authority was itself most readily available in the form of male rather than female figures: apostles and kings.

Apostles

Southern abbeys might draw the connection between their origins and supralocal authority through figures representing the primordial layer of Christianity, typically "apostles" who had known Christ (or his mother) or who had been entrusted by Saint Peter or an early pope with an evangelical mission to Gaul. The authority thus tapped, as we shall see, was that of the apostles' chief heir, the pope, although popes themselves, whether past or present, hardly ever appeared in the legends in the role of founder.

The transformation of local patron saints into apostolic figures had its roots in ninth-century traditions. During this earlier period, in the wake of the alliance between the Frankish rulers and the pope, churches began to compose *vitae* presenting their patron saint and founder as a missionary sent either by Pope Clement (Peter's successor), or by Peter himself.[19] In the eleventh century, the prized apostolicity could take another form, as we discover in interpolated, rewritten, or newly composed *vitae*. Although some of these texts retain the link with Rome through Peter or the pope, many also begin to depict their subject as having traveled to the Holy Land before going to Rome. Already by the tenth century, the legend of Front of Périgueux recounted how this saint had voyaged to the Holy Land from Gaul to learn from the desert fathers.[20] In the eleventh century, the links with the Holy Land became more direct, and the movement was reversed. Now saints came from the holy east and journeyed westward to Gaul—as did several of the saintly founders in the southern legends (Saint Gilles and Germier, Clovis's partner in the foundation of several of Lézat's priories).[21]

---

[19] In the ninth century, it may have been bishoprics (rather than monastic communities) that fostered legends of apostolic founders; see Goffart, *Le Mans Forgeries*, pp. 51–52, 195–196.

[20] "La vie ancienne de saint Front," ed. Maurice Coens, *AB* 48 (1930): 324–360.

[21] In this paragraph, I generally follow Emile Amann and Auguste Dumas, *L'église au pouvoir des laïques 888–1057* (Paris, 1948), pp. 179–186; and Richard Landes, "The Dynamics of Heresy and Reform in Limoges: A Study of Popular Participation in the 'Peace of God' (944–1033)," *Historical Reflections / Réflexions Historiques* 14 (1987): 473–474. See also the brief remarks of Geary, *Furta Sacra*, pp. 76–78.

These saints from the east might be given apostolic missions. For example, three mid to late eleventh-century *vitae* recount how Severus, patron saint of Saint-Sever, born somewhere in Asia Minor, converts to Christianity under Julian the Apostate.[22] After a brief spell as a hermit, he turns to the apostolic duty of preaching, unsuccessfully attempting to convert the Vandals. Eventually he and six companions arrive in Rome, where they spend a year "under the patronage of the apostles" and the tutelage of a Pope Eugenius. An angel then appears to Severus and tells him to make his way to Gascony, the region he is predestined to convert to Christianity.[23] There he constructs various churches and preaches with much effect; martyrdom at the hands of invading barbarians crowns his apostolic success. Saint-Sever's patron, sent by Peter's heir, the pope, thus becomes the apostle of Gascony, lauded as such in a panegyric at the close of the final version of the *vita*.[24]

In the apotheosis of this hagiographic development, local saints metamorphosed into one of Christ's intimates—not necessarily one of the twelve apostles themselves, but one of the seventy-two disciples who had witnessed the Last Supper and the Passion. In the south, the most spectacular example of the eleventh-century penchant for such saints is perhaps the early eleventh-century proclamation of Saint Martial of Limoges as an apostle.[25] In the early eleventh century, Martial's already extant *vita* was reworked and the new version attributed to Aurelianus, one of Martial's companions.[26] This text recounts how Martial, a Jew, converted to Christianity, was baptized by Peter, witnessed various of Christ's miracles, was present at the Last Supper and Pentecost, went with Peter to Rome, and was sent by the Prince of Apostles to evangelize Gaul. In the Limousin, he not only successfully wrested the populace and its prince from their pagan beliefs, but also founded a splendid basilica as his tomb, the future abbey of Saint-Martial.

[22] *Prima vita sancti Severi martyris; Secunda vita sancti Severi metrice scripta; Vita tertia sancti Severi martyris* (*AASS* November 1:220–233). I follow the text of the *Vita tertia* for the most part here.

[23] *Vita tertia sancti Severi martyris* (*AASS* November 1:229).

[24] *Prima vita sancti Severi martyris* (*AASS* November 1:225–226). Not only is Severus presented as the apostle of Gascony, but he is also implicitly made into the heir and successor of Saturninus, the bishop who, according to Gregory of Tours, had been sent to convert Toulouse. Here the Christianization of Gascony is genealogically linked with that of the rest of Gaul; see *Vita tertia sancti Severi martyris* (*AASS* November 1:229–230).

[25] See Daniel Callahan, "The Sermons of Adémar of Chabannes and the Cult of St. Martial of Limoges," *Revue Bénédictine* 86 (1976): 251–295; Landes, "Dynamics of Heresy and Reform," his *Relics, Apocalypse,* as well as his "A Libellus from St. Martial of Limoges Written at the Time of Ademar of Chabannes: Un faux à retardement," *Scriptorium* 37 (1983): 178–204; and Louis Saltet, "Un cas de mythomanie bien documenté: Adémar de Chabannes (988–1034)," *Bulletin de la Littérature Ecclésiastique* 32 (1931): 149–165. The development of the cult of Mary Magdalene in Burgundy and Provence is another striking example of this phenomenon; see Victor Saxer, *Le culte de Marie-Madeleine en Occident des origines à la fin du Moyen Age,* Cahiers d'Archéologie et Histoire, 3 (Auxerre 1959).

[26] Pseudo-Aurelianus, *Vita eiusdem B. Martialis.*

While Martial's cult was fostered under special circumstances and in an especially charged atmosphere, there were parallel developments in other southern saints' cults, or at least in their *vitae*.[27] Saint Austremonius, the first bishop of Clermont and, like Martial, one of the seven bishops sent to evangelize Gaul under Decius mentioned by Gregory of Tours, appears in the ninth- and tenth-century versions of his *vita* as a missionary sent by either Peter or Clement.[28] But in the *vita* composed in the mid-eleventh century by Issoire (the monastery that claimed Austremonius as its founder), this saint had become one of the seventy-two disciples who learned the rudiments of the faith from Christ's lips, attended the Last Supper, and grieved at the Passion—like Martial in the Pseudo-Aurelian *vita*.[29] After Christ's death, moreover, Austremonius was sent by Peter to evangelize not merely the Auvergne but all of Aquitania Secunda (including, this version of the *vita* pointedly specifies, the Limousin).[30] Although Austremonius was not explicitly given the title of "apostle" in his *vitae* or in calendars or liturgy, becoming at most "martyr," he was fashioned as the equal of Martial.[31]

Austremonius's new guise suggests not only rivalry with Martial but also more generally how monasteries came to value the role of apostolic missionary for their founder and patron.[32] Other founding figures receive this sort of gilding by becoming intimates of the Holy Family. For example, Amator, the eponymous hermit upon whose body Rocamadour was founded, was a companion to the Virgin, according to Robert of Torigny's late twelfth-century chronicle.[33] By the fourteenth century, when Bernard Gui found time among his more official duties to collect local legends of the south, Amator's prestige had been heightened further; he was now one of Martial's associates and had acquired a wife, Veronica, a dear friend of the Virgin.[34]

Whether or not the saint in question was made into a member of the living Christ's own circle of disciples, such apostolic claims served to place

[27] On the particular circumstances surrounding Martial's cult and legend, see Landes, "Dynamics of Heresy and Reform," and his *Relics, Apocalypse.*

[28] Gregory of Tours, *Historia Francorum* 1.30 (*MGH SSRM* 1.1:48); *Vita prima S. Austremonii* and *Vita secunda S. Austremonii* (*AASS* November 1:49–61).

[29] *Vita tertia S. Austremonii* (*AASS* November 1: 62–63).

[30] *Vita tertia S. Austremonii* (*AASS* November 1: 66).

[31] For Austremonius as martyr, see *Vita tertia S. Austremonii* (*AASS* November 1:61–77); Paris, BN Latin 9085, f. 51rb-va; and Clermont-Ferrand, BM 63, f. 98r (marginal addition). The monks of Issoire were probably very aware of the Limoges traditions; in the eleventh century their monastery had many connections with the Limousin.

[32] Indeed, in their *vitae*, both extant in early twelfth-century manuscripts, two Auvergnat patron saints respectively play Austremonius's role as the saint who introduces Christianity to the Auvergne. Saint Necterius: *Vita Necterii*, Clermont-Ferrand, BM 149, ff. 119va–122va (perhaps composed before the *Vita tertia* of Saint Austremonius). Saint Marius: *Vita [Marii]* (*AASS* June 2:114–126; cf. Clermont-Ferrand, BM 732, pp. 103–104, 108–109). This latter text postdates the *Vita tertia* of Austremonius.

[33] Robert of Torigny, *Chronica* (*MGH SS* 6:519).

[34] For the relevant passage from Bernard Gui, see the citation in *De sancto Amatore eremita* . . . (*AASS* August 4:16–17).

the church which bore the saint's name and which enshrined his or (rarely) her relics into direct contact with the primordial layer of Christianity. Other patron saints—one of the original twelve apostles, for example, or the Virgin, or Mary Magdalene—could and did have this meaning. In the case of a local saint endowed with an apostolic function, however, the dynamic of the patron–church relationship is particular. The church, through its relics, becomes coterminous with and embodies both the local introduction of Christianity and the integration of the region into the larger entity of the Church. It thus becomes a center from which Christianity emanates, and creates for itself a connection with the authority represented by the apostles and their imitators. The apostles, then, did not appear as foci for what we might anachronistically call Gallican separatism. When these monasteries remembered their origins, they depicted them with figures who were local, but shaped to represent a connection with a supralocal authority of the past and, indeed, of the present: papal Rome.

For the contemporaneous incarnation of this larger authority represented by the apostles was not episcopal but papal. Although many of these apostolic figures were bishops—such as Martial of Limoges, Front of Périgueux, and Austremonius of Clermont—not all of them were. Furthermore, the cults of these apostolic bishops were often fostered by monasteries, and sometimes, as in the case of Martial, in the face of at least the initial resistance of the local bishop.[35] There is no evidence that the eleventh-century bishops of Clermont were instrumental in the heightening of Austremonius's image that occurred at the abbey of Issoire, although later prelates may have appropriated the enhanced saint for themselves.[36] Nor have I found any indication that the monks of Saint-Sever intended Severus as a commemoration of the power of the archbishop of Bordeaux or of any other Gascon prelate. Indeed, in the legendary charter that relates this abbey's (re)foundation in the late tenth century, Guillaume-Sanche, duke of Gascony, places Saint-Sever under the authority of the Roman church alone, a disposition strengthened by a string of most monastic comminatory clauses.[37]

These apostolic cults placed the monastery in a relationship with one bishop above all, the bishop of Rome. Various popes send Severus, Austremonius, and Martial on their missions, and in the *acta* of Saint Amator (an undatable text), the saint now not only associates with the Virgin, but

---

[35] For a northern parallel, see Farmer's discussion of how the canons of Saint-Martin of Tours fashioned Martin as an apostle in order to rival and challenge their archbishop: *Communities of Saint Martin*, pp. 235–244.

[36] For some suggestive remarks on the later bishops of Clermont and Austremonius, see Catherine Brissac, "Le sacramentaire ms. 63 de la Bibliothèque municipale de Clermont-Fd: Nouvelles données sur l'art figuré à Clermont autour de 1200," *Bulletin Historique et Scientifique de l'Auvergne* 86 (1974): 303–315.

[37] On this text, see below, Chapter 4 at nn. 7–10.

spends two years hobnobbing with Peter in Rome.[38] Furthermore, according to the Pseudo-Aurelian *vita*, Peter gives his staff to Martial, surely a gesture symbolic of transmission of authority.[39] Hence, the shaping of local saints in the mold of apostles could establish a sometimes tacit, sometimes articulated connection between the churches they founded and the vicar of the prince of apostles—the pope, whom eleventh-century ecclesiastical reform had created as the transcendent guarantee of monastic liberty from *all* other human domination, never mind that of other bishops.[40] In other words, the apostolicity of these saints in eleventh-century texts relates in part to the monastic desire for *libertas* which informs the southern foundation legends and which was indeed a general preoccupation of western European monasteries in this era. A monastery founded by and upon a saint who was himself apostolic possessed intrinsically (although not necessarily effectively) apostolic liberty.

I say "himself" deliberately, for the conduits of this apostolic authority were by and large male. I have discovered only one instance in which a local female founder has even a hint of apostolic aura. According to the early thirteenth-century *Chronique Saintongeaise,* a vernacular prose text composed by a cleric from either Bordeaux or Saintes, Saint Martial and his contemporary, a woman known as Saint "Benedicte" to whom he had lent Peter's staff, founded various churches at Bordeaux.[41] Here Martial's apostolic authority implicitly rubs off onto his temporary female partner. But of course, even in legend she could not herself technically be part of the chain of apostolic succession, no more than any woman could.

Benedicte, like most female founders in the southern legends, is given a male partner. But she is overshadowed not so much by Martial as by other male founders who in the *Chronique Saintongeaise* also tower over Martial himself. The text repeats twice the tale of the foundations made by Benedicte and Martial—but each time it frames the story within the context of royal refoundation. Clovis comes to Bordeaux and founds various churches, including those which Martial and Benedicte had established; later, Charlemagne and his epic cronies refound the churches whose apostolic

---

[38] *Acta [sancti Amatoris]* (*AASS* August 4:24–25).

[39] Pseudo-Aurelianus, *Vita eiusdem B. Martialis,* p. 366.

[40] See Farmer, *Communities of Saint Martin,* pp. 158–160. On the pope and monastic liberty, see Chapter 6 below.

[41] The two halves of *Chronique Saintongeaise* have been edited separately. In each, the foundations at Bordeaux are mentioned: *Tote Listoire de France (Chronique Saintongeaise),* ed. F. W. Bourdillon (London, 1897), pp. 16–17; *Chronique dite Saintongeaise: Texte franco-occitan inédit "Lee": A la découverte d'une chronique gasconne du XIIIe siècle et de sa poitevinisation,* ed. André de Mandach (Tübingen, 1970), pp. 288–290 (on the manuscripts, author, and dating of the entire text, see de Mandach's remarks, pp. 1–197). Benedicte (as Benedicta) appears in the Pseudo-Aurelian *vita* of Martial, but there she does not explicitly have the role of founder; see Pseudo-Aurelianus, *Vita eiusdem B. Martialis,* pp. 370–371.

origins the text reiterates.[42] The apostolic beginnings provide the lineage of the royal foundations, and Benedicte and Martial appear as the precursors of the kings whose actions as founders (and warriors) structure the text.

Royalty

The narrative progression in the *Chronique Saintongeaise* places kings as founders on center stage, a position they had enjoyed in the legends since the later eleventh century. There they appeared without female consorts or rivals, for, almost without exception, the southern abbeys to claim royal founders invoked kings—not princesses, not queens, not even the royal couple.[43] Now female apostles such as Mary Magdalene were per se anomalies, but queens and princesses were not. Furthermore, actual queens, Merovingian, Carolingian, and Capetian, directed much of their patronage toward churches, acting as founders and donors (although I have found no evidence of queenly favor bestowed particularly upon southern ecclesiastical communities).[44] Southern monasteries could have chosen to celebrate such women as founders but most often did not.

This marked preference for male over female royalty has the rhetorical effect of almost erasing the latter as a locus of royal authority. Indeed, even in the one instance I have discovered of a queen represented as founder, she is upstaged by kings. The *Chronique Saintongeaise* attributes the establishment of one southern church to Clotild, but it ascribes a plethora of such foundations to various kings.[45] Furthermore, the only legend to depict a royal princess as the primary founder provides her with male partners who make cameo but crucial appearances. Enimia, Merovingian princess and saintly hermit, designates as sacred the site of the monastery that would bear her name. It is she who decides to build a monastery in which to house her increasingly numerous followers. But when a dragon appears and disturbs the work of the stonemasons, Enimia appeals to her male friend, Bishop

---

[42] See the references in n. 41 above.

[43] Frances Terpak, however, suggests there was a legend of Charlemagne and Hildegard as founders at Saint-Caprais of Agen; see "The Romanesque Architecture and Sculpture of Saint Caprais in Agen" (Ph.D. diss., Yale University, 1982), pp. 223–240. I thank Dr. Terpak for allowing me to read this manuscript.

[44] For ecclesiastical patronage of early medieval queens, see Pauline Stafford, *Queens, Concubines, and Dowagers: The King's Wife in the Early Middles Ages* (Athens, Ga., 1983), pp. 123–124. On Capetian queens, see Marion Facinger, "A Study of Medieval Queenship: Capetian France, 987–1237," *Studies in Medieval and Renaissance History* 5 (1968): 3–48; and Louis L. Honeycutt, "Images of Queenship in the High Middle Ages," *Haskins Society Journal* 1 (1989): 61–71. I have not made a detailed study of the question of queenly patronage of southern churches; but among the authentic diplomas that mention as an intercessor or coactor Hildegard, one of Charlemagne's wives, none is for a southern church (*MGH Diplomata Karolinorum* 1:115–117, 202–204, 210, nos. 81, 149, 155). Interestingly, none of the forged diplomas that mention Hildegard relates to a southern church (*MGH Diplomata Karolinorum* 1:292–294, 296–298, 315–319, 481–482, nos. 219, 222, 231, 232, 318).

[45] For Clotild's foundation, see *Tote Listoire*, p. 17.

Hilarus, who defeats the monster.[46] Although the episode symbolically glorifies episcopal authority, does it not also insinuate that this female founder, even though she was of royal blood, needed the help of male power to carve out sacred space from secular, to defeat the unclean force that threatened the nascent abbey? Moreover, it is not Enimia who endows the new community with property, but rather her father, a certain King Clovis, and her brother Dagobert.[47] Through their actions, not hers, Sainte-Enimie's institutional status is guaranteed. Enimia might have royal blood, but in this episode, her male relatives represent royal authority and power. Like Hilarus, Clovis and Dagobert are clothed with (male) official authority, while Enimia has instead (female) charismatic and prophetic power.

Indeed, while actual queens participated in royal rule to a greater or lesser degree, depending on the era and the region, greater authority always rested with the king.[48] To be sure, there were women who reigned alone in the twelfth century. But clerical writers were reluctant to describe even those queens as exercising power and authority in their own right.[49] Perhaps the absence of royal women from southern legends springs from the same source as this reluctance. For, in general, the monasteries of the south desired to associate their origins with a power that they, like these twelfth-century writers, constructed and interpreted as far greater than that of any queen or royal princess: the king, the male incarnation of royalty.

This presence of kings, the embodiments of precisely the supralocal authority absent in the south, is one of the most striking characteristics of the legends. By the late eleventh century, southern abbeys favored kings not only above queens, but above all other types of legendary founders. Certainly there were exceptions to this general predilection, and in different versions of its legend a monastery might appeal both to royal and to non-royal founders. Nonetheless, in most legends, a royal partner appeared or was implied. Often a monastery even fashioned a royal founder for itself where originally there was none. In such instances imaginative memory selected the qualities with which to adorn a figure originally lacking them, or even obliterated founders deemed unsuitable, replacing them with personages inherently royal.

For example, according to the original version of the eighth- or ninth-century *vita* of Desiderius of Cahors (630–655), the abbey of Moissac had been founded at some time during this bishop's lifetime by two "praisewor-

---

[46] For this episode, see "Vita, inventio et miracula sanctae Enimiae," pp. 270–72, and above, Chapter 2 at nn. 94–97.

[47] "Vita, inventio et miracula sanctae Enimiae," p. 273.

[48] No study I have read suggests that a medieval queen's official power and authority ever equaled that of the king.

[49] See Louis L. Honeycutt, "Female Succession and the Language of Power in the Writings of Twelfth-Century Churchmen," in *Medieval Queenship*, ed. John Carmi Parsons (New York, 1993), pp. 189–201.

thy men, Ansbertus and Leothadius."⁵⁰ Although Moissac's early twelfth-century martyrology commemorated Ansbertus and Leothadius, it denied both of them the title of founder, characterizing Ansbertus merely as abbot and Leothadius as bishop and confessor.⁵¹ Even more striking, Moissac doctored its eleventh-century copy of the *vita* in order to endow itself with founders who were antecedent to the unremarkable Leothadius and Ansbertus and, perhaps more important, who were royal. In the early twelfth century someone, presumably a denizen of the abbey, taking scraping knife and pen in hand, erased and added words to the passage relating the foundation. Henceforth it would read: "Now in his [Desiderius's] time the monastery of Moissac, begun shortly before with royal revenues, was competently brought to completion by the praiseworthy men Ansbertus and Leothadius."⁵² Ansbertus and Leothadius as founders were thus preempted by a royal—although vague—figure.⁵³

By the first quarter of the thirteenth century, the monks of Moissac seem to have developed extensive liturgical commemorations for the king, their "patron and founder" (*patronus et fundator*), and his successors.⁵⁴ By the later thirteenth century, this tradition of royal foundation had become pub-

⁵⁰ *Vita sancti Desiderii episcopi Cadurcensis*, edited by Bruno Krusch in a composite volume, *Liber Scintillarum*, ed. H. Rochais, Corpus Christianorum Series Latina, 117 (Turnholt, 1957), pp. 343–401, here 370–371. On the foundation see Friedrich Prinz, *Frühes Mönchtum im Frankenreich: Kultur und Gesellschaft in Gallien, den Rheinlanden und Bayern am Beispiel der monastischen Entwicklung (4. bis 8. Jahrhundert)* (Munich, 1965), pp. 269–270; and Magnou-Nortier, *La société laïque*, p. 90.

⁵¹ "Moysiaco sancte ansberti abbatis" and "sancti leotadii episcopi et confessoris" (the latter a marginal note, probably a twelfth-century addition), in Paris, BN Latin 5548, ff. 64r and 70r. On this manuscript, see Dufour, *La bibliothèque*, p. 144, no. 94. On Ansbertus, see Axel Müssigbrod, "Der heilige Abt Ansbertus von Moissac," *AB* 99 (1981): 279–284.

⁵² The text (with the additions and changes in italics) reads: "Nam et M*oy*ssiacense cenobium *paulo ante regiis expensis* inicitium huius tempor*is* a viris laudabilis Ansberto et le*athadio competenter expletum est*" (Paris, BN Latin 17002, f. 212ra). Krusch reconstructed the original text (no doubt using some of the later manuscripts of the *vita*, for some of the erasures in Latin 17002 are so complete that even my examination of the passages in question under ultraviolet light did not reveal the missing words) as follows: "Nam et Mussiacense cenobium huius tempore a viris laudabilibus Anseberto et Leuthado iniciatum est" *Vita sancti Desiderii*, pp. 370–371). Dufour dates the manuscript to the eleventh century: *La bibliothèque*, pp. 147–148, no. 100.

⁵³ In Aymeric de Peyrat's *Chronicon*, Ansbertus and Leothadius appear as two abbots of the monastery. Aymeric intimates that kings are the founders: "serenissimi reges francorum specialem affectionem ad eosdem [Ansbertus and Amandus] gerebant et dictum cenobium diligebant tamquam fundatores et ipsi peculiares protectores" (Paris, BN Latin 4991A, f. 153ra; and Paris, BN Latin 5288, f. 61va). On Amandus's place in Moissac's legend, see below, Chapter 4 at nn. 88–91.

⁵⁴ The liturgical devotions included a daily mass in honor of the kings as well as an annual solemn mass and commendation of the king of France. These are recorded (as far as I have been able to discover) only in Aymeric de Peyrat's *Chronicon*, (Paris, BN Latin 4991A, ff. 104vb–105ra, 165va–vb). Aymeric cites his sources: an old manuscript (*quodam libro antiquissimo;* f. 104vb) and a letter the monks sent to Philip II sometime after the siege of Moissac in 1212 (ff. 165va-vb). The letter has been edited in A. Lagrèze-Fossat, *Etudes historiques sur Moissac*, 3 vols. (Paris, 1870, 1872, 1874), 1:373–374.

lic enough that Philip III recalled it in his privilege for the monastery.[55] As we shall see, at various moments Moissac shaped this generic royal foundation with the molds of specific kings;[56] here I want to underline that the desire to acquire a king—any king—had begun to permeate the legend and the monastery's image of itself by at least the twelfth century.

In other cases, the legendary creation of a royal founder took the guise of a simple but significant amplification of a hagiographic topos of this era: a *vita* would endow its subject with not noble but royal blood.[57] Thus Enimia, a princess whose genealogy as outlined in her *vita* is most suspect, becomes founder of Sainte-Enimie;[58] and Alboynus/Albodenus, of equally difficult but equally royal descent, effects the peace-bringing foundation of the monastery of Clairvaux-d'Aveyron.[59] Of course, such foundations were not true regalian foundations; they were royal only genealogically and indirectly. Nonetheless, such legendary founders indicate these monasteries' preference for associating a royal rather than merely aristocratic figure with their origins.

Indeed, while in the legends nobles are often celebrated as donors and patrons, as founders they are, with very few exceptions, placed in the shadow of the king—even when the foundation was actually due to the initiative of a noble and no king had any part in the process.[60] Legends could adopt various narrative strategies to lend a predominantly royal tone to what had been merely aristocratic foundations. An aristocratic founder could be shaped as such a close associate of a king that he could come to symbolize the monastery's connection with and loyalty to the ruler, as is the case with Guillaume, epic hero and founder of the abbey of Gellone.[61] More frequently, legends presented the monastery as first having been founded by a king, typically Charlemagne or Pippin the Short, and then refounded much later by a noble. For example, in the legends of La Réole (actually founded in the tenth century by the duke of Gascony) and Saint-Savin of Bigorre (founded in the same period by the count of Bigorre), Charlemagne was mentioned as founder in order to form a prologue to these monasteries'

[55] Philip III's privilege of 1272 describes Moissac as the monastery "a praedecessoribus nostris franciae regibus fundatum" (Paris, BN Doat 130, f. 75r). Cf. the confirmation of royal privileges made by Charles VIII in 1487: *Ordonnances des rois de France de la troisième race, recueillies par ordre chronologique*, 21 vols. (Paris, 1723–1849), 20:58–64. Despite Colette Beaune's assertions to the contrary (*Naissance*, p. 67), these royal letters do not specify that Clovis was the founder of Moissac.

[56] See below, Chapter 4 at nn. 72–94.

[57] See the version of the *History of the Seven Sleepers* composed at the northern monastery of Marmoutier (Saint Martin becomes a direct descendant of the kings of Hungary): Farmer, *Communities of Saint Martin*, pp. 167–173.

[58] Enimia's confused genealogy: "Vita, inventio et miracula sanctae Enimiae," p. 253.

[59] See above, Chapter 2 at nn. 38–41.

[60] For exceptions, see n. 11 above.

[61] See below, Chapter 5 at nn. 164–175.

refoundation by duke and count respectively.[62] Here the desire to extend the monastery's history backward coincided with that to characterize the monastery as originally constituted by a royal figure, thereby diminishing the significance of the local noble as founder. Alternatively, an abbey could present itself as a noble foundation that had later been delivered into royal possession, or refounded by a king.[63] This is the case in what seems to be a clear instance of celebration of a nonroyal foundation: the legendary establishment of Mozac by a "duke of Aquitaine."

This "duke" is Calminius, also claimed as founder by Saint-Chaffre, an abbey some one hundred seventy kilometers to the southeast of Mozac and part of the same monastic network. Perhaps originally a Merovingian noble of the sixth century, perhaps a contemporary and friend of Sidonius Apollonaris, perhaps originally nothing more than a place name, Calminius was gradually elevated at Mozac and Saint-Chaffre as duke—and, at Mozac, as we have seen, also as saint.[64] By the late eleventh century, sometimes accompanied by his wife, Namadia, he was celebrated at Mozac as the abbey's founder and as a Roman "senator."[65] His emergence as founder at Saint-Chaffre was more gradual. First he was nothing but a toponymic; the monastery was known in its charters of the ninth, tenth, and early eleventh centuries as Calmilius or Calmiliense, a place name meaning fallow or uncultivated land.[66] By the later eleventh century, though, the abbey had assumed the name of Saint-Chaffre (*monasterium sancti Theofredi*), and Calmilius was no longer a feature of the landscape. Rather, he was "senator of the city of

---

[62] La Réole: *Recueil des chartes de l'abbaye de Saint-Benoît-sur-Loire*, 1:39–43, no. 18; "Cartulaire du prieuré de Saint-Pierre de La Réole," pp. 144–145, no. 99. Saint-Savin: *Cartulaire de l'abbaye des Bénédictins de Saint-Savin*, p. 2, no. 2. Such a device appears also in Uzerche's legend although the king in this case is Pippin the Short (see below, Chapter 4 at nn. 149–150).

[63] See the twelfth-century foundation narrative of the monastery of Vabres: *Cartulaire de l'abbaye de Vabres au diocèse de Rodez: Essai de reconstitution d'un manuscrit disparu*, ed. Etienne Fournial, (Rodez and Saint-Etienne, 1989), pp. 23–28, no. 1. In some instances, royal *traditio* is combined with an implicit extension of the abbey's history backward. The early eleventh- or late tenth-century *miracula* of Saint Genou open with a long prologue that describes the history of Gaul and then relates the reigns of, most particularly, the Carolingians up through Louis the Pious. After this most royal preface, the *miracula* describe Saint-Genou's foundation, thus placing it in the context of royal history. Although the original founders of the church are two nobles, the text takes pains to present them as close relatives of Pippin I of Aquitaine—whom the founders ask not only for a grant of immunity, but to whom they also deliver the abbey in a *traditio*. The text then recounts the continuing patronage of the Carolingians. This monastery is thus presented as royal rather than noble from its inception. *Miracula S. Genulphi episcopi* (*AASS* January 2:97–107).

[64] On Calminius as a place name, see Fournier, "Saint Austremoine," p. 442. On the fifth-century Calminius, friend of Sidonius Apollinaris, see Herwig Wolfram, *History of the Goths*, trans. Thomas J. Dunlap (Berkeley, 1988), p. 451 (n. 129) and pp. 475–476 (n. 519).

[65] *Recueil des actes de Pépin*, pp. 227–242, (here 239), no. 58. *Vita tertia S. Austremonii* (*AASS* November 1:79).

[66] For the charters, see *Cartulaire de l'abbaye de St-Chaffre*. On the meaning of the place name, see Fournier, "Saint Austremoine," p. 442, n. 91.

Clermont and prince"—and the abbey's founder.[67] In twelfth-century sources, Calmi(l)(n)ius's elevation is complete. For in this period, both Mozac and Saint-Chaffre proudly presented their founder as the powerful and most Roman duke of Aquitaine, and Mozac called him saint.[68] By at least the fourteenth century, the church of Laguenne, which too claimed Calminius (but as its patron saint), styled him in similar fashion.[69]

Calminius's elevation to the status of duke and saint implied neither a commemoration of the contemporary Poitevin dynasty nor positive reminiscences of the seventh- and eight-century dukes of Aquitaine, figures who eventually styled themselves as kings and attempted to resist the early Carolingians. As we shall see, these latter historical personages were excoriated as traitors in the legends. Nor is there any hint that Calminius was imagined as a counterweight to royal power—nor, in the context of the political world of the twelfth century, any reason that he would have been so imagined. Beginning in 1137 the title of duke of Aquitaine was borne by kings, first Louis VII and then a long succession of English rulers. The title assigned to Calminius might thus have had royal echoes.

In any case, Calminius was overshadowed by a king in the twelfth century, at least at Mozac. Glorious Duke Calminius established the "royal monastery" (*monasterium regale construxit*) of Mozac, the twelfth-century *Vita S. Calminii* produced by this abbey asserted.[70] But why was Mozac royal if its founder was a duke? The answer is to be found in another and much more developed strand of Mozac's legend: the celebration of Pippin the Short as the abbey's refounder. In a series of richly embroidered texts, Pippin was gradually acquiring this role while at the same time, in more spare (and sparse) documents, Calminius was becoming duke and saint.[71] This emerging tale of royal refoundation quite literally framed the emerging saintly duke: Calminius first appeared at Mozac in a late eleventh-century forged diploma of Pippin the Short in which that king confirms the abbey's possession of the properties granted by its noble founder. Even though the diploma made no explicit reference to royal refoundation, Pippin called Mozac "our monastery" (*nostrum coenobium*).[72] Thus, already implicit in the

---

[67] *Cartulaire de l'abbaye de St-Chaffre*, pp. 3–5. The cartulary's author reiterates several times that although the abbey was now known as Saint-Chaffre, it had originally borne its founder's name: pp. 5, 8, 44–45, nos. 9, 50. Cf. Fournier, "Saint Austremoine," pp. 444–445.

[68] Mozac: *Vita S. Calminii confessoris* (*AASS* August 3:759–762). Saint-Chaffre: *Vita S. Theofredi* (*AASSosB* 3.1:476–485) and a narrative charter, which is virtually undatable (extant only in a seventeenth-century copy), *Cartulaire de l'abbaye de St-Chaffre*, pp. 167–168, no. 429.

[69] "Calminius dux aquitanie apud aquinam requiescit cuius gesta partim habentur." Bernard Gui, *Nomina sanctorum lemovicensis dyocesis*, in Paris, BN n.a. Latin 1171, ff. 214ra-rb, and Toulouse, BM 450, f. 243ra.

[70] *Vita S. Calminii confessoris* (*AASS* August 3:760).

[71] See below, Chapter 4 at nn. 127–146.

[72] *Recueil des actes de Pépin*, pp. 227–242, no. 58.

diploma was the sentiment that informed the later *Vita S. Calminii*'s striking proleptic statement rendering the duke a prelude to the king. The monarch provided the framework for the community's self-definition: despite its legendary elevation of Calminius, Mozac saw itself as no mere ducal abbey, but rather as a *monasterium regale* from its inception.

Like the various other narrative strategies used in legend to place aristocratic founders in the shade of kings, Mozac's legend reveals that by the twelfth century, royal was the flavor of foundation preferred by the monasteries. Perhaps this does not seem surprising. The king always held a privileged place in medieval imagination, retaining both his distinctness from the aristocracy and his role as sovereign even when he was effectively only one among many princes and needed their support as much as if not more than, they needed his.[73] Accordingly, medieval society appears to have engaged often in the practice of what Marshall Sahlins has called "heroic history": the production of a vision of the past in which the actions of certain heroes, generally kings, represent and provide the structure for the history of the whole society.[74]

Yet these legends are not merely an example of how in the Middle Ages the remembered social past was often the royal past. This predilection for kings as founders was not a trait of medieval monastic foundation legends in general. In the eleventh and twelfth centuries, the legends of many German abbeys focused upon noble rather than royal figures, and some from northern France explicitly celebrated a noble instead of the king; for these latter monasteries, the ruler appears rather as a problematic patron who could metamorphose into oppressor an at any moment.[75] Why, then, in the foundation legends of the kingless land south of the Loire were royal figures magnified and exalted?

The very fact that this question is raised by texts coming from a region that historians often define as part of the political "periphery" during this period itself poses a larger methodological question. Studies of medieval images of kingship (and of the processes of modern "nation building") tend to focus on how the ruler and his intimates shaped and produced the monarch as a charismatic center.[76] Implicit in such examinations of how the monarchy

---

[73] On the distinctiveness of the king even during the period when Capetian power was very limited, see for example Koziol, *Begging Pardon*.

[74] Sahlins, *Islands of History*, pp. 35–52.

[75] On the German legends, see Patze, "Adel und Stifterchronik." Marmoutier's legend glorified the Angevins to the detriment of the Capetians; see Farmer, *Communities of Saint Martin*, pp. 79–88. At the northern French abbey of Morigny, a noble was celebrated as founder while the king appeared often as an oppressor; see *La chronique de Morigny (1095–1152)*, ed. Léon Mirot (Paris, 1912). Among the southern legends I have found no instance of even the slightest negative shadow being cast upon the king for the benefit of a noble.

[76] See the articles by medievalists in *Lieux de mémoire*. In her *Naissance*, Beaune explicitly intends to examine how symbols and images of country and king corresponded to currents of popular belief (e.g., pp. 188–206). Nonetheless, she treats the center as the impetus (e.g., p.

(or state) elaborates and manipulates images of itself is thus a distinctly centrist bias. By analytically privileging the king, this approach adopts and accepts the perspective of the ruler it purports to explain: that the monarch is the generative symbolic center, and all else is peripheral.[77]

As some scholars have recently suggested, there are other analytic possibilities.[78] What, for example, if one looks from the perspective of the so-called periphery, in this case the monasteries south of the Loire? As soon as one does so, the bias implicit in language such as "center" and "periphery" is thrown into relief. Using the figure of the king (and apostles), these monasteries constructed themselves as centers of the larger map, not as its periphery. Furthermore, creating in their legends a vibrant image of the king—but for their own and not royal purposes—these abbeys demonstrate that the significance of the royal image is not produced or defined only by the monarch and his intimates.[79] How the "periphery," in this case the abbeys of the kingless south, imagines its relationship with the "center" is as important as how the "center" views the "periphery."

---

348) and the expansion of the monarchy as the vehicle of national sentiment. For further specific examples, see below, Chapter 5 at nn. 30–32. Also see Peter Alter, *Nationalismus* (Frankfurt, 1985), pp. 27–28, and Clifford Geertz's "Centers, Kings, and Charisma: Reflections on the Symbolics of Power," in his *Local Knowledge: Further Essays in Interpretive Anthropology* (New York, 1983), pp. 121–146.

[77] This is clear in Graus's disappointment to find that in France Charlemagne was a figure celebrated "only" in local legends and "literary" traditions: *Lebendige Vergangenheit*, pp. 182–198 (cf. his *Volk, Herrscher und Heiliger*, p. 426). The assimilation of a local figure by the center may actually mean its demise as a living tradition, rather than its apotheosis; see Edward L. Davis, "Arms and the Tao: Hero Cult and Empire in Traditional China," in *Sodai no shakai to shukyo* (Society and Religion in the Sung) (Tokyo, 1985), pp. 1–55, esp. 37–46.

[78] Julia Smith has argued that the experience of provinces is as important as that of the central government for an understanding of empire; see her *Province and Empire: Brittany and the Carolingians* (Cambridge, 1992). Gabrielle Spiegel shows how an image of the king was produced and manipulated by the aristocracy: *Romancing the Past: The Rise of Vernacular Prose Historiography in Thirteenth-Century France* (Berkeley, 1993). For a later period, see Sahlins's innovative *Boundaries*, and for a brief critique of "the myth of the center," see Cohen, *The Symbolic Construction*, pp. 36–37.

[79] Even the historical writing of those abbeys very much associated with rulers did not necessarily reflect royal interests, but rather those of the monastic community itself. See Althoff, "Gandersheim und Quedlinburg," pp. 136–144.

4

Translatio:
From Rome to the Franks

W ho were the authoritative representatives of royal power invoked by the abbeys? Two sorts of chronologies will structure my answer. The chronology of the southern past itself will be the framework; I will consider these rulers separately in the order in which they historically succeeded one another, beginning with those who embodied Roman imperial power and then turning to the Frankish rulers. As I examine each set of rulers, I will be most attentive to the chronology of legendary development itself, that is, to the way in which these images metamorphosed, and waned or waxed over time. Of course, I could invert the relation of the two chronologies, looking first at the eleventh century and how all types of founders were imagined in that period, then proceed to the twelfth century and so on. But that would lead to a continual cross-sectioning and juxtaposition of the images of the founders and would detract from the point I am trying to make: to create the community's identity in the past and present, monasteries selected specific figures and, in doing so, reshaped the founders themselves, ascribing to them over time increasingly significant roles, drawing them ever closer to the sacred center represented by the abbey.

Roman-style Rulers

The most ancient garb in which the southern abbeys clothed their founders was that of imperial Rome, certainly a source of great authority and one that possessed much allure throughout the Middle Ages. The meaning of this slice of the past was particularly potent in the land south of the Loire. Despite the successive waves of Gothic and Frankish kings, the deep imprint of centuries of Roman rule remained upon this region. The southerners conceived of themselves institutionally and culturally as Roman, a sentiment that lingered into the eleventh century and took many forms, including legends of Roman-style rulers who founded monasteries.[1]

The imaginative sway of *Romanitas* was so great that it even spilled out of its historical period to color the entire vision of the non-Frankish past as elaborated by southern abbeys; in those few instances in which a monastery imagined for itself a pre-Frankish but non-Roman ruler as founder, this figure was nonetheless clothed in Roman attributes. This legendary Romanization of, as we shall see, Gothic and Gascon figures may stem in part from the fact that many barbarian kings had actually drawn upon Rome as the model of rulership. Equally, and here more important, it reveals the desire that characterizes these monasteries' legends: that for a founder who represented supralocal authority, authority that went beyond the bounds of the south. A distinctly Gothic or Gascon king could not serve in this fashion.

The portrait of Stephen, duke of Aquitaine, provided by the Pseudo-Aurelian *vita* (ca. 1010) of Saint Martial is the earliest instance among the southern legends of the invocation of the Roman past.[2] This text paints Stephen, the saint's lay partner in the foundation of the future Saint-Martial, as unmistakably an incarnation of *Romanitas*. Under Stephen's command are four legions, the *vita* specifies. He reports directly to Rome, for at one point Emperor Nero summons him and his legions to the imperial capital.[3] Furthermore, Stephen rules Aquitaine, a land not only of pagans whom the apostolic Martial converts, but also of functioning "theaters" where the saint makes of himself a public spectacle.

This Roman leader in this Roman setting is a duke, not a monarch. Nonetheless, the preference for rulers shapes Saint-Martial's legend. Declaring that the duke ruled as king in all but name, and was second in power only to Nero himself, the *vita* configures Stephen as royal.[4] Furthermore, this passage is a deliberate echo of, or perhaps preface to, a famous one in Ademar of Chabannes's *Chronicon*. There Ademar described the contemporaneous duke of Aquitaine and patron of Saint-Martial, William III, as a "king rather than a duke," a man who fittingly consorted not with other

---

[1] Lauranson-Rosaz attributes "une certaine Romanité" to the eleventh-century south; see his *L'Auvergne,* and his "La romanité du Midi de l'an mil: Le point sur les sociétés méridionales," in *Catalunya i França,* pp. 45–58. Cf. Poly and Bournazel, *Feudal Transformation,* pp. 221–227. On the persistence of Roman culture and self-representation in the Midi in earlier periods, see Magnou-Nortier, *La société laïque;* and Rouche, *L'Aquitaine.*

[2] Pseudo-Aurelianus, *Vita eiusdem B. Martialis.*

[3] Pseudo-Aurelianus, *Vita eiusdem B. Martialis,* p. 368.

[4] Pseudo-Aurelianus, *Vita eiusdem B. Martialis,* pp. 368, 370. For discussion, see Bernard S. Bachrach, "'Potius Rex quam Dux esse putabatur': Some Observations Concerning Ademar of Chabannes' Panegyric on Duke William the Great," *Haskins Society Journal* 1 (1989): 11–21.

princes, but rather with kings and popes.[5] At each end of Saint-Martial's history, then, was a duke, but one who was a decidedly kinglike figure. In between were years of patronage by just those figures whom the dukes equal; Ademar lists donations by Pippin the Short (surely here citing legendary traditions), and tells with pride of the visits of other Carolingian rulers to Saint-Martial, the church he even calls a "royal basilica" (*basilica regalis*).[6]

This combination of aristocratic founder and king(s) occurs, though in a different pattern, in another eleventh-century legend celebrating Roman-style origins: that of Saint-Sever. Saint-Sever seems to celebrate above all its refoundation circa 988/989 by a powerful local noble, Guillaume-Sanche, count-duke of Gascony.[7] In a narrative charter most probably composed late in the eleventh century and copied onto the blank folios at the end of the abbey's sumptuous *Beatus* manuscript, Guillaume-Sanche recounts the fabulous circumstances surrounding his reestablishment of the ruined monastery.[8] Using this explicitly comital framework, Saint-Sever nonetheless succeeds in tinging its origins with royal—and Roman—colors.[9] For two kings lurk in the background and both, even the one who is supposedly Gascon, are shaded into images of imperial *Romanitas*. It is this latter theme, rather than one of Gascon ethnicity, that informs the abbey's eleventh-century image of its origins.

The narrative charter recounts how Guillaume-Sanche established Saint-Sever as a thanksgiving offering for a victory in battle (against the Normans) achieved with the saint's aid, a trope often used for royal foundations.[10] Indeed, when Guillaume-Sanche approaches Severus's tomb before the bat-

---

[5] Ademar, *Chronicon* 3.53–54 (*Chronique*, pp. 176–177). Cf. Bachrach, "'Potius Rex.'"

[6] Ademar, *Chronicon* 1.58, 3.18, 3.22, 3.57 (*Chronique*, pp. 60–61, 134, 142, 182–183).

[7] This legend cannot represent an effort to associate the abbey with a contemporaneous noble lineage, for by the time it was recorded in writing, the evanescent "greater" Gascon dynasty had already vanished; see Dunbabin, *France in the Making*, pp. 87–89, 173–179. On the circumstances of the actual foundation, see Higounet and Marquette, "Les origines de l'abbaye de Saint-Sever," pp. 27–37.

[8] For an edition of the foundation charter copied in the *Beatus* (Paris, BN Latin 8878), see "Documents transcrits à la fin du *Beatus*," in *Saint-Sever*, pp. 114–116. Higounet and Marquette ("Les origines de l'abbaye de Saint-Sever") date the composition of this text to the abbacy of Suavius (1092–1107).

[9] In her unconvincing *Les princes de Gascogne, 768–1070* (Marsolan, 1982), Renée Mussot-Goulard argues that the Gascon princes fostered a production of commemorative texts in which they figured as quasi-regal figures. But most of her evidence comes from monastic sources not necessarily controlled by the dukes. Her evidence points rather to the fact that *monasteries* sought to shape their founders as kings. Given the unreliability of her work, Mussot-Goulard's discussion of the Gascon texts treated here will not be used. See Bisson's remarks on her argumentation: "Unheroed Pasts," p. 295.

[10] On such foundations, see Elizabeth Hallam, "Monasteries as 'War Memorials': Battle Abbey and La Victoire," in *The Church and War*, ed. W. J. Shields, Studies in Church History, 20; (Oxford, 1983), pp. 47–57. Severus appears at the battle on a white horse; see Frantisek Graus, "Die Heilige als Schlachtenhelfer: Zur Nationalisierung einer Wundererzählung in der mittelalterlichen Chronistik," *Festschrift für Helmut Beumann zum 65. Geburtstag*, ed. Kurt-Ulrich Jäschke and Reinhard Wenskus (Sigmaringen, 1977), pp. 330–348.

tle in order to entreat the saint, he explicitly invokes a king as his model. The count promises that in return for intercession, he will subject himself and all the territory under his authority to Severus "just as the former king of this country, Hadrian, . . . submitted himself and his whole kingdom to the . . . martyr's *dominatio*." The charter thus shapes the abbey's origins as royal, making the actions of the present founder correspond to those of a past king.

Just who was this royal prototype for the count of Gascony? The three versions of the *vita* of Saint Severus, composed in the mid to late eleventh century (probably just before the narrative charter) provide the legendary answer. The *vitae* relate how Severus arrived in Gascony with his apostolic mission. There he discovered the country's king, Hadrian, suffering from a lingering illness. In return for his cure, Hadrian promised Severus that he would subject himself and his kingdom to the saint's power. This is the Hadrian whom the narrative charter has Guillaume-Sanche imitate explicitly. The desired relationship between monastery and the secular power represented by both the count and his royal type is made clear.

Despite his role as king of the Gascons and exemplar for the tenth-century count of Gascony, Saint-Sever's Hadrian is no incarnation of Gascon-ness. His name conjures up images of emperors rather than of Gascon rulers. Furthermore, according to the *Vita tertia sancti Severi*, the seat of Hadrian's kingdom was an ancient and "most celebrated fortified town" which the Romans had established to defend the whole province.[11] This royal city with the Roman past was called Palaestrion—no Gascon name that. This Greek word common in classical Latin sources was no doubt chosen by the composer(s) of Severus's *vitae* to underline the Roman-ness of Hadrian and his city (as well as to presage Severus's martyrdom on this site; as the *Vita tertia* specifies, Palaestrion means *luctatorium*: place of wrestling or exercise).[12]

It is not only through this king that Saint-Sever gives itself Roman and royally colored beginnings. Its patron saint himself bears a good imperial name. Indeed, according to the *vitae*, Severus was royal. Born to the king of the (mythic?) *gens Ambligonia*, he renounced the crown upon becoming a Christian. Nonetheless, the *Vita prima* often refers subsequently to him as "King Severus"; in other hagiographic texts from the abbey, he always ap-

---

[11] *Vita tertia S. Severi* (*AASS* November 1:230).

[12] *Vita tertia S. Severi* (*AASS* November 1:230). Or was the name suggested by an extant place name? F.-J. Bourdeau, *Manuel de géographie historique de l'ancienne Gascogne et de Béarn . . .* (Paris, 1861) and Auguste Longnon, *Atlas historique de la France depuis César jusqu'à nos jours . . .* (Paris, 1912), p. 219, mention the existence of a viscounty of Palestre in the eleventh-century, but they cite only the legendary documents from Saint-Sever. I have not been able to find a modern place name that corresponds to Palaestrion. The *castrum* that appears next to Saint-Sever on the map in the *Beatus* of Saint-Sever is Palestrion, according to François de Dainville, "La *Gallia* dans la mappemonde de Saint-Sever," *Actes du 93e congrès national des sociétés savants . . .* (Paris, 1970), p. 395. Was it therefore a real place, or does this make the map even more legendary?

pears with the epithet "martyr king" (*rex martyr*).[13] This Roman and royal saint suffers martyrdom at the hands of the Vandals on the site where the monastery bearing his name would be built; his body became the foundations of the monastery.[14] Moreover, the site of his death and of the future abbey was Palaestrion, King Hadrian's royal seat with its venerable Roman history.

This Roman and royal past seeps into the present of the comital foundation. According to the narrative charter, not only does Guillaume-Sanche explicitly establish the same relationship with Severus (and therefore by implication with the monastery under this saint's patronage) that Hadrian had, but he also gives to his foundation the *castrum* of Palaestrion, Hadrian's legendary royal seat.[15] Admittedly, the charter also frames Guillaume-Sanche's role to echo that of an earlier prince. According to the *Vita tertia*, not King Hadrian but a certain Sebastian, "prince (*princeps*) of the region," had been the original founder of the abbey church.[16] But while the eleventh-century charter describes Guillaume-Sanche as refounding the monastery, it does not mention Sebastian. The princely echo is thus very muted, while the Roman and royal resonance is predominant. The *vitae* make the abbey's origins Roman and royal thrice over, through the patron saint, the king who aids him, and the site itself.

This *Romanitas* created at Saint-Sever may have the ring often sounded by the elaboration of Roman identity in the eleventh-century south by aristocrats: a conscious rejection of things Frankish.[17] Indeed, Saint-Sever depicted the Franks as destructive invaders from the north; according to the *Vita tertia* and Guillaume-Sanche's charter, the Franks destroyed the magnificent church that Sebastian founded in honor of Severus.[18] In contrast to these marauders who bring ruin upon the abbey, Roman-style rulers and saints (and Gascon princes) appear as the legendary patrons of the abbey, a juxtaposition that is perhaps not surprising given Saint-Sever's location in an area that historians generally consider to have been a bastion of resistance to representatives of Frankish royal authority.

This use of a Roman-style ruler to express anti-Frankishness appears in the one case I have found in which a Gothic king figures as a founder. As we

---

[13] See the account of the translation of Severus's head edited in Pierre Daniel Du Buisson, *Historiae monasterii S. Severi libri x* (Vicojulii ad Atturem, 1876), pp. 89–100. Du Buisson notes that a bust reliquary seen at the abbey in the sixteenth century depicted a crowned Severus.

[14] Severus carried his severed head to what would be his burial place and the site of the monastery. *Vita tertia S. Severi* (*AASS* November 1:233).

[15] "Documents transcrits," pp. 114, 116.

[16] This particular passage appears only in Du Buisson's edition of the *Vita tertia S. Severi: Historiae*, pp. 126–127.

[17] See the references in n. 1 above.

[18] Again, this passage appears only in Du Buisson's edition of the *Vita tertia S. Severi: Historiae*, pp. 126–127. For the passage in the charter, see "Documents transcrits," p. 115.

have seen, according to the *vita* of Saint Gilles, a certain Flavius, "king of the Goths," decided to found and endow a monastery with the saintly hermit's aid.[19] In the other legendary sources for Saint-Gilles, Flavius is graced with the same title.[20] This king probably owes his origins to the transformation of a toponymic into a personal name. Numerous documents, from a diploma of Louis the Pious (814) to charters and privileges from as late as the twelfth century, describe the monastery as located in the "vallis Flaviana."[21] Flaviana could easily have suggested to the monks the Roman personal name Flavius.[22] But why assign this name, rather than one that was recognizably Gothic, to a king of the Goths? The answer involves Rome and empire. "Flavius" had been used as a title first by the Gothic kings and then by the Lombard rulers (Frankish monarchs never adopted it).[23] As "Flavii," the kings of the Visigoths and the Ostrogoths had ruled the territory that included the (future) Saint-Gilles.[24] Yet this was a title derived from a Roman *praenomen* that was above all imperial. "Flavius" designated kings claiming Roman *imperium* and an association with the Roman imperial dynasty. It did not signify Gothicness (or for that matter any other non-Roman ethnicity) but rather *Romanitas* and Gothic pretentions to the imperial dignity.

All these resonances of the name "Flavius" echo in Saint-Gilles's legend, clearly transmitting the message that the abbey owed its foundation in part to a ruler who embodied a certain *Romanitas*—a glorious past that preceded the Franks. To be sure, a Charles, "king of the Franks," appears in the *vita* of Gilles, yet the text not only literally keeps him at a distance from the abbey's foundation, but also casts aspersions on his character.[25] Flavius appears as the positive counterweight to the ambivalent portrait of the Frankish ruler.

[19] *Vita S. Aegidii: AB* 8 (1889): 102–120; *AASS* September 1:299–304; Jones, *Saint Gilles*, pp. 98–111. See also above, Chapter 2 at nn. 84–92.

[20] In a manuscript of the 1130s or 1140s containing forged papal privileges copied along with authentic papal documents, Flavius appears in two privileges of John VIII dated 878. The first text calls Flavius merely "quondam rex," but the second specifies "quondam Gothorum rex" (Paris, BN Latin 11018, ff. 3r–7r, 7r–12v; *Bullaire de l'abbaye de Saint-Gilles*, pp. 5–17, nos. 2 and 3). Flavius appears in exactly the same spare terms in one passage of yet another of the monastery's legendary productions: the continuation of the *Liber pontificalis* composed (by 1142) by Petrus Guillermus, a monk of Saint-Gilles. See *Liber pontificalis*, ed. Louis Duchesne, 3 vols. (Paris, 1886–1957), 2:221–222.

[21] Louis's diploma: *HL* 2:93–94, no. 30.

[22] Jones believes that the place name itself derived from an inscription containing the word "Flaviano" found in the (Roman?) ruins at Espeyran, a village some two or three kilometers southwest of Saint-Gilles. *Saint Gilles*, pp. 37–38.

[23] For this point and those following, I draw on Herwig Wolfram's detailed study of the title and its use by Gothic and Lombard kings—*Intitulatio* I: *Lateinische Königs- und Fürstentitel bis zum Ende des 8. Jahrhunderts*, MIÖG suppl. 21 (Graz, 1967), pp. 56–176—and his *History of the Goths*, pp. 284–288. See also the brief remarks of Rouche, *L'Aquitaine*, pp. 374 and 674, n. 267.

[24] Wolfram, *History of the Goths*, pp. 309, 315.

[25] See below, Chapter 5 at nn. 131–143.

Through this Romanized Gothic ruler, Saint-Gilles ensured that it owed its foundation and independence to a ruler who clearly preceded the monarchs claimed by the bishops of Nîmes by at least the later eleventh century if not much earlier as the source of their rights over the monastery: Charlemagne and his son.[26]

In late tenth- and eleventh-century legends, *Romanitas* might thus have anti-Frankish overtones, although as the legend of Saint-Martial shows, it did not have to. By the twelfth century, Roman attributes seem to have lost any such connotation; in this period, those abbeys which associated Roman-style rulers with their origins did so with little if any anti-Frankish bias. Instead, Roman attributes now merely heightened a founder's prestige. For example, in the late eleventh or early twelfth century, the composer of the *Vita Menelei* declared that Meneleus, founder of Menat, was a great-great grandson of Emperor Heraclius—a stupendous inflation of the sober statement in the ninth-century *vita* of Benedict of Aniane: "Saint Meneleus sprang from royal seed."[27] This is certainly an indication of the desire for founders of the greatest possible authority, but no implication of anti-Frankishness.

Calminius, legendary founder of Mozac and Saint-Chaffre, also had his stature raised through *Romanitas*. In late eleventh-century sources he was characterized as a Roman senator;[28] and in the twelfth-century *vita* composed at Mozac, although he was given all the necessary attributes of a medieval duke, he appeared in so many words as the incarnation of glorious *Romanitas*. Born to a senatorial family, from his birth illuminated by "the light of Roman clarity" and raised as a Christian, Calminius was appointed senator of Rome and then *dux* of Aquitaine by Emperor Justinian.[29] Quitting the Eternal City, Calminius came to the Auvergne where he founded Saint-Chaffre and Mozac. He even provided the latter with Roman relics; here, as in the Pseudo-Aurelian *vita* of Martial, imperial and papal *Romanitas* work together. But there is no indication that Calminius's Roman qualities were the vehicle for any anti-Frankish sentiment. As we have seen, in Mozac's legend, Calminius's actions as founder formed a preface to those of a Frankish king, Pippin the Short, celebrated as the abbey's refounder. Here the role played by the Franks at Saint-Sever—as destroyers of the abbey with Roman origins—has been turned inside out; now the Frankish king restores rather than ruins.

At Saint-Sever itself there are hints that in the twelfth century the anti-

---

[26] See below, Chapter 6 at nn. 48–49.

[27] *Vita Menelei abbatis Menatensis* (*MGH SSRM* 5:135–136); Ardo, *Vita Benedicti* (*MGH SS* 15.1:214).

[28] See above, Chapter 3 at nn. 64–69.

[29] The *vita* specifies that there were seventy senators—surely a number which recalls that of Christ's disciples (seventy or seventy-two). *Vita S. Calminii confessoris* (*AASS* August 3:760). The number thus elevates the Senate as more than a merely political assembly.

Frankish tone lessened if not vanished: an entry of 1139 in a necrology from this monastery commemorated Charlemagne in positive terms, describing his death *in senectute bona* ("in good old age") and using it as a point from which to reckon the present date.[30] To be sure, a Frankish king did not become part of this Gascon abbey's foundation legend. In the eleventh century, however, Charlemagne had already appeared as founder in the legends of two other Gascon abbeys, Saint-Savin of Bigorre and La Réole. In the twelfth century, legends of many other churches from this same region would assign him the same role.[31]

Not only had secular *Romanitas* lost its previous connotations, but it was gradually losing its power as the authority with which southern monasteries sought to gild their origins. Of the instances I have found of this appeal to founders made Roman, only that of Calminius certainly postdates the eleventh century. Furthermore, I have found only these few cases of the invocation of Roman-style founders—hardly a deep coloring of the past as imaginatively remembered by southern abbeys. Instead, the primary coloring came from just those rulers rejected at Saint-Gilles, but celebrated at Mozac, Saint-Savin, and La Réole: Frankish kings.

For as the image of secular imperial Rome waned, southern abbeys increasingly turned in their legends toward a set of rulers drawn from the Frankish layer of the meridional past. By the later eleventh century, these latter towered over the tiny minority of fictionalized and generic Romanized rulers. When claiming a royal founder, the vast majority of the monasteries chose to embroider the memory of a Frankish rather than a non-Frankish king. This may, of course, be explained by historical facts; many of these monasteries were founded after the destruction of the Visigothic kingdom of Toulouse in 508 and indeed after Pippin the Short's decisive victories in the south during the 760s. But legendary production and imagination are not hemmed in by this type of fact (although they are by others). Rather, the predilection for Frankish rulers shows (among other things) how the consciousness of this southern land or at least that of its monasteries had shifted by the later eleventh century.[32] If abbeys chose to situate their origins in the pre-Frankish past, they Romanized that past—but most chose instead to create their identity through Frankish royal founders.

---

[30] After giving the number of years Charlemagne reigned, the entry reads: "in senectute bona obiit Vᵒ kalen. februarii, octingesimo XIIII anno ab incarnatione domini. Nunc vero millesimus CXXXVIII est, sicque ab obitu ejus usque nunc CCCXXV anni sunt" (cited by Du Buisson, *Historiae,* p. v).

[31] See below, Chapter 5 at nn. 176–184.

[32] From a brief survey of naming patterns in tenth- and eleventh-century Provence, Poly concludes that although consciousness of the distinction between Romans and Franks persisted throughout the tenth century, by the end of the century it had waned. See Poly, *La Provence,* pp. 50–53.

Frankish Kings: Dynastic Origins

By the later eleventh century, in southern monastic imaginative memory, the secular Roman past had ceded to a new vision of history in which the Frankish kings ruled supreme. The abbeys, however, did not choose at random from the plethora of Merovingian and Carolingian kings, nor did they necessarily select the same rulers who were embellished in legends north of the Loire. The monasteries claiming Frankish royal founders selected those kings who had brought about the south's integration (whether permanently or not) into the greater Frankish realm. Kings of Francia, kings of Aquitaine, and subkings of all sorts were generally ignored, swept under the carpet or transformed into those illustrious rulers under whom the south, willy-nilly (usually nilly), had become Frankish: Clovis, Pippin the Short, Charlemagne. Like the local saints turned apostles, these rulers represented the abbey's inclusion within a sphere of larger authority, an authority that in turn transmitted itself to the abbey. In imaginative memory, the often destructive historical actions of these rulers in the south thus became increasingly constructive—of monastic identity.

As we shall see, as southern abbeys celebrated Frankish kings with increasing ardor, they reshaped the royal role in foundation, ascribing ever more importance to the monarch. Those legends predating the end of the eleventh century hold the Frankish king at arm's length, usually locating him in his northern palace. Physical space thus separates the community from the royal patron; king and monastery connect but do not come into direct contact. Furthermore, these early texts celebrate the king not as primary founder but as patron. While the king stays in his palace and grants property to the new community, it is most often a saint with ties to the south who actually effects the foundation, delineating monastic space with his or her body. This physical and symbolic distancing of the king may echo Carolingian hagiographic traditions which created boundaries between king and community across which the actual ruler, a possibly domineering patron, might not step.[33] In the context of the eleventh-century south, however, these vestiges of implicit warnings directed to the ruler (if such they were) read as indications of how dimly imagined the king as founder was.

Yet, toward the end of the eleventh century and increasingly in the twelfth, the imagined Frankish king was no longer pale, absent, or overshadowed by a saint. From now on, the legends place the foundation within the context of a royal journey or expedition to the south (sometimes imagined, sometimes historically authentic). The contact between community and royal founder, no longer attenuated by space, is immediate. Further-

---

[33] On such Carolingian traditions, see Goffart, *Le Mans Forgeries*, pp. 75–78.

more, in the later legends, the role of the saintly partner is diminished or vanishes altogether; the king is commemorated as the sole founder. This displacement of the saint reveals a new focus on the king as the legitimating and delineating principle of monastic identity. It also suggests that these legendary kings had begun to take on the attributes of the figures they replaced. An image of the saintly king was thus adumbrated.

No longer distanced but embraced, these kings—and not saints—increasingly create the textual space of legend. Earlier legends often appeared in the form of hagiographic texts; saints were the subjects, kings the supporting actors. To be sure, legends in the form of hagiography did not then disappear. But just as the saint as founder yielded to the king, by the twelfth century the hagiographic text as foundation legend was displaced in favor of texts that were intrinsically royal in structure and content: diplomas. By at least the thirteenth century, legends might appear in the guise of long prose narrative texts (both in Latin and in the vernacular) which, whether masquerading as epic, *vita,* or history, were every bit as centered on the king as were the diplomas.[34] These narratives might interweave the actions of kings with those of saints, but the narrative thread was the tale of how the Frankish kings traversed the south, establishing churches as freely as Johnny Appleseed sowed trees.

These then are the general parameters within which the legends reshaped the Frankish kings. But Clovis, Pippin the Short, and Charlemagne did not therefore emerge as exact replicas of one another, any more than portraits of medieval kings in manuscripts, although generic, were identical. Instead, monastic imaginative memory fixed on different qualities of each ruler, while increasingly ascribing to each the aura implicit in the role of founder.

Clovis

When southern monasteries chose a Merovingian as their legendary founder, it was almost invariably Clovis, the first of the Frankish kings to rule in the south. Thus, when Figeac, a community largely preoccupied with a different royal founder (Pippin the Short), sought in the late eleventh and early twelfth centuries to extend its history back even further, it chose not just any Merovingian but Clovis for the cameo role of founder of Lunan, the

[34] Lagrasse's *Gesta Karoli Magni,* the prologue to the chronicle of Conques, and the *Chronique Saintongeaise* were among these longer and later texts. For a Provençal example, see the mid-thirteenth-century reworking by a monk of Lérins of the fifth-century life of the abbey's founder, Saint Honoratus: *Die vita sancti Honorati.* An equally fabulous foundation legend, featuring the epic Charlemagne, was composed (although in the vernacular) sometime in the thirteenth century, probably at the abbey of Montmajour; see "Le roman de saint Trophime," edited by N. Zingarelli in *Annales du Midi* 13 (1901): 297–345. Also see J. Gazay, "Le roman de saint Trophime et l'abbaye de Montmajour," *Annales du Midi* 25 (1913): 5–37.

community to which Figeac owed its origins.[35] Clovis possessed traits that rendered him a most appealing choice as a founder. He was both the first Frankish king to adopt Christianity and the first king of a unified Frankland. He incarnated origins. By incorporating him into its legend of foundation, the monastery thus made its own beginnings—and rights—coterminous with those of the Christian Frankish rulers.

Southern churches were far from being the only ecclesiastical communities to succumb to this king's charm as a legendary founder. Many traditions recorded in *vitae* and other types of texts paint Clovis as the munificent founder of churches and monasteries scattered throughout the Frankish realm.[36] There was not even a particular concentration of Clovis legends south of the Loire. Yet the southern legends merit special attention. They reveal how the king who made orthodox Christianity official in the south was commemorated there. Furthermore, they suggest that in order to understand the full-blown image of Clovis that appeared in the fourteenth and fifteenth centuries, we must look not only north to the royal realm itself, but also south.

Colette Beaune, the scholar most recently and thoroughly to study the legendary Clovis, has traced how this king was woven into the complex of centralized monarchist myths crystallizing in the late Middle Ages.[37] In northern and royal(ist) sources, Clovis appears as the first French king, the first "roi très chrétien," the first crusader, the paradigm and model for contemporary kings whose nation he had founded—a royal ideal created by the royal center. But alongside this exemplary Christian king emerged another Clovis, one perhaps more vibrant and alive: "Saint Clovis," to whom

[35] The earlier documents (two ninth-century texts) relating to Lunan make no mention of Clovis; see *Recueil des actes de Pépin*, pp. 5–9, 132–151, nos. 2 and 32. In a diploma forged in the name of Pippin the Short in the late eleventh century, Lunan appears as a monastery built by unnamed kings; see Wolff, "Note sur le faux diplôme," p. 298. Then, in a version of the same diploma fabricated in the twelfth century (Wolff, "Note sur le faux diplôme," p. 309), and in a privilege for Figeac forged in the name of Pascal I during the same period (*GC* 1, instr. 44), Clovis finally appears—but as the donor of certain properties to Lunan. Only in an interpolation of the 1170s to Ademar of Chabannes's *Chronicon* does Clovis appear as the founder of Lunan; see Paris, BN Latin 5926, ff. 36r-v, and *Chronique*, p. 58, note s*. Prinz believes that Clovis actually founded Lunan, but bases his statement on the interpolation in Ademar; see Prinz, *Frühes Mönchtum*, p. 32. On Figeac's legend of Pippin the Short, see below at nn. 117–123.

[36] Godefroid Kurth, *Clovis*, 2 vols. (Brussels, 1923), 2:265–295. The only other treatments I have found of these texts as a group merely cite Kurth: Georges Tessier, *Le baptême de Clovis. 25 décembre . . .* (Paris, 1964), pp. 154–161; Beaune, *Naissance*, p. 56. Of the southern saints or traditions Kurth cites in addition to those discussed here, several (Cesarius of Arles, Hilary of Poitiers, Severinus of Agaune, Maixent, Sacerdos) were associated with Clovis either in ways that are too limited to permit us to speak of a legend or in texts that largely predate the eleventh century (or postdate the fourteenth). They will therefore not be discussed here.

[37] In this paragraph I follow Beaune's "Saint Clovis: Histoire, religion royale et sentiment national en France à la fin du Moyen Age," in *Le métier d'historien au Moyen Age: Etudes sur l'historiographie médiévale*, ed. Bernard Guenée (Paris, 1977), pp. 139–156; as well as her *Naissance*, pp. 55–74.

monastic churches were dedicated and veneration was offered, a development that postdated 1300. This "saint" leads south of the Loire and away
from the development of a monarchist ideology at the center, for the three
cases of "Saint Clovis" discussed by Beaune all involve southern monasteries:
Moissac, Dorat, and Sainte-Marthe of Tarrascon.[38]

What are the implications of Saint Clovis's localization primarily in the
south rather than in the royal north? Beaune argues that the cult represents
the efforts by monasteries located on the fringes of royal power to integrate
themselves into the expanded Capetian realm—certainly a probable explanation. But was the legendary Clovis nurtured in the south only in the later
Middle Ages and only in conjunction with the territorial expansion of the
Capetians, as Beaune implies? She makes no effort to explore the southern
prehistory of this king's image, merely noting the presence of some antecedent southern legends focusing on Clovis. For Beaune as for other scholars,
the royal north remains the generative center of royal myth: Saint Clovis
represented a southern reaction to, and adaptation of, the image of the king
developed in the north.[39] An examination of the meridional prehistory of
Beaune's Saint Clovis, however, tells a different story.

This prehistory is composed of the four cases of developed Clovis legends
I have found: Saint-Léonard of Noblat, Saint-Germier, Auch, and Moissac
(Clovis, as we saw, also appeared in legend at Figeac, but very briefly). To be
sure, two of these instances involve nonmonastic communities: Noblat was a
house of canons, and Auch was an archbishopric. But their legendary Clovis
coincides with the king of monastic imaginative memory. Furthermore, Noblat and Auch shaped Clovis in accord with the general patterns of change
in the image of royal founders that characterized the monastic legends.
Their legends too are part of the imaginative history of the king as founder.

For example, the *vita* (composed in approximately 1030) of Saint Leonard
of Noblat, the earliest of the Clovis legends under consideration here, creates
a king who, although vital for the foundation, is in certain ways distanced
from the community.[40] The *vita* establishes first a most intimate relationship
between Clovis and this saint. In its opening words the *vita* proclaims that
Leonard, born in Francia to noble parents who were among Clovis's most
favored retainers, was the king's godson, a binding kinship tie of manifold
significance.[41] Next the *vita* relates how Leonard refused to join the king's
military entourage, preferring instead "to follow in Archbishop Remi's

[38] Beaune, *Naissance,* pp. 66–74; Beaune, "Saint Clovis."

[39] "[C]ette croyance [that Clovis was a saint], apparue dans les domaines royaux . . . "
(Beaune, *Naissance,* p. 73).

[40] *Vita sancti Leonardi confessoris* (*AASS* November 3:150–155). On the *vita*'s date, see
Steven Sargent, "Religious Responses to Social Violence in Eleventh-Century Aquitaine,"
Historical Reflections / Réflexions Historiques 12 (1985): 228–232.

[41] *Vita sancti Leonardi confessoris* (*AASS* November 3:150). On the significance of godparents, see Joseph Lynch, *Godparents and Kinship in Early Medieval Europe* (Princeton, 1986).

footsteps" and become a cleric. The parallel between Leonard and Remi is extended further; the text describes a privilege granted to Leonard by Clovis that would later adorn Noblat, Leonard's foundation. Blessed Remi had persuaded the "Frankish kings" to agree that whenever they visited Reims, all the prisoners in the city would be freed (thus establishing the ceremonial practice of pardon associated with royal entry).[42] Imitating his master, Remi's "disciple" Leonard obtained a similar privilege from the king; whenever Leonard visited prisoners in their places of confinement, they would be liberated. The effect of the saint's entry was thus made analogous to that of the king's, underlining the association of Leonard and Clovis.[43]

The *vita* maintains the royal note in its description of the foundation of Leonard's monastery, the episode with which it culminates. Obeying instructions he received in a vision, Leonard went south to Aquitaine. Some ten miles outside Limoges he came to a forest, a hunting preserve of the "kings of Gaul and the dukes of Aquitaine." In this princely landscape (a favorite of foundation legends), Leonard eased the labor pains of an unnamed king's wife.[44] In gratitude, the king offered Leonard a goodly portion of the royal forest. Establishing himself there as a hermit, the saint eventually collected a group of followers and founded a monastic community. Noblat was thus made into a distinctly royal as well as saintly foundation. Indeed, according to the *vita*, the monastery's very name recalls its royal nature: Leonard called it Noblat (*Nobiliacum*) "because it had been given to him by a very noble king."[45]

Although Clovis does not appear in this episode, is the ruler who characterizes the foundation really the faceless king of Gaul? Certainly the latter gave the land upon which the monastery would be built, but he himself is so generic that he serves primarily to lend a royal cast to the foundation. On the other hand, the abbey's patron saint is unmistakably attached to the very specific Clovis who introduces and sets the tone for the *vita*. By a series of analogies and transfers, Clovis's sheen rubs off onto the unspecific royal foundation. Nonetheless, this early eleventh-century text distances Clovis in certain ways, literal and symbolic. He is located only in the north, and his realm is Francia. When Leonard ventures south of the Loire, he enters a world governed by kings "of Gaul" who might be intended to represent the

[42] On this practice, see Lawrence M. Bryant, *The King and the City in the Parisian Royal Entry Ceremony: Politics, Ritual, and Art in the Renaissance* (Geneva, 1986), pp. 24–27; and the more detailed discussion of Richard A. Jackson, *Vive le roi! A History of the French Coronation from Charles V to Charles X* (Chapel Hill, N.C., 1984), pp. 94–114, esp. 98–102. Clovis and the establishment of the royal pardon appear in conjunction with another saint as well, Severinus of Agaune; see Kurth, *Clovis*, 2:182.

[43] *Vita sancti Leonardi confessoris* (*AASS* November 3:150–151).

[44] *Vita sancti Leonardi confessoris* (*AASS* November 3:152–153).

[45] *Vita sancti Leonardi confessoris* (*AASS* November 3:154).

Merovingians, but might not;[46] the power of the king explicitly identified as Frankish is northern-based. Furthermore, the saint—not Clovis or the nameless king—plays the main role in the foundation. It is Leonard's step and not royal will that delineates the monastery's boundaries, making its territory firmly his own.[47]

In a somewhat later foundation legend (late eleventh or possibly early twelfth century) we find a similar configuration of saint and king in foundation, but here the associated yet distanced royal partner is explicitly Clovis. This is the *vita* of Saint Germerius, patron saint of the powerful and wealthy priory of the abbey of Lézat just south of Toulouse at Muret.[48] According to this text, Germerius came to Gaul from Jerusalem and was ordained a deacon. An angel instructed him to go to Paris where he was to be made a bishop. After the consecration, as Germerius was making his way toward Toulouse, his designated see, King Clovis summoned him to the palace and invited him to dine. During the meal, Germerius exercised his sacerdotal function, giving "bread which he had blessed" (*eulogias*) to the king and his princes and then hearing their confession. Finally, Clovis asked for the bishop's prayers and offered him in exchange whatever he would like. Germerius responded: "I ask nothing except that you give me as a reward an estate (*potestatem*) in the region of Toulouse, that is, as much as the shadow of my cloak can cover in the territory of Ducorum."[49] Clovis granted him the territory for six miles around Ducorum, confirming the donation with a written charter of liberty. Then Germerius, upon the king's request, spent twenty days in his palace. Later he returned to the south and founded two churches at Ducorum, one dedicated to Saint Martin and the other to Saint Saturninus. The identity of the latter church remains uncertain.[50] The car-

---

[46] On the use of the term "Gallia" in the tenth and eleventh century to indicate the whole realm, including the south (as opposed to "Francia," which designated the north), see Bernd Schneidmüller, *Nomen patriae: Die Entstehung Frankreichs in der politisch-geographischen Terminologie (10.–13. Jahrhundert)* (Sigmaringen, 1987), pp. 34–61.

[47] The king wished to give him the whole forest; Leonard accepted only as much of it as he himself could circumambulate on his mule during one night. *Vita sancti Leonardi confessoris* (*AASS* November 3:153). On other such delineations of property, see above, Chapter 2 at nn. 117–121.

[48] Several versions of the *vita* are extant (see Appendix 2). Here I rely primarily on the version in the earliest manuscript, Lézat's cartulary (the outlines of the story are the same in all the versions); see *Cartulaire de l'abbaye de Lézat*, 2:411–414, no. 1584. Germerius was possibly a seventh-century bishop of Toulouse, possibly a completely fictive person; see Rouche, *L'Aquitaine*, p. 425, and Louis Saltet, "Saint Germier: Etude critique sur sa vie," *Annales du Midi* 13 (1910): 171–175. The church of Saint-Germier had been Lézat's priory since 948; see *Cartulaire de l'abbaye de Lézat*, 1:239–240, no. 303. On the power of its priors, see *HL* 4:708–711.

[49] *Cartulaire de l'abbaye de Lézat*, 2:411–412.

[50] Trying to locate Germerius's legendary foundations has led to a quagmire of scholarly discussion. See Douais, "Saint Germier, évêque," pp. 42–51; Victor Fons, "Mémoire historique sur les prieurés de Saint-Germier et de Saint-Jacques de Muret," *Mémoires de la Société*

tulary of the abbey of Lézat, however, permits us to identify the former as either Saint-Martin of Ox (a village some four kilometers southwest of Muret) or Saint-Martin of Roziniac, both of which in the 1090s passed into the possession of the monastic community established under the patronage of Germerius: Saint-Germier.[51]

The *vita* thus presents Germerius as the first Christian Frankish king's intimate and intercessor, and Clovis as the lay partner in the saint's southern foundations and the guarantor of their liberty.[52] Clovis bestowed upon Germerius not only land, liberty, and much gold and silver, but also those objects which founders in fact and legend typically provided: rich vestments as well as crosses, chalices, patens, staffs, and crown candelabra, all made of gold and silver. But, as in the case of Noblat's foundation, the saint designated with his own body the fiscal land he wished to acquire from the king. Germerius consecrated and organized the monastic space, whereas the king's role was limited to that of provider of material property.

Nonetheless, let us not underestimate the importance of Clovis in this foundation legend. The king's significance becomes clear in light of the appearance in Lézat's compendious cartulary of the section of the *vita* that relates Germerius's encounter with Clovis and the subsequent foundations. According to a *vidimus* of 1245, the monks of Lézat had deliberately chosen to include this portion of the *vita* in the cartulary, copying it from a manuscript that belonged to the monastery and contained many saints' lives.[53] Why had they done so? The location of the *vita* in Lézat's cartulary provides the answer; in this cartulary, tidily organized according to estates, the *vita* is one of the first pieces that deal with Saint-Germier's properties.[54] The cita-

---

archéologique du Midi de la France 8 (1861–1865): 76–82; and Saltet, "Saint Germier," pp. 156–157.

[51] The text of the *vita* in the Lézat cartulary identifies the church of Saint-Martin with Roziniac (*Cartulaire de l'abbaye de Lézat*, 2:413) as does Bernard Gui (see the edition in Douais, "Saint Germier, évêque," p. 98), although he calls it Roviniacum. I have been unable to find this village either on a map or in the *Dictionnaire national des communes de France* (Paris, 1984). For Saint-Germier's possession of Saint-Martin of Roviniac, see *Cartulaire de l'abbaye de Lézat*, 2:406–409, 410–411, nos. 1576–1579, 1581–1583 (N.B.: the next document is the extract from the *vita* discussed below, at nn. 53–55). Ox or d'Ox appears in 1:232-233, 244, nos. 295 and 307; 2:373–374, 432–433, 473–478, nos. 1514, 1608–1609, 1611, 1658–1664, 1666–1668.

[52] In later traditions, Germerius, like Leonard, becomes interwoven with the figure of Archbishop Remi, certainly the saint most often depicted as Clovis's intimate. By at least the fifteenth century, the church of Saint-Rémi at Toulouse possessed relics of Saint Germerius, and by the sixteenth century a legend had developed relating that the archbishop of Reims had left his gloves, miter, and rings to his friend Germerius, who then founded the church in his honor at Toulouse. See Douais, "Saint Germier, évêque," pp. 61–63. The "gloves of Saint Remi" are now preserved at Saint-Sernin of Toulouse; see *Les trésors des églises de France: Musée des Arts Décoratifs, Paris, 1965* (Paris 1965), p. 272, no. 501.

[53] For the *vidimus*, see *Cartulaire de l'abbaye de Lézat*, 2:414.

[54] See *Cartulaire de l'abbaye de Lézat*, 2:411–414, no. 1584. According to the editors (1:xv), quire 38 deals with Muret, Ox, Seysses. and Saint-Germier.

tion of the *vita* thus serves as title to and justification for Saint-Germier's possession of Ox and Roziniac: they are foundations made upon land granted by the first Christian king to the church's patron saint himself, ancient and incontestable. Indeed, Lézat and Saint-Germier may have had good reason to defend their possession of Ox. In the 1170s, a certain Pons d'Ox reclaimed the church of Saint-Martin which his parents had given to Saint-Germier; the matter was finally settled in Saint-Germier's favor in 1194/1195.[55]

The legends of Noblat and Saint-Germier demonstrate that by the eleventh century Clovis could be invoked as an authority in the south, although in each case a saint and not the king enjoyed the limelight as founder. Clovis's role, however, is not the same in both cases. In the later legend, Clovis participates directly in the foundation, whereas in the earlier one he does not and the royal foundation is made by a nebulous "king of Gaul." Although in neither case does Clovis himself come south, being clearly located in northern palaces, in the later legend the Frankish king is at least depicted as controlling fiscal land in the south. Though it is hazardous to draw conclusions about chronological developments from only two texts, I am tempted to suggest that by the time the *vita* of Saint Germerius was recorded, the Frankish king had become a more commanding presence in meridional monastic imagination. Perhaps this development explains why a glimpse of Clovis can be caught in certain late eleventh- and twelfth-century layers of the abbey of Figeac's legend.[56]

More important, by the mid-twelfth century there was at least one southern legend that celebrated not only Clovis's authority but also his actual presence in the south: that of the powerful archbishopric of Auch. This legend intertwines the establishment of Auch's primacy with Clovis's meridional sojourns, that is, with his campaigns against the Visigoths which culminated in the battle of Vouillé (507) and the capture of Toulouse (508).[57] It presents Clovis as having brought an ecclesiastical golden age to the south by defeating the heretical Arians and establishing orthodox Christianity—a picture not too far removed from the historical circumstances of this king's victory over Alaric II. The southern episcopate (overwhelmingly orthodox) and the local population (itself orthodox) bitterly resented and resisted the rule of the Arian Goths and hence welcomed the Frankish kings with open

---

[55] *Cartulaire de l'abbaye de Lézat*, 2:373–374, 433, 473–476, nos. 1514, 1611, 1659–1661, 1666. Given that in 1210 Pons appears as a monk of Lézat (*Cartulaire de l'abbaye de Lézat* 2:476–477, no. 1667), he and his family seem to have a relationship of give and take with the abbey like those discussed by Rosenwein, *To Be the Neighbor of Saint Peter.* On property conflicts and legends, see Chapter 6 below.

[56] See above at n. 35.

[57] On this legend as evidence of southern commemorative history, see Bisson, "Unheroed Pasts," pp. 281–308. Jacques Clémens finds in it evidence of a Gascon consciousness: "La Gascogne est née à Auch au XIIe siècle," *Annales du Midi* 98 (1986): 165–184.

arms. After his triumph, Clovis hastened to consolidate an alliance with the southern bishops which culminated in the council of Orléans of 511. Although this was an evanescent amity, dissolving into strife upon Clovis's death, it was commemorated and gilded in Auch's twelfth-century legend.[58]

This legend survives in two texts, recorded in the three extant versions (all copied in the thirteenth century) of the cathedral's cartulary; the first of the texts was probably composed in the first half of the twelfth century and the second in approximately 1175.[59] The later text is essentially another version of the first, providing a similar but flatter portrait of Clovis. The earlier text occupies a prominent place in the extant versions (which are expansions of an earlier one) of the cartulary. The original cartulary seems to have terminated in a table of contents.[60] The Clovis document in question immediately follows this table; it was thus the text that headed and set the tone for the new section of the cartulary.[61]

This text begins by describing how Clovis liberated Auch and the surrounding area from the oppression of the Muslims(!).[62] In gratitude for this divinely conferred victory, the text continues, Clovis endowed the church of Auch with lands, precious objects, immunity, and "royal dominion" (*dominium regale*). After this preface, which already sets up the relation between the king and Auch, the text describes how Clovis defeated the heretic Alaric. Then Perpetuus, archbishop of Auch at the time, hearing of the presence of this Christian Frankish king, came out joyfully to meet Clovis "and offered to him bread and wine, just like another Melchisedech to another Abraham" (cf. Gen. 14.18–20). Here the opposition between the (bad) Visigothic Arian kings and the (good) Frankish orthodox king is underlined, and Auch is lined up on the correct side. The later Auch text also locates the archbishops on the correct (royal) side, thus placing them in a special relationship of loyalty to the Frankish king.[63] This theme of fidelity

[58] On Clovis's campaigns against Alaric II, and the Frankish king's alliance with anti-Visigothic southern bishops, see Rouche, *L'Aquitaine*, pp. 43–52; Wolfram, *History of the Goths*, pp. 190–193, 243–246.

[59] *Cartulaires du chapitre de l'église métropolitaine Sainte-Marie d'Auch*, ed. C. Lacave La Plagne-Barris, Archives Historiques de la Gascogne, 2d ser., 3 (Paris, 1899), pp. 77–86, no. 77 (AD Gers G.17 ff. 31r–34v), and pp. 157–64, no. 134 (AD Gers G.17, ff. 72r–76r); no. 134 is the earlier of the two texts.

[60] AD Gers G.17, ff. 69r–71v.

[61] This table of contents is in the same hand (in AD Gers G.17) as the text in question. See the analysis of the manuscripts in Clémens, "La Gascogne."

[62] On other twelfth-century southern French examples of confusion between the Visigoths and the Muslims, see Etienne Delaruelle, "Les saints militaires de la région de Toulouse," in *Paix de Dieu et guerre sainte en Languedoc au XIIIe siècle*, Cahiers de Fanjeaux, 4 (Toulouse, 1969), pp. 181–182. There are possible epic overtones in this confusion: not only were the Muslims the generic foes of the kings in the *chansons de geste*, but in a twelfth-century *chanson* the hero, one of Clovis's sons, helps his father defend Paris against the infidel. See *Floovant, chanson de geste du XII siècle*, ed. Sven Adolf (Uppsala, 1941).

[63] See Bisson's analysis of the Auch text in "Unheroed Pasts," p. 296.

to the king, we will find, marks other ecclesiastical communities' legends celebrating other Frankish rulers.

In the earlier of the Auch texts, the meeting (or communion) of king and prelate was followed by various gifts that Clovis made to Auch. First he conferred his special affection and grace upon Perpetuus, thus emblazoning Auch as a royal archbishopric.[64] Next he granted to the archbishop, present and future, the city and its suburb as well as the church of Saint-Martin which he, Clovis, had founded there at Clotild's instigation.[65] Due to Clovis's generosity, Auch also became the metropolitan see of "Gascony"—a nice anachronism since nearby Eauze had actually enjoyed that honor until the middle of the ninth century.[66] Finally, the king granted to the archbishop the church (and *villa*) of Saint-Pierre of Vic (presumably Vic-Fezensac, thirty kilometers northwest of Auch); the rest of the document relates the long and embroiled confict between Auch and several aristocratic families for control of this estate. Here Clovis is used in a most evident fashion to establish Auch's possession of the contested priory and property at Vic-Fezensac, as he is by the later Auch text to claim the right of burial which the archbishops disputed with the monastery of Saint-Orens.[67] Furthermore, in both texts, Clovis legitimates the see's primacy. The metropolitan's origins coincide with the primeval and golden age represented by the establishment of Christian Frankish rule in the south.

Auch's legend thus celebrates a Frankish king not only as the distributor of rights and property, as in Saint-Germier's legend, but also as a ruler who exercises his power in person south of the Loire. Furthermore, Clovis is at least Perpetuus's equal partner in the foundation of Auch's primacy; he is not overshadowed by a saint as he is at Saint-Germier and as is the faceless king at Noblat. The earlier Auch text even crowns Clovis with a hint of a halo. Among the other gifts that the king made to the archbishopric were "his tunic and cloak (*clamys:* the purple military mantle) and also the small golden pitcher (*urceolus*) from which water was poured to wash the hands of the queen and the king."[68] Surely the former are the garments emblematic of the consulship that, according to Gregory of Tours, Clovis wore at Tours

---

[64] In the twelfth century, Auch was not a royal archbishopric; see the archbishoprics discussed in Pacaut, *Louis VII.*

[65] This latter foundation may be a reworking of the passage in the eighth-century *Liber historiae Francorum* in which Clovis, exhorted by Clotild, founded Saint Peter of Paris before the battle of Vouillé (*MGH SSRM* 2:267). The legend of Clovis's foundation of Saint-Martin of Auch is elaborated upon by two texts (unfortunately impossible to date) copied by an eighteenth-century abbot; see Auch, BM 73, pp. 175, 181. On the spread of Martin's cult in the wake of the Frankish kings after they had adopted him as their patron in the sixth century, see Prinz, *Frühes Mönchtum,* pp. 19–46.

[66] On the vicissitudes of the history of Auch and Eauze, see Rouche, *L'Aquitaine,* p. 274.

[67] On the conflict with Saint-Orens, see also *Cartulaires du chapitre de l'église métropolitaine Sainte-Marie d'Auch,* pp. 49–51, 55–57, 204–210, 211–214, nos. 52, 56, 164–165, 171.

[68] *Cartulaires du chapitre de l'église métropolitaine Sainte-Marie d'Auch,* p. 159, no. 134.

when this honor was conferred upon him.[69] The clothes and the pitcher are thus objects intimately associated with the king, and seem like nothing so much as relics. Clothes saints had worn and objects they had touched were often transformed into relics—enshrined in churches, venerated, and considered to be conduits for the saint's power or *virtus*. Do not the royal garments and pitcher of Auch's legend suggest that, already by the early twelfth century, colors of sanctity had tinged Clovis's image in the south?

The Auch tradition, then, intimates that well before the fourteenth century ecclesiastical establishments could imagine and claim as founder a Clovis who came south and not only distributed rights and gifts, but also left behind relics of his presence. Here is the Clovis who preceded and presaged the saint-king celebrated in the south in the later Middle Ages. The latter was no pale reflection of the Clovis elaborated in the royal north but rather the apotheosis of a figure long integrated into the meridional imaginative landscape. Indeed, when in the thirteenth century a cleric composed the patchwork vernacular *Chronique Saintogeaise,* he naturally made Clovis into the proud founder of dozens of southern churches.[70]

Clovis was thus a vivid imaginative presence for southern communities well before he appeared as a saint at the three examined by Beaune: Dorat, Sainte-Marthe of Tarascon, and Moissac. The first two of these monasteries seem not to have commemorated this king previously—but they hardly invented the saint from thin air, nor simply because the Capetians were now present. Both probably drew on the anterior southern invocations of the legendary Clovis.[71] At Moissac, Saint Clovis had his own prehistory. By the twelfth century, as we have seen, Moissac had fostered a tradition of its royal foundation.[72] An artful alteration of a passage in the vita of Desiderius of Cahors asserted that the monastery had been "begun" with royal moneys; left tantalizingly imprecise was the identity of the king or kings in question.

Several fragments of evidence suggest that a Clovis was forming behind this generic façade. An inscription, originally in the cloister and now located on the interior wall of the apse, commemorates the dedication of the abbey church in 1063. The last two lines proclaim: "King Clovis established (*instituit*) this church for you, Christ, [our] God. / After him, munificent Louis enriched it with gifts (*donis*)."[73] Nineteenth-century historians tried to make

[69] Gregory of Tours, *Historia Francorum* 2.38 (*MGH SSRM* 1.1:88–89); cf. Rouche, *L'Aquitaine,* pp. 49–50.
[70] *Tote Listoire,* pp. 16–18.
[71] The Saint Clovis of Dorat probably represented that monastic community's attempt to rival nearby Noblat. Beaune makes this observation without drawing out its implications: "Saint Clovis," pp. 151–152, and *Naissance,* pp. 69–71.
[72] See above, Chapter 3 at nn. 50–55.
[73] The inscription is reproduced in Dufour, *La bibliothèque,* pl. 78, and in Rupin, *L'abbaye,*

this Clovis accord with the early seventh-century foundation described in the unadulterated *vita* of Desiderius; hence, they proposed that he was Clovis II (638–657).[74] Certainly this is possible, but no extant documents link this king in any way with Moissac.[75] It seems much more likely that in this consecration inscription (often, we have seen, a locus of memory and of such claims both in legend and in history) the abbey invoked the far more powerful image of the first Clovis.[76]

The inscription was certainly read in this fashion by the monks of later centuries. Moissac's abbot cited it in a letter sent to Philip Augustus complaining about both Raymond VI of Toulouse's abuse of the monastery's rights and the destruction wrought upon the town during the siege of 1212—in so many words, the monastery's loss of *potestas*.[77] The letter begs the king to restore the monastery's immunity and *libertas*. It begins by evoking Moissac's royal foundation:

we read that your ancestors founded this most ancient monastery . . . and endowed it all around with . . . possessions, just as is contained in the deeds (*gestis*) of the kings of the Franks and of blessed Ansbertus, archbishop of Rouen and abbot of our monastery. And in the consecration [inscription] of our church is written among other things: "King Clovis built this church for you, Christ, [our] God. / After him, munificent Louis enriched it with gifts (*donis*)."[78]

Although the letter does not make explicit which Clovis the monks thought the first king of the inscription was, the context (the appeal to the present monarch) suggests that the illustrious Clovis I was being set forth as an example to Philip.[79] In any case, the implication and exhortation are obvious. This Clovis had seen fit to found the monastery, and Louis to enrich it

p. 50. On the church dedicated in 1063, see Durliat, "L'église abbatiale de Moissac," pp. 155–177.

[74] See Jules Marion, "L'abbaye de Moissac: Notes d'un voyage archéologique dans le sud-ouest de France," *Bibliothèque de l'Ecole des Chartes* 11 (1849): 89–147.

[75] The earliest document extant for Moissac is a charter of 680, in which no Clovis appears; see *HL* 2:42–45, no. 4.

[76] On dedication inscriptions, see above, Chapter 1 at nn. 75–77.

[77] The abbot's letter was composed after the 1212 siege of Moissac (by Simon de Montfort) and before 1223, since it was addressed to Philip II, who died in that year.

[78] Aymeric de Peyrat, *Chronicon* (Paris, BN Latin 4991A, f. 165va); cited in Lagrèze-Fossat, *Etudes*, 1:373.

[79] Clovis might also be proposed to Philip as an archetype in Guillaume Le Breton's *Philippidos*. The section called "De origine Francorum" ends with a long description (bk. 1, ll. 176–216) of Clovis's conversion. The text then jumps immediately to Philip II's accession to the throne (although in one manuscript there is a genealogical tree which extends from Marcomir to Dagobert). *Philippidos* 1.171–223, in *Œuvres de Rigord et de Guillaume Le Breton, historiens de Philippe-Auguste*, ed. H.-F. Delaborde, 2 vols. (Paris, 1882–1885), 2:14–15.

with gifts; Philip should follow in his august predecessors' footsteps and protect the monastery from its enemies.

Aymeric de Peyrat, the only source I have found for this letter, framed it in his *Chronicon* with a reference to a Clovis unmistakably the First. Aymeric wrote that in the 1230s, Raymond VII of Toulouse "held the monastery in much hatred" because of the abbey's legend that it had been founded by "Clovis, the first king of the Franks, and certain of his successors, the kings of France."[80] Certainly for Aymeric, the Clovis of the inscription cited in the letter was Clovis I. Earlier in the *Chronicon*, Aymeric himself had proposed the inscription as evidence that "the most illustrious Clovis was the first and principal founder of the monastery of Moissac. . . . [He] was the first Christian king of the Franks."[81]

This statement linking Moissac's origins with those of the Christian Frankish monarchy forms the refrain of Aymeric's *Chronicon*, serving as an epithet to characterize Clovis and claim him for the monastery.[82] As we saw in Chapter 2, Aymeric writes that Clovis decided to found the monastery on the eve of the battle of Toulouse when he had a vision of two griffins carrying stones in their beaks and depositing them in the valley of the Tarn.[83] He and his men began to build a church there in honor of Saint Peter, and completed it after the victory, the text hints, with Alaric's fabulous treasure. Like the establishment of Auch's primacy, the foundation of Moissac was linked intimately to the golden age symbolized by the Clovis who came south to defeat the Goths.

Indeed, Aymeric grandly proclaimed: "the monastery of Moissac was begun miraculously with this triumph. Therefore it was prominent henceforth under the name of a royal monastery (*regale monasterium*)."[84] He resisted any intimation that the royal founder could have been other than Clovis, as his citation—or rather alteration—of Pierre Des Vaux-Cernay's description of Moissac shows. Pierre had actually written that in the fortified town of

[80] Aymeric de Peyrat, *Chronicon* (Paris, BN Latin 4991A, f. 165rb; cf. the similar statement on f. 122va). For details of the rivalry between count and monastery, and the role of legend, see below: Chapter 6 at nn. 146–159.

[81] In full the passage reads: "Idemque illustrissimus clodoveus Moyssiacensis cenobii fuit primus et principalis fundator unde ab olim in hoc [f. 103ra] monasterio conscribuntur hoc nempe cenobium quingentisimo vi fundatum anno quo christus nascitur propheta in orbem. I . . . [ink blot making text illegible] . . . habuit clodoveo france tenenti qui primus fuit rex francorum christianus. Et in quodam lapide sculpti de littera difficili et antiquissima, tales versus perleguntur" (Paris, BN Latin 4991A, ff. 102vb–103ra).

[82] The passages describing or mentioning Clovis that I have found in the *Chronicon* (Paris, BN Latin 4991A) include ff. 7vb, 102vb–103rb, 103vb–104va, 104vb–105rb, 120vb–121ra, 136ra, 162ra, 164va, 165rb, 170va-vb, and 175rb. I have found only one reference to Clovis in the fragmentary autograph Paris BN Latin 5288 (f. 61va).

[83] See above, Chapter 2 at nn.63–65.

[84] Aymeric de Peyrat, *Chronicon* (Paris, BN Latin 4991A, f. 103vb).

Moissac, "as it is said, the king of France, Pippin, had made a monastery of a thousand monks."[85] In the *Chronicon,* the king had of course become Clovis.[86] For Aymeric, the monastery could only be the fruit of the first Christian king's decisive victory which had made the south Frankish. Monastery was coterminous with monarchy.[87]

This preference for Clovis led Aymeric to reject not only other kings, but also a saint as founder for Moissac. In an authentic diploma (818) of Pippin I of Aquitaine, Moissac is described as the abbey that "Saint Amandus, abbot, built in the distant past."[88] According to his *vita,* Saint Amandus, bishop of Maastricht in the seventh century, did spend some time south of the Loire in his natal land.[89] All his monastic foundations, however, were located in the north.[90] Indeed, at Moissac itself, there is no evidence of any cultivation of the image of Amandus as founder; an eleventh-century hagiographic manuscript from the abbey includes a copy of his *vita* which is not interpolated to ascribe to the saint any participation in Moissac's establishment.[91] Still, Aymeric, who as the monastery's historian cited Pippin's diploma in the *Chronicon,* had to resolve the apparent contradiction, and did so, not surprisingly, in favor of Clovis. Appointed by Dagobert to restore the abbey, Amandus was not Moissac's founder; he merely completed what Clovis had begun.[92]

Furthermore, in Aymeric's account of the foundation, Clovis has no contemporaneous saintly partner to cast him in the shadow. Once the site has been revealed by the wondrous griffins, the king's presence is enough for

---

[85] *Petri Vallium sarnarii monachi Historia Albigensis,* ed. Pascal Guébin and Ernest Lyon, 2 vols. (Paris, 1926–1930), 2:40. I have found no evidence that Moissac itself ever considered any king Pippin its founder. A Pippin I of Aquitaine, however, does confirm the monastery's immunity; see below at n. 88.

[86] "Et in predicta villa Clodoveus rex Francorum nuper fecerat quoddam nobile monasterium monachorum" (Paris, BN Latin 4991A, f. 164va). It is possible that Aymeric was not the author of this alteration but was simply reproducing an anterior interpolation.

[87] Aymeric at one point draws an explicit parallel between the chronology of the Frankish kings and the monastery's history, implying an analogy between monastery and monarchy: "sane sicut in regno Francie et regibus francorum trina legitur generacionis successio prima a Clodoveo fundatore predicti monasterii usque ad karolum magnum, a karolo magno usque ad hugonem chapet, tertia ab hugone usque nunc, sic hoc monasterium potuit habere trinam mutacionem temporum" (Paris, BN Latin 4991A, ff. 162ra-rb). The first era began with the abbey's foundation by Clovis; the second with Odilo of Cluny, in whose time Moissac became Cluniac; and the third comprised the depredations of the counts of Toulouse and the *abbates milites* (see below, Chapter 6 at nn. 146–159).

[88] *Recueil des actes de Pépin,* pp. 3–4, no. 1.

[89] Baudemundus, *Vita S. Amandi* (*AASS* February 1:852).

[90] See Auguste Molinier's remarks: *HL* 1:707–708, n. 4; *HL* 2:260–269.

[91] Paris, BN Latin 2627, ff. 56r–65v. Nor does the sermon for Amandus's feast day which follows (ff. 72r–83r) attribute to him Moissac's foundation.

[92] Aymeric de Peyrat, *Chronicon* (Paris, BN Latin 4991A, ff. 135rb, 136ra; cf. ff. 152vb–153ra).

the foundation. No bishops, no abbots, but rather Clovis and his troops are the actors who create the sacred space of the abbey. Perhaps this is partly because of the way the *Chronicon* shapes Clovis as a king who radiates piety: Aymeric describes Clovis as an exemplary Christian (and prototype crusader?) who had made a pilgrimage to the Holy Land.[93]

For Aymeric, Clovis was even more than an excellent Christian. In one passage Aymeric addresses to this king a prayer of an intercessory tone. Why was Clovis worthy of such supplication? In this prayer Aymeric lauds Clovis for his defeat of the Arian Goths, his bringing of baptism's grace to the Frankish kings, and his foundation of the abbey—the traits associated with Clovis throughout the *Chronicon* and in the other legends. Immediately after the prayer, Aymeric bestows upon Clovis the title of saint: "And I have heard that in some regions churches are discovered which have been founded in honor of Saint Clovis."[94] The abbot thus believed that the king had sufficient celestial merit to warrant his prayer for intercession. The metamorphosis was complete; the shadowy Clovis of Saint-Germier and the Clovis who left relics at Auch had become a patron saint. This process may have been stimulated by, but was not caused by, the expansion of Capetian power. Clovis became a saint because of the way these ecclesiastical communities imagined their own origins. This vision may have accorded with images crystallizing in the royal realm itself, but was nonetheless independent from them.

Certainly none of Clovis's descendants who ruled in the south enjoyed any such legendary apotheosis. I have found little evidence that monasteries of the south appropriated or embellished the memory of other Merovingians as founders.[95] The sole exception I have discovered is the legend of Sainte-Enimie. The eponymous founder of this monastery was, her twelfth-century *vita* proclaims, the sister of Dagobert and the daughter of

---

[93] "Hic fertur in oriente fuisse ac loca sanctorum visitasse ipsumque adivisse iherosolimam et loca passionis ac resurectionis dominice que in evvangelio legimus sepe vidisse" (Paris, BN Latin 4991A, f. 104va). On Clovis as proto-crusader in this passage, see Beaune, *Naissance*, p. 60. Given the popularity of the story of Charlemagne's voyage to Jerusalem, it is also possible that Aymeric or his sources were casting Clovis in Charlemagne's image. Aymeric wrote a work on Charlemagne that I have been unable to consult: *Stromatheus tragicus de planctu Caroli Magni* (Cahors, BM 37).

[94] "Et percepi quod in aliquibus partibus ecclesie reperiuntur fundate in honore sancti clodovei," (Paris, BN Latin 4991A, f. 104vb). Beaune cites other passages in which Aymeric refers to Saint Clovis (*Naissance*, p. 65, n. 42), but my consultation of them did not reveal any mention of King Clovis, only King Clovis.

[95] There was a legend in existence by the eleventh century that associated Clovis and a Princess Theodochilda (supposedly his daughter) with the origins of Mauriac. This tradition, however, was created not by Mauriac but by the northern abbey of Saint-Pierre-le-Vif (Sens) in an effort to uphold its claims to land in Auvergne; see Jean Le Guillou, "La reine Theod-Hilde: Tentative d'identification," *Bulletin du Comité d'Histoire et Traditions Populaires de Mauriac et sa Région*, 2 (n.d.): 1–42, esp. 14–23.

King Clovis, son of Dagobert, who himself was the grandson of the first Clovis–a most impossible but also a most Merovingian genealogy.[96] Not only did this princess establish the abbey (after she had solved the problem of the destructive dragon), but her father and brother endowed it with property, thus deepening the foundation's Merovingian tint.[97]

More typically, while Clovis could be exalted and commemorated as a beneficent founder, his descendants were excoriated—sometimes within the same text. For example, in the prologue to the chronicle of Conques, Clovis is remembered favorably (he supposedly refounded the monastery on his way to fight Alaric), but Theudebert, "the older son of Childeric, king of the Franks," is castigated for the woe he brought upon the churches of Aquitaine.[98] Certainly many of the Merovingians who succeeded Clovis in the south wreaked destruction, causing a ferment of Aquitainian rebellion that lasted nearly a century.[99] They were thus perhaps unlikely to be remembered favorably—but, as we shall see, one king who destroyed more than he constructed in the south, Pippin the Short, was exalted in legend. The absence of Clovis's descendants in the legends is due rather to the processes of selective and imaginative memory. It was not the Frankishness of Clovis's successors but their non-Clovisness that caused the monasteries to elide them. None of these rulers could match his qualities of primacy and antiquity; nor could they take credit for having introduced Christianity to the kings and for having vanquished the Arians in the south. It was the combination of these latter achievements that encouraged southern ecclesiastical establishments to transform Clovis in their memory from conquering warrior into saintly and heroic founder. Churches who could attach their foundation to the campaign that brought him south not only acquired for themselves a king who incarnated beginnings, but also became a part of the heretics' defeat—an event that signaled both the triumph of orthodoxy and Aquitaine's entrance into the Frankish realm.

---

[96] "Vita, inventio et miracula sanctae Enimiae," p. 253. Is Enimia's father supposed to be Clovis II, whose father was Dagobert I but whose grandfather was not Clovis I but Clotar? Clovis II did not have a son named Dagobert. See the genealogy in Patrick Geary, *Before France and Germany: The Creation and Transformation of the Merovingian World* (Oxford, 1988), pp. 232–233. Perhaps Enimia is made a distant rather than an immediate descendant of Clovis I in order to associate her (monastery) with the contemporaneous traditions concerning relic translations from the Gévaudan to Saint-Denis; see "Vita, inventio et miracula sanctae Enimiae," pp. 241–242, 278–279.

[97] "Vita, inventio et miracula sanctae Enimiae," p. 273.

[98] "Chronique du monastère de Conques," pp. 392–393. This Theudebert is perplexing. Neither Theudebert I nor II was a son of Childeric (II?). Furthermore, Theudebert I was a ruler who generally pleased the Aquitanians; perhaps the reference is to the campaigns by which he took Rodez and Lodève before he became king in 533. Theudebert II of Austrasia mounted an expedition against the Basques in 602, but otherwise did not intervene in meridional affairs. Rouche, *L'Aquitaine*, pp. 57–58, 89.

[99] Rouche, *L'Aquitaine*, pp. 51–85.

Pippin the Short

After the Merovingians came the Carolingians, a dynasty to whom the south remained loyal for some years after the advent of the Capetians in 987, as historians have long been aware. This lingering meridional fidelity manifested itself perhaps most strikingly in a number of charters that continued to be dated according to Carolingian regnal years. *Formulae* of other southern (most notably Catalonian) charters from this period also betray the sentiment that the Capetians, as non-Carolingian rulers, were not legitimate: *iesu christo regnante; rege expectante* ("with Jesus Christ reigning"; "awaiting a king"). By at least the middle of the eleventh century (if not much earlier) such *formulae* and the Carolingian dating had disappeared.[100] But did the loyalty represented by these earlier diplomatic forms, unreal and idealistic though it was, evaporate as well? It seems rather to have been transmuted into an extraordinary development and cultivation of the image of the Carolingian kings as monastic founders and benefactors, in legends from the second half of the eleventh century onward. As we shall see, this legendary version of loyalty to the Carolingians had a meaning unlike that of the charters' *formulae:* the legendary invocation of the Carolingians did not imply rejection of the present rulers. Yet, in its extent and complexity, this imaginative commemoration of the Carolingians rivaled that occurring contemporaneously north of the Loire in which historians have found evidence of an emerging "national consciousness" focused on (and fostered by) the Capetian king.[101]

Meridional loyalty to the Carolingians as expressed in foundation legends was not indiscriminate; no Pippinid mayors of the palace were celebrated, nor was Charles Martel. The elision of this latter is perhaps to be expected, for Charles was the Hammer not only of the Arabs but also of the south and more particularly of churches. Hence, monasteries hardly had much reason to remember him favorably or to transform him into a legendary benefactor. Nonetheless, monastic imagination could work wonders; in hagiographic sources from other regions and times, Martel is praised as an ecclesiastical patron.[102] The factor that impeded his legendary commemoration by southern monasteries was perhaps quite simply that he had been a king only de

[100] See Bernd Schneidmüller, *Karolingische Tradition und frühes französisches Königtum: Untersuchungen zur Herrschaftslegitimation der westfränkisch-französichen Monarchie im 10. Jahrhundert* (Wiesbaden, 1979), pp. 194–199. Also see Michel Zimmermann, "La datation des documents catalans du IXe au XIIe siècle: Un itinéraire politique," *Annales du Midi* 93 (1981): 345–375. For a recent reappraisal of the evidence, which puts the disappearance of such *formulae* much earlier (by Robert the Pious's reign), see Jean Dufour, "Obédience respective."

[101] See below, Chapter 5 at nn. 30–32.

[102] On the range of images of Martel, see Ulrich Nonn, "Das Bild Karl Martells in den lateinischen Quellen vornehmlich des 8. und 9. Jahrhunderts," *Frühmittelalterliche Studien* 4 (1970): 70–137.

facto and not in name.[103] An abbey celebrating him as its founder would not thereby have been able to clothe itself with the coveted status of a royal monastery.

The first Carolingian embellished as a founder by the southern legends was himself the first official king in the family: Pippin the Short, who shared with Clovis the appealing attribute of primordiality. Pippin figured as founder or refounder in the legends of nine southern monasteries (Saint-Pierre of Uzerche, Figeac, Sorèze, Mozac, La Règle, Saint-Quintin of Gaillaguet, Saint-Pierre of Joncels, Conques, Saint-Michel-de-Cuxa) and one house of canons (Saint-Yrieix-de-la-Perche).[104] Interestingly, all but two of these communities were located in Auvergne and its periphery—exactly the area that Pippin had traversed so frequently in his multiple campaigns of the 760s. Did some memory of his passage linger? In this ultimately successful attempt to integrate Aquitaine into his kingdom, however, Pippin had burned rather than founded churches.[105] Like Clovis, he came to the south as a warrior and was remembered by monasteries as a benefactor; unlike Clovis, his conquest had not been associated with an expulsion of heretics or an exaltation of the episcopate. Here the transformative power of monastic imaginative memory is evident, for not only had Pippin wreaked havoc in the 760s, but throughout his reign his actual patronage of churches south of the Loire had been minimal. Among Pippin's thirty-one authentic diplomas, only one was issued for a southern establishment, a diploma of 768 granting immunity to Saint-Hilaire of Poitiers.[106] And this latter was dated at Saint-Denis, not at Poitiers—no attestation, then, of benefits accorded while the king was campaigning in the south.

But the diplomas forged in Pippin's name reveal that it was in the south rather than in the north that monasteries most particularly cultivated the memory of this king. Among the twelve forged diplomas of Pippin collected

[103] Nonn points out that in various sources Martel acquires kingly attributes, even the title of king, but is nonetheless not considered to be royal: "Das Bild Karl Martells," pp. 72–74, 80–82, 90–99.

[104] In addition, two southern monasteries claim Pippin as (re)founder in texts that are not definitively datable any earlier than the fifteenth century: Clairac (near Agen) and Marcillac, a priory of Moissac. The legend of Clairac takes the form of a forged diploma; see MGH Diplomata Karolinorum 1:53–54, no. 38 (the Chronique dite Saintongeaise, p. 268, presents Charlemagne as this community's founder). For the Marcillac legend, see the charter of 1496 (Paris, BN Doat 123, ff. 149v–150r) and the legend of Saint Namphasius ("De sancto Namfasio eremita Marciliaci apud Cadurcos," in AASSosB 3.2:447–448). I have been unable to identify the breviary of Cahors cited by Jean Mabillon; Namphasius appeared in liturgical manuscripts from the twelfth century onward (Paris, BN Latin 944, ff. 31vb, 75v, 113vb, 145v; Paris, BN 13236, ff. 186r, 440ra-rb). On the history of Marcillac, see Edmond Albe and Armand Viré, L'Hébrardie, 3 vols. (Brive, 1924–1925), vol. 1. I thank Pierre Bonnassie for bringing the Marcillac legend to my attention.

[105] On the campaigns of Charles Martel and Pippin, see Rouche, L'Aquitaine, pp. 111–132 (125 for a map of Pippin's campaigns).

[106] MGH Diplomata Karolinorum 1:32–33, no. 24.

in the most critical edition of his acts, fully one-third (four) relate to southern monasteries, and all of them pertain to (re)foundations effected by the
king.[107] To these can be added five other diplomas formerly attributed to
Pippin I or II of Aquitaine, but which Léon Levillain has correctly identified
as forgeries in the name of the first Carolingian king.[108] Of these, two are for
the same monastery and relate to its foundation by Pippin; as for the other
three, only one (a grant of tolls to Saint-Sulpice of Bourges) does not deal
with a refoundation in which the king participated. Overall, then, southern
monasteries forged more than half (nine) of the seventeen diplomas known
to have been fabricated in Pippin's name. Moreover, of the other eight
diplomas, six were created by ecclesiastical establishments in the eastern
Frankish realm, one deals with Rome, and only one was fabricated by a
northern French establishment—predictably the self-appointed guardian
of the royal past, Saint-Denis.[109] The concentration of the forgeries south
and not north of the Loire is thus unmistakable.

These meridional forgeries depict Pippin not as a king who issued
diplomas from some distant northern royal seat(s), but as one who was
active south of the Loire; five of the nine diplomas are dated at or near the
monastery in question, or they mention the king's presence there. Not
unexpectedly, these diplomas were fabricated in just the epoch when, as I
have argued, legends began increasingly to bring Frankish kings as founders
south of the Loire: the last decades of the eleventh century and the first half
of the twelfth century.

Most of these diplomas relating to foundation are fulsome narratives,
rather than spare and sober diplomatic instruments. They present not a
mere royal subscription, but a Pippin interwoven into a tale, a king who has
been imaginatively remembered. Only two abbeys used Pippin to gild their
foundation by simply claiming him without much elaboration as a
(re)founder. Sometime in the twelfth century, the monks of Saint-Pierre of
Joncels, a monastery that is first mentioned in the *Notitia de servitio monasteriorum* of 817, created for themselves a refoundation by this king.[110] In a
diploma fashioned from bits of authentic Carolingian royal precepts, Pippin
declared that at the request of Abbot Benedict, he (the king) had decided to
rebuild the abbey and endow it with fiscal properties. In case any doubt
existed as to which King Pippin had issued the diploma, someone, presumably a monk of Joncels, added after the regnal year the Incarnation dating
that would clarify the matter: 762.[111] Texts relating to the foundation of

[107] *MGH Diplomata Karolinorum* 1:45–49, 53–54, 59–60, nos. 33, 34, 38, 42.

[108] *Recueil des actes de Pépin*, pp. 269–293, nos. 62–66.

[109] *MGH Diplomata Karolinorum* 1:42–60, nos. 31 (Cröv), 37 (Gorze), 36 (Trier), 39
(Saint-Maximin of Trier), 32 and 41 (Fulda), 40 (Rome), 35 (Saint-Denis).

[110] *Notitia de servitio monasteriorum*, in *MGH Capitularia regum Francorum* 1:351, no. 171.

[111] *Recueil des actes de Pépin*, pp. 127–132, no. 30; cf. p. 286, no. 65. The diploma is extant
in a twelfth-century "copy" which I have been unable to consult (it is part of a private

Sorèze, actually established by a count during the reign of Charlemagne, hint only slightly more at an integration of Pippin into a legendary world.[112] Probably between the late eleventh and the mid-twelfth century, this monastery forged two diplomas in the name of Pippin. In the first, dated 753/754, the king recounts how, at the behest of the Virgin who had appeared to him in a vision, he founded Sorèze in her honor and granted it property and certain privileges.[113] In the second diploma (758/759), Pippin reiterates and expands upon these privileges and donations.[114]

Although they do not reveal a legendary king, these diplomas from Joncels and Sorèze do demonstrate the authority that Pippin the Short's name possessed by the twelfth century in the south. But why did these monasteries decide to confer upon this king rather than another the honor of being their founder? The other diplomas fabricated in Pippin's name, as well as legends taking an explicitly narrative form, reveal the qualities that made this king appealing as a legendary founder. Given the relative synchronicity of these texts, I shall consider them according to the various dimensions they added to Pippin's image, asking how and why these monasteries embellished this bellicose king's image to such an extent that the meaning of his presence in the south was utterly transformed.

Monastic communities could choose in their legends to play subtly upon Pippin's anointing as the first Carolingian king and its relation to the abbey's own consecration, as did the monastery of Figeac. Figeac's legend, developed in the 1090s and embellished over the course of the following century, consists of a number of forged diplomas and papal privileges as well as several narrative sources. Two diplomas of Pippin the Short, both dated 755 (the first probably fabricated in the 1090s, the second in the course of the twelfth century), relate how Pippin had decided to refound the monastery of *Jonante* (Lunan) built by his predecessors (whose names are not given).[115] Changing the abbey's site (perhaps to avoid the floods that had ruined the old monastery), he changed its name as well. The king then endowed the new abbey, henceforth known as Figeac, with various properties—including the cella of Saint-Quintin at Gaillaguet. This latter

---

collection). The A.D. date was added in a hand that "seemed" different to Léon Levillain and that he does not date. On the circumstances of this forgery, see below, Chapter 6 at nn. 233–239.

[112] Sorèze was founded by Count Atticus under Charlemagne; see Josef Semmler, "Karl der Grosse und das fränkische Mönchtum," in *Karl der Grosse: Lebenswerk und Nachleben*, ed. Wolfgang Braufels et al., 5 vols. (Düsseldorf, 1965–1968); 2:270. This monastery appears in the *Notitia de servitio monasteriorum*, in *MGH Capitularia regum Francorum* 1:351.

[113] *Recueil des actes de Pépin*, pp. 269–275, no. 62.

[114] *Recueil des actes de Pépin*, pp. 276–85, no. 63. Levillain believes that both these documents were intended as forgeries in the name of Pippin the Short, not in that of either Pippin of Aquitaine.

[115] See the critical edition and discussion of these two texts by Wolff, "Note sur le faux diplôme," pp. 298–311. On Lunan's legendary foundation, see above at n. 35.

donation was framed as a complementary royal foundation in a diploma of Pippin probably fabricated at Figeac in the same period as the others.[116] Rich in picturesque details, this diploma creates a Pippin who acts in the world of legend. But it does not provide a portrait of Pippin himself.

The main strand of Figeac's legend, however, does. The two forged diplomas relate how in 755, accompanied by Pope Stephen II, Pippin came (most unhistorically) to Figeac where he and the pope witnessed the abbey's miraculous consecration.[117] Other documents, probably composed in conjunction with or just after the first of the Pippin diplomas, mention the miracle.[118] This sequence of events culminating in the consecration—as we have seen, a defining moment of foundations, real and legendary—provides the key to understanding Figeac's Pippin. This importance of the consecration is underlined by a forgery no doubt specifically intended to complement the earlier version of the royal diploma: a privilege of Pope Stephen II also dated 755.[119] This text illuminates the meaning of the consecration's date: the year after Pippin's anointing by this very pope. In the privilege, Stephen proclaims that after the "consecration" at Saint-Denis, he went south with the king to consecrate the new royal foundation of Figeac. This "consecration" at Saint-Denis was Pippin's (second) anointing. Was this term selected deliberately to emphasize the continuum between the anointing of the king and that of Figeac's altar, at both of which Stephen officiated?[120]

This implicit parallel becomes explicit in the privilege's description of the miracle that (rather than the pope) actually effects the abbey church's consecration. Before the eyes of the pope and the recently anointed king, a cloud fills the sanctuary, like the *nebula* that consecrated Solomon's temple (3 Kings 8.10–12; 2 Paralipomenon 5.13–14, 6.1–2). This biblical type which often informed miraculous dedications here is given special resonance.[121] As in the Book of Kings, the anointing of the king is associated with the miraculous dedication of the church he had constructed. Hence,

[116] On this diploma, see above, Chapter 2 at nn. 112–113.

[117] See the critical edition and discussion of these two texts by Wolff, "Note sur le faux diplôme," pp. 298–311. On miraculous consecrations, see above, Chapter 2 at nn. 163–171.

[118] These include a privilege of Pope Pascal I (purporting to date from 822), and the chronicle of Figeac (which identifies Pippin as the founder). The privilege is edited in *GC* 1, instr. 43–44. The chronicle is edited by Etienne Baluze as *Historia monasterii Figiacensis in Dioecesi Cadurcensi*, in *Miscellanea novo ordine digesta et non paucis ineditis monumentis* (re-ed. J. D. Mansi), 4 vols. (Lucca, 1764), 4:1–2.

[119] *GC* 1, instr. 43. I have found no manuscript of this text other than the copies from the seventeenth century in Paris, BN Doat 126, ff. 18v–20v, 15r–17r. Wolff dates this text as late eleventh or early twelfth century; see his "Note sur le faux diplôme," pp. 321–322.

[120] Admittedly, other texts used *consecratio* in reference to royal anointing; see *Vita Meinwerci episcopi Patherbrunnensis*, ed. Franz Tenckhoff (Hannover, 1921), p. 29. But the term usually referred to ordination or to the consecration of an altar or church; see "consecratio" in Niermeyer, *Mediae Latinitatis lexicon*, p. 253.

[121] See above, Chapter 2 at nn. 163–165.

the anointings echo one another; the church—whether Figeac or the temple—inaugurates the reign and is made indubitably royal. This version of Figeac's foundation passed into a source that was widely diffused and used both in southern and in northern monasteries; a late twelfth-century interpolation in Ademar of Chabannes's *Chronicon* essentially rephrases the forged privilege of Stephen.[122] Figeac would henceforth be known as a monastery both founded by the first anointed Carolingian king, and consecrated in the presence of this new Solomon as his temple—a transcendent status whose significance in the context of rivalry with nearby Conques we shall explore later.[123]

As the monastery becomes quintessentially linked to the establishment of the new dynasty, the dynasty itself is exalted. The mechanism is Pippin's status as the first anointed Frankish king. More frequently, however, southern monasteries celebrated Pippin as a founder for a reason that seems paradoxical: his military expeditions of the 760s. In these other legends, Pippin's intention to subdue the south was not ignored, but it was translated into a mission with beneficent results for the monasteries. From destruction came legendary construction. Furthermore, in the process of this transformation, the monasteries shaped themselves as monuments expressing Pippin's victory and, even more important, the Carolingian loyalty of their inhabitants.

The complex legend of the abbey of Mozac, developed in many documents composed beginning in the last decade of the eleventh century and continuing throughout the next century, shows how this image of Pippin as monastic founder while on military campaign crystallized. In this series of texts, intertwined with a foundation legend developing contemporaneously at the abbey of Issoire, a royal translation of relics was gradually fashioned into a royal refoundation. Indeed, part of the foundation legend of each of these abbeys related to their eventually conflicting claims to possess the relics of Saint Austremonius, "apostle of the Auvergne."[124] According to the seventh-century core of the *Vita prima S. Austremonii,* this saint-bishop was buried and venerated at Issoire, the monastery he had founded.[125] But a ninth-century addition to the *Vita prima* composed at Mozac describes a series of translations, each provoked by neglect of Austremonius's cult. The relics traveled first from Issoire to Volvic, a monastery about ten kilometers

---

[122] Ademar of Chabannes, *Chronicon* (Paris, BN Latin 5926, ff. 36r-v; *Chronique,* p. 58, note s*). On the dating of the interpolation, see above: Chapter 2, n. 31.

[123] See below, Chapter 6 at nn. 246–263.

[124] On Austremonius's apostolicity, see above, Chapter 3 at nn. 28–31.

[125] *Vita prima S. Austremonii* (*AASS* November 1:49–54). On Austremonius's foundation of Issoire and burial there, see *Vita prima S. Austremonii* (*AASS* November 1:50, 52); *Vita secunda S. Austremonii* (*AASS* November 1:57); and the greatly inflated account of the *Vita tertia S. Austremonii* (*AASS* November 1:67, 73–74). Fournier characterizes this tradition of Issoire's foundation as "mythique" (*Le peuplement,* p. 450).

southwest of Mozac, and then finally from Volvic to Mozac, where, assured proper reverence, they remained.[126]

This latter translation was gradually shaped in Mozac's textual tradition into a refoundation of the monastery by King Pippin. The ninth-century section of the *Vita prima* composed at Mozac relates the translation in the following fashion. Mozac had suffered from the wars devastating Aquitaine (no doubt the prolonged wrangles between Louis the Pious's sons in which Aquitaine was often at stake and Pippin II deeply embroiled).[127] Presumably in order to restore his monastery's fortunes, the abbot, Lamfred, asked a certain King Pippin for permission to translate a saint's body to Mozac. Pippin not only acceded to this request, but personally assisted at the translation, even carrying the relics himself.[128] This implicit reference to David and the translation of the Ark (1 Paralipomenon 13.1–8, 15.15–16, 25–29) becomes explicit in the *Vita secunda S. Austremonii*, an unremarkable reworking of the *Vita prima* composed at Mozac sometime in the late ninth or early tenth century. According to the *Vita secunda,* "joyful like David who once played before the ark of the Lord, the king [Pippin] exulted before the holy martyr's relics and carried the sacred limbs on his own shoulders"—a description repeated almost verbatim by later versions of the *translatio.*[129] In the biblical text, only priests were allowed to touch and transport the Ark; David merely played and sang in the procession. At Mozac, though, King Pippin is elevated to the sanctified role of a priest who may safely handle the sacred.[130]

But which King Pippin? The translation probably occurred in 848 and involved Pippin II, king of Aquitaine.[131] Indeed, a thirteenth-century manuscript of the *Vita prima* identifies Pippin as "king of the province of Aquitaine."[132] Pippin remains the king of Aquitaine in the *Vita secunda.*[133] In a tenth-century manuscript of the *Vita Prima,* however, the *Aquitanie* qualifying

---

[126] *Vita prima S. Austremonii* (*AASS* November 1:53).

[127] On the years of strife between the Pippins and other Carolingians, the most comprehensive treatment is still that of Auzias, *L'Aquitaine.*

[128] *Vita prima S. Austremonii* (*AASS* November 1:53).

[129] *Vita secunda S. Austremonii* (*AASS* November 1:59). Cf. *Revelatio corporis Austremonii et ejusdem duplex translatio* (*AASS* November 1:79–80).

[130] Louis VII carries the reliquary of Saint Denis at the consecration of Suger's new church, but Suger is careful to emphasize that the king received it from the bishops: *Libellus alter de consecratione ecclesiae sancti dionysii,* ed. and trans. in Erwin Panofsky, *Abbot Suger: On The Abbey Church of St.-Denis and Its Art Treasures,* 2d ed. (Princeton, 1979), p. 116. In other *translatio* texts, it is bishops who carry relics "propriis . . . humeris"; see the ninth-century *Miracula S. Mauri sive restauratione monasterii Glannafoliensis* (*MGH SS* 15.1:464).

[131] See Levillain's comments in *Recueil des actes de Pépin,* p. 238, no. 58 (revising his earlier opinion that the translation occurred in 863, expressed in his "La translation des reliques de saint Austremoine à Mozac et le diplôme de Pépin II d'Aquitaine [863]," *Le Moyen Age* 17 [1904]: 281–337).

[132] Clermont-Ferrand, BM 148, as cited by Fournier, "Saint Austremoine," p. 426, n. 26.

[133] *Vita secunda S. Austremonii* (*AASS* November 1:59).

rex Pippinus has been erased.[134] With the elimination of the incriminating *Aquitanie*, this king becomes Pippin the Short, ruler of the Franks. Although it is impossible to pinpoint this erasure's date more precisely than sometime before the sixteenth or seventeenth century (when the *Aquitanie* was reinserted), it may well have occurred in just the period when Pippin the Short explicitly replaced the errant Pippin II in Mozac's legend and at Issoire: the later eleventh and twelfth centuries.[135]

The *Vita tertia S. Austremonii*, an amalgam of texts produced in the (later?) eleventh century by the two monasteries claiming this saint's body, Mozac and Issoire, proclaims in no uncertain terms that Pippin the Short had presided at Austremonius's translation. The section of the text composed at Issoire describes how a certain "king of the Franks" named Pippin convoked a council to combat trinitarian heresies.[136] This was the council of Gentilly (767), which immediately preceded Pippin's fifth campaign against Waïfre and at which, as Ademar of Chabannes relates, matters relating to the Trinity were aired.[137] According to the *vita*, though, this council was primarily the occasion for royal munificence toward monasteries; Pippin opened his treasure chest and distributed funds earmarked for the restoration of churches. The text then mentions Abbot Lamfred's petition for the precious relics (although, unsurprisingly, Mozac is not mentioned). Unfortunately, the manuscript breaks off before describing the translation itself.

In any case, this Pippin is unmistakably king of the Franks, not of Aquitaine, just as he is in the Mozac layer of the *Vita tertia*.[138] According to the latter, Lamfred approached "the most serene lord king Pippin," who at that time was "staying" (*morabatur*) at Clermont accompanied by a host of "his magnates." A *rex serenissimus*, *augustus*, and even *augustissimus* wearing a diadem—this must be Pippin the Short, not a mere subking.[139] And surely, despite the euphemism ("staying"), this was a memory of the king who had repeatedly laid siege to Clermont in the 760s.

Another document produced at Mozac (in the last decade of the eleventh century or the early years of the twelfth) leaves no doubt that this monastery was claiming for itself Charlemagne's father. This text is a diploma of Pippin II which was altered and interpolated to ascribe to Pippin the Short not only the translation of Austremonius's relics, but also generous donations of

---

[134] Clermont-Ferrand, BM 147, f. 4v.

[135] See Fournier's description of the erasure (although he does not remark on its implications) in "Saint Austremoine," p. 426, n. 26.

[136] The section of the *vita* composed at Issoire (and later recopied and reworked at Mozac) is to be found in *AASS* November 1:61–77. Also see Fournier, "Saint Austremoine," pp. 456–462.

[137] Ademar of Chabannes, *Chronicon* 1.59 (*Chronique*, p. 61).

[138] The portion of the *Vita tertia S. Austremonii* composed at Mozac is the *Revelatio corporis Austremonii* (*AASS* November 1:77–80). Cf. Fournier, "Saint Austremoine," pp. 462–464.

[139] *Revelatio corporis Austremonii* (*AASS* November 1:79). On the *intitulatio* used for Pippin II in his diplomas, see *Recueil des actes de Pépin*, pp. cxliv–cxlv.

royal estates and the reconfirmation of Mozac's privileges.[140] The diploma is dated 764 at Clermont, a year in which Pippin the Short actually had been in the north.[141] This text, like the Mozac version of the *Vita tertia*, seems to recall Pippin's presence at Clermont in 760 and 761. Thus, not only had Mozac's legend transmuted Pippin II of Aquitaine into Pippin the Short, it had also transformed the latter from a ravaging warrior into a glorious ecclesiastical patron.

In a slightly later layer of Mozac's legend, a text composed sometime after the *Vita tertia* and probably in the twelfth century, the various transformations of king, relic translation, and battle at Clermont reach their culmination. The translation of Austremonius's relics fades into a mere epilogue to Mozac's refoundation by the king. Even more important, this refoundation is perhaps the apotheosis of the inversion of Pippin the Short's campaigns in the Auvergne. This document, the account of a vision Lamfred had before the translation, interweaves, as we saw in Chapter 2, Pippin's munificence with a revelatory miracle of refoundation.[142] Abbot Lamfred seems to see himself recounting the vision he had to "the glorious lord king Pippin." Pippin in exchange relates a complementary vision he himself had the same night.[143] The tradition of the king's vision first appeared in the Mozac section of the *Vita tertia*, but there it functions as a prefiguring of the king's participation in the translation of Austremonius's relics to Mozac.[144] In the Lamfred text, refoundation informs Pippin's vision. A splendidly garbed old man (Austremonius) shows Pippin deer tracks in the snow of Mozac's cemetery and tells him that he is to build a church there. Refoundation by the king, a purely royal gesture, thus replaces a focus on (the relics of) the saint, a displacement whose importance we have seen before and will again.

After this sequence of interlocking visions, the king comes to Clermont, and this time the text makes his intention explicit: he was to battle Waïfre. Having taken Bourbon l'Archambault and laid siege to Clermont, Pippin remembers his vision and accomplishes the refoundation just as he had been instructed by Saint Austremonius. The victorious king orders that a church of "wondrous size" be built, and for its construction sends back cartloads of cut stone salvaged from his destruction of the city of Clermont.[145] Here the

---

[140] For an edition and discussion of this diploma, see *Recueil des actes de Pépin*, pp. 227–242, 285–286, nos. 58 and 64; and Levillain's earlier discussion in "La translation des reliques de saint Austremoine."

[141] He was in the Ardennes; Levillain, "La translation des reliques de saint Austremoine," p. 293.

[142] The text is edited by Krusch, "Reise nach Frankreich," pp. 24–25. On the site's revelation, see above, Chapter 2 at nn. 70–71.

[143] *Revelatio corporis Austremonii* (*AASS* November 1:79).

[144] Pippin had a vision of himself in the church at Volvic. He saw Austremonius clad as if for a journey and was assigned to the saint as a traveling companion for a trip to Mozac. *Vita tertia S. Austremonii* (*AASS* November 1:79).

[145] Krusch, "Reise nach Frankreich," pp. 24–25.

meaning of Pippin's campaigns is completely transmogrified. Not only does the king restore the abbey during a military expedition, but he rebuilds it with the concrete evidence of his ruinous warfare, the stones of Clermont. Constructed from destruction, the abbey thus literally becomes a monument to Pippin's triumph. Furthermore, the stones that might have been construed as symbols of Auvergne's resistance to Frankish domination become instead signs of Mozac's royal foundation and, by implication, its royal allegiance.[146]

Two other legends invoking Pippin as founder use the pair destruction-regeneration to express Carolingian loyalty in a similarly striking fashion. Furthermore, as these legends lionize the Carolingian ruler, they concurrently denigrate his adversary, Waïfre, the would-be leader of an independent Aquitaine. These themes are etched in bold relief in the foundation legend of Saint-Pierre of Uzerche, a narrative text of the early twelfth century which formed the preface to the monastery's cartulary.[147] The text's first words set up the royal frame: "While King Pippin was ruling." The rest of the sentence relates what Ademar of Chabannes's *Chronicon* also tells us: Pippin destroyed the city of Limoges on his second Aquitainian campaign. Ademar ascribes the king's action to the refusal of the city's inhabitants to receive him "in peace."[148] The Uzerche text sharpens this in order to underline the misplaced loyalty of the Limogeois which justified the city's destruction: "Waïfre, the duke of Aquitaine, incited the inhabitants of the Limousin, particularly the city of Limoges, to rebellion." Thus the syntax of the text's first sentence sets up clearly the opposition between legitimate ruling king and illegitimate rebelling Waïfre and his special adherents, the inhabitants of Limoges.[149]

This scourging royal vengeance is balanced in the Uzerche narrative by Pippin's construction of a city that incarnates from its inception Frankish loyalty. Having ravaged Limoges, Pippin wished to build another city in the same region and chose the site that would become Uzerche. There the king constructed an impregnable and proud walled city, establishing it as a "royal and episcopal seat." The claim to replace Limoges exactly is transparent (Pippin wanted Uzerche to be in no way dissimiliar to Limoges, the text tells us), as is the pretension to preeminence underlined by the proposed etymology of Uzerche (Latin: *Userca*): *Us* means the earth, and *archos* prince. Yet, Uzerche's glory was ephemeral even in legend. According to the narrative, sometime after Pippin's death the bishop of Limoges successfully

---

[146] For another possible (and complementary) reading of this passage, see below, Chapter 6 at nn. 138–142.

[147] *Ex historia monasterii Usercensis*, in *Cartulaire de l'abbayed' Uzerche*, pp. 13–50.

[148] Ademar of Chabannes, *Chronicon* 1.58 (*Chronique*, p. 60).

[149] The whole sentence reads: "Regnante Pipino rege, Gaiferus dux Aquitaniae Lemovicenses, praesertim urbem Lemovicensem incitavit" (*Ex historia monasterii Usercensis* in *Cartulaire de l'abbaye d'Uzerche*, p. 12).

stripped Uzerche of its primacy and subjected this legitimate royal and episcopal city to the ultimate humiliation, transferring it into the power (*ditio*) of a layman. Limoges once again had betrayed the Frankish king, this time by upsetting his ordering of the hierarchy.

The focus of the text then shifts from the city of Uzerche to its monastery, Saint-Pierre, which had not been mentioned before. Several generations after Uzerche's despoliation, a certain nobleman, Arbertus of *Chavanno,* decided to restore the "most noble monastery which King Pippin had built" and which had been abandoned by all but one lone cleric. This abbey, despite its refoundation, remained distinctly royal; not only did Arbertus petition permission for its restoration from the king, but he promised that its monks would "supplicate God day and night for the king and the stability of the kingdom"—a duty of Carolingian royal monasteries. Thus the power and prestige of Pippin's evanescent bishopric were translated to and concentrated in its refounded monastery, which in turn embodied the city's loyalty to its Frankish royal founder.

This narrative manipulated the memory of Pippin's campaigns in order to endow Uzerche with illustrious Carolingian royal origins and a brief moment of primacy—and to blacken rebellious Limoges and its bishops. Even though the late tenth-century bishop of Limoges, Hildegarius, who at Arbertus's request actually had participated in the refoundation and had issued the abbey's charter of privileges in 977, is granted his rightful role in the text, his predecessors are cast as usurpers of Uzerche's rightful status.[150] Although some of Hildegarius's successors enjoyed good relations with the abbey, several, particularly those contemporaneous with or just preceding the narrative text's composition, most decidedly did not. Hence, in this rewriting of history, Pippin's campaigns against Waïfre became the means of distinguishing those who in the future, as in the past, could slide from good to bad (rebels and antagonists of the monastery) from those who were intrinsically good (faithful to the king and the monastery itself). As in Mozac's legend, destruction generated the creation of royal space in the form of a monastery.

Limoges, too, manipulated history to situate itself among the faithful and to gain a monastic monument to the Carolingian's victory. The foundation legend of the female monastery of Sainte-Marie de la Règle of Limoges (a community mentioned in the *Notitia de servitio* of 817) depicts this church as rising, literally, from the ashes of the clash between Pippin and his adversary.[151] This legend takes the form of a diploma in Pippin's name, extant by 1175 when it was confirmed by Louis VII, and probably composed sometime

---

[150] See below, Chapter 6 at nn. 166–172.

[151] *Notitia de servitio monasteriorum,* in *MGH Capitularia regum Francorum* 1:351. The Astronomer includes this monastery among those which Louis the Pious restored as king of Aquitaine; see *Vita Hludowici imperatoris* (*MGH SS* 2:616).

in the twelfth century.[152] Exalted as "emperor" in the *invocatio*, Pippin relates how he had destroyed Limoges with "sword and flame" in order to punish "Duke Waïfre [who was] most fiercely rebelling against me." Here the opposition between Pippin—not just a king but an emperor—and the ducal traitor is made most clear. Furthermore, the text exalts Limoges as it had Pippin; Pippin describes Limoges as "such a great and such a noble city . . . which was the head and leader of the Aquitainian cities." In flagrant contradiction to historical fact, Limoges is thus clearly distinguished from the duke who used it as a base for his revolt.

Indeed, far from punishing this city, Pippin expresses his regret for having burned down its churches and monasteries. He most particularly laments the destruction of the church of the Virgin. This church, he states, had been built by Martial, and it was there that Christ had appeared to the saint and predicted his death (a scene the Pseudo-Aurelian *vita* of Martial mentioned, but did not locate in a specific church).[153] In other words, this was a special church, hallowed by its founder, the saintly apostle of the Limousin. Now it would have a new founder and one who was royal, for Pippin proceeded to reestablish the church magnificently. La Règle thus becomes an expression of Limoges's loyalty to the Carolingian, both during and after the rebellion of the treacherous duke of Aquitaine. Destruction becomes regeneration—as well as a transformation of the monastery's nature. La Règle's primitive history was characterized by its association with its saintly apostolic founder; its subsequent history took on instead the coloration of its Frankish royal founder. Here again king displaces saint, just as in Mozac's legend royal refoundation had replaced royal translation of relics.

Unlike Clovis, Pippin does not become himself a saint; rather, as he becomes more prominent as a legendary founder, he plays roles earlier reserved to saints. Nonetheless, I would suggest, he implicitly acquires the sanctifying attributes with which, as we have seen in Chapters 2 and 3, legends necessarily and typically endow founders. This subtle transformation of Pippin's image in monastic imaginative memory was accompanied by another: from Pippin I (or, more rarely, II) of Aquitaine to Pippin the Short, king of the Franks. Around the year 1000, monasteries seeking to endow themselves with a royal founder might choose Pippin I of Aquitaine, as is the case at Saint-Jean-d'Angély. This abbey was refounded in approximately 942 by two nobles, as a diploma of that date in which Louis IV confirmed their actions relates.[154] The diploma makes no mention of royal origins for the abbey. By the time Ademar of Chabannes (d. 1034) wrote his *Chronicon,*

---

[152] *MGH Diplomata Karolinorum* 1:59–60, no. 42. For Louis VII's confirmation, see the eighteenth-century copy in Paris, BN Latin 9194, p. 191.

[153] Pseudo-Aurelianus, *Vita eiusdem B. Martialis,* p. 373.

[154] *Cartulaire de Saint-Jean d'Angély,* 2 vols. Archives Historiques de la Saintonge et de l'Aunis, 30 and 33 (Paris, 1901–1903), 1:11–12, no. 1.

however, the monastery had acquired a royal founder: Ademar includes
Angély among Pippin I of Aquitaine's foundations.[155] As his source for this
assertion, he cites—but only to reject as a fairy tale (*frivola . . . pagina*) filled
with chronological impossibilities—a text from Angély that recounts the
royal foundation.[156]

The text to which Ademar refers so scornfully was produced by Angély in
conjunction with the celebrated *inventio* of John the Baptist's head at the
abbey (1016). This narrative interweaves the abbey's royal foundation with
an elaborate tale of how the relic had originally arrived on the nearby
Atlantic coast.[157] The text begins by relating how John's head ended up in
Alexandria after various post-decapitation peregrinations. Then a group of
monks, directed by a vision, brings the relic to the western shore of Aquitaine. There they encounter Pippin, king of Aquitaine, who has just slaugh-
tered thousands of Vandals (*sic*). After various miracles which associate the
relic's advent and the royal victory, the king and the monks process to
Angély, site of the royal residence. There Pippin presides over the construction, endowment, and consecration of a church in which the relics are
gloriously enshrined: Saint-Jean. Founded by a king next to his palace, the
abbey was thus indubitably royal.

For the monks of Angély in the early eleventh century, then, Pippin I of
Aquitaine could provide the desired royal aura. So too in the ninth- and
tenth-century layers of Mozac's legend, Pippin I could play the critical royal
role. But as we have seen, by the later eleventh century at Mozac, Pippin had
lost the qualifying "Aquitaine" to become Pippin the Short, king of the
Franks. A twelfth-century *notitia* from Angély hints at a similar tranformation: it explains how William, duke of Aquitaine, refounded Angély, an
abbey "built by King Pippin."[158] Can this "glorious king," as the text later
calls him, still be Pippin I? It seems more likely that the omission of "Aquitaine" was as deliberate in this later layer of Angély's legend as it was at
Mozac (and perhaps elsewhere).[159]

For by the later eleventh century, any Pippin other than Charlemagne's
father was unimaginable as legendary founder; those abbeys whose legends
first emerge in the second half of the eleventh century or later automatically
transformed Pippin I into Pippin the Short. Thus, only the latter ever ap-

---

[155] Ademar says that Pippin acted at the behest of his father (Louis the Pious). *Chronicon*
3.16 (*Chronique*, p. 132).

[156] Ademar of Chabannes, *Chronicon* 3.56 (*Chronique*, pp. 179–80).

[157] *Angeriacensium de translatione capitis [S. Joannis baptistae]* (*AASS* June 5:650–652).

[158] *Cartulaire de Saint-Jean d'Angély*, 1:13, no. 2.

[159] Pippin I also underwent a transformation at the abbey of Saint-Antonin of Rouergue.
In 825 the king of Aquitaine had made donations to this monastery; see *Recueil des actes de
Pépin*, pp. 12–16, no. 4. A *notitia* concocted by the thirteenth century (the date of the
manuscript), however, ascribes these grants to "domno Pipino, rege serenissimo francorum
et Aquitanorum"; see *HL* 5:45–47 (here 45), no. 5.

pears in their legends. Figeac, for example, probably owed its foundation to Pippin I of Aquitaine according to a diploma of this king (838), doubtless the source upon which the monks drew to create those more splendid acts of Pippin the Short.[160] Similarly, the diploma recounting Pippin the Short's refoundation of La Règle still bears traces of its original nature as one issued by Pippin I of Aquitaine.[161] Yet Figeac and La Règle mention only Pippin the Short in the role of legendary founder.

This growing tendency to hide the Pippins of Aquitaine behind Pippin the Short might be explained quite simply. Pippin the Short had one clear advantage over the Pippins of Aquitaine. He predated them both by approximately a century. The older the foundation, we have seen, the better and the more authoritative. Precedence was to preside.[162] This, however, can be only a partial explanation of the glorification of Pippin the Short and his destructive campaigns. Why did monastic imaginative memory not choose to exalt kings of the Aquitaine, "southern" kings? If not the Pippins, why not those incipient rulers of the eighth-century Aquitaine: Odo, Hunald, and Waïfre? The occlusion of the Pippins of Aquitaine may reflect a desire to efface the memory of kings who in their own times had not inspired the Aquitainians' undivided allegiance.[163] But why the elision of Pippin the Short's opponents? The obvious slurring of Waïfre and the underlining of his "treachery" that we saw in the legends of La Règle, Uzerche, and Mozac contrast oddly with the Aquitainian solidarity that, Michel Rouche argues, actually had been engendered by this leader (as well as by Odo and Hunald).[164]

I would suggest that the invocation of Pippin the Short demonstrates that the southern monasteries imaginatively remembered their past not against the background of a politically independent Aquitaine, but rather in terms of loyalty to the great early Carolingians who had traversed the region. These monasteries wished to identify their foundation with kings who incar-

---

[160] See the comments of Levillain in *Recueil des actes de Pépin*, pp. 6, 144, nos. 2 and 32; and Wolff, "Note sur le faux diplôme," pp. 327–329.

[161] This diploma mentions as abbess Guntrada, who appears in another diploma of Pippin I of Aquitaine; see *GC* 2:610–614. Furthermore, in an eighteenth-century copy of the La Règle diploma, the date given to "Emperor" Pippin's subscription is 837; see Paris, BN Latin 9194, p. 191 (omitted in the edition in *MGH Diplomata Karolinorum* 1:59–60, no. 42).

[162] See below, Chapter 6 at nn. 245–246.

[163] See Auzias, *L'Aquitaine*. .

[164] Rouche, *L'Aquitaine*, pp. 111–132. Rouche points out that these would-be kings were remembered and celebrated in three (mostly lost) *chanson* cycles. But Pippin the Short, too, was assimilated into the charmed world of the *chansons*. See Gaston Paris, "La légende de Pépin le Bref," in his *Mélanges de littérature française du Moyen Age*, ed. Mario Roques, 2 vols. (Paris, 1912), 1:183–215; and, most particularly, the *chanson* extant only in Adenet Le Roi's late thirteenth-century version as *Berte as grans piés*, ed. Albert Henry (Geneva, 1982). To be sure, this poem evokes no meridional landscapes or campaigns, but it does demonstrate that the southern monasteries were not alone in their embellishment of the memory of the first Carolingian king.

nated the center, not with those who represented peripheral or centrifugal forces. Pippin the Short, as the first anointed Frankish king and as the ruler of the realm that would form the core of his son's empire, was thus a more appealing founder than any king of Aquitaine, too local and particular whether or nor Carolingian. Furthermore, Pippin the Short's presence in the south, his campaigns, had resulted in decisively (though certainly not permanently) bringing this region into the greater realm. His campaigns thus could be remembered and celebrated imaginatively as symbolizing the establishment of a relationship between the king and the south—the same sort of positive integrating relationship that the legendary Romanized founders, the apostles, and the Frankish Clovis created between monastery and larger authority. The destruction Pippin actually wrought was transformed aptly and easily into reconstruction and regeneration. The monasteries south of the Loire, an area into which the Capetians rarely ventured before the thirteenth century, desired the absent royal authority and, in the eleventh and twelfth centuries, created a legendary Pippin who brought it to them.

The most prestigious representative of royal authority and the one most subject to legendary embroidery throughout the medieval west was not Pippin but his son, the king who would become emperor: Charlemagne. Two of the southern legends combine father and son for maximum effect–that of Conques and that of the canons at Saint-Yrieix (a third legend, that of Saint-Michel-de-Cuxa, does so in a less interesting fashion).[165] Pippin makes the foundation more ancient, for he is intrinsically and inevitably antecedent to his son. In these legends, though, Pippin basks in the reflected glory of his son; his main quality is being his son's father. It is Charlemagne who adds the crucial finishing touches that create the monastery's identity. These two legends not only permit us to explore another facet of Pippin, but lead us to consider how Charlemagne himself was being shaped as a monastic patron.

The earlier of these two foundation legends emerged contemporaneously with those which invoke Pippin alone. This legend, much discussed by modern literary scholars for reasons that will become apparent, depicts the foundation of Saint-Yrieix-de-la-Perche. This house of canons was located some forty kilometers south of Limoges: that is, in the area through which Pippin probably passed early in the 760s. Furthermore, Uzerche with its Pippin legend lay no more than thirty kilometers to the southeast of Saint-Yrieix; La Règle was only a bit further away and to the north. It is not difficult to imagine contact between these houses in which the subject of foundation

---

[165] In Cuxa's twelfth-century legend—two diplomas forged in the name of Charlemagne—the abbey presents itself as having received privileges from Pippin which Charlemagne confirms when he refounds the abbey. See d'Abadal, "Com neix i com creix," pp. 167–171.

might have been mentioned.[166] In any case, in approximately 1090, the canons of Saint-Yrieix fabricated a diploma of Charlemagne purporting to date from 794.[167] In this text Charlemagne announces that on his way to Spain (an expedition that actually occurred in 778) he stopped at a certain royal estate, Saint-Yrieix. He then relates how his "most serene and pious sire Pippin" formerly had decided with the counsel of his magnates to restore Saint-Yrieix, a royal monastery that had enjoyed the patronage of the Merovingian kings but then apparently had been abandoned.[168] The rest of the diploma describes Pippin's sedulous provisions for the canons, including the establishment of their *libertas* from secular (and, by implication, ecclesiastical) lords.

The diploma contains what may be a very oblique reference to Pippin's campaigns (*adiens hunc locum*), but does not play upon the theme of regenerative destruction as do the legends of Uzerche, Mozac, or La Règle. Nor does it exalt Pippin as the first anointed Frankish king, as Figeac's forged diplomas did. The only characteristic that distinguishes Pippin as anything other than a generic king is his relationship to Charlemagne. This latter monarch himself plays a minor role in the text, merely confirming the privileges of his Merovingian predecessors and of his father. The canons of Saint-Yrieix chose, however, to fabricate the diploma not in the name of their supposed refounder but in that of his son, certainly an indication of the coloring with which they wished to tint their past. They evidently preferred that Charlemagne's subscription, rather than his father's, substantiate their legend and privileges.

In this subscription, Emperor (already in 794!) Charlemagne suddenly springs forth as the specific and charismatic persona that his father is not—and one that any medieval reader or audience probably would have recognized immediately. Accompanying his own illustrious name were those of five witnesses, among them "Lord Turpin, Otgerius Palatinus, Guillaume Curbinasus, and the most valiant Bertrand," four of the celebrated peers who second Charlemagne on his epic expeditions to Spain and Jerusalem.[169] Legend thus justified legend. Saint-Yrieix's authority for its refoun-

[166] See below, Conclusion at nn. 11–17, for abundant evidence that ecclesiastical communities were well aware of one another's foundation legends.

[167] *MGH Diplomata Karolinorum* 1:355–57, no. 251.

[168] The abbot showed Charlemagne diplomas of various Merovingian rulers.

[169] The witness list of the Saint-Yrieix diploma has understandably titillated generations of scholars of the *chansons de geste,* for here are four of Charlemagne's epic peers present in a document predating the earliest manuscript of the *Chanson de Roland.* See, for example, Ramón Menéndez Pidal, *La chanson de Roland et la tradition épique des Francs,* trans. I.-M. Cluzel, 2d rev. ed. (Paris, 1960), pp. 401–404. None of them, however, has examined the document specifically for what it is—a foundation legend.

Jean-Pierre Poly and Eric Bournazel have suggested recently that the fifth witness, a certain "Roger Cornvalto" represents the Roger appointed count of Limoges by Charlemagne, a touch they interpret as intended to anchor the document in local history.

dation was the Charlemagne of the *chansons*. When the canons imagined this ruler, it was as an emperor on his way to Spain, adorned with heroic trappings and companions. Charlemagne thus raises the refoundation to an epic level while the Merovingians and Pippin perform the less glorious task of assuring its royal antiquity.

Pippin as founder is again dwarfed by his towering imperial son in a text that depicts another aspect of Charlemagne as monastic patron: the prologue to the chronicle of Conques.[170] This text establishes Conques as indubitably and anciently royal (like Saint-Yrieix) by describing a series of royal refoundations occasioned by successive discontinuities.[171] First Clovis restores the monastery during his expedition against Alaric. Then, after other destructive catastrophes, Pippin the Short refounds Conques and entrusts it to his son Charlemagne, who in turn passs it on to Louis the Pious. After Louis, the text states, his son, Pippin (I) of Aquitaine, becomes the abbey's patron.

Conques thus appears as an abbey "cherished" (*diligebant*) by the Frankish kings from their Christian beginnings. But which of this chain of royal refounders lends his persona to Conques's self-image, projected and felt? Clovis is an artificial and flat figure, a device to acquire Merovingian roots that this (Carolingian?) monastery probably did not have. Pippin is the active agent of the Carolingian refoundation, deciding to restore the monastery after its most recent destruction (by the Muslims fleeing from the victorious Charles Martel). Is Pippin, however, magnified and celebrated as legendary founders generally were? The text betrays an awareness of his specificity, interweaving the king's project to recover Aquitaine with his interest in Conques.[172] The theme of campaign/construction is explicit. Nonetheless, the text introduces Pippin as the "father of Charles the Great" and refers to him later as the "king and *emperor* of the Gauls" (my emphasis)—thus defining him doubly in terms of his son.

Charlemagne, then, lurks behind Conques's Pippin. Indeed, as we shall see, the earlier layers of Conques's legend celebrated Charlemagne as founder, without breathing a word about his father.[173] No doubt the pro-

---

Poly and Bournazel, *Feudal Transformation*, p. 323. If this is indeed Roger of Limoges, his subscription invokes yet another dimension of the legendary emperor, for Roger was a principal character in the well-known Charlemagne foundation legend developing contemporaneously at the Poitevin abbey of Charroux, approximately one hundred kilometers to the northwest of Saint-Yrieix; see below, Chapter 5 at nn. 57–70.

[170] See "Chronique du monastère de Conques," pp. 391–394.

[171] See above, Chapter 2 at n. 28.

[172] The text paints Pippin's interest in Conques as military: "animabatur rex ad istum locum Conchas diligendum quia in recuperatione Aquitaniae, locus is Conchas sua natura tutissimus et ad defendum aptissimus ad invadendum paratissimus multum sibi adfuerat"; "Chronique du monastère de Conques," p. 393. Conques, set into the escarped hillside above the River Doudou, certainly possesses some of these strategic qualities.

[173] See below, Chapter 5 at nn. 33–41.

logue represents a triumphant flourish in the face of the elaborate Pippin legend of the abbey's rival and former dependent, Figeac.[174] Here Conques not only subsumes its adversary's founder but claims a king far antecedent, Clovis, and a king far more glorious, Charlemagne. As in the case of Saint-Yricix, it is this latter king and not his father who grants the foundation its distinguishing characteristics. The Conques prologue relates that on his deathbed Pippin enjoined his son to "love" the abbey. This relationship of (implicit) *amicitia* does not manifest itself only in the way it does with the other kings mentioned in the text: donations and privileges. Charlemagne's *amicitia* also takes a form that we have seen to be characteristic for founding figures: magnificent gifts of relics and reliquaries. Charlemagne comes to the abbey and bestows upon it very significant relics: Christ's umbilical cord and his foreskin. A sentence then follows which compresses a claim both to this king as founder and to a very special status: "He gave to this monastery, first (*prima*) among all those monasteries founded by him, the letter *A* of the alphabet made from gold and silver."

These emblems given by Charlemagne—the gleaming letter symbolizing precedence in time (and, by implication, in the emperor's affections) and the two most intimate relics of the newborn Christ—characterize the Carolingian refoundation of Conques. Pippin is again eclipsed by his son, this time not because of the latter's epic dimensions but rather because of his provision of special and precious objects of manifest significance which create the monastery's identity. As we shall see, by the thirteenth century one of the qualities considered intrinsic to these objects was their provenance from Charlemagne. Their resonance with the legendary Charlemagne was as unmistakable as that of his epic peers cited by the Saint-Yrieix diploma. In order to demonstrate fully the importance of the Carolingian invocation in the legends of Conques and Saint-Yrieix, I shall turn from the image of the first Carolingian king to that of his more illustrious son: Charlemagne.

---

[174] On the rivalry between Conques and Figeac, see below, Chapter 6 at nn. 248–265.

5

Epics and Royal Relics

Charlemagne, unlike his father, was widely celebrated in legends, monastic and otherwise, throughout western Europe; he held a privileged place in medieval memory.[1] Within a generation or so of his death, Charlemagne had passed into legend. In this realm his stature grew continuously. This monarch became a source of authority and legitimation invoked by groups and individuals, who, as they claimed him, further enhanced his symbolic value. By the eleventh and twelfth centuries, popes and kings might claim Charlemagne as the foundation for their opposing positions in contests with each other, while urban communities presented him as the source of their rights and privileges, and noble families created genealogies for themselves tracing their origins back to a member of his family.[2] Nor were ecclesiastical communities immune to his allure; churches and monasteries throughout western Europe retrospectively associated their origins with this Frankish king crowned emperor on Christmas Day 800.

Indeed, the monarch as founder was an integral part of the Charlemagne legend—at least according to the *Historia Karoli Magni et Rotholandi,* better known as the "Pseudo-Turpin." A vastly popular text, which circulated in numerous Latin and vernacular versions, the Pseudo-Turpin was originally

---

[1] See Fentress and Wickham, *Social Memory,* pp. 153–162, 171; Robert Folz, *Le souvenir et la légende de Charlemagne dans l'empire germanique médiéval* (Paris, 1950); Gaston Paris, *Histoire poétique de Charlemagne,* 2d ed. (Paris, 1906).

[2] On these various uses (and others) of the legendary Charlemagne, see especially Folz, *Le souvenir et la légende;* Freedman, "Cowardice, Heroism"; and Gabrielle M. Spiegel, "*Pseudo-Turpin,* the Crisis of the Aristocracy and the Beginnings of Vernacular Historiography in France," *Journal of Medieval History* 12 (1986): 207–223, as well as her *Romancing the Past,* pp. 69–98.

composed in Latin in either the late eleventh century or the first half of the twelfth, perhaps in southern France or Spain, but more probably in northern France.[3] It lauds Charlemagne as founder of an indescribable number (*scribere nequeo* . . .) of churches and abbeys, a role to which the *Vita Karoli Magni,* composed under the auspices of Frederick Barbarossa shortly after Charlemagne's canonization in Germany (post 1165), devotes two chapters.[4] More strikingly, the Pseudo-Turpin also describes how in a vision, Archbishop Turpin saw black knights going off to Aachen to seize the dying Charlemagne's soul. Observing them returning empty-handed, the archbishop asked what had happened and received the following report. When Charlemagne's merits were being weighed, the archangel Michael and his host had placed on the scales so many "stones and beams of churches" founded by the king that they tipped in favor of the good.[5] The message could not be clearer: Charlemagne escaped the demons' clutches and merited Paradise because he had established so many churches. Perhaps it is not surprising, then, that in the early thirteenth-century window at Chartres cathedral which narrates the highlights of the legendary Charlemagne's life, one roundel depicts the monarch overseeing the construction of a church.[6]

In its trumpeting of Charlemagne as founder, the Pseudo-Turpin enumerates the five churches he established in honor of Saint James, three of which were located in southwestern France (at Béziers, Toulouse, and somewhere between Dax and Saint-Jean of Sorde); it also attributes to the monarch the foundation of a Spanish monastery.[7] The list of these churches is interpolated in different ways in the various versions of the Pseudo-Turpin, but the southern predominance remains.[8] The German canonization *vita* of

---

[3] Most scholars assign the Pseudo-Turpin northern French origins and date it to the first half of the twelfth century. See Meredith-Jones's editorial comments in *Historia Karoli Magni,* pp. 33–84; Poly and Bournazel, *Feudal Transformation,* pp. 195–199; and Spiegel, *Romancing the Past,* p. 343, n. 56. For an argument that the original text was composed in the late eleventh century in Spain by a cleric with intimate knowledge of southwestern France (perhaps Peter, bishop of Pampelona and originally a monk of Conques), see André de Mandach, *Naissance et développement de la chanson de geste en Europe,* 1: *La geste de Charlemagne et de Roland* (Paris, 1961), pp. 22–73.

[4] See the *Historia Karoli Magni,* p. 179; and the *Vita Karoli Magni,* 1.14–15, in Rauschen, *Die Legende Karls des Grossen,* pp. 36–39.

[5] *Historia Karoli Magni,* pp. 229, 231 (variant 335–336). Beaune suggests that this vision may have been borrowed from a text describing the death of Henry II of Germany: *Naissance,* p. 100.

[6] The Pseudo-Turpin was one of the sources drawn upon by the window's designers. On the window in general, see Clark Maines, "The Charlemagne Window at Chartres Cathedral: New Considerations on Text and Image," *Speculum* 52 (1977): 801–823 (on this roundel, 811–812).

[7] For the foundations dedicated to Saint James, see *Historia Karoli Magni,* pp. 103, 105; for the Spanish monastery (dedicated to Saints Facundus and Primitivus on the River Ceia), pp. 109, 295–296.

[8] Henri Treuille, "Les églises fondées par Charlemagne en l'honneur de Saint Jacques d'après le Pseudo Turpin," in *La chanson de geste et le mythe carolingien: Mélanges René Louis . . . ,* 2 vols. (Saint-Père-sous-Vézelay, 1982), 2:1151–1161.

Charlemagne locates him as a monastic founder in southern France even more strikingly, almost completely ignoring the rich traditions of the numerous German communities that associated this monarch with their own origins.[9] One chapter of the canonization *vita* even names the twenty-odd monasteries that Charlemagne founded.[10] They are exactly those abbeys located in Aquitaine or Septimania whose foundation or refoundation is attributed to Louis the Pious in the Astronomer's ninth-century biography.[11] The clerics in Barbarossa's service did not invent this legend; Charlemagne's usurpation of his son's role as founder of the abbeys in Septimania and Aquitaine had already appeared in the early twelfth-century *Historia ecclesiastica* composed by a northern French monk, Hugh of Fleury.[12] These northern French and imperial German texts thus situate the legendary Charlemagne's activity as a founder in especially (though not exclusively) the region south of the Loire.

Indeed, the ecclesiastical communities of this area themselves created a particularly vibrant image of this Carolingian as patron of their origins. For although southern French monasteries were hardly alone in attributing the role of founder to Charlemagne, the territory south of the Loire does seem to have been particularly rich in such traditions.[13] Charlemagne figured in the legends of almost half the monasteries considered here; fourteen abbeys developed legends in which he enjoyed the limelight as founder, three others had legends in which the founders were part of the legendary emperor's entourage, and several others introduced Charlemagne in various important roles.[14] Perhaps these numerous southern legends—and the localization of Charlemagne as founder in the south by the Pseudo-Turpin, the German canonization *vita,* and Hugh of Fleury—reflect in part historical realities; Charlemagne's actual monastic patronage had been particularly directed to Septimania and Aquitaine (as well as to the region east of the Rhine).[15] Here, then, monastic imaginative memory had merely to

---

[9] On the German foundation legends invoking Charlemagne, see Folz, *Le souvenir et la légende.*

[10] *Vita Karoli Magni* 1.15, in Rauschen, *Die Legende Karls des Grossen,* p. 38.

[11] Astronomer, *Vita Hludowici imperatoris (MGH SS* 2:616–617).

[12] Hugh of Fleury, *Historia ecclesiastica (MGH SS* 9:362). The *Vita Karoli Magni* cites this passage almost verbatim.

[13] A point emphasized by Paris, *Histoire poétique,* p. 109. Schneidmüller found a concentration of forgeries in the name of Charlemagne in southern as opposed to northern France; see his *Karolingische Tradition,* pp. 26–30.

[14] Charlemagne as (re)founder: Aniane, Brantôme, Charroux, Conques, Saint-Michel-de-Cuxa, Gerri, Lagrasse, Psalmodi, La Réole, Saint-Polycarpe, Saint-Savin of Lavedan, Sarlat, Sorde, Vabres (also the cathedral of Narbonne). Monasteries founded by members of Charlemagne's entourage: Alet, Gellone, Perse. Legends in which Charlemagne played a significant role: Moissac and Saint-Gilles (also at Saint-Yrieix-de-la-Perche). Frances Terpak suggests that there was a Charlemagne legend at Saint-Caprais of Agen: "The Romanesque Architecture," pp. 223–240.

[15] Semmler, "Karl der Grosse und das fränkische Mönchtum."

pand and embellish; there was no need to invert the image of the king as in
the case of the destructive Pippin the Short.

The appearance of Charlemagne in southern legends, however, also indicated deliberate choice; not all the abbeys to claim Charlemagne had really
been founded by him, nor had all even been in existence during the
Carolingian era. Furthermore, neither Charlemagne's son Louis (who had,
after all, been king of Aquitaine and a great patron of its monasteries) nor
his grandson Charles the Bald (who enjoyed legendary repute in northern
monasteries) was a focus of southern monastic imaginative memory.[16] In
some legends Charlemagne even usurped the role of founder that in historical reality these two descendants of his had played.[17] Louis may have been
elided in part for the same reason that the Pippins and other kings of
Aquitaine were; as a regional king, or subking, he did not represent the
desired link with the larger source of authority. Charles the Bald probably
suffered from a variant of the same phenomenon. He was seen as a king of
the north, not as a ruler of the integrated realm.[18] The other Carolingians
postdating Charlemagne too were largely ignored by southern abbeys in
their legends.

Thus, southern monasteries molded Charlemagne, along with his father
but to the exclusion of his imperial descendants, into the emblematic
founder. Charlemagne lent to these communities' legendary origins the
desired qualities, not only Carolingian but also charismatic. For in these
legends, Charlemagne progressively (though unofficially) acquires an aura
of sanctity that communicates itself in turn to the abbey. He does so through

[16] The sole exception I have found is Saint-Martial of Limoges, which in a forged
diploma of the early eleventh century presented Louis the Pious as its refounder; see Andreas
Sohn, *Der Abbatiat Ademars von Saint-Martial de Limoges (1063–1114): Ein Beitrag zur Geschichte
des cluniacensischen Klösterverbandes* (Münster, 1989), pp. 53–54, 87–88. On Charles the Bald
and northern monasteries, see the brief remarks of Koziol, *Begging Pardon*, pp. 168–169.

[17] At Conques, Louis the Pious disappeared behind his father (see below at nn. 40–41).
In texts confected in the twelfth century at Saint-Michel-de-Cuxa, Charlemagne replaced
Charles the Bald as the king who confirmed the foundation; see d'Abadal, "Com neix i com
creix," pp. 165–171. A similar process seems to have been at work at Vabres. A diploma,
copied almost word for word from one in the name of Charlemagne created at Aniane, ends
with an eschatocol of Charles the Bald (the monarch under whom the abbey was probably
founded). *Cartulaire de l'abbaye de Vabres*, pp. 29–33, no. 2; for the Aniane diploma, see below,
Chapter 6 at n. 174. Fournial uses the eschatocol to argue that the Vabres forger intended
the diploma to be read as one of Charles the Bald (see his remarks in *Cartulaire de l'abbaye de
Vabres*, pp. 33–34). But why would the forger have used the celebrated diploma of
Charlemagne from Aniane unless he had intended to invoke this monarch? Nor is the
presence of the Charles the Bald eschatocol decisive; at La Règle, a diploma very definitely
invoking Pippin the Short ends with an eschatocol of Pippin I of Aquitaine (see above,
Chapter 4 at n. 161).

[18] See Schneidmüller, *Nomen patriae*, pp. 140–208. This is not to say that southern
monasteries ignored Charles the Bald's prestige; several of them (including Charroux and
Lagrasse) in the tenth and eleventh centuries forged or interpolated diplomas in his name.
See Jean Dufour, "Etat et comparaison des actes faux ou falsifiés, intitulés au nom des
Carolingiens (840–987)" in *Fälschungen im Mittelalter*, 4:171–180, 205–208.

the two guises in which he appears in all but six of the legends.[19] Charlemagne is the donor of special objects, most often relics of patron saints (particularly special relics of Christ), or he is the epic king of the *chansons de geste* who, accompanied by his shimmering peers, founds monasteries on his way to and from Spain—the ruler we have already encountered in legends of Saint-Yrieix and Conques.

At first glance, though, it seems that to understand these aspects of Charlemagne as monastic founder—saint, epic king, and provider of precious objects—we must turn away from the south and its abbeys and toward legendary traditions fostered elsewhere (and in conjunction with contemporary rulers). Scholars generally believe, for example, that Charlemagne was officially made a saint by various monarchs seeking to legitimate their own reigns, most particularly Frederick Barbarossa and Frederick II of Germany.[20] According to this line of argument, Charlemagne's cult, officially established first in Germany under Barbarossa's aegis in 1165, did not appear in France until the fourteenth century, when it was introduced by Charles V; fostered by royal initiative, the cult remained until the seventeenth century a strictly Parisian phenomenon.[21]

The Charlemagne who gives precious objects also seems to reflect an image developed elsewhere—and, once again, often in conjunction with actual rulers' ambitions. For example, the official canonization *vita* of Charlemagne, composed by a cleric perhaps from Aachen, perhaps from Saint-Denis, but certainly at Frederick Barbarossa's behest, states that Charlemagne founded some twenty-three monasteries. To distinguish them, the king had inscribed above the lintel of each the letter of the alphabet representing the relative order in which they had been founded.[22] Here then seems to be the source for the assertion in the legend of Conques that Charlemagne had emblazoned this abbey as the first of his foundations by bestowing upon it a gold and silver *A*.

At Conques, Charlemagne also makes gifts even more highly charged than golden letters: relics of Christ, including the Holy Foreskin. The role as donor of such relics (which the legendary Charlemagne grants to southern abbeys far more frequently than he does letters) itself seems to derive from

---

[19] Only six monasteries do not explicitly present Charlemagne in these ways: Gerri, Psalmodi, La Réole, Saint-Savin of Lavedan, Saint-Polycarpe, and Vabres. Yet they do not endow him with any other characteristics; in their legends (all in diplomatic forms and all most probably created between the eleventh and the twelfth century), all that seemingly distinguishes Charlemagne from any other king is his name. That name, however, is quite significant.

[20] On Charlemagne's canonization in Germany, see Folz, *Le souvenir et la légende*, pp. 159–234.

[21] Robert Folz, "Aspects du culte liturgique de saint Charlemagne en France," in *Karl der Grosse*, 4:77–99.

[22] *Vita Karoli Magni* 1.15, in Rauschen, *Die Legende Karls des Grossen*, p. 38.

Latin traditions emanating from the capital of Barbarossa's counterparts, Capetian Paris. "It is said that the Lord's foreskin was brought down by an angel to Charlemagne in the temple of the Lord and that it was translated by him [Charlemagne] to Aachen and afterward it was placed by Charles the Bald in the church of the Savior at Charroux," proclaims a gloss found in a significant number of late twelfth- and thirteenth-century manuscripts of the widely diffused and used *Historia scholastica* of the Parisian master Peter Comestor.[23]

This scholastic tradition itself seems to be based on another associated with the French royal capital: that of Charlemagne's "voyage" to Constantinople and Jerusalem where he received various relics. In a Latin text composed probably between 1080 and 1095 at Saint-Denis of Paris, this most celebrated imperial journey, nascent in earlier texts from elsewhere, appears full-blown for the first time.[24] This work, the *Descriptio qualiter Karolus Magnus clavum et coronam domini a Constantinopoli Aquisgrani detulerit . . .*, relates how Charlemagne, in the guise of a crusader, liberated Jerusalem and then received his pious recompense at Constantinople: pieces of Christ's crown of thorns as well as a nail and a fragment of the True Cross.[25]

---

[23]   "Dicitur quod preputium domini delatum est ab angelo Karolo magno in templum domini et translatum ab eo apud aquis grani et post a Karolo calvo positum in ecclesia salvatoris apud carosium" (with minor variants) in at least the following seven thirteenth-century glossed manuscripts of the *Historia Scholastica:* Paris, BN Latin 15254, f. 120va; Paris, BN Latin 16033, f. 137rb; Paris, BN Latin 16034, f. 117va; Paris, BN Latin 16037, f. 109vb; Paris, BN Latin 16040, f. 110va; Paris, BN Latin 16042, f. 178va; Paris, BN Latin 18279, f. 128rb. I thank Philippe Buc, who shared with me his list of the glossed *Historia scholastica* manuscripts at the Bibliothèque Nationale. He also kindly verified for me that the following seven Vatican manuscripts of the same text carry the gloss: Latin 1972 (late twelfth century); Latin 1973; Ottob. Latin 632; Reg. Latin 303, f. 120vb; Ross. 570, f. 185r(a); Ross. 511, f. 115vb; Lat. 9336, f. 138va (the last six are thirteenth-century manuscripts). This gloss also appears in the Migne edition of the *Historia scholastica*, but there it ends "alii dicunt Antuerpiam delatum, nam illic in summa veneratione habetur" (*PL* 198:1541). This latter phrase is no doubt an addition that does not predate the fifteenth century, when the cult of the Holy Foreskin at Antwerp is first attested. See *Commemoratio sacrosancti praeputii Christi Antuerpiae, et alibi* (*AASS* January 1:6–8); and the late fifteenth-century *Historia de translatione carnis dominicae circumcisionis . . .* , written by a canon regular of Antwerp, in *De codicibus hagiographicis Ioannis Gielemans canonici regularis in rubea valle prope Bruxellas adiectis anecdotis*, Subsidia Hagiographica, 3 (Brussels, 1895), pp. 429–430.

[24]   The tradition of Charlemagne's pilgrimage/crusade to the Holy Land did not originate at Saint-Denis; on its development from the ninth century onward, see Folz, *Le souvenir et la légende*, pp. 134–142, and Benedict of Soracte, *Chronicon* (*MGH SS* 3:710–711).

[25]   The *Descriptio qualiter Karolus Magnus clavum et coronam domini a Constantinopoli Aquisgrani detulerit qualiterque Karolus Calvus hec ad sanctum Dyonisium retulerit* has been edited in Rauschen, *Die Legende Karls des Grossen*, pp. 103–125. On the dating and circumstances of composition of this text, see Beaune, *Naissance*, p. 94; and Folz, *Le souvenir et la légende*, pp. 179–181 (also 134–142 on the ninth-century roots of the tradition). On the manuscripts, see Elizabeth A. R. Brown and Michael Cothren, "The Twelfth-Century Crusading Window of the Abbey of Saint-Denis: Praeteritorum enim recordatio futurorum est exhibitio," *Journal of the Warburg and Courtauld Institutes* 49 (1986): 14–15, n. 65.

He then translated these relics to Aachen; later his grandson, Charles the Bald, gave some of them to Saint-Denis. Despite the difference in the relics' specific identity, the general outline is the same as that of the *Historia scholastica* gloss: Charlemagne's acquisition of relics associated with Christ, his translation of them to Aachen, and Charles the Bald's subsequent endowment of a western Frankish monastery—this time a monastery itself unmistakably royal. A mid-twelfth-century *chanson de geste* recounts a playful version of much the same story, but insists that Charlemagne himself brought the relics to Saint-Denis.[26]

The origins of this *chanson,* like those of most vernacular epic poems, appear to lie in the north. The epic Charlemagne, so prominent in many of the legends, thus seems also to have been borrowed from elsewhere. For scholars have generally argued that despite the often strikingly accurate southern settings, the *chansons de geste* had their roots in Burgundy, Normandy, and so on—anywhere but south of the Loire.[27] Indeed, with the exceptions of *Girart de Roussillon* (ca. 1173) and some fourteenth-century Provençal versions of the Charlemagne and Roland cycle, the *chansons* are extant for the most part in northern dialects.[28]

Here then seem to be the traditions from which southern monasteries drew in their depiction of Charlemagne as donor of special relics, as epic king, and as a saint. This series of texts—the *vita* produced to accompany Charlemagne's canonization which Frederick Barbarossa engineered, the *chansons,* the gloss on a text composed by a twelfth-century master at the University of Paris which would by the next century claim not only royal protection but also Charlemagne as its founder,[29] the *Descriptio qualiter* fabricated at Saint-Denis, center for the production of much royal ideology with a Carolingian cast—all seem to indicate that it is to the imperial sphere of influence and to the royal north of France, most particularly to that domain under the Capetians' direct control, that we should look to understand the development of the legend of Charlemagne as a monastic patron.

[26] *Le voyage de Charlemagne à Jerusalem et à Constantinople,* ed. Paul Aebischer (Paris, 1965).

[27] See, for example, René Louis's remarks in his magisterial *De l'histoire à la légende: Girart comte de Vienne . . . ,* 3 vols. (Auxerre, 1946–1947), 2:266–288, 3:177; and Poly and Bournazel, *Feudal Transformation,* pp. 319–324. Rita Lejeune's theory that the *chanson* of Aymeric de Narbonne was originally southern (see her "La question de l'historicité du héros épique Aimeri de Narbonne," *Economies et Sociétés au Moyen Age: Mélanges offerts à Edouard Perroy* [Paris, 1973], pp. 50–62) has not gained much credence. But Alice Colby-Hall has recently (and convincingly) suggested that at least the Guillaume cycle originated in the south: "In Search of the Lost Epics of the Lower Rhône Valley," in *Romance Epic: Essays on a Medieval Genre,* Studies in Medieval Culture, 14 (Kalamazoo, Mich., 1987), pp. 115–127. I thank Joseph Duggan for his help in this matter.

[28] My thanks to Michel-André Bossy for help on this point.

[29] On this latter legend and that of the *translatio studii,* see Folz, "Aspects du culte liturgique," pp. 81–83. Cf. Beaune, *Naissance,* pp. 301–302.

Such a northern- and royal-centered perspective certainly would accord with the vast majority of work that has been done on the development of the Carolingian legend in Capetian (and later) France. Scholars have been interested above all in the moments at which the French kings and their intimates, northern ecclesiastical establishments particularly and traditionally associated with the Frankish kings, adopted Charlemagne (and other rulers of the past) as symbols of monarchy.[30] Here, they proclaim, we see the engendering of a "nation" and a "national consciousness" centered on the Capetian kings, themselves proclaimed in the early thirteenth century the genealogical descendants of the Carolingians.

With few exceptions, the history of the legendary Charlemagne thus becomes a centrist examination of how the kings and their associates invoked and manipulated the memory of this monarch.[31] But what about the southern monasteries' legends? These legends fall into the category of what are often labeled "local legends," a term that reveals an implicit hierarchy of value influencing much scholarly consideration. Despite some nuanced remarks about the importance of such local traditions, most historians have generally relegated them to a subordinate position of some sort.[32] Does the Charlemagne of the southern legends thus represent a mere borrowing, a pale reflection of the image of Charlemagne elaborated by Parisian, royalist, imperial, and northern traditions?

That is too simple. Southern abbeys did not slavishly and passively copy from elsewhere the traits with which they commonly endowed Charlemagne; rather, these communities actively fashioned the legendary monarch. Consider, for example, the ABCs of Charlemagne as founder: the legend of this ruler's monastic alphabet. Was the monarch's role as provider of the golden letters decorating and distinguishing such abbeys as Conques

---

[30] The bibliography on this question is vast. See, for example, Beaune, *Naissance;* Elizabeth A. R. Brown, "La notion de la légitimité et la prophétie à la cour de Philippe Auguste," in *La France de Philippe Auguste: Le temps des mutations. Actes du colloque international organisé par le C.N.R.S. (Paris, 29 septembre–4 octobre 1980),* ed. Robert-Henri Bautier (Paris, 1982), pp. 77–111; Ehlers, "Kontinuität und Tradition"; Schneidmüller, *Nomen patriae;* Percy Ernst Schramm, *Der König von Frankreich,* 2 vols. (Weimar, 1939), esp. 1:138–139; Gabrielle M. Spiegel, "The *Reditus regni ad stirpem Karoli Magni:* A New Look," *French Historical Studies* 7 (1971): 145–174; and Karl Ferdinand Werner, "Die Legitimität der Kapetinger und die Entstehung des *Reditus regni francorum ad stirpem Karoli,"Die Welt als Geschichte* 12 (1952):203–225. See also Jacques Le Goff's recent summary and overview in *Histoire de la France: L'état et les pouvoirs,* ed. Jacques Le Goff (Paris, 1989), pp. 58–60.

[31] Spiegel's approach is an exception; see her *"Pseudo-Turpin,"* pp. 207–223, as well as her *Romancing the Past,* pp. 69–98. For noncentrist approaches, see also the discussion of the Charlemagne legend in Germany by Folz, *Le souvenir et la légende,* and in late medieval Catalonia by Freedman, "Cowardice, Heroism."

[32] Poly and Bournazel do accord importance to local traditions in the formation of the *chansons de geste: Feudal Tranformation,* pp. 319–324 (following in the footsteps of Louis's *De l'histoire à la légende*).

really created by the German canonization *vita?* At Conques, the assertion that Charlemagne had granted to the abbey the first letter of the alphabet appears in a text that is annoyingly difficult to date: the prologue to this abbey's chronicle.[33] The most logical time for the prologue's composition would be the years around 1100, but certain passages make me wonder whether it was written rather in the late twelfth or early thirteenth century.[34] In other words, the prologue either pre- or postdates the canonization *vita*. If the former is true, then it seems that the clerics working for Barbarossa borrowed from Conques, rather than the other way round.

But what if the Conques text was later than the official *vita?* Did the alphabet have its genesis in German traditions? Perhaps, but not necessarily. Comments in the canonization *vita* suggest that the legend of the monastic alphabet (like so much else in this text) may have been borrowed from elsewhere. The "diligent reader," asserts the *vita*, will notice that Charlemagne's many other (read: German) foundations are not mentioned, including that most famous church of Aachen. The awkward explanation provided is that only some of the churches Charlemagne founded were graced with letters.[35] Why would this text, intent on claiming Charlemagne for the German emperor, highlight the legendary Carolingian's special favor toward non-German monasteries unless the tradition was already such a part of the imaginatively remembered Charlemagne that it could not be omitted? Where should we look for the monastic alphabet's origins if not among those monasteries which it ornaments: according to the canonization *vita*, "Charlemagne's foundations" in Septimania and Aquitaine?[36] Conques is named as one—and perhaps it was there, at this monastery which claimed the first letter of the alphabet and thus the most prestigious position, that the tradition began. After all, if this tradition had come from another abbey, surely that monastery would have claimed the premier place for itself. I have found only one, maybe two (southern) ecclesiastical communities besides Conques that claimed a letter—Lagrasse, and perhaps the canons of Brioude—and neither rivaled Conques for possession of the *A*.[37]

Furthermore, the only monastery I have found that produced gleaming physical proof of the alphabet was Conques. At the abbey today is a reliquary

---

[33] "Chronique du monastère de Conques," pp. 391–394.

[34] On the dating of this text, see Appendix 2 below.

[35] *Vita Karoli Magni* 1.15, in Rauschen, *Die Legende Karls des Grossen*, pp. 38–39.

[36] *Vita Karoli Magni* 1.15, in Rauschen, *Die Legende Karls des Grossen*, p. 38.

[37] Lagrasse claimed to be the twenty-first of the abbeys Charlemagne founded–but that only in conjunction with its foundation had the king established the alphabet. *Gesta Karoli Magni*, p. 84. A charter of the early thirteenth century from Saint-Julien of Brioude thunders a curse against a thief who stole "auream literam beati Juliani, videlicet C"—but the text itself does not mention Charlemagne in association with the letter (the editor does). *Spicilegium Brivatense: Recueil des documents historiques relatifs au Brivadois et l'Auvergne*, ed. Augustin Chassaing (Paris, 1886), pp. 22–23 (here 22), no. 12.

FIGURE 4. Reliquary known as "Charlemagne's *A*" (Conques, ca. 1100). Photograph by permission of Igor Gorevich.

still known as "Charlemagne's *A*" (see Figure 4). Shaped like a triangle, it is made of panels of beaten gilded silver covering a wooden frame. At its apex is a large crystal boss, the container for the relic—probably of the Cross. Like so many of the abbey's other treasures, this reliquary was fashioned under the patronage of abbot Bego III (1087–1108).[38] It is easy to identify this

---

[38] On this reliquary, see Adolf Reinle, "Das 'A Karls des Grossen,' im Kirchenschatz von Conques," in *Variorum Munera Florum: Latinität als prägende Kraft mittelalterlicher Kultur: Festschrift für Hans F. Haefele zu seinem sechzigsten Geburtstag*, ed. Adolf Reinle, Ludwig Schmugge,

this reliquary with the prologue's *A* of Charlemagne; it has the appropriate shape and is made of the appropriate materials (surely its panels of gilded silver are the prologue's "silver and gold").

But when was this reliquary first identified as the initial letter of the royal alphabet? Since at least the eleventh century, Conques had claimed Charlemagne as its founder; it seems perfectly plausible that the *A* was in some way part of this already developed legend. The earliest evidence of Charlemagne as founder at Conques is the verse account of the translation of Saint Faith's relics from Agen to Conques (probably composed in the late eleventh century).[39] According to this text, after the first church at Conques was destroyed by Muslims, a hermit, Dado, came to inhabit the escarped hillside. He eventually requested Charlemagne to restore the monastery. The king agreed and ordered his son Louis to carry out the task. A prose version of the translation, written probably in the twelfth century, amplifies the royal tone.[40] Here the monastery is given a vague royal past anterior to the Carolingians; Dado is not mentioned, and the restoration is ascribed solely to Charlemagne and his son. In legend, Charlemagne thus replaced Louis the Pious, who, in an authentic diploma of 819, had confirmed the foundation of the abbey.[41]

In the twelfth century, Conques seems even to have emblazoned its association with Charlemagne upon the façade of its church, gazed upon by multitudes of medieval pilgrims.[42] In the middle register of its celebrated Last Judgment tympanum, to the right of Christ, a prelate, probably an abbot, leads by the hand a bearded and crowned king holding a scepter (see Figure 5).[43] The very specific claims to Charlemagne made in the *translatio* texts strongly suggest that this royal figure with the *barbe fleurie* was the legendary founder himself.[44] And curved delicately along an archivolt of the twelfth-century tympanum at one of Conques's nearby priories, Perse, is a monarch with the same attributes (see Figure 6). This king is probably Charlemagne himself, for both Perse's tympanum and its foundation leg-

---

and Peter Stotz (Sigmaringen, 1985), pp. 129–140. Also see *Trésors des églises de France*, pp. 304–305 and pl. 41.

[39] *Translatio metrica S. Fidis virginis et martyris* (*AASS* October 3:290).

[40] *Translatio altera* (*AASS* October 3:295–296).

[41] *Cartulaire de l'abbaye de Conques*, pp. 409–410, no. 580.

[42] The dating of the tympanum is a matter of dispute. See the discussion and bibliography in Jean-Claude Bonne, *L'art roman de face et de profil: Le tympan de Conques* (Paris, 1984), pp. 313–317.

[43] Preceding the prelate, in the group of figures closest to Christ, is a bearded man in a short cape leaning on a staff, a figure usually identified as the hermit Dado; see Bonne, *L'art roman de face et de profil*, p. 233.

[44] Bonne has argued that this figure is not a representation of any particular king, but rather a multivalent reference to royal foundation and donations: *L'art roman de face et de profil*, pp. 233–235. But Georges Gaillard believes that it is Charlemagne: *Rouergue Roman* (La Pierre-Qui-Vire, 1963), p. 49.

FIGURE 5. Bearded and crowned king (Charlemagne?) holding scepter. From the tympanum of Conques, first half of the twelfth century. Photograph by permission of Philippe Buc.

end (the latter unfortunately undatable) strongly echo those of the mother abbey in which he figured so explicitly.[45] Charlemagne as founder was thus very present at Conques and perhaps at one of its priories before the canonization *vita* was composed. Was the legend of his donation of the golden *A* to Conques part of this presence? If so, then the tradition of the alphabet had its roots in Conques's Charlemagne legend but was first written down in the canonization *vita*.

Given the connections between Conques and the Hohenstaufen, it is easy to imagine how the legend could have passed from this abbey to Frederick Barbarossa's clerics who composed Charlemagne's official *vita*. Among the pilgrims to Conques in the last years of the eleventh century were several

[45] Perse claimed to have been founded by Saint Hilarianus, supposedly Charlemagne's confessor and companion. On this legend (for which I have found no documents), see the discussion in *AASS* June 2:1068–1069. On the Perse tympanum, see Louis Saltet, "Perse et Conques: Rapport entre deux portails voisins du douzième siècle," *Bulletin de la Société Archéologique du Midi de la France*, 2d ser., 46–47 (1926): 72–92 (Saltet identifies the king as Charlemagne).

FIGURE 6. King (Charlemagne?) from the twelfth-century tympanum of Perse, a priory of Conques. Photograph by permission of Philippe Buc.

Hohenstaufen brothers. Upon their return home, they founded the church of Sainte-Foy in Sélestat and gave it to Conques as a priory.[46] Hohenstaufen patronage of the priory seems to have continued until at least 1137 in the person of Frederick (II) of Swabia, Frederick Barbarossa's father.[47] It is most likely that Barbarossa himself patronized this church, given that it was so intertwined with his immediate ancestors. This Hohenstaufen priory remained very aware of the traditions of the mother abbey; the most complete manuscript of Saint Faith's *miracula* is one that by the twelfth century was in Sélestat's possession, perhaps sent from Conques itself.[48] This priory then could have served as the conduit by which a tradition from Conques could have ended up in the canonization *vita*.

Perhaps, though, the alphabet did originate with the canonization *vita* and not at Conques. Even so, Conques did not merely copy the *vita;* instead, it actively reshaped the royal alphabet. Consider the discrepancy between the form of the letters described in the canonization *vita*—inscriptions—and the three-dimensional form they have in every other text I have found to describe them. Like the Conques prologue, all later sources to mention the alphabet (not only writers from the German realm, but also the fourteenth-century Aymeric de Peyrat of Moissac and Bernard Gui) consider the letters to have been wrought from gold.[49] Even if the canonization *vita* and not the prologue is the earliest textual reference to the alphabet, I would suggest that the plastic nature of the letters was determined by the reliquary present at the monastery that claimed the first letter of the alphabet and thus first place in Charlemagne's affections: Conques. For where else would the transformation from inscribed letter to golden object have occurred if not at the only monastery I have found that actually boasted such a treasure?

A metamorphosis of this sort at Conques would have been all the more natural, given that the golden reliquary already seems to have been associated with Charlemagne by 1155: that is, before Charlemagne's canonization. A text composed at Sainte-Foy of Sélestat by this date connects this

---

[46] See the charter of 1095 in *Cartulaire de l'abbaye de Conques*, pp. 405–406, no. 575; and the legendary *De fundatione monasterii S. Fidis Sletstadtensis* (*MGH SS* 15.2:996–1000). Cf. Ernst Klebel "Zur Abstammung der Hohenstaufen," *Zeitschrift für die Geschichte des Oberrheins* 102 (1954): 151–163.

[47] At least according to the *De fundatione monasterii S. Fidis Sletstadtensis* (*MGH SS* 15.2:996–1000).

[48] Sélestat, BM Latin 95. See the description and analysis of the manuscript in *Liber miraculorum sancte Fidis*, ed. A. Bouillet (Paris, 1897), pp. xx–xxi, xxv–xxvii.

[49] "[T]ot monasteria construxit quod sunt littere in alphabeto et in quolibet monasterio unam litteram auream valorem C. librarum ad dignoscendum pro tempora que ipse fundacionis exordium eorundem extiterat" (Aymeric de Peyrat, *Chronicon;* Paris, BN Latin 4991A, f. 128ra). "Deinde ad numerum elementorum alphabeti xxiiii coenobia fundavit et in unoquoque per ordinem litterarum unam ex auro fabricatam reliquit ad tempus fundationis uniuscuiusque monasterii dinoscendum" (Bernard Gui, *Cathalogus pontificum Romanorum;* Paris, BN Latin 4976, ff. 52vb–53ra). Cf. the fourteenth-century texts from Germany and Flanders cited by Rauschen, *Die Legende Karls des Grossen*, p. 38, n. 44.

reliquary to the monarch, although describing it as his stirrup rather than as an *A*.[50] The canonization *vita*, then, did not determine the reliquary's identification with Charlemagne, but rather may have lent the relationship between this object and Conques's legendary founder a new shape. In turn, the canonization *vita*'s alphabet may have gained a new form as it was appropriated by Conques and attached to the reliquary.

Whichever of these scenarios corresponds to historical reality, Conques's image of Charlemagne as provider of golden letters was no mere derivative of the canonization *vita*—no more than the other traits of Charlemagne as monastic founder in the southern legends were mere reflections of traditions elaborated elsewhere. Instead, the southern images of Charlemagne and those created in the royal north and imperial realm intertwined and interreacted in a complex symbiosis. As I explore how in southern monastic imaginative memory Charlemagne was elevated to the stature of saint in his role as provider of relics or as the heroic king of the *chansons*, it will become clear that while these aspects of Charlemagne may appear in northern (and royal or royalist) legends, they were equally—if not more—indigenous to the south, as was the saintly Charlemagne himself. Let me turn southward, beginning with the king who donated relics, because the legends celebrated this Charlemagne earlier than they did the epic ruler.

King, Christ, and Relics

By the eleventh century, several southern churches claimed Charlemagne had provided them with the sacred objects that were constitutive of a monastic community's identity and without which no foundation was complete: relics. For example, in the late eleventh or early twelfth century, the monks of Saint-Michel-de-Cuxa composed an embellished tale of their abbey's foundation in which their forefathers travel to Paris and successfully petition the mythic Carolingian for the relics of Saint Germain, patron of the original community.[51] A similar Charlemagne appears in a probably interpolated if not forged charter attributed to an early tenth-century count of Périgord. The king establishes Brantôme, an abbey probably founded by Pippin I of Aquitaine;[52] he then endows it with relics of one of the Inno-

---

[50] *De fundatione monasterii S. Fidis Sletstadtensis* (*MGH SS* 15.2:999). For the suggestion that the "stirrup" referred to by the text is the reliquary at Conques, and for the dating of the text, see Jean-Claude Schmitt, *Les revenants: Les vivants et les morts dans la société médiévale* (Paris, 1994), pp. 125, 274–275, nn. 24, 27.

[51] See the forged diploma of Charlemagne and the forged charter, which takes Protasius's voice, published in d'Abadal, "Com neix i com creix," pp. 167–171.

[52] I have found only a seventeenth-century copy of this charter: Paris, BN Collection Périgord 33, ff. 187–188. Ademar of Chabannes grouped Brantôme with the foundations made by Pippin I of Aquitaine: (*Chronicon* 3.16; *Chronique*, p. 132). The monastery is mentioned in the *Notitia de servitio monasteriorum* of 817: (*MGH Capitularia regum Francorum* 1:351).

cents, the oddly named Sicarius ("Assassin").[53] These cases and others like them suggest that largesse in the form of donations of relics had become part of the imaginatively remembered Charlemagne's persona.[54] Hence, in the mid-thirteenth-century *Chronique Saintongeaise* this king naturally not only founds southern churches right and left, but also bestows holy remains upon many of them.[55] Furthermore, such legends hint that ecclesiastical communities sought to give their relics meaning as memorials of more than just the patron saint; the relics acquired the patina of the legendary Charlemagne by whom they had been given.

The reverse dynamic was equally possible. Not only could Charlemagne lend his aura to the relic, but the relic in turn could lend its own to the king, as another layer of Brantôme's legend, an interpolation (eleventh century?) in the *Annales* of Lorsch, hints.[56] Pippin the Short had earlier received from the pope the relics of the Innocent that Charlemagne would grant to Brantôme, the text specifies, thus furnishing the relics with a two-generation Carolingian genealogy and Roman origins. More important perhaps is the tenor of the association between Charlemagne and relic sketched in the text's next words: Charlemagne had been victorious in battle "many times" owing to the relic's aid. Thus the abbey's patron saint is presented as the protector of the king, himself the patron of the abbey he both founded and endowed with the relic. A parallel is adumbrated between the patronage of the saint and that of Charlemagne, for the relic representing the saint and the community also signifies and identifies the king.

Hence, as Charlemagne became intimately linked with these precious objects through which the saints exercised their patronage, his role as patron became imaginatively intertwined and in many ways assimilated to theirs. Such reciprocal transferences of meaning became increasingly com-

---

[53] Sicarius is mentioned in a generic fashion as a martyr (and not an Innocent) in prayers in an early eleventh-century manuscript from Limoges (Paris, BN Latin 821, f. 59va–vb) and in a twelfth-century text belonging to Aurillac (Paris, BN Latin 944, f. 63v). In a charter from Conques (between 1060 and the mid-twelfth century), he was identified as an Innocent; see *Cartulaire de l'abbaye de Conques*, p. 19, no. 15. By at least the seventeenth century this oddly named saint was even more strangely identified as a son (and victim) of Herod—and conflated with Sicarius, a (ninth-century) bishop of Bordeaux who was buried at Saint-Romain of Blaye; see the discussion in the seventeenth-century Paris BN Latin 12751, p. 194, and the marginal note in the seventeenth-century Paris BN Collection Périgord 33, f. 188.

[54] According to a diploma forged in perhaps the late twelfth century, Charlemagne gave relics of patron saints to the abbey of Sorde; see *MGH Diplomata Karolinorum* 1:567–568 (cf. below at n. 180). According to an inscription of uncertain date at Sainte-Eulalie of Bordeaux, Charlemagne had brought relics of Saint Sever's companions to that church. Du Buisson, *Historiae*, pp. 85–86. The legendary Charlemagne founded the cathedral church of Narbonne and brought back relics from Spain with the intention of granting them to his new foundation. For this legend, see the *querimonia* (ca. 1059) of the viscount of Narbonne, Berengar: HL 5:497–502, no. 251. On this legend and its context, see Frances Terpak, "Local Politics: The Charlemagne Legend in Medieval Narbonne," *Res* 25 (1994): 96–110.

[55] *Chronique dite Saintongeaise*, pp. 267–268, 279–280, 281, 282, 283, 284.

[56] *Annales Laurissenses et Einhardi* (*MGH SS* 1:146).

mon by the twelfth century, occurring strikingly and suggestively with relics of Christ, most particularly the True Cross and the Holy Foreskin.

I shall begin with the Cross, a relic that, unlike the Foreskin, had been popular in western Europe for centuries. By the twelfth century, Charlemagne's donation of the former relic had become almost a literary topos; according to the widely read Pseudo-Turpin, when this ruler founded a church he almost inevitably endowed it with a fragment of the Cross.[57] Earlier texts (including Ademar of Chabannes) had transmuted the gifts Charlemagne actually received from the patriarch of Jerusalem into relics of the Passion, but the motif of Charlemagne's donation of a fragment of the Cross seems to have developed first in the southern abbeys' legends.[58] The earliest evidence comes from the Poitevin monastery of Saint-Sauveur of Charroux. Although according to the *Historia scholastica* gloss this abbey was the home of the Holy Foreskin, Charlemagne first appears in its legend as the donor of another special relic of Christ: a fragment of the True Cross, a type of relic that had been especially venerated by Poitevin churches since the seventh century.[59]

The earliest evidence of this Charroux tradition is found not in the sources of the abbey itself but in those composed by third parties—surely an indication that Charroux had publicized its legend in some fashion.[60] In his *Chronicon*, Ademar of Chabannes relates that Charroux had been founded by Roger, count of Limoges, and then endowed by Charlemagne with a piece of the Holy Cross sent by the patriarch of Jerusalem.[61] There is no reason to doubt that Ademar, despite his "mythopoetic" tendencies, was

---

[57] *Historia Karoli Magni*, p. 179.

[58] Whether or not Charlemagne actually had received relics from the patriarch revolves around one's interpretation of a passage of the *Annales Laurissenses et Einhardi: MGH SS* 1:188, 189. See Berent Schwineköper, "Christus-Reliquien-Verehrung und Politik," *Blätter für deutsche Landesgeschichte* 117 (1981): 201–205. By at least the time Ademar of Chabannes was writing, the objects had become relics of the Passion; see his *Chronicon* 2.15 (*Chronique*, pp. 89–90). Various other European abbeys elaborated legends focusing on Charlemagne's donation of some of these relics. In none of them, though, is the True Cross particularly identified with Charlemagne; see, for example, the early eleventh-century *Liber de sancti Hidulphi sucessoribus in mediano monasterio* (*MGH SS* 4:188). Furthermore, of the fifteen instances of Charlemagne as donor of the Cross listed by A. Frolov, only two are both earlier than the Charroux tradition and not from a southern French monastery: Saint-Riquier and Reichenau; Frolow, *La relique de la Vraie Croix: Recherches sur le développement d'un culte* (Paris, 1961), pp. 198–210, no. 75. For Saint-Riquier, the evidence is an eighth- or early ninth-century inventory of relics that the abbey acquired through the generosity and aid of Charlemagne and various prelates. The Cross is not specifically identified with any one of the many donors, nor is it singled out; see Angilbert, *De ecclesia centulensis libellus* (*MGH SS* 15.1:174, 176). In the tenth-century (?) legend of Reichenau, the Cross shares the limelight with the Holy Blood, and Charlemagne does not give these relics directly to the abbey but rather to a noble family; see *Ex translatione sanguinis domini* (*MGH SS* 4:446–449).

[59] Carol Heitz, "*Adoratio crucis*: Remarques sur quelques crucifixions pré-romanes en Poitou," in *Etudes de civilisation médiévale (IXe–XIIe siècles): Mélanges offerts à Edmond-René Labande* (Poitiers, 1975), pp. 395–405.

[60] On the publicity of legends in general, see below, Conclusion at nn. 11–40.

[61] Ademar of Chabannes, *Chronicon* 3.40 (*Chronique*, p. 162, note x).

in this instance recording a tradition that came from Charroux itself.[62] The eleventh-century *miracula* of Saint-Genou repeated essentially the same story.[63] These two sources reveal that already by the early eleventh century, Charroux was known to possess a fragment of the Cross of royal provenance.

In the earliest extant layer of Charroux's own legend, a narrative text probably composed not long after 1045, the abbey celebrated its acquisition of this royal relic.[64] The text opens by describing how Charlemagne, passing through the territory of Roger, count of Limoges, encountered a pilgrim returning from Jerusalem with a relic of the Cross. The king wheedled from him this relic with the explicit intention of founding a monastery in which to enshrine it. Count Roger, at Charlemagne's command, then built the church on the exact spot where the king acquired the relic. Thus, from its inception, the abbey church was a commemoration of the moment when the relic became paired with the king.

The text reiterates this importance of the Cross for Charroux—and for Charlemagne. Count Roger and his wife, Eufrasia, endowed the monastery with land, and then Charlemagne provided the property that the text clearly considers more important: a wealth of relics, among them twelve fragments of the Holy Cross that the patriarch of Jerusalem had sent to the king.[65] Thus Charlemagne completed the foundation as he began it. Furthermore, these same relics and the others mentioned in the text appear in a non-legendary inventory of the abbey's relics composed in 1045.[66] Hence the legend attaches a genealogy to all the relics actually present at Charroux in the eleventh century, but especially to its famous and distinctive fragments of the Cross.

By the mid-eleventh century, then, Charroux had elaborated for itself a coherent legend in which its real founder, Roger of Limoges, was over-shadowed by Charlemagne, the king who had actually only confirmed his count's foundation with a routine grant of immunity.[67] In its legend the abbey also chose effectively to ignore Louis the Pious, a ruler to whom it had

---

[62] There would have been plenty of opportunity for Ademar to hear the legends from the monks of Charroux themselves; he relates that in the early eleventh century, those monks had brought their piece of the Cross to his home monastery, Saint-Cybard of Angoulême (*Chronicon* 3.40; *Chronique*, p. 162).

[63] *Miracula S. Genulphi episcopi* (*AASS* January 2:99).

[64] *Chartes et documents pour servir à l'histoire de l'abbaye de Charroux*, pp. 1–7.

[65] Here the text conflates various passages of Ademar's *Chronicon* (2.15, 2.17, 2.19; *Chronique*, pp. 89–90, 93–94, 96–97) in order to present these relics as those sent to Charlemagne by the patriarch of Jerusalem.

[66] *Chartes et documents pour servir à l'histoire de l'abbaye de Charroux*, pp. 41–44.

[67] On Charroux's actual foundation, see the diploma of Charlemagne (785–800): *MGH Diplomata Karolinorum* 1:260–261, no. 194 (also in *Chartes et documents pour servir à l'histoire de l'abbaye de Charroux*, pp. 10–11). Cf. the poem by Theodulf of Orléans, *Carmina* no. 50, in *MGH Poetae Latini aevi Carolini* (Hannover, 1880), 1.1:550–551. On Roger of Limoges, see Robert de Lasteyrie, *Etude sur les comtes et vicomtes de Limoges antérieurs à l'an 1000* (Paris, 1874), pp. 12–15.

close ties. Louis had (re)founded the monastery, which consequently had been his loyal supporter and advocate during the troubles of the late 820s.[68] In Charroux's legend, Louis was granted merely the pedestrian role of rebuilding in stone the church his father had made from wood, and Roger was made into the executor of Charlemagne's will.[69] Only Charlemagne was celebrated, and he was characterized above all as the provider of relics, especially those of the Cross. These latter relics became as much the monarch's seal upon the foundation as they were a symbol of the abbey's celestial patron, Christ.[70]

By the early twelfth century, other abbeys south of the Loire claimed Charlemagne's stamp upon their foundation in a similar fashion.[71] Early twelfth-century texts at Sarlat and Moissac claim that Charlemagne had granted them a relic of the Cross (although at Moissac, the context was not foundation—as we have seen, Moissac associated its origins with Clovis).[72] Gellone too had such a relic. Its fragment of the Cross appeared in sources antedating the twelfth century; these texts however, did not specify the relic's provenance.[73] By at least the twelfth century, though, the abbey had reinterpreted the relic in order to give it a Carolingian coloring.[74] According to the early twelfth-century *vita* of Guillaume, who was this abbey's legendary (and probably actual) founder, Charlemagne accedes to his favorite duke's decision to embrace the monastic life, but on one condition: that Guillaume accept a gift from him. Guillaume requests and receives the relic

---

[68]   On Louis's relations with Charroux, see Robert Favreau and Marie-Thérèse Camus, *Charroux* (Poitiers, 1989), pp. 6–7. Charroux appears on the Astronomer's list of abbeys founded or refounded by Louis when he was king of Aquitaine; see *Vita Hludowici imperatoris* (*MGH SS* 2:616–617).

[69]   Louis does not appear in the narrative text under discussion here, but rather in a text probably composed at the same time: *Chartes et documents pour servir à l'histoire de l'abbaye de Charroux*, pp. 11–13.

[70]   Beginning in 989, Charroux was the setting for a series of so-called peace councils. At such councils, relics often presided along with human beings as sources of powerful authority. Charroux's piece of the Cross, given by a ruler of legendary authority, would have been a potent symbol in such a context.

[71]   See Frolow, *La relique de la Vraie Croix*, pp. 203–210, no. 75.

[72]   A relic list of 1102 from a reliquary at Moissac identifies the contents as relics given by "the king Charles," all of them relating to the Passion and among them a fragment of the Cross. The thirteenth-century (?) copy of this text (AD Tarn-et-Garonne, Montauban G.585) is cited by Alexander Gieysztor, "The Genesis of the Crusade: The Encyclical of Sergius IV (1009–1012)," *Medievalia et Humanistica* 5, 6 (1948, 1950): 24, n. 97. For Sarlat, see Hugh of Fleury, *Vita S. sacerdotis* (*PL* 163:992).

[73]   Charters attest to the Cross's presence at Gellone as early as the late 870s: *Cartulaires des abbayes d'Aniane et de Gellone*, 1:15–16, 99, nos. 12, 113.

[74]   The prologue to the *miracula* that celebrate the *virtus* of both Guillaume and the Cross specify the latter's Carolingian provenance: *Historia miraculorum [S. Willelmi ducis]* (*AASS*, May 6:822). Victor Saxer has argued that this text dates from the first half of the eleventh century; see his "Le culte et la légende hagiographique de saint Guillaume à Gellone," in *La chanson de geste*, 2:572–576. This may be so, but the earliest manuscript of these *miracula* (Montpellier, BM 16) dates from the twelfth century.

of the Cross that Charlemagne had been sent from Jerusalem; the duke then enshrines it at Gellone.[75] Gellone's prized relic is thus vested with a double layer of Carolingian veneer, passing from the hands of the legendary ruler to those of the no less legendary Guillaume.

So definitely a symbol of Charlemagne had this relic become that Gellone's rival, Aniane, in its effort to present the king as its cofounder, announced in its highly interpolated and colorful version of the Carolingian chronicle of Moissac that it too possessed fragments of the Cross. These, moreover, came not through the agency of an intermediary, even one so illustrious as Guillaume, but rather had been willed to the monastery directly by Charlemagne in his famous testament.[76] Yet another monastery, Alet, announced its piece of the Cross as a gift from the pope who was associated with Charlemagne in Latin legend: Leo III. In the charter (composed probably by the twelfth century) describing the abbey's foundation by Count Bera, styled son of Count William (no doubt Guillaume of Gellone is intended), Bera petitions the pope for this relic for Alet.[77] Finally, Charlemagne not only had founded the Périgordin abbey of Paunat on a site distinguished by miracles, but he had given it relics of the Cross—at least according to the thirteenth-century *Chronique Saintongeaise.*[78]

Hence, by the twelfth century, the Cross had become a tangible symbol of Charlemagne as well as of Christ. Words put in Charlemagne's mouth by the *vita* of Guillaume make explicit this new nature of the Cross. Charlemagne tells Guillaume: "these [relics] will always be true and most certain symbols (*signa*), an eternal memorial (*memoria*), a means of frequently recalling our affection [for you]. For without doubt, as often as you gaze upon . . . or touch . . . these holy objects, you will not be able to forget your lord Charles."[79]

Before considering the implications of this pairing of Charlemagne and Cross, let me remark on the independence of this tradition from developments at the Capetian center. At Saint-Denis of Paris, a legend was embroidered in the late eleventh century celebrating Charlemagne's indirect dona-

[75] *Vita [S. Willelmi ducis] (AASS* May 6:815–816).

[76] The passage in question is an interpolation of Einhard's description of Charlemagne's division of his goods in his testament: "Unam partem sibi reservavit quam dedit benedicto abbati sancti salvatoris anianensis archisterii videlicet crucis dominicis [*sic*]" (Paris, BN Latin 5941, f. 33v). The Cross is also emphasized in the probably contemporaneous text by Pseudo-Ardo Smaragdus, *Sermo sancti Ardonis, cognomento Smaragdi . . . (AASSosB* 4.1:225).

[77] *HL* 2:79–80, no. 23. Bera was not among Guillaume's children. See Constance B. Bouchard, "Family Structure and Family Consciousness among the Aristocracy in the Ninth to Eleventh Centuries," *Francia* 14 (1986): 641–642, 653–654; Joseph Calmette, "La famille de Saint Guilhem," *Annales du Midi* 18 (1906): 145–165, esp. 149; and Tisset, *L'abbaye de Gellone,* pp. 23–38.

[78] *Chronique dite Saintongeaise,* pp. 267–268.

[79] *Vita [S. Willelmi ducis] (AASS* May 6:815–816).

tion of relics of Christ: the *Descriptio qualiter*.[80] But this text is very different. It presents the piece of the Cross as only one among a host of relics given by the king and upon which the abbey prided itself. Furthermore, Charlemagne's acquisition of the relics and their subsequent arrival at the monastery are not at all like what we have seen. According to the Saint-Denis text, Charlemagne journeyed to Jerusalem, delivered the Holy City from the Muslims and received his recompense, the relics, at Constantinople. Here the royal abbey proposes Charlemagne as crusader—a significant development, to be sure, but one that influenced only one of the southern abbeys' legends. The early twelfth-century legend of Gellone specifies that the relic of the Cross had been brought by the patriarch's messengers; the Moissac text mentions no journey to Jerusalem; Alet's relic is from Rome; and Charroux's comes from a wondrous pilgrim and/or the patriarch's envoys. Only at Sarlat was the relic of the Cross described as the fruit of a royal journey to the Holy Land, but the author of the relevant text, Hugh of Fleury, was a monk of an abbey as royal as Saint-Denis and was doubtless aware of the latter's traditions.[81] Thus we find no northern tradition imposing itself, but rather southern monasteries themselves shading the Cross into an emblem of their royal founder.

But why this relic in particular? Charlemagne's association with it was more than a mere manifestation of the general efflorescence of devotion to the Cross in the eleventh and twelfth centuries.[82] The Cross was a royal, indeed imperial, relic per se, evoking the crowned and triumphant Christ and his eternal victory. Hence rulers often employed fragments of it as personal talismans; Byzantine emperors had carried such relics into battle since the sixth century.[83] Enclosed in reliquaries with inscriptions proclaiming the Cross's potency, such relics became part of the battle equipment of the Visigothic rulers, then of the German and Slavic kings.[84] Whether or not the historical Charlemagne wielded a relic of the Cross in this fashion—or

[80]   See above at nn. 24–25.
[81]   Hugh even writes that he had read "in quibus actibus" of Charlemagne how this ruler had brought back the Cross and other relics from Jerusalem—probably a reference to Saint-Denis's *Descriptio qualiter*. See Hugh of Fleury, *Vita S. sacerdotis* (*PL* 163:992).
[82]   Frolow argues that the eleventh and twelfth centuries witnessed most of the translations of relics of the Cross to churches in France: *La relique de la Vraie Croix*, pp. 143, 145.
[83]   Michael McCormick, *Eternal Victory: Triumphal Rulership in Late Antiquity, Byzantium and the Early Medieval West* (Cambridge, 1986), pp. 216, 247, 249; Schwineköper, "Christus-Reliquien-Verehrung," pp. 197–199.
[84]   For an inventory of instances of the Cross carried as a talisman by rulers in battle, see Frolow, *La relique de la Vraie Croix*, pp. 77–80, 238, 245–246, 263–264, 271, 287–290. For the Visigothic *profectio bellica*, see *Liber ordinum* . . . , ed. Marius Férotin, Monumenta Ecclesiae Liturgica, 5 (Paris, 1904), pp. 149–156. Concerning Visigothic use of the relic of the Cross in the context of royal ceremony, see McCormick, *Eternal Victory*, pp. 297–326, esp. 302–314. On the German emperors and the Cross, see Schwineköper, "Christus-Reliquien-Verehrung."

whether he even possessed such a relic at all—is a matter of some debate.[85] In the imaginative memory of at least one of the southern monasteries, however, he did.[86] The second layer of Charroux's legend, a narrative text composed early in the twelfth century, presents the fragment of the Cross given by Charlemagne to the abbey as a "small reliquary hanging from a chain (*filacterium*) adorned with a fragment of the Lord's cross, which he called 'Warrior' (*Bellator*) because he was accustomed to using it in battle."[87] Here the name makes explicit the triumphal tenor of the relationship between Charlemagne and Cross.

The continuum between eternal and mortal royal victory thus helps to explain how the identification between Charlemagne and the True Cross had become one of essence. By the twelfth century, the Cross had a dual nature for southern monasteries. It was a reminder of two lords: the celestial king, Christ, and the paradigmatic terrestrial king, Charlemagne. More than a hint of the Christomimetic ideal of kingship which probably postdated the historical Charlemagne comes to color the legendary monarch.[88] For surely in this pairing of king with Christ through the mediation of relic, an analogy was established between the heavenly ruler and the earthly monarch—and Charlemagne elevated to at least the rank of holy.

[85] Schwineköper argues that that there is no evidence that Charlemagne actually possessed any relics of the Cross himself: "Christus-Reliquien-Verehrung," pp. 201–205.

[86] Legend also linked Charlemagne's father with this relic; according to Benedict of Soracte, Pippin the Short had worn a fragment of the Cross around his neck. See Benedict's *Chronicon* (*MGH SS* 3:707).

[87] *Chartes et documents pour servir à l'histoire de l'abbaye de Charroux*, p. 30. Perhaps this passage indicates that the early Carolingian pendant made of two pieces of crystal sheltering between them a fragment of the Cross and supposedly found in Charlemagne's tomb in the nineteenth century deserves the title by which it is known: "Charlemagne's talisman" (on this pendant, see Schramm, *Herrschaftszeichen*, 1:309–312). But it is equally if not more likely that both the "talisman" and Charroux's *Bellator* represent stages in the legendary adornment of Charlemagne's neck with a cross pendant of some sort. This process began by at least the early eleventh century, when Thietmar of Merseburg described the golden cross pendant Charlemagne was wearing when Otto III opened his tomb. See Thietmar of Merseburg, *Chronicon*, in *Die Chronik des bischofs Thietmar von Merseburg und ihrer korveier Uberarbeitung*, MGH Scriptores Rerum Germanicarum Nova Series, 9; (Berlin, 1935), pp. 185–186. Ademar of Chabannes's account of the same event mentions rather a crown which bore a relic of the Cross; see Ademar, *Chronicon* 2.25 (*Chronique*, p. 105). The legendary *Chronique Saintongeaise* (pp. 279–280) depicted Charlemagne granting his cross-shaped reliquary pendant to one of his southern French foundations, a certain Sainte-Marie de l'Ile sur Seugne.

[88] See also Stephen Nichols's discussion of how Charlemagne is made Christlike in various Romanesque sources: *Romanesque Signs: Early Medieval Narrative and Iconography* (New Haven, 1983), pp. 66–94. On the Christomimetic ideal of kingship, see Lothar Bornscheuer, *Miseriae Regum: Untersuchungen zum Krisen- und Todesgedanken in den herrschaftstheologischen Vorstellungen der ottonisch-salischen Zeit* (Berlin, 1968); Robert Deshman, "*Christus rex et magi reges*: Kingship and Christology in Ottonian and Anglo-Saxon Art," *Frühmittelalterliche Studien* 10 (1976): 367–405; Kantorowicz, *The King's Two Bodies*, pp. 42–86; and Koziol, *Begging Pardon*, pp. 138–173.

Such an analogy informs the relationship between Charlemagne and the other relic of Christ for which Charlemagne was famed by the later twelfth century: the Holy Foreskin. As we have seen, a gloss found in many manuscripts of the *Historia scholastica* proclaims that in the Church of the Holy Sepulcher at Jerusalem, Charlemagne received this relic from an angel and then translated it to Aachen; Charles the Bald gave it to Charroux. This story was repeated almost verbatim in many other late twelfth- and thirteenth-century texts, including Gervase of Tilbury's *De otiis imperialibus,* Innocent III's treatise on the mass, and Jacobus of Voragine's vastly popular *Legenda aurea.*[89] Although all these writers base their tale upon the Parisian gloss, this tradition was not Parisian in origin. It represented a reinterpretation of the legend of the southern abbey where, the gloss tells us, the Foreskin reposed: Charroux.

As we have seen, Charroux claimed that Charlemagne had given it a fragment of the Cross. In the early twelfth-century layer of this abbey's legend, however, the Cross, although present in the guise of *Bellator,* had been superseded by another relic as the symbolic embodiment of the patronage of king and Christ.[90] According to this text, after having founded Charroux and overseen its consecration by Leo III, Charlemagne regrets not having relics of the quantity and quality befitting a monastery dedicated to such a "great king" (Christ). On the pope's advice, Charlemagne travels to Jerusalem in order to acquire relics for his new abbey. There he attends mass at the Church of the Holy Sepulcher. Lo and behold! The hand of God appears and places on the corporal covering the chalice an object called by the text the "Holy Virtue" (*sancta virtus*). Then a little boy—the Christ child—suddenly appears from the right (and hence positive) side of the altar and addresses Charlemagne: "Most noble prince, accept with veneration this small gift (*munusculum*) which, it is sure, [comes] from my true flesh and my true blood."[91] The rest of the text relates how Charlemagne carefully chaperoned the precious relic back to Charroux, where he placed it on the altar as an offering.

This text never makes explicit the exact nature of the Holy Virtue. The first document I have found from Charroux that does so is a privilege of Clement VII (1380); in it, the pope grants indulgences to all who come to the septennial *ostensio* of the "foreskin of Jesus Christ our Lord, called the

---

[89] Gervase of Tilbury, *De otiis imperialibus* 3.24 (*MGH SS* 27:386); Jacobus of Voragine, *Legenda aurea,* p. 86; Innocent III, *De sacro altaris mysterio* (*PL* 217:876–877). Also see Alberic of Trois-Fontaines, *Chronica* (*MGH SS* 23:721); John of Würzburg's late twelfth-century (?) *Descriptio terrae sanctae* (*PL* 155:1061); and Fretellus's twelfth-century *Descriptio locorum circa hierusalem adiacentium* (Paris, BN Latin 5129, ff. 61va–vb, a manuscript of the late twelfth or early thirteenth century; better than the edition in *PL* 155:1047–1048).

[90] *Chartes et documents pour servir à l'histoire de l'abbaye de Charroux,* pp. 29–41.

[91] This miraclous apparition of Christ during mass is a eucharistic miracle reflecting the preoccupation in the later eleventh century with the doctrine of the real presence.

Holy Virtue."[92] But surely the Holy Virtue was already the Holy Foreskin in the twelfth-century layer of Charroux's legend. After all, what else could the "small gift" miraculously granted to Charlemagne by the youthful Christ be if not flesh and blood which the Savior had lost as a child—his umbilical cord or his foreskin?[93] The latter is more likely, for would the late twelfth-century cleric who composed the *Historia scholastica* gloss have arbitrarily invented the label of "Holy Foreskin" for the relic Charlemagne received at Jerusalem and gave to Charroux? Certainly the Holy Foreskin was in circulation by the early twelfth century. In his treatise (ca. 1125) distinguishing legitimate from illegimate relics, Guibert of Nogent fulminated against "those" who claimed they possessed Christ's foreskin; he may even have been referring to Charroux (of whose traditions this inquisitive monk might well have been aware).[94] Charroux's "Holy Virtue," which by the late eleventh or early twelfth century had stolen the place of the True Cross as Charlemagne's seal and as the embodiment of the abbey's patrons, king and Christ, was thus the Holy Foreskin.[95]

Before considering the meaning of Charlemagne's association with this startling relic, let us wonder whether Charroux's legend is an imitation of Saint-Denis's account of Charlemagne's pilgrimage-crusade during which the king obtained relics. Not only does Charroux's Charlemagne now voyage to Jerusalem to receive the significant relic, but specific passages of the legend even echo the exact wording of Saint-Denis's *Descriptio qualiter;* at moments, the text even switches from "king" to the Dionysian "emperor."[96]

---

[92] *Chartes et documents pour servir à l'histoire de l'abbaye de Charroux*, pp. 318–319, no. 190.

[93] Jean Cabanot argues that the *sancta virtus* was first the relic of the Cross, and that only later was the name attached to the Foreskin; see "Le trésor des reliques de Saint-Sauveur de Charroux, centre et reflet de la vie spirituelle de l'abbaye," *Bulletin de la Société des Antiquaires de l'Ouest,* 4th ser., 16 (1981): 103–123. If the relic had been the Cross with a new name, however, why would Christ have appeared in the guise of a young boy? And why would he have explicated his "little gift" to the emperor as his flesh and blood? Other historians are willing to believe that the *sancta virtus* was already the Holy Foreskin in the late eleventh or early twelfth century. See Favreau and Camus, *Charroux,* p. 24; and Gisela Schwering-Illert, *Die ehemalige französische Abteikirche Saint-Sauveur im Charroux (Vienne) im 11. und 12. Jh.: Ein Vorschlag zur Rekonstruktion und Deutung der romanischen Bauteile* (Düsseldorf, 1963), pp. 30–34. I have been unable to consult Georges Chapeau, "Les grandes reliques de l'abbaye de Charroux," *Bulletin de la Société des Antiquaires de l'Ouest,* 3d ser., 8 (1928): 101–128.

[94] Guibert of Nogent, *De pignoribus sanctorum* (*PL* 156:629, 631–632).

[95] The Holy Virtue literally replaces the Cross; some of the miracles ascribed to it are ones that Ademar of Chabannes had ascribed solely to Charroux's relic of the Cross (cf. Ademar of Chabannes, *Chronicon* 3.23, *Chronique,* pp. 144–145, and *Chartes et documents pour servir à l'histoire de l'abbaye de Charroux,* pp. 34–35). Another Charroux text (which probably represents an intermediate stage of the legend and which relies heavily on Ademar) attributes the same miracle to both relics given by Charlemagne: *Chartes et documents pour servir à l'histoire de l'abbaye de Charroux,* pp. 48–50.

[96] See Schwering-Illert, *Die ehemalige französische Abteikirche,* pp. 31–34. Georges Chapeau errs in asserting that Charroux's text exactly copies the *Descriptio qualiter,* but he points out useful parallels; see his "Fondation de l'abbaye de Charroux: Etudes sur les textes," *Bulletin de la Société des Antiquaires de l'Ouest* 7 (1926): 471–508.

Nonetheless, Charroux's new legend was no literary pastiche of the Saint-Denis text. There are great differences in the nature of Charlemagne's voyage and in the relation of the king to the monastery in question.[97] Furthermore, the relic that the Charroux text focuses on is startlingly different from those traditional ones of the Passion which figure in the Saint-Denis legend.

Indeed, there are traces of the crystallization at Charroux of the Holy Foreskin's legend and cult that predate or are contemporaneous with the Saint-Denis text (composed, remember, between 1080 and 1095). The beginning of the cult can probably be identified with the council of 1082 held at Charroux during which an altar was consecrated and the monastery's "precious relics" were displayed, at least according to the chronicle of nearby Saint-Maixent.[98] According to the early twelfth-century layer of Charroux's legend, it was at this council that the Holy Virtue, which Aldebert III, count of the March and "protector" of the abbey, had formerly secreted away, was revealed to an attentive audience of bishops and abbots.[99] A miracle even manifested the relic's authenticity and its fleshy nature; the Holy Virtue oozed blood—just as hosts, other pledges of Christ's corporeal presence, began to do increasingly in this period.[100] This newly found relic also appeared in somewhat less dramatic late eleventh- and early twelfth-century texts from Charroux. A charter composed between 1061 and 1095 recorded a donation made to "God and the Holy Virtue of Charroux."[101] In a confirmation of the abbey's privileges by the bishop of Perigueux in 1101, the relic and Charlemagne were mentioned as a pair: "Charroux was built by lord Charlemagne especially before all other [monasteries] in honor of the highest virtue (*summe virtutis*) of the Holy Savior."[102] Thus, Charroux may have borrowed certain elements from Saint-Denis's *Descriptio qualiter,* but only in order to adorn its own incipient legend of the Holy Foreskin.

[97] There is no suggestion that Charlemagne goes to Jerusalem for any purpose other than the pacific one of acquiring relics, and no hint of a subsequent journey to Constantinople or a translation of the relics to Aachen.

[98] *La chronique de Saint-Maixent, 751–1140,* ed. and trans. Jean Verdon, (Paris, 1979), p. 144.

[99] *Chartes et documents pour servir à l'histoire de l'abbaye de Charroux,* pp. 39–40. Cabanot, in "Le trésor des reliques," provides a useful summary of the texts and events involved in the establishment of the cult.

[100] On such eucharistic miracles and the increasing devotion to the Host in this period, see Miri Rubin, *Corpus Christi: The Eucharist in Late Medieval Culture* (Cambridge, 1991), esp. pp. 108–129.

[101] *Chartes et documents pour servir à l'histoire de l'abbaye de Charroux,* p. 95, no. 5.

[102] *Chartes et documents pour servir à l'histoire de l'abbaye de Charroux,* p. 126, no. 24. The Latin admittedly is ambiguous. "[A] domno karolo magno augusto pre ceteris honori summe virtutis sancti salvatoris jesu christi . . . fuisse constructum" could simply be a reference to Christ's power, but given the charter previously cited, it seems probable that *virtus* is the relic. Later in the twelfth century, the abbey's charters referred regularly to the *sancta virtus;* see, for example, *Chartes et documents pour servir à l'histoire de l'abbaye de Charroux,* pp. 145, 161–162, 166, nos. 37, 45, and 48.

In any case, by the late twelfth century, Charlemagne, the Holy Foreskin, and Charroux were such a celebrated trio that word of them had reached Paris and its schools. There they sprang to the mind of some cleric as he read Peter Comestor's account in the *Historia scholastica* of the Circumcision. This unknown cleric added the gloss, which, as we have seen, was copied into a large number of manuscripts of this widely used school text. But he interpreted Charroux's legend through the lens of the Charlemagne tradition with which as a cleric in Paris he probably would have been more familiar: Saint-Denis's *Descriptio qualiter* (which he might have read, heard about, or even seen recounted in the stained glass of Suger's splendid new church).[103] When he thought of relics brought back by Charlemagne from the Holy Land, it was of those which, according to the Saint-Denis legend, the king had deposited at Aachen and which Charles the Bald brought to France. In his gloss, therefore, the cleric assigned Charroux's endowment with the Foreskin to Charlemagne's grandson, not to Charlemagne himself.[104] The interpolation of Charles the Bald into the tradition of the Foreskin where he had never been is yet more evidence that this king enjoyed a legendary stature in the north that he lacked south of the Loire. At Charroux, the only king ever associated with this relic was Charlemagne.

With this latter restructuring, the Holy Foreskin passed from the realm of monastic legend to that of the *Historia scholastica* and its large audience. Thus wrested from its context, Charroux's Foreskin not only became a subject of scholastic debate but was celebrated far beyond Poitou.[105] Nonetheless, even in this scholastic tradition, the relic remained associated with Charroux—and with Charlemagne. It was Charroux's legend, not Parisian traditions, that had made the Foreskin into a relic emblematic of the legendary king.[106]

[103] On the window at Saint-Denis, see Brown and Cothren, "The Twelfth-Century Crusading Window."

[104] The citation of the gloss that appears in John of Würzburg's *Descriptio terrae sanctae* shows how endowment with relics was seen naturally as an act by the founder. John writes that Charles the Bald translated the Foreskin from Aix to the monastery of Charroux which he himself (!) had built; see *PL* 155:1061.

[105] The gloss about Charroux's Foreskin was accompanied by another, which addressed the problem of the Foreskin and the Resurrection and concluded that Christ's foreskin would return to its "place," "glorified" like the rest of Christ's body: Paris, BN Latin 16034, f. 117va; Paris, BN Latin 16040, f. 110va; Vatican Reg. Latin 303, f. 120vb; Vatican Ross. 570, f. 185ra (mentioning Rome instead of Charroux and omitting Charlemagne). A commentary attributed to Stephen Langton also discusses the problem, mentioning Charroux but not Charlemagne; see *In Historia scholastica* (Paris, BN Latin 14414, f. 135rb). I am grateful to Philippe Buc for bringing this manuscript to my attention. Both Innocent III (*De sacro altaris mysterio; PL* 217:876–877) and Jacobus of Voragine (*Legenda aurea,* p. 86) mention the problem in their description of the Charroux Foreskin. This discussion did not originate as a reaction to the gloss: see, for example, Guibert of Nogent's ponderings about Christ's resurrection and his relics (*De pignoribus sanctorum; PL* 156:651–653).

[106] Both relic and king remained associated with the monastery. When Calvin fulminated against those churches which dared claim the impossible relic of the Foreskin, Charroux

But why did the Foreskin replace the Cross in Charroux's legend as the embodiment of the abbey's patrons, king and Christ? Perhaps by the late eleventh century there were too many churches that claimed fragments of the Cross, and Charroux wished to distinguish itself with something different. Furthermore, this monastery's new relic tapped into certain spiritual trends, just as the Cross did; the Foreskin accorded with the increasing interest in the real presence, and in the incarnated and youthful Christ. Indeed, the Foreskin might have been a natural choice for an abbey that already possessed the Cross, for these two relics form a symbolic continuum. They represent, as it were, the alpha and omega of the Incarnation— Christ's infancy and his death. Since at least Jerome in the late fourth century, medieval writers had interpreted Christ's suffering at the Circumcision, the blood he shed as a child, as a prefiguration of his suffering on the Cross and the blood he would shed as an adult.[107] According to this logic, the True Cross and Holy Foreskin complement each other as relics, and form a fitting frame for a king increasingly considered saintly.

By at least the later eleventh century a reliquary guarded in the palace of Rome's cathedral articulated this complementarity. According to the *Descriptio sanctuarii Lateranensis ecclesie*, a text composed between 1073 and 1118, in the Lateran's Saint Lawrence chapel was a golden, gem-studded cross in the "middle" of which were enshrined Christ's foreskin and umbilicus.[108] The rituals in which this cross was used and the way in which it was physically adapted to contain the relics demonstrate the unity of significance of the container and its contents.[109]

---

headed his list of offenders; see his *Traité des reliques, ou advertisement tres utile au grand profit qu'il reviendroit à la Chrestienté . . .* (Geneva, 1863; reprint of 1599 ed.), pp. 12–13, 83. Calvin, however, does not connect this relic with Charlemagne, even though the *Historia scholastica* gloss was still in circulation as late as the seventeenth century; see Alfonso Salmeron's citation of it in his *Comentarii in evangelicam historiam et in acta apostolorum*, 16 vols. (Cologne, 1602– 1604), 3:320–321. On later legends of the Holy Foreskin, see Pierre Saintyves, *Les reliques et les images légendaires . . .* (Paris, 1912), pp. 143–144, 179–184, 274–275.

[107] See Jerome, *In evangelium secundum Lucam* (*PL* 30:569). This tradition is certainly remembered in the eleventh century. See Jotsald's explicit citation of Jerome: *De vita et virtutibus sancti Odilonis abbatis* (*PL* 142:910–911). In earlier exegetical traditions, the Circumcision was interpreted as prefiguring the Resurrection: Augustine, *Epistula clvii*, in *Epistulae* (CSEL 44.3), pp. 461–462; Pseudo-Alcuin, *De divinis officiis liber* (*PL* 101:1176–1177). Also see Caroline Walker Bynum, "The Body of Christ in the Later Middle Ages: A Reply to Leo Steinberg," in her *Fragmentation and Redemption: Essays on Gender and the Human Body in Medieval Religion* (New York, 1991), pp. 86–92.

[108] See the long passage reproduced in Hartmann Grisar, *Die römische Kapelle Sancta Sanctorum und ihr Schatz* (Freiburg, 1908), p. 59. On the dating, composition, and manuscripts of the *Descriptio sanctuarii*, see Giovanni Baptista de Rossi, *Inscriptiones christianae urbis Romae septimo saeculo antiquiores*, 2 vols. (Rome, 1857–1888), 2:222–223 (app. 1).

[109] For the rituals and the physical design of the reliquary, see the descriptions in Grisar, *Die römische Kapelle*, pp. 82–89 and fig. 42. On the veneration of the Foreskin at the Lateran in general (with some comparative material) see also Grisar's "Die angebliche Christusreliquie im mittelalterlichen Lateran (Praeputium domini)," *Römische Quartalscrift für christliche Altertumskunde und für Kirchengeschichte* 20 (1906): 109–122.

At Charroux itself there is evidence suggesting such juxtaposition of Cross and Foreskin (although nothing indicates that the monks were influenced by, or even knew of, the Lateran tradition). A reliquary still at the abbey today consists of a thirteenth-century gold and silver frame on a pedestal. Two facing angels hold up between them an oval box, the compositional focus of the object. Within the oval is a lidded reliquary, which has been dated most recently as late eleventh century—the period when the cult of the Holy Foreskin emerged at Charroux. On the cover is Christ, flanked by the alpha and omega. Written around the side of the container are words that recall those with which the youthful Christ presented the Holy Foreskin to Charlemagne: "here the flesh of Christ's blood is contained" (*hic caro sanguinis christi continetur*). Given what we know about the significance of the Circumcision, the eucharistic reference would suggest that this reliquary indeed was intended for the Holy Foreskin.[110]

This inscription, however, might also have been intended to recall the other relic for which Charroux was famous. Inside this Romanesque hinged reliquary was a Byzantine one that in the nineteenth century was found to contain a cruciform piece of wood stained with red (blood?).[111] It is almost impossible to know if the cross-shaped wood was originally enclosed in this way (or another) in the Romanesque reliquary or if it was added only later. Nonetheless, it is tempting to believe that the Holy Foreskin and the Cross were enshrined within the same object in the twelfth century—or that the shrine proclaiming itself to hold the Foreskin actually held the Cross, thus inverting the Lateran reliquary which announced itself a cross but contained the Foreskin and Umbilicus.

Furthermore, the fabric of the largest container of Charroux's relics—that is, the abbey church—may also have expressed the continuum of meaning between Cross and Foreskin. After a series of disastrous fires (1022, 1029, post 1047), this church was rebuilt in the late eleventh and early twelfth centuries. Its new and very unusual design combined the traditional cruciform plan with a much less common rotunda, consisting of an octagon of pillars surrounded by a triple ambulatory.[112] The rotunda, the composi-

110   Other scholars have also identified this reliquary as that of the Holy Virtue. See A. Frolow, "Le medaillon byzantin de Charroux," *Cahiers Archéologiques* 16 (1966): 40; and Schwering-Illert, *Die ehemalige französische Abteikirche*, p. 33. Although the inscription might apply to the Eucharist, monstrances began to be used only in the fourteenth century; see Michel Andrieu, "Aux origines du culte du Saint-Sacrement: Reliquaires et monstrances eucharistiques," *AB* 68 (1950): 397–418.

111   Frolow, "Le medaillon," pp. 40–41. On the Byzantine reliquary, see also *Les trésors des églises de France*, pp. 185–186, no. 344 and pls. 108–109. Madame Clément, the current *présidente* of the Syndicat d'Initiatif of Charroux (which manages the remains of the abbey church), was kind enough to inform me that when she recently opened the reliquary, it contained a wooden cross, two bones, and a piece of thorn.

112   On the eleventh-century design and building campaign, see Favreau and Camus, *Charroux*, pp. 12–19 and fig. 4; Raymond Oursel, *Haut-Poitou roman* (La Pierre-Qui-Vire,

tional as well as ritual center of the Church, had a symbolic meaning as explicit as that of the cruciform plan; it recalled and imitated the Anastasis, the Church of the Holy Sepulcher at Jerusalem (see Figure 7).[113] Thus, in its very structure Charroux's church both announced the patron to whom it was dedicated, the Savior, and articulated the church's nature as a shrine for the two relics that had been granted by the abbey's other patron, Charlemagne. The cruciform shape evoked the fragment of the True Cross, and the rotunda with its octagon the Holy Foreskin, for, let us remember, Charlemagne had received this latter relic in the Church of the Holy Sepulcher.[114]

Now one might object that the cult of the Foreskin at Charroux developed too late in the eleventh century to have influenced the design of the abbey church.[115] But the invention and elevation of the Holy Virtue occurred in conjunction with the 1082 consecration of one of the new church's altars. The ceremony most probably had been planned well in advance (the twelfth-century layer of the legend indicates various preparations). Could not the architectural plan have been conceived in part to celebrate this relic which would be associated with the ritual constitution of the material church as sacred space? In any case, the relics' legendary donor, Charlemagne, infused Charroux's interpretation of the ultimate and most significant consecration of its new church. A contemporaneous text likened the dedication of the new church by Pope Urban II in 1096 to the legendary consecration of Charlemagne's church performed by his pope, Leo III.[116] Ritual and architectural design thus combined to shade the church into an expression of the abbey's relics, their complementarity, and the legend surrounding them.

By the later twelfth century, these relics whose complementarity was embodied in Charroux's church—the True Cross and the Holy Foreskin—thus

---

1975), pp. 135–138 and pls. 28–35; and Schwering-Illert, *Die ehemalige französische Abteikirche*, pp. 56–82. Unfortunately, all that remains of the Romanesque church is the proud octagon of pillars.

[113] See Schwering-Illert, *Die ehemalige französische Abteikirche*, pp. 85–102. For a very stimulating general consideration of such imitations of the Anastasis, see Richard Krautheimer, "Introduction to an 'Iconography of Mediaeval Architecture,'" *Journal of the Warburg and Courtauld Institutes* 5 (1942): 1–33.

[114] If Charroux's church was intended primarily to celebrate the relic of the Cross, as some have argued (see Cabanot, "Le trésor des reliques," p. 111; Favreau and Camus, *Charroux*, pp. 18–19), then why was the rotunda included? It was neither a common architectural feature of churches in Poitou nor particularly associated elsewhere with the Cross. See Krautheimer, "Introduction to an 'Iconography,'" esp. p. 21.

[115] This is Schwering-Illert's argument, but she dates the abbey's plan to 1047 or earlier; see her *Die ehemalige französische Abteikirche*, pp. 17, 56–82. After the 1047 dedication, however, the abbey church was destroyed by fire; see *Chroniques des églises d'Anjou*, ed. Paul Marchegay and Emile Mabille (Paris, 1869), p. 396. Favreau and Camus date the abbey's plan to the later eleventh century: *Charroux*, pp. 12–18.

[116] *Chartes et documents pour servir à l'histoire de l'abbaye de Charroux*, pp. 25–27.

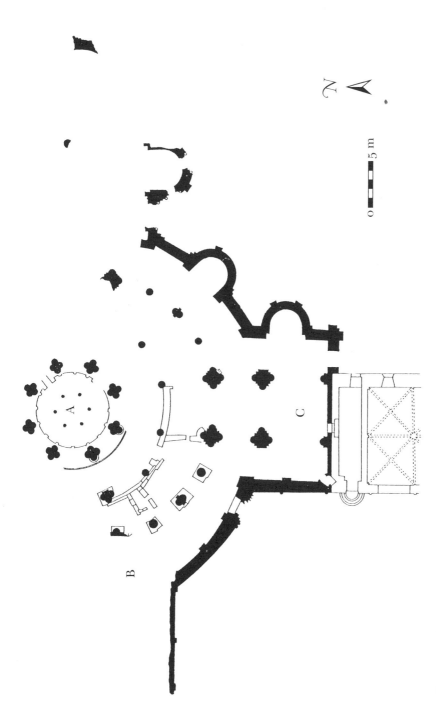

FIGURE 7. Ground plan of Saint-Sauveur of Charroux. This plan shows only what remains today of the Romanesque structure. Visible are the rotunda (A), part of the nave (B), and one transept (C). From Zodiaque, *Haut-Poitou roman*.

symbolically not only encompassed Christ's incarnation and passion but also signaled the emperor's own sanctifying presence and patronage. These relics had become so much a part of the legendary Charlemagne's identity that a monastery which possessed them could claim the king as its patron, thereby making itself a participant in the Carolingian legend. Alternatively, a monastery that already claimed the king as founder could reinvent its relics as those more special ones.

It is the latter principle that seems to have been operative in creating Conques's claim that Charlemagne had given this abbey Christ's foreskin (and umbilical cord). As we have seen, this claim was first articulated in the prologue to the abbey's chronicle. But it had a prehistory. According to the early eleventh-century *Liber miraculorum sancte Fidis* of Bernard of Angers, Conques possessed a golden reliquary which the monks believed was a gift of Charlemagne.[117] Bernard provides no details about this reliquary's appearance, other than that it was made from gold and was portable. One reliquary still at Conques fits this description and was extant at the time of Bernard's visit: a shrine-shaped reliquary of gold plaques on a wooden frame, an amalgam of Merovingian and Carolingian elements assembled into its present form around 1000.[118] Significantly, according to ninth- and tenth-century entries on the relic list (an authentic) inside the reliquary, the shrine contained relics of various saints, the Virgin, and even some generic ones "from Christ's flesh (*sanctis . . . ex carnie Christi* [*sic*])."[119] If this reliquary is the one mentioned by Bernard, then Charlemagne was associated with relics of the incarnated Christ at Conques as early as the first decades of the eleventh century.

To be sure, the authentic made no explicit reference to the Holy Foreskin and Umbilicus. By the time the prologue was composed, however, the monks reinterpreted the generic relics of Christ mentioned by the list as specifically those two.[120] But why? Only a certain number of corporeal relics of Christ were plausible or possible, and most of them were necessarily things he would have shed as a child: baby teeth, foreskin, umbilical cord, and so on. Why did the monks at Conques select from among these the two that they did?

[117]　*Liber miraculorum sancte Fidis* 2.4, p. 100.

[118]　For a detailed analysis of this reliquary, see Marie-Madeleine Gauthier's description in *Rouergue roman* (La Pierre-Qui-Vire, 1963), pp. 102–103, 115, 117, 125–126, 138–139, and pl. 44–48; and *Les trésors des églises de France*, pp. 296–299. This reliquary is often known today as the "Reliquary of Pippin the Short." It has that label in a *procès-verbal* of 1889 describing the reliquary; see the transcription of this text in Dominique Taralon, "'Le reliquaire de Pepin' du trésor de Conques," Maîtrise, Paris IV, 1988/89, pp. 94–95, n. 168.

[119]　The authentic is edited in A. Bouillet and L. Servières, *Sainte Foy: vierge et martyre* (Rodez, 1900), p. 214. The editors assign to each entry a date (all ranging from the seventh to the tenth century and presumably based on paleographic criteria).

[120]　Even though she interprets the authentic as referring directly to the Holy Foreskin and Umbilicus, Gauthier does not connect the reliquary of Pippin with the one mentioned in the prologue as enshrining these two relics; see *Rouergue roman*, pp. 115, 117.

When the prologue to the chronicle was composed, the Charroux tradition associating Holy Foreskin and Charlemagne may already have been in circulation. Indeed, the monks at Conques may have been aware of this tradition.[121] Perhaps it influenced them as they contemplated their reliquary and read the list of its contents. They knew the reliquary had been given by Charlemagne, and they knew that he had been the recipient of the Holy Foreskin. What else could the "holy things from Christ's flesh" mentioned by the authentic be than the Foreskin? They may have added the Umbilicus because it, like the Foreskin, was fleshly proof of Christ's childhood. Furthermore, the very design of the Conques reliquary may have suggested the relics' identification as those of the infant Christ; the reliquary clearly depicts Christ on the Cross. Reinterpreted as the container for Foreskin and Umbilicus, this reliquary thus makes concrete the same symbolic continuum—Passion, Circumcision, and Christ's childhood—that informed both Charroux's church and reliquary, and the Lateran's reliquary.[122] Using the lens of the legendary Charlemagne, the monks of Conques engaged in a process of rereading; accordingly, their generic relics of Christ metamorphosed into some of those more special ones which had become emblematic of the king as founder.

We have found, then, that as Charlemagne was celebrated as the donor of relics, he came to participate in the sacral charge they carried, and in turn lent his own increasing aura to them. Let me underline two features of this phenomenon. First, it did not depend on or even reflect developments in the Capetian center. Rather, it was engendered by the way in which southern monasteries constructed images of their origins. Second, by the twelfth century, as the reciprocal transferences of meaning between Charlemagne and relics became increasingly common, there are hints that in legends the relics of patron saints were increasingly eclipsed in favor of relics emblematic of, and granted by, the legendary Carolingian. For example, at Conques in the early eleventh century, the golden reliquary supposedly given by Charlemagne was the attendant companion of a more glorious and famous

---

[121] A verbal echo of the gloss may appear in the prologue. The prologue claims that the Foreskin had been given to Charlemagne by his *avunculus*—perhaps a misreading (either of the original scribe or the seventeenth-century copy) of *angelus?* See "Chronique de l'abbaye de Conques," p. 393. If so, then the prologue must postdate the appearance of the gloss (late twelfth century). On the other hand, Charlemagne's uncle was Carlomann, who had founded the monastery of Soracte near Rome (see Einhard, *Vita Karoli Magni,* in *Vie de Charlemagne,* p. 12). According to a late tenth-century legend, Charlemagne gave some relics to Soracte; see Benedict of Soracte, *Chronicon (MGH SS* 3:710–711). Does the prologue's *avunculus* represent some confused memory of this tradition?

[122] Although eventually losing its identification with Charlemagne, this reliquary retained its identification with the Holy Foreskin until the nineteenth century, as two inventories (1812, 1889) of the abbey's treasure show. Taralon, "'Le reliquaire de Pepin,'" pp. 94–95, n. 168.

one: the statue containing the relics of the abbey's patron saint, Saint Faith.[123] But by the time the prologue was composed, precious objects granted by the royal founder—the *A* and the Foreskin and Umbilical Cord—were the focus; the prologue does not mention Saint Faith's reliquary at all, and its description of the acquisition of her relics reads like a perfunctory afterthought.[124] Thus, a shift of emphasis had occurred in the constitution of the monastery's identity: from traditional saint to king. This same subtle but important change in the king's role also shaped the other legendary incarnation of Charlemagne as founder, the Charlemagne of the *chansons de geste.*

Charlemagne and the Epic Landscape

Beginning in the last years of the eleventh century, many southern monasteries began to see the landscape of their origins through the frame of the *chansons de geste.* Such epic envisioning also occurred in several abbeys located elsewhere in France—but in these cases, the epic heroes interwoven with the monasteries' foundation were often those postdating or predating Charlemagne, such as Raoul of Cambrai or Girart of Roussillon.[125] Southern abbeys instead focused on Charlemagne and his epic contemporaries such as Roland or Guillaume. These legends creating a past in which the epic Charlemagne figured prominently are evidence that southern monks were certainly very familiar with such epics as the *Chanson de Roland.* These epics, then, must have been sung in the south as well as the north, even if they are now extant largely in northern and not southern dialects. Perhaps these monastic legends suggest that epics once circulated in Provençal versions, as did the *chansons* sung of saints;[126] perhaps they even provide support for those lone scholarly voices arguing for the southern origins of certain

---

[123] *Liber miraculorum sancte Fidis* 2.4, p. 100. On Bernard of Angers and the *majestas,* see my "Un problème de cultures ou de culture," pp. 357–368.

[124] "Chronique du monastére de Conques," pp. 391–394. I am certainly not suggesting that Saint Faith had ceded her place to Charlemagne as the object of the devotion of monks and pilgrims, but rather that in the narrative describing Conques's origins and history, royal patronage had become more important. Interestingly, Beaune notes that at Saint-Denis, all cures were attributed to the Crown of Thorns and the Holy Nail brought from Aachen by Charles the Bald; that is to say, they were ascribed to the "royal relics," rather than to the relics of Denis. Beaune, *Naissance,* p. 94.

[125] On monastic legends celebrating Girart, see Louis, *De l'histoire à la légende;* and Victor Saxer, "Légende épique et légende hagiographique: Problème d'origines et d'évolution des chansons de geste," *Revue des Sciences Religieuses* 33 (1959): 372–395. On those invoking Raoul of Cambrai, see Misonne, *Eilbert de Florennes.* In general on such legends, see Joseph Bédier, *Les légendes épiques: Recherches sur la formation des chansons de geste,* 2d ed., 4 vols. (Paris, 1914–1921).

[126] Paris long ago made a similar suggestion; see his *Histoire poétique,* pp. 79–91. On *chansons des saints,* see Zaal, "*A lei francesca.*"

epic cycles such as those of Guillaume and Aymeric de Narbonne.[127] In any case, when southern monks introduced the epic king into their legends, they were invoking a tradition that was already very present in some shape in the south, and through their legends they made it even more present.

Indeed, Joseph Bédier long ago suggested that the *chansons* were firmly rooted in local soil, northern and southern, and that monasteries were key players in the development of the genre.[128] Although Bédier was probably not correct about the manner of composition of the chansons, his work suggests that monasteries did not merely siphon off information from the *chansons* but rather existed in some sort of symbiosis with the epic tradition.[129] For not only was the monastic world resonant with epic characters, events, and imagery, but monastic tradition also contributed to epic.[130] The nature of the relationship that we shall discover between the Charlemagne of epics and the king of the foundation legends, then, is much like that between the king of relics in southern legends and the king of the Saint-Denis tradition: a maze of mutual borrowings and transformations.

The *vita* of Saint Gilles, although it expressly denies to Charlemagne the role of founder, leads us into this maze. For Gilles's peculiar association with this king was celebrated not only by other Latin traditions, as were Charroux's Charlemagne and Holy Foreskin, but also by the *chansons* sung in courts and town squares throughout France. Indeed, the pairing of this saint with the Carolingian ruler captured the medieval imagination and became an integral part of the Charlemagne legend. The fate of the *vita* thus underlines how southern abbeys could create traits of the imaginatively remembered king that became part of his persona elsewhere.

As we have seen, the *vita* assigns to Gilles a royal partner in the abbey's foundation, but one who most definitely is not Frankish and who precedes the Franks historically: Flavius, "king of the Goths."[131] Nonetheless, the paradigmatic Frankish ruler, Charlemagne, appears in an episode that became the best-known feature of the *vita*. After the monastery's foundation and endowment by Flavius, Gilles's fame as a holy man spreads, finally

---

[127] For arguments that these cycles originated in the south, see Colby-Hall, "In Search of the Lost Epics"; and Lejeune, "La question de l'historicité."

[128] Bédier, *Les légendes épiques.*

[129] More recent research has shown how the *chansons* in their extant form show signs of oral formulaic composition and evolved over several centuries in a complex interaction between written texts and sung poems. See for example René Louis, "L'épopée française est carolingienne," *Coloquios de Roncevalles, agosto 1955* (Saragossa, 1956), pp. 327–460; Menéndez Pidal, *La chanson de Roland,* and even more recently, Joseph Duggan, "Social Functions of the Medieval Epic in the Romance Literatures," *Oral Tradition* 1 (1986): 727–766.

[130] For debate about the nature of the interaction between monastic and epic tradition, see Bédier, *Les légendes épiques;* Louis, *De l'histoire à la légende,* esp. 2:169–175, 3:89–153, 156–240; and Saxer, "Légende épique et légende hagiographique."

[131] See above, Chapter 4 at nn. 19–26.

reaching the ears of Charles, king of the Franks. This ruler might be Charles Martel, but is more probably Charlemagne; in any case, by approximately 1096, he was considered to have been the latter.[132] Summoned by Charles, the saint travels north. Arriving at an unidentified palace, Gilles finds the king in spiritual anguish, tormented by memory of a sin so heinous that he cannot bring himself to confess it even to the saint.[133] Then one day, as Gilles celebrates mass, an angel places on the altar a *carta* which describes the royal sin and proclaims that the king will be forgiven if he confesses to Saint Gilles. In secret, the saint urges Charles to confess, but the ruler, still fearful, will only commend himself to Gilles's prayers. Gilles then shows him the carta, and the king, admitting that "those things which were written were true," begs for Gilles's intercession. The saint then prays for Charles and admonishes him never to repeat his sin—which remains tantalizingly unnamed.[134]

This episode of Charlemagne's sin and its absolution was neither simply a hagiographic topos nor an already extant motif of the Charlemagne legend which Saint-Gilles appropriated. Rather, it seems to have appeared first in this *vita,* but probably resulted from the combination of two antecedent traditions. The idea that the glorious Charlemagne might have gravely sinned appeared in three ninth-century Latin texts from Reichenau that relate visions of this ruler in partial torment in the other world.[135] The motif of an unnamed sin (although not a king's) and its absolution through a *carta* that materializes during mass may have been borrowed from the *vita* of John the Almoner, a seventh-century patriarch of Alexandria, which apparently had been translated from the Greek by the eleventh century.[136] It is not clear

---

[132] Given the confusion that often prevailed concerning Charles Martel and Charlemagne, and the fact that some scholars have argued that Gilles really lived during the reign of the former, the *vita* may have intended the king to be Martel. Furthermore, Martel passed through the area in the 730s, burning Nîmes; see Rouche, *L'Aquitaine,* pp. 116–117. Still, there is an important factor which would hinder such an interpretation. In the *vita* of Saint Gilles, the Frankish king is clearly located in the north; he never comes to the region surrounding the monastery. Whichever Charles this was originally, by the later eleventh century he had clearly become Charlemagne. The first layer of the chronicle of Saint-Sernin of Toulouse (ca. 1096) asserts of the year in which Charlemagne died "eodem anno vivebat sanctus Aegidius" (*Chronicon sancti Saturnini Tolosae,* in *HL* 5:49, no. 10).

[133] Later Latin traditions identify Orléans as the site of the palace (and mass), but the *vita* does not. See the editors' remarks in Guillaume de Berneville, *La vie de saint Gilles par Guillaume de Berneville, poème du XIIe siècle,* ed. Gaston Paris and A. Bos (Paris, 1881), p. xiv.

[134] For the entire episode, see the three versions of the *Vita S. Aegidii: AB* 8 (1889): 118; *AASS* September 1:302–303; and Jones, *Saint Gilles,* pp. 108–109.

[135] See Baudoin de Gaiffier, "La légende de Charlemagne: Le péché de l'empereur et son pardon," in *Recueil de travaux offerts à M. Clovis Brunel,* 2 vols. (Paris, 1955), 1:490–503. In these texts there may be some conflation of Charlemagne with his grandfather, Charles Martel. According to ninth-century texts composed at Saint-Denis, the souls of other Frankish kings were seen to suffer postmortem punishment; on this tradition and its implications, see Beaune, *Naissance,* pp. 98–104.

[136] See de Gaiffier, "La légende de Charlemagne," p. 498.

how (and indeed if) Saint-Gilles had learned of the sinful king from the vision texts, or of the mass and *carta* from the *vita* of John the Almoner; it is evident, however, that the transformation of these two motifs into one episode involving Charlemagne first appeared in the *vita* of Gilles.

This *vita* was a wildly popular text, to judge from the large number of manuscripts still extant (approximately eighty), and the core of its appeal appears to have been Charlemagne's sin and its absolution by Gilles.[137] The "mass of Saint Gilles" rapidly became one of the most popular and constant episodes of the legendary Charlemagne's life. Vernacular texts celebrating Charlemagne—beginning with the Oxford manuscript (twelfth century) of the *Chanson de Roland*—often refer to the mass or associate Gilles in some way with this ruler.[138] The episode was so famous that by the late twelfth century, masters in Parisian schools began to debate how Saint Gilles could have been accorded the power to absolve an unconfessed sin.[139] Gilles and the mass were even assimilated into the iconography of the epic emperor. The mass was portrayed in a stone relief at Notre-Dame of Paris, as well as in one at Chartres. In the latter cathedral the absolution figured in the gleaming colors of the thirteenth-century Charlemagne window, crowning the story of the king.[140] Gilles, Charlemagne, and the *carta* also appeared in various frescoes, and perhaps even on sculpted capitals of southern pilgrimage churches.[141] The Germanic realm too knew of Gilles's relationship with Charlemagne; the official *vita* of the emperor devoted a chapter to the mass, and Saint Gilles and the *carta* adorned one panel of the massive reliquary in which Frederick II enshrined Charlemagne's relics in 1215.[142]

Saint Gilles then was a well-known figure of the imaginative landscape, coupled with the legendary king in text, image, and song. But as the motif of the mass of Saint Gilles was diffused and embellished in these sources, which did not emanate from the monastery known by the saint's name, its original meaning was turned inside out. Saint-Gilles had introduced King Charles into its legend—but only to hold him at arm's length from the foundation

[137] See the list of the manuscripts in Jones, *Saint Gilles*, pp. 95–98.

[138] Rita Lejeune, "Le péché de Charlemagne et la *Chanson de Roland*," in *Homenaje ofrecido a Dámaso Alonso . . .* 3 vols. (Madrid, 1961), 2:339–371. The passage in the Oxford manuscript of the *Chanson de Roland* (laisse 155; in Segre's edition, 1:197–198) is subject to different interpretations; Lejeune and others believe it refers to the mass.

[139] See de Gaiffier, "La Légende," p. 497, n. 4. This debate is reminiscent of the contemporaneous discussion about Charlemagne and Charroux's Foreskin in the same schools.

[140] Maines, "The Charlemagne Window."

[141] Germaine Demaux, "Une fresque inédite du XIIIe siècle en l'abbaye d'Aiguevive (Loire-et-Cher): Saint Gilles remettant à Charlemagne la 'chartre' apportée par un ange," in *La chanson de geste*, 1:279–292; Jacques Dubois, "Trois bas-reliefs du portail du Couronnement de Notre-Dame à Notre-Dame de Paris," *Cahiers de la Rotonde* 11, pp. 19–28; Rita Lejeune and Jacques Stiennon, *La légende de Roland dans l'art du Moyen Age*, 2 vols. (Brussels, 1966), 1:145–152.

[142] *Vita Karoli Magni* 1.14, in Rauschen, *Die Legende Karls des Grossen*, pp. 35–36. On the reliquary of Charlemagne, see Folz, *Le souvenir et la légende*, p. 282.

itself. Thus the *vita* of Gilles accords with what we have found in other very early legends: the king is distanced. This text, however, goes beyond creating a protective boundary between king and abbey. In the *vita*'s presentation of the mass, there is a definite suggestion that the ruler is subordinated to Gilles, for only with the saint's aid can Charlemagne be absolved. The roots of this negatively slanted representation of Charlemagne may lie in the abbey's protracted struggle with the bishops of Nîmes who, we shall see, claimed Charlemagne as the source of their lordship over the abbey.[143] The *vita*'s portrait of Charlemagne implicitly undermines these claims; instead of the king exercising power over the community, the community's patron saint exercises power over Charlemagne.

This potentially negative meaning of the mass in the *vita* was turned into a positive one by the vast majority of other sources that describe the episode. The mass became a celebration of Gilles's association with Charlemagne, a mark of the closeness between king and saint. Hence, by the twelfth century, as abbeys sought to bring the king closer to their origins, monastic foundation legends could even borrow the episode for that effect. Aniane, for example, replaced Gilles with Benedict, to whom Charlemagne, in gratitude for his absolution, then granted privileges and property.[144] The mass had become a trait of Charlemagne not dissimilar to the relic of the True Cross, or to the epic peers of France, and the ecclesiastical institution that claimed it could also thereby claim the king. When outsiders looked back at the history of Saint-Gilles, they even altered it accordingly. Some thirteenth-century writers in the Capetian circle omitted Flavius in their summaries of the life of Saint Gilles. Others explicitly made Charlemagne, precisely the Carolingian king the Rhône abbey had wished to distance from its founding saint and foundation, into the founder.[145]

The epic tradition also changed the significance of the association of Gilles and Charlemagne by, not surprisingly, focusing upon the king's sin rather than upon the saint and his power of absolution. Indeed, it was in vernacular epic that the nature of Charlemagne's unconfessed and unmentionable sin was first identified. By the twelfth century (if not already the eleventh), everyone knew that Charlemagne had committed incest with his sister, and that the fruit of their sin was Roland—for the *chansons de geste* and frescoes upon church walls alluded unmistakably to the forbidden union.[146]

---

[143] See below, Chapter 6 at nn. 47–48.

[144] Pseudo-Ardo Smaragdus, *Sermo sancti Ardonis, cognomento Smaragdi . . .* (*AASSosB* 4.1:225–226). This motif was also appropriated by an ecclesiastical community not located in southern France; see Folz, *Le souvenir et la légende*, pp. 478–479.

[145] See the relevant texts cited by the editors of Guillaume de Berneville's *La vie de saint Gilles*, pp. xci–xcv.

[146] See Lejeune, "Le péché," pp. 342–347. The name of Charlemagne's sister, Gisela according to Einhard (*Vita Karoli Magni*, in *Vie de Charlemagne*, p. 58), thus Gisle in the vernacular, raises some tantalizing possibilities about the association of Gilles and

This theme of the king's sexual sin, embroidered upon sometimes fantastically, became a constant of the vernacular Charlemagne legend.[147] And almost always Gilles appeared in some role.

The epic Charlemagne had thus gained as a companion this saint who performed the mass that saved the royal soul. This association indicated that yet another metamorphosis had occurred as the mass passed from Saint-Gilles's legend to other contexts. There is no evidence that in the *vita* the monks of Saint-Gilles imagined the king in epic garb, although their patron saint rapidly became a companion of just this version of Charlemagne. For these monks, Charlemagne was not the glorious warrior-king of the *chansons*, nor was he for those communities which claimed him as founder before the very late eleventh century.

The epic streak in the foundation legends of southern abbeys begins to appear only in the years around 1100, well after the era in which Gilles's *vita* was composed.[148] Previously, although monks were certainly aware of the Charlemagne of the *chansons*, they did not explicitly invoke him as a founder, nor celebrate their foundation in epic terms. Of those forgeries made in Charlemagne's name by the southern monasteries considered here, none that can be considered with any certainty to precede the later eleventh century endows the royal founder with any epic traits; at Saint-Polycarpe, Psalmodi, Gerri, La Réole, and Saint-Savin of Bigorre he is simply the illustrious Carolingian ruler who presides over the abbey's (re)foundation.[149]

This is not to suggest that before the later eleventh century the monks were deaf to the *chansons* already being sung in France and Spain; indeed, we know they were not.[150] But in the legends extant from this earlier period,

---

Charlemagne's sin. If the legend identifying the nature of the sin was already exant in the tenth and eleventh centuries, was Gilles associated with it because of the coincidence of names? Alternatively, did Gilles's name suggest that the sin might have to do with Charlemagne's sister of similar name? The homophony, however, exists only in the vernacular, Aegidius in no way recalling Gisela. Furthermore, only some of the texts relating to Charlemagne's sin name the sister Gisle (Lejeune, "Le péché," p. 366, n. 72; Guillaume de Berneville, *La vie de saint Gilles*, p. lxx; Adenet Le Roi, *Berte aux grans pieds*, laisse 130, p. 130); others call her Berte.

[147] See the texts cited by Lejeune, "Le péché," pp. 342–347; and by the editors of Guillaume de Berneville's *La vie de saint Gilles*, pp. lxxii–lxxxv.

[148] The same seems to be true for monastic legends from other regions. See Louis, *De l'histoire à la légende*, 2:105–106; and Saxer, "Légende épique et légende hagiographique," pp. 389–390.

[149] Saint-Polycarp: *MGH Diplomata Karolinorum* 1:458–460, no. 305. Psalmodi: *MGH Diplomata Karolinorum* 1:455–456, no. 303. Gerri: *MGH Diplomata Karolinorum* 1:464–466, nos. 308 and 309. La Réole: *Recueil des chartes de l'abbaye de Saint-Benoît-sur-Loire*, 1:39–43, no. 18; "Cartulaire du prieuré de Saint-Pierre de La Réole," pp. 144–145, no. 99. Saint-Savin: *Cartulaire de l'abbaye des Bénédictins de Saint-Savin*, p. 2, no. 2.

[150] The earliest written versions of the *chansons* are two fragmentary Latin texts, certainly from the hands of clerics or monks: the so-called Fragment of the Hague (ca. 980–1030) and the *Nota Emilianense* (third quarter of the eleventh century). See Menéndez Pidal, *La chanson*

although epic "facts" may appear, they can be stripped of their intrinsic significance. Such omission of the epic could characterize even secular descriptions. For example, when in approximately 1059 Berengar, viscount of Narbonne, recounted Charlemagne's foundation of that city's cathedral, the frame was an epic rather than a historical "event," and one of which the viscount was certainly aware: Charlemagne's taking of Narbonne in conjunction with his expedition to Spain.[151] Nonetheless, the viscount mentioned the king's Spanish campaign only obliquely and without epic overtones. Berengar merely states that Charlemagne had brought back from Spain the relics of Just and Pastor, intending to give them to the church he founded at Narbonne. Charlemagne's expedition is presented not as combat with the infidel but as a translation of relics pure and simple. His presence in the city and his Spanish campaign thus resolve into the endowment of the cathedral with relics rather than with an overtly epic genealogy.

By the late eleventh century, though, as we have seen in the case of Saint-Yrieix, ecclesiastical communities might appeal openly to the epic Charlemagne as founder. Indeed, by the early years of the twelfth century, many of the southern monasteries to claim Charlemagne as founder rendered him in epic tones. These legends were part of the process by which the *chansons* were captured in written form; the appearance of epic in such legends coincides approximately with the first manuscripts extant of *chansons de geste* celebrating secular subjects.[152] But the chronology of epic's assimilation into foundation legends has yet another layer of significance. With their borrowings from and transformations of the *chansons,* southern abbeys created a connection for themselves with the epic past and the Carolingian king. Thus these legends have much to tell us, not only about the nurturing of the Carolingian memory in the south, but also about the way in which these monasteries' image of themselves changed, becoming explicitly royal. This process of the penetration of epic into monastic written sources and its consequences can be traced most easily at Gellone, a monas-

---

de Roland, pp. 372–381, 384–447; and Martín Riquer, *Les chansons de geste françaises,* trans. I. Cluzel, 2d ed. (Paris, 1968), pp. 70–73, 134–138, 322–331.

[151] For the text: *HL* 5:500, no. 251 (see also Terpak's discussion of this text in her "Local Politics"). Narbonne was won back from the Muslims not by Charlemagne but by his father, Pippin the Short, in 759 and previously had been besieged by Charles Martel (737). By the twelfth century, the taking of Narbonne mentioned in the *Chanson de Roland* (laisse 268; in Segre's edition, 1:277–279) had been elaborated into its own *chanson,* that of Aymeric de Narbonne. See *Aymeri de Narbonne: Chanson de geste . . . ,* ed. Louis Demaison, 2 vols. (Paris, 1887). On the awareness of this epic tradition in the Narbonnais from the tenth century onward, see Lejeune, "La question de l'historicité," pp. 50–62.

[152] On the manuscripts of the *chansons,* see Joseph J. Duggan, "Die zwei 'Epochen' der *Chansons de geste,*" in *Epochenschwellen und Epochenstruktur im Diskurs der Literatur- und Sprachhistorie,* ed. Hans Ulrich Gumbrecht and Ursula Link-Heer (Frankfurt, 1985), pp. 389–408.

tery that probably had been founded by an authentic member of the Carolingian imperial aristocracy, Guillaume, appointed count of Toulouse by Charlemagne in the late eighth century.[153] Although Gellone celebrated primarily Guillaume, as the abbey increasingly framed him in epic terms as Charlemagne's famous peer, its legend came to encompass the king of the *chansons* as well.

In the eleventh century, there is no evidence that the monks of Gellone imagined an epic hero as their founder, although there are indications that Guillaume was increasingly important for the abbey and its conception of itself.[154] For, beginning in the first quarter of the eleventh century, Guillaume, mentioned as a saint in charters of donation since the 870s, began to lend his name to the abbey.[155] Charters came to refer to the abbey as Gellone or the "monastery of Saint Guillaume." By the mid-twelfth century the former appellation vanished, and the abbey would henceforth be called Saint-Guilhem-le-Désert.[156] Furthermore, starring in a spate of texts produced at Gellone in the eleventh century is Guillaume, to whom one of the abbey's altars was dedicated in 1076.[157]

In these eleventh-century texts, however, Guillaume appears in the garb of a conventional saint, without even an epic fillip. For example, in liturgical texts, he is described often as a confessor, once as "the soldier (*miles*) . . . of Christ, glorious and most saintly Guillaume"[158] and once, in the later eleventh century, as having spurned worldly honor for the company of angels— a reference to his monastic conversion?[159] So too the posthumous miracles for which Guillaume began to be celebrated in the early part of the century,

[153]   On the historical Guillaume, see among others Auzias, *L'Aquitaine*, pp. 34–38, 48–52; and Bouchard, "Family Structure," pp. 641–642, 653–655.

[154]   Saxer suggests that Guillaume's epic personality was the decisive factor in attracting eleventh-century pilgrims to the abbey, but I have found no evidence to support such a view; see his "Le culte et la légende hagiographique de Saint Guillaume."

[155]   On references to Guillaume in donations predating the eleventh century, see *Cartulaires des abbayes d'Aniane et de Gellone*, 1:15–16, 31–32, 99, nos. 12, 30, 113.

[156]   On the appearance of Saint-Guilhem as the abbey's name, see Pierre Tisset, *L'abbaye de Gellone au diocèse de Lodève des origines au XIIIe siècle* (Paris, 1933), pp. 129–130.

[157]   On the altar's dedication, see below: Chapter 6, n. 195.

[158]   "Mile . . . christi . . . gloriose Guilelme sanctissime" (Montpellier, BM 6, f. 135r). Folios 133r–135v have been added to this tenth-century manuscript; folio 135, written in an eleventh-century hand, was originally an isolated folio. An ex libris in a seventeenth-century hand identifies this manuscript as one of Aniane's (f. 1r); it may have been originally a Gellone manuscript, or it may be a sign that at Aniane too Guillaume was venerated in the eleventh century.

[159]   Montpellier, BM 18, f. 98r–v (the office for Guillaume's feast appears on ff. 97v–100r). Folios 1r–8v of this sacramentary are in various twelfth-century hands (prayers for the vigil of Guillaume's feast, ff. 7v–8r); folios 9r–200v are in eleventh-century hands. The office of Guillaume also appears in the eleventh-century Paris BN Latin 1877, f. 13r. See Saxer's discussion (unfortunately lacking exact references) of evidence of Guillaume's cult in liturgical manuscripts: "Le culte et la légende hagiographique de Saint Guillaume," pp. 568–570.

and which were recorded probably sometime before 1050, were nothing out of the hagiographic ordinary.[160] They tell us little more about Guillaume than that he worked wonders and hence attracted pilgrims to the abbey.

In the first section of Gellone's large and copiously decorated cartulary, compiled in approximately 1066, Guillaume is no more epic.[161] He appears in a manifest forgery: a document that purports to be a list composed in 807 (?) by Juliofredus, abbot of Gellone, enumerating the fiscal properties conceded by the "emperors" Charlemagne and Louis to "Saint Guillaume, prince of the marches of Gaul (*princeps Gallie finibus*)."[162] In this Carolingian past, Guillaume figures as a glorious prince, beneficiary of the emperors' largesse, and already a saint—but not as an epic hero (and not even explicitly the abbey's founder). Indeed, Juliofredus's supposed Carolingian connections receive almost more attention than Guillaume; the eschatocol characterizes the abbot most improbably as "a blood relative of emperor Charles."[163] Guillaume thus appears largely as a conduit, albeit an illustrious one, for donations made by Carolingian rulers to an abbey governed by a member of their family; and the frame is not their donations to Guillaume, but rather an abbot's testament.

By 1122, however, when a whole new layer was added to the cartulary, Guillaume had become the frame for the monastery's presentation of itself as an institution. The eleventh-century section of the cartulary had opened with a privilege of Alexander II; in the twelfth-century section, it is Guillaume, not a pope, who sets the tone. In this later section of the cartulary, the first document—a most significant position in any medieval manuscript—is Guillaume's charter of foundation, dated December 14, 804, but forged in either the very late eleventh or the early twelfth century.[164] This charter's importance is announced as well by its presentation. It

---

[160] *Historia miraculorum [S. Willemi ducis]* (*AASS* May 6:822–826). Saxer has proposed a date of 1030–1048 for the *miracula*, based on internal evidence (the extant manuscript is twelfth century); see his "Le culte et la légende hagiographique de Saint Guillaume," pp. 572–576.

[161] Cassan and Meynial's edition of this cartulary (*Cartulaires des abbayes d'Aniane et de Gellone*, vol. 1), while containing accurate transcriptions, is very misleading; it changes the order of the documents, and ignores not only changes of hand but also codicological facts that alter one's reading of the manuscript. Here I will refer to the texts as they are edited and will also offer my own analysis of the manuscript: AD Hérault 5.H.8.

[162] AD Hérault 5.H.8, f. 3v; *Cartulaires des abbayes d'Aniane et de Gellone*, 1:5–6, no. 4. These properties are actually estates held by the abbey in the eleventh rather than the ninth century; hence the text assures them a Carolingian history. For critical discussions of this document, see Pückert, *Aniane und Gellone*, pp. 145–148; Tisset, *L'abbaye de Gellone*, pp. 56–59. Tisset argues that the text may have been forged even before 1066 but that it shows signs of having been reworked in the heat of the later eleventh-century conflict with Aniane. The only authentic document in which Juliofredus appears is a charter of 926; see *Cartulaires des abbayes d'Aniane et de Gellone*, 1:15–16, no. 12.

[163] See Pückert, *Aniane und Gellone*, p. 148; and Tisset, *L'abbaye de Gellone*, p. 58.

[164] The charter is the first entry in the table of contents that heads this section of the cartulary: AD Hérault 5.H.8, f. 59v; *Cartulaires des abbayes d'Aniane et de Gellone*, 1:135, no. 157.

does not begin in the space left blank below the end of the table of contents, but at the top of the next folio. Furthermore, its first letter, the *I* of *In nomine dei*, is nine lines tall and decorated with interlacing highlighted with a yellow wash.

Not only is Guillaume thus emphasized, but he has also acquired a new nature. The monks had evidently begun to inflect the portrait of their founder to make him accord with the epic Guillaume, the hero who according to the *chansons* had driven the Muslims from southern France and married the lovely infidel princess, Guiborc. According to the charter, Guillaume gives various properties to this monastery, which he constructed at Charlemagne's behest (*in causa domni et senioris mei Karoli iussi*). Here Guillaume, seconded by Charlemagne, plays the leading role in Gellone's Carolingian past—now an epic past. For written in highlighted capitals which catch the reader's eye are the names of the relatives Count Guillaume wishes the foundation to benefit spiritually. At the end of the list are his second wife, "Guitburg," and his "nephew Bertrand." Surely these are the converted Saracen princess and the hotheaded Bertrand who appear at Guillaume's side in the *chansons de geste*.

Epic permeates even more markedly the *vita* of Guillaume composed at Gellone during the same era: that is, in the first quarter of the twelfth century.[165] This text opens with a rhetorical question that immediately introduces the hero of the *chansons:* Is there any kingdom, province, city, or people that does not celebrate Guillaume's deeds of prowess against the Saracens and in the service of glorious King Charles? Then, although the prologue insists that the *vita's* subject will not be Guillaume's famous battles against the "barbarians" but rather his "spiritual deeds" (*spiritualia gesta*), the first third of the text describes just those epic events.[166]

But when the monks came to imagine their Guillaume in epic garb, they did not simply translate the *chansons* into Latin. While this *vita* flourishes its saintly subject's epic nature, it very distinctly associates Guillaume *not* with the king whom he most often serves in the *chanson* cycle, Louis the Pious, but with Charlemagne, the ruler to whom the epic hero devoted his early years.[167] In the *vita*, Guillaume is characterized as having supported

---

Guillaume's charter: AD Hérault 5.H.8, ff. 64r–v (it exactly fills both sides of the folio); *Cartulaires des abbayes d'Aniane et de Gellone*, 1:144–146, no. 160. For the codicological reasons explained in Appendix 2 below, this charter no longer immediately follows the table of contents, although it did originally. For critical analyses of the charter, see Pückert, *Aniane und Gellone*, pp. 124–145; and Tisset, *L'abbaye de Gellone*, pp. 42–56.

[165] *Vita [S. Willelmi ducis]* (*AASS* May 6:811–820).

[166] The *vita* is so epic that scholars of the *chansons* have long cited it as an evidence for the development of various elements of the Guillaume cycle: that is, that it already included a version of the *Prise d'Orange*.

[167] Charlemagne appears in the *chansons* that describe Guillaume's youth; otherwise the king is Louis. Elsewhere Guillaume appears as one of Charlemagne's peers, accompanying him, for example, to Jerusalem in the *Voyage de Charlemagne*.

Charlemagne like silver columns that carry the golden seat of a throne, as always having been ready to fight for this king, and as having favored among all the monasteries in Aquitaine those which Charlemagne had built or restored.[168] Charlemagne's grief at seeing Guillaume depart for the monastery is described in lengthy detail, underlining the king's affection for him. Finally, when Guillaume endows Gellone, he asks Charlemagne to confirm the foundation; Louis plays only the minor role we have often seen ascribed to him, granting to the completed foundation various fiscal properties—and only as king of Aquitaine, not yet as emperor.[169] Gellone wished to be connected to the king who was most important in southern monastic memory, and it shaped the epic Guillaume accordingly.

In turn, matters of great concern to Gellone in the early twelfth century—a heated conflict with the abbey of Aniane, which was trying to enforce its claims to Gellone as a daughter and hence a subject monastery—shaped the epic image of Guillaume as it was constructed in at least one *chanson*. The *Moniage Guillaume* (which scholars agree was sung in its extant form by the third quarter of the twelfth century) relates how Guillaume became a monk at Aniane but found its community ungenerous and mean-spirited.[170] The monks of Aniane, for their part, were appalled by Guillaume's enormous appetite and tried various ruses to rid themselves of the voracious novice. After a violent confrontation in which Guillaume killed the prior, the hero left the monastery and established himself in a hermitage which the *chanson* identifies as Saint-Guilhem-le-Désert. Here we find not antimonastic gibes pure and simple, but a distinctly anti-Aniane bias—and a transposition of the conflict between the two monasteries. This is not to suggest that there was no version of the *Moniage* before the two monasteries clashed in the second half of the eleventh century, but rather that the *Moniage* as we know it, characterizing Aniane in terms that probably echoed the sentiments of the monks of Gellone, was shaped by this conflict.[171] Thus, once Gellone had explicitly adopted the Guillaume of the *chansons,* the abbey's experiences inflected the epic image of this hero, now its patron saint.

Sometime in the very late eleventh or early twelfth century, then, Gellone began to paint its founder and foundation in epic terms, adapting and changing the hero of the *chansons* to fit its own situation and to integrate itself into the "poetic history" of the glorious Charlemagne.[172] Here we see a

---

[168]   *Vita [S. Willelmi ducis]* (*AASS* May 6:802).

[169]   *Vita [S. Willelmi ducis]* (*AASS* May 6:807).

[170]   *Les deux rédactions en vers du Moniage Guillaume,* vol. 1; on the identification of the abbey to which Guillaume first repaired as Aniane, see the editor's comments, 2:102–104.

[171]   When the cleric Gerold of Avranches related to William the Conqueror's men edifying and inspiring tales of holy knights, Guillaume's conversion was one of his subjects. Orderic Vitalis, *Ecclesiastical History of Orderic Vitalis,* ed. Marjorie Chibnall, 6 vols. (Oxford, 1969–1980), 3:217. This may be a reference to an extant version of the *Moniage.*

[172]   By the seventeenth century at least, the abbey was in possession of a thirteenth-

reworking of the abbey's past in order to make it even more Carolingian similar to the way in which, as we have seen, relics in this period were increasingly given Carolingian connotations. Indeed, at Gellone the connection to the world of the *chansons* was made at least in part through the relics that reposed in the abbey: the fragment of the Cross given by Charlemagne to Guillaume as a pledge of friendship and, equally important, the saintly body of Guillaume, now recognized as one of Charlemagne's heroic peers. It is no accident that in 1138, Guillaume's relics were elevated, making the presence of the Carolingian hero at the monastery manifest.[173] The monks trumpeted these relics as those of the epic Guillaume. In a sermon composed for the saint's feast day no later than the mid-twelfth century, the writer reminds his audience that Guillaume was the most distinguished among all the counts of Emperor Charlemagne's court, a valiant opponent of the Saracens and, finally, the monk whose body now reposed in the abbey.[174] Pilgrims too knew by now that at Gellone they would find the holy remains of Guillaume of the *chansons*. The so-called *Pilgrim's Guide* (ca. 1139) tells those on their way to Compostela to stop and venerate the relics of this "most valiant knight . . . [who] subjugated Nîmes . . . and Orange."[175]

In other southern legends dating from approximately this same period, monasteries wove themselves into the world of the *chansons* in a similar fashion. Let me begin with a monastery from that stronghold of resistance to the Frankish kings, Gascony. The abbey of Saint-Jean of Sorde, actually founded sometime in the late tenth century, had appropriated in no uncertain terms the epic Charlemagne as its founder by the first half of the twelfth

century illuminated manuscript executed in the north of France and containing almost the entire cycle of *chansons* about Guillaume. See Guillaume Catel, *Histoire des comtes de Tolose* (Toulouse, 1623), p. 50. The manuscript is today in Paris (BN Français 774). On the history and contents of this manuscript, see Paulin Paris, *Les manuscrits françois de la Bibliothèque du roi* . . . , 7 vols. (Paris, 1836—1848), 6:135–144, no. 7186; and Hermann Suchier, "Le manuscrit de Guillaume d'Orange anciennement conservé à Saint-Guilhem du Désert," *Romania* 21 (1873): 335–336.

[173] The *elevatio* or *translatio* of 1138 is described in a martyrology of Gellone: Paris, BN Latin 12773, p. 394. Cf. the slightly different text, also from one of Gellone's martyrologies, in *AASSosB* 4.1:88. Mabillon also reproduces the inscription on a lead shrine (found in a stone sarcophagus at Gellone in 1679) which describes the *elevatio;* see *AASSosB* 4.2:556.

[174] "[E]nim sicut vestra dilectio bene novit cum cunctorum in aula serenissimi imperatoris caroli comitum clarior haberetur, seculi dignitatibus relictis, habitu veri monachi decentissime compertus [?] religionis sacre ad quibusdam peritis imbutus in hac se carcerali custodia cunctis suis diebus domino christo vero regi inclusit militaturus ut qui diu in seculo luerat commoratus atque cum sarracenis fortiter proliatus devictis superatisque hostibus." This sermon, probably composed at Gellone, follows Guillaume's *vita* and precedes the *miracula* in a mid-twelfth-century manuscript from the abbey: Montpellier, BM 16, ff. 205r–v and 207r–v (there is no f. 206), here 205v.

[175] *Guide du pèlerin de Saint-Jacques de Compostelle: Texte latin du XIIe siècle, édité et traduit en français d'après des manuscrits de Compostelle et de Ripoll,* ed. Jeanne Vielliard (Paris, 1984), pp. 46, 48.

century.[176] The earliest datable evidence of this tradition is a charter from approximately 1120 in which William IX of Aquitaine confirmed the abbey's estates. These lands, he specified, had been granted by Charlemagne, who had endowed Sorde on his way to fight the infidel in Spain.[177] A forged diploma (probably composed in the first half of the twelfth century), dated at Dax in the fateful year 778, recounts the circumstances of this foundation.[178] Charlemagne solemnly decides to found Sorde in order to gain divine grace and Saint John's help in his upcoming battles with the Muslims.[179] The monastery explicitly is made a part of the expedition, disastrous but glorious, that would culminate at Roncevaux.

The epic integration is even more striking in another forged and even more colorful diploma, probably composed somewhat later in the twelfth century.[180] Charlemagne and Archbishop Turpin establish Sorde and then proceed to Spain. After various victories, Charlemagne brings back the bodies of the dead for burial, choosing Sorde as Turpin's eternal resting place. Here the monks were clearly imagining the king not in terms of the Latin Pseudo-Turpin, but rather in terms of the *chansons* they must have heard sung, perhaps even in front of their own abbey. According to the Pseudo-Turpin, the archbishop survives Roncevaux and even Charlemagne's death and is then himself buried at Vienne.[181] But in the *Chanson de Roland*, Turpin dies a martyr's death along with Roland and Olivier, and is buried with them by Charlemagne at the church of Saint-Romain of Blaye (near Bordeaux).[182] The monks of Sorde simply altered the *chanson* slightly in order to claim for themselves the body of the archbishop who had consecrated their church. By means of the body—or rather the relics—of the bellicose archbishop, the abbey becomes a memorial to the epic Spanish campaign in which its foundation participated.

By the late twelfth century there are hints that other Gascon ecclesiastical communities created for themselves a concrete connection to epic, claiming not only to have been founded by Charlemagne or one of his peers, but also to enshrine the body of a fallen peer brought back by the epic king

---

[176] The earliest mention of Sorde is a charter, circa 975, recording a donation made by Guillaume-Sanche, duke of Gascony: *Cartulaire de l'abbaye de Saint-Jean de Sorde . . .* , pp. iv–v. The abbey had been founded perhaps under the aegis of Saint-Michel of Pessan, a monastery in the diocese of Auch; see below, Chapter 6, n. 197.

[177] *Cartulaire de l'abbaye de Saint-Jean de Sorde . . .* , pp. 65–66, no. 81.

[178] *MGH Diplomata Karolinorum* 1:314–315, no. 230.

[179] Charlemagne also endows the monastery with extensive fiscal lands and exemption from all episcopal authority.

[180] *MGH Diplomata Karolinorum* 1:567–568.

[181] *Historia Karoli Magni*, pp. 213, 215, 217.

[182] *Chanson de Roland*, laisse 268 (in Segre's edition, 1:278). The Latin *Pilgrim's Guide* of the later twelfth century mentions the presence at Blaye only of Roland's body, placing Olivier's body at Belin (forty kilometers south of Bordeaux) and not mentioning where Turpin rests: *Guide du pèlerin*, p. 80.

upon his return from Spain. Unfortunately, we can only view these traditions from the outside, that is from the perspective of twelfth-century texts not composed at the churches themselves but that surely reflect local traditions in some fashion: the *Chanson de Roland,* the *Pilgrim's Guide,* and the Pseudo-Turpin. According to these three texts, clustered around Bordeaux were churches that appropriated for themselves a place in the epic landscape by claiming the bodies of its heroes. Each text relates how the sorrowing Charlemagne brought back Roland's body from Roncevaux and laid it in a tomb at Saint-Romain of Blaye, a chapter of canons supposedly founded by the hero himself; the Pseudo-Turpin designates the church of Belin and the cemetery of Saint-Seurin of Bordeaux as the sacrosanct resting places of numerous other epic warriors.[183] In the same passage, the Pseudo-Turpin relates that many of Charlemagne's heroes were also buried at the cemetery of Les Aliscamps of Arles. But with the exception of this Provençal site, the claims to epic bodies made by non-southern churches are ignored by the *Chanson de Roland,* the *Pilgrim's Guide,* and the Pseudo-Turpin. [184] Accordingly, the twelfth-century audience of these very popular texts would have received the impression that the heroes' relics were concentrated south of the Loire. Perhaps this impression would not have been false; the texts' depiction of meridional churches as shrines for the heroes hints that southern ecclesiastical communities in particular cultivated a connection with the epic Charlemagne.

Two characteristics of this evident intertwining of foundation and epic are of particular relevance here. First, the epic streak in foundation legends appears in the same period when relics were increasingly given Carolingian connotations. Most often, in fact, an abbey was elevated as epic not so much through the circumstances of its foundation as through the relics that reposed there. These bodies articulated the Carolingian connection even more explicitly than the relics emblematic of Charlemagne, such as the True Cross and the Holy Foreskin. These latter had a double resonance, symbolizing Christ but recalling Charlemagne. But the bodies of the epic heroes intrinsically and primarily represented the epic world and its ruler. These "holy martyrs," as the *Pilgrim's Guide* calls them, dying in the service of the paradigmatic crusading Christian king, thus represented a new layer of

---

[183] On the tradition at Blaye, see the references in note 182 above; *Historia Karoli magni,* p. 213; and Camille Jullian, "La tombe de Roland à Blaye," *Romania* 25 (1903): 161–173. For Belin and Saint-Seurin of Bordeaux, see *Historia Karoli Magni,* pp. 215, 217. The Charlemagne legend at Saint-Seurin also appears in two forged charters which I have been unable to consult: AD Gironde G.1142 and G.1145 (noted but not edited in *Cartulaire de l'église collégiale Saint-Seurin de Bordeaux,* ed. Jean-Auguste Brutails [Bordeaux, 1897], p. lxix–lxx).

[184] By 1080, for example, Saint-Faron of Meaux claimed to have the body of Ogier. See *Conversio Otgarii duplex* (*MGH SS* 5:203–206); and Ferdinand Lot, "La légende d'Ogier le Danois," in his *Etudes sur les légendes épiques françaises* (Paris, 1970), pp. 280–292.

patron saints with a new significance.[185] Saint John the Baptist remained the
nominal patron of Sorde, as did Saint Romain for Blaye; but by the twelfth
century Turpin and Roland, present in their tombs as John and Romain
were in their reliquaries, had become just as much a part of these churches'
definition of themselves. Hence, the presence of their remains adumbrated
a change in the way these religious communities viewed and presented
themselves. By the twelfth century, Charlemagne and figures intrinsically
associated with him had begun to rival and displace traditional saints in
southern legends.

This brings me to a second point about the importance of epic in the
legends. I would propose that by claiming these new-style patron saints,
monasteries began to imagine themselves as part of—indeed, as the center
of—the royal Frankish past celebrated in the *chansons,* and hence as part of
the French realm. The twelfth-century legends only hint at this process. But
by the mid-thirteenth century it had become explicit. Now monasteries not
only associated their foundation with epic figures but envisioned it in epic
terms, as we see at the abbey of Lagrasse.

Already by at least the very early thirteenth century, Lagrasse considered
Charlemagne its founder; a document specifying the contributions of each
priory toward the rebuilding of the abbey church (ca. 1216) lauds Lagrasse
as Charlemagne's construction.[186] Several decades later, this legend was
flamboyantly articulated and expanded in two long narrative texts: one in
Provençal, known as the *Philomena,* and the other in Latin, called the *Gesta
Karoli Magni ad Carcassonam et Narbonam* (both extant by 1255 and the latter
after 1237).[187] Apart from language, these two texts are essentially identical;
in each, epic—and Charlemagne—create monastic space, and monastic
space becomes the setting for the actions of the king and his peers.

In its striking prologue the *Gesta Karoli Magni* announces itself to be
Charlemagne's own official history, recounting events that the king himself
wished to be remembered and not forgotten.[188] Lagrasse's imaginatively
remembered origins thus become Charlemagne's memory of his deeds at

---

[185] *Guide du pèlerin,* p. 80. On Roland as martyr, see also Nichols, *Romanesque Signs,* pp.
134–147, 192–203.
[186] "[E]cclesia, quam recolende memorie Karolus Imperator inclitus construxit in honore gloriosae Virginis Mariae et Apostolorum Petri et Andreae, eamque bonis ditavit plurimis
et dotavit." Here I cite from the copy of this document in the only manuscript of it I have
identified, the seventeenth-century annotated compilation of Dom Etienne Du Laura: *Sinopsis rerum memorabilium Crassensis Beatae Mariae ad Orbionem fluvium Carcassonensis diocesis in
Occitania Abbatia . . . ,* Paris, Bibliothèque Mazarine 3388, pp. 109–111 (here 109), with a
discussion of dating at pp. 434–435. Du Laura's date of 1216 is accepted by Claudine
Pailhes, "La crise de la communauté monastique de Lagrasse au XIIIe siècle," in *Sous la Règle
de saint Benoît: Structures monastiques et sociétés en France du Moyen Age à l'époque moderne (Abbaye
bénédictine Sainte-Marie de Paris 23–25 octobre 1980)* (Geneva, 1982), p. 268, n. 17.
[187] For facing edition, see the *Gesta Karoli Magni.*
[188] *Gesta Karoli Magni,* pp. 4, 6.

Narbonne and Carcassonne: epic battles and the foundation of Lagrasse, itself made epic.[189] For the text interweaves the tale of Lagrasse's foundation with a version of the *chanson* relating the king's taking of Narbonne.[190] These two strands of the *Gesta Karoli Magni*, the battle for Narbonne and the foundation of Lagrasse, are spliced together in part by the narrative technique. Charlemagne does not merely appear at the abbey before and after his military exploits, as he does in Sorde's legend. Rather, the action unfolds simultaneously; both text and king move back and forth between battles and building.

But the abbey and its denizens also participate actively in epic events. At Charlemagne's wish, a "good knight" is consecrated as abbot of Lagrasse, and then Archbishop Turpin selects as monks a hundred knights and squires.[191] These warriors in monks' robes form one of the valiant contingents in the siege of Narbonne. Bellowing as a battle cry the name of their abbey, they cleave Muslims with as much relish—and success—as any of Charlemagne's peers.[192] Here the usual topos of the monastic life as service in the spiritual army of God has been transformed into monastic life as active duty in Charlemagne's epic army.[193] Surely this imaginative transposition reveals how through epic, Lagrasse envisioned itself as part of royal history.

This integration is underlined in the way that the *Gesta Karoli Magni* presents the abbey itself, its patrimony, and the surrounding landscape as epic, royal space. As we have seen, Charlemagne and his heroes design the abbey's architectural plan and then help in the actual construction.[194] Furthermore, after the fall of Narbonne, the Muslim queen Oriunda, like so many other Saracen princesses in epic, wishes to convert and marry a Christian knight. At her express request, the baptism and marriage occur at Lagrasse, and afterward she makes rich offerings to the monastery.[195] Subsequently Charlemagne invests Aymeric with Narbonne and commands him to become Lagrasse's vassal; Aymeric humbly does homage to the abbot.[196]

---

[189] According to the prologue, the *Gesta Karoli Magni*'s textual history is that of the *chansons:* the text had been found in the abbey's archives and then translated into the appropriate language. The *chansons* too often begin by announcing that the *jongleur* is using as his source an old text found at the abbey of Saint-Denis. At Lagrasse, the same trope is used; but now this abbey, not Saint-Denis, is the repository of epic memory and the center of royal textual commemoration.

[190] The monks, however, did not follow exactly the version of this *chanson* as it is extant. See *Aymeri de Narbonne*, 1:ccxxxiii–ccxl and 22–50.

[191] *Gesta Karoli Magni*, pp. 74, 94.

[192] *Gesta Karoli Magni*, pp. 140, 142, 144, 210.

[193] The abbey itself becomes an appropriate setting for its epic inhabitants. Charlemagne eventually transforms it into a castle, complete with towers and moat; see *Gesta Karoli Magni*, pp. 42, 94.

[194] See above, Chapter 2 at nn. 98–100.

[195] *Gesta Karoli Magni*, pp. 182, 196, 198.

[196] *Gesta Karoli Magni*, pp. 198, 200.

The abbey is thus a focal point for the patronage of the epic figures—and in turn extends to them its own benefaction, spiritual and feudal.

Even more strikingly, the heroes' actions impregnate the landscape centered on the monastery with epic meaning. The text abounds in place names, which are almost always given an epic resonance as the site of a battle, the location of an ecclesiastical foundation by Charlemagne or one of his peers, or the burial place of a fallen hero.[197] The king and other heroes grant to Lagrasse many of these places as well as a tenth of their battle spoils, thus constituting the monastery's patrimony as above all epic and royal.[198] This royal endowment spills into the era of the *Gesta Karoli Magni*'s composition, for many of these places represented churches or estates that in the thirteenth century Lagrasse either owned or was trying to claim.[199]

Charlemagne and his companions thus usurp a role assigned to saints in the earlier legends: the physical delineation and organization of monastic space. As they do so, they also assume the saints' function of rendering it sacred. For example, they found a series of chapels and monasteries as memorials on the site of an epic battle or as shrines to the fallen heroes.[200] Lagrasse's territory, then, consists in sites consecrated by the blood of the epic martyrs and their permanent presence in the form of their holy relics. Lagrasse itself—the narrative, spatial, and epic center of the text—is consecrated with such relics; for the patriarch of Jerusalem, the abbot of Mont-Saint-Michel, and the bishop of Chartres along with various knights who, like these prelates, had fallen in battle in Charlemagne's service, were enterred with much solemnity at the abbey.[201] These new sacred figures eclipse the abbey's patron, the Virgin, whose association with Lagrasse had been famed in the eleventh century even among Muslims.[202] In the *Gesta Karoli Magni*, the Virgin appears essentially as a link between the abbey and the battling Charlemagne (who invokes her as his protector).[203] She plays no

---

[197] E.g., *Gesta Karoli Magni*, p. 72. For more detail, see above, Chapter 2 at nn. 127–131.

[198] *Gesta Karoli Magni*, pp. 38, 40, 44, 46, 48, 144.

[199] See below, Chapter 6 at nn. 310–311.

[200] The abbot of Saint-Denis was buried at Les Palais which he had founded; see *Gesta Karoli Magni*, p. 72. Roland founded Saint-André of Sorède as a resting place for Augier of Normandy (p. 48). Later, the bishop of Chartres and two monks, one from Saint-Germain-des-Prés and one from Saint-Denis, all of whom fell in battle with Marsilius, were buried at Sorède as well (p. 92).

[201] *Gesta Karoli Magni*, pp. 70, 72, 180, 196.

[202] On the eleventh-century pilgrimage to the Virgin at Lagrasse, see François Clément, "Le pèlerinage à Lagrasse, d'après une source arabe du XIe siècle," *Annales du Midi* 100 (1988): 489–495. I am certainly not suggesting that Charlemagne and his companions replaced traditional saintly patrons in other aspects of monastic life, textual or devotional. Devotion to the Virgin remained important at Lagrasse as late as the seventeenth century; see Dom Jean Trichaud's description of the veneration accorded the statue of the Virgin in his *Chronicon seu historia regalis Abbatiae Beatae Mariae de Crassa . . . ;* (Paris, BN Latin 12857, pp. 99–100).

[203] *Gesta Karoli Magni*, pp. 50, 52.

role in the foundation, neither appearing in a vision to the king nor indicating in any way the sacredness of the future monastery's site.

The king and the prelates and princes attached to him had thus become the legitimating and sanctifying principles structuring the monastery's image of its origins—no local saints, no trace (never mind embroidery) of Nibridius, the member of Benedict of Aniane's flock who had actually founded the monastery in the late eighth century and then became a not insignificant archbishop of Narbonne. Nor do the seven hermits, borrowed from the legend of the Seven Sleepers, represent full partners in the foundation. They are revelations of the site's sanctity, rather than participants in the abbey's establishment.

Lagrasse's legend represents the culmination of a process already incipient in twelfth-century texts invoking the epic Charlemagne. In the late twelfth-century layer of Sorde's legend, not only did Charlemagne found the abbey but "he, with the archbishop of Reims, Turpin, sealed the sacred altars with his own hand (*propria manu sigillavit*)."[204] Charlemagne's role as a sanctifier of space is underlined in no uncertain terms, for here he usurps what we have seen to be an episcopal prerogative: the right of consecration. But by the thirteenth century, as Lagrasse's legend shows, Charlemagne did not have to officiate at a ritual in order to consecrate the landscape. No mediation is necessary; the monarch's very presence has become sanctifying.

In the process, Charlemagne himself was crowned with a halo—not visible perhaps to modern historians focusing on developments in the Capetian center, but certainly apparent to the southern monks. By the thirteenth century, there is evidence of liturgical commemoration of this king at at least one southern abbey: Gellone. In a martyrology of this period and from this monastery, Charlemagne appears on January 28, his feast day.[205] He (as well as Louis the Pious) may even have been commemorated at this abbey in the eleventh century.[206] By 1351 at Lagrasse, moreover, masses were celebrated

---

[204] In the last entry of the abbey's thirteenth-century cartulary there is a reference to this legendary consecration, although here it is Pope Leo (given a garbled genealogy making him partly native to southern France) rather than Charlemagne who aids Turpin: "[M]iloleo fuit patre Stampensis inter italiam et apuliam, ubi est sanctus angelus matre vero petragoricensis de sancto asterio [et] de sancto leone. In consecratione sordensis ecclesie fuerunt hi apostolicus miloleo Turpinus Remensis archiepiscopus." *Cartulaire de l'abbaye de Saint-Jean de de Sorde . . .*, p. 158, no. 184 (with some minor changes per my transcription from the manuscript, Paris, BN Latin n.a. 182, f. 50v).

[205] "V kal. febr. (. . .) Item in gallis apud aquisgrani palacium transitus domini karoli piissimi imperatoris" (Montpellier, BM 13, f. 3v). For a consideration of Charlemagne in some earlier necrologies, see Schneidmüller, *Karolingische Tradition*, pp. 15–23. On the importance of liturgical celebrations of kings as potential indications of cult, see Robert Folz, *Les saints rois du Moyen Age en Occident (VIe–XIIIe siècles)*, Subsidia Hagiographica, 68 (Brussels, 1984), pp. 173–175.

[206] In the late seventeenth century, Estiennot copied entries for these two kings from a martyrology of Gellone which he dated as eleventh century: Paris, BN Latin 12733, pp. 394, 397.

daily in honor of Charlemagne, styled "founder" of the monastery—and, at some point before the seventeenth century, apparently with papal dispensation, these *suffragia* gave place to cult (*cultus*).[207] When Charles V confirmed Lagrasse's privileges in 1376, he not only mentioned the abbey's miraculous consecration but referred to its founder as "Saint Charlemagne."[208] Here Charles V speaks, not the abbey, and it was he who had introduced Charlemagne's cult into France.[209] Nonetheless, we have seen Charlemagne's stature in this monastery's legend, and by the sixteenth century, (at least) he figured in its liturgical calendar.[210] Charles V's "Saint Charlemagne" surely accorded with the image of the king presented by Lagrasse itself in the *Gesta Karoli Magni*.

Indeed, the official "Saint Charlemagne" appeared in the south at the same moment as he did in Paris—that is, in the fourteenth century—but not at the initiative of a king seeking to legitimate himself. In 1345 Charlemagne's official cult was introduced in Girona, a Catalonian city that in our period had more links with the monasteries of the south, particularly with Lagrasse, than did the Capetian capital. But why would the bishop of Girona have taken such a bold step if in southern imagination Charlemagne was not already considered saintly?[211] Surely the southern foundation legends played no small role in creating the ambience that made the bishop's action possible.

The liturgical office for the saint-king composed and used in Girona in the fourteenth century[212] bears no resemblance to the Office of Charlemagne created at Aachen and used in the Parisian commemoration of the king.[213] Instead, it presents a Charlemagne already familiar to us, even though he has assumed the title of saint. The king has taken Narbonne and decides to liberate Saracen-held Girona. After a vision in which the Virgin, Saint James, and Saint Andrew appear and assure him they will be at his side in battle, Charlemagne processes through the Pyrenees toward

---

[207] In 1677, Dom Trichaud copied the section relevant to Charlemagne of the *Rotulus Moysis* (1351), containing the customs of the monastery, and then remarked: "Desiit tandem mos ille ut licuit (probante suprema divi petri sede) non amplius suffragia sed cultum religiosissimo imperatori adhibere." See his *Chronicon* (Paris, BN Latin 12857, pp. 124–125). For a more complete copy of the *Rotulus Moysis*, see *Cartulaire de l'ancien diocèse et de l'arrondissement administratif de Carcassonne*, ed. A. Mahul, 7 vols. (1857–1882), 2:331.

[208] This privilege (dated at Senlis, 1376) is edited in *Cartulaire de l'ancien diocèse*, 2:351.

[209] See above at n. 21.

[210] Charlemagne's *obit* appears in a printed breviary of 1523: *Cartulaire de l'ancien diocèse*, 2:437.

[211] Bishops often recognized figures who had already been made into saints by local veneration.

[212] On this text and the introduction of the cult to Girona, see Jules Coulet, *Etude sur l'Office de Girone en l'honneur de saint Charlemagne*, Publications de la Société pour l'Étude des Langues Romanes, 20 (Montpellier, 1907). The text of the Office is edited on pp. 57–59.

[213] On the importation of the Office of Aachen for use in Paris, see Folz, "Aspects du culte liturgique."

Girona, stopping to defeat various Muslims and to found various churches. In the last lesson, he arrives at Girona and founds its cathedral on a site designated by a heavenly sign. Charlemagne's salient characteristic in the southern liturgy is thus that he founds churches in conjunction with his epic expeditions. He is the Charlemagne also celebrated at Lagrasse and other meridional monasteries, a saintly Charlemagne indigenous to the south. Indeed, the most recent editor of the Office of Girona argues convincingly that it was based not only on various Pyrenean legends emanating from the relevant churches themselves and on the epic tradition of Charlemagne's capture of Girona, but also explicitly on Lagrasse's *Gesta Karoli Magni*.[214] The sanctity of Charlemagne in France was created not only by the Capetian king's importation of the cult first officially established in Germany by Frederick Barbarossa, but also by churches far from the actual royal center but intent on fashioning one for themselves.

By the mid-thirteenth century, Frankish kings had come to dominate southern monasteries' imaginatively remembered origins. Without completely abandoning the region's Roman heritage, these abbeys anchored themselves imaginatively in a newer stratum of political authority: one represented by the Frankish rulers. In their desire to place their origins under the aegis of these kings, however, the abbeys remained in a sense as conservative as the south had been earlier in remembering itself as Roman. The rulers embellished and exalted in the southern legends represented the primordial layers of Frankish authority: Clovis and the early Carolingians. These rulers, not the later Carolingians or members of aristocratic dynasties, came to symbolize the new antiquity with which southern monasteries wished to clothe their origins.

These particular Frankish kings were selected in part because they were located in the more distant and hence more authoritative past. Other criteria, however, revealing the profound significance of the meridional monastic acceptance of the Frankish past, also informed this choice. Rulers such as Charles the Bald, glorious perhaps but a king of the north, and those such as the Pippins of Aquitaine or those would-be kings, Hunald and Waïfre, who represented the south as a separate but subkingdom, were rejected in monastic memory in favor of kings who had incorporated the south (even if violently) into a larger realm: Clovis, Pippin the Short, Charlemagne (even the Romanized Hadrian and Flavius). These latter kings permitted an imaginative exchange in which the monarch's symbolic role as center communicated itself to the monastery, and the monastery became part of the political entity represented by the monarch.

The growing desire to integrate the abbey with royal history took the form

214 Coulet, *Etude sur l'Office de Girone*, pp. 138–158.

of a displacement of traditional saints in foundation in favor of royal figures, and a metamorphosis of the king from distant patron to active and saintly presence. In the earlier legends, kings participated in foundations as material partners while an ecclesiastic or saintly figure played the more significant consecrating role. By the twelfth century, though, saints as founders often yielded to the Frankish kings. In the process, the king was elevated and clothed with qualities of the figures he had replaced; as the royal presence became sanctifying in foundation, the king became saintly.

Distanced in earlier legends from the highly charged moments of origins, the kings were now fully embraced in foundation's significance. To be sure, Gregory VII had thundered that less than seven secular rulers had ever achieved sanity; he had also wondered rhetorically whether kings or emperors had ever been known to cure the blind or revive the dead, and whether altars were ever dedicated to their names or masses said in their honor.[215] But in this age postdating the official divorce between kingship and priesthood occasioned by the Investiture Controversy, southern monasteries nonetheless increasingly imagined the monarch as the authority and consecrating presence that sanctified their origins.[216] This unofficial yet potent process of sanctification coincided with—but did not reflect—contemporaneous French kings' projection of images both of themselves (Louis VII for example, shaped himself in a saintly mold) and of the Carollingian kings they had begun to claim as their ancestors.[217] Indeed, this sanctification of legendary monarchs by southern monasteries suggests that an important element of later Capetian and Valois ideology, the notion of the sacred royal lineage and of the "roi très chrétien," was not exclusively a royal creation, but one to which the political "periphery" had contributed significantly.[218]

Why and in what context did this longing for the king, so apparent in the imaginative landscape of southern foundation legends, arise? And why did it become so marked beginning at the very end of the eleventh century? A combination of phenomena—both those which are general to this era and

[215] Gregory VII, *Epistolae* 8.21, in *Das Register Gregors VII.*, ed. Erich Caspar, MGH Epistolae Selectae 2 (Berlin, 1920), pp. 558–559.

[216] As Bernhard Töpfer points out, the effect of the Investiture Controversy on the image of the king was much less pronounced in France than in Germany. See his "Tendenzen zur Entsakralisierung der Herrscherwurde in der Zeit des Investiturstreiten," *Jahrbuch für Geschichte des Feudalismus* 6 (1982): 163–171.

[217] Unlike Louis VII and Louis IX (who was a saint because of his life), the royal saintly figures discussed here were celebrated not so much for their virtues as for their consecrating presence.

[218] For a thorough consideration of the idea of the sacred royal lineage, see Beaune, *Naissance*, pp. 216–225; also see Le Goff's brief remarks in *Histoire de la France*, p. 125. On the "roi très chrétien," see Joseph R. Strayer, "France: The Holy Land, the Chosen People, and the Most Christian King," in *Action and Conviction in Early Modern France: Essays in Memory of E. H. Harbison*, ed. T. E. Rabb and J. E. Siegel (Princeton, 1969), pp. 3–16.

those which are specific to these abbeys' situation—illuminates this predilection for royal founders and the forms it took. Here let me stress the
words "combination" and "illuminates." In relating imaginative changes and
constructions to their context, I do not mean to situate determinative causes
only in the latter. The causes for imaginative developments must be sought
within as well as outside the imagination. External factors illuminate rather
than explain monastic imaginative memory. Furthermore, no one answer,
no one factor suffices as an explanation; all these factors together wove the
context for the legends.

First of all, the legends and their embroidery of kings past arose in the
context of a broad renascence of historical writing. This desire to recuperate
and record the past characterized the twelfth century and, scholars increasingly argue, the eleventh as well.[219] The two facets of Charlemagne explored
here—the king of relics and the king of epics—are related to certain man-
ifestations of this flourishing curiosity about the past.

In the eleventh and twelfth centuries, during the remarkable welling of
devotion to saints' relics that had begun circa 1000, churches increasingly
felt the need to authenticate and identify the relics they possessed or invented. In this period, the practice of placing in reliquaries a document
(an authentic) that named the enclosed relics became increasingly common.[220] Furthermore, hagiographic texts such as *vitae* and *miracula* proliferated.[221] These had among their many purposes that of attaching to relics a
genealogy and a history that continued into the present. Associating relics
with Charlemagne had a similar effect: authenticating and identifying, his-
toricizing, and rooting in specificity.

This sort of historicization, however, does not help us understand the
abbeys' specific predilection for Frankish kings. The other type of historicization in which the southern monastic creation of Charlemagne partakes is
more telling. The monasteries' adoption and reshaping of the king of the
epics were contemporaneous with the production of the earliest extant
manuscripts of the *chansons de geste*.[222] Both phenomena—that is, the capturing in written form of oral epic and the coloration of written monastic
sources by these songs—relate to the general penetration of folkloric and
oral material into written sources in the twelfth century. But surely they
attest also to an awakening of interest in the past and, in turn, a desire to fix
it in writing. Moreover, this epic past, largely imagined but becoming in-

---

[219] Historians have generally attributed the efflorescence of historical writing to the
twelfth century "Renaissance," but more recent work is showing that the past was already of
vital concern by the eleventh century. See Landes, *Relics, Apocalypse,* and Geary, *Phantoms of
Remembrance.*

[220] Hermann-Mascard, *Les reliques,* pp. 120–124.

[221] Head, *Hagiography and the Cult of Saints,* pp. 58–60, 72, 285–287.

[222] On the chronological distribution of the manuscripts of the *chansons,* sec Duggan,
"Die zwei 'Epochen' der *Chansons de geste,*" pp. 389–408.

creasingly authoritative as it entered the world of written sources, was itself
royal and Carolingian. The southern legends thus function within a broader
context of renewed interest in the textual recording of the past and, more
specifically, within that of capturing on parchment the celebration in song
of the gilded Carolingian era.

The use of epic has another significance as well, one that coincides with
the meaning of other traits of the monastic creation of the royal past.
Invoking epic, abbeys created a connection between themselves and the
king, and expressed a certain loyalty to him.[223] Equally, the Carolingian
relics, both those of traditional saintly patrons given by Charlemagne and
those of the epic martyrs, incarnated the king's presence and placed the
monastery under his protection. In their selection of kings, abbeys chose
those who represented kingdoms larger than the south. Thus, in their legends, monasteries imagined themselves as under the protective wing of the
king who embodied the larger Frankish realm of the past. But did these
abbeys therefore imagine themselves as part of the Capetian present?

After all, the fashioning of images of a royal past does not necessarily
translate into acceptance of the present ruler.[224] As we have seen, the invocation of the Carolingians in the dating clauses of late tenth- and early
eleventh-century southern French charters indicated a rejection, rather
than an embrace, of the rulers actually on the throne: the Capetians. Furthermore, the Flemish aristocracy of the thirteenth century shaped
Charlemagne as a symbol of resistance to the Capetians, and the same king
appeared in the twelfth-century genealogies of many northern French noble
lineages that were busy making themselves as independent from royal control as possible.[225]

The situation of the northern aristocratic lineages was, however, quite
different from that of the southern abbeys; the latter were not competing
with the king for political power. Moreover, claims to royal foundation by an
abbey meant something quite different from aristocratic claims to a royal
ancestor. In the latter instance, loyalty to or even association with the king of
the present was hardly hinted at; rather, the royal ancestor heightened the

[223]   On how epic might create a sense of loyalty to the king, see Andreas Bomba, *Chansons
de geste und französisches Nationalbewusstsein im Mittelalter: Sprachliche Analysen der Epen des
Wilhelmzyklus* (Stuttgart, 1987). For a different but related argument, see D. Boutet, "Les
chansons de geste et l'affermissement du pouvoir royal (1100–1250)," *Annales E.S.C.* 37
(1982): 3–14.
[224]   See Janelle Greenberg's demonstration of how the legendary image of Edward the
Confessor was invoked as justification for the deposition of Charles I of England: "The
Confessor's Laws and the Radical Face of the Ancient Constitution," *English Historical Review*
104 (1989): 611–637.
[225]   On the Flemish aristocracy, see Spiegel, "*Pseudo-Turpin,*" pp. 207–223, and her *Romancing the Past*, pp. 55–98. On aristocratic genealogies and the use of the Carolingian past,
see for example Farmer, *Communities of Saint Martin*, pp. 85–88. The Saxons fashioned
Charlemagne as a symbol of resistance to German monarchs; see Folz, *Le souvenir et la légende*,
pp. 115–120.

prestige of the lineage, making it into a potential rival of the present ruler. Royal foundation, on the other hand, implied that an abbey's relationship with the contemporaneous king was the same intimate one it had once had with the (legendary) king of the past. For status as a royal abbey was permanent.[226] Thus, the king of the present inherited the role of the abbey's patron and protector. By claiming the king of the past, abbeys could embrace the king of the present.

There are indications that many southern abbeys capitalized to just that end on the royal pasts they had created for themselves: they used their legends to gain the Capetian king's protection. When in the twelfth century Louis VII extended a tentative royal presence into the south, he not only became embroiled in the conflict between the counts of Barcelona and those of Toulouse, but he took numerous bishoprics and monasteries into his protection—a measure that perhaps had a more lasting effect.[227] Among these churches were some of the monasteries we have seen busily building in legend an image of the king as founder and protector: Saint-Gilles (1163), Gellone (1162), Mozac (1169), and La Règle (1175).[228] Furthermore, Philip Augustus took Sarlat (1181) and probably Figeac under his protection, and he reconfirmed Louis's privilege for La Règle.[229] Not only did these abbeys actively petition the king for his protection (at least according to the texts), but in each of Louis's privileges the king indicates that he acts upon the precedent of earlier kings who had played the role of patron at the abbey in question. Perhaps Louis was alluding to these monasteries' legendary royal origins—a possibility underlined by his privilege for La Règle. There Louis states that he reconfirms the abbey's possession of all that "our predecessor, King Pippin" had given the community of nuns. Surely this is a reference to the monastery's legendary diploma of Pippin the Short.[230] Legend thus became the basis for a relationship with the contemporaneous king.

Similarly, the monks of Moissac, invoking their abbey's legendary royal foundation, appealed to Philip Augustus to remedy the effects of their bad treatment at the hands of the counts of Toulouse.[231] While there is no indication of any royal response to this desperate plea, the abbots readily did homage to the king after the capture of the town of Moissac by Simon of Montfort in 1212. Furthermore, upon Raymond VII's death (1249), as had

---

[226] See below at nn. 245–247.

[227] On Louis VII, see Pacaut, *Louis VII.*

[228] Gellone: *GC* 6, instr. 282–283. La Règle: an eighteenth-century copy in Paris, BN Latin 9194, p. 191. Mozac: *GC* 2, instr. 114–116. Saint-Gilles: *HL* 5:1279–1280, no. 657.

[229] For editions of Philip Augustus's privileges for La Règle, Figeac (classified by the editors as an "acte suspect"), and Sarlat, see *Recueil des actes de Philippe Auguste roi de France,* ed. H.-François Delaborde et al., 4 vols. (Paris, 1916–1989), 1:32–33, 199–200, 246–247, nos. 22, 167, 203.

[230] Paris, BN Latin 9194, p. 191. If Louis had been referring here to a diploma of Pippin I of Aquitaine, would he have considered this Pippin his predecessor?

[231] See above, Chapter 4 at nn. 77–79.

been stipulated by the Treaty of Paris (1229), Alfonse of Poitiers, Louis IX's brother and Raymond's son-in-law, became count of Toulouse and so held certain rights over Moissac.[232] After Alfonse died childless and the county of Toulouse became a royal *sénéchaussée,* Philip III and his successors issued a series of privileges for the abbey—some of which intoned solemnly that Moissac had been "founded by our predecessors, the kings of France."[233]

Moissac was not the only abbey to express its loyalty to the Capetians when they definitively arrived south of the Loire in the thirteenth century. Lagrasse did so most spectacularly, although for years it had been in the *mouvance* of the count-kings of Catalonia and retained even into the thirteenth century links with the kings of Aragon.[234] In 1226, this monastery's abbot, Benedict, urged Carcassonne to surrender to Louis VIII, and subsequently received the city consuls' pledges of submission and fidelity to king and pope.[235] More strikingly, under Abbot Bernard Imbert, at whose behest the *Gesta Karoli Magni* was written, a series of spectacular royal forgeries was fabricated at Lagrasse.[236] In these texts, the abbey claimed as its own a huge number of estates and churches, some of which had indeed been part of its patrimony and were then infeudated in the later twelfth century, as with so much monastic property everywhere in the south.[237] Lagrasse did so in the name of the king—for the vast majority of these forgeries purported to be royal privileges and donations. Many of the properties thus claimed are those which simultaneously were rendered royal in the *Gesta Karoli Magni.*[238] These diplomatic forgeries masqueraded not only under the name of the legendary king, Charlemagne, but also under those of the actual kings, Louis VIII and Louis IX.[239] The authoritative king was no longer just Carolingian and imagined, but Capetian and concrete.[240]

---

[232] Marion, "L'abbaye de Moissac," p. 126.

[233] See above, Chapter 3, n. 55, for these texts.

[234] On Lagrasse's links with Barcelona and the kings of Aragon, see for example Paris, BN Doat 66, ff. 221r–222v, 271r–272v, 273r–274r, 419–420v, 425r–427v; Du Laura, *Sinopsis rerum memorabilium,* Paris, Bibliothèque Mazarine 3388, ff. 125–126; and Mahul, *Cartulaire de l'ancien diocèse,* 2:231, 277.

[235] *HL* 8:846–847, no. 275.iv.

[236] See Pailhes, "La crise de la communauté monastique," pp. 265–276.

[237] On the circumstances of these forgeries, see below, Chapter 6 at nn. 310–319.

[238] Given the vast number of place names, both in these forgeries and in the *Gesta Karoli Magni,* it is impossible for reasons of space to provide here the details of how these claims coincide. Lagrasse also claimed many of these same properties in two other forgeries of the thirteenth century: one in the name of Gelasius II and the other in that of Bernard-Ato, count of Carcassonne. For these latter texts, see the forthcoming edition of Lagrasse's charters by Elisabeth Magnou-Nortier (who kindly provided me with copies of the texts in question).

[239] On forgeries in the name of Capetian kings and Charlemagne, see Pailhes, "La crise," and Magnou-Nortier's forthcoming edition of Lagrasse's charters.

[240] Interestingly, at Saint-Jean d'Angély, probably sometime in the twelfth century, a document was forged in Hugh Capet's name relating to the abbey's "refoundation"; see *Cartulaire de Saint-Jean d'Angély,* 1:22–25, no. 5.

The process by which the southern monasteries created an image of the king in their foundation legends thus had a resonance in reality. When the Capetians arrived, they found abbeys that, by nurturing the memory of Frankish rulers of the past, had created an image of the king. Was it the Capetians themselves who had provoked this imaginative process? Was the expanding role of kings in these legends a ripple caused by the ever widening circle that was actual royal authority? In the twelfth century, the Capetians began to extend their power beyond the Ile-de-France and to reappear south of Loire. Louis VI undertook several forays into the Auvergne in the 1120s, and Louis VII, after his marriage with Eleanor of Aquitaine, made a ceremonial entry into the land he had thus acquired. Even after his divorce, Louis VII continued to intervene in southern affairs and, as we have seen, to issue diplomas for southern ecclesiastical establishments. By 1154, through the marriage of his sister Constance to Raymond V of Toulouse, Louis had gained a southern ally and, eventually, a vassal. Philip Augustus would continue this pattern of the extension of royal power southward.

Perhaps, then, these kings cast their growing shadows upon the monasteries' images of themselves. I am reluctant, however, to postulate an exact correlation. Although the royal coloring of the legends deepened considerably during this period, it did not do so in the second half of the twelfth century but rather beginning in the last years of the eleventh—a period in which the Capetian king enjoyed relatively little power south of the Loire. Already in the early eleventh century, Charlemagne dominated Charroux's presentation of its origins. In other words, the legendary appeal to the Frankish kings was not precipitated by, but instead preceded, the augmentation of actual royal power. Furthermore, it is unclear whether the Capetians had established themselves so decisively in the south by the late twelfth century that these monasteries would necessarily have considered the king to be continuously or effectively present.[241] Although perhaps inflected by the increasing but still fleeting royal sojourns in the south, the monastic image of the king expressed a desire for the absent ruler rather than a celebration of one who dominated the constellation of political forces in the south. Hence, Lagrasse had not embroidered a Saint Charlemagne with the

[241] Basing his judgment on an examination of the dating of charters by Capetian regnal years in the later twelfth century, Charles Higounet concludes that the Midi had not lost the sentiment that it belonged to an "entité supérieure, confuse . . . qui était le royaume de France dont le Capétien était bien le roi" ("a larger, though perhaps indistinct, entity . . . which was the kingdom of France whose king was certainly the Capetian"); see his "Problèmes du Midi au temps de Philippe Auguste," in *La France de Philippe Auguste: Le temps des mutations: Actes du colloque international organisé par le C.N.R.S. (Paris, 29 septembre–4 octobre 1980)*, ed. Robert-Henri Bautier (Paris, 1982), pp. 311–320. Paul Ourliac, however, expresses some doubt as to how authentically recognized the Capetians were. Frequent misspellings of their names in charters would seem to indicate that they were not terribly familiar to the scribes and, thus, perhaps not to southern society in general. See his comments on Higounet's paper (p. 321).

intention of welcoming the Capetian king any more than La Règle had created Pippin the Short in order to win Louis VII's protection.

Yet in the constellation of southern forces there were royal figures besides the Capetians. Did they perhaps influence the legends more? The Catalonian count-kings ruled the counties of Carcassonne and Razès by the later eleventh century and, in the twelfth century, having gained Provence and other southern territories through a most advantageous marriage, they challenged the count of Toulouse. But it is unlikely that the monasteries that elaborated royally colored legends before 1162 would have conceived of the Catalonians as royal. Before that date, although they were by 1137 the effective rulers of the kingdom of Aragon, the Catalonians styled themselves counts and not count-kings.[242] These actual kings were present in the second half of the twelfth century, but legendary ones had emerged well before that period.

This chronological disparity is evident in the case of the other royal dynasty that appeared in the twelfth-century south: the Angevin kings. Henry II, having gained the title of Duke of Aquitaine and Gascony through his marriage to Eleanor, not only established his rule there, but also, as Louis VII had done, forcefully pressed his wife's dynastic claims to Toulouse. Nonetheless, again for chronological reasons, we cannot too closely tie the origins of the king's role in southern legends to Henry's presence. Yet another factor limits the possible effect of the Angevins upon these legends: they ruled their domains in the south not as the monarchs they were, but rather under various princely titles. For example, Henry II, a powerful and impressive king, was certainly recognized as such by monasteries such as Charroux, which accepted his protection in 1177 after he had acquired the county of La Marche. Although the first sentence of the document relating Henry's reception of Charroux into "his hand" calls him in no uncertain terms "king of the English," Henry was not a king in or of Aquitaine; he was its duke. The text makes Henry's dual status clear. When establishing the tenor of his relationship with the abbey, the documetn invokes "his predecessors, the counts of Poitiers."[243] Henry and his successors would be seen as kings, but as kings of another people. In Aquitaine and Gascony, they were princely vassals of the Capetian king.

[242] On the transition from count-king to king, see Percy Ernst Schramm, "Die Entstehung eines Doppelreiches: Die Vereinigung von Aragon und Barcelona durch Ramón Berenguer IV. (1137–1162)," in *Vom Mittelalter zur Neuzeit: Zum 65. Geburtstag von Heinrich Sproemberg*, ed. Helmut Kretzschmer (Berlin, 1956), pp. 19–50. On the various stages of the expansion of Catalonian power north of the Pyrenees, see among others the following: Thomas N. Bisson, *The Medieval Crown of Aragon: A Short History* (Oxford, 1986), pp. 26–27, 35–40; Charles Higounet, "Un grand chapitre de l'histoire du XIIe siècle: La rivalité des maisons de Toulouse et de Barcelone pour la prépondérance méridionale," in *Mélanges d'histoire du Moyen Age dédiés à la mémoire de Louis Halphen* (Paris, 1951), pp. 313–322; Poly, *La Provence*, pp. 320–340.

[243] *Chartes et documents pour servir à l'histoire de l'abbaye de Charroux*, pp. 164–165, no. 47.

Thus southern abbeys certainly were more exposed to actual kings in the twelfth century than they had been in the eleventh. But their legendary embellishment of royal founders was inflected by, rather than engendered by, political action at the royal level. This is not to deny the importance of the sociopolitical context. Once again, though, I would like to shift the emphasis from "center" to "periphery"—in this case, from the actual kings to the local, southern, and immediate sociopolitical context in which these abbeys were embedded. For the reasons behind the creation of the Frankish royal image lay in the needs of the abbeys themselves.

Kings and, by the eleventh century at least, the pope functioned as the juridical protectors of monastic property and, most particularly, liberty. This latter was the component of monastic identity that expressly delineated an abbey's position in the web of actual and local social relations.[244] Juridically speaking, the highest degree of liberty in the Middle Ages was not freedom from all subjection and constraint, but rather dependence on only king and pope, the highest human powers.[245] Such liberty was permanent, at least *en principe*. Abbeys were aware that kings and popes were not supposed to allow those monasteries which were peculiarly theirs to pass from their hands.[246] Or, to reverse the terms, as southern monasteries did: once a free or royal abbey, always a free or royal abbey.[247] Hence, legends that intertwined the acquisition of liberty with the abbey's origins—as did legends of royal foundation—had a peculiar force. Such legends enshrined liberty, an inalienable property of the abbey from the time it was granted, as an original, intrinsic characteristic of the monastic community. The legitimating aura of legendary royal origins combined with the juridical concept of *libertas* to form a bulwark intended to preserve the abbey's independence.

[244] See above, Chapter 1 at nn. 87–97, for a discussion of other aspects of the technical definition of monastic liberty.

[245] See Gerd Tellenbach's succint analysis of the medieval concept of liberty, in *Church, State and Christian Society at the Time of the Investiture Contest,* trans. R. F. Bennett (Oxford, 1948).

[246] King or pope could appoint a third party as guardian. On the inalienability of royal monasteries, see Ferdinand Lot and Robert Fawtier, *Histoire des institutions françaises au Moyen Age,* 3 vols. (Paris, 1957–1962), 3:244–246; and Semmler, "Traditio und Königsschutz," pp. 1–33. The privilege Louis VII granted in 1165 to Mozac specifies: "monasterium . . . sub regia protectione tali ratione et lege quod extra manum nostram mittere vel cuiquam feudatario dare neque nobis neque heredibus nostris liceat" (*GC* 2, instr. cols. 114–116). Also see the privilege granted by this same ruler in 1170 to Saint-Gilles: *HL* 5:1279–1280, no. 657. For striking evidence (though from a northern French monastery) that abbeys were very aware of this principle of inalienability, see Odo of Saint-Maur, *Vie de Bouchard le vénérable . . . ,* ed. Charles Bourel de la Roncière (Paris, 1892), p. 8. By the twelfth century, those abbeys belonging "specially to Rome" could be subject to no other power; see Schreiber, *Kurie und Kloster,* 1:47–56.

[247] *Abbatia libera* was a term increasingly used in the eleventh century (at least in Germany) for those abbeys given to the pope; see Hirsch, *Die Klosterimmunität,* p. 26. Although royal abbeys were granted *libertas,* this term does not seem to have been applied to them.

Inherent in the abbeys' predilection for royal founders was a thirst for this liberty—but also for something rather different: freedom from any sort of earthly subjection.[248] Certainly an ecclesiastical community might express this desire in the language of liberty assured by king and pope, that is, by interpreting such liberty as actual institutional independence. But pope and king were inclined to conceive of privileges of liberty as documents indicating a monastery's acceptance of their lordship—and they often acted on this inclination.[249] Southern abbeys, however, unlike their northern counterparts, did not have to worry that by using king and pope as their legendary guarantee, they might tempt the contemporaneous incarnations of those powers to transform protection or *tuitio* into effective domination.[250] The Capetian kings were too far away, their power in the south too theoretical. Furthermore, the eleventh- and twelfth-century popes were equally distant and in no position to establish themselves as lords of southern abbeys.[251] These monasteries could safely conjure up the image of the king in their legends because the liberty with which they thereby garbed their origins implied only theoretical dependence on distant protectors—and hence effective freedom.

The legends crowned the king's juridical value as guarantor of monastic liberty with their suggestion of his sanctity. A king with an aura of saintliness would be that much more an awesome protector. Imagined as a commanding and sanctifying presence, the legendary king (like a patron saint) could be invoked in the face of those powers which actively sought to dominate the abbey, to diminish its liberty, and to extinguish its identity.[252] It is no coincidence that this image of the king burgeoned in southern legends beginning

[248] Herbert Grundmann nicely demonstrates the existence of this urgent desire for a freedom that did not imply any subjection whatsoever: "Freiheit als religiöses, politisches und persönliches Postulat im Mittlelater," *Historische Zeitschrift* 183 (1957); 23–53.

[249] On the importance of distinguishing between the perspective of abbeys and that of the protector, see the compelling evidence in Hirsch, *Die Klosterimmunität*, pp. 36–39 (here papal abbeys). Cf. Grundmann's discussion, in "Freiheit."

[250] For northern abbeys, see the case of the canons of Saint-Martin of Tours who, geographically close to the king and juridically under his control, risked experiencing his "protection" as domination and who thus tailored their writings accordingly. Sharon Farmer, "Ambivalent Resistance: Martinian Responses to Capetian/Dionysian Hegemonies in the Twelfth and Thirteenth Centuries," paper presented at the *Maiestas* conference, Paris, June 1990. See also the remarks of Koziol, *Begging Pardon*, p. 207.

[251] Accordingly, from the point of view of pope and king, the actual privileges they granted southern monasteries in this period may have represented solicitations of the support of the abbey in question as much as they did extensions of royal/papal dominion. Certain popes, embroiled in controversy with emperors and with rival claimants to the papal throne, came to this region in the late eleventh and early twelfth century and sought the vital support of its powerful abbeys, alliances ratified by privileges. Louis VII himself traced out such a network of southern ecclesiastical allies with his privileges of the 1160s and 1170s; see Pacaut's analysis in his *Louis VII*.

[252] Here I am suggesting only an analogy between the way a legendary royal founder or a patron saint could be invoked in the abbey's defense. I am not proposing that these royal patrons defended their monasteries with miracles as did patron saints.

in the late eleventh or very early twelfth century. In exactly this period, meridional monasteries were increasingly involved in conflicts with potential lords who were not so far away as the king—but rather ominously present. Local contexts, not royal initiative, thus shaped the southern construction of the legendary monarch.

III

CONTEXTS

6

Community and Conflict

O ne of the most common matrices for the formation and invocation of legend was conflict, either protracted or short and sharp, between abbeys and individuals, groups, or institutions that, unlike king or pope, wielded effective power in the south and therefore menaced monastic liberty and identity. In these not infrequently violent clashes, the appeal to legendary origins and founders, particularly to a king or to grants of liberty by a pope, could figure prominently, even decisively. For the legendary founders (royal and apostolic), while symbolically connecting the abbey to sources of larger authority, also implicitly or even explicitly situated it in the network of immediate social relations. Through the image of its founder and foundation, a monastery might ward off and exclude powerful local agents while simultaneously projecting counterclaims: that is pretensions to increasing its own sphere of domination, to subsuming the surrounding landscape within its identity. But in situations of conflict and stress—that is, challenges to monastic identity—imaginative memory functioned above all in an oppositional sense, constructing the community as separate, as different.[1]

Often the sources unmistakably imply such a connection between legend and conflict. Sometimes, however, a legend and a conflict that appear in contemporaneous sources are linked in no explicit fashion. Synchronicity alone does not imply a causal nexus. In such cases, nonetheless, the conflict

---

[1] On the relation between threats to identity and the formation and invocation of imagined pasts (albeit in the context of ethnic and national rather than monastic identity), see Cohen, *The Symbolic Construction;* and Smith, *The Ethnic Origins of Nations,* pp. 37–41, 51–56, 74–76, 175–176. On "oppositional" identity formation (in the context of nationalism), see Alter, *Nationalismus,* pp. 24–26; and, more extensively, Sahlins, *Boundaries,* esp. pp. 269–274.

is significant for the interpretation of the legend. Revealing the atmosphere in which the legend was engendered, the tension tells of the abbey's concerns and interests—factors that surely shaped the legend in some degree. Alternatively, a monastery could perceive and interpret conflict from the vantage point of its already extant legend, conforming its actions accordingly. In either case, the legend became articulated as a structural principle reinforcing the abbey's identity. This self-definition might be subject to further elaboration in similar circumstances; different layers of one monastery's legend could reflect different phases of a conflict or even clashes with different opponents. These disparate, seemingly contradictory elements and versions form a unity, however, defining the abbey in the face of other powerful social actors, deflecting any possible claims of domination.

To be sure, this was not a fixed equation, nor a Pavlovian reaction. Not every such conflict in this period stimulated the production of foundation legends, nor did conflict inform every one of the legends under consideration here. In the cases of conflict, though, the interplay between past and present characteristic of imaginative memory is at its most patent and most tangible—and thus is most easily perceived. Such instances illuminate how legends actually figured in the lives of these monastic communities, how critical they could be as statements of identity at the local level. Furthermore, although legends could and did arise for other reasons, these other impulses lie along a spectrum of which conflict occupies a large segment: the desire to create and assure identity, and to order social relations.[2]

My consideration of this relationship between conflict and legend will focus on those instances in which the independence, relative or absolute, of the monastic community was at stake. Certainly other matters, particularly competing claims to property or to relics, could generate friction between abbeys and other social actors. Yet only infrequently do such tensions appear to be the primary cause of resort to legend among southern monasteries: Saint-Sever was impelled to make its legend concrete in the context of a property dispute with Sainte-Croix of Bordeaux; the archbishopric of Auch defended its possession of various churches through its legendary founder, Clovis; and Issoire's legend bears traces of a dispute with Mozac over the possession of the relics of Saint Austremonius.[3] Perhaps the rela-

---

[2] See below, Conclusion at nn. 1–10.

[3] The quarrel in the late eleventh and then again in the late twelfth century between Issoire and Mozac over the possession of the relics of Saint Austremonius caused Mozac to heighten the role that Pippin the Short played in the relics' translation to this abbey (which became a royal refoundation). At Issoire, possession of the relics became even more intimately intertwined with its foundation legend. See the *Additamentum de reliquiis S. Austremonii* (*AASS* November 1:80–82) (incomplete; complete in Paris BN n.a Françaises 7455, ff. 319r–322r). On these two legends, see above: Chapter 4 at nn. 124–146; and below at nn. 240–243. Also see Fournier, "Saint Austremoine," pp. 454–456, 461, 463. Saint-Sever disputed the possession of the church of Soulac with Sainte-Croix of Bordeaux. The course of this conflict was directly reflected in the structure of Saint-Sever's legend, although the disputed

tively small number of such cases indicates that threats to an abbey's independence menaced its identity more fundamentally than did those to its relics or property.

In any case, these other types of conflict have an essential similarity to those in which liberty was at issue. When elements of identity—whether the saintly patron, the material patrimony, or liberty—were threatened, abbeys might turn to their imaginatively remembered origins, thus affirming and asserting what was menaced. As they did so, monasteries most often painted integral portraits of themselves, not singling out the menaced element. The whole might stand for that part, or one element for another. In its legend, for example, Saint-Sever stressed liberty as much if not more than it did property; if its liberty was assured, so was its property. Similarly, in legendary debates over liberty and domination, relics and property might figure prominently, becoming metaphors to express the integrity of the threatened abbey.

Embodying these threats to monastic identity and liberty, and thus provoking the invocation and crystallization of images of the imaginatively remembered past, were certain social actors. Bishops and the secular nobility could fall into this category. This is hardly surprising. After all, as we have seen, certain motifs used in legends very explicitly hem in episcopal and secular power by delineating the abbey as a place of divinely sanctioned immunity.[4] Furthermore, the legends rarely celebrate bishops and lay members of the aristocracy as founders, usually relegating them to secondary roles at best.

But there was another enemy, perhaps the one seen by the abbeys as the most dangerous. The legends make no explicit statements about this social agent—but silences, we shall find, are as important as explicit statements in monasteries' imaginative construction and coloring of themselves. This shadowy enemy was domination by other abbeys, particularly (although not exclusively) those federating monasteries, such as Cluny, too often seen by historians as shining white knights that liberated religious communities in distress by benevolently taking them under their wing.[5] The southern leg-

---

church is not mentioned specifically. For example, a trial by battle which appears in the sources relevant to the conflict, is translated in the legend into both the comital founder's battle against the Normans and a trial by cold water (the latter related to his possession of a church). Furthermore, in the legend, the founder very consciously endows Saint-Sever with liberty from any archiepiscopal or episcopal control (the archbishop of Bordeaux was Sainte-Croix's champion). For the relevant texts, see "Documents transcrits," pp. 113–126; (also see Elisabeth Magnou-Nortier, "L'affaire de l'église de Soulac d'après les actes faux contenus dans le Beatus [XIe s.]," *Saint-Sever*, pp. 99–111. On Auch, see above, Chapter 4 at nn. 66–67.

[4] See above, Chapter 2.

[5] Among the historians who see Cluniac reforms as fostering the liberty of the reformed community, see Cowdrey, *The Cluniacs*, esp. pp. 108–112. Also see Lemarignier, "L'exemption monastique," pp. 322–323; and Lemarignier, "Political and Monastic Structures in France at the End of the Tenth and the Beginning of the Eleventh Century," in *Lordship and*

ends make it clear that monasteries resisted such incorporation. Abbeys saw (correctly) that subordination to another monastery implied just as much a loss of liberty as did subjection to a lay or episcopal lord.

One caveat, though. We must not envision a state of permanent warfare between the monasteries, on the one hand, and bishops, the secular aristocracy, and competing abbeys on the other. These social agents were bound together in various sorts of relations whose tenor depended on specific circumstances. Inimical relations could metamorphose into amity, return to the opposite pole, and then swing back again in a repetitive oscillation.[6] My focus here, however, will be the negative pole rather than the positive in order to trace how, threatened by the expanding lordship of these agents (particularly in the later eleventh century and the first half of the next), southern monasteries constructed themselves as sacred places sheltered by their legendary origins.

Saint-Gilles and the Three Enemies

I will begin by considering in some detail a series of profuse, rich, and explicit sources from one abbey—Saint-Gilles—that displays all three monastic enemies in their full colors. What we observe there will illuminate the situations of abbeys whose sparser sources relate tales of tension more obscurely. For although most monasteries faced one or two enemies instead of this triple menace, the traits of the clashes between Saint-Gilles and its antagonists—the bishops of Nîmes, the counts of Toulouse, and the abbey of Cluny—also characterized the tensions between other abbeys and each type of opponent.

The suggestion that Saint-Gilles's situation reveals the general pattern of conflict is not to deny this monastery's historical specificity. Indeed, Saint-Gilles was in one aspect different from the other abbeys. Most monasteries invoked the king of their origins, using him as the primary conduit for and symbol of their liberty. But although its legend had a distinct royal component—Flavius, "king of the Goths"—Saint-Gilles chose instead to appeal to its patron saint's legendary *traditio* of the new foundation to the pope.[7] Amplifying and embroidering this act, the monastery

Community in Medieval Europe: Selected Readings, ed. Fredric L. Cheyette (New York, 1968), pp. 111–121. The most vocal proponent of Cluny's status as a shining white knight dispensing liberty remains Joachim Wollasch; see his *Mönchtum zwischen Kirche und Welt*, pp. 136–171, and his "Questions-clé du monachisme européen avant l'an mil," in *Saint-Sever*, pp. 13–26.

[6] Here I borrow the apt terminology of friendship and enmity used in Barbara Rosenwein, Thomas Head, and Sharon Farmer, "Monks and Their Enemies: A Comparative Approach," *Speculum* 66 (1991): 764–796. See also Rosenwein, *To Be the Neighbor of Saint Peter*.

[7] On Flavius, see above, Chapter 4 at nn. 19–26; on the *traditio*, Chapter 2 at nn. 177–179.

made the pontiff into its transcendent source and guarantor of liberty. Saint-Gilles celebrated and welcomed its Roman protector in nonlegendary ways also: several popes visited the abbey during in the late eleventh and early twelfth centuries; its church and that of at least one of its priories were consecrated by papal hands; and its twelfth-century librarian, Petrus Guillermus, composed a reworking of the official history of the popes, the *Liber pontificalis,* which would be the basis for all subsequent versions of this text.[8]

Nonetheless, this focus on Rome rather than on royal figures does not invalidate Saint-Gilles's value as an example. Apostolic or papal *Romanitas* did color other southern abbeys' legendary images of themselves (although less strongly than did royal tones).[9] Furthermore, as we shall see, although monasteries appealed to the Frankish kings of the past, they often turned at the same time to the popes of the late eleventh and twelfth centuries, sometimes integrating them into their legends.[10] For these communities, legendary kings and contemporaneous popes functioned in tandem. Whether king or ecclesiastical *Romanitas* was the dominant color of a legend, the goal was the same: the assurance of monastic independence and the community's integrity.

Still another factor makes Saint-Gilles an appropriate introduction to the complex interaction between conflict, identity, and crystallization of legend and liberty. The abbey's narrative expression of its legend, the *vita* of Saint Gilles, is complemented and completed by a remarkable twelfth-century manuscript in which the dynamic of identity formation in the matrix of conflict is particularly transparent. A monk or monks of Saint-Gilles, sifting through the available documents, compiled this manuscript in order to present an interpretation of the clashes that threatened the community's integrity.[11] A small (16.5 cm x 11 cm) manuscript of seventy-six folios, Paris BN Latin 11018 originally consisted of only its first fifty-seven folios—folios of good quality white parchment, neatly written in one twelfth-century hand with red rubrics and ornate initial letters, some adorned with gold leaf.[12] The obvious care and expense lavished upon these folios signal the importance the contents—a chronologically ordered series of papal documents,

---

[8] On Petrus Guillermus, see *Liber pontificalis,* 2:xxiv–xxxiv. For descriptions of the visits of Gelasius II (1118) and Calixtus II (1119), see 2:317, 320–321, 322, 324. Gelasius consecrated Sainte-Cécile of Estagel; Urban II consecrated the main church in 1096 (see n. 67 below).

[9] See above, Chapter 3 at nn. 19–42.

[10] Folz remarked on a similar phenomenon in the German realm: *Le souvenir et la légende,* pp. 107–110, 148–156.

[11] Some documents present at the abbey were pointedly not included in the manuscript. See the edition of papal letters relevant to Saint-Gilles which includes texts not in Paris, BN Latin 11018: *Bullaire de l'abbaye de Saint-Gilles.*

[12] On this manuscript, see Appendix 2 below. Hereafter when I mention this manuscript, I am referring only to these first fifty-seven folios.

forged and authentic, beginning with an undatable privilege of a certain "Benedict" and ending with one of Innocent II from 1132—held for the monks.

Composed probably not long after 1132, a year whose significance will become apparent, Paris BN Latin 11018 represents more than a mere account of the abbey's struggles.[13] This manuscript asserts the abbey's legendary image of itself and its liberty—and thus itself becomes as legendary as the *vita* of Gilles. This occurs along two axes, one diachronic and the other synchronic. As the manuscript recounts the overlapping threats to the abbey's liberty and to its lordship over the burgeoning port town that had coalesced around its walls, the individual documents appeal to and develop Saint-Gilles's legendary identity. This narration of events in time thus reinforces the legend. But the manuscript as a whole is also a static portrait of the abbey's unchanging liberty derived from its legendary origins. This synchronic quality is evident in the language chosen for the manuscript: exclusively documents emanating from popes. This language presents Saint-Gilles as it imagined itself, as an abbey whose liberty was and always had been Roman. Indeed, the manuscript as a whole plays upon the implications of the legendary act that had established Saint-Gilles as first free and then papal: the saintly founder's *traditio* of his abbey to the pope. Through these texts that narrate conflict, an iconic vision of the abbey's origins is created and proclaimed as present reality.

To understand this, let us begin where a medieval reader leafing through the manuscript might have: with the rubrics that introduce each privilege. Rubrics were used to frame texts interpretatively. Telling the reader how to read, they thus reveal the composer's own intentions. If we ignore the privileges themselves, and read the rubrics as one continuous metatext, a rough rhythm becomes apparent: the declaration of the abbey's possession of a certain privilege (or, less frequently, a property), followed by the contesting of that right (or property), or vice versa.[14] In either case, the result is a proclamation of the privilege to all the princes and prelates of the surrounding land—thus making public the abbey's identity. The rubrics emphasize the abbey's privileges; the narrative of conflict is secondary, manipulated to reinforce these privileges and to create the abbey's identity.[15]

---

[13] On the manuscript's dating, see Appendix 2 below.

[14] It must be admitted that this is an approximate pattern; for example, see Paris, BN Latin 11018, ff. 32v–40r, 42r–53r.

[15] To describe conflict, the rubrics use the preposition *contra* (to describe a papal proclamation in favor of the monastery against its enemies) as often as they do a noun describing the enemies' action (e.g., *invasio*); each form appears six times. This first usage underlines implicitly the abbey's rights in the face of opposition—and is one more example of how the rubrics, rather than just presenting a narrative of conflict, also constitute the abbey as a place of privilege.

In its very structure the manuscript asserts that the abbey had always—
that is since its legendary origins—possessed these privileges. What can still
be read of the badly mutilated rubric of the first document in Paris BN Latin
11018 hints at Gilles's legendary act from which the abbey's liberty flowed:
"Saint Gilles [at?] Rome . . . brought."[16] The full rubric probably explained
that Saint Gilles had gone to Rome and delivered his new foundation into
the pope's hands—the act described by the text of this document, which
purports to be the very privilege that the saint received for his abbey in
return for having placed it under papal protection.[17] This document, which
was fabricated whole cloth in the late eleventh century as we shall see,
complements and elaborates upon (probably intentionally) the vita's more
colorful account of the *traditio*.[18] Paris BN Latin 11018 introduces Saint-
Gilles with this flamboyant proclamation that its legendary founder had
established it as a papal and free (*liber*) monastery, not to be subject to
episcopal or lay power. This privilege becomes the lens through which the
subsequent documents relating to the abbey's conflicts with those very
powers are to be read. From the beginning (of both manuscript and monastery), declares this text, the power that various lords attempted to exercise
over Saint-Gilles was illegitimate.

Immediately following this privilege, the manuscript relates the first
round of conflict with the abbey's most ancient enemy, its bishops ordinary,
the bishops of Nîmes. In this episode, the status with which the legendary
traditio (although certainly not in its eleventh-century form) endowed Saint-
Gilles figured prominently. In two privileges, dated July and August of 878
and included in Paris BN Latin 11018 immediately after Benedict's privilege, Pope John VIII proclaims that the abbey was a papal possession that
the bishops of Nîmes had usurped.[19] In each of these lengthy texts the pope
relates the same tangled tale.

Gilles, Pope John states, had been granted the "vallis Flaviana" by King
Flavius. The saint then donated this valley to the pope, and built there a
church in honor of the apostle Peter. In this very church the saintly
founder's body now reposed. But, John laments, because the church was far
distant from Rome and hence neglected by the popes, the bishop of Nîmes
had dared to seize (the verb used is a form of *invadere*) it as his own. The
bishop had even demanded confirmation of his new possession from the
king of the Franks. This royal *preceptum* John mentions so scathingly is perhaps the diploma of 814 addressed to Christianus, bishop of Nîmes, in

---

16   "Roma sanctus Aegidius . . . adtulit" (Paris, BN Latin 11018, f. 2v).
17   *Bullaire de l'abbaye de Saint-Gilles*, pp. 1–2, no. 1; Paris, BN Latin 11018, ff. 2v–3r.
18   On the *vita*'s presentation of the *traditio*, see above, Chapter 2 at nn. 177–179.
19   *Bullaire de l'abbaye de Saint-Gilles*, pp. 5–10, 11–17; Paris, BN Latin 11018, ff. 3r–7r, 7r–
12v.

which Louis the Pious refers to the church of Saint Peter in the "vallis Flaviana" as one of the bishopric's "cellae"—the earliest authentic source to mention the abbey.[20]

Furthermore, John indignantly relates, the bishop of Nîmes's possession of Saint-Gilles had also been confirmed by none other than his own predecessor on the papal throne. For the bishop, putting little stock in the royal *preceptum,* had slyly approached Nicholas (I) for a more authoritative recognition of his claims to the abbey.[21] Deceived by the bishop's wiles (John assures the reader), Nicholas had fulfilled this request. But, John states with evident relish, he himself had found in the archives at Rome a text that could trump both royal diploma and his predecessor's confirmation—the very privilege Gilles had received in return for his *traditio* of the abbey to the pope.

Thus, John states, in 878 on his way to the council of Troyes, he stopped off in Arles.[22] There an assembly of local bishops and archbishops judged invalid the privilege of Nicholas I that the current bishop of Nîmes, Girbertus, had proffered as proof of the legitimacy of his control of the abbey. Receiving the abbey into his hands, and granting it certain rights that made it very definitely a papal and not an episcopal possession, John appointed as caretakers its own abbot, Leo, and the powerful archdeacon of Uzès, Amelius.[23]

Thus, Paris BN Latin 11018 complements its first privilege with the second and the third. These latter two assert that the pope had vanquished the bishop of Nîmes and reestablished Saint-Gilles as the papal monastery that it had been from its origins—and the first privilege is there to prove it. Indeed, the link with legendary foundation is made explicitly. In order to free the abbey from its "illegitimate subjection" to the see of Nîmes, Pope John invokes the legendary act described in the first privilege: the *traditio.* This opening sequence of the manuscript thus places legend, conflict, and lib-

---

[20] *HL* 2:93–94, no. 30. Whether the church was also known as Saint-Gilles in this period is not evident. The *Notitia de servitio monasteriorum* (817) calls it "monasterium sancti Aegidii," but this text is extant in only two thirteenth-century manuscripts, both from Saint-Gilles. See Emile Lesne, "Les ordonnances monastiques de Louis le Pieux et la Notitia de servitio monasteriorum," *Revue d'Histoire de l'Eglise en France* 6 (1920): 161–175, 449–493. When copying the text, the scribes may have changed "Peter" into "Gilles."

[21] Here the bias of the pope appears—his privilege is worth more than that of the king— certainly an unusual opinion for the ninth century, but one that John VIII could very well have held. See Ulrich Winzer's somewhat different interpretation of John VIII: *S. Gilles: Studien zum Rechtsstatus und Beziehungsnetz einer Abtei im Spiegel ihrer Memorialüberlieferung,* Münstersche Mittelalter-Schriften, 59 (Munich, 1988), p. 42, n. 1.

[22] For the reasons behind John's actual journey to Gaul for the Council of Troyes, see Arthur Lapôtre, *L'Europe et le Saint-Siège à l'époque carolingienne: Première partie: Le pape Jean (872–882)* (Paris, 1895), pp. 316–350.

[23] The detailed provisions restricting the ordinary's rights over Saint-Gilles show John's privileges to be among those rare instances of papal grants of exemption (or its precursor) predating the tenth century.

erty on a continuum. Furthermore, if these documents of John VIII are authentic—and the majority opinion among diplomaticists is that, despite certain irregularities, they are—then they are the earliest extant evidence for the development of the abbey's legend.[24] Here are not only Gilles and the *traditio,* but also King Flavius, although not specifically identified as the king of the Goths as he will be in the *vita.* If this is the primordial layer of the legend, it seems that during the first round of conflict in which Saint-Gilles's status was at stake, the legend was first articulated. Hence the continuum of conflict, liberty, and legend was both textual and historical.

Interestingly, though, it is the pope, rather than the monks, who brandished the legendary *traditio* in the face of the bishops of Nîmes; these two privileges were probably dictated by John VIII himself, rather than being composed by the abbey and then confirmed by the pope as were so many papal privileges throughout the Middle Ages.[25] Here then the monks were not at work putting words in the pope's mouth or ascribing to him actions that would fulfill their own interests. Instead, in the privileges, John invokes the *traditio* in order to underline his *own* rights over the abbey, not the liberties it thus possessed.

This subtle accent on papal rights and not monastic freedoms characterizes what is known of the ninth- and tenth-century phase of the abbey's conflict with the bishops of Nîmes. By 879 Girbertus had "invaded" the abbey and expelled the monks, and the letters that follow John's privileges in Paris BN Latin 11018 show that this bishop of Nîmes continued to press

[24] Technically unusual aspects of John's privileges arouse some suspicion that these documents are forgeries or contain interpolations. The second privilege opens with an A.D. dating very unusual in privileges of this epoch, and both privileges end in extremely developed and lengthy comminatory clauses that recall those of monastic charters from the eleventh century more than they do the general, short, and sober anathemas of papal documents. On these problems and others, see Jones, *Saint Gilles,* pp. 21–28 (she concludes that the privileges are later forgeries, as do Jacques Dubois and Geneviève Renaud, "L'influence des vies des saints sur le développement des institutions," in *Hagiographie, cultures et sociétés, IVe–XIIe s.: Actes du colloque organisé à Nanterre et à Paris, 2–5 mai, 1979* [Paris, 1979], pp. 495–496). However, John's privileges for Saint-Védast of Arras, Saint-Médard of Soissons, and Tournus have lengthy anathemas—and the last also opens with an A.D. date of 878, the same year as the Saint-Gilles privileges; see *PL* 126:658–659, 660–662, 772–774. It is unlikely that all these privileges would have been tampered with in exactly the same fashion. Further ground for suspicion is the fact that these two privileges for Saint-Gilles are not included in the eleventh-century compilation of John's letters and privileges that is known as his *Register* (made at Monte Cassino in the 1070s). This omission of the two privileges *might* make them forgeries, but not necessarily so.

For the generally convincing arguments of those who believe that the Saint-Gilles privileges are authentic, see, among others, Paul Fabre, *Etude sur le Liber censuum de l'église romaine* (Paris, 1892), pp. 49–51; Hirsch, "Untersuchungen," pp. 374–377; Dietrich Lohrmann, *Das Register Papst Johannes' VIII. (872–882): Neue Studien zur Abschrift Reg. Vat. 1, zum verlorenen Originalregister und zum Diktat der Briefe* (Tübingen, 1968), pp. 268–269, 274–276; Magnou-Nortier, *La société laïque,* p. 406; and Winzer, *S. Gilles,* pp. 27–28, 41–44.

[25] Lohrmann, *Das Register Papst Johannes' VIII,* pp. 274–276.

his (perhaps rightful) claims over the abbey.[26] Hadrian III (884–885) wrote
to the archbishop of Narbonne proclaiming that Girbertus would be excommunicated if he continued to oppress the abbey that was "beneath our and
the apostle Peter's dominion (*ditione*) and lordship (*potestate*)."[27] Writing
directly to Girbertus and then to Amelius, protector of the abbey, Stephen V
(885–891) repeated the threat.[28]

These papal protests that the abbey belonged to Rome and not to Nîmes
related to lordship, not monastic freedom. As a papal abbey, Saint-Gilles was
neither independent nor free in the ninth and tenth centuries.[29] In his
privileges of 878, John VIII had entrusted his possession, the abbey, not to its
abbot alone, but also to Amelius, archdeacon of Uzès. The former quickly
disappeared and the latter came to dominate the abbey; in a letter included
in Paris BN Latin 11018, Marinus I (882–884) informed the monks of Saint-
Gilles that he had granted the abbey to Amelius to "hold" (*ad tenendum*), to
"govern" (*ad gubernandum*), and to "rule" (*ad regendum*).[30] Hadrian III reiter-
ated Amelius's status as the local papal agent controlling the abbey, as did
Stephen V in both his letters.[31] The exclusion of Girbertus, then, did not
preclude outside ecclesiastical control by an intermediary. Nor did it preclude an episcopal intermediary—for by 885/888, Amelius had been
elected bishop of Uzès.

Characterizing this first round of conflict between abbey and ordinary are
the actions of a series of popes seeking not to "liberate" the abbey but rather
to establish their rights over it. In these efforts to wrest the abbey from the
bishop of Nîmes, the popes appealed to the abbey's incipient legend for
their own benefit. Then they appointed as protector of their rights a local
intermediary who, after himself becoming bishop, was no more tractable
than Girbertus of Nîmes had been; according to angry letters of both Stephen V and Sergius III, Amelius had been recalcitrant about remitting Saint-
Gilles's annual *census,* the external sign that the abbey belonged to Rome
(and not to the bishop).[32] What about the abbey itself in this wrangling

---

[26] On Girbertus's "invasion," see John VIII's letter of 879: *PL* 126:845–846 (not included
in Paris BN Latin 11018).

[27] *Bullaire de l'abbaye de Saint-Gilles*, pp. 4–5, no. 2; Paris, BN Latin 11018, f. 12v–13v.
Abbé Goiffon identifies this pope as Hadrian II, but Winzer more plausibly sees in him
Hadrian III; see Winzer, *S. Gilles*, p. 46, n. 1. Indeed, given the manuscript's generally strict
chronological order, this privilege (placed after that of Marinus and before that of Stephen
V), must pertain to Hadrian III and not to Hadrian II.

[28] *Bullaire de l'abbaye de Saint-Gilles*, pp. 18–19, nos. 6–7; Paris BN Latin 11018, ff. 13v–
14v.

[29] The terms *liber* and *libertas* never appear in these ninth- and tenth-century documents.

[30] *Bullaire de l'abbaye de Saint-Gilles*, p. 17, no. 5; Paris, BN Latin 11018, f. 12v.

[31] Hadrian III: *Bullaire de l'abbaye de Saint-Gilles*, pp. 4–5, no. 2; Paris, BN Latin 11018, f.
12v–13v. Stephen V: *Bullaire de l'abbaye de Saint-Gilles*, pp. 18–19, nos. 6 and 7; Paris, BN Latin
11018, ff. 13v–14v.

[32] Stephen V: *Bullaire de l'abbaye de Saint-Gilles*, p. 18, no. 6; Paris, BN Latin 11018, f. 13v.
Sergius III: *Bullaire de l'abbaye de Saint-Gilles*, pp. 20–21, no. 8; Paris, BN Latin 11018, f. 14v–

between popes and local bishops? We might wonder whether, in the late ninth or early tenth century, Saint-Gilles coveted this status as a papal monastery which it gained almost willy-nilly; after all, it had essentially exchanged one bishop for another. Was its situation really much different from that of other southern abbeys that were technically subject to episcopal *potestas* in this period?[33]

Why, then, were these documents included in Paris BN Latin 11018 if they depicted not an independent Saint-Gilles but one under the thumb of outside agents? The answer lies in how such documents would have been interpreted not by a reader in the ninth or tenth century, but by one in the early twelfth century—that is, at the time of the manuscript's composition. By the later eleventh century, status as a papal monastery (which so clearly clothes Saint-Gilles in these early documents) had acquired a new luster and meaning. With a now territorial sense of their proprietary rights, popes, beginning with Leo IX, had come to conceive of those churches under their protection and in their possession as exclusively theirs.[34] From the monastic perspective, such status now implied liberty. As we shall see, beginning in the mid-eleventh century, Saint-Gilles developed the implications of its subjection to Rome in order to assert its possession of *libertas*—not just the highly prized exemption from episcopal jurisdiction, but freedom from domination by any worldly power, lay or ecclesiastical. Imbued with this spirit, the twelfth-century compiler(s) of Paris BN Latin 11018 would read the ninth- and tenth-century papal documents through an anachronistic lens as the foundations for and the early history of the abbey's *libertas*. Thus reinterpreted, these texts demonstrated that Saint-Gilles had always been recognized to possess this now very special status guaranteed by Rome, and their inclusion in the manuscript implied that it always should be in the future.

The eleventh- and twelfth-century documents in Paris BN Latin 11018 assert this continuity between origins and present liberty. In these privileges and letters, Saint Gilles's *traditio* is repeatedly cited as the basis for papal rights over the abbey.[35] Yet while the founder's legendary act remained the touchstone that John VIII's privileges had made it, it also gained a new meaning. By 1091, the monastery had produced its own version of the act that John had supposedly found several centuries earlier in the Roman

---

15r. Amelius was a partisan of the Burgundian rulers of Provence, so his support of Formosus was not surprising; see Poly, *La Provence*, pp. 19–21.

[33] On episcopal control of southern abbeys during this period, see Magnou-Nortier, *La société*, pp. 399–408.

[34] Hirsch, "Untersuchungen," pp. 363–433.

[35] *Bullaire de l'abbaye de Saint-Gilles*, pp. 21–24, 25–26, 29–30, 35–36, 37–38, 41–42, 47–48, 55–57, 73–75, nos. 9, 11, 14, 17, 19, 23, 29, 37,53; Paris, BN Latin 11018, ff. 15r–17v, 18r–v, 21r–22v, 25v–26r, 26v–27r, 30v–32r, 40v–41r, 43r–46r, 53v–57v.

archives.[36] That is, the monks fabricated the privilege that opens Paris BN Latin 11018 with such a flourish, purporting to be the *preceptum* Gilles had received upon delivery of his new foundation into the keeping of the pope, here named for the first time: "Benedict."

According to this privilege, not only were kings, dukes, and counts prohibited from wielding *dominatio* over the abbey, a right reserved for the pope himself, but no bishop could excommunicate or impose any *servicium* upon the monks and only the pope himself could bless the newly elected abbots. The abbey, proclaims "Benedict," was to remain perpetually "free (*liber*) and undisturbed . . . beneath the protection of the blessed apostles Peter and Paul and this apostolic see." The *traditio* had thus been transformed into a banner of the sweeping liberty from domination—lay or ecclesiastical—which the abbey sought during this period. The emphasis was now on the *libertas* that flowed from the original subjection to Roman jurisdiction, rather than on papal rights as it had been in the ninth century.

This legendary version of the *traditio* trumpets exactly that liberty which the monks demanded in the face of the bishops of Nîmes, who had resurfaced as the abbey's antagonists by at least the third quarter of the eleventh century. It seems more than likely that the document was fashioned in the thick of the debate in order to articulate the freedom Saint-Gilles sought from its ordinary—a freedom newly defined but one that the abbey believed it had always possessed. In a series of letters and privileges issued by Alexander II, Gregory VII, Urban II, and Pascal II (all included in Paris BN Latin 11018) we can trace the irruptions of tension between abbey and ordinary and their results: the negation of the prerogatives claimed by the bishops; the affirmation, based on the *traditio,* of the *libertas* enjoyed by Saint-Gilles.

At stake were the bishops' pretensions to several of the rights mentioned in "Benedict's" privilege: consecration of the newly elected abbot, ordination of those monks who became priests, and the right to excommunicate or place under interdict the monastic community (perhaps also the right to impose various *exactiones*).[37] Among these, the issue that seems to have been most important for the abbey was the matter of the abbot's consecration; also of great concern was the ordination of the monks. Of the six documents

[36] *Bullaire de l'abbaye de Saint-Gilles*, pp. 1–2, no. 1; Paris, BN Latin 11018, ff. 2v–3r. The language of this document (with its invocations of *libertas*) and its stipulations betray it as a forgery from no earlier than the eleventh century. It must have been extant by 1091, when Urban II specified that the pope to whom Gilles had given his abbey was Benedict (*Bullaire de l'abbaye de Saint-Gilles*, pp. 29–30, no. 14; Paris, BN Latin 11018, ff. 25v–26r). No earlier text names the pope; see Hirsch, "Untersuchungen," pp. 374–377.

[37] A privilege of Pascal II addresses the issue of episcopal exactions: *Bullaire de l'abbaye de Saint-Gilles*, pp. 47–48, no. 29; Paris, BN Latin 11018, ff. 40v–41r. There was also friction between the bishop and the abbey over certain of the latter's important properties—again evincing an episcopal desire for domination. See Urban II's letter of 1095: *Bullaire de l'abbaye de Saint-Gilles*, pp. 33–34, no. 16; Paris, BN Latin 11018, ff. 22v–24r.

dealing directly with the clashes with the bishop, four are framed by their rubrics as statements of the abbey's prerogatives in these matters.[38] Furthermore, Bishop Froterius II of Nîmes, who actively tried in the 1070s to obstruct Saint-Gilles's right (implied in John VIII's privileges) to send its abbot to Rome for his blessing, was pointedly not mentioned in the abbey's early twelfth-century necrology—although the two bishops who in the 1090s placed the abbey under interdict and disputed certain of its properties were.[39]

Why this concern with the bishop's power to consecrate, rather than with his ability to punish through excommunication and interdict? In general, the agent of consecration gains a certain power over that which is being consecrated, as we have seen in the consideration of both the ritual and the miraculous consecration of churches.[40] More specifically, the episcopal blessing of the newly elected abbot implied both the bishop's right to approve or reject the candidate and the elect's obligation to take a vow of obedience to the bishop.[41] Hence this ritual involved a submission to episcopal *ius*—a flagrant contradiction of both Saint-Gilles's nature as an abbey under papal jurisdiction and its effective independence.

The successive solutions reached and proclaimed in Paris BN Latin 11018 accord with those found for other abbeys enjoying the same status.[42] Fiery Gregory VII declared that the consecration of Saint-Gilles's abbot was a papal prerogative, and it was in these terms that Saint-Gilles was characterized in Cardinal Deusdedit's *Collectio canonum* (ca. 1087).[43] Urban II, while granting the monks the right to choose any bishop they liked for the purposes of consecration and ordination, urged that they select the bishop

---

[38] "Pro consecratione abbatis episcopo nemausensis missum," Paris, BN Latin 11018, f. 17v (text: ff. 17v–18r; *Bullaire de l'abbaye de Saint-Gilles*, pp. 24–25, no. 10); "De consecratione abbatis contra episcopum nemausensis," Paris, BN Latin 11018, f. 18r (text: ff. 18r–v; *Bullaire de l'abbaye de Saint-Gilles*, pp. 25–26, no. 11); "De abbatia hungario et ordinatione nostra," Paris, BN Latin 11018, f. 24r (text: ff. 24r–25v; *Bullaire de l'abbaye de Saint-Gilles*, pp. 27–29, no. 13); "De ordinatione fratrum huius monasterii," Paris, BN Latin 11018, f. 25v (text: ff. 25v–26r; *Bullaire de l'abbaye de Saint-Gilles*, pp. 29–30, no. 14). The other two privileges: *Bullaire de l'abbaye de Saint-Gilles*, pp. 33–34, 37–38, nos. 16 and 19; Paris, BN Latin 11018, ff. 22v–24r, 26v.

[39] On Froterius, see Alexander II's letter: *Bullaire de l'abbaye de Saint-Gilles*, pp. 24–25, no. 10; Paris, BN Latin 11018, ff. 17v–18r. Also that of Gregory VII: *Bullaire de l'abbaye de Saint-Gilles*, pp. 25–26, no. 11; Paris, BN Latin 11018, ff. 18r–v (cf. the papal version of this letter in Gregory VII, *Epistolae* 1.68 [*Das Register*], pp. 97–99). For bibliographic material on the bishops of Nîmes commemorated in the necrology, see Winzer, *S. Gilles*, pp. 309–317.

[40] See above: Chapter 1 at nn. 80–85; Chapter 2 at nn. 160–171.

[41] See Schreiber, *Kurie und Kloster*, 1:126–141; and Schwarz, "*Jurisdicio* und *Condicio*," pp. 51–53.

[42] See Schreiber, *Kurie und Kloster*, 1:128.

[43] Gregory VII (1074): *Bullaire de l'abbaye de Saint-Gilles*, pp. 25–26, no. 11; Paris, BN Latin 11018, ff. 18r–v. Cf. the papal version in Gregory VII, *Epistolae* 1.68 (*Das Register*, pp. 97–99). Deusdedit (who drew on Gregory's letter): *Die Kanonessamlung des Kardinals Deusdedit*, ed. Victor Wolf von Glanvell (Paderborn, 1905), 3.261, pp. 532–535.

of Nîmes.[44] Urban's stipulations did not rob the abbey of its *libertas,* for the oath of obedience was eliminated and the abbot's independence from the bishop was thus guaranteed.[45]

The other components of Saint-Gilles's exemption from the ordinary's jurisdiction were also defended by the popes, and the tension subsided by the second decade of the twelfth century. After this time, the bishop ordinary often appeared as the monastery's ally, although in no way its lord.[46] The abbey's independence from his jurisdiction was mentioned as a matter of course in the privileges of Calixtus II (1119) and Innocent II (1132) which are included in Paris BN Latin 11018 and which invoke the legendary *traditio.*[47] The manuscript thus tells of the progressive and finally successful articulation of Saint-Gilles's liberty in the face of attempts by the bishops of Nîmes to exercise what they saw as their legitimate rights.

Those rights were based on origins, asserted the bishops in their own legendary tradition which existed in some tension with that of Saint-Gilles. The Nîmes legend took the form of an episcopal list, extant in a late twelfth-century copy but based on a text composed by at least 1141. The text, the bishops' memory and commemoration of their predecessors (*hec sunt nomina Nemausensium episcoporum qui ad presens in nostra sunt memoria*), begins not with the Merovingian prelates, but rather with Girbertus.[48] This prelate, one of the archvillains in Paris BN Latin 11018, is assigned to the reign of Charlemagne, rather than that of Charles the Bald. Not only are the see's orgins thus implicitly placed in the time of the Charles who counted for more among southern ecclesiastical communities, but the bishopric is made

[44]   See Urban's two privileges of 1091: *Bullaire de l'abbaye de Saint-Gilles,* pp. 27–30, nos. 13 and 14; Paris, BN Latin 11018, ff. 24r–26r.

[45]   The profession or omission of the oath of obedience at the abbot's consecration could be what distinguished an abbey exempt from episcopal jursidiction from one subject to it. See Schreiber, *Kurie und Kloster,* 1:134–144.

[46]   On subsequent friendly relations with the bishops of Nîmes, see Winzer, *S. Gilles,* pp. 314–316. During the conflict with the counts of Toulouse/Saint-Gilles, the abbey called upon the bishops as its allies; see below at nn. 58–90.

[47]   Calixtus II: *Bullaire de l'abbaye de Saint-Gilles,* pp. 55–57, no. 38; Paris, BN Latin 11018, ff. 43r–46r. Innocent II: *Bullaire de l'abbaye de Saint-Gilles,* pp. 73–75, no. 53; Paris, BN Latin 11018, ff. 53v–57v. Hadrian IV not only placed Saint-Gilles under the jurisdiction of a legate sent *a latere,* but also conferred upon the abbot one of the coveted *iura pontificalia:* the right to wear the miter during the celebration of mass. *Bullaire de l'abbaye de Saint-Gilles,* pp. 77–78, no. 56; Paris BN Latin 11018, ff. 73v–74r. This latter right was confirmed by Alexander III and conceded in perpetuity by Innocent III; see *Bullaire de l'abbaye de Saint-Gilles,* pp. 89, 103–104, nos. 67 and 79.

[48]   This list (Nîmes, BM 14, f. 218va) is partially edited in *HL* 5:28–29, no. 5, and even less completely in Louis Duchesne, *Fastes épiscopaux de l'ancienne Gaule,* 3 vols. (Paris, 1894–1915), 1:311. According to Thomas Bisson (who very generously shared his transcription and analysis of the text with me) the first section of the list is written in one late twelfth-century hand and breaks off with Aldebertus (consecrated in 1141). The list then resumes with an entry for 1242 made in a contemporaneous hand; the hand changes continually thereafter and is contemporaneous with the date of the entries. Also see Bisson, "Unheroed Pasts," p. 305. On the earlier bishops of Nîmes, see Duchesne, *Fastes épiscopaux,* 1:312–313.

the beneficiary of the legendary Carolingian's largesse. The next entry continues the theme: Louis the Pious gave to Bishop Christianus the abbeys of Saint-Gilles and Tornac (perhaps a reference to Louis's diploma of 814 mentioning them as episcopal possessions).[49] Nîmes's rights over Saint-Gilles are thus anchored firmly in a royal gift—one that preceded and thus took precedence over any actions of the monastery's legendary patrons, Gilles and Flavius. For the list's next entry reads: "Bishop Crocus in whose time existed blessed Gilles and King Flavius." Here Gilles and Flavius are safely placed *after* the bishops' acquisition of rights over the monastery from the Carolingian king. No further kings appear as guarantors of episcopal rights over Saint-Gilles; instead, the next five entries intone that these rights were reconfirmed by a succession of popes, starting with Nicholas I.

In Paris BN Latin 11018, Saint-Gilles disputed the validity of these latter claims by presenting a seamless series of popes declaring that the abbey was papal and always had been. As for the authority of Louis the Pious, Saint-Gilles could draw upon the narrative component of its legend, the *vita* of Gilles, to retort that not only had a far more ancient and thus prestigious king, Flavius, ruler of the Goths, founded the abbey, but a Carolingian Charles (perhaps Louis's own father, Charlemagne) had been dependent upon Gilles for absolution.[50] Furthermore, through its manipulation of the hunt motif, the *vita* had suggested metaphorically that episcopal power over the abbey was illegitimate. As we have seen, at the climax of the hunt scene, the bishop of Nîmes prostrates himself before the wounded saint, begging forgiveness for the violence he has perpetrated upon the sacred body.[51]

The *vita* assigns to the bishop a partner in this sin and penitence: Flavius, representative of princely power. Secular lords were thus included in this metaphoric depiction of wounds inflicted upon the abbey by those who transgressed its boundaries. Indeed, as Saint-Gilles's sense of liberty and identity based on its legendary foundation expanded in the later eleventh century, the abbey also came into conflict with secular agents who were busy consolidating their own lordship in the lower Rhône valley. In these bitter and often violent clashes, the monastery would meet with less definitive success than it had in the face of episcopal power. But Paris BN Latin 11018 relates these conflicts in such a way as to hide the lack of triumph. The story becomes similar to the one in which the bishops had been the antagonists; it is the tale of Saint-Gilles's attempts, in the face of illegitimate claims, to defend its rightful *libertas* as established by its legendary founder.

The aspect of *libertas* at stake this time was immunity, both spatial and jurisdictional. The two eleventh-century legendary versions of the *traditio* stipulate that the abbey should not be subject to any lay power. Although

[49] On the diploma, see above at n. 20.
[50] See above, Chapter 5 at nn. 131–147.
[51] See above, Chapter 2 at n. 86.

probably forged during the tension with the bishops, the privilege of Pope
"Benedict" with which Paris BN Latin 11018 begins underlines the abbey's
freedom from secular *dominatio*.[52] The *vita*, moreover, describes the privilege Gilles receives from the pope solely in those terms, that is as a liberation of the abbey from any lay lordship.[53] This secular immunity was no
legendary invention: beginning in the late ninth century, popes (imitating
kings) granted immunity to monasteries they took into their jurisdiction.[54]
Nonetheless, the Benedict forgery and the *vita* accentuate what in John
VIII's privileges had been implied rather than stated—the illegitimacy of lay
control—and they link it explicitly to the abbey's legendary origins.

A forged privilege of a Pope Benedict (VIII) included in the manuscript
contains a direct appeal to the *traditio* in the face of lay challenges.[55] The
pope thunders recriminations at a certain Count Guilhem and his mother,
Adelaid, who have dared to consent to alienations of the abbey's property.[56]
At the end of a lengthy and vivid malediction, the pope declares that "no
bishop, nor any count nor any secular power should dare presumptuously to
usurp the monastery of Saint-Gilles into their lordship (*dominio*)"; any who
do shall be cursed because "blessed Gilles delivered that abbey with all
property belonging to it into the lordship (*dominio*) . . . of the blessed
apostle Peter."[57] This forgery serves as a generic warning against lay predators, and echoes the stipulations of the Benedict privilege opening the
manuscript. Furthermore, the text may be intended to be read in light of the
most important conflict with a secular enemy that Paris BN Latin 11018
describes: the clash between Saint-Gilles and the counts of Toulouse.

Before turning to the texts that narrate this conflict, I should point out
something they most deliberately conceal: by the second half of the eleventh
century, the counts of Toulouse evidently considered the abbey theirs to
dispose of as they wished.[58] Moreover, it was not just over the monastery that
the counts exercised their power, as is indicated by the appellation that
Raymond IV gained from his inheritance as Pons's younger son (1061) and

52   See above at nn. 16–17, 36.
53   See above, Chapter 2 at nn. 177–179.
54   See Cowdrey, *The Cluniacs*, pp. 5, 12–15.
55   Magnou-Nortier, in her discussion of this document's diplomatic impossibilities, suggests tentatively that it might have been forged circa 1000: *La société*, pp. 505–506. Given the
chronology of the abbey's conflict with the counts of Toulouse, though, I would suggest that
it was forged sometime later in the eleventh century. Harald Zimmermann also classifies this
text as a forgery: *Papsturkunden 896–1046*, 2:891–893, no. 468. Winzer, however, accepts the
privilege as authentic; see his *S. Gilles*, pp. 48–49.
56   For discussion of just who this count is, see references in n. 55 above.
57   *Bullaire de l'abbaye de Saint-Gilles*, pp. 21–24, no. 9; Paris, BN Latin 11018, ff. 15r–17v.
58   See the charter of 1037, in *HL* 5:428–429, no. 211; and that of 1066, in *HL* 5:542–
543, no. 276 (also edited by Alexandre Bruel in *Recueil des chartes de l'abbaye de Cluny*, 6 vols.
[Paris, 1876–1903], 4:517–519, no. 3410). For discussion of these texts, see Winzer, *S. Gilles*,
pp. 49–52.

that he did not renounce even upon his accession to the countship of Toulouse some thirty years later: count of Saint-Gilles.[59] This title encompassed claims not just to the abbey and its revenues, but also to the prosperous port town that had formed around the saint's shrine. By the twelfth century this town was an important center for trade, overland and maritime.[60] Raymond IV had not only several residences there, but a mint.[61] This mint would continue to produce coins into the later twelfth century, and under Alfonse-Jourdain and Raymond V (if not already under Raymond IV and Bertrand) those coins embodied the count's possession of the town: on one side was *onor sancti egidii*—the "seigneury of Saint-Gilles"—and on the other, the lord count's name.[62]

But there was another lord of Saint-Gilles: the abbey itself. The monastery claimed jurisdiction over the town and its inhabitants, just as other abbeys did over the bourgs that coalesced around their walls. This claim had been made patent in Gilles's *vita*: Flavius endowed the monastery with the territory that encircled it within a radius of five miles.[63] This space, defined by the patron saint's own step, surely embraced the port. Indeed, a letter of 1097 refers to Saint-Gilles as the abbot's "own bourg."[64] The two lords— monastic and comital—were bound to clash. On the one hand, as the count sought to establish Saint-Gilles as the seat of his power, the abbey countered in order to retain its jurisdiction over this increasingly rich and important town. As the abbey's sense of its *libertas* developed, on the other hand, Saint-Gilles, like other churches in the later eleventh century, fought to make its lay lords renounce their rights, now pronounced illegitimate.

Saint-Gilles used as a weapon its status as a Roman monastery. Despite the clear indications that the abbey was subject to comital control in the eleventh century, its nature as a papal possession had not been effaced; in a charter of 1066 Raymond IV and his mother, Almodis, specified that Saint-Gilles was an "allod of Saint Peter" which they held through a gift (*donum*) of

---

[59] On the transmission to and division between Pons's two sons of his possessions and titles, see Dunbabin, *France in the Making*, p. 170. On Raymond's use of the title, see Carra Ferguson O'Meara, *The Iconography of the Façade of Saint-Gilles-du-Gard* (New York, 1977), pp. 18–19.

[60] For an excellent analysis of Saint-Gilles as a trade center, see Hektor Ammann, "Die Deutschen in Saint-Gilles," in *Festschrift Hermann Aubin zum 80. Geburtstag*, ed. Otto Brunner et al., 2 vols (Wiesbaden, 1965), 1:185–220.

[61] On Raymond's residences, see the evidence assembled by Ferguson O'Meara, *The Iconography of the Façade*, p. 43, n. 49.

[62] Concerning these coins, see *De Toulouse à Tripoli: La puissance toulousaine au XIIe siècle (1080–1208): Musée des Augustins [Toulouse], 6 janvier–20 mars 1989* (Toulouse, 1989), pp. 208, 211.

[63] See above, Chapter 2 at n. 117. I am not suggesting that this motif appears in the *vita* because of the counts, merely that the legend endowed the abbey with control over its immediate surroundings.

[64] *Cartulaire de l'abbaye de Saint-Victor de Marseille*, ed. Benjamin Guérard, 2 vols. (Paris, 1857), 1:178–179, no. 152.

the pope.[65] This interesting ambiguity reveals that the abbey was still recognized as peculiarly Roman, even by those whose *dominatio* contravened the abbey's intrinsic immunity.

In a series of letters and privileges of popes Urban II, Pascal II, and Calixtus II, Paris BN Latin 11018 relates how the abbey drew upon and thus developed its Roman identity in order to contain the counts. The first round of the conflict is narrated by two letters of Urban II. According to the first (1095), at Saint-Gilles on the saint's feast day—certainly a public moment—Raymond IV had renounced his claims and those of his descendants to the offerings made at various of the abbey's altars.[66] A more complete *guerpitio* follows immediately in the manuscript; in a letter of 1096, Urban II relates that Raymond had renounced all the estates belonging to Saint-Gilles that he held, justly or injustly, as well as all "rightful or wicked customs (*pravas consuetudines*)" over the abbey.[67] This privilege's rubric is telling: "Concerning the renunciation of this town (*ville*) by [Count Raymond]."[68] On the eve of his departure for Jerusalem, the count had thus rendered to the abbey its revenues and its possessions—most notably, according to this rubric, the town of Saint-Gilles itself.[69]

But as Paris BN Latin 11018 describes in great detail, by the first decade of the twelfth century, relations between count and monastery had soured again. Raymond IV's son, the wayward Bertrand, reasserted the rights over Saint-Gilles that his father had renounced; these efforts are narrated in Paris BN Latin 11018 by twelve letters and privileges of Pascal II spanning the period from circa 1105 to circa 1108.[70] During these years, Bertrand would have had every reason to wish to establish himself as lord of Saint-Gilles. He had lost Toulouse in 1097 to William IX of Aquitaine, and regained control

[65] *HL* 5:543, no. 276.

[66] *Bullaire de l'abbaye de Saint-Gilles*, pp. 30–33, no. 15; Paris, BN Latin 11018, ff. 19r–21r. Raymond had apparently made this renunciation first in 1090 at a council held at Toulouse; see Ferguson O'Meara, *The Iconography of the Façade*, p. 20.

[67] *Bullaire de l'abbaye de Saint-Gilles*, pp. 35–36, no. 17; Paris, BN Latin 11018, ff. 21r–22v. In this privilege, dated at Saint-Gilles, Urban also states that he had consecrated the altar of the new abbey church—a definitive demonstration of the abbey's status as a papal and not comital possession. See above, Chapter 1 at nn. 82–85. For the text of the *guerpitio* at Nîmes, see *HL* 5:743–744, no. 393.

[68] "De dimmissione huius ville ab eodem" (Paris, BN Latin 11018, f. 21r).

[69] Raymond also patched up his relationship with Gilles, the saint who would be his patron during the crusade. See *Le "Liber" de Raymond d'Aguiliers*, ed. Laurita L. Hill and John Hugh (Paris, 1969), p. 46. In 1096, the count made a donation to the cathedral of Le Puy "ob honorem et amorem sancti Aegidii quem multis injuriarum modis frequenter offendi" (*HL* 5:747–748, no. 395). One of his stipulations was that the canons celebrate Gilles's feast annually. Interestingly, I have found no record of a similar comital donation to Saint-Gilles itself. Was there on Raymond's part a separation of devotion to saint from devotion to his shrine, indicating a continuing underlying tension between count and abbey?

[70] See Winzer's overview of the conflict with Bertrand: *S. Gilles*, pp. 233–238.

of that city only in 1108.[71] In the intervening years, he tried to transform Saint-Gilles into his seat of power.

According to the documents of Pascal II in Paris BN 11018, Bertrand's first move (ca. 1105) had been to reclaim (*invadere* is the term used in Pascal's indignant letter threatening excommunication) the altar offerings of Saint-Gilles.[72] As Pascal's subsequent letters (based upon a *querimonia* the monks had made at Rome before their papal protector in about 1107) attest, Bertrand then went from bad to worse.[73] The count and his henchmen, members of powerful local dynasties, "violently invaded" the town and the monastery, capturing some monks and wounding others, seizing the abbey's possessions, desecrating and destroying its buildings.[74] But it was not only by attacking the monks and their material base, the abbey, that Bertrand physically installed himself as lord of Saint-Gilles. According to Paris BN Latin 11018, the count had also constructed "new fortifications just next to (*iuxta*) the church of blessed Gilles," donjons (*turres*) that towered over (*super*) it.[75] The implication was that Bertrand had installed his own castle in such a way as to counterbalance or even negate the church as a symbol of power.

Pascal admonished Bertrand, but to no avail.[76] Finally the pope appealed to the local prelates and magnates to league against Bertrand and compel him to return what he had stolen and destroy the fortifications—under pain of excommunication.[77] By March 1107 Bertrand, obviously unrepentant, had suffered the threatened penalty, and Pascal wrote the burghers and monks of Saint-Gilles to tell them that they must not associate with the excommunicate.[78] By July, Bertrand seems to have caved in under the pressure; he promised reparations for the damages he had caused, and renounced claims to the abbey's properties in exactly the same terms as his father had done.[79]

The excommunication was relaxed, but not for long. A year later, Pascal wrote letters to various local bishops to inform them of Bertrand's new

[71] John Hine Mundy, *Liberty and Political Power in Toulouse, 1050–1230* (New York, 1954), p. 16.

[72] *Bullaire de l'abbaye de Saint-Gilles*, pp. 38–39, no. 20; Paris, BN Latin 11018, ff. 30r–v.

[73] For the *querimonia*, see *Bullaire de l'abbaye de Saint-Gilles*, pp. 42–43, no. 24; Paris, BN Latin 11018, ff. 33r–34r.

[74] See Pascal's letter to Bertrand's accomplices: *Bullaire de l'abbaye de Saint-Gilles*, pp. 42–43, no. 24; Paris, BN Latin 11018, ff. 33r–34r.

[75] *Bullaire de l'abbaye de Saint-Gilles*, pp. 40, 42–43, nos. 22 and 24; Paris, BN Latin 11018, ff. 32v–34r.

[76] *Bullaire de l'abbaye de Saint-Gilles*, p. 40, no. 22; Paris, BN Latin 11018, ff. 32v–33r.

[77] *Bullaire de l'abbaye de Saint-Gilles*, pp. 44–45, nos. 25 and 26; Paris, BN Latin 11018, ff. 34r–36v.

[78] *Bullaire de l'abbaye de Saint-Gilles*, p. 46, no. 27; Paris, BN Latin 11018, f. 37v.

[79] *Bullaire de l'abbaye de Saint-Gilles*, pp. 46–47, no. 28; Paris, BN Latin 11018, ff. 37v–38v.

transgressions, essentially the same acts of violence against the abbey and its monks that he had perpetrated earlier (the rubrics speak of the count's "second invasion").[80] Then Bertrand disappears from Paris BN Latin 11018—perhaps because in 1108 he was able to return to Toulouse and no longer pressed his claims to Saint-Gilles. Furthermore, he departed for the Holy Land in 1109, apparently in the pope's good graces (perhaps having made amends for past aggression against the abbey).[81]

Yet this was certainly not the end of comital expansion at Saint-Gilles. In the early 1120s, Alfonse-Jourdain would follow in his brother's path and try to make himself lord of Saint-Gilles in a series of spectacular violations of the abbey's liberty and integrity. This count's "invasions" (as the rubrics call them) occurred sometime in the early 1120s, the years during which Alfonse-Jourdain was embroiled in a struggle with the count of Barcelona for the control of Provence. Saint-Gilles seems to have been among Raymond Berengar III's allies.[82] Alfonse's invasions were probably an attempt to regain this town, so important politically and economically, from his enemy. But they also continued his family's policy of making Saint-Gilles a major comital seat—and it is in this light that the abbey presented them in Paris BN Latin 11018.[83]

In ten letters to various addressees, Calixtus II relates his attempts to protect Saint-Gilles from the count whom he paints as rapacious and sacrilegious. The abbot and his monks as well as Raymond (Berengar III?) had deposed a *querimonia* stating that (in 1121?) Alfonse had invaded the bourg and abbey with armed force, committing murder and setting fires—recognized, almost symbolic methods of announcing one's enmity.[84] Furthermore, he had forced the townspeople to swear fidelity to him, thus contravening the fidelity they had formerly pledged to the abbot of Saint-Gilles, their true lord.[85] Finally, as his brother had done, Alfonse imposed upon Saint-Gilles's topography the material sign of his power; he built a castle which loomed, Calixtus specified, "right beside (*iuxta*) the boundaries placed by our predecessors and confirmed by ourselves."[86] The proximity of

[80] *Bullaire de l'abbaye de Saint-Gilles*, pp. 48–49, 51, nos. 30 and 33; Paris, BN Latin 11018, ff. 38v–39r, 40r–40v. See also the letter Pascal sent to the monks and burghers of Saint-Gilles in the same year: *Bullaire de l'abbaye de Saint-Gilles*, pp. 50–51, no. 32; Paris, BN Latin 11018, ff. 39v–40r.

[81] Cf. Winzer, *S. Gilles*, p. 238.

[82] Poly, *La Provence*, p. 330; Winzer, *S. Gilles*, p. 240, n. 1.

[83] Alfonse, like Bertrand, may also have been focusing his attention on Saint-Gilles because he had lost control of Toulouse. Ousted from the latter city in 1113, he returned only in 1123. Mundy, *Liberty and Political Power*, p. 16.

[84] On *praedia, incendia* (Raub und Brand), and *homicidia*, see Otto Brunner, *Land und Herrschaft: Grundfragen der territorialen Verfassungsgeschichte Südostdeutschlands im Mittelalter*, 3d ed. (Munich, 1943), pp. 87–107.

[85] Forced homage also belonged to the sequence of *Raub und Brand* (see n. 84 above).

[86] *Bullaire de l'abbaye de Saint-Gilles*, pp. 60–61, no. 41 (see also pp. 59–60, 61–62, nos. 40 and 42); Paris, BN Latin 11018, ff. 47r–48r (see also 48v–50r). On the previous papal

the castle to the sacred boundaries of the abbey's space embodied the rivalry between count and monastery just as Bertrand's castle had some fifteen years earlier. Stressing repeatedly that he would tolerate no such affronts to a "monastery of the Roman church," Calixtus exhorted Alfonse and his henchmen to leave the town and abbey in peace, and to destroy the castle they had built (he also released the burghers from the oath made to the count).[87]

The pope's attempt to reinstate the abbey as lord of the town had little effect. A few months later, Alfonse-Jourdain decided to eliminate his rival once and for all. Capturing the abbot, Hugh, and incarcerating him in the comital castle at Beaucaire, Alfonse released him—but only after extorting a vow that he would never again enter the abbey of Saint-Gilles.[88] Furthermore, Alfonse expelled the monks and invaded the town again.[89] Once again intoning that Saint-Gilles was a Roman possession, Calixtus first threatened excommunication and then unleashed it upon the count and his accomplices (1122?). The pope insisted that the excommunication would not be lifted until Alfonse-Jourdain had not only made reparations and released the abbot from his vow, but had also destroyed the hated castle and left the abbey and its monks free (*liberi*).[90]

Here the tale ends, with comital power declared illegitimate and the abbey's liberty and lordship affirmed by the pope. The manuscript contains no further mention of relations with the counts who battled the abbey for control of Saint-Gilles. Other documents provide a postscript. The two remained rivals until at least the early thirteenth century, and the question of who would prevail was played out in much the same terms, at times violent, at times conciliatory. As they had done before, the monks would continue to appeal to their Roman protector, who in turn would threaten the count with excommunication for having dared infringe upon a papal abbey's liberty.[91]

establishment of the boundaries (*termini*), see *Bullaire de l'abbaye de Saint-Gilles*, pp. 52–53, 55–59, nos. 35, 37–39; Paris, BN Latin 11018, ff. 42r–v, 42v–46r.

[87] See references in n. 86 above and *Bullaire de l'abbaye de Saint-Gilles*, pp. 62–63, no. 43; Paris, BN Latin 11018, ff. 49r–v (also pp. 63–64, no. 44; ff. 48r–v).

[88] *Bullaire de l'abbaye de Saint-Gilles*, pp. 64–65, no. 45; Paris, BN Latin 11018, ff. 50r–51r.

[89] *Bullaire de l'abbaye de Saint-Gilles*, pp. 65–66, no. 46; Paris, BN Latin 11018, ff. 51r–v.

[90] See references in n. 89 above and *Bullaire de l'abbaye de Saint-Gilles*, pp. 66–68, nos. 47–49; Paris, BN Latin 11018, ff. 51v–53v.

[91] Although the abbey induced Raymond V and his wife, Constance, Louis VII's sister, to renounce their rights to its territories (and to the port and its revenues) in the early 1160s (Léon Ménard, *Histoire civile, ecclesiastique et littéraire de la ville de Nismes . . .* 7 vols. [Paris, 1744–1758], 1, *preuves*, no. 24, pp. 36–37), the town remained Raymond's seat of power. See Mundy, *Liberty and Political Power*, pp. 50–51, 115. The count's justice began to rival that of the abbey; see Alexander III's letter in *Bullaire de l'abbaye de Saint-Gilles*, p. 86, no. 64. In the last decade of the century, Raymond seized various of the abbey's properties and built a castle—this time inside the sacred *termini*. See *Bullaire de l'abbaye de Saint-Gilles*, pp. 96–101, 114–115, nos. 73–75, 82–83.

Paris BN Latin 11018 thus contains Saint-Gilles's interpretation of its relations with two of the powers that threatened its liberty and its lordship over the town: the bishops of Nîmes and the counts who claimed more than just the name of the abbey. These two conflicts caused the articulation and public proclamation of the abbey's special relationship to Rome which had originated in its founder's legendary *traditio*. This explicit message, also contained in the *vita* of Gilles, was reflected and amplified by the manuscript's language and form.

The manuscript's positive enunciation of Saint-Gilles's identity was accompanied by a negative one: the implicit refusal of a quality that many modern historians attribute to the Rhône abbey, that of being "Cluniac" (whatever that label, slippery and ambiguous at best, might mean).[92] This silence might seem puzzling. After all, Cluny has been considered by many historians as the hero that liberated monasteries from the distress of lay and episcopal control and shared with them its Roman liberty—the very liberty so strikingly asserted in Paris BN Latin 11018.[93] Why did Saint-Gilles never invoke its membership in the "Cluniac church" (*ecclesia Cluniacensis*) when confronted by bishops and counts?

The answer lies in the tenor of relations between Saint-Gilles and Cluny. These differed radically from the idealized image promulgated by the latter's partisans (medieval and modern). Cluny was as much an enemy of the Rhône abbey's liberty as were the counts and bishops. In 1066 the secular lords of Saint-Gilles, Raymond IV and his mother, Almodis, subjected the abbey to Hugh of Cluny, while retaining certain rights for themselves.[94] It appears that Saint-Gilles was not forced to accept a Cluniac abbot immediately.[95] In 1076, however, Gregory VII announced that the abbot of Saint-Gilles had been excommunicated (it is unclear why).[96] Delivering Saint-Gilles to Cluny for the purpose of reform, the pope stated that the Burgundian monastery was to appoint a new abbot. But Cluny's power of election was to be limited to this one instance; Gregory specified that Saint-Gilles was thereafter to exercise its right of free election.[97] This stipulation that Saint-Gilles's subjection was only temporary was ignored. Thus, from 1076 until

---

[92] Wollasch provides a definition of "Cluniac" in his *Mönchtum zwischen Kirche und Welt,* pp. 155–158. More recently, the difficulty of establishing a blanket definition for the variety of relations that could exist between Cluny and other abbeys has been recognized. See Constance B. Bouchard, "Merovingian, Carolingian and Cluniac Monasticism: Reform and Renewal in Burgundy," *Journal of Ecclesiastical History* 41 (1990): 365–388; and Rosenwein, *To Be the Neighbor of Saint Peter.*

[93] See n. 5 above.

[94] *HL* 5:542–543; another edition in *Recueil des chartes de l'abbaye de Cluny,* 4:517–519, no. 3410.

[95] Winzer, *S. Gilles,* p. 64.

[96] Gregory VII, *Epistolae* 3.10a, in *Das Register,* p. 269.

[97] *Bullaire de l'abbaye de Saint-Gilles,* pp. 26–27, no. 12; Paris, BN Latin 11018, ff. 18v–19r. See Winzer, *S. Gilles,* pp. 58–66.

1125 Saint-Gilles was ruled by abbots who came from the congregation at
Cluny; and in the papal confirmations of Cluny's possessions of 1076, 1100,
1118, and 1120, Saint-Gilles was listed as a dependent monastery. Although
Gregory VII, Pascal II, Gelasius II, Calixtus II, and Honorius II all seemed to
have believed that Saint-Gilles was subject in some fashion to Cluny, these
popes also characterized the Rhône abbey in various of their privileges as a
papal possession.[98] From the papal perspective, in other words, Roman
jurisdiction over the monastery and its subjection to Cluny were
compatible.[99]

From Saint-Gilles's perspective, though, they most certainly were not.[100]
Already in 1097 there was some strife between the two abbeys in which
Urban II intervened.[101] The pope did not specify the reason for the tension,
but might it not have been a certain resistance to Cluny at Saint-Gilles?[102] By
the first decade of the twelfth century, moreover, relations between the
abbot and the community of Saint-Gilles were difficult—a sign perhaps of
the community's reluctance to accept a Cluniac superior.[103] In any case,
Pascal II felt it necessary to exhort the monks to adhere more strictly to the
"disciplinary jurisdiction of Cluniac customs" (*Cluniacensis ordinis distric-
tionem*), surely a sign that the community at Saint-Gilles did not display
much ardor for Cluniac ways.[104]

Pascal's injunctions apparently had little effect. After the death of Hugh
(the abbot whom Alfonse-Jourdain had imprisoned at Beaucaire and then
shipped back to Cluny), Saint-Gilles elected for itself in 1124 a non-Cluniac
abbot, Peter, a member of the powerful Anduze family.[105] Surely this choice,
confirmed by Calixtus II just before his death, reveals that resistance to
Cluny had hardened at Saint-Gilles. The new pope, Honorius II, a firm
Cluniac partisan, may have interpreted it as such. In 1125, apparently at the
request of Peter the Venerable, Honorius restored Saint-Gilles to Cluny "for
the purposes of reform and maintaining it in the religious way of life"—
surely an affirmation that Saint-Gilles, although papal, was to remain

---

[98] For details of the Cluniac pancharts and the descriptions of Saint-Gilles as papal but
subject to Cluny, see Winzer, *S. Gilles*, pp. 66–96.

[99] Popes could entrust their abbeys to intermediaries and did so, especially to Cluny and
Saint-Victor of Marseilles. See Pfaff, "Sankt Peters Abteien," pp. 153–154.

[100] See the case of the papal monastery of Santa Maria di Termiti, which Gregory VII
entrusted to Desiderius of Monte Cassino. Although the pope had stipulated that Santa
Maria's *libertas* would remain intact, the monks forced Desiderius to withdraw, accusing him
of having intended to reduce the monastery to a *cella*. Szabó-Bechstein, "*Libertas Ecclesiae*," p.
183.

[101] *Bullaire de l'abbaye de Saint-Gilles*, pp. 36–37, no. 18; Paris, BN Latin 11018, f. 30r.

[102] Winzer comes to the same conclusion: *S. Gilles*, pp. 77–78.

[103] *Bullaire de l'abbaye de Saint-Gilles*, p. 39, no. 21; Paris, BN Latin 11018, ff. 32r–v.

[104] *Recueil des chartes de l'abbaye de Cluny*, 5:223–224, no. 3871.

[105] Oddly, Peter is not mentioned in the abbey's early twelfth-century necrology, but five
members of his family are—and in the entries for four of them, their relation to Peter is
specified. Winzer, *S. Gilles*, pp. 384–385.

in Cluny's control.[106] In that same year, Honorius wrote a stern letter to Peter Anduze, declaring that although the abbey was a papal possession, it had been entrusted to Cluny. Therefore, commanded the pope, under no circumstances was Peter to fail to appear at Cluny within the next forty days in order to profess his "subjection and obedience" to Peter the Venerable.[107]

It is unclear whether Peter Anduze bowed his neck and made the vow of obedience that would have marked him and his community as Cluny's dependents. But it is likely he did not, for when in 1132 the matter of Saint-Gilles's relation to Cluny was brought before Innocent II and settled once and for all, the vow of obedience was clearly at stake. The prologue to one of the documents containing the resulting *compositio* underlines how, for Saint-Gilles, this vow—like that which a bishop might wish to extract at the abbot's consecration—was antithetical to the abbey's Roman liberty.[108] The settlement resolved the contradiction in favor of Saint-Gilles's image of its *libertas*, permitting Cluny only limited influence over the abbey it had tried to subjugate.[109] Saint-Gilles had thus obtained recognition that the "special privileges" (*specialia privilegia*) Cluny had exercised over it were illegitimate, and that its own "ancient liberty" (*antiqua libertas*) would endure.[110]

Should we persist, then, in calling Saint-Gilles "Cluniac," as most historians do? If we wish to emphasize the (atrophied) rights that Cluny retained after 1132, we may. We would do so, however, at the expense of the abbey's image of itself—for the course of relations between the two monasteries suggests that Saint-Gilles would have vehemently rejected such an appellation, just as it had refused Cluny's domination. Indeed, Paris BN Latin 11018 reveals that Saint-Gilles's conception of itself as a papal monastery enjoying *libertas* precluded any identification with the *ecclesia Cluniacensis*.

Only three times is Cluny's name even breathed in the manuscript. Gregory VII's letter of 1076, stating that he has given Saint-Gilles to Cluny for a one-time reform appears in the manuscript, but under the rubric "Concerning the liberty of election of our abbots."[111] In other words, the rubric subverts and inverts the temporary subjection to Cluny implied in the text, making the reader perceive the letter instead as a papal statement of the

---

[106] *Bullaire de l'abbaye de Saint-Gilles*, pp. 69–70, no. 50 (not in Paris BN Latin 11018).

[107] *Bullaire de l'abbaye de Saint-Gilles*, pp. 70–71, no. 51 (not in Paris BN Latin 11018).

[108] *Recueil des chartes de l'abbaye de Cluny*, 5:384, no. 4029.

[109] The conditions are spelled out in two very similar documents of 1132, one preserved at Cluny (*Recueil des chartes de l'abbaye de Cluny*, 5:384–388, no. 4029) and the other presumably at Saint-Gilles (*Bullaire de l'abbaye de Saint-Gilles*, pp. 71–73, no. 52; not in Paris BN Latin 11018).

[110] Both versions of the 1132 *compositio* refer to Cluny's renunciation of its *specialia privilegia;* that addressed to Saint-Gilles referred to the abbey's *antiqua . . . liberta[s].* See the references in n. 109 above.

[111] *Bullaire de l'abbaye de Saint-Gilles*, pp. 26–27, no. 12; Paris, BN Latin 11018, ff. 18v–19r: "De libertate electionis abbatum nostrorum."

abbey's liberty to choose its own superior. Cluny surfaces a second time in a letter of 1098 in which Urban II appoints Hugh, archbishop of Lyon, as the arbiter in an unspecified dispute between Cluny and Saint-Gilles. But Urban's words do not even hint at Saint-Gilles's subjection to Cluny. Furthermore, in this letter the pope briefly mentions that the privileges he had formerly granted Saint-Gilles should remain unchanged. This stipulation is the reason the letter was included in the manuscript, as the rubric makes clear: "The confirmation of certain privileges."[112] Neither text lets the reader even suspect Cluny's lordship over Saint-Gilles. To the contrary, the rubrics that frame these documents as papal guarantees of Saint-Gilles's *libertas* render Cluny innocuous. Finally, Cluny is mentioned as Abbot Hugh's place of exile after his release by Alfonse-Jourdain—not a statement that could alter Saint-Gilles's presentation of its nature as a papal and free abbey.[113] Obliterated by this resounding silence, the period of Cluniac domination was not allowed to cloud the image the abbey created of itself in the manuscript.

Nor did the Burgundian abbey appear in Saint-Gilles's necrology (composed in 1129), a document in which one would certainly expect to find affinity with Cluny expressed if any existed. The monks of Saint-Gilles did not commemorate with their prayers either members of the Cluniac congregation or Cluny's supporters. Rather, the names selected were those of the members of Saint-Gilles's own congregation and those individuals who had defended the abbey's *libertas*. The necrology was a subtle but clear statement of the monastery's refusal to incorporate Cluny into its vision of itself and its liberty.[114]

Saint-Gilles thus recognized, as many other southern abbeys did, that subjection to another monastery contravened liberty just as fundamentally as lay or episcopal lordship. But one might object that the conflict with Cluny played a lesser role in the abbey's proclamation of its legendary identity and liberty. After all, no statement about Saint-Gilles's liberty from other abbeys appears in the *vita,* nor in the forged privilege of Benedict with which Paris BN Latin 11018 opens. Furthermore, unlike the strife with the counts or with the bishops, the tale of the abbey's resistance and eventual triumph over Cluny is not related in the manuscript.

Such silence was not peculiar to Saint-Gilles. As we shall find in other cases, there was little language—legendary or otherwise—with which to counter directly the menace posed by Cluny or, indeed, by any abbey intent

---

[112] *Bullaire de l'abbaye de Saint-Gilles*, pp. 36–37, no. 18; Paris, BN Latin 11018, f. 30r: "Confirmatio quorundam privilegiorum."

[113] On Alfonse-Jourdain and the abbot, see above at n. 88.

[114] In this paragraph I follow Winzer, *S. Gilles*, esp. pp. 225–228, 386–414. In general on the use of necrologies to discern an ecclesiastical community's self-image, see Wollasch, *Mönchtum zwischen Kirche und Welt*, pp. 53–135.

on subjecting another. Abbeys could create themselves as immune to the control imposed by another monastery only through subtle manipulations, insinuations, and omissions. Such tactics may have resulted from a certain lack of coincidence between the monasteries' desire to be free from domination by another abbey and the concept of liberty as evolved in the reforming circles of the late tenth through the twelfth century. According to the ideals of reform, monastic liberty had come to comprise freedom from lay and episcopal control. A language was developed in order to express these concepts. Hence, in the privilege that sets the tone for Paris BN Latin 11018, the legendary Pope Benedict could explicitly grant to Gilles's new foundation such freedom. But how could he endow Saint-Gilles with the liberty from Cluny that it so desired? There was no official language to express this aspect of liberty. For the reformers, lay and ecclesiastical alike, were often engaged in a contrary project: that is, delivering one abbey into the control of another (ostensibly superior morally and spiritually) for the purpose of "reform."[115] This basic tenet of reform contravened the liberty the abbeys sought: freedom from any lord, whether in the guise of another monastery or not.

There were thus no specific words with which Saint-Gilles could express its liberty as including freedom from any other abbey, no positive legendary motif it could employ. All Saint-Gilles could do was to underline its liberty as freedom from all subjection by invoking in legend one of the human guarantors of such liberty: the pope. Paris BN Latin 11018 is a stunning statement of this sort of liberty, elaborated as much against the threat represented by Cluny as against those posed by bishop and count. Indeed, Saint-Gilles choice to use exclusively the medium of papal privileges speaks as much of the conflict with Cluny as it does of the others. While explicitly warding off the claims of the bishops and counts, this language was also peculiarly apt for meeting and contesting Cluny on its own ground—that is, as an abbey enjoying the special protection of the pope.[116]

Furthermore, the manuscript's very construction shows the special importance of the conflict with Cluny in the enunciation of Saint-Gilles's Roman identity. The manuscript concludes with a privilege of Innocent II dated from 1132, a document containing no reference to the settlement between Cluny and Saint-Gilles that this pope had effected one month earlier. Innocent, invoking the abbey's status as a Roman possession founded on Gilles's legendary *traditio*, confirms "all liberty and immunity granted . . . by our

---

[115] On how by the later eleventh century, such "reforms" were often also veiled extensions of lordship, see below, at nn. 203–219.

[116] The Burgundian abbey of Vézelay chose a similar language in its late twelfth-century presentation of its liberty in the face of various enemies, including Cluny. See *Monumenta Vizeliacensia: Textes relatifs à l'histoire de l'abbaye de Vézelay*, ed. R. B. C. Huygens, Corpus Christianorum Continuatio Medievalis, 42 (Turnholt, 1976), pp. 243–393.

predecessors' privileges." Surely this general and sweeping papal statement of liberty which Abbot Peter Anduze had specifically requested was Saint-Gilles's way of affirming its newly won independence from Cluny. Moreover, it was with this statement that the compiler of Paris BN Latin 11018 chose to terminate the manuscript. Why select this privilege rather than another as the endpiece if not because the date had a special significance in the context of the manuscript's subject: Saint-Gilles's legendary liberty? Echoing the opening privilege of the legendary Benedict, the final piece was, like it, a banner of the abbey's identity and liberty. Complementing the Benedict privilege, the final document demonstrated that the abbey's original and legendary liberty continued into the present, the present of the triumph over Cluny. The manuscript thus announces Saint-Gilles as papal and free—explicitly in the face of the counts and bishops, and implicitly, but just as strikingly, in the face of Cluny.

By binding together into a single entity the abbey's legendary origins and its present liberty, Paris BN Latin 11018 functions analogously to the cypress doors sculpted with the figures of Peter and Paul which in the *vita* Gilles receives from the pope on the occasion of the *traditio*.[117] In legend, these doors, the public face of the church, memorialized the *traditio* while proclaiming to all who saw the abbey that it was guarded by the apostles. The manuscript may even have had an actual physical monumental complement as well as this legendary one: the complex and extensive program of the abbey church's west façade, probably sculpted between about 1120 and about 1150, during the period of the manuscript's composition (see Figure 8).[118] No matter what interpretation they propose of its iconography, scholars agree that the façade betrays a remarkable reliance upon Roman and Late Antique models, both in its style and in its architectural disposition.[119] Actual Roman columns were even incorporated into the façade. Is this extreme emphasis on classical models yet another instance of Saint-Gilles's expression of its nature as a Roman abbey? Let us remember the threat represented by the series of comital castles built to tower above the

[117] See above, Chapter 2 at nn. 177–179.

[118] The dating of the façade has been much debated. The general consensus at present is that the crypt wall was built by the 1120s; construction was then halted and the program of the façade redesigned. Among others, see Ferguson O'Meara, *The Iconography of the Façade*, pp. 53–62, 95–161; Ferguson O'Meara, "Saint-Gilles-du-Gard: The Relationship of the Foundation to the Façade," *Journal for the Society of Architectural Historians* 39 (1980): 57–60; and Whitney Stoddard, *The Façade of Saint-Gilles: Its Influence on French Sculpture* (Middletown, Conn., 1973), pp. 127–159.

[119] On the classicizing style, see Ferguson O'Meara, *The Iconography of the Façade*, pp. 63–84; Victor Lassalle, *L'influence antique dans l'art roman provençal* (Paris, 1970); and Stoddard, *The Façade of Saint-Gilles*. On the iconography, see the different interpretations of Marcia L. Colish, "Peter of Bruys, Henry of Lausanne, and the Façade of St.-Gilles," *Traditio* 28 (1972): 451–460; and Ferguson O'Meara, *The Iconography of the Façade*. Also see Walter Cahn's reevaluation of both interpretations: "Heresy and the Interpretation of Romanesque Art," in *Romanesque and Gothic: Essays for George Zarnecki* (Woodbridge, Eng., 1987), pp. 27–34.

FIGURE 8. West façade of Saint-Gilles, first half of the twelfth century. Photograph by permission of Sheila Bonde.

abbey church. Next to these rude constructions, the church with its elegant west front would have been a sophisticated and powerful reminder of the abbey's legitimate lordship (and certainly not a celebration of the exploits of the counts, as some art historians have seen it to be).[120] Far from being the expression of Cluniac ideology that some art historians, misinterpreting Saint-Gilles's relation with the Burgundian abbey, have considered it to be, the façade with its deliberate echoes of Roman triumphal architecture may even proclaim the victory Saint-Gilles felt it had achieved over Cluny.[121] In any case, like Paris BN Latin 11018 and the cypress doors of the *vita,* the façade makes plain the results of the legendary *traditio,* announcing Saint-Gilles as peculiarly Roman.

Impelled by what it defined and thus experienced as pressure from episcopal, lay, and monastic lords, Saint-Gilles unfolded its legendary identity in these various forms. Invoking the pope as the transcendent sanction of its liberty and therefore its integrity, the abbey very distinctly weighted the equation between papal jurisdiction and Roman liberty in favor of the latter, interpreting it as effective independence. Other abbeys, facing similar en-

---

[120] For the argument that the façade celebrated the counts, see Ferguson O'Meara, *The Iconography of the Façade.* Her argument is made even more unlikely by the fact that the abbey did not incorporate the counts—except for possibly Raymond (IV?)—into its liturgical memory, that is its necrology. See Winzer, *S. Gilles,* pp. 364–366, 416–417.

[121] Concerning the façade as a reflection of Cluniac ideology, see Ferguson O'Meara, *The Iconography of the Façade,* pp. 148–157.

emies, likewise constructed themselves through their legends as independent, although coloring their liberty first royal and then papal. As I explore this process, it will become evident in which context of stress the abbeys were most likely to forge concrete foundation legends from extant but vague traditions: that is, which of the three enemies seemed most to threaten southern monasteries' image of themselves.

Lay Lords

The lay aristocracy, painted in older scholarship as the villain of a play entitled *The Eleventh-Century Church in the Hands of the Laity*, might seem at first a likely suspect.[122] Indeed, recent reassessments of ecclesiastical attitudes toward lay ownership of churches and the nobility's role in motivating monastic reform have found that there was a symbiosis between monasteries and the lay aristocracy, but that this relationship was not maintained without friction.[123] Such tension could irrupt into conflict, and could stimulate abbeys to resort to legendary self-definitions.

The tempestuous relations between the counts of Clermont and the monastery of Mozac during the twelfth century demonstrate the repercussions that conflicts could have on already extant legendary traditions. Confronting the counts, Mozac turned to two legendary guarantees of its immunity, one of whom was the legendary Pippin the Short. The actual king also played a role in the clash; legend and reality came to echo each other. Perhaps because of the traditional royal rights in the Auvergne and Velay, first Louis VI (1120s) and then Louis VII (1130s, 1160s–1170s) intervened in a complicated series of struggles in which the counts of Clermont and the viscounts of Polignac, seeking to expand their power, were aggressors not only against Mozac but also against the cathedral of Clermont, the canons of Brioude, and the abbeys of Manglieu and Issoire.[124]

---

[122] See Amann and Dumas, *L'église au pouvoir des laïques.*

[123] On ecclesiastical attitudes toward lay ownership of churches, see Hans-Erich Mager, "Studien über das Verhältnis der Cluniacenser zum Eigenkirchenwesen," in *Neue Forschungen über Cluny und die Cluniacenser,* ed. Gerd Tellenbach (Freiburg, 1959), pp. 169–217. For the aristocracy's role in "reform," see (among others) Bouchard, *Sword, Miter, and Cloister;* Karl Schmid, "Adel und Reform in Schwaben," in *Investiturstreit und Reichsverfassung,* ed. Josef Fleckenstein, Vorträge und Forschungen, 17 (Sigmaringen, 1973), pp. 296–319; Gerd Tellenbach, "Das Reformmönchtum und die Laien im elften und zwölften Jahrhundert," in *Cluny: Beiträge zu Gestalt und Wirkung der cluniazensischen Reform,* ed. Helmut Richter, Wege der Forschung, 241 (Darmstadt, 1975), pp. 371–400; and Joachim Wollasch, "Adel und Reform in Burgund," in *Investiturstreit und Reichsverfassung,* pp. 277–293. For a recent summary of these views, see John Howe, "The Nobility's Reform of the Medieval Church," *American Historical Review* 93 (1988): 317–339. An excellent discussion of symbiosis and tension between monastery and aristocracy is to be found in Rosenwein, *To be the Neighbor of Saint Peter.*

[124] For general remarks on these conflicts, see Dunbabin, *France in the Making,* p. 357; and Pacaut, *Louis VII,* pp. 85–87. Clerics, too, were aggressors in these conflicts. The deans of

In the 1120s, responding to the entreaties of the bishop of Clermont, Louis VI descended into the Auvergne to subdue the count. Suger, in his *vita* of Louis, relates that the count had occupied Clermont, but the twelfth-century *Vita S. Calmilii* written at Mozac accents a different comital offense.[125] This latter text accused Guillaume VI of having fortified Mozac's church.[126] Here the castle appears explicitly as the material embodiment of noble power, directly challenging the abbey just as it had at Saint-Gilles. But as the king mastered both the situation and the count, the church seems to have been restored to its original function, possibly even acquiring a new magnificence. The Carolingian church at Mozac was rebuilt in the Romanesque style at some point during the twelfth century, probably in those years immediately following the count's attack.[127]

Relations between Mozac and the counts remained difficult throughout the twelfth century, despite a reconciliation between the two parties in 1147 (the terms of which made it clear that the count and the abbot shared and thus vied for control of the *villa* of Mozac).[128] By the 1160s the count, allied with the viscount of Polignac, had created enough new difficulties for the Auvergnat churches that Louis VII was provoked to intervene in person. In 1169, during the second of his campaigns, Louis issued a diploma of royal protection for Mozac, specifying that no ecclesiastical or secular person would have the right "to build a tower (*turrem*) or a castle (*castellum*) within the abbey's boundaries."[129] This phrase, although not unusual in privileges, has a particular resonance of reality, given the preceding events. Was it directed specifically against the counts who at least once before had sought to transform Mozac into their castle? In any case, the counts' turbulence was not dammed for long. In 1211, Count Guy II, embroiled in a prolonged *guerra* with his brother, Bishop Robert of Clermont, invaded and destroyed the town and abbey of Mozac, carrying off the relics of Saint Austremonius in the bargain and thus symbolically stripping the community of its iden-

---

Clermont fortified the cathedral of Clermont against the bishop in the 1120s (Suger, *Vita Ludovici. Vie de Louis VI*, p. 232), and in the 1150s and 1160s the dean of Brioude, brother of the viscount of Polignac, aided his family's attempt to gain control of the town and chapter by transforming the deanery into a castle (see the series of letters in *Recueil des historiens des Gaules et de la France*, ed. M. Bouquet et al., 24 vols [Paris, 1738–1904], 16:43, 45–46, nos. 139, 145, 147).

[125] Suger, *Vita Ludovici. Vie de Louis VI*, pp. 232, 234, 236, 238, 240.

[126] Louis captured "Mosiacensem ecclesiam quam adversus eum Arvernicus comes munierat" (*Vita S. Calminii confessoris [AASS* August 3:761]).

[127] Bernard Crapelet suggests tentatively the abbacy of Eustache of Montboissier (1131– post 1147) for the church's reconstruction; *Auvergne romane* (La Pierre-Qui-Vire, 1965), p. 206.

[128] See the text in *Bibliotheca Cluniacensis . . .* , ed. Martin Marrier and Andreas Quercetanus (Macon, 1915; reprint of 1614 ed.), no. 229, cols. 1411–1412.

[129] *GC* 2, instr. 116. Also see Achille Luchaire, *Etudes sur les actes de Louis VII* (Paris, 1885), pp. 282–283, no. 580.

tity.[130] As in the 1120s and 1160s, this comital incursion occasioned royal wrath, intervention, and victory.[131]

This tension between count and abbey, irrupting over the span of some one hundred years, played a role in the crystallization of Mozac's identity in several ways. During the twelfth century, the monastery recuperated the shadowy figure of Calminius, its aristocratic founder, fleshing him out in order to endow itself not only with more antique roots, but with a saintly and exemplary aristocratic protector. As the representation of imperial *Romanitas*, Calminius was a powerful imaginative counterpart to the counts, rendering their pretensions puny.[132] Furthermore, Calminius, founder and protector of Mozac as well as of Saint-Chaffre, demonstrated the correct aristocratic attitude toward monasteries.[133] Was the twelfth-century *Vita S. Calminii* thus an implicit admonishment and lesson directed toward the count who had threatened the abbey? Moreover, was the clash with the counts the immediate context, if not the catalyst, for this new embellishment of Calminius—indeed, for his transformation into a saint?

The *Vita S. Calminii* presents the events as such, intertwining the *inventio* (or at least elevation) of the new saint, the conflict with the count in the 1120s, and Louis VI's victory. According to the *vita*, Calminius's remains had reposed "for very many years" in a wooden coffin-shrine behind the main altar, remaining hidden (*lat[ere]*) (and by implication forgotten?) in this humble place until Louis VI's reign.[134] Although vaguely ascribing to Calminius's intercession some generic miracles previous to this time, the text leaves little doubt that the founder's sanctity was revealed only during the royal resolution of the conflict with the count. Searching the church for booty, Louis's *satellites* open the shrine, and find celestial rather than material treasure. They are reprimanded for their sacrilege (and cupidity) by punitive miracles: Mozac did not intend to trade one form of domination for another. The invented sanctity of the founder, associated with the victory of

130 For several slightly different versions of Guy's attack on Mozac, see the *Chronicon Bernardi Iterii armarii monasterii S. Marcialis*, in *Chroniques de Saint-Martial de Limoges*, ed. Henri Duplès-Agier (Paris, 1874), pp. 83, 84; and *Ex chronico Cluniacensis coenobii*, in *Recueil des historiens des Gaules*, 18:743. Cf. the account of the violent conflict between the brothers in Etienne Baluze, *Histoire généalogique de la Maison d'Auvergne*, 2 vols. (Paris, 1708), 1:71–72.

131 See Guillaume Le Breton, *Philippidos* 8.452–485, in *Œuvres de Rigord et de Guillaume Le Breton*, 2:227–228.

132 On Calminius, see above: Chapter 3 at nn. 1–7, 64–72; Chapter 4 at nn. 28–29.

133 See Farmer's elucidation of how in their legendary traditions the monks of Marmoutiers shaped various of their patrons as models for aristocratic behavior: *Communities of Saint Martin*, pp. 78–116.

134 *Vita S. Calminii confessoris* (*AASS* August 3:761). Although this passage does not use the topos of the saint's body whose presence was forgotten until it was revealed, the structure of the narrative and its use of the verb *latere* suggest that there was no previous cult of Calminius and that this is an *inventio* rather than an *elevatio*. The earliest definitively datable documents to refer to Calminius as a saint at Mozac date from the 1160s; see above, Chapter 3 at nn. 5–6.

king and abbey over count, is presented as a guarantee of the monastery's liberty from all oppression or unjust exercise of domination—even on the part of its royal protector.

Whether or not in reality the origins of Calminius's cult at Mozac were linked this neatly to the conflict with the count, the abbey imaginatively commemorated them as being so. The appeal to this founder, hitherto a minor figure in the abbey's legend but suddenly saintly and significant, thus informed the abbey's own image of its crisis and triumph. Indeed, on the eve or perhaps even during the conflict between bishop and count in which Mozac would suffer a third time at the count's hands, the abbey added a further layer to its image of Calminius. As we have seen, sometime at the very end of the twelfth century, Mozac commissioned an impressive and eloquently narrative enamel shrine for the relics of its founder.[135] Did this new way of rendering manifest the saint's presence reveal the abbey's continuing need to define itself in the face of the count?

In any case, as it recuperated Calminius, Mozac did not thereby glorify contemporaneous nobility or fashion itself as an abbey subject to aristocratic jurisdiction.[136] Instead, in the twelfth century Mozac insisted in a new way upon its nature as a royal monastery. It did so partly through Calminius himself; as we have seen, the *Vita S. Calminii* characterized Mozac as already a "royal monastery" (*monasterium regale*) at the time of its foundation by Calminius.[137] Furthermore, this text highlighted the association of the king's victory over the count with the saint's revelation-elevation. As this latter link between king and saint hints, Mozac's nature as a royal abbey established by previous layers of its legend had taken on a new dimension in the context of the conflicts with the counts.

Indeed, Mozac made such conflict part of its legendary royal identity in the twelfth-century vision of Lamfred, the culmination of the textual re-fashioning of the translation of Saint Austremonius's relics into a refoundation of the abbey by Pippin the Short.[138] After describing Pippin's decision to rebuild and richly endow Mozac, the vision text concludes by describing how the king vanquished Waïfre. Certainly Pippin's campaigns against this renegade duke and would-be king were a topos of the southern legends— but given the twelfth-century situation at Mozac, might there not be in this episode a reference to the contemporaneous counts who, bent on domination of the region (and abbey), had been subdued by the Capetian king?[139]

---

[135] See above, Chapter 3 at nn. 1–3.

[136] Use of an aristocratic figure in an abbey's legend did not necessarily translate into a celebration of contemporary aristocrats. See above, Introduction, n. 24.

[137] See above, Chapter 3 at nn. 70–72.

[138] The text is edited by Krusch, "Reise nach Frankreich," pp. 24–25. For further discussion, see above: Chapter 2 at nn. 70–71; Chapter 4 at nn. 142–146.

[139] This reading is justified by the tendency the legends have to use Waïfre, a rebel against legitimate royal power, in a negative fashion.

Furthermore, in this text, Pippin rebuilds Mozac with the stones of Clermont, the city so ominously close to Mozac and the site where the counts of Clermont had their primary castle until Louis VI dislodged them in the 1120s.[140] Are the *visio's* "stones of Clermont" an oblique reference to the comital castle whose menace had been neutralized by the king? If so, this legendary appropriation of the stone construction emanating power—Clermont—as the fabric for Mozac's architectural expression of itself is a triumphant textual inversion of the count's actual transformation of the abbey church into a fortification in the 1120s.[141]

The vision text thus introduced details into Mozac's legend that made the royal refoundation equally a triumph over a noble oppressor and a destruction of his stronghold.[142] Conflict became integrated into the abbey's image of its origins in such a way as to make the king not merely its patron but also an active protector from the beginning. Legend and reality coincided as they did at Saint-Gilles. Not only had the Capetians thrice rescued the abbey from the counts but, following their interventions, Louis VII and Philip II had endowed Mozac with privileges of royal protection—and hence with the status of a royal monastery.[143] This dovetailing of legendary and actual identity appears in Louis's diploma. The king states that he is "following the example of our predecessors." The only extant document that could have served as his exemplar is Mozac's diploma of Pippin the Short, a legendary fabrication of the late eleventh century.[144] Here the king, at the abbey's request, confirms and thereby realizes its legend, while branding as illegitimate any comital pretensions.

Mozac, like Saint-Gilles, thus suffered primarily from comital pretensions to physically control monastic space. This sort of violent clash between abbey and nobility may have been the product of the intensification and expansion of territorial lay lordship during the late eleventh and twelfth centuries. In this period, though, a less violent process was at work that could create friction between monasteries and secular lords. In the eleventh century, lay rights—particularly those of proprietorship—over churches be-

---

140   On the castle, the counts, and Louis VI, see Gabriel Fournier, *Châteaux, villages et villes d'Auvergne au XVe siècle d'après l'Armorial de Guillaume Revel* (Paris, 1973), pp. 68, 78.

141   On the architectural dialogue between castle and church in legend, see above, Chapter 2 at nn. 105–109; in reality (at Saint-Gilles), see above at nn. 75–76, 86–87.

142   The eleventh-century *Vita tertia S. Austremonii* already had made Mozac into a royal refoundation (see above, Chapter 4 at nn. 136–139), but the details pertaining to Waïfre and Clermont discussed here are unique to the vision text.

143   Philip II's privilege (1217) confirms that of Louis VII (1169). Philip's privilege: *Recueil des actes de Philippe Auguste*, 4:127–129, no. 1503. For Louis's, see n. 144 below.

144   Louis VII: *GC* 2, instr. 111. Pippin the Short: *Recueil des actes de Pépin*, pp. 227–242, 285–286, nos. 58 and 64. Philip I's diploma of 1095 is unlikely to have been the exemplar invoked by Louis VII, for it is above all a *traditio* of the abbey to Cluny. See *Recueil des actes de Philippe Ier, roi de France (1059–1108)*, ed. Maurice Prou (Paris, 1908), pp. 342–343, no. 135. Also see Appendix 1 below.

came the target of certain reformers' attacks. Despite the rash of *guerpitiones* (renunciations) made in the late eleventh century by lay nobles cowed or convinced by the reformers' proclamations, lay rights over abbeys often remained a reality.[145] Although the aristocracy had hardly been persuaded that such rights were illegitimate, monasteries began to define them as such. This process of redefinition was evident at Saint-Gilles: only in the late eleventh century did the abbey grow restive over the rights that the counts of Toulouse had exercised since at least the early part of the century. Perhaps, too, this process was mirrored in the legend of Moissac, the other case in which there is an interplay—this time most delicate—between legendary identity and conflict with the secular aristocracy.

In the eleventh century, Moissac seems to have maintained essentially good relations with the lords who held the title of "secular abbot" (*abbas secularis*). First the counts of Toulouse and then various members of local aristocratic families fulfilled this function, which entailed an oath of fidelity to the abbot, certain fiscal prerogatives, and the defense (*defensio*) of the monastery.[146] Only in the 1090s was there any sign of strain between Moissac and these abbots. Bertrand de Fumel was accused of having inflicted *violentia* and *injuria* upon the abbey—perhaps a formula that alluded to usurpations of property, perhaps a protest against an attempt to impose conditions the abbey saw as onerous.[147]

All remained quiet until 1130. In that year, the monks appealed to Alfonse-Jourdain of Toulouse to support their claims to a certain property that their secular abbot had tried to usurp. There are also indications that this abbot, Bertrand of Monte Incensi, had attempted to extend his prerogatives over the abbey while at the same time refusing to profess his fidelity. Significantly, the title now used for the office that Bertrand had tried to metamorphose into lord of Moissac was not *abbas secularis,* but *abbas miles.* Perhaps in reaction to this Bertrand's pretensions, Moissac obtained from Alfonse-Jourdain a permanent renunciation of the comital right to impose an *abbas miles.* After this implicit transfer of the right to the abbey itself, there

[145] Cf. Hirsch's conclusion, with respect to twelfth-century Germany, that although the names used for the lay lords of abbeys may have changed (from *Eigenherren* [proprietary lord] to *Vögte* [stewards]), their power had not been effectively diminished. Hirsch, *Die Klosterimmunität.*

[146] Here I follow the convincing revisionist analysis of the "secular abbots" in Axel Müssigbrod, *Die Abtei Moissac 1050–1150: Zu einem Zentrum cluniacensischen Mönchtums in Südwestfrankreich,* Münstersche Mittelalter-Schriften, 58 (Munich, 1988), pp. 39–59. For a very different interpretation of the secular abbots and the tenor of their relations with Moissac, see Magnou-Nortier "Abbés séculiers," pp. 123–132, and her *La société laïque,* pp. 501–504.

[147] Nonetheless, this secular abbot was commemorated in the abbey's necrology, an indication perhaps that his altercation with the abbey had not been too acrimonious. Müssigbrod, *Die Abtei Moissac,* pp. 49–50.

seem to have been no further *abbates seculares* or *milites*—perhaps because the abbey no longer needed such protection, perhaps because it now saw any lay lordship as illegitimate.[148]

Recently it has been suggested that the iconography of the celebrated twelfth-century tympanum of the abbey church be read as a statement of Moissac's "triumph" over its secular abbots.[149] But perhaps this suggestion, which implies that Moissac had long suffered from these abbots, needs to be modulated; the tympanum may have been instead an expression of the abbey's growing sense of its independence from lay tutelage. The inklings of legendary development discernible at Moissac during this period were perhaps stimulated by the same crystallization of identity. The abbey had claimed that it was a royal foundation since at least the eleventh century. Then, sometime in the twelfth century, Moissac interpolated its copy of the *Vita sancti Desiderii* in order to obliterate the textual traces of its actual nonroyal foundation.[150] Was this legendary reassertion of a royal foundation part of Moissac's definition of itself as free from control of local lay aristocrats?

These are speculations at best, based on relative chronological coincidence. In the early thirteenth century, however, there was a tight weave between legend and Moissac's relations with local secular lords, at least according to the chronicle written by Moissac's late fourteenth-century abbot, Aymeric de Peyrat. Aymeric's descriptions should be taken with a grain of salt, though, for this abbot firmly believed (in good Gregorian fashion) that any lay person who exercised any form of control over the abbey was its enemy. Thus, in a black portrait that has mislead many historians, he shaped the "secular abbots" of the eleventh century as oppressors and villains.[151] We must be mindful of this slant as we read Aymeric's description of how the counts of Toulouse slipped between the poles of enmity and amity with the monastery.[152]

During the period of social tensions and rifts created by the political struggle that had coalesced around the Cathars, this abbey and the counts of

---

[148] On Bertrand of Monte Incensi's relations with Moissac, and on Alfonse-Jourdain's renunciation which resulted in the disappearance of this office, see Müssigbrod, *Die Abtei Moissac*, pp. 54–56. Here I give a somewhat different and more pointed interpretation of the abbey's evident decision to appoint no further secular abbots.

[149] Peter Klein, "Programmes eschatologiques, fonction et réception historiques des portails du XIIe siècle: Moissac–Beaulieu–Saint-Denis," *Cahiers de Civilisation Médiévale* 33 (1990): 328.

[150] See above: Chapter 3 at nn. 50–52, on the interpolation, and Chapter 4 at nn. 73–94 on Moissac's legend in general.

[151] See the perceptive remarks of Müssigbrod, *Die Abtei Moissac*, pp. 57–58.

[152] Aymeric devotes the last section of the *Chronicon* entirely to the counts of Toulouse (Paris, BN Latin 4991A, ff. 167rb–178va). The counts also surface frequently in the section dealing with the abbots of Moissac (ff. 152ra–167rb).

Toulouse appear to have come into conflict. In this conflict, the abbey's
legendary origins figured in various ways. As we have seen, Aymeric de
Peyrat relates that the abbey, suffering from what it saw as usurpations and
invasions by successive counts of Toulouse (first Raymond VI, who had
arrested the abbot, and then Simon of Montfort, who proved no better a
lord), sent a letter to Philip Augustus appealing for aid sometime in the
second decade of the thirteenth century.[153] The letter explicitly invoked the
abbey's royal foundation and implored the monarch to restore the privileges, most particularly the *libertas,* which his predecessors had granted.[154]
The "servitude" (*servitus*), as the letter calls it, imposed by the count thus
provoked the abbey to enunciate clearly and publicly its legend, or at least
Aymeric saw it as having done so.

Aymeric, with some chronological confusion, used this letter as the cen-
terpiece in his account of a round of conflict between Moissac and Raymond
VI's son, Raymond VII. First, Aymeric complains that the latter had inflicted
various injuries upon the abbey.[155] The count's motivation, Aymeric insists
repeatedly, was in part precisely Moissac's legend: "it is true that [Raymond
VII] held the monastery, its abbot and its community, in great hatred" not
only because his father had been besieged in the town of Moissac (1214?),
but most particularly because "it was said publicly that Clovis, the first king of
the Franks, and certain of his successors, the kings of France" had founded
the abbey.[156] Given the situation of the 1220s and 1230s, it is not hard to
imagine how Raymond VII's hackles would have been raised by Moissac's
proud claims to royal origins. The kings of France were perhaps the last
people to whom the counts of Toulouse felt well disposed in this era. Nor
were the counts particularly fond of the abbey, which, unlike the townspeo-

---

[153] For the abbey's relations wth Raymond VI and Simon of Montfort, see Lagrèze-Fossat,
Etudes historiques, 1:143–58.

[154] See above, Chapter 4 at nn.77–79.

[155] "Post hunc raymundus de monte pensato [an abbot of Moissac] de quo legitur quod
anno domini millesimo ccxxxiiii raymundus pessimus omnium raymundorum et loquitur de
raymundo ultimo quod tunc erat mortuus raimundus pater suus senior (ut dicetur infra)
disrupit et dissipavit minime dans honorem deo vero genitori sue nec sanctis eius petro et
paulo famosissimum monasterium quod sit in toto suo comitatu ministrante raymundo
meliori omnium raymundorum [the abbot]. Hic raymundus abbas conquestus fuit regi
francie de malis per ipsum comitem contra suum monasterium perpetratis et commissis"
(Aymeric de Peyrat, *Chronicon;* Paris, BN Latin 4991A, f. 165rb). On Raymond VII's relations
with the abbey, see Lagrèze-Fossat, *Etudes historiques,* 1:164–170.

[156] "[E]t verum est quod dictus comes [Raymond VII] multum odium habebat monasterium, abbatem et conventum, quia predecessor suus fuerat in obsidione facta per sym-
onem comitem montiffortis predicte ville tempore patris sui et qui dicebatur publice quod
clodoveus primus rex francorum et quidam successores sui reges francie dictam abbatiam
fundaverunt" (Aymeric de Peyrat, *Chronicon;* Paris, BN Latin 4991A, f. 165rb). "Maiorem
idignationem [sic] quem habuit comes tholosanus contra abbatem moyssiacy et suum monasterium fuit quia asserebant clodoveum primum regem francie christianum fundasse dictum monasterium" (f. 122va).

ple of Moissac, had generally supported the crusading invaders from the north.[157]

After this stunning statement of the reasons behind Raymond VII's enmity, Aymeric cites the letter to Philip Augustus which laments this count's father's mistreatment of the abbey.[158] This conflation of counts is not without significance: here again, although at the level of narrative structure rather than of actual appeal, legend was linked with conflict. Aymeric, as he wrote the early thirteenth-century monks had done, conducted his discourse about comital domination at least partly through the medium of Moissac's legend of royal foundation (which by his day had been translated into actual royal protection).[159]

Other than these three instances—Moissac, Saint-Gilles, and Mozac—I have found no cases in which the evidence suggests that legend related in any fashion to identifiable tension with secular lords. Perhaps this is because such conflicts were less rather than more frequent, and blended into the symbiosis that scholars now perceive in the relations between abbeys and the lay aristocracy. Or perhaps the paucity of cases is simply a matter of which sources have survived. After all, the legends in general focus on creating the monastery as a place that is free from outside control. Various motifs even circumscribe lay power with various motifs, thus relegating it to the domain outside the sacred space of the monastery.

But must this legendary emphasis on freedom from secular lords necessarily have been engendered by specific conflicts? After all, freedom from lay control was one of the banners waved by ecclesiastical reformers beginning in the second half of the eleventh century; it was a pillar of the ideal of liberty they promulgated. In their legends, many southern abbeys took part in this tantalizing redefinition of the network of social relations by ascribing to themselves such independence—whether or not they experienced actual conflict with lay lords.[160] Nonetheless, the reformers' ideals did not govern completely the monasteries' imagination. Only rarely did the pope, or his representative in the shape of a figure endowed with ecclesiastical *Romanitas,* appear as the primary transcendent guarantee of immunity from secular control. Rather, as at Mozac and Moissac, the king most often enjoyed this role.

---

[157] During the siege of 1212, the abbot of Moissac appears to have taken sides with the crusaders from the north; see Lagrèze-Fossat, *Etudes historiques,* 1:153.

[158] Aymeric de Peyrat, *Chronicon* (Paris, BN Latin 4991A, f. 165va–vb). Although Aymeric implies that the letter was written in this context, the letter addresses "King Philip" and hence could not have been written in the 1230s.

[159] On the thirteenth-century recognition of Moissac's status as a royal abbey (and thus the realization of its legend), see above, Chapter 5 at nn. 231–233.

[160] See Goffart's caution against assuming that conflict lies behind an emphasis on certain privileges or rights: *Le Mans Forgeries,* pp. 192–199.

Episcopal Lords

Given that I have found only two cases besides Saint-Gilles in which the lay aristocracy was the threat that stimulated the legendary impulse, it might seem that bishops, the other social agent from whose control "reformed" abbeys sought to escape, were the real villains. Indeed, recent studies of eleventh-century monasticism have tended to shift the onus from the lay to the ecclesiastical aristocracy—that is, to the episcopate. We have come to understand the eleventh and twelfth centuries as a time in which monasteries attempted to win partial if not full exemption from the jurisdiction of the diocesan bishop or at least to liberate themselves from his *potestas*.[161] This welling rejection of episcopal domination, which had a long if obscure prehistory, may have a twofold significance similar to that I suggested for the contemporaneous monastic refusal of lay lordship. On the one hand, these efforts may represent a reaction to a change in the nature of episcopal lordship, which like other forms of lordship, intensified and became expressed in increasingly hierarchical terms in the late eleventh and twelfth centuries.[162] On the other, the desire for exemption may also relate to the reformers' redefinition of monastic liberty as involving at least some freedom from episcopal control—a definition certainly absorbed by (if not evolved within) monastic milieus.

In their quest for this sort of liberty, as in that for freedom from lay lordship, monasteries could draw upon their legendary resources.[163] Moreover, as they defined their liberty from ordinaries, southern abbeys appealed first and foremost to the bishops' distant Roman counterpart, the pope, as might seem natural. As we shall see, though, the king could play an imaginative role in this debate between abbey and bishop. In monastic imagination the liberty he assured was continuous with that affirmed by the pope, even in the age of the Gregorian splitting of secular and ecclesiastical jurisdictions.[164]

---

[161] See the works cited above in Chapter 1, nn. 94–97. In the eleventh century, the term *libertas* did not yet imply full exemption from episcopal jurisdiction as it would by the later twelfth century. See Schreiber, *Kurie und Kloster,* 1:32–47; and Szabó-Bechstein, *"Libertas Ecclesiae,"* pp. 179–183. Nor did freedom from episcopal *potestas* imply exemption; see, for example, the privilege of Leo IX for Chiusa (1050) in Paul I. Kehr, *Regesta Pontificum Romanorum: Italia Pontifica,* 9 vols. (Berlin, 1906–1962), 6.2:122–123, no. 2.

[162] For an interesting related suggestion, see Cowdrey, *The Cluniacs,* p. 23, n. 2 (although I would emphasize more the role of changes in episcopal lordship).

[163] See the discussions of three northern French abbeys and their relations with their ordinary. Fécamp: Lemarignier, *Etude sur les privilèges d'exemption,* pp. 192–204. Fleury: Head, *Hagiography and the Cult of Saints,* pp. 202–234. Marmoutier (and Saint-Martin of Tours): Farmer, *Communities of Saint Martin,* pp. 38–62, 157–165.

[164] Compare the way in which several German and Italian abbeys used earlier royal diplomas granting immunity as the basis for their claims of exemption in the eleventh and twelfth centuries. Hirsch, *Die Klosterimmunität,* pp. 6–9; Schreiber, *Kurie und Kloster,* 1:41, n. 1.

The instances in which abbey opposed bishop reveal several permutations of the relationship between legend and conflict. But in each case, episcopal jurisdiction as embodied by the right and rite of consecration (whether of church or abbot) played a significant role, as it had at Saint-Gilles. This ritual was multivalent both for monks and bishops, symbolizing monastic subjection—or monastic liberty.[165] For example, in 1095/1096, when the abbot of Uzerche, Geraldus, asked Urban II to consecrate the abbey church—according to the twelfth-century prologue to this abbey's cartulary—the bishop ordinary, Humbaldus of Limoges, angrily intervened to prevent what he obviously saw as a usurpation of his rights and a freeing of the abbey from his control.[166] The subsequent abbot of Uzerche, Gaubertus Malafaida, effected a reconciliation with the ordinary by means of the same ritual; he asked Humbald's successor, Wido (as well as the archbishop of Lyon and the bishop of Perigueux), to consecrate the abbey's altars.[167]

This is but one of the ambivalent episodes that, according to the prologue, characterized relations between Uzerche and its bishop in the twelfth century. Bishop Eustorgius (d. 1137), whom the text praises as "most pious" (*piissimus*), appears as an ally and patron who enriched the abbey.[168] The situation changed, however, under his successor and nephew, Geraldus of Cher, whom Eustorgius had entrusted to the abbot of Uzerche for his education.[169] The *nutritus* turned against the abbey where he had been raised; Geraldus "armed himself against the church of Uzerche." This generic accusation of violent lordship prefaced the specific charge that Geraldus had usurped two of the abbey's properties and had even allowed one of them, a priory, to make itself into an abbey. The abbot of Uzerche appealed to Rome for a settlement—an indication, like the 1095/1906 request that Urban II

---

[165] See the case of the northern abbey of La Trinité (Vendôme) which fabricated documents proclaiming that it had the right to choose whatever bishop it liked for the abbot's consecration. Johnson, *Prayer, Patronage*, pp. 121–122.

[166] *Ex historia monasterii Usercensis,* in *Cartulaire de l'abbaye d'Uzerche,* p. 35. Tension between abbot and bishop existed before 1095; Geraldus had contested the legitimacy of Humbaldus's election in 1087, and was active in his eventual removal as bishop; see Sohn, *Der Abbatiat Ademars,* pp. 241–266. Humbaldus's refusal to let Urban consecrate the abbey may have been legitimate. According to the privilege (ca. 977) that the bishop of Limoges issued at Uzerche's foundation, the abbey was to have the right of free election, but it was not granted any exemption from episcopal jurisdiction, spiritual or disciplinary; see *Cartulaire de l'abbaye d'Uzerche,* pp. 60–65.

[167] On this incident, see above, Chapter 1 at n. 82.

[168] The abbot had Eustorgius released from the captivity in which William IX was holding him; the bishop gave *multa bona* to Uzerche. Furthermore, intervening as a mediator in a disputed abbatial election at Uzerche (ca. 1133), Eustorgius was physically attacked but nonetheless praiseworthily continued to strive for a settlement. *Ex historia monasterii Usercensis,* in *Cartulaire de l'abbaye d'Uzerche,* pp. 37, 40, 42.

[169] *Ex historia monasterii Usercensis,* in *Cartulaire de l'abbaye d'Uzerche,* p. 40.

consecrate the church, that the abbey considered itself papal.[170] Not only did Uzerche triumph, but it obtained privileges from Lucius II and Eugenius III stating its "immunity" and its relation to Rome; although the prologue's language is ambiguous, it suggests these pontiffs stated that the abbey was a papal possession and under Roman jurisdiction.[171]

Uzerche thus affirmed its identity as a papal abbey in the context of opposition to some of its bishops ordinary. But what of its legend? Certainly there is not the same tight weave that was discernible at Saint-Gilles, or even at Mozac and Moissac; Uzerche did not call upon its origins to sanction the liberty it sought. The relation between conflict and legend was even more subtle, and perhaps wholly unconscious. Remember that Uzerche presented itself in the prologue as a foundation of Pippin the Short, who intended thus to replace the rebellious see of Limoges. The way in which the narrative constructs Limoges's fall from grace, Uzerche's ascension, and Limoges's eventual unjust reclamation of primacy casts a shadow upon the bishops of Limoges. Their lordship was questionable, the legend hints. It might be good or it might be bad, according to the circumstances.[172] Is this another form of the ambivalence with which the abbey evidently viewed the bishops of the twelfth century?

In the second instance I have found of clash between abbey and ordinary in which legend plays a role, legend was invoked—but only faintly—during the conflict. But documents fashioned during the conflict that were not intrinsically legendary became so afterward. The core of the tension between this abbey, Aniane, and its ordinary was again the balance between episcopal lordship and monastic liberty as embodied by consecration and resulting obedience. By the 1060s, Aniane began to refuse to accept benediction—either of its abbots or of those monks who entered orders—from the hands of the bishops of Maguelone.

This clear denial of subjection to episcopal power manifested itself in a series of privileges of Popes John XV, Nicholas II, Alexander II, Urban II, and Pascal II, all forged or interpolated at Aniane between the later eleventh and the mid- to early twelfth century.[173] Through these documents, the

---

[170] The appeal to Rome did not necessarily mean that Uzerche was exempt from episcopal jurisdiction; see Schreiber, *Kurie und Kloster,* 1:206–207.

[171] "Eam sub protectione Romanae ecclesiae posuerunt, ut tanquam filiam eam omni tempore diligat, regat, defendat, nec jure suo defraudari patiatur." Uzerche was also to pay an annual *census,* a sign of being a papal possession. For the course of the conflict between Geraldus and the abbey, see *Ex historia monasterii Usercensis,* in *Cartulaire de l'abbaye d'Uzerche,* pp. 44, 46–48 (here 48).

[172] On this mechanism in the legend, see above, Chapter 4 at nn. 147–150.

[173] *Cartulaires des abbayes d'Aniane et de Gellone,* 2:78–90, nos. 1–6. For an even more daring forgery of John XV, with essentially the same contents as that of "Nicholas," see *Papsturkunden 896–1046,* 1:599–601, no. 309 (Zimmermann also provides an edition of the John privilege included in the cartulary: 1:597–599, no. 308). On the possible dates of these forgeries, see Pückert, *Aniane und Gellone,* pp. 44, 54–102; and Tisset, *L'abbaye de Gellone,* pp.

abbey claimed that it possessed the rights of free election and of choosing the bishop it wished for ordinations and the abbot's consecration, as well as certain other prerogatives. Aniane reinforced the authority of these claims, particularly to the important right of selecting the bishop for abbatial consecration, by appealing to a most significant king: Charlemagne. Whether through interpolation or forgery, by late in the eleventh century the abbey had produced a diploma in which the monarch granted this right as well as that of free election.[174] While clothing Charlemagne with no clearly legendary garb, this text lends to the desired liberty the aura of the Carolingian ruler whose very name, as we have seen, had legendary echoes by the later eleventh century. Certainly those echoes would have resonated at Aniane, for it was in this period that the abbey began to press claims in legend to foundation by this monarch.[175] Indeed, Aniane made this diploma explicitly a part of its legend; it was inserted into the middle of the ninth-century *vita* of the monastery's primary founder, Benedict of Aniane. This interpolation, one of several introduced into the *vita* in the late eleventh or early twelfth century, deliberately associated the right of freedom from episcopal interference in abbatial election and consecration with Aniane's legendary origins.[176] Such liberty thus became intrinsic and permanent.

While thus constructing itself as a place utterly immune to episcopal lordship, Aniane presented itself as a locus of an equal power. The forged and interpolated papal privileges purported to endow the abbey with the right to dispense penance to its own monks and to lay people, and with the power to bind and loose, that is to pronounce excommunication and absolution—very unlikely rights for a monastery.[177] These startling and unusual pretensions to rival or indeed to replace the ordinary in his pastoral function, as well as those more familiar claims of liberty from his jurisdiction, were of course violently rejected by the bishops of Maguelone. Injured in their right, these prelates brought their case before Alexander II and Urban II, who decided in their favor. The abbots owed "subjection and reverence" to the ordinary, Alexander insisted, and at the council of Clermont in 1095 Urban obliged the current abbot, Peter, to swear then and

72–81. While it is likely that the forgeries and interpolations were done in several stages (some in the late eleventh century and others in the twelfth), Pückert's suggestion that several date from no earlier than the 1160s seems unlikely, given the structure of the cartulary's manuscript; see below at nn. 181–185.

    174 This diploma appears twice in the abbey's cartulary: *Cartulaires des abbayes d'Aniane et de Gellone*, 2:14–15 (in the middle of the *vita* of Benedict of Aniane) and 41–43, no. 1 (heading a series of royal diplomas). Pückert convincingly demonstrates that this text is a forgery; see his *Aniane und Gellone*, pp. 10–40, 47–52.

    175 See below at nn. 295–298.

    176 On the interpolations, see below at nn. 283–285.

    177 According to canon 18 of the First Lateran Council (1123), monks were not to dispense penance: *MGH Libelli de Lite* 2.2:183. Cf. Schreiber's brief remarks, *Kurie und Kloster,* 2:29, n. 2.

there his obedience to the bishop.[178] A *convenientia* of 1109 between abbot
and bishop showed that the former still had to be constrained to swear his
obedience to the latter, although now the primary issue seemed to be certain
churches that Aniane held but the bishop claimed as his own.[179] A promise
of obedience would be required of future abbots also, as privileges of
Calixtus II (1119) and Hadrian IV (1155) for Maguelone stated.[180]

Thus, the forgeries had not succeeded in liberating the abbey from the
ordinary's power. As authentic privileges of Innocent II (1130), Eugenius
III, and Anastasius IV (1154) show, Aniane was recognized as enjoying papal
protection, but not exemption from episcopal jurisdiction, either complete
or partial.[181] Nonetheless, the forgeries and the extraordinary liberty they
delineated became part of the abbey's legendary presentation and conception of itself. All the forgeries and interpolated documents are to be found
in Aniane's cartulary, compiled from the mid-twelfth through the early thirteenth century.[182] This does not seem terribly significant until we consider
the organization of the manuscript.[183] Heading the cartulary is the *vita* of
Benedict, Aniane's founder; this text, we have seen, includes the forged or
interpolated diploma of Charlemagne.[184] Following it are several letters of
Benedict and then two tables of contents, one listing the royal diplomas and
the second the papal privileges.[185] Next are the diplomas, all Carolingian
and headed by yet another copy of Charlemagne's diploma, and then the
papal privileges, the first six of which are the forgeries.[186] Tellingly, the

---

[178] Alexander's letter to the monks of Aniane: *Bullaire de l'église de Maguelone*, ed. J.
Rouquette and A. Villemagne, 2 vols. (Montpellier, 1911–1914), 1:4–5, no. 2. Urban's
privilege of 1095 for Maguelone recounting the events at Clermont: *Cartulaire de Maguelone*,
ed. J. Rouquette and A. Villemagne, 2 vols. (Montpellier, 1912–1913), 1:22–23, no. 7.

[179] *Cartulaire de Maguelone*, 1:65–69, no. 31. The bishop granted some of the disputed
churches to Aniane, but the abbot was forced to remit far more of them to the bishop.

[180] *Bullaire de l'église de Maguelone*, 1:33, 82, nos. 16 and 52.

[181] *Cartulaires des abbayes d'Aniane et de Gellone*, 2:96–100, nos. 10–12. In a privilege of
1120, Calixtus II states that Aniane is "specialiter sub beati Petri jure et proteccione"—a
phrase that could very well imply exemption. See *Cartulaires des abbayes d'Aniane et de Gellone*,
2:95, no. 9. This phrase, however, may be an interpolation; it is not repeated by any later
popes. Aniane did appear in the list of monasteries "of Saint Peter" in Cencius's redaction of
the *Liber censuum*, but a papal abbey was not necessarily exempt. See *Le Liber censuum de l'église
romaine*, ed. Paul Fabre and Louis Duchesne, 3 vols. (Paris, 1889–1952), 2:243.

[182] On the manuscript containing the cartulary, see Appendix 2 below.

[183] On the importance of the organization of material in cartularies, see Patrick Geary,
"Entre gestion et *gesta*," in *Les cartulaires: Actes de la table ronde organisée par l'Ecole nationale des
chartes et le G.D.R. 121 du C.N.R.S. (Paris, 5–7 décembre 1991)*, ed. Olivier Guyotjeannin et al.
(Paris, 1993), pp. 13–26.

[184] AD Hérault 1.H.1, ff. 1r–13v; *Cartulaires des abbayes d'Aniane et de Gellone*, 2:1–35.

[185] Letters of Benedict: AD Hérault 1.H.1, ff. 13v–14r; *Cartulaires des abbayes d'Aniane et de
Gellone*, 2:36–38. Table of royal diplomas: AD Hérault 1.H.1, ff. 14r–14va; *Cartulaires des
abbayes d'Aniane et de Gellone*, 2:39–40. Table of papal privileges: AD Hérault 1.H.1, f. 14vb;
Cartulaires des abbayes d'Aniane et de Gellone, 2:40–41.

[186] AD Hérault 1.H.1, ff. 15r–27r; *Cartulaires des abbayes d'Aniane et de Gellone*, 2:41–97.

rubrics used to describe these six privileges in the table of contents all include the word *libertas*.

The cartulary continues with more documents (privileges and charters). As these latter are not listed in the table of contents, however, it is possible that the manuscript was originally intended to end with the last privilege listed in the table, a privilege of Innocent II from 1130.[187] If this is so, then the original cartulary as a whole had a structure linking legend and liberty akin to what we have seen before. The foundation and founder (the *vita* and letters of Benedict) introduce and frame the other two pillars of monastic freedom: kings (Carolingian) and popes (eleventh and twelfth century, with one exception). This vision of Aniane's identity, partially predicated upon the documents forged during the conflict with the ordinary, strongly stamps the cartulary even in its present extended form; the cartulary becomes a text commemorating legendary foundation and legendary liberty.

At Uzerche and Aniane, as at Saint-Gilles, conflicts with the bishop ordinary in which the ritual of consecration was manipulated by one party or by both thus influenced in some fashion the abbeys' legendary perception of themselves. Given the general desire of abbeys to escape from episcopal jurisdiction in this era, it may seem surprising that I have not found more such cases among southern monasteries. Even in those instances just examined, the connections between legend and this sort of tension were often oblique rather than direct. Perhaps behind some of these legends lay conflicts that are obscured by lack of sources. After all, the legends in general accord much importance to establishing the abbey as a place as free as possible from episcopal domination. But then, the legends also delineate the monastery as free from lay control—and I have found equally few instances where actual clashes with this latter potential enemy stimulated the legendary impulse. The reason is probably the same in each case.

Legends that emphasize liberty—even those which take the form of a papal privilege (or a run of such privileges) guaranteeing certain rights in relation to the diocesan—do not always have as their core specific clashes with bishops.[188] The example of Charroux is illuminating. Its early twelfth-century *Liber de constitutione* contains a series of such papal privileges, beginning with one granted by Leo III in his legendary garb and ending with one in which Urban II, explicitly recalling the legend, consecrates the abbey and

---

[187] Given that there seems to be no paleographic caesura after Innocent's privilege (AD Hérault 1.H.1, ff. 34r–v), perhaps the cartulary now extant is partially a copy of another manuscript that contained only the privileges and the diplomas listed in the tables (and perhaps Benedict's *vita* and letters?). In any case, after Innocent's privilege, the principle of organization changes from strict chronology to what may be a grouping of properties by region but is certainly not chronological. This certainly bespeaks a change in the cartulary's function. Geary points out that chronological organization was commemorative, while organization by estates was an aid in managing the abbey's lands; see his "Entre gestion et *gesta*."

[188] See Goffart, *Le Mans Forgeries*, pp. 192–199.

thus establishes it as free.[189] The importance to Charroux of such liberty is underlined by another element of its legendary dossier: the supposedly eighth-century "testament" of Count Roger of Limoges, wildly interpolated if not created whole cloth sometime early in the eleventh century.[190] Here Roger, styled as the abbey's founder and builder (under Charlemagne's orders), stipulates that no bishop of Poitiers shall wield *potestas* over the abbey, nor celebrate mass there unless asked, nor require from the monks any price for consecrations and benedictions he performs for them.[191]

Yet behind these legendary assurances of Charroux's liberty, it is difficult to discern any hint of actual conflict with the ordinary over the abbey's status. There are no references to any such tensions in the abbey's charters until the mid-thirteenth century, well after the composition of the *Liber de constitutione*.[192] Instead, the bishop of Poitiers consecrated the church in 1028 and probably in 1047; and if he was not present at the council of 1082 when the abbey's new central relic, the Holy Foreskin, was revealed, he was when Urban II solemnly dedicated the main altar of the magnificent new church in 1096.[193] In light of the apparently amicable relations between abbey and bishop, this selection of Urban as the officiating prelate should not be read as an act of belligerent defiance of the ordinary, but rather as an indication of Charroux's desire for the liberty that the anointing of the altar by papal hands enunciated.[194] There is no evidence that the bishop of Poitiers took umbrage at this declaration of independence expressed by

[189] The popes are Leo III, John VIII, Benedict VII/VIII, Leo IX, Alexander II, and Urban II. There is some variation in the privileges' stipulations, that of Leo III being the simplest statement of protection and that of Alexander II introducing the important phrase "salva . . . reverencia sedis apostolice," which implied that the abbey was under papal jurisdiction. *Chartes et documents pour servir à l'histoire de l'abbaye de Charroux*, pp. 65–85. Leo III's (and possibly Leo IX's) privilege is a forgery, while those of John VIII, Alexander II, and Urban II seem to be authentic; see Hirsch, "Untersuchungen," pp. 384–387. Zimmermann considers the privilege of Benedict (VII) a probable forgery; see *Papsturkunden 896–1046*, 1:473–474, no. 238.

[190] *Chartes et documents pour servir à l'histoire de l'abbaye de Charroux*, pp. 53–62.

[191] Roger adds that if any bishop or archdeacon dare inflict *graves* or *superstitiones iniustas* (the equivalent of *malae consuetudines?*) on the abbey, he shall lose his office—a most unusual pretension to power within the ecclesiastical hierarchy on a count's part and, thus, yet another indication that the document is not authentic. *Chartes et documents pour servir à l'histoire de l'abbaye de Charroux*, pp. 58–59.

[192] The dispute about visitation in the mid-thirteenth century: *Chartes et documents pour servir à l'histoire de l'abbaye de Charroux*, pp. 251–258, nos. 109 and 110. There were two churches disputed between the abbey and the bishop in the twelfth century, but again probably after the *Liber*'s composition (pp. 137–138, 154–165; nos. 32 and 43).

[193] Consecration of 1028: Favreau and Camus, *Charroux*, p. 12. Consecration of 1047: *Chronique de Saint-Maixent*, p. 124.

[194] The link between papal consecration and restriction of episcopal rights in favor of papal rights (which from the monastic perspective meant liberty) is made explicitly in Urban's privilege: "quia ipsius aecclesie altare . . . nostris est manibus consecratum, adicientes statuimus ut preter apostolice sedis pontificem, nullus deinceps audeat in idem altare excommunicationis aut interdictionis proferre sententiam" (*Chartes et documents pour servir à l'histoire de l'abbaye de Charroux*, pp. 81–82).

papal consecration; nor did the bishop of Lodève seem to bridle when an altar at Gellone was consecrated by the papal legate, Amatus of Oloron, in 1076.[195]

Thus, every bishop did not react aggressively when an abbey attempted to gain the liberty symbolized by papal consecration; behind every legend stressing liberty from episcopal power, there was not necessarily a conflict with the ordinary. Such legends attest instead to the general monastic enthusiasm for drawing out the *libertas* defined by the reformers to its logical conclusions: in this case, exemption from all episcopal power. But the liberty proclaimed by such legends—and by such papal consecrations—was multivalent. Gellone's consecration by Amatus was a statement directed not at the bishop of Lodève, but rather at a monastic rival: the abbey of Aniane. The legate's act declared that Gellone was not a *cella* of nearby Aniane, as the latter monastery would have had it. As we shall see, Gellone's foundation legend was carefully crafted as a similarly proud and defiant proclamation of a liberty that would not admit of domination by another monastery.[196]

Monastic Lords

Such tensions in which abbey opposed abbey stimulated the legendary impulse at least as often as did friction between monasteries, on the one hand, and the lay or ecclesiastical aristocracy, on the other. Indeed, more of the legends seem to have arisen in the former context than in the latter. Again, perhaps this pattern is a product of chance—a matter of which documents happened to survive until the present day—but it might also be explained by the nature of hostile relations between abbeys. Did domination by another abbey challenge a monastic community's identity more fundamentally than episcopal or lay lordship, and hence more often prompt recourse to legend, the delineation and affirmation of that identity? The answer to this question is predicated in part on the nature of such domination.

Beginning in the late tenth century and reaching a crescendo in the late eleventh and early twelfth centuries were two monastic impulses that were complementary but bound to clash. This convergence of factors was similar to that in the case of monastic relations with bishops or the lay aristocracy. On the one hand was the desire for liberty from all domination, and on the

[195] For the consecration of the altar (dedicated to Guillaume) see the entry in thirteenth-century martyrology from Gellone (which then became an Aniane manuscript?): Montpellier, BM 13, f. 22v. There is no evidence of an actual struggle between this monastery and its bishop ordinary (the bishop of Lodève). Tisset dates Montpellier BM 13 as twelfth century (*L'abbaye de Gellone*, pp. 82–83, n. 157), but an entry for Saint Francis (f. 28r) is in the same hand as the rest of the manuscript.

[196] See below at nn. 299–307.

other a will to expand and strengthen monastic lordship, whether over estates, priories, or other abbeys. Although before the eleventh century there had been monasteries subject to others, abbeys would now feel more keenly the contradiction between such a subordinate status and their developing sense of independence and integrity. Finding, as did a monk of Saint-Jean of Sorde (according to a *notitia* purporting to date from the first half of the eleventh century), that it was unworthy to "be subject to the power (*potestas*) of another monastery," many abbeys tried in the later eleventh and twelfth centuries to rid themselves of ties that they had accepted previously.[197] Indeed, the colorful *notitia* relating to Sorde announces that the monk in question had stolen the charter that delineated his abbey's domination by another (Pessan) and lit fire to it with a candle. Whether or not this actually occurred, the charter's reduction to ashes symbolizes the hatred with which many abbeys came to regard another monastery's lordship. Thus, as in the cases of lay and episcopal control, the desire for liberty caused monasteries to redefine and to reorganize their relations with external social agents.

But it was not just the striving for liberty that led to this alteration and, inevitably, to conflict. The nature of one abbey's subordination to another had also changed. By the later eleventh century, monasteries, like lay and episcopal lords, envisioned relations in increasingly hierarchical terms.[198] Bonds between abbeys, which in the ninth and tenth centuries had been loosely defined and expressed in terms of affiliation between equals, became explicitly ones of lordship and subjection.[199] More onerous, such ties

---

[197] *GC* 1, instr. 167. This *notitia* was composed not from the perspective of Sorde, but from that of the abbey claiming domination over it: Pessan. That the abbey seeking to maintain domination would attribute such a sentiment to its subordinate underscores how prevalent the desire for independence was. The text purports to be the judgment rendered in the matter (thus Pessan appears as the winner) at a council over which Raymond, archbishop of Auch (ca. 1030) presided. This is the only text I have found relating to the controversy; the early thirteenth-century cartulary of Sorde (*Cartulaire de l'abbaye de Saint-Jean de Sorde . . .*) makes no reference to it (or, unsurprisingly, to the abbey's subjection in any way to Pessan). Already in the tenth century, some monasteries had rebelled against the imposition of the tutelage of another, as the celebrated case of Odo of Cluny's reform of Fleury shows. John of Salerno, *Vita sancti Odonis* (*PL* 133:80–81).

[198] Although abbots had always functioned as lords in monastic culture (see Koziol, *Begging Pardon*, pp. 184–185, 189–194), in the later eleventh century abbots began to style themselves more consciously as such, borrowing from secular ritual and insignia. See Wollasch, *Mönchtum zwischen Kirche und Welt*, p. 157; and Johnson, *Prayer, Patronage*, pp. 50–51. Also see Bernard of Clairvaux's pestiferations against abbots who rode in state like "domini castellorum": *Apologia*, in *Sancti Bernardi opera*, 3:102–103.

[199] Kassius Hallinger points out that Benedict of Aniane had no intention of creating a system of mother abbey and subject daughter, unlike the Cluniacs of the eleventh century; see his *Gorze-Kluny: Studien zu den monastischen Lebensformen und Gegensätzten im Hochmittelalter*, 2 vols. (Graz, 1971; 1st publ. 1950), 2:741, 743–744. Magnou-Nortier argues that only in the eleventh century did precise juridical ties begin to make one abbey subject to another; see her *La société laïque*, p. 491.

would be increasingly rejected and resisted in struggles that were perhaps even more bitter than those between abbeys and secular or episcopal lords.

In privileges and other diplomatic sources, such subjection often was expressed simply by a proprietary formula; monastery X appears among the list of monastery Y's possessions. Behind this simple statement lay an array of possible relations between the two monasteries: control of abbatial elections, selection of the subject community's abbot from the dominant house, an oath of obedience from one abbot to the other, the right to intervene in internal affairs of the subject house, control over the property of the subject house, elimination of the office of abbot and installation of a mere prior, and so on.[200] Such were the conditions that Saint-Pons-de-Thomières, Lagrasse, Saint-Victor of Marseilles, Moissac, and Cluny tried (often unsuccessfully) to impose upon a number of southern abbeys in order to build for themselves a chain of dependencies in the eleventh and early twelfth centuries.[201]

This phenomenon was not limited to a few large abbeys; such appetites characterized southern monasteries in general. Conques, Aniane, Psalmodi—these are just a few of the abbeys we shall find struggling to maintain or extend control over monasteries they defined as dependencies, although these latter certainly conceived of themselves as free. Indeed, an abbey that fought bitterly for its own liberty could be engaged simultaneously in defending its lordship over another monastery; Psalmodi, which had managed to extricate itself from Saint-Victor's grasp by the early twelfth century, accepted only willy-nilly Joncels's declaration of independence in the 1130s.[202]

Both perspectives, that of liberty and that of lordship—and thus the conflicts themselves—were fueled by various of the diverse currents of eleventh-century ecclesiastical reform. Liberty was a tenet of reform, especially by the later eleventh century. So, however, as we saw in the case of Saint-Gilles, was the subjection of one abbey to another for the purposes of spiritual and moral discipline (that is, for the introduction of the more rigorous ideals of communal life promulgated by the reformers).[203] Whether or not Cluny's motivations in its reforms of the tenth century were purely spiritual, accompanying its "reforms" of the eleventh century was

[200] On the configuration of relations between Cluny and its properties, see Rosenwein, *To Be the Neighbor of Saint Peter.*

[201] See E. Griffe, "La réforme monastique dans les pays audois (seconde moitié du XIe siècle)," in *Moissac et l'Occident*, pp. 133–145; Magnou-Nortier, *La société laïque*, pp. 491–512 (she points out the evanescence of the "federations" thus created); Anscari M. Mundo, "Monastic Movements in the East Pyrenees," in *Cluniac Monasticism in the Central Middle Ages*, ed. Noreen Hunt (Hamden, Conn., 1971), pp. 111–122; and Paul Schmid, "Die Entstehung des Marseiller Kirchenstaates," *Archiv für Urkundenforschung* 10 (1928): 176–207, and 11 (1930): 138–152.

[202] See below at nn. 233–329.

[203] See above at nn. 114–116.

often a barely concealed desire to subjugate and dominate—a desire that characterized Saint-Victor of Marseilles, the other great "reformer" in the south, from the beginning of its expansion in the mid-eleventh century.[204]

By this period, then, reform had two edges: the introduction of genuine spiritual reform went hand in hand with the incorporation of the monastery into the reformer's sphere of lordship. Both aspects were profoundly disturbing to the monastery thus reformed. The moral and disciplinary component of reform caused a radical and often bewildering change in the rhythm of life and the structure of the community, doing violence to its identity. Although many historians have seen such reforms as fostering monastic liberty (which they define only as freedom from lay control and exemption from episcopal jursidiction), from the perspective of the "reformed" abbey the one often precluded the other.[205] A "reformed" abbey became a dependent, a status hardly consonant with the monastic definition of liberty, which involved independence from *all* lordship, not just secular or episcopal.

Thus, despite the views of some modern historians—and of those agents (popes, bishops, and secular lords) who gave monasteries into the power of reforming abbeys—reform often amounted to a profound disruption of the community's ways. Equally, like subjection to any other monastery whose desire to extend or maintain its lordship was not masked behind the name of "reform," reform could promise the loss of liberty, rather than its assurance.[206] There were no neat and benevolent monastic federations contrasting with secular, "feudal" disorder and violence.[207] Monasteries could

[204] Hallinger argues that Cluny was rapacious from the mid-tenth century on; see his *Gorze-Kluny*, 2:743–761, 766–767. Jacques Hourlier argues that it was only under Odilo that Cluny became interested in *dominatio* ("Cluny et la notion de l'ordre religieux" in *A Cluny*, pp. 219–226), as does Wollasch (*Mönchtum zwischen Kirche und Welt*, pp. 152–153, 170–171). On Saint-Victor's methods, see Schmid, "Die Entstehung." Cf. Odo of Saint-Maur's famous statement that when a new abbot was appointed for Saint-Maur after its reform by Cluny, the Cluniacs "valde tristes effecti sunt quia cupiebant sibi ipsum locum ad cellam redigere" (*Vie de Bouchard le vénérable*, p. 13). For the view that Cluny should not be labeled as expansionist, see Bouchard, *Sword, Miter and Cloister*, p. 101, and her "Merovingian, Carolingian and Cluniac Monasticism."

[205] For historians who see Cluniac reforms as fostering monastic liberty, see n. 5 above.

[206] Several historians have made similar remarks specifically about Cluniac reform: Charles Dereine's comments on Lemarignier, "Aspects politiques," pp. 48–49; Jacques Dubois's comments on Wollasch, "Questions-clé," in *Saint-Sever*, p. 26; and Hallinger, *Gorze-Kluny*, 2:57–67 (mentioning Cluny but focusing on resistance to Hirsau). For a more general statement, see Mundo, "Monastic Movements," pp. 98–99 (whose chronology differs from the one presented here). On specific instances of resistance to Cluny, see Paul Ourliac, "L'abbaye de Lézat vers 1063," *Moissac et l'Occident*, pp. 167–177; Sohn, *Der Abbatiat Ademars*, esp. pp. 56–71, 302–305, 308; and, for the thirteenth century, Florent Cygler, "L'ordre de Cluny et les *rebelliones* au XIIIe siècle," *Francia* 19 (1992): 61–93. See also Thomas W. Lyman, "The Politics of Selective Eclecticism: Monastic Architecture, Pilgrimage Churches and 'Resistance to Cluny,'" *Gesta* 27 (1988): pp. 83–92.

[207] Lemarignier proposes that in the context of the political anarchy of the eleventh century, a model for order was created through monastic structures, most particularly the

and did clash in ways very similar to the often violent interactions between aristocratic lineages; at issue for abbeys as for aristocrats were domination and subordination. To be sure, southern abbeys sought order, but an order predicated on independence and lordship, not on subjection.

Striking texts composed between the last decade of the eleventh century and the middle of the twelfth century reveal in vivid terms how monastic lords were hated and resented as predators every bit as dangerous to liberty as any lay or episcopal lord. These texts describe Cluny's reform of Saint-Martial in the 1060s, Saint-Victor's reform of Psalmodi in the late eleventh century, and Lagrasse's attempt to acquire for itself the Catalan abbey of Guixols sometime early in the twelfth century.[208] To these can be added two texts pertaining to the reform of houses of canons; their subjects are Saint-Victor's reform of Saint-Martin of La Canourgue (Gévaudan) in 1060 and the late eleventh-century reform of Vieux (Albigeois) in which Aurillac was implicated.[209] These latter relate the same tale (and in the same language) of violent imposition of external lordship that appears in the sources relating to the abbeys.

Except for that pertaining to Guixols, each of these texts was composed in the form of a *notitia*, a descriptive notice, and written by the community that stood to lose its liberty at the hands of the aggressor. Even in the case of Guixols, the perspective of the threatened abbey is not completely obscured, for the document, a charter of 1118, was written by the bishop of Girona, apparently Guixols's partisan and defender.[210] With the exception of the Guixols text, all were composed from a retrospective of some twenty to one hundred years. These explications of events in the abbey's recent past were often composed with the obvious intention of rendering the other monastery's domination illegitimate. Here, however, it is not the polemical function of these texts that is of interest, but rather their perspective: how these communities remembered and characterized the imposition, whether or not in the guise of reform, of another abbey's power.

Cluniac congregation; see his "Political and Monastic Structures." Perhaps this is so—but it was an image of order that was often rejected by monasteries that would not be at the apex of the pyramid.

[208] Saint-Martial: a *nota* composed between 1120 and 1156, edited in de Lasteyrie, *L'abbaye*, pp. 427–429 (on its dating and composition, Sohn, *Der Abbatiat Ademars*, pp. 46–56). Psalmodi: a *notitia* composed by the abbey, in *GC* 6, instr. 184–186 (see Schmid, "Die Entstehung," pp. 202–206). Guixols: the bishop of Gerona's proclamation (1118) of interdict imposed on all of Lagrasse's possessions in his diocese; see De Marca, *Marca Hispanica*, col. 1251.

[209] Saint-Martin of La Canourgue: an account written in the early to mid-twelfth century by the canons themselves, "Un récit inédit de la prise de Saint-Martin of La Canourgue par les moines de Saint-Victor de Marseilles," ed. Robert Barroux, *Bulletin Philologique et Historique du Comité des Travaux Historiques* (1924): 190–191. Vieux-en-Albigeois: a long *notitia* written by the canons during the episcopate of Bertrand, bishop of Albi (1115–1125); edited in *Miscellanea novo ordine*, 1:124–126.

[210] See the reference in n. 208 above.

"By violence, by lay force, by the shedding of blood, by the expulsion of the monks, and finally by the granting of money"—this was how the monks of Saint-Victor gained control of Psalmodi, according to the *notitia* composed circa 1099 by the latter abbey.[211] The acts sketched in this brief formulaic phrase appear in the other texts. All, with the exception of the *notitia* relating to Vieux, emphasize the violence of the aggressor monastery, accusing the antagonist of having actually employed bands of *milites* to take the church in question.[212] "Occupation," "invasion," "violence"—these words scattered through the texts frame the events as occurring "against the will" of the abbey, as the bishop of Girona explicitly stated in the case of Guixols.[213] Commonly used to stigmatize those who broke the peace, this language of violence branded the aggressor as a violator of ecclesiastical sanctuary. It set up an implicit opposition between the innocent and unarmed (*inermes*) abbey and its armed opponent, which was exercising a power that certainly did not accord with monastic ideals, particularly those promulgated by the reformers.

Furthermore, very often the antagonist is accused of having acted in collusion with laymen. The *nota* of Saint-Martial, for example, recounts how Hugh of Cluny relied on the aid of the viscount of Limoges (and his *milites*) in order to insinuate himself into Saint-Martial and then carry out a coup.[214] Such descriptions expose the aggressor abbey as scheming to introduce a foreign, not purely monastic power into the victim monastery—and remember that by the later eleventh century, lay control of churches had been redefined as illegitimate.

These texts insinuate that the antagonist also engaged in even more tainted dealings in order to establish its domination. Two of the texts relate that lay collaborators were won to the cause through money and gifts.[215] An aggressor might bribe clerics as well in the effort to gain the object of its

211   *GC* 6, instr. 185.
212   See the spectacular description of the capture of Guixols by the abbot of Lagrasse and his men: de Marca, *Marca Hispanica,* col. 1251. The *nota* from Saint-Martial even refers to violent occupation in its title; see de Lasteyrie, *L'abbaye,* p. 427. The text from Saint-Martin of La Canourgue describes how the monks of Saint-Victor descended upon the canons with *multitudine militum* and took the comunity *per violentiam;* see "Un récit inédit," p. 191. At one stage of a bitter dispute between Aniane and La Chaise-Dieu about the possession of Goudargues, Honorius II in 1125/1129 accused the monks of La Chaise-Dieu of having "invaded" (*invaserunt*) Goudargues "violenter et per potestates externas" (*Cartulaires des abbayes d'Aniane et de Gellone,* 2:110, no. 22).
213   "Contra voluntatem ipsius loci abbatis": de Marca, *Marca Hispanica,* col. 1251.
214   See de Lasteyrie, *L'abbaye,* pp. 427–429. The *notitia* of Vieux gives particularly rich details about the involvement of various local *milites;* see *Miscellanea novo ordine,* 1:124–126. Also see the text relating to Guixols (de Marca, *Marca Hispanica,* col. 1251) and Honorius II's description of the attack on Goudargues by La Chaise-Dieu (n. 212 above).
215   The viscount of Limoges is offered a great sum of gold and a very swift horse; see de Lasteyrie, *L'abbaye,* p. 428. The *milites* involved in Vieux's "reform" are promised money and mules; see *Miscellanea novo ordine,* 1:125.

desire. According to the text from Saint-Martin of La Canourgue, the bishop of Mende had been angry that the monks of Saint-Victor had dared "occupy" La Canourgue without his permission, but he was pacified by the offer of a white mule. And thus, "by the mediation of a gift (*munere interveniente*)"—the standard if elliptic phrase for simony—"they obtained the church from the bishop."[216] These hints of simony, like the language of violence and the accusations of lay collaboration, discredited the aggressor, characterizing its domination as founded on acts contradicting the ideals of reform.[217]

The final act ascribed to the aggressor by these texts is shaped differently. While blackening the antagonist, it also reveals what these events meant for the abbey in question: the destruction of the community, the utter loss of its identity. Invariably these texts relate how the aggressor violently expelled the monks or canons and replaced them with its own personnel. The meaning of this act is made particularly clear by the Saint-Martial *nota*. Hugh of Cluny drove out the "natural monks" (*monachos naturales*), "who were serving God and Saint Martial." The original monks were thus the only true community of the patron saint while the Cluniacs were unnatural invaders. The Psalmodi text, moreover, used the metaphor of exile for the monks whom Richard of Saint-Victor forced to leave the abbey.[218] These texts imply that after reform, after the imposition of another abbey's lordship, the true monastery no longer existed; usurpers, outsiders occupied its physical shell but could not replace or re-create it.

The *notitiae* thus frame the aggressor abbeys as illegitimate lords whose domination was fatal for the community and certainly contradicted whatever liberty it possessed. The Saint-Martial text even declares that upon taking possession of the abbey, the Cluniacs tore up its charters of liberty granted by king and pope.[219] Whether or not this accusation was founded on fact, it functions in the text as a symbolic expression of how such "takeovers" (an anachronistic yet perhaps appropriate term) were remembered not as the liberation but rather as the destruction of the abbey in question.

I would suggest that, as such, these monastic takeovers were seen as much more threatening than either episcopal or aristocratic lordship and could provoke at least as much resistance.[220] The latter two certainly menaced

[216] "Un récit inédit," p. 191. The Psalmodi text does not specify whom the monks of Saint-Victor bribed, but levels the charge: *GC* 6, instr. 184–186.

[217] See Rudolf Schieffer's discussion of how charges of simony were used by cathedral chapters to discredit their bishop: "*Spirituales Latrones:* Zu den Hintergründen der Simonieprozesse in Deutschland zwischen 1069 und 1075," *Historisches Jahrbuch* 92 (1972): 19–60.

[218] Richard of Saint-Victor had expelled the monks from Psalmodi and "in externas nationes abire et mori fecerit" (*GC* 6, instr. 185).

[219] See de Lasteyrie, *L'abbaye*, p. 429.

[220] Johnson remarks that monasteries' relations with other monasteries tended to be more acrimonious than those with the laity; see her *Prayer, Patronage*, pp. 103–114, 127.

liberty, but the former could consume the abbey's very identity as well. Engulfed by another monastery, the abbey risked losing its abbot and being reduced to the status of a priory—a status that in and of itself negated any liberty or autonomy.[221] Even if it did retain its abbot, the monastery risked losing its identity, just as a modern corporation does when threatened by a takeover.[222] Indeed, it has been remarked that several of the abbeys that Lagrasse and Saint-Pons-de-Thomières subjugated in the later eleventh century ceased to exist soon after being taken over.[223] Does their fate perhaps suggest that when their sense of being an autonomous community had been lost, these abbeys could no longer function? The threat posed by other monasteries—by social agents that had the same nature—was one to essence as well as to independence.[224]

Hence, abbeys did not always look for or accept the "protection" of other monasteries; such "protection" could mean entering into a relation of subjugation that contravened liberty and identity.[225] To resist such domination, abbeys could seek the protection of their legendary origins and could appeal to the liberty, intrinsic and permanent, established by their founders. Apostles or, more frequently, legendary Frankish kings (seconded by various popes) sheltered these monasteries against not only bishops and lay aristocrats, but also against other abbeys.[226] The Saint-Martial *nota* commences with a resounding proclamation of the abbey's status as totally independent, a condition resulting from its foundation:

> [W]e wish it to be known to all men, that the monastery of blessed Martial of Limoges, was established by that same most saintly father in the beginning with the liberty (*libertas*) which he had received from the lord Jesus Christ,

221 See also the case of Muri, which refused to become a priory of the "reforming" abbey of St. Blasien by appealing to one of its lay founders, saying that "locum esse liberum, hic debere esse abbatem." See Schmid, "Adel und Reform in Schwaben," pp. 310–313, here 312 (he underlines how "reform" hardly brought liberty to Muri).

222 Jacques Hourlier very nicely describes this threat as one of "perdre son individualité" ("losing its individuality"); see his "L'entrée de Moissac dans l'ordre de Cluny," in *Moissac et l'Occident*, p. 29.

223 Griffe, "La réforme monastique," pp. 133–145.

224 Cf. Cohen, *The Symbolic Construction*, pp. 40–45, 50, 86.

225 Because reform entailed such subjection, monasteries rarely submitted themselves voluntarily to either Cluny or Saint-Victor. The case of Figeac, which actively sought Cluny's tutelage, is an exception that proves the rule; see below at nn. 253–254. Consider also the case of Vézelay, a monastery that violently rejected Cluniac domination in the eleventh century, only to accept it in the early twelfth century in order to escape the bishop of Autun. But by the 1170s, Vézelay had proclaimed its freedom from Cluny as well. Louis, *De l'histoire à la légende*, 1:156–157, 175–177, 180–182, 186.

226 Wollasch argues that in the eleventh century, neither pope nor king was considered an effectual guarantor of liberty—but Cluny was. See his "Questions-clé," p. 25 (cf. his *Mönchtum zwischen Kirche und Welt*, pp. 9–52, 136–171). Perhaps this was the view of the bishops and nobles who delivered abbeys to Cluny, but it certainly was not that of southern monasteries.

and, confirmed in the same by his successors, remained always free and unrestricted and without the yoke of subjection to any mortal up until the time of the sixth abbot of Cluny, Saint Hugh.[227]

This juxtaposition of foundation and liberty occurs at a textual level. But during their efforts in the first half of the twelfth century to liberate themselves from Cluny, might not the monks have actually called upon the gift of liberty made to them by Saint Martial, reproclaimed an apostle with new fervor in just this period?[228]

Psalmodi seems to have invoked its legend in this way during a successful struggle to wrest itself from Saint-Victor's lordship.[229] The *notitia* (probably composed by Psalmodi) declares that Saint-Victor had dared to invade the abbey even though "according to apostolic privileges, namely of John and Stephen, and through royal diplomas, that is of Charles, Louis and the acts of other kings [which] we have here, [Psalmodi] was free (*liber*) and ought to be subject to no one except the Roman church."[230] Purporting to be the record of the proceedings of a council held at Le Caylar in 1096/1098, the *notitia* then relates that the assembled ecclesiastics examined these documents, both pontifical and royal, and decided in favor of Psalmodi's liberty. Indeed, in their decision, the *notitia* specifies, they cited the diplomas and privileges as the basis for their judgment.[231] Given that Psalmodi probably wrote this text, it is impossible to know whether the privileges really played a role in the abbey's liberation. The community, however, obviously saw them as the basis and the proof of its liberty. Furthermore, although in this use of popes and Carolingian kings as guarantors there is nothing obviously legendary, the liberty Psalmodi claimed at Le Caylar may nonetheless stem from the abbey's legendary image of itself. The diploma of Charlemagne referred to in the *notitia* may be that extant forgery in which the king agrees to the refoundation of Psalmodi in a place more secure from Muslim raids, and even entrusts his (fictitious) nephew, Theodemir, to the abbey in order that

---

[227] See de Lasteyrie, *L'abbaye*, p. 428.

[228] Richard Lardes kindly provided me with information relevant to the renascence of the cult of Saint Martial's apostolicity in the twelfth century.

[229] On Psalmodi's freeing of itself from Saint-Victor, see Schmid, "Die Entstehung," pp. 195, 202–206.

[230] A forged or at least interpolated privilege of Stephen VI for Psalmodi is extant in which the pope places the abbey and all its possessions under Roman jurisdiction and prohibits it from being subjected to "alterius aecclesiae iurisdiccionibus." The privilege refers twice to royal diplomas granted the abbey—in a fashion that Zimmermann considers "ungeschickt wenn nicht interpoliert" ("awkward if not interpolated"); see *Papsturkunden 896–1046*, 1:3–5, no. 1. No privilege of any Pope John is extant for Psalmodi; see Schmid, "Die Entstehung," p. 204, n. 1.

[231] *GC* 6, instr. 184–186 (here 185). The royal diplomas are also mentioned in a forged privilege of Gelasius II. *Papsturkunden in Frankreich: Reiseberichte zur Gallia Pontifica*, ed. Wilhelm Wiederhold, 2 vols., Acta Romanorum Pontificum, 7 and 8 (Vatican, 1985), 1:316–318, no. 11.

he might become a monk there—a special mark of favor that creates an intimate tie between this special king and the abbey.[232]

It was not only abbeys suffering from a takeover that might appeal to legend. The welling desire to gain liberty from old bonds of submission could also prompt recourse to legend. Indeed, one of Psalmodi's prize possessions, the monastery of Saint-Pierre of Joncels (located some ninety kilometers to the northwest of Psalmodi in the diocese of Béziers), in its turn drew upon the legendary possibilities of the Carolingian rulers to assert its freedom from the mother abbey's tutelage. The document that first mentions the relationship between Joncels and Psalmodi speaks in terms of two equals that formed one entity. A diploma of Charles the Simple of 909 addresses Regembaldus, abbot "from (ex) Psalmodi . . . and Joncels."[233] By the later eleventh century, though, the bonds had become hierarchical. Joncels appeared as Psalmodi's possession, not its partner, in the privileges of Urban II (1099), Pascal II (1115), and Honorius II (1125) for the latter abbey.[234]

Furthermore, certain documents hint that Joncels began to resent its subjection to Psalmodi. From Gregory VII, Joncels gained a privilege of liberty including the right of free election and appeal to Rome—not necessarily a sign of resistance to Psalmodi but certainly an indication of the abbey's crystallizing sense of independence.[235] The privileges of Pascal II and Honorius II for Psalmodi introduce a phrase (an interpolation?) that perhaps suggests Joncels's attempts to evade this abbey's control as well as Psalmodi's determination that it would not: "certainly it is not permitted that anyone should extract the monastery of Joncels from union with the monastery of Psalmodi (a cenobii Psalmodiensis unitate)."[236]

A notitia relating the proceedings of a council over which Arnold, archbishop of Narbonne (ca. 1121–1149), presided, makes clear that there was indeed such tension between the two abbeys. This text also demonstrates in remarkably explicit terms how legendary origins could create and sanctify present liberty. According to the notitia, Psalmodi produced "some royal diplomas" which granted it Joncels, and a privilege of Pascal (II) which included Joncels among the churches belonging to it (probably the extant

---

[232] MGH Diplomata Karolinorum 1:455–456, no. 303. But the document does not mention liberty and seems to focus instead on certain of the abbey's estates (see above, Chapter 2 at n. 22); it may thus have been invoked during, rather than composed for, the conflict. A Theodemir, abbot of Psalmodi, was mentioned in two diplomas of Louis the Pious; see GC 6, instr. 169–170. For another claim of blood relations between Charlemagne and an abbot, see above, Chapter 5 at n. 163.

[233] HL 5:127–130 (here 128), no. 37.

[234] Papsturkunden in Frankreich, 1:307–310, 313–316, 324–326, nos. 6, 10, 16.

[235] GC 6, instr. 128–129.

[236] Papsturkunden in Frankreich, 1:315, 326, nos. 10 and 16. Unitas could also mean spiritual confraternity, but as subsequent documents show, it is unlikely that it is used in this sense here.

privilege of 1115). The monks of Joncels vehemently disputed the authority of these documents. They claimed "free and undisturbed possession of their monastery from its very beginning and foundation (*ab exordio fundationis*) and defended it with the authority of the royal diplomas of the most Christian princes Pippin and Charles and further also with privileges of Gregory and Pascal of glorious memory, which seemed authentic to those present."[237] The diploma of Charlemagne referred to is no longer extant (if indeed it ever was), but that of his father is. This twelfth-century forgery presents Joncels as free since its origins—or, rather, since its legendary Carolingian refoundation. In this diploma, Pippin refounds Joncels and endows it with *libertas*, explicitly using this word which never appeared in authentic Carolingian diplomas.[238]

Faced with the authority of origins, of the great Carolingian rulers, and of the contemporaneous popes, the council decided unanimously in favor of Joncels's liberty. This decision, recounted in the *notitia*, was reinforced by a privilege of Innocent II (1139). Not only did Innocent command the abbot and monks of Psalmodi to remain thenceforth silent about "subjection (*subjectio*) and the other things which they claimed" from Joncels, but he proclaimed Joncels's freedom in sweeping (and perhaps pointed) terms: it was to be "subject to no human whatsoever (*omnino humanum*) besides the Roman church."[239] Ultimately settled by the pope, the matter had led Joncels to articulate a legendary identity for itself. Seeking to shake off the old "union" with Psalmodi which had evolved into lordship, Joncels created itself as an abbey whose liberty was not evanescent and recent, but permanent and ancient, arising from its very foundation.

In circumstances similar to those experienced by Joncels and Psalmodi, many southern monasteries elaborated legends that proclaimed their freedom. We must be careful, however, not to reduce such legends to the status of mere bulwarks in defense of independence. As we have seen, monastic takeovers and monastic lordship struck at an abbey's nature even more fundamentally than episcopal or lay control. In such situations, the threatened community sought particularly to reinforce and reaffirm its identity, to delineate itself as an entity separate from the aggressor—or indeed from the

---

[237] *GC* 6, instr. 134.

[238] "[S]ub nostro mundeburdo nostreque libertatis defensione . . . hec largitio et libertas nostre magnificentie" (*Recueil des actes de Pépin,* pp. 127–132, no. 30; here 132). On this text, see above, Chapter 4 at nn. 110–111. On the avoidance of the word *libertas* in Carolingian diplomatic sources, see Szabó-Bechstein, "*Libertas Ecclesiae,*" pp. 45–47.

[239] *Papsturkunden in Frankreich,* 2:768–770, no. 21. The latter phrase may very well reveal Joncels's hand (this document may very well be an *Empfängerschrift,* a text written by the recipient); neither Wiederhold nor Schreiber (*Kurie und Kloster,* 2:299, n. 3) expresses doubts as to its authenticity. The entire privilege was reconfirmed verbatim by Lucius III in 1183; see *Papsturkunden in Frankreich,* 2:879, no. 125.

abbey to which it had traditionally been subject. Through their legends, monasteries made such statements of identity and of liberty.

Issoire's legend of refoundation explicitly makes such a declaration in the face of domination by another abbey: Charroux. By the later eleventh century, Charroux claimed as its dependent this Auvergnat abbey first mentioned by Gregory of Tours. Philip I (1077) and Popes Urban II (1096–1099), Anastasius IV (1154), and Innocent III (1211) all recognized Issoire's subordinate status.[240] But the monastery hardly saw itself in those terms. Although in the (very scanty) sources there is no indication that this abbey managed to shake off Charroux's lordship, Issoire created for itself a legend in which its refoundation took the shape of liberation from precisely this domination.[241] This legend is transmitted in a text (ca. 1197) that Mozac probably composed to relate its triumph over Issoire in their rivalry for the relics of Saint Austremonius, but the first half recounts a tradition that must be from Issoire.[242] According to this text, under Pippin the Short, Roger, "duke of Aquitaine" (promoted by the legend from his actual position as count of Limoges), founded Charroux and endowed it with the *castrum* of Saint-Yvoine.[243] During the Norman invasions, the monks sought refuge in their Auvergnat possession. Establishing themselves in the *castrum,* they assured their future by making monks of the local peasants. After a "long time," Bernard, a monasticized native who had become the abbot of this offshoot community, felt the desire to free himself and his brother monks from their subjection to Charroux. The text distills this longing for independence into a very clear expression: "they began to ponder how . . . they might extract themselves from subjection (*subjectio*) to the abbot and monks of Charroux." Bernard proposed that they overthrow (*evertere*) the *castrum* and refound Issoire, the abbey Austremonius himself had founded. Receiving approbation for this plan (and thus for their independence) in a vision of the saint, the abbot and the monks destroyed the castle and con-

---

[240] *Chartes et documents pour servir à l'histoire de l'abbaye de Charroux,* pp. 64, 81, 146, 174. Issoire seems to have remained in Charroux's possession. An *enquête* of 1567 spelled out the rights that Charroux had claimed over Issoire until twenty-five years previously: confirmation of newly elected abbots, profession of all monks at Charroux (p. 394). See also Pierre-François Fournier and Roger Sève, "Les biens de l'abbaye de Charroux en Auvergne," *Bulletin Historique et Scientifique de l'Auvergne* 85 (1972): 267–278.

[241] Yet Issoire had gained some measure of recognition of its independence, appearing on Cencius's list (1192) of "Saint Peter's monasteries" in the *Liber censuum.* Cf. Pfaff's puzzlement over the implications for the abbey's status: "Sankt Peters Abteien," p. 193.

[242] *Additamentum de reliquiis S. Austremonii (AASS* November 1:80–82) (complete in Paris, BN n.a Françaises 7455, ff. 319r–322r).

[243] Here Issoire draws on Charroux's legendary traditions. Sometime in the eleventh century this latter abbey fabricated or interpolated the testament of Roger. In it, the count's wife, Euphrasia, endows Charroux with the *castrum* of Saint-Yvoine. *Chartes et documents pour servir à l'histoire de l'abbaye de Charroux,* p. 57. Whether or not Saint-Yvoine had been part of Charroux's original endowment, it was recognized as the abbey's possession by Leo IX, Alexander II, and all the subsequent popes who confirmed Charroux's estates (pp. 73, 77).

structed the monastery "from the stones of that very castle." The castle, symbol of Charroux's power and hated domination, was thus eradicated and appropriated—and Issoire was established as independent from its rebirth.

Rarely, however, was the profound thirst for independence and the corresponding desire to escape from another abbey's grasp formulated in such an explicit legendary statement. Indeed, perhaps the word "statement" is misleading. As we have seen in the case of Saint-Gilles, the language employed was rather one of indirection, of a heightening of liberty such that it excluded *all* lordship—or, as the *nota* of Saint-Martial so nicely stated, the domination of "any mortal"—except for the benign tutelage of the legendary founders (or their contemporary representatives).[244]

Nonetheless, this silence, expressive in and of itself, could be accompanied by a symbolically significant (if often subtle) discourse that reveals the conflict. Competition could be played out in legendary terms. For example, Joncels's choice of Pippin rather than Charlemagne as legendary (re)founder was probably influenced by Psalmodi's previous embellishment of Charlemagne. After all, by appealing to Pippin Joncels thus established itself—and its liberty—as chronologically prior to Psalmodi.[245] It claimed the authority of antiquity in an age in which, as the Anglo-Norman Anonymous proclaimed, the oldest church was the most independent and had the most right to dominion.[246] Similarly, Figeac's selection of Charlemagne's father as its founder was influenced no doubt not only by the fact that a Pippin (I of Aquitaine) had actually established the abbey, but also by its conflict with Conques, a monastery that by the eleventh century claimed Charlemagne as its own founder.[247] Indeed, this case hints at an actual two-sided debate conducted through legend in which claims of domination could be expressed directly, but those of liberty only indirectly.

The tension between Conques and Figeac was much like that between Psalmodi and Joncels—but with a twist. Figeac had been founded by 838 as the "New Conques" on a site (along the River Célé) less difficult to provision than Conques, clinging to its precipitous hillside. But, cautioned Pippin I of

[244] The thirst for independence did not prevent a monastery from shaping its legend to include ties to another abbey. When a legend did not depict an abbey's relation with the other as one of domination, it certainly did not therefore render the abbey in question subordinate. Legends, then, might be associative—but in such a way as to remove any taint of subjection.

[245] Compare the legend of Saint-Leonard of Noblat (above, Chapter 4 at nn. 40–47), which may have been structured in order to make Leonard more prestigious than Saint Martial.

[246] Anglo-Norman Anonymous, *Tractatus Eboracenses (MGH Libelli de Lite* 3:657–658), and Corpus Christi College 415, Cambridge University, f. 265, both cited with incisive discussion by Lemarignier, *Etude sur les privilèges d'exemption*, pp. 196–198, 300. Cf. his comments on Dubois and Renaud's "Influence des vies des saints," p. 513. See also Goffart, *Le Mans Forgeries*, pp. 51–52, 61–65, 207–239.

[247] On the legends of Conques and Figeac, see above: Chapter 4 at nn. 117–123, 170–174; Chapter 5 at nn. 35–50.

Aquitaine in his diploma of 838, although many of the monks of Conques were to migrate to the "New Conques," the older abbey was to retain the "dignity of priority and the reverence of antiquity."[248] This phrase would become a bone of contention between the old and the new Conques in the later eleventh century, when it would be read anchronistically as establishing a hierarchy of domination and subjection.[249] At this point, Figeac, although it had certainly had its own abbots since the tenth century, if not the ninth, sought to renounce any "reverence" whatsoever that it might owe Conques and, turning the tables, claimed that Conques owed it obedience.[250]

The first datable evidence of this friction between the two abbeys is a privilege of Gregory VII from 1084. Addressed to both communities, the pope declares that after much discussion, it had been decided that "Figeac ought to be subjected to the monastery of Conques and to adhere to it as a limb to the head, *according to the dispositions of those who built the abbeys* [my emphasis]."[251] Despite this statement, Gregory had taken Figeac's claims seriously. With an evident concern for ecclesiastical unity and harmony, he stipulated that if the present abbot of Conques should die before that of Figeac, Conques would be united to Figeac and must accept its abbot on pain of excommunication—and vice versa. According to Urban II's declaration at the Council of Nîmes (1096), where the conflict was finally resolved, Conques's abbot had died first. Yet the community elected for itself a new abbot rather than accept Figeac's, thus sparking a bitter altercation. At Nîmes, Urban decreed that henceforth both monasteries were to have their own abbots—but that Figeac was to accept the tutelage of Cluny.[252] Urban

[248] *Recueil des actes de Pépin,* pp. 132–151 (here 150), no. 32.

[249] Levillain, however, suggests that this phrase might reveal tension between the two already in the ninth century; see *Recueil des actes de Pépin,* pp. 139–140, no. 32. Wolff develops this theory ("Note sur le faux diplôme," pp. 327, 330), but there is no explicit evidence of such friction.

[250] An abbot of Figeac, Calsto, is mentioned in a testament of 972 (*HL* 5:268–269, no. 122). A privilege of Benedict (VI) of 973 refers to this same abbot and "all his successors." See *Papsturkunden 896–1046,* 1:442–443, no. 225 (Zimmermann identifies this privilege as a forgery, but believes that it was based on an authentic one; hence the mention of the abbot may not be suspect). The *Translatio sancti Viviani episcopi in coenobium Figiacense et ejusdem ibidem miracula,* composed at Figeac in the late tenth or early eleventh century, mentions three abbots of Figeac, one, Aigmarus, from the early ninth century; see *AB* 6 (1889): 258, 267, 272. The late eleventh-century chronicle of Figeac lists abbots beginning with Aigmarus, but this is a highly polemical text; see *Historia monasterii Figiacensis,* pp. 1–2.

[251] *GC* 1, instr. 241–242. This phrase is similar to that in a charter of Conques which dates itself as "eo tempore quo papa Gregorius VII convocavit Romae magnum sinodum . . . adversus Haeenrici [*sic*] regis placitum, et quo tempore Stephanus abbas Conchensis Figiaci monasterium ab eodem papa impetravit . . . ut sicut praecepta regalia monstrabant, perpetuo abbati Conchensis esset subditum et serviet sicut membra capiti" (*Cartulaire de l'abbaye de Conques,* p. 54, no. 53). This eschatocol does not necessarily mean that in 1076 Gregory had already dealt with Conques and Figeac. Rather, it may conflate two things for which Gregory would have been known at Conques: his conflict with Henry (1076) and his declaration of 1084 relating to Figeac.

[252] *Recueil des chartes de l'abbaye de Cluny,* pp. 57–58, no. 3710.

gave as the reason for this latter stipulation a declaration by the abbot of Cluny that the 1084 privilege of Gregory was a forgery and that the pope had actually granted Figeac to the Burgundian abbey. No such text has survived (if it ever existed), but in an extant late eleventh-century charter, Bego of Calmont, a member of a family that had been among Conques's lay patrons since the early eleventh century, delivered Figeac to Cluny.[253] In any case, it is clear that Figeac accepted (perhaps even had solicited) Cluny's rule in order to escape from the lordship of an abbey too threateningly close.[254]

This acrimonious conflict over precedence translated into a dialogue in the rich legendary texts produced by Conques and Figeac during the late eleventh century.[255] Figeac's bridling at subjection to Conques was most strongly expressed in the development of its identity as a foundation of the newly anointed and resplendent Pippin the Short. The dominant theme of its cluster of fabrications was that Pippin, seconded by various popes, had proclaimed the abbey "free from all human power" except for the mild *tuitio* of king and pontiff.[256] Thus, Figeac had translated its foundation as the "New Conques" by a king of Aquitaine into its establishment as an utterly independent and free abbey by a much more prestigious ruler. Furthermore, its founder and foundation now preceded the legendary (re)founder, Charlemagne—and thus the legendary (re)foundation—of its rival, Conques.

As this chronological manipulation implies, through its legend Figeac sought not only liberty but preeminence, thus inverting the original relationship between the two abbeys. Here liberty and the appetite to dominate appear hand in hand; in order to achieve independence, a monastery could claim lordship. In each of Figeac's legendary texts, Conques appears—but only as a mere "colony of hermits" that Pippin and pope had placed under

[253] *GC* 1, instr. 44. On relations between the family of Calmont and Conques, see Jacques Miquel, *Calmont d'Olt en Rouergue: Château médiéval de la vallée du Lot* (Rodez, n.d.), p. 4; also see *Cartulaire de l'abbaye de Conques*, pp. 78, 390, 401–403, nos. 82, 556, 572.

[254] This is an exception that proves the rule. There is no evidence of resistance to Cluny by Figeac.

[255] The rivalry between the two abbeys also appeared in the form of a competition in legend over who had acquired its relics in the most spectacular fashion—a contest whose prize was not only predominance but the attention of pilgrims en route to Compostela. See Geary, *Furta Sacra*, pp. 58–63, 86, 138–141.

[256] See the forged diploma of Pippin, edited in Wolff, "Note sur le faux diplôme," p. 300. In legendary privileges, Stephen II and Pascal I make similar declarations (Stephen's adds various clauses about freedom from episcopal jurisdiction); see *GC* 1, instr. 43–44. The late twelfth-century interpolation in Ademar of Chabannes's *Chronicon* concludes the account of Figeac's foundation: the king and pope "ab omni humano servitio liberam fieri [Figeac] nisi sola romani pontificis tuitione propriis privilegiis sancxerunt" (Paris BN Latin 5926, ff. 36v; edited in *Chronique*, p. 58, note s*). On the relationship between the conflict and Figeac's forgeries, see Wolff, "Note sur le faux diplôme," pp. 322–325. For further discussion of these texts, see above, Chapter 4 at nn. 117–125.

the governance of their new foundation's abbot.[257] Figeac's late eleventh-century or early twelfth-century chronicle—filled with accusations that Conques had engaged in simony and other unsavory dealings—is marked by this same parlaying of precedence in time into dominance.[258] It opens by trumpeting the abbey's foundation by Pippin the Short and its miraculous consecration "by the almighty Lord Himself," and continues with a tale of refoundation that makes the pretension to lordship crystal clear. Figeac's refounder, the ninth-century abbot Aigmarus, was the patron of two large crucifixes adorned with gold and precious stones, proclaims the chronicle. The largest of these he granted to Figeac, and the smaller (*minor*) to Conques "so that by this it should be clear to all which of those monasteries should rule (*praesse*) the other."[259] This patent statement of the order between the two rivals is complemented by the text's accusation that Conques, originally subject to Figeac, had freed itself by making its prior into an abbot in the early ninth century; it was to the present day "without a rightful head."[260] Thus, Figeac's chronicle delegitimizes Conques's present state, rendering it a perversion of the original hierarchy established by Pippin the Short.

Evidently quite aware of its opponent's legendary pretensions, Conques responded in its own traditions, even meeting Figeac on the latter's terms: through the figure of Pippin. The late eleventh-century portion of Conques's chronicle emphasized Pippin of Aquitaine's donation of Figeac, a grant it stated had been confirmed by successive kings.[261] The verse *translatio* of Saint Faith composed in the same period mentions Figeac as the "monastery . . . [that] Pippin, who was king, had long ago ordered to be built there [and to be] beneath the lordship (*dominio*) of Conques."[262] In this text, it is no longer evident which Pippin is at stake, the king of Aquitaine or the king of the Franks.

But in a charter purporting to date from the first half of the eleventh century, and confirming Figeac's subordinate status, the king is Pippin the Short.[263] This text, surely forged by Conques in the late eleventh century, opens with a flourish: "the great king Pippin ruling the realm of the Franks built many monasteries from their foundations and rebuilt many which had

---

257 See references in n. 256 above.
258 The motif of precedence in time could also be used as a trope for actual and not just desired domination. See Alexandre Grandazzi's discussion of the legendary traditions relating to Rome's origins, in his *La fondation de Rome: Réflexion sur l'histoire* (Paris, 1991), pp. 218–220.
259 *Historia monasterii Figiacensis*, p. 1.
260 *Historia monasterii Figiacensis*, p. 1.
261 *Chronicon monasterii Conchensis*, pp. 1387–1388.
262 *Translatio metrica S. Fidis virginis et martyris* (*AASS* October 3:291).
263 *GC* 1, instr. 44.

been destroyed."[264] It then relates how Pippin came to Conques, found the hermit Dado living there with a community, and endowed the monastery with many gifts and estates. Perceiving the harshness of the site, the king decided to found a "New Conques," calling it Figeac. Not only does this charter draw upon Pippin I's diploma of 838 to stress the "dignity and reverence of the most ancient abbey"—that is, Conques—but it surpasses the diploma by declaring that Pippin had actually subjected Figeac to Conques. It even relates how Figeac's present state of illegitimate independence had occurred: "most nefarious" counts and *principes* had separated the two abbeys and placed an abbot in "the subject monastery." The supposed agent of the charter, Bego of Calmont (whom we have met before as the donor of Figeac to Cluny), proposed to remedy their misdeed and restore the hierarchy so that "dignity and reverence would remain to Conques, just as the kings had decreed." Bego further stipulated that when the abbot of Figeac died, his replacement should be chosen from among the monks of Conques by the abbot of this latter monastery—a right that made clear Figeac's subordinate status. Was this document a reply to and a negation of Bego's donation of Figeac to Cluny? In any case, this forgery shows that Conques accepted Figeac's transformation of Pippin from king of Aquitaine to king of the Franks, but not the significance with which its rival had endowed him. It negated and inverted that new meaning. The twice-transformed legendary Pippin the Short clothed Conques with the dignity of antiquity, and thus precedence, as the historical Pippin of Aquitaine had done.

Well aware of each other's traditions, Conques and Figeac expressed their rivalry in the symbolic terms of legend. Indeed, they competed within a shared framework of foundation by the same legendary personae—the great early Carolingians—just as we saw in the case of Psalmodi and Joncels. This play of identities within one system of representations is not without significance. For these figures representing the larger authority became the space for local rivalries. The existence of such competition may even have contributed to the extraordinary development of the royal image in these legends.[265]

[264] Gustave Desjardins accepts this text as authentic; see *Cartulaire de l'abbaye de Conques,* p. xvii. This document, however, could hardly be authentic; in it Bego, not even a count or a *princeps,* reconfirms Pippin's privilege and then restructures relations between the abbeys by giving Conques the power to elect Figeac's abbot—highly unusual pretensions for a lay aristocrat, even in this period. The abbot mentioned in the document is Odolric (1031–1060), clearly an attempt to antedate Conques's supposed regaining of control over Figeac. The text was probably forged sometime in the 1080s or 1090s when the dispute between the two abbeys had broken out.

[265] For a similar dynamic, see S. R. F. Price's discussion of the celebration of the Roman imperial cult by Greek cities of Asia Minor: *Rituals and Power: The Roman Imperial Cult in Asia Minor* (Cambridge, 1984), pp. 64, 126–132.

Although involved in an oppositional relationship, these monastic communities did not create themselves as opposites. Each abbey sought to differentiate itself, but did so by making itself closer than its opponent to the significant king(s): that is, by choosing from the same set of elements rather than selecting completely different ones.[266] Indeed, not only did these monasteries often couch their identity in terms of the same legendary figures, but they often borrowed from and recast for themselves their opponent's legend as Conques did with Figeac's Pippin.[267] This certainly shows how familiar monasteries were with one another's legends; more important, though, it also relates directly to the issue of identity and conflict. We have seen how in their legends Mozac and Issoire seized the castles representing their opponent's power and transformed them into their own architectural expressions of identity and dominance. In a similar fashion, monasteries that took the legend of their opponent stripped their rival metaphorically of its separate identity (and thus its independence or its lordship) and, investing this identity with new meaning, appropriated it for themselves.

One further case demonstrates these mechanisms at work between two abbeys that were keenly aware of each other's legend. Each, using the medium of legendary figures, tried to create for itself an identity that would either subsume the other or specifically exclude it, according to whether the goal was dominance or liberty. The late eleventh-century conflict between Aniane and Gellone, Carolingian foundations spaced only six kilometers apart along the River Hérault, revolved around Gellone's original—and thus current—status. Had Gellone been founded by Guillaume with or without the aid of Benedict, Aniane's equally famous founder, and as a *cella* of Benedict's monastery or not? Although the heavily interpolated and forged sources make it impossible to divine what the actual roles of Benedict and Guillaume were, it is probable that Gellone had never been Aniane's *cella*.[268] In any case, charters of the tenth and eleventh centuries mention Gellone's abbot as a matter of course, and there is no sign that Aniane raised any pretensions to domination until the second half of the eleventh century.[269] Indeed, in the first half of that century, relations between the two abbeys were sufficiently friendly to permit them to build together a graceful

---

[266] See Claude Lévi-Strauss's discussion of systems of transformation of one essential structure: *The Savage Mind*, (Chicago, 1966), pp. 75–90 (he remarks briefly that such transformations can express competition between communities or individuals, p. 90). Also see Cohen, *The Symbolic Construction*, p. 49.

[267] Nonetheless, Charlemagne remained the focus of Conques's foundation legend.

[268] See the various hypotheses of Pückert, *Aniane und Gellone*, pp. 198–234; Tisset, *L'abbaye de Gellone*, pp. 84–85, 131–133; and Jean Mabillon, *Annales ordinis sancti Benedicti occidentalium monachorum patriarchae*, 6 vols. (Lucca, 1739–1745), 4:622, bk. 62, chap. 105.

[269] The earliest authentic document to name Gellone's abbot is a diploma of Charles the Simple dating from 913 (*Cartulaires des abbayes d'Aniane et de Gellone*, 1:229–230, no. 278). The only two authentic ninth-century documents in the cartulary (1:99, 230–231, nos. 113 and 279) do not mention the abbot by name, although the first refers to an abbot.

bridge (still standing) over the Hérault, and to divvy up rights over the placement of fishing weirs without any apparent quarrel.[270]

By the 1060s, though, Aniane had begun machinations to gain control of Gellone and reduce it to a *cella*. The abbot of Aniane, Emmeno, wrote to both Alexander II and Gregory VII to set forth his monastery's claims, basing them on origins. He complained to Alexander that from its foundation Gellone had been subject to Aniane, but that the monks of Gellone had nonetheless dared to elect their own abbots.[271] In his letters addressed to Gregory, Emmeno's attack sharpened; he specified that Louis the Pious— with the counsel of Guillaume—had delivered Gellone into Aniane's power. Only recently had Aniane lost control of Gellone when the *cella*'s community elected for itself abbots (by simoniac means, Emmeno specifies, thus smearing Gellone).[272]

Despite these vehement letters (which may or may not have been sent), Aniane did not gain its objective. Instead, in two privileges granting papal protection, Alexander II reaffirmed Gellone's right to free election, and Urban II in a privilege no longer extant stated explicitly that Gellone was in no way to be subject to Aniane.[273] The reconfirmations of Urban's privilege by Popes Calixtus II (1123), Eugenius III (1146), and Alexander III (1162) might indicate that Aniane did not easily renounce its pretensions—or simply that Gellone wished to have its independence proclaimed as often as possible.[274] This is the context in which the legate Amatus of Oloron in 1076 consecrated Gellone's altar dedicated to its saintly founder Guillaume—yet another expression of papal protection in the face of the menace posed by Aniane.[275]

In the course of this conflict (and even afterward if Urban's privilege really settled the matter) each abbey, besides having recourse to contemporaneous popes, fabricated a foundation legend that, intentionally or not, announced its position. Since Aniane's *libido dominandi* appears to have sparked the affair, I shall first examine how this abbey promulgated its

[270] On the bridge and the weirs, see *Cartulaires des abbayes d'Aniane et de Gellone*, 1:21–23, nos. 18–20.

[271] This letter exists only in Mabillon's paraphrase: *Annales ordinis sancti Benedicti*, 4:622, bk. 62, chap. 105.

[272] Like Emmeno's letter to Alexander II, these letters are extant only in Mabillon's description: *Annales ordinis sancti Benedicti*, 5:73–74, bk. 64, chap. 68. Tisset seems to believe that all of Emmeno's letters were forgeries; see his *L'abbaye de Gellone*, pp. 81–83. His primary reason is that these letters cited forgeries, but surely texts appealing to forgeries can themselves be authentic.

[273] Alexander's privileges, significantly, head Gellone's first version of its cartulary (*Cartulaires des abbayes d'Aniane et de Gellone*, 1:1–3, nos. 1 and 2). See above, Chapter 5 at n. 164.

[274] On these privileges and the length of the conflict, see Tisset, *L'abbaye de Gellone*, pp. 40–42, 87–90. Alexander III's privilege indicates that the reconfirmations were a preventive measure against Aniane's continued pretensions to lordship over Gellone; see Tisset's edition, *L'abbaye de Gellone*, p. 221.

[275] On this consecration, see above at n. 195.

claims over Gellone by invoking origins. In a series of texts, Aniane openly announced that Gellone had been founded as its *cella*. Tailoring to its liking Guillaume's charter of his foundation donations to Gellone—a document that may never have existed in an original form but that became a structure through which the two abbeys expressed their rivalry—Aniane presented the count as having explicitly subjected the new community to Benedict and his monastery.[276] Extant now in a late twelfth- or early thirteenth-century copy, but purporting to date from December 15, 804, this version of the charter was probably composed in the later eleventh century in the heat of the contest.[277] Gellone's founder proclaims that he gives to Aniane all that he had granted to "that *cella* Gellone which I . . . built with the counsel and help of lord abbot Benedict and which the lord abbot Benedict himself is seen to govern." Repeating twice more that Gellone is a *cella* subject to Aniane, Guillaume adds an extraordinary stipulation that barely veils Aniane's pretensions to absolute control over Gellone's institutional identity: if anyone dare separate the *cella* from Aniane, all the possessions Guillaume granted to Gellone are to fall to Aniane.[278]

These direct assertions of Gellone's subordination occur in simpler form in several forged or heavily interpolated texts, all included in Aniane's twelfth-century cartulary, itself a document that, through its structure, states the abbey's legendary identity.[279] In two diplomas of Louis the Pious probably forged by the 1070s (Emmeno referred to their contents in his letter to Gregory VII), the monarch grants to Aniane various properties, among them "a certain little cell (*cellula*) called Gellone, in the *pagus* of Lodève, with all its appurtenances and whatever Guillaume, formerly count, who built that cell (*cella*) as representative of our lord father, and other good men gave to it."[280] A letter of this ruler, heavily interpolated if not completely fabricated, implies the same thing no less clearly if more subtly.[281] The eleventh-century popes, the other member of the duo of the abbeys' favorite guarantors, add their weight to that of the Carolingians. In two forged privileges, Nicholas II and Alexander II state that no bishop is to presume to bless an abbot elected by Gellone, because the *ordinatio* of this

[276] Tisset expresses some doubt as to whether there ever was an original; see his *L'abbaye de Gellone*, pp. 152–154.

[277] The extant copy is AD Hérault 1.H.2.

[278] On how these properties function as a representation of the abbey itself, see above, Chapter 2 at nn. 110–116.

[279] On this cartulary's structure, see above at nn. 182–187.

[280] This grant is reconfirmed in a forgery of Charles the Bald: *Cartulaires des abbayes d'Aniane et de Gellone*, 2:53–60, nos. 9 and 10 (Louis the Pious), no. 11 (Charles the Bald). For critical analyses of these forgeries, see Pückert, *Aniane und Gellone*, pp. 161–179; and Tisset, *L'abbaye de Gellone*, pp. 62–67.

[281] *Cartulaires des abbayes d'Aniane et de Gellone*, 2:75–77, no. 19. For critiques of this document, see Pückert, *Aniane und Gellone*, pp. 179–197; and Tisset, *L'abbaye de Gellone*, pp. 68–72.

"cell" (*cella*) belongs to Aniane alone (and had from times of old, Nicholas specifies).[282]

But it was not only through forgeries that Aniane sought to proclaim Gellone's original subjection. Gellone's foundation as a *cella* is enshrined in the narrative text that frames and introduces all the documents in Aniane's cartulary: Ardo's celebrated *vita* of Benedict. This *vita* is generally considered to be an authentic production of one of Benedict's disciples. It very well may have been. But the image it presents is not entirely trustworthy; the original version of the *vita* was embellished in the late eleventh and/or early twelfth century with several interpolations.[283] Its description of Guillaume's foundation of Gellone has long been recognized as one—perhaps the most flamboyant—of these.[284] According to the *vita,* upon his conversion Guillaume came to Aniane and then spent the rest of his life at Gellone, the *cella* whose construction he had previously ordered. Not only does the text emphasize Gellone's physical proximity to Aniane, but it states that Benedict populated the *cella* with his own monks (who instructed Guillaume in the ways of the religious life).[285]

The so-called *Chronicle* of Aniane, extant in a very late eleventh- or twelfth-century copy and probably composed in the same period, repeats this passage rendering Gellone an appendage of Aniane. In its confused narrative, the *Chronicle* also provides another version of Gellone's foundation, one that sharpens the message of subjection: "with the counsel of the emperor, the lord abbot Benedict with all his clergy began to build a *cella* there."[286] Here Gellone becomes Benedict's project, and its status as a *cella* is sanctioned by the emperor (Louis). The same message is transmitted by the

---

[282] *Cartulaires des abbayes d'Aniane et de Gellone,* 2:80–85, nos. 2 and 3. These documents also contained stipulations relative to the rights Aniane claimed in its dispute with the bishops of Maguelone.

[283] E.g., the reworked version of Charlemagne's diploma; see above at n. 174.

[284] Most scholars who have studied the Guillaume tradition or the conflict between Aniane and Gellone have recognized this passage as an interpolation. See, for example, Joseph Bédier, "Recherches sur les légendes du cycle de Guillaume d'Orange," *Annales du Midi* 19 (1907): 16–17. Although Saxer more recently expressed his opinion to the contrary, he gives no supporting evidence; see his, "Le culte et la légende hagiographique," p. 571. Pückert is the only scholar I know of who expresses some awareness that the rest of the *vita* may therefore be less trustworthy than most historians consider it; see his *Aniane und Gellone,* p. 107.

In a study of the *vita*'s description of the altar dedicated to the Trinity, René Feuillebois points out that the word *ara* is used. He finds only one pre-eleventh-century instance of this word outside of Carolingian poetry; see his "Essai de restitution de l'autel érigé par saint Benoît dans l'abbatiale d'Aniane," *Archéologie du Midi Médiéval* 3 (1985): 21–22, 23 (n. 35). This is perhaps suggestive of some sort of later reworking but is certainly not conclusive; Benedict, as a member of Charlemagne's circle and one of Alcuin's correspondents, doubtless was very familiar with poetic language.

[285] Ardo, *Vita Benedicti,* in *Cartulaires des abbayes d'Aniane et de Gellone,* 2:23–24.

[286] "Ibique dominus benedictus abbas cum omni clero suo construere cepit cellam cum consilio imperatoris" (Paris, BN Latin 5941, f. 45v).

Chronicle's alteration of the *Vita Benedicti*'s list of monasteries under Benedict's regime. The *vita* simply included Gellone in this list without comment, but the *Chronicle* insists on the monastery's subordinate status: "the *cella* of Gellone which the pious father Benedict built."[287] In the margin, drawn next to this list was a symbol of Benedict's authority, and of the power Aniane wished to wield over Gellone: an abbot's crozier.[288]

Aniane reinforced these direct claims with more subtle ones. In several texts, the abbey associated Guillaume so closely with itself and with its own saintly founder that Gellone disappeared. This appropriation of Guillaume—venerated as a saint not only at Gellone but at Aniane (perhaps already by the eleventh century) as well—appears in the interpolated passage of Ardo's *Vita Benedicti*.[289] According to this text, upon his conversion Guillaume went first to Aniane, and, endowing the abbey with many rich gifts, was received there into the monastic life. Even when Guillaume had fixed himself at Gellone, his intimate connection with Aniane did not vanish; the passage relates that Benedict guided and regulated his ascetic practices.[290] That such association between Guillaume and Benedict might have existed is of course plausible and possible—but in the context of the conflict between the abbeys, the passage reads as an oblique but definite attempt to assimilate Guillaume.

The appropriation of Guillaume is even more striking in the *Chronicle* of Aniane. This text repeats the passage from the *Vita Benedicti* twice, and the first time leaves out any mention of Gellone. Thus, the passage now reads that Guillaume came to Aniane, gave the abbey many precious gifts, and "delivered himself to serve Christ there for all of his life"—a phrase that in the *vita* relates to Gellone.[291] With the *Chronicle*'s omission of Gellone, Guillaume becomes a monk of Aniane pure and simple. Furthermore, the *Chronicle* presents its own version of the 804 charter of Guillaume's dona-

---

[287] "Gellonem cellam quod hedificavit benedictus pius pater" (Paris, BN Latin 5941, f. 41r).

[288] Paris, BN Latin 5941, f. 41r.

[289] A hymn to Guillaume written in an eleventh-century hand appears on a folio glued into a tenth-century manuscript of Paul's Epistles (Montpellier, BM 6, f. 135r). In the seventeenth century the manuscript belonged to Aniane according to an ex libris on folio 1r; it may always have been in the same monastery's possession. Guillaume appears in the calendar of a later century breviary from Aniane (Montpellier, BM 118).

[290] On Guillaume's arrival first at Aniane and then *conversatio* at Gellone, see Ardo, *Vita Benedicti,* in *Cartulaires des abbayes d'Aniane et de Gellone,* 2:23–24.

[291] The entire entry comes from Ardo's *Vita Benedicti* but omits the *vita*'s description of Guillaume's removal to Gellone: "Anno dcccᵒviᵒ. In isto anno Wielmus condam comes ad anianum monasterium qui est constructus [*sic*] in honore domini ac salvatoris nostri ihesu christi et gloriose matris eius semper virginis pervenit cum omnibus muneribus auri argentique ac preciosorum vestium se tradidit christo omni vite sue tempore serviturum. Nec more in deponendi comam fieri passus est quin pocius die natalis apostolorum petri et pauli auro textis depositis vestibus christicolarum induit habitum seseque celicolarum adscisci numero quantocius congaudens efficitur" (Paris, BN Latin 5941, f. 22v; cf. the unaltered quotation of the passage, ff. 43r–v).

tions to Gellone, but this time there is no word of Gellone at all. Guillaume donates in perpetuity the properties to Aniane "where lord abbot Benedict rules," and pronounces a ringing *anathema maranatha anathemate* against any transgressors.[292] Gellone's founder is transformed into Aniane's benefactor—and through the very act with which he was supposed to have established Gellone. Gellone itself disappears, not only because its name is replaced by that of Aniane, but because the estates that composed its original patrimony (and thus institutional identity) belong to Aniane.[293] The *Chronicle* even hints at an assimilation of another of the components of Gellone's identity and fame: its relic of the True Cross. Among the fabulously rich gifts that this text claims Charlemagne had left Aniane, there seems to have been such a relic.[294]

Aniane's attempts to present Gellone as its subordinate thus affected and inflected the former abbey's image of itself. Perhaps the way in which Aniane began weaving for itself intimate legendary connections with Charlemagne reveals this same dynamic. The sermon ascribed to Ardo but composed no doubt in the same era as the *Chronicle* commemorates Charlemagne as founder, and as witness of the abbey's miraculous consecration.[295] The rubric that introduces the *Chronicle* makes clear Aniane's focus on Charlemagne: "The genealogy, birth and acts or life of Charlemagne, glorious and most pious emperor."[296] This text mingles Charlemagne's history with that of Aniane's foundation and its saintly founder, Benedict, to such an extent that these latter are subsumed under and become part of the shimmering figure of the monarch. Furthermore, the text describes various symbolically significant objects the king had bestowed upon to Aniane. These gifts distinguished the abbey as special in the royal affections, and, we have seen, formed the counterpart to Gellone's fragment of the Cross; they embodied the position of eminence Aniane sought.[297] Clothing itself with as much of Charlemagne's aura as possible, Aniane thus fashioned itself as "the head (*capud*) of all monasteries, not only of those which were built in the region of Gothia, but also of those which were built in other regions at that time and through his [Benedict's] example and endowed with his treasures," as the *Vita Benedicti* proclaims. This statement so strikingly ex-

---

[292] Paris, BN Latin 5941, ff. 41v–42v. This text gives a date of 806, rather than 804, to the document.

[293] On close identity of foundation endowment with community, see above, Chapter 2 at nn. 110–116.

[294] "Unam vero partem sibi reservavit quam dedit benedicto . . . videlicet crucis dominicis [*sic*]" (Paris, BN Latin 5941, f. 33v).

[295] See above, Chapter 2 at n. 165.

[296] "Genealogia ortus vel actus sive vita karoli gloriosi atque piissimi imperatoris" (Paris, BN Latin 5941, f. 2r).

[297] On Charlemagne's gifts to Aniane, see above, Chapter 2 at nn. 135–139.

presses Aniane's aspirations in its conflict with Gellone that it may very well be yet another of the *vita*'s eleventh- or twelfth-century interpolations.[298]

In Aniane's legendary texts, three mechanisms dovetailed: the direct proclamation of Gellone's subordination; the appropriation of Gellone's founder and traditions; and, finally, the intensification of Aniane's relation to Charlemagne, translating into an elevation of the abbey and its claims to domination. Gellone developed its own legend using some similar mechanisms—but in the name of exclusion and liberty, not inclusion and lordship.

Gellone stated its original and thus permanent independence by denying that any figures other than Guillaume, his family, Charlemagne, and Louis the Pious were involved in its foundation. Gellone had its own version of Guillaume's charter of 804. Heading the early twelfth-century section of Gellone's cartulary, this document declares that the epic Guillaume gave the properties listed to the "monastery" of Gellone which he himself had built at Charlemagne's behest.[299] No mention of Aniane or of its Benedict is allowed to mar this vision of Gellone's origins as an independent abbey. Indeed, Guillaume specifies that according to "the teaching of venerable father Benedict"—most decidedly the saint of Nursia and not of Aniane— he had provided the foundation not only with monks but with an abbot. At the end of the document, Gellone again appears as a "monastery" with its own abbot, not a *cella* as in one of Aniane's versions. This image of Gellone's origins is reinforced by a diploma of Louis the Pious forged sometime before its inclusion in the same section of Gellone's cartulary. In this document purporting to date from 807, Louis, king of Aquitaine, relates how Guillaume, "who had been a most renowned count in the palace of our august father Charles" but who then renounced worldly glory for the monastic life, had asked him to grant to Gellone certain fiscal properties.[300] Gellone is described in the same terms as in the charter of 804—as a "monastery" founded by Guillaume serving as a representative for Charlemagne.

The early twelfth-century *vita* of Guillaume, composed no doubt in part as a counterpoint to Aniane's *vita* of its founder, heightens this picture of an

---

[298] Ardo, *Vita Benedicti*, in *Cartulaires des abbayes d'Aniane et de Gellone*, 2:13. Whether or not this was a tendentious interpolation, the phrase's polemical potential was recognized in the twelfth century. In a foundation legend that expressed in part its desire to free itself from Saint-Victor, the abbey of Vabres borrowed this phrase for itself; see Appendix 1 below.

[299] *Cartulaires des abbayes d'Aniane et de Gellone*, 1:144–146, no. 160. For further discussion of this text, see above, Chapter 5 at nn. 164–165.

[300] *Cartulaires des abbayes d'Aniane et de Gellone*, 2:209–210, no. 249. This diploma mentions Juliofredus as abbot and was originally, therefore, probably a companion piece to the apocryphal *testamentum Juliofredi* found in the first half of the cartulary (see above, Chapter 5 at nn. 162–163). For analyses of Louis's diploma, see Pückert, *Aniane und Gellone*, pp. 148–160; and Tisset, *L'abbaye de Gellone*, pp. 40 (n. 16), 59–61.

independent abbey founded by an intimate of Charlemagne.[301] In its account of Gellone's establishment and construction, the *vita* of Guilluame very pointedly grants no role to anyone but this saint and his sons, Charlemagne, and Louis the Pious.[302] The same exclusion of Aniane occurs in its description of Guillaume's conversion. Bearing the precious fragment of the Cross granted by Charlemagne, the count is received into the monastic life directly at Gellone without stopping at Aniane, and his largesse benefits only Gellone.[303]

These pointed if oblique assertions of Gellone's original and intrinsic independence are accompanied by a portrayal of Guillaume as a figure who overshadows Aniane's founder. The hero who appears in the first half of the *vita* resonated in a way Benedict never could with the growing interest of the late eleventh and twelfth centuries in the epic past.[304] Indeed, perhaps the conflict was what encouraged Gellone to articulate the epic nature of its founder, thus endowing itself with as much Carolingian sheen as possible. The *vita*'s Guillaume, moreover, could even compete with Benedict on the saintly abbot's own turf. After his conversion, Guillaume becomes a humble, hardworking, pious ascetic. His asceticism is even described in terms borrowed from Ardo's descriptions of Benedict's self-macerations.[305] This appropriation of Benedict's characteristics for Gellone's own founder serves both to elevate Guillaume and to deny Aniane's preeminence based on its founder's special qualities.

Gellone conducted its dialogue with Aniane through the figure of Charlemagne as well. In the *vita*, Guillaume's intimacy with Charlemagne— and Charlemagne's affection for Guillaume and thus his foundation—were highlighted.[306] This was perhaps an unconscious insinuation that no abbey (read: not Aniane) could have been closer to the magnificent Carolingian than Gellone had been at its foundation. Further, through its relationship with Charlemagne, Gellone affirms its possession of that most special relic, the fragment of the True Cross.[307] This relic becomes the symbol particularly of Charlemagne's *amicitia* with Gellone's founder. No room is left for any possible competition.

---

[301] *Vita [S. Willelmi ducis] (AASS* May 6:811–820). Perhaps the first scholars to remark on how this *vita* was a riposte to Aniane's *vita* of Benedict were Pückert, *Aniane und Gellone,* pp. 110–119; and C. Revillout, "Etude historique et littéraire sur l'ouvrage latin intitulé *Vie de saint Guillaume,"* *Mémoires de la Société Archéologique de Montpellier* 6 (1870–1876): 517–518.

[302] See above, Chapter 2 at nn. 101–104, and *Vita [S. Willelmi ducis] (AASS* May 6:817).

[303] *Vita [S. Willelmi ducis] (AASS* May 6:817).

[304] See above, Chapter 5 at nn. 165–169.

[305] Pückert, *Aniane und Gellone,* pp. 110–119; Revillout, "Etude historique et littéraire," pp. 524–535. Bédier summarizes their observations, but exaggerates when he asserts that *all* of Gellone's traditions (including the fragment of the Cross!) were imitations of those of Aniane. See his "Recherches sur les légendes," pp. 19–22.

[306] See above, Chapter 5 at nn. 167–169.

[307] See above, Chapter 5 at n. 79.

The principle at operation for Gellone was thus exclusion (of Aniane and Benedict), and that for Aniane was inclusion (of Gellone and Guillaume). Nonetheless, each monastery borrowed from and reshaped the traditions of the other. Their creation of legendary identity was predicated not on difference but on an intensification of the same characteristics and a heightening of the relationship to two central figures: Charlemagne and Guillaume. The interplay between the two monastic impulses generative of conflict in the late eleventh century and the first half of the twelfth—liberty and domination—expressed itself in terms of legendary appropriation of, and competition for, those Carolingian personages.

Unnamed by the southern legends but underlying many of them was thus a specific danger: that of being engulfed by another monastery and subsumed into its identity. Vabres in its efforts to free itself from Saint-Victor's lordship, Sorèze in order to ward off first Saint-Victor and then Moissac, and perhaps Mozac and Sarlat in the face of Cluny—these were some of the other communities who turned to their imaginatively remembered origins when so threatened.[308] Equally, abbeys bent on incorporating another monastery into their sphere of power expressed their intentions by integrating the object of their desire into their own legendary identities. Monasteries, then, were not only institutions that could be bound together by fraternal and spiritual ties, but were places of competing lordships. In the interstices of their rivalries for *dominatio* and *libertas*, foundation legends flourished.

Such legends, as well as those (less numerous) for which the background was tension with bishops or the secular aristocracy, were clustered in the late eleventh through the mid-twelfth century—a period of significant social reordering caused in part by the ideals of ecclesiastical reform, in part by changes in lordship.[309] On the one hand, "reform" fueled abbeys' thirst for independence from episcopal and lay lordship; on the other, friction between monasteries might be generated when one was subjected to another for purposes of reform. An abbey's legends, its statements of identity, sketched out its desired place in this world of changing social relations.

By the end of this period—that is, by the early to mid-thirteenth century—abbeys still might invoke their legendary origins in the context of conflict and lordship, although now against a new background: the social turmoil of the Albigensian Crusade and its aftermath. Remember how Moissac turned to its legendary founder, Clovis, when confronted by the counts of Toulouse. And Lagrasse, profiting from the effects of the Albigensian Crusade (landholders branded as heretics had been stripped of their rights and property), attempted both to regain estates that had been infeu-

---

[308] For these cases, see Appendix 1 below.

[309] I do not mean to reduce the changes during this period to these two phenomena, but they are the most relevant here.

dated to the local aristocracy over the course of the later twelfth century and
to expand its holdings by claiming as its own certain properties it had never
held.[310] For, as we have seen, the *Gesta Karoli Magni* and the spate of stunning forgeries that poured forth from Lagrasse in the 1240s and 1250s
complement each other in their efforts to color royal, delineate, and organize as this abbey's patrimony a vast number of estates.[311] Thus the monastery attempted to repair its financial situation, which like that of many other
abbeys, had become difficult toward the end of the twelfth century.[312] But
behind this legendary flamboyance was more than an effort to expand
Lagrasse's territorial lordship. New factors, a new process in the ordering of
monastic institutions, inflected the *Gesta's* composition. In this new type of
reform, which differed from that of the late eleventh and early twelfth
centuries, lay the final enemy of monastic identity, the final challenge to
monastic integrity: internal stress.

Lagrasse: The Internal Enemy

Late in the twelfth century and continuing into the thirteenth, monastic
discipline in many of the great old Benedictine abbeys degenerated, or at
least was perceived as doing so. In response came a new round of reform,
often imposed by bishops or cardinals rather than by another monastic
house. Indeed, one of the great "reformers" of the earlier period, Saint-
Victor of Marseilles, itself required reform by 1195.[313] The background for
the *Gesta Karoli Magni* was a situation of internal disorganization and crisis
that was particular to Lagrasse but symptomatic of these more general problems of southern Benedictine monasticism.[314]

Under Bernard Imbert (1237–1255), the abbot at whose behest the Latin
version of the *Gesta* was composed, the monastery was rocked by a series of

---

[310] See Paris, BN Doat 66, 313r–316v, 318r–322r, 326r–328r. Many of these texts deal
with estates also claimed as the abbey's own in the *Gesta Karoli Magni.*

[311] See above, Chapter 5 at nn. 237–240.

[312] On Lagrasse's financial crisis in the late twelfth century, see Pailhes, "La crise," pp.
265–276. Other southern abbeys, too, appeared to have suffered from such problems during
this period; papal and episcopal decrees prohibiting the abbot from infeudating monastic
land appear in numerous cartularies.

[313] For the document recounting the reform imposed by the bishop of Fréjus and a
cardinal named Bernard, see *Cartulaire de l'abbaye de Saint-Victor de Marseille,* 2:249–251, no.
856. Cluny itself had been reformed in the first half of the twelfth century under Peter the
Venerable, and then again in the thirteenth (on this latter, see Cygler, "*Rebelliones,*" pp. 66–
68). There is evidence that Saint-Gilles underwent some sort of reform in the first quarter of
the thirteenth century; see the texts in *Bullaire de l'abbye de Saint-Gilles,* pp. 101–102, no. 76
and pp. 115–116, no. 85.

[314] Ironically, Lagrasse's Abbot Benedict had been one of those who proposed and
instituted monastic reforms under Gregory IX's direction; see the text from 1226 discussed
in *Cartulaire de l'ancien diocèse,* 2:265.

intense crises detrimental to the community's sense of itself.[315] Abbot Bernard and various factions of monks were at violent odds with one another by 1245. By 1248 the situation had deteriorated to such an extent that the archbishop of Narbonne, prompted by the pope, introduced a strict moral reform. This involved not only the imposition of greater discipline within the abbey, but also the partial and temporary dissolution of the monastic community; twenty-eight monks were sent to live in other abbeys for varying periods of time.

Subsequent to the reform, matters seem to have become worse. Not only did the abbot create more enemies for himself within what was left of the community, but the abbey experienced a great loss of face. Rumors that various of the royal confirmations of property were forgeries began to circulate, eventually reaching the ears of Louis IX and Blanche of Castille, themselves benefactors of the abbey. In 1253 the king established a new agreement with Lagrasse concerning its properties and revenues, one that was much less advantageous to the abbey than his earlier grants. Moreover, the king demanded the return of the earlier diplomas. Because many of these diplomas were in fact forged, however, the abbot was reluctant to do so. Then, in 1255, one of the monks, professing great hatred for Bernard Imbert, confessed that he himself had made the forgeries and had attributed them to the abbot in an attempt to harm his enemy.[316]

This confession rounds out our image of the dimensions of the crisis at Lagrasse. The abbey was suffering the effects of actions by an ambitious and unscrupulous abbot, rifts within the community, an outside imposition of reform which further fragmented the community (indeed, physically dispersed it), and a great scandal provoked by a series of forgeries revealed as such. Yet the sweeping portrait of the abbey created in the *Gesta Karoli Magni* is the diametrical opposite, resolving the tension of the present into the glory of the past. In the legend, Lagrasse experiences no loss of prestige, no loss of royal favor, no moral crisis, no internal divisions.[317] Instead, as we

---

[315] In this paragraph and the next, I rely on the discussion of these crises in Pailhes, "La crise," esp. pp. 269–275.

[316] The text, rife with fascinating details about the methods of forgery and the tangle of personal relations within the abbey, was copied by Etienne Du Laura in the seventeenth century into his *Sinopsis rerum memorabilium* (Paris, Bibliothèque Mazarine 3388, pp. 128–130). Claudine Pailhes suggests that the monk's confession may represent an effort to save the abbot by providing a scapegoat: "La crise," p. 273.

[317] There is, however, a curious incident in which Charlemagne kills the abbot and tears out the prior's eyes as punishment for having attempted to usurp property he had given to the *magister* who built Lagrasse. The king then appoints a new abbot. *Gesta Karoli Magni*, pp. 106, 108, 110, 112, 114. This incident may reflect some of the tensions within Lagrasse under Bernard Imbert, or it may relate to other incidents at Lagrasse not revealed in the extant sources—or it may be an invention intended to underline dramatically Charlemagne's role as constitutor and protector of the abbey. The property in question was the mill of Boyssède, of which I have found no mention in any text predating the *Gesta Karoli*

have seen, the abbey is triumphant, inhabited by monks as loyal to the king as they are brave in his battles, a worthy recipient of royal magnaminity, the apple of the royal eye and the center of the royal landscape—a position achieved in part through the text's extraordinary focus on property.[318]

Furthermore, the integrative quality that characterized the legend's treatment of space contradicted and remedied the reality of the dispersed and fragmented community.[319] The *Gesta Karoli Magni*'s Lagrasse is the center from which all emanates and to which all returns, the generative force of a web that embraces and integrates–not an abbey that was manifestly incapable of maintaining even the most fundamental unity, that of the community itself. Through the manipulation and characterization of space as its patrimony and as royal, Lagrasse thus created a shimmering image that could tell the outside world (including the king) just what the abbey was, as well as remind the community itself of what it should be.

The *Gesta Karoli Magni* and the context of its composition thus reveal some of the changes in the invocation of legendary foundation that had occurred between the eleventh and the mid-thirteenth century. This legend, like so many others, precipitated in a medium of stress. But this stress was of a different sort. In the earlier period, the tension had been engendered by conflict or friction with an external social agent, whether episcopal, noble, or monastic. By the thirteenth century, the stress, while external in the form of the social uncertainty provoked by the Albigensian Crusade, could also be internal. Now the recourse to legend might function within the context of a certain degeneration and internal disorganization of the community, rather than within that of threats, implicit or explicit, posed by neighbors and rivals.

Nonetheless, we should not underestimate the similarities that unite these tensions and these legends. In this later period, as in the earlier, the friction sprang from the process of defining and then maintaining the abbey's position in the social hierarchy at the local level. Accordingly, the legends traced monastic identity in shifting patterns of lordship and liberty—or, as we saw in Chapter 2, motifs of inclusion and exclusion.

Magni. Nor has Gauthier Langlois: "Moulins, forges et établissements hydrauliques de l'Aude (Xe–XVe siècle)," D.E.A., Paris I, 1988–1989, Répertoire, no. 11.1.18.185.

[318] See above, Chapter 5 at nn. 186–204.

[319] I am influenced by Farmer's discussion of how the increasing dispersal of the community at Marmoutier among distant priories fostered a need to create some kind of imaginative "adhesive" that could bind the monks together. See her *Communities of Saint Martin,* pp. 127–136. Lagrasse, too, had many priories; see the list in the early thirteenth-century document copied by Du Laura in his *Sinopsis rerum memorabilium* (Paris, Bibliothèque Mazarine 3388, p. 109). What I am suggesting here, though, is that the integrating function of the legend was related not just to this general situation but especially to a particular moment in which even the core community resident at the mother abbey had been scattered.

Whether in the face of bishops, the secular nobility, other abbeys, or even internal distress, the legends and the legendary founders announced the monastery's integrity and permanence. Its roots firmly planted in the soil of the legendary past, the monastery was assured of its identity as the unique and (to borrow from the *nota* of Saint-Martial) "natural" community able to survive all challenges.

Conclusion

Through their legendary origins, abbeys articulated series of boundaries, inclusive and exclusive, symbolic and concrete. Hence, situations in which a monastery's position in the social hierarchy was
threatened were particularly apt to provoke the invocation of legendary
foundation. In my explanation of why abbeys had recourse to the imaginative past, I have stressed this conflictual context—and not only because it
was the most common setting. In a sense, the legends themselves oblige me
to do so. Structuring monastic identity in relational terms, whether negative
or positive, they direct attention not only to the abbey itself but to its position in the social web, its dealings with its neighbors. These latter were often
characterized by a degree of tension (natural perhaps in an era of expansion
and territorialization of lordship, lay and ecclesiastical), and by the emergence of new ideals of social order.

Such friction—whether over liberty, relics, property, or status—allows us
to observe "in action" the implicit social ordering that the legends in general
accomplish. But tension was not the least common denominator of situations that engendered the assertion and affirmation of monastic identity
through beginnings. As we have seen, legends delineated the abbey's independence, relative or absolute, whether or not in cases of actual conflict
with a noble, a bishop, or another monastery. Equally, legends could focus
on relics when there was no explicit rivalry, and on property when there was
no identifiable dispute. For the legends were no mere reactions to stress.
Rather, they participated in a general restructuring of monastic institutional
identity that began around the year 1000 and involved (among other
things) not only liberty, but also relics and property.

In reality and in legend, relics were crucial expressions of an abbey's identity, but the legends themselves were equally important for the relics. By providing them with a past, legends named relics—and thereby rendered them significant in the present. For the sacredness and the efficacity of relics depended on the construction of their identity.[1] Unidentified bones were just that—bones. Foundation legends were certainly not the only way in which relics could acquire their meaning. But the intertwining of a relic (or living saint) with foundation was peculiarly suitable for proclaiming the relationship of identity between relic and community. Through association with the abbey's origins, the relics participated in the constitution of the community and thereby became irrevocably part of the monastery. An abbey seeking to invent, reinterpret, or promote its relics might well choose to express these needs in a foundation legend.

For example, the various layers of Charroux's legend focusing on the relics brought by Charlemagne—first the fragment of the True Cross and then the *sancta virtus,* or Holy Foreskin—very clearly relate to the abbey's development and promotion of the cult of these sacred objects.[2] In the case of the True Cross, the legend functioned to reinterpret an object that had already been significant for the abbey. By becoming a gift of Charlemagne, the Cross was reinvested with meaning, and its cult presumably was boosted. In the case of the Holy Foreskin, the context of promotion is even clearer, and the constitutive power of legends of origins particularly evident. This relic, remember, was "invented" (both in the medieval and the modern sense of the word) at Charroux in the late eleventh century. The legend participated in this invention, creating an identity for an object that had not existed before. As it did so, the legend helped to launch the cult, endowing the Foreskin with Charlemagne's aura. Other cases suggest that the invention of new relics or the desire to gild extant ones with new prestige could precipitate the crystallization of legends.[3]

Legends thus could relate to the need to invent or reinvent sacred remains. To be sure, devotion to relics was not a new phenomenon, nor one limited to the period of the eleventh through the thirteenth century. But the enhanced social significance acquired by relics beginning in the eleventh century may have stimulated the legendary impulse. Relics excited a newly intense popular devotion which manifested itself in an explosion of pil-

---

[1] Geary, *Furta Sacra,* pp. 5–9.

[2] On this legend, see above: Chapter 5 under "Charlemagne and the Epic Landscape."

[3] At Rocamadour in the second half of the twelfth century, the invention of relics occasioned the need for legend, resulting in the creation of the holy hermit and servant of the Virgin, Amadour (see above, Chapter 2 at n. 43). Perhaps the same thing occurred in the eleventh century at Brantôme where relics were discovered and then created through the legend of Charlemagne's donation of the relics of Sicarius, the paradoxical Innocent (see above, Chapter 5 at nn. 52–53, 56). Also see the case of Narbonne: Terpak, "Local Politics." Various of the legends that appear in *vitae* also may have been related to (among other things) the desire to promote the saint's cult.

grimages to saints' shrines, local and distant.[4] A flurry of inventions and translations occurred as relics began to figure in the lives of ecclesiastical communities in new ways. These communities began to compose collections relating miracles (vengeful and beneficent) that had occurred through the relics' *virtus,* to build churches that could accommodate crowds of pilgrims, and to construct ambulatories and elevated crypts in order to display the sacred objects. Furthermore, relics increasingly became channels through which ecclesiastical communities might express and regulate their relations with the outside world. Relics were turned outward. While remaining the abbey's internal core, they also became more and more its public face. Hence, as they shaped the relics, foundation legends also molded this face.

As relics proliferated, so did the need to identify them—and to distinguish them from those possessed by other communities, particularly from other relics of the same saint or sacred object.[5] In this context, foundation legends could serve as both identity and principle of differentiation. Through its history, its indelible association with this abbey, Charroux's fragment of the True Cross was implicitly defined as different from the multitude of other pieces of the Holy Wood. This need to tie the representation of the sacred to a specific place and to render local the possibly generic is not unlike that which resulted in the multiplicity of the Virgin Mary; she was the Virgin of Loreto, of Rocamadour, of Le Puy, of Walsingham—and each was different from the next. Such individuation was important not only to imbue the abbey with a sense of self, but also to proclaim to the outside world who the abbey was in relation to other shrines. Distinguishing a relic with a special history might elevate the abbey above its competitors, luring pilgrims, prestige, and wealth.

Thus, the new importance of relics in this period could provide the context for recourse to the imaginatively remembered past, as could changes in yet another aspect of monastic identity that was important to foundation both in legend and reality: property. Many southern legends— including those of Aniane, Gellone, Uzerche, Saint-Chaffre, Saint-Germier, and the cathedral of Auch—appear as prologues to cartularies or as part of the cartulary's structure.[6] Although the first three of these instances related to highly charged conflictual situations, they had a further dimension of

---

[4] Bernhard Töpfer's "Reliquienkult und Pilgerbewegung zur Zeit der Klosterreform im Burgundisch-Aquitanischen Gebiet," in *Vom Mittelalter zur Neuzeit: Zum 65. Geburtstag von Heinrich Sproemberg,* ed. Hellmut Kretzschmar (Berlin, 1956), pp. 420–439 remains a compelling statement (abbreviated English version in *The Peace of God,* pp. 41–57).

[5] Surely this is one of the factors behind the renewed production of hagiography beginning in the eleventh century. See Head, *Hagiography and the Cult of the Saints,* pp. 58–60, 72, 285–287.

[6] Cluny's foundation legend also appeared in one of its cartularies; see Iogna-Prat, "La geste des origines." On foundation narratives as prologues to northern French cartularies, see Benoît-Michel Tock, "Les textes non diplomatiques dans les cartulaires de la province de Reims," in *Les cartulaires,* pp. 45–58.

significance. Here the legendary impulse coincided with and indeed was part of the new organization, expansion, and territorialization of monastic lordship that occurred in the eleventh and twelfth centuries. For the development of the cartulary, a form that in France first appeared tentatively in the late tenth century and swelled into a great river in the twelfth century and later, relates to (among other things) new attitudes toward monastic property.[7] The cartularies evince the desire to delineate the physical boundaries of the abbey's patrimony and jurisdiction. The legends participate in this same process of institutional definition; hence they complement the cartularies, whether as prologues or not.

This process is particularly evident in the case of Saint-Chaffre, an abbey that in the later eleventh century experienced a certain reorganization. First, its abbey church, like so many others in this era, was rebuilt, a project begun under Abbot William III (1074–1086) and finished under William IV (1087–ca. 1136). William IV embarked upon further restructuring. At his behest, the abbey's cartulary chronicle was composed, making the community's patrimony tangible in a new way, just as the fabric of the church had been renewed. This document begins with a discussion of how the charters would be organized, continues with a brief description (typical of charter preambles) of the expulsion from Paradise, the Incarnation, salvation, and the Church as Mary and Martha—and then turns to the tale of Saint-Chaffre's foundation by Calminius, "senator and prince" of Auvergne.[8] Grounded in sacred and then in specific history, the charters follow. The articulation of the legend thus occurred in the context of the statement and organization of the abbey's lordship. The imaginatively remembered past becomes the foundations of this exclusive lordship in the present, lending its authoritative weight to that of the collected charters, literally framing and thus implicitly characterizing these monasteries' relations with their dependents. Legends colored monastic territorial lordship not only as it was established over the course of the eleventh and twelfth centuries, but also as it was reorganized toward the middle of the thirteenth century as in the *Gesta Karoli Magni*.[9]

The ideal of liberty, new functions of relics, the territorialization of monastic lordship—these were some of the specific factors in the crystallization of the legends and of a new sense of monastic identity. This framework of change helps to explain why the legends proliferated when they did and not earlier. Beginning in the eleventh century, monasteries had perhaps more reasons to appeal to their origins than they had had before. Monasteries had become conscious of themselves as institutions in new ways, and needed to

---

[7] On cartularies, see the collected articles in *Les cartulaires*.
[8] *Cartulaire de l'abbaye de St-Chaffre*, pp. 1–4. On Calminius, see above: Chapter 3 at nn. 1–7; Chapter 4 at nn. 28–29.
[9] See above, Chapter 6 at nn. 310–312.

distinguish themselves as such, just as the aristocratic lineages that emerged in this period felt the need to create distinguishing historicized genealogies for themselves. The constitutive authority of origins—especially those origins located in the golden age (which the legends helped gild) before the caesura of the late ninth and tenth centuries—became this principle of distinction.

Here I do not mean to suggest that the legends were mere façades for deeper interests, mere strategies for arriving at certain ends in new situations. Such mechanical and materialist equivalences miss the importance of the imaginatively remembered past. For the legends were part of the deep changes during this period, not merely reflective of them. Whether establishing exclusive boundaries of independence, or the inclusive ones of lordship and association, or even the neutral ones of mediation (remember the foundation of Clairvaux-d'Aveyron which instituted peace between two castles), the legends participated in the process of implicit social ordering, creating a past that could inflect the present.[10]

This general process by which the abbey told itself who it was, structured its relations with others, and distinguished itself from others was subject to chronological inflections. Those legends (or layers thereof) which emerged in the first half of the eleventh century seem to have been the least polemical. They represent an awakening to the importance of the past, a concern to historicize relatively new foundations and to recuperate the past of those houses which had roots in the pre-tenth-century era. In the second half of the eleventh century and continuing well into the first half of the twelfth, new situations predominated: those of conflict in which liberty and lordship were at stake. In this context of explicit reordering, which borrowed from and transformed the ideals of various ecclesiastical reformers, legends particularly blossomed. After this great concentration of legendary production in the era of reform, the legendary ferment diminished. In the later twelfth century and the first half of the next, some new layers, sometimes explanatory, sometimes polemical were added to extant traditions. But the legendary landscape seemed to be firmly in place, only needing further elaboration. Few new legends appeared. Those that did were often situated in the familiar contexts of conflict and lordship, although by the thirteenth century they were played out against the turbulent background of the Albigensian Crusade and its aftermath. Here, too, as a setting was a new and different phase of monastic reform in which abbeys appealed to legend not in the face of external challenges, but rather in an effort to deal with internal crisis.

The situations impelling abbeys to reaffirm their identity through imaginatively remembered origins thus altered between the beginning and the

---

[10] On Clairvaux-d'Aveyron, see above, Chapter 2 at nn. 38–41.

end of the period considered here. So did the way in which these communities represented and shaped the past. There was a shift from secular
Rome to the sacred Rome represented by the apostles and their chief heir,
the pope. This new Rome was flanked—often even overshadowed—by the
Frankish kings who appear in the legends with increasing frequency by the
twelfth century. Although hints of imperial Rome lingered, the past had
become Frankish—and most royally so. For Clovis, Pippin the Short, and
especially Charlemagne began to occupy an ever larger portion of the limelight, almost replacing the saints who dominated in earlier legendary layers.
As Frankish kings became associated with the constitutive time of origins, its
power and its sanctity began to rub off on them.

Through the legends, then, there occurred a certain imaginative reconstitution and reconfiguration of royal power in the guise of particularly the
early Carolingians. The so-called political periphery thus actively created the
center: that is the king. I have explored this process from its stirrings in the
early eleventh century to its blossoming in the thirteenth century, showing
how the king gradually emerged as an active presence. In the very early
eleventh century, a community such as Noblat might imagine a faceless and
shadowy king who reigned south of the Loire, but it would confine the
named (although equally substanceless) king, in this case Clovis, to the
north. By the thirteenth century, the specific king could be imagined as
exuberantly present, as a character full and rounded through epic, functioning to delineate or even sanctify the southern landscape, as did
Lagrasse's Charlemagne.

Not only had the shape of the imagined king changed, but so had the
implications of his presence in the legends. I have argued that as these
abbeys constructed the king, they implicitly placed themselves in an integrative relationship with the greater authority he represented. By the mid-
thirteenth century, the melding of past and present implied in imaginative
memory was realized in a new way. The king was now part of the present and
not just of the past. Now if southern abbeys chose to create royal founders
for themselves in legend, they would have to contend with a king whose
power no longer resided only in their imagination, but in their backyard in
the form of the royal seneschals. Equally, they might now expect—even
demand—active royal protection.

If the coloring and configuration of imagined origins had changed, certain structural constants remained. From the beginning to the end of the
period, the legends made the abbey a (if not *the*) sacred center of the
landscape. This is one of the underlying meanings of foundation both in
legend and in ritual: the monastery must be revealed and constructed as a
porta caeli and a prefiguration of paradise. Furthermore, the legends
mapped the world, local and larger, around this sacred center. Through
their legendary origins, abbeys constructed themselves not in isolation, but

in relation to the surrounding world; or, rather, they constructed that world in relation to themselves. Southern monasteries imagined a past—and a present—in which sacred boundaries assured lordship, independence, and position in the social hierarchy, in the world.

Legends were thus statements of monastic identity turned both inward and outward. As the abbey's private face, the legend assured the monks of their history, rooting them in continuity with the constitutive and sacred moment of origins. As a public face, the legend proclaimed to all both the abbey's identity as a sacred center and its vision of the social order. But did this imaginatively remembered past also inform how the outside world saw these southern monasteries? In other words, was anyone outside the monastery walls aware of these legends?

Much evidence indicates that the answer is yes. Abbeys themselves often knew of one another's legends.[11] In the heat of their dispute in the eleventh and twelfth centuries, Aniane and Gellone were keenly aware of each other's legends—sometimes even down to the letter of the texts—as were Conques and Figeac, in a similarly charged context, and Psalmodi and Joncels.[12] It did not take a quarrel, however, for one monastery to communicate its legend to another. The first traces of Charroux's legend appear in the *miracula* relevant to the abbey of Saint-Genou and in Ademar of Chabannes's *Chronicon*.[13] Somehow, then, knowledge of Charroux's traditions had seeped out. Vabres was familiar enough with Aniane's version of the *Vita Benedicti* (especially the forged diploma of Charlemagne it included) to be able to reproduce passages almost verbatim in its own legend.[14] And in the *Gesta Karoli Magni*, Lagrasse's Charlemagne complained about the "abbots of Sorèze and of Gaillaguet (*Gaillacus*) . . . because they had not come to his aid at [the siege of] Narbonne. He asserted that because his own father Pippin had built the monastery of Sorèze and he himself had rebuilt it and given much to it, the abbot should have come to him with all his military force (*posse*)."[15] Lagrasse thus had learned in some fashion of Sorèze's foundation legend invoking Pippin the Short.[16] The passage also implies obliquely that Lagrasse was not unfamiliar with the legend of Gaillaguet's foundation by the same Carolingian, for otherwise why would the *Gesta Karoli Magni* have mentioned this abbey in the same

---

[11] Here I disagree with Hans Patze, who argues that monastic archives were private, almost secret, and that monasteries did not consult one another's documents (he calls cases in which abbeys were aware of one another's privileges and charters "ungewöhnlich" [unusual]); see his "Adel und Stifterchronik," pp. 30–31, 75.

[12] See above, Chapter 6 at nn. 233–239, 248–265.

[13] See above, Chapter 5 at nn. 60–63.

[14] See Appendix 1 below.

[15] *Gesta Karoli Magni*, p. 146.

[16] See above, Chapter 4 at nn. 112–114.

breath with Sorèze?[17] Legends thus circulated among monasteries—
perhaps in the form of oral stories, perhaps because monastic visitors were
shown the texts or objects that related the tale of origins.

Knowledge of the legends was not confined to monks. By the mid-
fourteenth century, the people of the bourg of Moissac believed that the
regal Christ who sat solemnly on the abbey's tympanum was King Clovis
himself—surely because they knew the abbey had been founded by that
mortal ruler.[18] In a period difficult to fix precisely (later than the mid-
fourteenth century but certainly by the late seventeenth century), the townspeople of Lagrasse knew about their abbey's legendary foundation. They
were reminded every year when the abbey celebrated Charlemagne's feast
day (January 28), for on this occasion all within the parish were prohibited
from working.[19] It seems unlikely that these were the only monastic bourgs
whose inhabitants were aware of the legendary origins of the abbeys that
exercised lordship over them.

Abbeys also drew their legends to the attention of local people who
wielded much authority. Bishops, for example, might know of these traditions. In a confirmation of Charroux's possessions of 1101, the bishop of
Périgueux referred to that abbey's foundation by Charlemagne and its consecration by Leo III.[20] The bishops of Nîmes, reminded frequently by popes,
were only too aware of Saint-Gilles's legendary origins. Indeed, those prelates inflected their own commemorative tradition partly in response to the
legend of this abbey over which they tried to exercise jurisdiction.[21] Furthermore, Moissac's loud and evidently public (*dicebatur publice*) claims to royal
foundation were heard not only by the townspeople, but apparently also by
at least one count of Toulouse, Raymond VII (whose ill will toward the
monastery was thereby fanned, Aymeric de Peyrat specifies).[22]

Some of the abbeys communicated their legends to an even more exalted
social group: the kings they sought as their protectors. Remember how La
Règle and Mozac showed to Louis VII documents relevant to their legendary
foundation by Pippin the Short, and how according to Aymeric de Peyrat
the monks of Moissac supplicated Philip Augustus by invoking Clovis as

[17] For the legend of Gaillaguet, see above, Chapter 2 at nn. 112–113.

[18] Beaune, *Naissance*, p. 69.

[19] After remarking on the change from *suffragia* to *cultus* in the abbey's veneration of
Charlemagne (see above, Chapter 5 at n. 210), Dom J. Trichaud remarks: "Quo ex tempore
sacrae eius memoriae dicata mensis januarii dies 28 ab opere feriata in tota Crassensis
paroecia, rituque solemnissimo festorum primae classis cum octava ab coenobitis celebrata"
(*Chronicon*, Paris, BN Latin 12857, p. 125). I date this practice as possibly post 1351, for it did
not appear in the abbey's customs compiled in that year (Trichaud's remark cited above
follows his copy of those customs). Certainly the practice appeared before 1677, the year in
which Trichaud was writing.

[20] *Chartes et documents pour servir à l'histoire de l'abbaye de Charroux*, pp. 126–127, no. 24.

[21] See above, Chapter 6 at nn. 48–49.

[22] See above, Chapter 6 at n. 156.

founder. Furthermore, when a mid-thirteenth-century (?) archbishop of Auch appealed to Louis (IX?) for protection, this prelate invoked his see's foundation by Clovis.[23] Likewise, in his confirmation of Lagrasse's status as a royal abbey in 1376, Charles V not only mentioned various of Charlemagne's diplomas (which were forged at Lagrasse) but also clearly referred to elements of the foundation legend as it appears in the *Gesta Karoli Magni* (miraculous consecration, Charlemagne's battles against the Muslims).[24] These instances attest to the realization of the imaginative creation of the king—but also to the fact that these legends were far from being traditions sealed in monastic silence. Finally, let us not forget that by the twelfth century an element of Saint-Gilles's legend—the mass—had migrated from this abbey's sources to multitudes of texts and images scattered across Europe, and that by the thirteenth century Charroux's legend of Charlemagne and the Holy Foreskin was famed in Paris and beyond.[25]

The very forms in which southern abbeys represented their imaginatively remembered origins suggest the nature of the legends as both private and public faces for these communities. Only infrequently did these monasteries' legends appear as independent narrative accounts. Such accounts were primarily intended to be read silently, although they might be diffused through being copied, and their contents relayed in oral forms. But this textual form itself was not overtly public—unlike those types of texts which frame most of the southern monastic legends.[26] Most often these legends were incarnated in shapes that were exposed to eye and ear.

Vitae and such diplomatic texts as privileges, whether papal or royal, were meant to be read not only silently but also out loud—and often on occasions

[23] On Mozac, see above, Chapter 6 at nn. 143–144; on La Règle, Chapter 5 at n. 230; on Moissac, Chapter 4 at nn. 77–79. On the Auch legend, see above, Chapter 4 at nn. 58–69; the archbishop's invocation of Clovis as founder appears in an intriguing if grammatically enigmatic document copied in the eighteenth century by the Abbé Louis Daignan de Sendat in his *Mémoires historiques*. The piece is entitled "Extrait d'un arret rapporté par Chopin [?] au sujet de l'archevesque hyspar [?] concernant l'homage du comte d'armagnac à l'église d'Auch" and dated 1245. It reads: "Visa informatione facta super homagio pro temporali ecclesiae auscitanae faciendo repertum est per testes dictum homagium a quodam archiepiscopo auxitano regibus francis factum est, ei nominum [?] hispanum quondam archiepiscopum Ludovicum regem francia [*sic*] requisivisse tanquam dominum temporalem, quod ecclesiam Auxitanicam fundatum et dotatum a Clodoveo rege francorum iuvaret, ei deffenderet sicut tenebatur. Item quod Arnaldus de armaniaco fecit homagio hyspano archiepiscopo pro comitatibus armaniaci et fezenciaci et de iis loquendum est domino regi" (Auch, BM 70, p. 645). Here the royal foundation not only establishes a relationship between king and archbishop, but implicitly structures the ruler's relations with his own vassals.

[24] In the seventeenth century, Trichaud copied part of Charles's diploma into his *Chronicon* (Paris, BN Latin 12857, pp. 81–83). See also the partial edition in *Cartulaire de l'ancien diocèse*, 2:351.

[25] See above, Chapter 5 at nn. 23, 89, 105.

[26] Farmer, however, suggests that the late eleventh-century narrative legend of Marmoutiers might have been prepared as a brief for the council of Clermont (1095); see her *Communities of Saint Martin*, p. 157.

when others besides the monks might hear. *Vitae* were used as readings on the major feast days of the community's patron saint, moments when pilgrims and other visitors were especially likely to be present.[27] At mass (with the Gospel reading or with the sermon), charters and diplomas were often read aloud, a practice known as *carta recitata*.[28] Indeed, one of the charters that form Saint-Sever's legend explicitly assumes a listening audience (*vestris auribus pandam*).[29] Particularly important charters or privileges—including perhaps those legendary ones in which the abbey's identity and boundaries were enunciated—would be selected as readings on solemn and very public occasions such as the saint's feast day. Written on the back of a late twelfth-century papal privilege guaranteeing Saint-Gilles's *libertas* was the following stipulation: "this privilege is read [out loud] annually at the greater feast of Saint Gilles."[30] Granted, this is no legendary text. But it is not difficult to believe that Sorèze, for example, would have chosen for such an occasion the diploma relating its foundation by Pippin the Short.

Legends in the shape of diplomas, charters, and privileges—like those in *vitae*—thus served within ritual contexts, affirming the abbey's identity not only for its monks, but for whomever else might be present. Those outsiders (mainly clerics, monks and nuns) and insiders who could understand Latin would now know the tale of the monastery's origins. Any illiterates present (whether of high or low status) might learn it from them or from the special parts of the service involving brief translations into the vernacular.[31]

Furthermore, as the legends in charter form demonstrate, legendary forms were predicated not only on telling but on showing. We have already seen how certain of the abbeys must have shown their legendary texts to various kings to obtain their ratification, and how monks might bring their charters of legendary foundation to councils where conflicts were adjudicated.[32] The manuscript (Paris BN Latin 11018) that contains Saint-Gilles's papal privileges and proclaims the abbey's legendary liberty, although of beautiful manufacture, was very small (only 16.5 cm × 11 cm)—possibly so

[27]   For a nice statement of the relationship between *vitae* and *lectiones,* see Head, *Hagiography and the Cult of the Saints,* pp. 121–129.

[28]   For two examples, see *Cartulaire de l'abbaye de Conques,* pp. 86–87, 187–188, nos. 92 and 222. On this practice in general, see Joachim Studtmann, "Die Pönformel der mittelalterlichen Urkunden," *Archiv für Urkundenforschung* 12 (1932): 251–374.

[29]   See "Documents transcrits," p. 120.

[30]   *Bullaire de l'abbaye de Saint-Gilles,* p. 93, n. 1.

[31]   On these parts of the service (*prone*), see Head, *Hagiography and the Cult of the Saints,* p. 132.

[32]   On kings and privileges, see above at nn. 23–24. On charters and conflicts, see Chapter 6. The early twelfth-century texts relating to a dispute between Aniane and La Chaise-Dieu over the possession of Goudargues show very nicely how documents were actually examined (and judged) in such cases. *Cartulaires des abbayes d'Aniane et de Gellone,* 2:90–95, nos. 7–9.

that it might easily be carried about and displayed to whomever, whether the pope, the counts of Toulouse, the monks of Cluny, or various councils.[33]

Display might be implied in other ways by the manuscripts into which legends were often copied. As we have seen, legendary texts—whether in the form of prologues, *vitae*, or diplomatic texts—might head cartularies. Rather than being collections designed for consultation only by the monks of the abbey in question, cartularies may also have been intended as documents that could be shown (as statements of the abbey's identity and rights) to important visitors.[34] Might not the rich decoration of the twelfth-century portion of Gellone's cartulary (which opens with Guillaume's legendary charter of December 14) suggest that this manuscript was intended for display in some way, whether or not in the context of conflict?[35] Remember, too, that the diplomatic documents composing Saint-Sever's legend were copied onto the very last folios of its glorious *Beatus*. There is much debate about the function of this sumptuous manuscript.[36] But perhaps this codex which certainly had liturgical and ritual functions for the monastic community itself was also shown to outsiders in some fashion. If such manuscripts were revealed to eyes other than those of the monks, so were the legendary beginnings they contained.

The nontextual forms in which southern abbeys sometimes expressed their legends were even more explicitly public. Reliquaries received much attention, not only from the monks but from pilgrims who came to venerate the relics. Would not the custodian, or a guide, have proudly related the story of the abbey's origins explicit or implicit in many of these (such as the late twelfth-century enamel shrine of Calminius at Mozac, Charlemagne's *A* at Conques, and the reliquary that might have contained the *sancta virtus* at Charroux)? Equally, a guide or a monk might have pointed to the king on the tympanum at Conques or at Perse and announced his identity as the abbey's founder. Sculpted capitals, too, sometimes even graced with inscriptions identifying who the significant figures were, could depict scenes of foundation visible to any visitor to the church willing to gaze upward.[37] We have seen how in its very architecture, Charroux's church recalled the Holy Cross and the Holy Sepulcher, thus announcing the abbey's legendary iden-

---

[33] On this manuscript and its importance for Saint-Gilles, see above, Chapter 6 under "Saint-Gilles and the Three Enemies."

[34] See Tock's brief discussion of how foundation narratives that opened cartularies thus became public: "Les textes non diplomatiques," p. 53.

[35] AD Hérault 5.H.8, ff. 59v–176r. In this section of the manuscript, there are numerous decorated initials both figurative and abstract (line drawing with color). On Guillaume's charter, see above: Chapter 5 at nn. 164–165; Chapter 6 at nn. 299–300.

[36] See "Table ronde: Le *Beatus*," in *Saint-Sever*, pp. 335–339.

[37] For such capitals, see Swiechowski, *Sculpture romane d'Auvergne*, pp. 149–152, 228, 253, figs. 117, 244–249, 254. One (p. 228) has an inscription quoting apparently from the foundation charter.

tity.[38] Indeed, one thirteenth-century inscription in the nave of this church proclaimed that Charroux's founder and lord was Charlemagne, and another declared that Roger had completed the royal project.[39] Here, inscribed upon the structure that itself expressed the legend, was the abbey's legendary identity. Such inscriptions, whether in stone or on wooden plaques, often lined nave walls, proclaiming to all and sundry the tale of the church's foundation, legendary or otherwise.[40]

The forms that legends might take thus hint at an answer to the question, particularly difficult perhaps for the Middle Ages, of how a group might communicate its identity—the symbolic boundaries it fabricates—to others. Southern abbeys did not capture their imaginatively remembered pasts only in narrative texts destined to be stored in a book cupboard, recopied and consulted perhaps but not integrated into the rhythm of their existence. More often, they articulated these legendary traditions in forms that, privately and publicly, made of their past a presence. This past commanded respect and often belief, for many of these forms carried an intrinsic authority which complemented and reinforced that of legendary origins. Privileges and diplomas added the veneer of pope and king. Reliquaries, *vitae,* and the material fabric of churches lent their intrinsic aura of the sacred to the legends. Authoritative and often tangible, the imaginatively remembered past thus suffused the present of the abbey, coloring both how it saw itself and how it was seen.

Not only was the world outside the cloister made aware of the abbey's identity created through imaginatively remembered origins, but that world, both local and larger, was implicitly embraced in the legend. As sacred center, the abbey created and ordered its periphery, the surrounding world. Furthermore, these legends were symbolic remakings, imaginative recreations of the world as it should be. To be sure, this is true of tales and myths of origins in general—but the foundation of a monastery, an enclosed and defined community, allowed a specific play between microcosm and macrocosm. The monastery was human society writ small, something that François Rabelais recognized in the sixteenth century.

---

[38]   See above, Chapter 5 at nn. 112–114.

[39]   These inscriptions were found in the nineteenth century. The one relating to Charlemagne reads: "rex iuris lator karolus / probitatis amator / huius fundator templi / fuit et dominator" (for a photograph, see Favreau and Camus, *Charroux,* p. 6, fig. 1). The other (in an identical script) reads: "rogerius comes et / princeps aquitanorum / perfecit hoc templum / imperante rege francorum" (my transcription). Among the fragments of sculpture that remain from the elaborate thirteenth-century portal are three large heads of laymen. Favreau and Camus identify two of these as Charlemagne and Roger, citing the inscriptions as evidence (*Charroux,* p. 34); this is a tantalizing theory, to be sure, but there is nothing to indicate that the inscriptions are glosses on statues.

[40]   For inscriptions relating to dedication, see above, Chapter 1 at nn. 75–77, and the intriguing evidence and discussion of Huyghebaert, "Une légende de fondation," pp. 200–208.

Rabelais chose to end his *Gargantua* with a mock monastic foundation legend, a parodic tale concerning the establishment of the abbey of Thélème, whose Rule consisted of the phrase "Do what you will" (*fay ce que vouldras*).[41] In these richly complex chapters, Rabelais, while poking fun at the monastic way of life, used the process of monastic foundation as a metaphor with which to express a restructuring of the world and of social relations according to humanist ideals. Of course, this literary image of foundation and the legendary ones I have considered are separated not only by centuries but by vast differences, not the least of which is that Rabelais's tale was invested with none of the meaning inherent in imaginative memory. Nonetheless, the description of Thélème underlines how reflection on the foundation of a monastery could be a locus for the expression of ideals of social order. Invoking the transformative power of their imaginatively re-membered origins, southern monasteries became makers of themselves, makers of kings, and makers of the world in their own image.

[41] François Rabelais, *Gargantua*, chap. 47, in *Œuvres complètes*, ed. Jacques Boulenger (Bruges, 1942), p. 181. The entire tale of Thélème's foundation occupies chapters 52–57 (in this edition, pp. 169–182).

1

Monasteries versus Monasteries

This appendix is intended as a supplement to the discussion in Chapter 6 concerning conflicts between abbeys in which legend played a role.

Vabres/Saint-Victor

The Events

Vabres was subjected to Saint-Victor for reform in 1060.[1] It then appeared as one of Saint-Victor's dependents in the following papal privileges (for Saint-Victor): Gregory VII (1079); Urban II (1095); Pascal II (1113); Innocent II (1135); Eugenius III (1149).[2] By 1120, however, Vabres had begun to resist and reject Saint-Victor's domination.[3] In that year Calixtus II wrote to the bishop of Rodez, presenting the abbot of Saint-Victor's complaint that Vabres had been "unjustly" freed of its "subjection" to Saint-Victor. The pope decreed that the abbots of both monasteries should come to Rome in order that the affair be adjudicated.[4] A *convenientia* of 1127 stipulated that

---

[1] *Cartulaire de l'abbaye de Saint-Victor,* 2:181–184, no. 827.

[2] *Cartulaire de l'abbaye de Saint-Victor,* 2:215, 208, 234–240, 220–230, 269–270, nos. 843, 840, 848, 844, 885.

[3] A privilege of Pascal II (1116) which exists only in a copy of a copy in the Vabres cartulary may show the abbey already trying to escape Saint-Victor. The pope confirms Vabres's possessions, stipulates that the abbey must pay an annual *census* to Rome, and grants it the right of appeal to the *curia*. See *Papsturkunden in Frankreich,* 2:754–756, no. 11. If it is authentic (Wiederhold expresses no doubts), this document may show the abbey successfully receiving confirmation of its status as a papal abbey; if it is forged, it shows Vabres trying to present itself as a papal abbey.

[4] *Cartulaire de l'abbaye de Saint-Victor,* 2:159–160, no. 811.

the abbot and monks of Vabres should return to the state of "subjection and obedience" to Saint-Victor (symbolized by the abbatial oath of obedience) that they had shaken off. Vabres was also to render to Saint-Victor a certain *monasterium* in return for which Saint-Victor would grant certain estates.[5] Despite this *convenientia*, Vabres had evidently not given in. In 1154 Pope Anastasius wrote a menacing letter to the abbot, warning him to show the obedience to Saint-Victor that thus far he had refused.[6]

The Legend

The struggle to escape Saint-Victor's grasp in the first half of the twelfth century seems clearly to have been the context for the elaboration of Vabres's foundation legend, at least in the version now extant.[7] This legend appears in the form of a narrative text that gives Vabres a long and distinguished history.[8] The text opens by describing how the *Marcomanni* (a misreading by the seventeenth-century transcriber of the more plausible *Nortmanni?*) had destroyed and devastated Gaul. One result was the degeneration of monastic discipline, and Vabres's foundation is shaped as beginning the instauration. The abbot of Paunat (Périgord), one of the remaining abbeys maintaining proper discipline, decided to remove his flock from the nefarious combined influence of the *Marcomanni* and the lax monks. The new site was provided by the count of Toulouse (who was the actual lay founder of Vabres).[9] Here Vabres is depicted as a house that, far from needing reform, was a bastion of proper monastic discipline and had a genealogy to prove it. Moreover, its lineage associated it not with Saint-Victor, but with Paunat.

Next the legend slips into a series of literal citations from the *vita* of Benedict of Aniane (the version presented in this abbey's cartulary). The count of Toulouse gives his foundation to Charlemagne. The emperor grants it immunity, his protection, and various privileges as per the diploma inserted into the Aniane *vita*—with the exception of the insertion of one word. Now not only counts and bishops are prohibited from exercising their justice over the abbey, but so are abbots (obviously external abbots).[10] Thus Vabres not only proclaims its status as a royal and inalienable abbey, but specifically renders Saint-Victor's lordship illegitimate. The other citations

---

    [5] *Cartulaire de l'abbaye de Saint-Victor,* 2:134–136, no. 785 (for Vabres's submission); 2:277–278, no. 890 (for Saint-Victor's grant of the stipulated properties to Vabres).

    [6] *Cartulaire de l'abbaye de Saint-Victor,* 1:635–636, no. 640.

    [7] Pückert comes to this same conclusion in his *Aniane und Gellone,* pp. 13, 44–45.

    [8] *Cartulaire de l'abbaye de Vabres,* pp. 23–28, no. 1.

    [9] On relations between the counts of Toulouse and the abbey in the ninth and tenth centuries, see Magnou-Nortier, *La société laïque,* p. 233.

    [10] *Cartulaire de l'abbaye de Vabres,* p. 31, no. 2. For the passage in the Aniane text, see *Cartulaires des abbayes d'Aniane et de Gellone,* 2:14–15. The diploma as it appears in the Vabres text has also been edited in *MGH Diplomata Karolinorum* 1:352–354, no. 249.

from the Aniane *vita* are equally revelatory; Vabres is proclaimed the *caput* of all abbeys not only in Gothia but elsewhere.[11] The legend then ends with yet another passage of the *Vita Benedicti* which in this context is made to read as a comminatory clause: "sedulo considerare libet quanta humilitate ac reverencia isdem metuendus sit locus, qui tot principibus videtur esse munitus" (a list of patron saints follows, almost the same as that in the *Vita Benedicti*).[12] Here Vabres's status as an independent monastery and its identity are given sacred boundaries.

Sorèze/Saint-Victor and Moissac

The Events

In a charter of 1062, Froterius, bishop of Nîmes, accompanied by his nephew the viscount (of Nîmes?) submitted Sorèze to Saint-Victor, granting the latter the permanent right to control abbatial elections at the former.[13] Some historians believe this document is authentic; others see in it a forgery on the part of rapacious Saint-Victor.[14] In any case, Sorèze is listed as an abbey subjected to Saint-Victor for matters of reform in the privileges granted to Saint-Victor by Gregory VII (1079) and Urban II (1095).[15] Sorèze appears in no further privileges for Saint-Victor. Then, in a charter dated 1119 and extant in an early twelfth-century copy, Viscount Bernard-Ato (presumably the Trencavel viscount of Béziers) submits Sorèze to Moissac for reform.[16] No mention is made of Saint-Victor's rights.

But Sorèze seems not to have remained Moissac's dependency, if indeed Bernard-Ato's charter had made it one. The abbey did not appear in any of Moissac's lists of its priories until the late fourteenth century, when Aymeric de Peyrat mentioned it as such in his *Chronicon*.[17] Rather than indicating that by the fourteenth century Sorèze belonged to Moissac, though, this reference more likely reveals that Aymeric, in his work as the abbey's historian, had come across the copy of the charter preserved in one of Moissac's manuscripts; there is no other evidence showing Sorèze as a dependency. In

[11] On this passage in the Aniane text, see above, Chapter 6 at n. 298.
[12] *Cartulaire de l'abbaye de Vabres*, p. 25–26, no. 1; Ardo, *Vita Benedicti*, in *Cartulaires des abbayes d'Aniane et de Gellone*, 2:13.
[13] *HL* 5:519–520, no. 263.
[14] Magnou-Nortier argues that it is a forgery; see her *La société laïque*, pp. 494–496. Schmid accepts it as authentic; see his "Die Entstehung," p. 183.
[15] *Cartulaire de l'abbaye de Saint-Victor*, 2:216, no. 843; 2:208, no. 840.
[16] The edition of this document in *HL* 5:875–876, no. 467, mentions as the original a text from the archives of Foix. I have identified instead an early twelfth-century copy written onto the last folio of a Moissac manuscript (Jerome, *Adversus Jovinianum*) of this period: Paris, BN Latin 1797, f. 79v. This copy entitles itself *carta de soreze* and is identical to that in *HL* 5—except that in the latter edition "nullus comes Tolosanus" reads "ullus comes Tolosanus."
[17] Müssigbrod, *Die Abtei Moissac*, p. 157.

1143, Sorèze received a privilege from Innocent II in which neither Moissac
nor Saint-Victor appeared. Was Bernard-Ato's charter therefore a forgery?
Or had Sorèze's legendary presentation of itself been convincing?

The Legend

Sorèze's legend consists of two diplomas presenting Pippin the Short as
the abbey's founder.[18] In these texts, Sorèze becomes a royal and hence
inalienable abbey. Its independence is made even more precise, for in one
of the diplomas, Pippin declares that "cenobium illud nullius alterius ecclesie juri preterquam Romane sujaceat ditioni." We have found this phrase in
other legends—and it is often intended as the exclusion not so much of
episcopal power as of that of another abbey.

It seems therefore logical to date these texts (which exist only in
seventeenth-century copies) to either the late eleventh century (the brush
with Saint-Victor) or the early twelfth (the one with Moissac). In any case,
some version of the legend was in circulation by the mid-thirteenth century,
when Lagrasse's *Gesta Karoli Magni* mentioned Sorèze as one of Pippin's
foundations.[19]

Mozac/Cluny

The Events

In 1095, Mozac was submitted to Cluny for reform by Durandus, bishop of
Clermont (Mozac's ordinary) and by count Robert of Auvergne (the abbey's
secular lord, according to one of the texts). Philip I approved this act in the
same year. According to the bishop's charter, Mozac was to be in Hugh of
Cluny's *potestas et ordinatio*.[20] There are more than mere hints that Mozac did
not happily accept the imposition of Cluny's lordship in the shape of this
"reform." In his *vita* of Hugh of Cluny, Hildebert of La Mans wrote: "is
[Hugh] itaque totus propagandi monasticam religionem studiis occupatus,
dum eam in monasterio Maudiacensi reformare contendit, nonnullorum
pertulit invidiam, convicia sustinuit, seductor et hypocrita, tyrannus et in-
vasor acclamatus."[21] The editors of this text emend "Maudiacensi" to
"Moysiacensi" (Moissac).[22] But a paleographical much more logically emen-
dation, involving only one letter change, would be to "Mauziacensi"

---

[18] On Sorèze's legend, see above, Chapter 4 at nn. 112–114.

[19] See above, Conclusion at n. 15.

[20] Two documents relate Mozac's submission to Cluny: a charter of Durandus and Philip
I's diploma (*Recueil des chartes de l'abbaye de Cluny*, 5:45–48, nos. 3697–3698. Philip's diploma
is also edited in *Recueil des actes de Philippe Ier*, pp. 342–343, no. 135.

[21] Hildebert of Le Mans, *Vita sanctissimi patris Hugonis abbatis Cluniacensis,* in *Bibliotheca
Cluniacensis . . .* , cols. 428–429.

[22] I have not been able to check the manuscript of this text myself.

(Mozac). This reading makes more sense, as well, when we consider the circumstances of the introduction of Cluniac reform to Moissac. The reform occurred in 1048 under Abbot Odilo—not under Hugh—and seems in any case to have provoked little resistance (perhaps because Moissac retained an abbot of its own).[23] Thus it is extremely unlikely, if not impossible, that the passage in the *vita* of Hugh refers to Moissac. Rather, it reveals Mozac's resistance to Hugh of Cluny.

Nonetheless, Mozac did not escape integration into the *ecclesia Cluniacensis*. In 1147, for example, when Count William wished to make peace with Mozac, the text of the *concordia* reads: "ego Willelmus arvernorum comes, reformando pacem cum domino Petro Clun. [*sic*] abbate et eius fratribus pro iniuriis, quas Mauziacensi monasterio . . . iniuriose intuli."[24] But in the 1260s, Mozac's resistance surfaced again and, in the context of a complicated situation (the abbot of Mozac and his monks appear to have been at war with each other), the abbey tried to rid itself of Cluny's domination—the flashpoint was Cluny's attempt to enforce its rights of visitation—although to no avail.[25]

The Legend?

It is possible that one layer of Mozac's legend of its refoundation by Pippin the Short was fabricated in conjunction with the late eleventh-century resistance to Cluny: the diploma in which Pippin the Short, mentioning Calminius and Namadia, confirms the abbey's properties and its diplomas granted by various of his Merovingian predecessors and endows it himself with further estates.[26] To be sure, this diploma, unlike others that we have found produced in contexts of resistance, is not a clear statement of royal protection. In it, however, Pippin does clearly state that the abbey is royal (*nostrum monasterium*). For this reason, I agree with Léon Levillain who, in his edition of the diploma, argued that it was fabricated in the late eleventh century in an attempt to ward off Cluny.[27] Pierre-François Fournier, however, scoffs at this theory, pointing to the lack of a precise statement of royal protection. But his assertion that the phrase *nostrum monasterium* hardly sufficed to make Mozac a royal abbey is surely exaggerated.[28]

Levillain suggested that the "vision" of Lamfred in which Pippin is magnified as the abbey's refounder could be interpreted also as a statement of

---

23 On the circumstances of Cluny's reform of Moissac, see Müssigbrod, *Die Abtei Moissac*, pp. 65–74.

24 *Bibliotheca Cluniacensis . . .* , no. 229, col. 1411.

25 This bitter and complicated struggle stretched from 1264 through 1266. See the documents in *Recueil des chartes de l'abbaye de Cluny*, 6:538–543, 552–553, 566–567, 573–576, nos. 5076–5077, 5087, 5116, 5121.

26 On Calminius and Namadia, see above, Chapter 3 at nn. 1–7. For the diploma, see *Recueil des actes de Pépin*, pp. 227–242, no. 58. Also see above, Chapter 4 at nn. 140–141.

27 *Recueil des actes de Pépin*, pp. 135–136.

28 Fournier, "Saint Austremoine," pp. 438–439, n. 74.

Mozac's royal nature (and hence independence) directed at Cluny.[29] This is possible, but I tend to situate this text rather in the context of Mozac's ambivalent relations with the counts of Auvergne.[30]

Sarlat/Cluny?

The Events? The Legend?

Given the ambiguity and slimness of the evidence, it is not at all clear what the tenor of the relationship between Cluny and Sarlat was. In a charter purporting to date from the 930s, Bernard, count of Périgord, performs a *traditio* of Sarlat to Odo of Cluny, granting Cluny the right to hold the abbey and to elect its abbot.[31] Is this charter authentic or a later Cluniac forgery? Robert Folz believes it is the latter, for Sarlat appears in none of the tenth-century papal confirmations of Cluny's estates[32] (nor in any other list of Cluniac properties I have consulted). Indeed, Folz argues that the charter was forged in the twelfth century, when Sarlat's legend of its foundation by Charlemagne appeared.

The legend, as we have seen, was first recorded by Hugh of Fleury in his *Historia ecclesiastica* and his *Vita S. sacerdotis*.[33] Folz argues that Sarlat claimed Charlemagne and royal foundation at this particular moment because of Cluny's attempts to subjugate it (represented by the charter of Bernard of Périgord).[34] He also argues that the privilege of "Pope Leo" for Sarlat mentioned by Hugh in the *Vita S. sacerdotis* is a legendary privilege of Leo III (again directed against Cluny).[35] Thus Sarlat would have created for itself Charlemagne and his equally shimmering papal companion as guarantees of its liberty. But, as Hugh makes clear in an abbreviated version of the *Historia ecclesiastica* that he composed expressly for the monks of Sarlat, this was Leo V and not Leo III.[36] The evidence of possible resistance through legend to a possible menace by Cluny is nowhere near as coherent as Folz argues. The chain of events and their relation to legend are far from definite—and, indeed, remain in the shadowy domain of the only possibly imaginable.

[29] On the vision text, see above: Chapter 2 at nn. 70–71; Chapter 4 at nn. 142–146.
[30] See above, Chapter 6 at nn. 124–144.
[31] *GC* 2, instr. 495.
[32] Folz, "Aspects du culte liturgique," p. 90, n. 78.
[33] See above, Chapter 5 at n. 12.
[34] Folz, "Aspects du culte liturgique," pp. 90–91.
[35] Folz, "Aspects du culte liturgique," pp. 90–91. See the relevant passage of the *Vita S. sacerdotis (PL* 163:995–996).
[36] See the text edited by Camille Couderc, "Note sur une compilation inédite de Hugues de Sainte-Marie et sa vie de saint Sacerdos évêque de Limoges," *Bibliothèque de l'Ecole des Chartes* 54 (1893): 468–474 (here 474).

2

The Most Frequently
Cited Legendary Sources

Included here are only the most frequently cited texts that compose each community's legend; I discuss many other texts in the course of this book. Most technical details pertaining to the dating of the texts can be found here.

Alet

Forged charter of "Count Bera," supposedly son of Guillaume: *HL* 2:79–80, no. 23. On the diplomatic irregularities that make this charter a forgery, see Magnou-Nortier, *La société laïque*, pp. 99–100. She has recently adduced further such irregularities and now believes the document is entirely forged, as she was kind enough to inform me. A version of the charter seems to have been in existence by 1119 or so. In that year, Calixtus II delivered a privilege for Alet (or is this, too, a forgery?) in which he mentioned this monastery "quod videlicet ab ipso fundatore nobilis memorie Bera comite beato Petro sub censu libre unius argenti singulis triennis persolvenda oblatum est" (*HL* 5:876–878, no. 468) (a privilege of Eugenius III contains a similar phrase: *Papsturkunden in Frankreich*, 2:780, no. 27). This is exactly the *census* stipulated in the forged charter of Bera.

Aniane

A sermon attributed to Ardo Smaragdus: Pseudo-Ardo, *Sermo sancti Ardonis, cognomento Smaragdi . . .*, in *AASSosB* 4.1:225–226. Mabillon edited this text from an Aniane manuscript, which I have been unable to identify among those preserved today at the Bibliothèque Municipale of Montpellier and the Archives Départementales de l'Hérault. This text was in existence by at least the mid-twelfth century, for the official canonization *vita* of Charlemagne cites passages from it; see *Vita Karoli Magni* 3.10, in Rauschen, *Die Legende Karls des Grossen,* pp. 77–78.

A much interpolated version of the Carolingian chronicle of Moissac, often known as the "*Chronicle* of Aniane": Paris, BN Latin 5941, ff. 2r–49v. This manuscript, which has been attributed to the scriptorium of Arles-sur-Tech (Dufour, *La bibliothèque,* p. 145), dates from either the late eleventh or the very early twelfth century. See François Avril et al., *Manuscrits enluminés de la péninsule ibérique* (Paris, 1982), no. 47, p. 50. In other words, it dates from the years of the controversy between Aniane and Gellone. For editions of the text, see Edmond Marténe and Ursin Durand, *Veterum scriptorum et monumentorum historicum dogmaticorum moralium . . . collectio amplissima* (Paris, 1729), 5:883–916; also *PL* 98:1409–1434.

A version of Guillaume's charter of 804: AD Hérault 1.H.2 (a late twelfth-century copy). Revillout provides what appears to be a transcription of this copy in his "Etude historique et littéraire," pp. 563–567. AD Hérault 1.H.2 is probably a copy of a document composed somewhat earlier; the logical time for this charter's fabrication would not be the late twelfth century but rather the later eleventh or early twelfth century, when Aniane was pressing its claims to Gellone. For critical analyses of this version of the charter, see Pückert, *Aniane und Gellone,* pp. 130–145; and Tisset, *L'abbaye de Gellone,* pp. 47–51. Revillout also provides a transcription of another version of the charter which he considered to be the original ninth-century document. The two versions differ by certain interpolations that are of little relevance here. I have not been able to locate this so-called ninth-century document (Revillout specified that it was in the possession of a Marquis de Prunarède), but both Pückert and Tisset remark that it contains passages not found in charters predating the eleventh century; thus, Revillout's "ninth-century original" was probably yet another forgery.

A cartulary, edited (but without any attention to changes of hand) as the second volume of *Cartulaires des abbayes d'Aniane et de Gellone.* The manuscript, AD Hérault 1.H.1, now consists of 136 folios written in hands ranging from the first half of the twelfth century to the mid-thirteenth century. Folios 1r–31v are in one hand which changes only slightly at 31v–32v; folios 33r–45v are written in a late twelfth-century hand; the changing hands thereafter are thirteenth century.

A diploma of Charlemagne forged in the late eleventh or early twelfth century. This text appears twice in the abbey's cartulary: *Cartulaires des abbayes d'Aniane et de Gellone,* 2:14–15 (in the middle of the *vita* of Benedict of

Aniane) and 2:41–43, no. 1 (heading a series of royal diplomas). On this diploma, see Pückert, *Aniane und Gellone*, pp. 10–40, 47–52.

The *vita* of Benedict of Aniane by Ardo (783–843) which contains several passages interpolated in the eleventh or twelfth century. For editions see *Vita Benedicti abbatis* (*MGH SS* 15.1:198–220); and *Cartulaires des abbayes d'Aniane et de Gellone*, 2:1–35.

Auch

Two texts in which Clovis appears. Both are included in the cathedral's cartulary, which exists in three versions (AD Gers G.16, G.17, and G.18), all edited as *Cartulaires du chapitre de l'église métropolitaine Sainte-Marie d'Auch*. I have been unable to consult the earliest of these manuscripts (AD Gers G.16); hence, my references here are to the slightly later "premier cartulaire blanc" (AD Gers G.17, I follow the older foliation). The documents containing the Clovis legend are no. 77, pp. 77–86 (AD Gers G.17 ff. 31r–34v), and no. 134, pp. 157–164 (AD Gers G.17, ff. 72r–76r). No. 134 is the earlier of the documents; Lacave La Plagne-Barris dates it to 1110, whereas Clémens ("La Gascogne est née," p. 171) situates it in the mid-twelfth century. Clémens's dating seems more plausible. In addition to Clémens's reasons, I would argue that the charter refers not only to a Peter of Vic who made a donation in 1090 (*Cartulaires du chapitre de l'église métropolitaine Sainte-Marie d'Auch*, no. 6, pp. 81–10), but also to Peter's son Arnaldus and his death as a grown man, and finally to Arnaldus's own son who became a canon. Given this succession of generations, 1110 is a rather early date for the text.

Bisson dates the later text (no. 77) to approximately 1175; see his "Unheroed Pasts," pp. 295–296, 305. The complete text of this document is not included in any of the manuscripts of the cartulary; the first section (including the description of Clovis) is missing in each. Lacave La Plagne-Barris reconstructed it from a *vidimus* of 1332 (which he identifies as Auch BM 62 but my consultation of this manuscript did not reveal the document in question). Hence, the exact wording may be incorrect. Nonetheless, Clovis did make an appearance in the original document; this text was listed in the cartulary's original table of contents as piece lxxvii, under the rubric "De Clodoveo rege francorum" (AD Gers G.17, f. 70v; in *Cartulaires du chapitre de l'église métropolitaine Sainte-Marie d'Auch*, p. 156).

Brantôme

An interpolation in the *Annales Laurissenses: MGH SS* 1:146. According to the editors, the interpolation appears only in one manuscript copied by

Duchesne; they do not attempt to date the no longer extant manuscript itself. But Charles Higounet proposes that the legend of Brantôme first appeared in an eleventh-century interpolation in the *Annales regni Francorum* (which he does not specifically identify but which is probably this passage of the annals of Lorsch). He gives no reason for this proposed dating; see his article "Brantôme," in *Lexikon des Mittelalters* ed. Robert Autry et al., 6 vols. to date (Munich and Zurich) 2:577.

A pared-down version of this legend appears in an authentic found in the seventeenth century in the reliquary of Saint Sicarius at Brantôme. This text exists in copies made by the Maurists in the seventeenth century: Paris, BN Latin 12633, ff. 137v–138r, 158r; Paris, BN Latin 12759, pp. 191–192. The latter copy is the clearest and most complete; the copyist entitled it "Vetus inscriptio inventa in capsa ss. innocentis sicharii et ante annos (ut ex charactere conjicere licet) quingentos exarata." Was the original thus from the twelfth century? I have found no other information on the abbey of Brantôme that would permit me to date this text any more definitively. Compare the versions of the text (and some misleading discussion) in "De S. Sichario martyre Brantolmae in Petragorico," *AASS* May 1:187–188.

A probably interpolated if not forged charter attributed to Bernard, an early tenth-century count of Périgord, also mentions Charlemagne's foundation of the abbey. I have found only a seventeenth-century copy of this charter: Paris, BN Collection Périgord 33, ff. 187–188.

Charroux

A compilation of narrative texts, diplomas, charters, and papal privileges known as the *Liber de constitutione, institutione, consecratione, reliquiis, ornamentis et privilegiis Karoffensis coenobii . . . (Chartes et documents pour servir à l'histoire de l'abbaye de Charroux,* pp. 1–85). Although extant only in two fifteenth-century manuscripts (Paris, BN Latin 5448, and a manuscript at the Société Eduenne of Autun), the most probable date for the *Liber's* compilation is the first half of the twelfth century; no text in it postdates Urban II.

Among the texts contained in the *Liber,* those which are most frequently referred to here are two narrative texts relating the abbey's foundation by Charlemagne. The first (*Chartes et documents pour servir à l'histoire de l'abbaye de Charroux,* pp. 1–7) I date as shortly after 1045; it contains a list of relics actually composed in that year. It does not postdate the 1080s, for by then a new layer of the legend was crystallizing: another narrative text included in the *Liber (Chartes et documents pour servir à l'histoire de l'abbaye de Charroux,* pp. 29–41). I date this text to the early twelfth century for the following reasons. It postdates Ademar of Chabannes because it contains passages that are reworkings of his *Chronicon*. It also probably postdates Saint-Denis's *Descriptio qualiter* (ca. 1095); in both texts, Charlemagne goes to the Holy Land, and parts of his voyage are described in almost identical language. But the Charroux text cannot be much later than the *Descriptio qualiter*, for the author of the former tells us that he witnessed the events at the council of Charroux held in 1082 (p. 38). This second Charroux text also exists in a much abbreviated form (*Chartes et documents pour servir à l'histoire de l'abbaye de Charroux*, pp. 7–9), which adds no new information; it was probably composed slightly later (for convenience's sake?) as summaries often were.

A gloss found in numerous late twelfth- and thirteenth-century manuscripts of the *Historia scholastica*, and recounting Charlemagne's acquisition of the Holy Foreskin (see above, chapter 5, n. 23).

Clairvaux-d'Aveyron

Two narrative charters: one dated 1062, the other 1060. Both are included in the twelfth-century cartulary of Conques: *Cartulaire de l'abbaye de Conques*, nos. 14 and 15, pp. 16–21.

Conques

The prologue to chronicle of Conques. The prologue has been edited as "Chronique du monastère de Conques . . . " by de Gaujal, *Etudes historiques*, 4:391–394. Given that this text concludes by stating (erroneously) that Gregory VII had subjected Figeac to Conques, the most logical time for its composition would be the years around 1100, the years during which Conques and Figeac were in the thick of their dispute. Indeed, historians have most often assigned this text to the end of the eleventh or the beginning of the twelfth century. But certain passages (such as the repeated use of Anno Domini dating and the possible verbal echo of the late twelfth-century *Historia scholastica* gloss on the Holy Foreskin; see above, Chapter 5, n. 121) make me wonder whether the prologue was composed later in the twelfth century. In any case, if the golden *A* given by Charlemagne and mentioned in the prologue was indeed (as I have argued) the triangular reliquary still at Conques today, the text must postdate the fabrication of this shrine (1087–1108). Unfortunately, manuscripts cannot resolve the matter of the prologue's date; the only manuscript I have been able to locate is the seventeenth-century copy in Paris, BN Doat 143, ff. 2r–5r, where it is attached (with no transition) to the abbey's *Chronicon*. There is also a macaronic version in the seventeenth-century Paris, BN Français 5456, pp. 1–6.

Conques's chronicle, edited (without the prologue) as *Chronicon monasterii Conchensis* by Martène and Durand, *Thesaurus novus anecdotorum . . . ,*

3:1387–1388. The text ends with Abbot Bego (1087–1108) and was probably composed early in the twelfth century. Again, the only manuscript I have
found is the seventeenth-century copy in Paris, BN Doat 143, ff. 5v–9v.

Figeac

Two versions of a forged diploma attributed to Pippin the Short. The first
was composed circa 1095, and the second in the twelfth century. For critical
editions (and discussion) of these two texts, see Wolff, "Note sur le faux
diplôme," pp. 298–311.

Figeac's legendary foundation appears in two other forgeries probably
contemporaneous with the first version of Pippin's diploma. These include
a privilege of Pope Stephen II: *GC* 1, instr. 43 (I have found no manuscript
of this text other than the seventeenth-century copies in Paris, BN Doat 126,
ff. 18v–20v, 15r–17r). Wolff dates this text as late eleventh or early twelfth
century; see his "Note sur le faux diplôme," pp. 321–322. The second of
these forgeries is a privilege of Pope Pascal I purporting to date from 822:
GC 1, instr. 43–44. I have found no manuscript other than the seventeeth-
century copy in Paris, BN Doat 126, ff. 22v–24v.

The very late eleventh- or early twelfth-century chronicle of Figeac, edited
as *Historia monasterii Figiacensis in Dioecesi Cadurcensi* by Baluze, *Miscellanea
novo ordine*, 4:1–2. The only manuscript I have found is the late copy in Paris,
BN Doat 126, ff. 26v–27r.

Gaillaguet

A diploma fabricated late in the eleventh or early in the twelfth century
and attributed to Pippin the Short (*MGH Diplomata Karolinorum* 1:48–49,
no. 34) extant in an early twelfth-century manuscript: Paris, BN Latin 5219,
no. 2.

Gellone (Saint-Guilhem-le-Désert)

The abbey's cartulary, AD Hérault 5.H.8, has been edited as volume 1 of
Cartulaires des abbayes d'Aniane et de Gellone. It consists of several layers, although the editors do not make this clear. The earliest section was compiled
at the behest of Abbot Peter (ca. 1066). The first section of the cartulary
comprises folios 1r–59v. Folios 1r–32v are in the same mid-eleventh-century
hand; halfway down 32v the hand changes (although it is still eleventh
century) and remains constant to 58r. Folios 58r–59v are written in con-

tinually changing hands probably contemporaneous with the documents they add (the latest of which dates from the first decade of the twelfth century). The organized part of this first section thus ends at folio 58r.

The second section of the cartulary was compiled by 1122 under Abbot William. This section begins on folio 59v in a twelfth-century hand announcing in highlighted capitals Abbot William's decision to compile a *testamentum* of the abbey's properties, and it is followed by a table of contents in the same hand (ff. 59v–61v). It is interrupted by folios 62 and 63, which are written in an eleventh-century hand and glued and sewn into the cartulary; folio 64r thus contains the first document (Guillaume's charter) listed in the table of contents and is in the same twelfth-century hand, which continues to folio 64v. Folio 65 has also been inserted; folios 66r–133r are in essentially the same hand as the table of contents (with occasional changes). Folios 133r–194v are written in various hands, all roughly contemporaneous (second half of the twelfth century). Here the original section seems to end; the rest of the cartulary (ff. 194v–215v) is written in numerous hands contemporaneous with the documents (late twelfth century onward).

The version of Guillaume's charter of 804 contained in this portion of the cartulary (f. 64r) probably does not predate the early twelfth century. For if this text had been extant by then, would it not have been included in the earlier portion of Gellone's cartulary?

The early twelfth-century *Vita [S. Willelmi ducis] (AASS* May 6:811–820). The manuscripts of this *vita* include the twelfth-century Montpellier, BM 16, ff. 189v–205r (a Gellone manuscript) and the less well known twelfth-century gathering added to an earlier Saint-Martial manuscript: Paris, BN Latin 1240, ff. 175r–181v (in the late fourteenth century Bernard Gui also included a summary of it in his *Sanctorale:* Paris, BN Latin 5406, ff. 92vb–96vb). The text certainly existed by 1130–1135, when Orderic Vitalis summarized it; see his *Ecclesiastical History*, 3:218–226. Most scholars argue that the vita was composed as a "companion piece" to the second layer of the abbey's cartulary, hence between approximately 1120 and 1135: Pückert, *Aniane und Gellone;* Revillout, "Etude historique et littéraire"; Saxer, "Le culte et la légende hagiographique de Saint Guillaume"; and Tisset, *L'abbaye de Gellone.* It is unlikely that the *vita* was composed much before this time, for no trace of its image of Guillaume colors any of the abbey's earlier sources.

Gerri

Two forged diplomas of Charlemagne (*MGH Diplomata Karolinorum* 1:464–466, nos. 308 and 309), dated to the tenth century by Schneidmüller, *Karolingische Tradition*, p. 29.

Issoire

The original version of the *Vita tertia S. Austremonii (AASS* November 1:61–77) composed at Issoire in the late eleventh century, but then recopied and partly retouched by Mozac; see Fournier, "Saint Austremoine," pp. 456–464. It exists in manuscripts of the late eleventh and twelfth centuries.

The *Additamentum de reliquiis S. Austremonii* (partially edited in *AASS,* November 1:80–82; complete in Paris, BN n.a Françaises 7455, ff. 319r–322r). This text, which dates from circa 1197, included Issoire's legend of refoundation but seems to have been composed at Mozac—or, like the *Vita tertia S. Austremonii,* it was originally composed by Issoire, but then reworked at Mozac. The text focuses on the location of Saint Austremonius's relics, a matter evidently disputed by the two abbeys. The first part of the text implies that the relics were in Issoire's possession; however, the bulk of the text (notably a passage that does not appear in the *AASS* edition) asserts that Issoire had faked these relics and that the true Austremonius reposed at Mozac.

Joncels

A forged diploma attributed to Pippin the Short: *Recueil des actes de Pépin,* no. 30, pp. 127–132; cf. no. 65, p. 286. The diploma is extant in a twelfth-century "copy," which I have been unable to consult (it is part of a private collection).

La Règle

A forged diploma attributed to Pippin the Short: *MGH Diplomata Karolinorum* 1:59–60, no. 42. This diploma is extant in seventeenth-century copies made from a *vidimus* of 1263; cf. Paris, BN Latin 9194, pp. 189–191. It was most probably extant by 1175, when Louis VII reconfirmed privileges given to the abbey by "Pippinus rex et predecessor noster" (Paris, BN Latin 9194, p. 191).

La Réole

A privilege of Gregory IV (*Recueil des chartes de l'abbaye de Saint-Benoît-sur-Loire,* 1:39–43, no. 18) and a charter of refoundation of 977 ("Cartulaire du prieuré de Saint-Pierre de La Réole," no. 99, pp. 144–145) mentioning the community's foundation by Charlemagne. Both were either fabricated or

interpolated sometime in the eleventh century. Although these texts refer to
La Réole's status as Fleury's priory, they were composed (or interpolated) by
La Réole itself, not Fleury; see the remarks of Prou and Vidier in *Recueil des
chartes de l'abbaye de Saint-Benoît-sur-Loire*, 1:159–165. In other words, the
Charlemagne tradition emanated not from the northern mother abbey but
from its southern priory.

La Sauve-Majeure

The *Vita S. Geraldi Silvae-majoris primi abbatis et fundatoris* (*AASSosB*
6.2:866–892), composed in the early twelfth century at this abbey.

Lagrasse

The *Gesta Karoli Magni ad Carcassonam et Narbonam,* extant in both a Latin
and a Provençal version. The author of the *Gesta* tells us that he is writing at
the behest of Abbot Bernard (p. 6). The editor, Schneegans, argues that this
is Bernard II, attested as abbot in 1205 (by 1208 there was another abbot),
pp. 39–40. But other scholars have suggested instead Bernard Imbert (abbot 1237–1255): Claude Fauriel in *Histoire littéraire de la France,* 41 vols.
(Paris, 1865–1981), 21:373–382; Paris, *Histoire poétique*, pp. 89–90. This
latter hypothesis is much more plausible given the flurry of royal forgeries
made at Lagrasse at Bernard III's command; the *Gesta Karoli Magni* was the
perfect complement to these fabrications.

Numerous forged diplomas, charters, and privileges masquerading under
the names of Charlemagne, Louis VIII, Louis IX, Gelasius II, and Bernard-
Ato of Carcassonne. The vast majority of these were created in the thirteenth century, particularly during Bernard Imbert's abbacy. For these texts,
see the forthcoming edition of Lagrasse's charters by Elisabeth Magnou-
Nortier and Claudine Pailhes.

Laguenne

An authentic from the late twelfth century describing Calminius's *inventio*
(1172) at this church: edited in Thomas d'Aquin de Saint-Joseph, *Histoire de
la vie de sainct Calmine,* pp. 293–294.

A thirteenth-century enamel reliquary depicting Calminius standing next
to Saint Martin. See Rupin, "La chasse de saint Calmine"; Costa, *Catalogue du
Musée Dobrée* (Nantes, 1961), fasc. 1:32–35, no. 35 and pl. 35.

Langogne

A forged or interpolated charter describing this priory's foundation: complete in a seventeenth-century copy, Paris, BN Latin 12767, ff. 61r–64r (partial editions in *HL* 5:331–333, no. 156, and *Papsturkunden 896–1046*, 2:731–732, no. 378). This version of the foundation charter does not appear in the cartulary of Saint-Chaffre (composed between 1087 and ca. 1136). Instead, a much more sober document with no mention of visions or journeys to Rome describes the priory's origins: *Cartulaire de l'abbaye de St-Chaffre*, no. 376, pp. 130–132. It is difficult to date the charter; the eleventh (or perhaps twelfth) century would seem the most logical time for its composition.

Maillezais

Sometime in the 1060s, Peter of Maillezais composed the *Qualiter fuit constructum Malliacense monasterium et corpus sancti Rigomeri translatum:* Paris, BN Latin 4829, ff. 246ra–255vb (edited as *De antiquitate et commutatione in melius Malleacense insulae sive qualiter fuit constructum Malleacense monasterium et corpus sancti Rigomeri translatum,* in *PL* 146:1247–1272). A new edition of this text is being prepared by Georges Pon.

Menat

This abbey's legend emerges in a cluster of *vitae,* all of which appear to exist in only one twelfth-century manuscript, Clermont-Ferrand, BM 150: *Vita Menelei abbatis Menatensis,* ff. 1r–27r (*Liber miraculorum sancti Menelei,* ff. 28v–46r); *Vita sancti Saviniani abbatis,* ff. 47r–55v; *Vita sancti Vincentiani confessoris,* ff. 72v–84v; *Vita sancti Genesii,* ff. 84v–86v (incomplete). The *Vita sancti Vincentiani* and the *Vita Menelei* have been edited in *MGH SSRM* 5:112–128, 129–157. Because all these texts relate to Menat, I believe that this manuscript was copied there and that all these *vitae*—with the exception of the *Vita sancti Vincentiani*—were composed there, probably in the first half of the twelfth century. The *Vita Menelei,* for example, opens with an elaborate genealogy that seems characteristic of late eleventh- and twelfth-century concerns. The *Vita sancti Vincentiani,* although it was retouched at Menat, seems to have been written earlier. This *vita* focuses on a church known as Saint-Viance in the mid-eleventh century when it was given to Saint-Pierre of Uzerche by the count of La Marche and certain viscounts (of Limoges?), although in the texts in Clermont-Ferrand BM 150 this church is called instead Avolca. For the donation to Uzerche, see *Cartulaire de l'abbaye d'Uzerche*, no. 52, pp. 90–97.

When Menat decided to claim Saint-Viance as its own (or at least to do so in the *Vita Menelei* where Barontus gives Avolca to Meneleus: *MGH SSRM* 5:148), it usurped and embroidered upon the *Vita sancti Vincentiani*. I have been unable to find other sources that would illuminate Menat's pretensions to Saint-Viance; Uzerche's cartulary is mute on the subject, as are those scarce extant sources for Menat which I have been able to discover (a few documents copied by the Maurists in the seventeenth century: Paris, BN Latin 12684, ff. 307r–309v).

Moissac

The *Chronicon* written by Aymeric de Peyrat (1377–1406), abbot of Moissac. The complete version of the *Chronicon* (Paris, BN Latin 4991A) represents a slightly later reworking of Aymeric's original text. Paris BN Latin 5228, ff. 60ra–67vb, contains fragments of the original and is probably an autograph. I thank Luc Ferrier, who is preparing an edition of the *Chronicon,* for sharing with me his analysis of the manuscript tradition. Extensive citations from Paris BN Latin 4991A appear in three studies of Moissac: Lagrèze-Fossat, *Etudes historiques sur Moissac;* Marion, "L'abbaye de Moissac"; Rupin, *L'abbaye et les cloîtres de Moissac.* Because these citations are often incomplete, and inaccurate in content as well as foliation, I have used my own transcriptions of the *Chronicon.*

Mozac

Various versions of the *Vita S. Austremonii.* Sometime during the second half of the ninth century, chapters 12–20 were added at Mozac to the seventh-century core of the *Vita prima S. Austremonii* (see the edition of the whole *vita* in *AASS* November 1:49–54). The *Vita secunda S. Austremonii* (*AASS* November 1:55–61) was composed at Mozac sometime in the late ninth or early tenth century. In the late eleventh century, Mozac added various touches to the *Vita tertia S. Austremonii,* which had been composed at Issoire (*AASS* November 1:61–77). In this same period, Mozac also added to the *Vita tertia* a text which has been edited separately as the *Revelatio corporis S. Austremonii et ejusdem duplex translatio* (*AASS* November 1:77–80). There has been much controversy over the dating of the three versions of the *vita:* Duchesne, *Fastes épiscopaux,* 2:118–222; Krusch, "Reise nach Frankreich," pp. 20–24; A. Poncelet, "La plus ancienne vie de S. Austremoine," *AB* 13 (1894): 33–46. Here I follow the chronology proposed in the most recent and most detailed analysis of these texts (based on an examination of the manuscripts): Fournier, "Saint Austremoine," pp. 423–434, 456–464.

A diploma attributed to Pippin the Short, forged in the late eleventh or early twelfth century. For an edition and discussion of this diploma, see *Recueil des actes de Pépin*, nos. 58 and 64, pp. 227–242, 285–286; and Levillain, "La translation des reliques de saint Austremoine."

The *Vita S. Calminii confessoris (AASS* August 3:760–761). This *vita* dates from approximately the mid-twelfth century; it mentions Louis VI's campaign of 1126 at Montferrand (see Suger, *Vita Ludovici. Vie de Louis VI*, pp. 236, 238, 240). The only manuscript of this text I have been able to identify is a copy made in 1636: Paris, BN Latin 11762, ff. 10r–11r.

A text recounting the visions of Abbot Lamfred and Pippin the Short: Clermont-Ferrand, BM 147, f. 147v. The text is written in a twelfth-century hand on a folio left blank (or inserted?) in this manuscript (otherwise written largely in a tenth-century hand) in the middle of the *passio* of Saint Lucy. Here I use the edition in Krusch, "Reise nach Frankreich," pp. 24–25. On the date of the text's composition, see Fournier, "Saint Austremoine"; and Levillain, "La translation des reliques de saint Austremoine," pp. 324–328.

The enamel reliquary of Saint Calminius and his wife Namadia made in the last years of the twelfth century. Gauthier, *Emaux du moyen âge occidental* (Fribourg, 1972), no. 58, pp. 333–335.

Noblat (Saint-Léonard)

The *Vita sancti Leonardi confessoris (AASS* November 3:150–155). Sargent argues that this *vita* and Léonard's cult were created whole cloth between 1030 and 1031; see his "Religious Responses," pp. 228–232.

Perse

The twelfth-century tympanum of this community's church depicts a king—perhaps Charlemagne, who figures in Perse's legend. I have been unable to locate any written medieval sources for this legend (summarized in *AASS* June 2:1068–1069).

Psalmodi

A forged diploma attributed to Charlemagne: *MGH Diplomata Karolinorum* 1:455–456, no. 303. This document exists in a twelfth-century copy but may have been composed somewhat earlier.

Rocamadour

This abbey's origins as the retreat of the hermit Amator were first mentioned in Robert of Torigny's *Chronica* (ca. 1184): *MGH SS* 6:519. By the fourteenth century, Amator was discussed by Bernard Gui (see *De sancto Amatore eremita . . .* , in *AASS* August 4:16–17). The *Acta [sancti Amatoris] (AASS* August 4:24–25) exists only in a seventeenth-century copy; it is impossible to know when this text was composed. On this text and a fifteenth-century version of Amator's *vita*, see E. Albe, "La vie et les miracles de S. Amator," *AB* 28 (1909): 57–90.

Saint-Chaffre

The *Vita S. Theofredi abbatis Calmeliacensis, martyris in Gallia (AASSosB* 3.1:476–485). Mabillon copied this *vita* from a Saint-Chaffre manuscript which he does not date; I have been able to find only a seventeenth-century copy by the Maurists in Paris, BN Latin 11773, ff. 119r–121v. Mabillon argued that the *vita* was composed in the tenth century. I suggest that it dates rather from the very late eleventh or the twelfth century, in part because the compiler of the narrative cartulary of Saint-Chaffre (1087–ca. 1136) seems to have been unaware of any such *vita*. He wrote: "non sint gesta ejusdem sanctissimi viri certa relatione ad nos usque plenius transmissa" (*Cartulaire de l'abbaye de St-Chaffre du Monastier,* p. 6). Furthermore, this *vita* exhibits many of the same features and much of the same language as the *vita* of Meneleus composed at Menat in the eleventh or twelfth century (although this could mean merely that one *vita* copied from the other, rather than that they were composed contemporaneously).

The abbey's cartulary, compiled sometime between 1087 and approximately 1136; edited as *Cartulaire de l'abbaye de St-Chaffre du Monastier.*

Saint-Genou

The prologue to the early eleventh- or late tenth-century *miracula* of Saint Genou relates this abbey's legend: *Miracula S. Genulphi episcopi: (AASS* January 2:97–107).

Saint-Germier

The *vita* of this community's patron saint, Germier, exists in four forms: a long version in Toulouse, BM 477, ff. 162va–165vb (early fourteenth-century); an abbreviation in the mid-thirteenth-century cartulary of Lézat (Paris, BN Latin 9189, ff. 268r–v); and two abbreviations by Bernard Gui, Toulouse BM 450, ff. 227rb–228rb and 247vb (fourteenth century). The first three texts (i.e., excepting Gui's last abbreviation) have been published in Douais, "Saint Germier," pp. 81–99; for a better edition of the cartulary's version of the *vita*, see *Cartulaire de l'abbaye de Lézat*, 2:411–414, no. 1584. Saltet, who combined and reworked these texts in his effort to re-create the "primitive version," argues that the *vita* was composed after the late eleventh century (when certain properties mentioned in the text were donated to Saint-Germier) and before the transfer of the saint's relics to a new church at Muret in 1156; see his "Saint Germier," pp. 167–170. Saltet's dating is probably accurate, but his analysis of the relation between the manuscripts is not irreproachable. Here I have followed the text of the *vita* in the Lézat cartulary.

Saint-Gilles

The *Vita S. Aegidii* exists in approximately ten versions extant in eighty or so manuscripts (see Jones, *Saint Gilles*, pp. 2–9, 95–98). Three versions have been published: *AASS* September 1:299–304; *AB* 8 (1889): 102–120; Jones, *Saint Gilles*, pp. 98–111. The earliest manuscripts date from the late tenth or early eleventh century; the text would not seem to have been composed much before that time. A version of the *vita* (perhaps that edited in *AASS*) served as the basis for the office of Saint Gilles composed by Fulbert of Chartres (d. 1029); for the most recent edition of this office, see R. Merlet and A. Clerval, *Un manuscrit chartrain du XIe siècle: Fulbert, évêque de Chartres* . . . (Chartres, 1893), pp. 198–229. For further discussion of the *vita* and varying hypotheses as to the era of its composition, see Anna Maria Luiselli Fadda, "Sulle tradizioni altomedievali di testi agiografici: Considerazioni in margine alla versione anglosassone della *Vita* di sant'Egidio abate," in *Culto dei santi, istituzioni e classi sociali in età preindustriale*, ed. Sofia Boesch Gajano and Lucia Sebastiani (Rome, 1984), pp. 11–53; Jones, *Saint Gilles*, pp. 18–35; and Winzer, *S. Gilles*, pp. 302–303.

A collection of papal privileges (some forged, some interpolated, some authentic) for Saint-Gilles copied into one manuscript probably not long after 1132: Paris, BN Latin 11018 (16.5 cm × 11 cm, 76 folios). The paleographic and codicological evidence indicates that the manuscript probably consisted originally of the first fifty-seven folios only. Folio 1r–v is blank, 2r is damaged; folios 2v–53v are written in the same hand, dated by François Avril (personal communication) as second quarter of the twelfth century. The privilege of Innocent II which occupies folios 53v–57v is in this hand or one very similar to it, although the ink is lighter. Each text in this section is introduced with red rubrics. Initial letters are ornamented. The hand is careful and neat. The remaining folios 58r–76v are written in continually changing hands, dating from the thirteenth century and later (ff. 66v, 67v–68r, 74v, 75v, 76v are blank; ff. 67r and 76v contain only a few notations or lines of practice text). Little care seems to have been taken in the copying of these heterogeneous texts, a great contrast to the first fifty-seven folios.

Furthermore, there are quire endmarks for only the first fifty-seven folios (ff. 9v, 17v, 25v, 33v, 41v, 49v, 57v). The last one is on 57v—which therefore was probably the last folio of the manuscript as it was originally bound. The parchment of these first fifty-seven folios is relatively white and of good and even quality. The remaining folios are of thicker parchment of lesser quality; the hair follicles are quite noticeable black points. The first fifty-seven folios are all of the same length, the remaining folios vary in length, and the bottom edge is therefore not uniform. Furthermore, the system of ruling changes after folio 57v. These codicological facts would seem to indicate that folios 58r–76v were added to the original fifty-seven folio, twelfth-century manuscript at some later (thirteenth century?) date.

These first fifty-seven folios were probably written between 1132 and 1154. The last document of this section is a privilege of Innocent II of 1132. Furthermore, the privilege in which Hadrian IV (1154–1159) granted the abbot the right to wear the miter was not included in the original section of Paris BN Latin 11018; it was copied in the thirteenth century onto the penultimate folios of the extant manuscript (ff. 73v–74r; *Bullaire de l'abbaye de Saint-Gilles*, no. 56, pp. 77–78). Why did this document, which accords so well with one of the messages of the original manuscript—Saint-Gilles's freedom from the bishops of Nîmes—not appear there? The most probable answer is that the original manuscript had been composed before the abbey obtained this important privilege.

It is possible that the scribe-author of this manuscript was Petrus Guillermus, a monk of Saint-Gilles who was very active in producing sources relevant to the abbey in the third and fourth decades of the twelfth century. As well as the reworking of the *Liber pontificalis,* he composed the *miracula* of Saint Gilles in the 1120s ("Liber miraculorum sancti Aegidii," *AB* 9 [1890]: 393–422) and was the scribe for its martyrology (pre 1129) and its necrology (1129). For an edition and critical discussion of the latter two texts, see Winzer, *S. Gilles,* pp. 97–116, 119–125, 148–214. Unfortunately, I have not been able to compare the hand of Paris BN Latin 11018 with that of any of the manuscripts known to have been written by Petrus Guillermus.

Most of the texts included in Paris BN Latin 11018 (including ff. 58r– 76v) have been published in *Bullaire de l'abbaye de Saint-Gilles.* But Goiffon's edition provides no codicological or paleographic information, does not include the rubrics, and mixes in with texts from Paris BN Latin 11018 others from the abbey's archives and elsewhere.

The entry for John VIII in the continuation of the *Liber pontificalis* composed (by 1142) by Petrus Guillermus of Saint-Gilles: *Liber pontificalis*, 2:221–222. Petrus's long entry for this pope is essentially a transposition into the third person of the two letters of John VIII in Paris BN Latin 11018.

Saint-Jean-d'Angely

The *Angeriacensium de translatione capitis [S. Joannis baptistae]* (*AASS* June 5:650–652). This text was probably composed in conjunction with the *inventio* of John the Baptist's head at Angély in 1016. It was in existence by the time Ademar of Chabannes composed his *Chronicon;* he cited a passage from it almost verbatim.

A twelfth-century *notitia* included in the abbey's cartulary mentions the community's legendary origins: *Cartulaire de Saint-Jean d'Angély*, 1:13, no. 2.

Saint-Martial of Limoges

The *Vita prolixior S. Martialis,* edited as Pseudo-Aurelianus, *Vita eiusdem B. Martialis episcopi Lemovicensis et Galliarum apostoli.* This text was composed either in the very last decade of the tenth century or the first decade of the eleventh; it existed by the 1010s. On its dating, see Landes, "Dynamics of Heresy and Reform," pp. 473–478.

A *nota* composed between 1120 and 1156 relating the abbey's takeover by Cluny, edited in de Lasteyrie, *L'abbaye de Saint-Martial,* pp. 427–429.

Saint-Michel-de-Cuxa

A forged diploma attributed to Charlemagne and a forged charter, both of which were fabricated in the twelfth century. See the discussion and edition of these texts in d'Abadal, "Com neix i com creix," pp. 165–172.

Saint-Polycarpe

A forged diploma attributed to Charlemagne in which this monarch confirms the abbey's foundation: *MGH Diplomata Karolinorum* 1:458–460, no. 305. This text was probably fabricated in the eleventh century.

Saint-Savin

A narrative charter from the *Cartulaire de l'abbaye des Bénédictins de Saint-Savin,* no. 2, pp. 2–8. This text was probably composed either under Abbot Bernard II (1059–1080) or just after his abbacy; see Durier's editorial comments.

Saint-Sever

Three versions (two prose and one verse) of the *vita* of Saint Sever: *Prima vita sancti Severi martyris; Secunda vita sancti Severi metrice scripta; Vita tertia S. Severi (AASS* November 1:220–233). The *Prima vita* mentions Abbot Gregory as still living, and hence was composed during his abbacy (1028–1072). The *Vita tertia* preceded or was contemporaneous with the *Prima vita;* the latter contains cryptic and truncated passages that are best explained if this text was an abbreviation of the *Vita tertia.* In any case, the *Vita tertia* does not have the characteristics of a much later reworking: if it does not precede the so-called *Vita prima,* it follows it closely in time. See Jacques Dubois, "L'observance monastique à l'abbaye de Saint-Sever et dans la province d'Auch," in *Saint-Sever,* p. 39.

Saint-Yrieix

A diploma of Charlemagne purporting to date from 794 but, according to its editor, probably fabricated around 1090: *MGH Diplomata Karolinorum* 1:355–357, no. 251.

Sainte-Enimie

The very early twelfth-century *Vita, inventio et miracula sanctae Enimiae,* edited by Brunel in AB 57 (1939): 237–298 (on the text's dating, see pp. 244–245).

Sarlat

The *Vita S. sacerdotis (PL* 163:980–1004), composed around 1107 by Hugh of Fleury. On its dating and composition, see Head, *Hagiography and the Cult of the Saints,* pp. 91–93.

Sorde

Two forged diplomas attributed to Charlemagne. The earlier of the two (*MGH Diplomata Karolinorum* 1:314–315, no. 230) exists only in a seventeenth-century copy; its editors date it as no later than the second half of the twelfth century. A charter of William IX of Aquitaine (ca. 1120; *Cartulaire de l'abbaye de Saint-Jean de Sorde . . .*, no. 81, pp. 65–66) refers to the abbey's epic foundation by Charlemagne; hence this diploma may have been in existence by this date. The second diploma, too, exists only in late copies (Paris, Collection Baluze 46, pp. 421–422, 425; BN Latin 12697, f. 247r–v [incomplete]), edited in *MGH Diplomata Karolinorum* 1:567–568. Its editors believe it to be not later than the second half of the twelfth century. This diploma ends with an enumeration of the privileges granted by Charlemagne which include exemption and the right to be subject only to Rome, and specifies that Sorde is to pay an annual *census* of five *solidi*. Indeed, in the post-1236 layer of the *Liber censuum* (2:207), Sorde owes this amount. The word *exemptum* employed by this charter to describe the abbey's status would be a very unusual usage for the eleventh or early twelfth century; see Schreiber, *Kurie und Kloster,* 1:28 (esp. n. 1). Hence this text is probably later, rather than earlier.

Sorèze

Two diplomas forged in the name of Pippin the Short, probably in the late eleventh or early twelfth century: *Recueil des actes de Pépin,* nos. 62 and 63, pp. 269–285. On the dating of these texts, see Appendix 1 above.

Uzerche

The twelfth-century narrative prologue opening this abbey's cartulary: edited by J.-B. Champeral as *Ex historia monasterii Usercensis,* in *Cartulaire de l'abbaye d'Uzerche,* pp. 13–50. This edition reproduces the text in Etienne Baluze, *Historiae Tutelensis libri tres* (Paris, 1717), cols. 825–850. This latter is itself an edition of a seventeenth-century or very early eighteenth-century transcription of the prologue (by Baluze himself?): Paris, BN Baluze 377, ff. 3r–14r. I have found no earlier manuscript containing this text. But M. de Chiniac, who apparently saw what remained of the original manuscript, published an engraving of the torn first folio and a transcription of the mutilated text; see *Histoire des capitulaires des rois françois . . .* (Paris, 1779), pp. ix-xvi (xii for the text, xv for the reproduction of the folio). The hand appears to be early twelfth century. This poses an interesting problem, for the text as published by Champeval, although incomplete (ending with the transcriber's note: "foliis III abscissis"), continues through Pope Eugenius III (1145–1153). Presumably, new entries were continually added to the original early twelfth-century text.

Vabres

A narrative text composed as a prologue in the early twelfth century for the abbey's cartulary, compiled in the same period: *Cartulaire de l'abbaye de Vabres,* no. 1, pp. 23–28.

Selected Bibliography

All manuscripts I have consulted are listed. In the case of printed primary sources and secondary works, however, only those which are frequently cited in the course of this book are included. All edited collections (whether of texts or articles) are listed under the title of the work. When two or more articles from the same edited collection are cited, the collection's title is abbreviated in each article entry and the collection is given its own separate entry.

Primary Works

Manuscripts
Archives Départementales de l'Hérault (Montpellier)
    1.H.1
    1.H.2
    5.H.8
Archives Départementales du Gers (Auch)
    G.16
    G.17
    G.18
Auch, Bibliothèque Municipale
    MS. 62
    MS. 70
    MS. 73
Clermont-Ferrand, Bibliothèque Municipale
    MS. 63
    MS. 147
    MS. 149
    MS. 150
    MS. 732

Montpellier, Bibliothèque Municipale
  MS. 6
  MS. 13
  MS. 16
  MS. 18
  MS. 118
Paris, Bibliothèque Mazarine
  MS. 3388
Paris, Bibliothèque Nationale
  MS. Collection Baluze 46
  MS. Collection Baluze 377
  MS. Collection Périgord 33
  MS. Doat 66
  MS. Doat 123
  MS. Doat 126
  MS. Doat 130
  MS. Doat 143
  MS. Français 774
  MS. Français 5456
  MS. Latin 821
  MS. Latin 933
  MS. Latin 944
  MS. Latin 1240
  MS. Latin 1275
  MS. Latin 1797
  MS. Latin 1877
  MS. Latin 2469
  MS. Latin 2627
  MS. Latin 3783.2
  MS. Latin 4829
  MS. Latin 4976
  MS. Latin 4991A
  MS. Latin 5219
  MS. Latin 5288
  MS. Latin 5291
  MS. Latin 5365
  MS. Latin 5406
  MS. Latin 5448
  MS. Latin 5548
  MS. Latin 5926
  MS. Latin 5941
  MS. Latin 9085
  MS. Latin 9189
  MS. Latin 9194
  MS. Latin 11018
  MS. Latin 11762
  MS. Latin 11773
  MS. Latin 12633
  MS. Latin 12684

MS. Latin 12697
MS. Latin 12733
MS. Latin 12751
MS. Latin 12759
MS. Latin 12767
MS. Latin 12773
MS. Latin 12857
MS. Latin 13236
MS. Latin 14414
MS. Latin 15254
MS. Latin 15431
MS. Latin 16033
MS. Latin 16034
MS. Latin 16037
MS. Latin 16040
MS. Latin 16042
MS. Latin 17002
MS. Latin 18279
MS. n.a. Françaises 7455
MS. n.a. Latin 182
MS. n.a. 1171
MS. n.a. 1872
MS. n.a. 1203
Toulouse, Bibliothèque Municipale
MS. 450
MS. 477
Vatican
MS. Latini 1972
MS. Latini 1973
MS. Latini 9336
MS. Ottoboniani Latini 632
MS. Reginensi Latini 303
MS. Rossiani 511
MS. Rossiani 570

Printed Sources

Acta [sancti Amatoris]. AASS August 4:24–25.

Les actes de consagracions d'esglésies de l'antic bisbat d'Urgell (Segles IX–XII). Edited by Cebrià Baraut. La Seu d'Urgell: 1986.

Additamentum de reliquiis S. Austremonii. AASS November 1:80–82.

Ademar of Chabannes. *Chronicon. Chronicon d'Ademar de Chabannes.* Edited by Jules Chavannon. Paris: 1897.

Adenet Le Roi. *Berte as grans piés.* Edited by Albert Henry. Geneva: 1982.

Ado of Vienne, *Martyrologe d'Adon: Ses deux familles, ses trois recensions.* Edited by Jacques Dubois. Paris: 1984.

Angeriacensium de translatione capitis [S. Joannis baptistae] ad suum monasterium. AASS June 5:650–652.

Annales Laurissenses et Einhardi. MGH SS 1:124–218.

Ardo. *Vita Benedicti abbatis Anianensis et Indensis. MGH SS* 15.1:198–220.

Astronomer. *Vita Hludowici imperatoris. MGH SS* 2:607–648.

Benedict of Soracte. *Chronicon. MGH SS* 3:695–719.

Bernard of Clairvaux. *Apologia.* In *S. Bernardi Opera* 3: *Tractatus et Opuscula*, pp. 53–108. Edited by Jean Leclercq and Henri M. Rochais. 8 vols. Rome: 1957–1977.

Bibliotheca Cluniacensis . . . . Edited by Martin Marrier and Andreas Quercetanus. Macon: 1915 (reprint of 1614 ed.).

Brevis historia monasterii Rivipullensis. In Pierre de Marca, *Marca Hispanica sive Limes Hispanicus . . . ,* cols. 1295–1301. Paris: 1688.

Bullaire de l'abbaye de Saint-Gilles. Edited by Abbé Goiffon. Nîmes: 1882.

Bullaire de l'église de Maguelone. Edited by J. Rouquette and A. Villemagne. 2 vols. Montpellier: 1911–1914.

Cartulaire de Brioude: Liber de honoribus sancto Juliano collatis. Edited by Henry Doniol. Paris: 1863.

Cartulaire de l'abbaye de Conques en Rouergue. Edited by Gustave Desjardins. Paris: 1879.

Cartulaire de l'abbaye de Lézat. Edited by Paul Ourliac and Anne-Marie Magnou. 2 vols. Paris: 1984–1987.

Cartulaire de l'abbaye de Saint-Jean de Sorde . . . . Edited by Paul Raymond. Paris: 1872.

Cartulaire de l'abbaye de Saint-Victor de Marseille. Edited by Benjamin Guérard. 2 vols. Paris: 1857.

Cartulaire de l'abbaye de St-Chaffre du Monastier, suivi de la Chronique de St-Pierre-du-Puy. Edited by Ulysse Chevalier. Paris: 1884.

Cartulaire de l'abbaye de Vabres au diocèse de Rodez: Essai de reconstitution d'un manuscrit disparu. Edited by Etienne Fournial. Rodez: 1989.

Cartulaire de l'abbaye des Bénédictins de Saint-Savin en Lavedan (945–1175). Edited by Charles Durier. Paris: 1880.

Cartulaire de l'abbaye d'Uzerche (Corrèze) du Xe au XIVe siècle avec tables, identifications, notes historiques. Edited by J.-B. Champeval. Paris: 1901.

Cartulaire de l'ancien diocèse et de l'arrondissement administratif de Carcassonne. Edited by A. Mahul. 7 vols. 1857–1882.

Cartulaire de l'église collégiale Saint-Seurin de Bordeaux. Edited by Jean-Auguste Brutails. Bordeaux: 1897.

Cartulaire de Maguelone. Edited by J. Rouquette and A. Villemagne. 2 vols. Montpellier: 1912–1913.

Cartulaire de Saint-Jean d'Angély. 2 vols. Archives Historiques de la Saintonge et de l'Aunis, 30 and 33. Paris: 1901–1903.

Cartulaire de Silvanès. Edited by P.-A. Verlaguet. Archives Historiques de Rouergue, 1. Rodez: 1910.

Cartulaire des abbayes de Tulle et de Rocamadour. Edited by J.-B. Champeval. Brive: 1903.

"Cartulaire du prieuré de Saint-Pierre de La Réole." Edited by Charles Grellet-Balguerie. *Archives Historiques de la Gironde* 5 (1863): 99–186.

Cartulaires des abbayes d'Aniane et de Gellone publiés d'après les manuscrits originaux. Edited by A. Cassan and E. Meynial. 2 vols. Montpellier: 1898–1900.

Cartulaires du chapitre de l'église métropolitaine Sainte-Marie d'Auch. Edited by C. Lacave La Plagne-Barris. Archives Historiques de la Gascogne, 2d ser., 3. Paris: 1899.

Cartulario de San Juan de la Peña. Edited by Antonio Ubieto Arteta. Textos Medievales, 6. Valencia: 1962.

Catalunya carolíngia. Edited by Ramon d'Abadal y de Vinyals. 3 vols. Barcelona: 1926–1955.

La chanson de Roland. Edited by Cesare Segre. 2 vols. Geneva: 1989.

Chartes et documents pour servir à l'histoire de l'abbaye de Charroux. Edited by Pierre de Monsabert. Archives Historiques de Poitou, 93. Poitiers: 1910.

Chronicon monasterii Conchensis. In *Thesaurus novus anecdotorum . . .* , 3:1387–1388. Edited by Edmond Martène and Ursin Durand. 5 vols. Paris: 1717.

La chronique de Morigny (1095–1152). Edited by Léon Mirot. Paris: 1912.

Chronique de Saint-Maixent, 751–1140. Edited and translated by Jean Verdon. Paris: 1979.

Chronique dite Saintongeaise: Texte franco-occitan inédit "Lee": A le découvete d'une chronique gasconne du XIIIe siècle et de sa poitevinisation. Edited by André de Mandach. Tübingen: 1970.

"Chronique du monastère de Conques . . . ." In *Etudes historiques sur le Rouergue,* 4:391–394. Edited by Marc Antoine François de Gaujal. 4 vols. Paris: 1858–1859.

De antiquis ecclesiae ritibus libri tres . . . editio novissima. Edited by Edmond Martène. Venice: 1783.

Descriptio qualiter Karolus Magnus clavum et coronam domini a Constantinopoli Aquisgrani detulerit qualiterque Karolus Calvus hec ad sanctum Dyonisium retulerit. In Rauschen, *Die Legende Karls des Grossen,* pp. 103–125.

Durand, Guillaume. *Pontifical.* In *Le pontifical romain au Moyen-Age.* Edited by Michel Andrieu. 3 vols. Studi e Testi, 86–88. Vatican: 1938–1940.

Einhard. *Vita Karoli Magni.* Edited by Louis Halphen. *Vie de Charlemagne.* 2d ed. Paris: 1981.

Erzählungen des Mittelalters in deutscher Übersetzung und lateinischen Urtext. Edited by Joseph Klapper. Wort und Brauch. Volkskundliche Arbeite . . . , 12. Breslau: 1914.

Ex historia monasterii Usercensis. In *Cartulaire de l'abbaye d'Uzerche,* pp. 13–50.

Gervase of Tilbury. *De otiis imperialibus.* MGH SS 27:359–394.

Gesta Dagoberti I. regis Francorum. MGH SSRM 2:396–425.

Gesta Karoli Magni ad Carcassonam et Narbonam. Edited by F. E. Schneegans. Romanische Bibliothek, 15. Halle: 1898.

Gregory of Tours. *Historia Francorum.* MGH SSRM 1.1.

———. *Liber in gloria confessorum.* MGH SSRM 1.2:294–370.

Gregory VII. *Das Register Gregors VII.* Edited by Erich Caspar. MGH Epistolae Selectae, 2. Berlin: 1920.

Guibert of Nogent. *De pignoribus sanctorum.* PL 156:607–680.

Guide du pèlerin de Saint-Jacques de Compostelle: Texte latin du XIIe siècle, édité et traduit en français d'après des manuscrits de Compostelle et de Ripoll. Edited by Jeanne Vielliard. Paris: 1984.

Guillaume de Berneville. *Vie de saint Gilles par Guillaume de Berneville, poème du XIIe siècle.* Edited by Gaston Paris and A. Bos. Paris: 1881.

Guillaume Le Breton. *Philippidos.* In *Œuvres de Rigord et de Guillaume Le Breton, historiens de Philippe-Auguste.* Edited by H.-F. Delaborde. 2 vols. Paris: 1882–1885.

"Histoire anonyme de la fondation du prieuré de Lavoûte-Chilhac par Odilon, abbé de Cluny." Edited by Pierre-François Fournier. *Bulletin Philologique et Historique (jusqu'à 1715) du Comité des Travaux Historiques et Scientifiques, 1958* (1959): 103–115.

Historia de translatione carnis dominicae circumcisionis . . . . In *De codicibus hagiographicis Ioannis Gielemans canonici regularis in rubea valle prope Bruxellas adiectis anecdotis,* pp. 428–430. Subsidia Hagiographica, 3. Brussels: 1895.

Historia Karoli Magni et Rotholandi, ou Chronique du Pseudo-Turpin. Edited by Cyril Meredith-Jones. Paris: 1936.

Historia miraculorum [S. Willelmi ducis]. AASS May 6:822–826.

Historia monasterii Figiacensis in Dioecesi Cadurcensi. In *Miscellanea novo ordine,* 4:1–2.

Hrotsvit of Gandersheim. *Primordia coenobii Gandeshemensis.* In *Opera,* pp. 440–472. Edited by H. Homeyer. Munich: 1970.

Hugh of Fleury. *Vita S. sacerdotis. PL* 163:980–1004.

Innocent III. *De sacro altaris mysterio. PL* 217:773–916.

Jacobus of Voragine, *Legenda aurea vulgo Historia Lombardica dicta.* Edited by Th. Graesse. Warsaw: 1890.

John of Salerno. *Vita sancti Odonis. PL* 133:43–48.

Le Liber censuum de l'église romaine. Edited by Paul Fabre and Louis Duchesne. 3 vols. Paris: 1889–1952.

Liber de apparitione sancti Michaelis in Monte Gargano. MGH Scriptores rerum Langobardicorum et Italicarum saec. VI–IX, pp. 540–543. Hannover: 1878.

Liber miraculorum sancte Fidis. Edited by A. Bouillet. Paris: 1897.

Liber pontificalis. Edited by Louis Duchesne. 3 vols. Paris: 1886–1957.

Miracula S. Genulphi episcopi. AASS January 2:97–107.

Miscellanea novo ordine digesta et non paucis ineditis monumentis. Edited by Etienne Baluze; re-edited by J. D. Mansi. 4 vols. Lucca: 1764.

Moniage Guillaume. In *Les deux rédactions en vers du Moniage Guillaume, chanson de geste du XIIe siècle* . . . . Edited by Wilhelm Cloetta. 2 vols. Paris: 1906–1911.

Monumenta Vizeliacensia: Textes relatifs à l'histoire de l'abbaye de Vézelay. Edited by R. B. C. Huygens. Corpus Christianorum Continuatio Medievalis, 42. Turnholt: 1976.

Notitia de servitio monasteriorum. MGH Capitularia regum Francorum 1:349–352, no. 171.

Odo of Cluny, *De vita sancti Geraldi Auriliacensis comitis. PL* 133:639–704.

Odo of Saint-Maur. *Vie de Bouchard le vénérable, comte de Vendôme, de Corbeil, de Melun et de Paris (Xe et XIe siècle).* Edited by Charles Bourel de la Roncière. Paris: 1892.

Orderic Vitalis. *Ecclesiastical History of Orderic Vitalis.* Edited by Marjorie Chibnall. 6 vols. Oxford: 1969–1980.

Ordonnances des rois de France de la troisième race, recueillies par ordre chronologique. 21 vols. Paris: 1723–1849.

Papsturkunden 896–1046. Edited by Harald Zimmermann. 3 vols. Vienna: 1984–1989.

Papsturkunden in Frankreich: Reiseberichte zur Gallia Pontifica. Edited by Wilhelm Wiederhold. 2 vols. Acta Romanorum Pontificum, 7 and 8. Vatican: 1985.

Peter of Maillezais. *Qualiter fuit constructum Malliacense monasterium et corpus sancti Rigomeri translatum.* Edited as *De antiquitate et commutatione in melius Malleacense insulae sive qualiter fuit constructum Malleacense monasterium et corpus sancti Rigomeri translatum. PL* 146:1247–1272.

Petrus Comestor. *Historia scholastica. PL* 198:1045–1722.

Pontifical romano-germanique du dixième siècle. Edited by Cyrille Vogel and Reinhard Elze. 3 vols. Studi e Testi, 226, 227, 269. Vatican: 1963–1972.

Prima vita sancti Severi martyris. AASS November 1:220–226.

Pseudo-Ardo Smaragdus. *Sermo sancti Ardonis, cognomento Smaragdi* . . . . *AASSosB* 4.1:225–226.

Pseudo-Aurelianus, *Vita eiusdem B. Martialis episcopi Lemovicensis et Galliarum apostoli.* In *De probatis sanctorum vitis* . . . , 2:365–374. Edited by Laurentius Surius. 4 vols. Cologne: 1618.

Pseudo-Hermenbertus. *Vita Vincentiani confessoris Avolcensis. MGH SSRM* 5:112–128.

"Un récit inédit de la prise de Saint-Martin de la Canourgue par les moines de Saint-

Victor de Marseilles." Edited by Robert Barroux. *Bulletin Philologique et Historique du Comité des Travaux Historiques* (1924):187–191.

Recueil des actes de Charles III le Simple, roi de France (893–923). Edited by Ferdinand Lot and Philippe Lauer. Paris: 1949.

Recueil des actes de Pépin Ier et Pépin II rois d'Aquitaine (814–848). Edited by Léon Levillain. Paris: 1926.

Recueil des actes de Philippe Auguste roi de France. Edited by H.-François Delaborde et al. 4 vols. Paris: 1916–1989.

Recueil des actes de Philippe Ier, roi de France (1059–1108). Edited by Maurice Prou. Paris: 1908.

Recueil des chartes de l'abbaye de Cluny. Edited by Alexandre Bruel. 6 vols. Paris: 1876–1903.

Recueil des chartes de l'abbaye de Saint-Benoît-sur-Loire. Edited by Maurice Prou and Alexandre Vidier. 2 vols. Paris: 1907–1912.

Recueil des historiens des Gaules et de la France. Edited by M. Bouquet et al. 24 vols. Paris: 1738–1904.

Revelatio corporis S. Austremonii et ejusdem duplex translatio. AASS November 1:77–80.

Robert of Torigny. *Chronica. MGH SS* 6:475–535.

"Roman de saint Trophime." Edited by N. Zingarelli. *Annales du Midi* 13 (1901): 297–345.

Suger. *Vita Ludovici. Vie de Louis VI le Gros.* Edited and translated by Henri Waquet. Paris: 1929.

Thesauri hymnologici hymnarium: Die Hymnen des Thesaurus Hymnologicus H.A. Daniels . . . . Edited by Clemens Blume. Analecta Hymnica Medii Aevi, 51. Leipzig: 1908.

Tote Listoire de France (Chronique Saintogeaise). Edited by F. W. Bourdillon. London: 1897.

Translatio altera [S. Fidis virginis et martyris]. AASS October 3:294–299.

Translatio metrica S. Fidis virginis et martyris. AASS October 3:289–292.

Vita Carileffi abbatis Anisolensis. MGH SSRM 3:386–394.

"Vita, inventio et miracula sanctae Enimiae." Edited by Clovis Brunel. *AB* 57 (1939): 237–298.

Vita Karoli Magni. In Rauschen, *Die Legende Karls des Grossen,* pp. 17–125.

Vita Menelei abbatis Menatensis. MGH SSRM 5:129–157.

Vita prima S. Austremonii. AASS November 1:49–54.

Vita S. Aegidii. Three versions have been edited. *AASS* September 1:299–304. *AB* 8 (1889): 102–120. In Jones, *Saint Gilles,* pp. 98–111.

Vita S. Calminii confessoris. AASS August 3:759–762.

Vita S. Geraldi Silvae-majoris primi abbatis et fundatoris. AASSosB 6.2:866–892.

Vita S. Theofredi abbatis Calmeliacensis, martyris in Gallia. AASSosB 3.1:476–485.

Vita [S. Willelmi ducis]. AASS May 6:811–820.

Vita sancti Desiderii episcopi Cadurcensis. Edited by Bruno Krusch. In *Liber Scintillarum,* pp. 343–401. Edited by H. Rochais. Corpus Christianorum Series Latina, 117. Turnholt, 1957.

Vita sancti Honorati nach drei Handschriften herausgegeben. Edited by Bernhard Munke, Wilhelm Schäfer, and Adolf Kretteck. Beihefte zur Zeitschrift für Romanische Philologie, 32. Halle: 1911.

Vita sancti Leonardi confessoris. AASS November 3:150–155.

Vita secunda S. Austremonii. AASS November 1:55–61.

Vita tertia S. Austremonii. AASS November 1:61–77.
Vita tertia S. Severi. AASS November 1:227–233.
Vita Vincentiani confessoris Avolcensis. MGH SSRM 5:112–128.

Secondary Works

A Cluny: Congrès scientifique: Fêtes et cérémonies liturgiques en l'honneur des saints abbés Odon et Odilon, 9–11 juillet 1949. Dijon: 1950.
Alter, Peter. *Nationalismus.* Frankfurt: 1985.
Althoff, Gerd. "Gandersheim und Quedlinburg: Ottonische Frauenklöster als Herrschafts- und Uberlieferungszentrum." *Frühmittelalterliche Studien* 25 (1991): 123–144.
———. "Genealogische und andere Fiktionen in mittelalterlicher Historiographie." In *Fälschungen im Mittelalter,* 1:416–441.
Amann, Emile, and Auguste Dumas. *L'église au pouvoir des laïques 888–1057.* Paris: 1948.
Anderson, Benedict. *Imagined Communities: Reflections on the Origin and Spread of Nationalism.* New York: 1983.
Appelt, H. "Die Anfänge des päpstlichen Schutzes." *MIÖG* 62 (1954): 101–111.
Auzias, Léonce. *L'Aquitaine carolingienne (778–987).* Paris: 1937.
Avril, François, et al. *Manuscrits enluminés de la péninsule ibérique.* Paris: 1982.
Bachrach, Bernard S. "'Potius Rex quam Dux esse putabatur': Some Observations Concerning Ademar of Chabannes' Panegyric on Duke William the Great." *Haskins Society Journal* 1 (1989): 11–21.
Beaune, Colette. *Naissance de la nation France.* Paris: 1985.
———. "Saint Clovis: Histoire, religion royale et sentiment national en France à la fin du Moyen Age." In *Le métier d'historien au Moyen Age: Etudes sur l'historiographie médiévale,* pp. 139–156. Edited by Bernard Guenée. Paris: 1977.
Bédier, Joseph. *Les légendes épiques: Recherches sur la formation des chansons de geste.* 4 vols. 2d rev. ed. Paris: 1914–1921.
———. "Recherches sur les légendes du cycle de Guillaume d'Orange." *Annales du Midi* 19 (1907): 5–205.
Benz, Suitbert. "Zur Geschichte der römischen Kirchweihe nach den Texten des 6. bis 7. Jahrhunderts." In *Enkainia: Gesammelte Arbeiten zum 800 jährigen Weihegedächtnis der Abteikirche Maria Laach am 24. August 1956,* pp. 62–109. Edited by Hilarius Emonds. Düsseldorf: 1956.
Bisson, Thomas N. *The Medieval Crown of Aragon: A Short History.* Oxford: 1986.
———. "Nobility and the Family in Medieval France: A Review Essay." *French Historical Studies* 16 (1990): 597–613.
———. "Unheroed Pasts: History and Commemoration in South Frankland before the Albigensian Crusade." *Speculum* 65 (1990): 281–308.
Bomba, Andreas. *Chansons de geste und französisches Nationalbewusstsein im Mittelalter: Sprachliche Analysen der Epen des Wilhelmzyklus.* Stuttgart: 1987.
Bonnassie, Pierre. *La Catalogne du milieu du Xe à la fin du XIe: Croissance et mutations d'une société.* 2 vols. Toulouse: 1975–1976.
Bonne, Jean-Claude. *L'art roman de face et de profil: Le tympan de Conques.* Paris: 1984.
Bouchard, Constance Brittain. "Family Structure and Family Consciousness among the Aristocracy in the Ninth to Eleventh Centuries." *Francia* 14 (1986): 639–658.

———. "Merovingian, Carolingian and Cluniac Monasticism: Reform and Renewal in Burgundy." *Journal of Ecclesiastical History* 41 (1990): 365–388.

———. *Sword, Miter, and Cloister: Nobility and the Church in Burgundy, 980–1198.* Ithaca, N.Y.: 1987.

Bouillet, A., and L. Servières. *Sainte Foy: Vierge et martyre.* Rodez: 1900.

Bousquet, Jacques. "La fondation de Villeneuve d'Aveyron (1053) et l'expansion de l'abbaye de Moissac en Rouergue." In *Moissac et l'Occident*, pp. 195–215. Toulouse: 1964.

Brown, Elizabeth A. R., and Michael Cothren. "The Twelfth-Century Crusading Window of the Abbey of Saint-Denis: Praeteritorum enim recordatio futurorum est exhibitio." *Journal of the Warburg and Courtauld Institutes* 49 (1986): 1–40.

Buc, Philippe. *L'ambiguïté du livre: Prince, pouvoir, et peuple dans les commentaires de la Bible.* Paris: 1994.

———. "Pouvoir royal et commentaires de la Bible (1150–1350)." *Annales E.S.C.* 44 (1989): 691–713.

Cabanot, Jean. "Le trésor des reliques de Saint-Sauveur de Charroux, centre et reflet de la vie spirituelle de l'abbaye." *Bulletin de la Société des Antiquaires de l'Ouest*, 4th ser., 16 (1981): 105–116.

Callahan, Daniel. "The Sermons of Adémar of Chabannes and the Cult of St. Martial of Limoges." *Revue Bénédictine* 86 (1976): 251–295.

Calmette, Joseph. "La famille de Saint Guilhem." *Annales du Midi* 18 (1906): 145–165.

Carruthers, Mary. *The Book of Memory: A Study of Memory in Medieval Culture.* Cambridge: 1990.

Les cartulaires: Actes de la table ronde organisée par l'Ecole nationale des chartes et le G.D.R. 121 du C.N.R.S. (Paris, 5–7 décembre 1991). Edited by Olivier Guyotjeannin et al. Paris: 1993.

Catalunya i França meridional a l'entorn de l'any mil / La Catalogne et la France méridionale autour de l'an mil. Edited by Xavier Barral i Altet et al. Barcelona: 1991.

La chanson de geste et le mythe carolingien: Mélanges René Louis . . . . 2 vols. Saint-Père-sous-Vézelay: 1982.

Chapeau, Georges. "Fondation de l'abbaye de Charroux: Etudes sur les textes." *Bulletin de la Société des Antiquaires de l'Ouest.* 3d ser., 7 (1926): 471–508.

Chibnall, Marjorie. "Charter and Chronicle: The Use of Archive Sources by Norman Historians." In *Church and Government in the Middle Ages: Essays presented to C. R. Cheney . . .*, pp. 1–17. Edited by C. N. L. Brooke et al. Cambridge: 1976.

Clanchy, M. T. *From Memory to Written Record: England, 1066–1307.* 2d ed. London: 1993.

Clémens, Jacques. "La Gascogne est née à Auch au XIIe siècle." *Annales du Midi* 98 (1986): 165–184.

Clément, Pierre A. *Eglises romanes oubliées du Bas-Languedoc.* Montpellier: 1989.

Cohen, A. P. *The Symbolic Construction of Community.* New York: 1985.

Colby-Hall, Alice. "In Search of the Lost Epics of the Lower Rhône Valley." In *Romance Epic: Essays on a Medieval Genre*, pp. 115–127. Studies in Medieval Culture, 14. Kalamazoo, Mich.: 1987.

Constable, Giles. "Monasticism, Lordship and Society in the Twelfth-Century Hesbaye: Five Documents on the Foundation of the Cluniac Priory of Bertrée." *Traditio* 33 (1977): 161–173. Reprinted in Constable, *Cluniac Studies* (London: 1980).

Costa, Dominique. *Catalogue du Musée Dobrée*. Nantes: 1961.

Coulet, Jules. *Etude sur l'Office de Girone en l'honneur de saint Charlemagne*. Publications de la Société pour l'Etude des Langues Romanes, 20. Montpellier: 1907.

Cowdrey, H. E. J. *The Cluniacs and the Gregorian Reform*. Oxford: 1970.

Crapelet, Bernard. *Auvergne romane*. La Pierre-Qui-Vire: 1965.

Crozet, René. "Le voyage d'Urbain II en France (1095–1096) et son importance au point de vue archéologique." *Annales du Midi* 49 (1937): 42–69.

Culture through Time: Anthropological Approaches. Edited by Emiko Ohnuki-Tierney. Stanford: 1990.

Cygler, Florent. "L'ordre de Cluny et les *rebelliones* au XIIIe siècle." *Francia* 19 (1992): 61–93.

d'Abadal, Ramon. "Com neix i com creix un gran monestir pirinec abans de l'an mil: Eixalada-Cuixa." *Analecta Montserratensia* 8 (1954/55): 125–337.

d'Aquin de Saint-Joseph, Thomas. *Histoire de la vie de sainct Calmine Duc d'Aquitaine . . . .* Tulle: 1646.

de Gaiffier, Baudoin. "La légende de Charlemagne: Le péché de l'empereur et son pardon." In *Recueil de travaux offerts à M. Clovis Brunel*, 1:490–503. 2 vols. Paris: 1955.

de Lasteyrie, Charles. *L'abbaye de Saint-Martial de Limoges . . . .* Paris: 1901.

de Lasteyrie, Robert. *Etude sur les comtes et vicomtes de Limoges antérieurs à l'an 1000*. Paris: 1874.

de Mandach, André. *Naissance et développement de la chanson de geste en Europe*. 1: *La geste de Charlemagne et de Roland*. Paris: 1961.

de Marca, Pierre. *Marca Hispanica sive Limes Hispanicus . . . .* Paris: 1688.

Debidour, V.-H. *Le bestiaire sculpté du Moyen Age en France*. Grenoble: 1961.

Delhommeau, L. *Notes et documents pour servir à l'histoire de l'abbaye de Saint-Pierre de Maillezais*. Paris: 1961.

Dimier, Anselm. "Quelques légendes de fondation chez les Cisterciens." *Studia Monastica* 12 (1970): 97–107.

"Documents transcrits à la fin du Beatus." In *Saint-Sever*, pp. 113–127.

Douais, C. "Saint Germier, évêque de Toulouse au VIe siècle: Examen critique de la vie." *Mémoires de la Société Nationale des Antiquaires de France* 50 (1889): 1–134.

Du Buisson, Pierre Daniel. *Historiae monasterii S. Severi libri x*. Vicojulii ad Atturem: 1876.

Dubois, Jacques. "L'observance monastique à l'abbaye de Saint-Sever et dans la province d'Auch." In *Saint-Sever*, pp. 39–53.

Dubois, Jacques, and Geneviève Renaud. "L'influence des vies des saints sur le développement des institutions." In *Hagiographie, cultures et sociétés IVe–XIIe s.: Actes du colloque organisé à Nanterre et à Paris, 2–5 mai, 1979*, pp. 491–511. Paris: 1979.

Duchesne, Louis. *Fastes épiscopaux de l'ancienne Gaule*. 3 vols. Paris: 1894–1915.

Dufour, Jean. *La bibliothèque et le scriptorium de Moissac*. Paris: 1972.

———. "Etat et comparaison des actes faux ou falsifiés, intitulés au nom des Carolingiens (840–987)." In *Fälschungen im Mittelalter*, 4:167–210.

———. "Obédience respective des Carolingiens et des Capétiens (fin Xe siècle–début XIe siècle)." In *Catalunya i França*, pp. 21–44.

Duggan, Joseph. "Social Functions of the Medieval Epic in the Romance Literatures." *Oral Tradition* 1 (1986): 727–766.

———. "Die zwei 'Epochen' der *Chansons de geste*," pp. 389–408. Edited by Hans Ulrich

Gumbrecht and Ursula Link-Heer. In *Epochenschwellen und Epochenstruktur im Diskurs der Literatur- und Sprachhistorie*. Frankfurt: 1985.

Dunbabin, Jean. *France in the Making, 843–1180*. Oxford: 1985.

Durliat, Marcel. "L'église abbatiale de Moissac des origines à la fin du XIe siècle." *Cahiers Archéologiques* 15 (1965): 155–177.

——. *Roussillon roman*. 4th ed. La Pierre-Qui-Vire: 1986.

Durliat, Marcel, and Victor Allègre. *Pyrénées romanes*. La Pierre-Qui-Vire: 1969.

Ehlers, Joachim. "Kontinuität und Tradition als Grundlage mittelalterlicher Nationsbildung in Frankreich." In *Beiträge zur Bildung der französischen Nation im Früh- und Hochmittlalter*, pp. 16–47. Edited by Helmut Beumann. Sigmaringen: 1983.

Eliade, Mircea. *Le sacré et le profane*. Paris: 1965.

Fabre, Paul. *Etude sur le Liber censuum de l'église romaine*. Paris: 1892.

Fälschungen im Mittelalter: Internationaler Kongress der Monumenta Germaniae Historica, München, 16.–19. September 1986. 5 vols. MGH Schriften, 33.1–5. Hannover: 1988.

Farmer, Sharon. "Ambivalent Resistance: Martinian Responses to Capetian/Dionysian Hegemonies in the Twelfth and Thirteenth Centuries." Paper presented at the *Maiestas* conference, Paris, June 1990.

——. *Communities of Saint Martin: Legend and Ritual in Medieval Tours*. Ithaca, N.Y.: 1991.

Favreau, Robert, and Marie-Thérèse Camus. *Charroux*. Poitiers: 1989.

Fentress, James, and Chris Wickham. *Social Memory*. Oxford: 1992.

Ferguson O'Meara, Carra. *The Iconography of the Façade of Saint-Gilles-du-Gard*. New York: 1977.

Folz, Robert. "Aspects du culte liturgique de saint Charlemagne en France." In *Karl der Grosse* 4:77–99.

——. *Le souvenir et la légende de Charlemagne dans l'empire germanique médiéval*. Paris: 1950.

Fournier, Gabriel. *Le peuplement rural en Basse Auvergne durant le haut Moyen Age*. Paris: 1962.

Fournier, Pierre-François. "Saint Austremoine, premier évêque de Clermont." *Bulletin Historique et Scientifique de l'Auvergne* 89 (1979): 417–471.

Freedman, Paul. "Cowardice, Heroism and the Legendary Origins of Catalonia." *Past and Present* 121 (1988): 3–28.

Frolow, A. "Le medaillon byzantin de Charroux." *Cahiers Archéologiques* 16 (1966): 39–50.

——. *La relique de la Vraie Croix: Recherches sur le développement d'un culte*. Paris: 1961.

Gaillard, Georges. *Rouergue Roman*. La Pierre-Qui-Vire: 1963.

Galbraith, V. H. "Monastic Foundation Charters of the Eleventh and Twelfth Centuries." *Cambridge Historical Journal* 4 (1934): 205–222, 296–298.

Gauthier, M.-M. *Emaux du Moyen Age occidental*. Fribourg: 1972.

——. *Emaux méridionaux: Catalogue international de l'œuvre de Limoges*. 6 vols. to date. Paris: 1987–.

Gazay, J. "Le roman de saint Trophime et l'abbaye de Montmajour." *Annales du Midi* 25 (1913): 5–37.

Geary, Patrick. *Before France and Germany: The Creation and Transformation of the Merovingian World*. Oxford: 1988.

——. "Entre gestion et gesta." In *Les cartulaires*, pp. 13–26.

——. *Furta Sacra: Thefts of Relics in the Central Middle Ages.* 2d ed. Princeton: 1990.

Geertz, Clifford. "Centers, Kings, and Charisma: Reflections on the Symbolics of Power." In Clifford Geertz, *Local Knowledge: Further Essays in Interpretive Anthropology,* pp. 121–146. New York: 1983.

Goffart, Walter. *The Le Mans Forgeries: A Chapter from the History of Church Property in the Ninth Century.* Cambridge, Mass.: 1966.

Gransden, Antonia. "The Growth of the Glastonbury Traditions and Legends." *Journal of Ecclesiastical History* 27 (1976): 337–358.

Graus, Frantisek. *Lebendige Vergangenheit: Überlieferung im Mittelalter und in den Vorstellungen vom Mittelalter.* Cologne: 1975.

——. *Volk, Herrscher und Heiliger im Reich der Merowinger: Studien zur Hagiographie der Merowingerzeit.* Prague: 1965.

Greenberg, Janelle. "The Confessor's Laws and the Radical Face of the Ancient Constitution." *English Historical Review* 104 (1989): 611–637.

Griffe, E. *Histoire religieuse des anciens pays de l'Aude.* Paris: 1933.

——. "La réforme monastique dans les pays audois (seconde moitié du XIe siècle)." In *Moissac et l'Occident,* pp. 133–145.

Grisar, Hartmann. "Die angebliche Christusreliquie im mittelalterlichen Lateran (Praeputium domini)." *Römische Quartalscrift für christliche Altertumskunde und für Kirchengeschichte* 20 (1906): 109–122.

——. *Die römische Kapelle Sancta Sanctorum und ihr Schatz.* Freiburg: 1908.

Grundmann, Herbert. "Freiheit als religiöses, politisches und persönliches Postulat im Mittelater." *Historisches Zeitschrift* 183 (1957): 23–53.

Guenée, Bernard. *Histoire et culture historique dans l'Occident médiéval.* Paris: 1980.

Halbwachs, Maurice. *Les cadres sociaux de la mémoire.* 2d ed. Paris: 1955.

——. *La mémoire collective.* 2d ed. Paris: 1968.

Hallinger, Kassius. *Gorze-Kluny: Studien zu den monastischen Lebensformen und Gegensätzten im Hochmittelalter.* 2 vols. Graz: 1971 (1st published 1950).

Hauck, Karl. "Haus- und sippengebundene Literatur mittelalterlicher Adelsgeschlechter." *MIÖG* 62 (1954): 121–145.

——. "Tiergärten im Pfalzbereich." In *Deutsche Königspfalzen,* 1:30–73. 3 vols. Veröffentlichungen des Max-Plancks-Instituts, 11.1–3. Göttingen: 1963–1965.

Head, Thomas. *Hagiography and the Cult of Saints: The Diocese of Orléans, 800–1200.* Cambridge: 1990.

——. "Hrotsvit's Primordia and the Historical Traditions of Monastic Communities." In *Hrotsvit of Gandersheim: Rara Avis in Saxonia?* pp. 143–164. Edited by Katharina M. Wilson. Medieval and Renaissance Monograph Series, 7. Ann Arbor: 1987.

Heinzelmann, Martin. *Translationsberichte und andere Quellen des Reliquienkultes.* Turnhout: 1979.

Hermann-Mascard, Nicole. *Les reliques des saints: Formation coutumière d'un droit.* Paris: 1975.

Higounet, Charles. "Un grand chapitre de l'histoire du XIIe siècle: La rivalité des maisons de Toulouse et de Barcelone pour la préponderance méridionale." In *Mélanges d'histoire du Moyen Age dédiés à la mémoire de Louis Halphen,* pp. 313–322. Paris: 1951.

Higounet, Charles, and Jean-Bernard Marquette. "Les origines de l'abbaye de Saint-Sever: Révision critique." In *Saint-Sever,* pp. 27–37.

Hirsch, Hans. *Die Klosterimmunität seit dem Investiturstreit: Untersuchungen zur Verfassungsgeschichte des deutschen Reiches und der deutschen Kirche.* Cologne: 1967 (reprint of 1913 ed.).

——. "Untersuchungen zur Geschichte des päpstlichen Schutzes." *MIÖG* 54 (1942): 363–433.

Histoire de la France: L'état et les pouvoirs. Edited by Jacques Le Goff. Paris: 1989.

Hourlier, Jacques. "Cluny et la notion de l'ordre religieux." In *A Cluny,* pp. 219–226.

Huyghebaert, Nicholas. "Une légende de fondation: Le Constitutum Constantini." *Le Moyen Age* 85 (1979): 177–209.

The Invention of Tradition. Edited by Eric Hobsbawm and Terence Ranger. Cambridge: 1983; rpt. 1988.

Iogna-Prat, Dominique. "La geste des origines dans l'historiographie clunisienne des XIe–XIIe siècles." *Revue Bénédictine* 102 (1992): 135–191.

Johnson, Penelope. "Pious Legends and Historical Realities: The Legends of La Trinité Vendôme, Bonport and Holyrood." *Revue Bénédictine* 91 (1981): 184–193.

——. *Prayer, Patronage, and Power: The Abbey of La Trinité, Vendôme.* New York: 1981.

Jones, E. C. *Saint Gilles: Essai d'histoire littéraire.* Paris: 1914.

Kantorowicz, Ernst H. *The King's Two Bodies: A Study in Medieval Political Theology.* Princeton: 1957.

Karl der Grosse: Lebenswerk und Nachleben. Edited by Wolfgang Braufels et al. 5 vols. Düsseldorf: 1965–1968.

Kastner, Jörg. *Historiae fundationum monasteriorum: Frühformen monastischer Institutionsgeschichtsschreibung im Mittelalter.* Münchener Beiträge zur Mediävistik und Renaissance-Forschung, 18. Munich: 1974.

Kienast, Walther. *Deutschland und Frankreich in der Kaiserzeit (900–1270): Weltkaiser und Einzelkönig,* 3 vols. 2d ed. Monographien zur Geschichte des Mittelalters, 9.1–3. Stuttgart: 1974–1975.

——. "Wirkungsbereich des französischen Königstums von Odo bis Ludwig VI. (888–1137) in Südfrankreich." *Historische Zeitschrift* 209 (1969): 529–565.

Kirk, G. S. *Myth: Its Function and Meaning in Ancient and Other Cultures.* Cambridge: 1970; rpt. 1971.

Knapp, Steven. "Collective Memory and the Actual Past." *Representations* 26 (1989): 123–149.

Kolb, Herbert. "Der Hirsch, der Schlangen frisst: Bermerkungen zum Verhältnis von Naturkunde und Theologie in der mittelalterlichen Literatur." In *Mediaevalia litteraria: Festschrift für Helmut de Boor zum 80. Geburtstag,* pp. 583–610. Edited by Ursula Hennig and Herbert Kolb. Munich: 1971.

Koziol, Geoffrey. *Begging Pardon and Favor: Ritual and Political Order in Early Medieval France.* Ithaca, N.Y.: 1992.

Krappe, Alexander H. "Guiding Animals." *Journal of American Folklore* 5 (1942): 228–246.

Krautheimer, Richard. "Introduction to an 'Iconography of Mediaeval Architecture.'" *Journal of the Warburg and Courtauld Institutes* 5 (1942): 1–33.

Krusch, Bruno. "Reise nach Frankreich im Frühjahr und Sommer 1892. Fortsetzung und Schluss. 3. Aufzeichnung des Abtes Lamfred von Mozac über König Pippins Beziehungen zu seinem Kloster." *Neues Archiv der Gesellschaft für ältere deutsche Geschichtskunde* 19 (1894): 24–25.

Kurth, Godefroid. *Clovis.* 2 vols. Brussels: 1923.

Lagrèze-Fossat, A. *Etudes historiques sur Moissac.* 3 vols. Paris: 1870, 1872, 1874.

Landes, Richard. "The Dynamics of Heresy and Reform in Limoges: A Study of Popular Participation in the 'Peace of God' (944–1033)." *Historical Reflections / Réflexions Historiques* 14 (1987): 467–511.

———. *Relics, Apocalypse and the Deceits of History: Ademar of Chabannes (989–1034)*. Cambridge, Mass.: 1995.

Lauranson-Rosaz, Christian. *L'Auvergne et ses marges (Vélay, Gévaudan) du VIIIe au XIe siècle: La fin du monde antique?* Le Puy: 1987.

Lejeune, Rita. "Le péché de Charlemagne et la *Chanson de Roland*." In *Homenaje ofrecido a Dámaso Alonso . . .* , 2:339–371. 3 vols. Madrid: 1961.

———. "La question de l'historicité du héros épique Aimeri de Narbonne." In *Economies et Sociétés au Moyen Age: Mélanges offerts à Edouard Perroy*, pp. 50–62. Paris: 1973.

Lejeune, Rita, and Jacques Stiennon. *La légende de Roland dans l'art du Moyen Age.* 2 vols. Brussels: 1966.

Lemarignier, Jean-François. "Aspects politiques des fondations de collégiales dans le royaume de France au XIe siècle." In *La vita comune del clero nei secoli XI e XII*, pp. 19–49. Miscellanea del Centro di Studi Medioevali, 3.1. Milan: 1962.

———. *Etude sur les privilèges d'exemption et de juridiction ecclésiastique des abbayes normandes depuis les origines jusqu'en 1140.* Paris: 1937.

———. "L'exemption monastique et les origines de la réforme grégorienne." In *A Cluny*, pp. 288–340.

———. *Le gouvernement royal aux premiers temps capétiens (987–1108).* Paris: 1965.

———. "Political and Monastic Structures in France at the End of the Tenth and the Beginning of the Eleventh Century." In *Lordship and Community in Medieval Europe: Selected Readings*, pp. 100–127. Edited by Fredric L. Cheyette. New York: 1968.

Lesne, Emile. *Histoire de la propriété ecclésiastique en France*, 6 vols. Paris: 1910–1945.

Levillain, Léon. "La translation des reliques de saint Austremoine à Mozac et le diplôme de Pépin II d'Aquitaine (863)." *Le Moyen Age* 17 (1904): 281–337.

Lévi-Strauss, Claude. "The Structural Study of Myth." *Journal of American Folklore* 28 (1955): 428–442.

Les Lieux de mémoire. Edited by Pierre Nora. 3 vols. to date. Paris: 1984–1993.

Lohrmann, Dietrich. *Das Register Papst Johannes' VIII. (872–882): Neue Studien zur Abschrift Reg. Vat. 1, zum verlorenen Originalregister und zum Diktat der Briefe.* Tübingen: 1968.

Lot, Ferdinand. *Etudes sur les légendes épiques françaises.* Paris: 1970.

Lot, Ferdinand, and Robert Fawtier. *Histoire des institutions françaises au Moyen Age.* 3 vols. Paris: 1957–1962.

Louis, René. *De l'histoire à la légende: Girart comte de Vienne . . . .* 3 vols. Auxerre: 1946–1947.

Luchaire, Achille. *Etudes sur les actes de Louis VII.* Paris: 1885.

Lugand, Jacques, Jean Nogaret, and Robert Saint-Jean. *Languedoc roman: Le Languedoc méditerranéen.* 2d ed. La Pierre-Qui-Vire: 1985.

Mabillon, Jean. *Annales ordinis sancti Benedicti occidentalium monachorum patriarchae.* 6 vols. Lucca: 1739–1745.

Magnou-Nortier, Elisabeth. "Abbés séculiers ou avoués à Moissac au XIe siècle." In *Moissac et l'Occident*, pp. 123–132.

———. "L'affaire de l'église de Soulac d'après les actes faux contenus dans le Beatus [XIe s.]." In *Saint-Sever*, pp. 99–111.

———. "Etude sur le privilège d'immunité du IVe au IXe siècle." *Revue Mabillon* 60 (1984): 465–512.

———. *La société laïque et l'église dans la province ecclésiastique de Narbonne (zone cispyrénéenne) de la fin du VIIIe à la fin du XIe siècle.* Toulouse: 1974.

Maines, Clark. "The Charlemagne Window at Chartres Cathedral: New Considerations on Text and Image." *Speculum* 52 (1977): 801–823.

Malinowski, Bronislaw. "Myth in Primitive Psychology." In his *Magic, Science, and Religion and Other Essays*, pp. 93–148. New York: 1948.

Marion, Jules. "L'abbaye de Moissac: Notes d'un voyage archéologique dans le sud-ouest de France." *Bibliothèque de l'Ecole des Chartes* 11 (1849): 89–147.

Martimort, Aimé-Georges. *La documentation liturgique de Dom Edmond Martène: Etude codicologique.* Studi e Testi, 279. Vatican: 1978.

McCormick, Michael. *Eternal Victory: Triumphal Rulership in Late Antiquity, Byzantium and the Early Medieval West.* Cambridge: 1986.

Menéndez Pidal, Ramón. *La chanson de Roland et la tradition épique des Francs.* Translated by I.-M. Cluzel. 2d rev. ed. Paris: 1960.

Michalowski, Roman. "Il culto dei santi fondatori nei monasteri tedeschi dei secoli XI e XII: Proposte di ricerca." In *Culto dei santi, istituzioni e classi sociali in età preindustriale*, pp. 105–140. Edited by Sofia Boesch Gajano and Lucia Sebastiani. Rome: 1984.

Misonne, Daniel. *Eilbert de Florennes: Histoire et légende, la geste de Raoul de Cambrai.* Louvain: 1967.

Moissac et l'Occident au XIe siècle: Actes du colloque international de Moissac, 3–5 mai 1963. Toulouse: 1964.

Mundo, Anscari M. "Monastic Movements in the East Pyrenees." In *Cluniac Monasticism in the Central Middle Ages*, pp. 98–132. Edited by Noreen Hunt. Hamden, Conn.: 1971.

Mundy, John Hine. *Liberty and Political Power in Toulouse, 1050–1230.* New York: 1954.

Müssigbrod, Axel. *Die Abtei Moissac 1050–1150: Zu einem Zentrum cluniacensischen Mönchtums in Südwestfrankreich.* Münstersche Mittelalter-Schriften, 58. Munich: 1988.

Nichols, Stephen. *Romanesque Signs: Early Medieval Narrative and Iconography.* New Haven: 1983.

Niermeyer, J. F. *Mediae Latinitatis lexicon minus.* Leiden: 1984.

Nora, Pierre. "Between Memory and History: *Les lieux de mémoire.*" *Representations* 26 (1989): 7–25.

Ogle, M. B. "The Stag-Messenger Episode." *American Journal of Philology* 37 (1916): 387–416.

Oursel, Raymond. *Haut-Poitou roman.* La Pierre-Qui-Vire: 1975.

Pacaut, Marcel. *Louis VII et son royaume.* Paris: 1964.

Pailhes, Claudine. "La crise de la communauté monastique de Lagrasse au XIIIe siècle." In *Sous la Règle de saint Benoît: Structures monastiques et sociétés en France du Moyen Age à l'époque moderne (Abbaye bénédictine Sainte-Marie de Paris 23–25 octobre 1980)*, pp. 265–276. Geneva: 1982.

Paris, Gaston. *Histoire poétique de Charlemagne.* 2d ed. Paris: 1906.

Patze, Hans. "Adel und Stifterchronik: Frühformen territorialer Geschichtsschreibung im hochmittelalterlichen Reich." *Blätter für deutsche Landesgeschichte* 100 (1964): 8–81; 101 (1965): 67–128.

The Peace of God: Social Violence and Religious Response in France around the Year 1000. Edited by Thomas Head and Richard Landes. Ithaca, N.Y.: 1992.

Pfaff, Volkert. "Sankt Peters Abteien im 12. Jahrhundert." *Zeitschrift der Savigny Stiftung für Rechtsgeschichte: Kanonistische Abteilung* 57 (1971): 150–195.

Poly, Jean-Pierre. *La Provence et la société féodale 879–1166: Contribution à l'étude des structures dites féodales dans le Midi.* Paris: 1976.

Poly, Jean-Pierre, and Eric Bournazel. *The Feudal Transformation, 900–1200.* Translated by Caroline Higgitt. New York: 1991.

Poncelet, A. "La plus ancienne vie de S. Austremoine." *AB* 13 (1894): 33–46.

Prinz, Friedrich. *Frühes Mönchtum im Frankenreich: Kultur und Gesellschaft in Gallien, den Rheinlanden und Bayern am Beispiel der monastischen Entwicklung (4. bis 8. Jahrhundert).* Munich: 1965.

Prinz, Friedrich. *Gründungsmythen und Sagenchronologie.* Zetemata. Monographien zur klassischen Altertumswissenschaft, 72. Munich: 1979.

Pschmadt, Carl. *Die Sage von der verfolgten Hinde: Ihre Heimat und Wanderung, Bedeutung und Entwicklung mit besonderer Berücksichtigung ihrer Verwendung in der Literatur des Mittelalters.* Greifswald: 1911.

Pückert, Wilhelm. *Aniane und Gellone: Diplomatisch-kritische Untersuchungen zur Geschichte der Reformen des Benedictinerordens im IX. und X. Jahrhundert.* Leipzig: 1899.

Rauschen, Gerhard. *Die Legende Karls des Grossen im 11. und 12. Jahrhundert.* Publikationen der Gesellschaft für Rheinische Geschichtskunde, 7. Leipzig: 1890.

Reinle, Adolf. "Das 'A Karls des Grossen' im Kirchenschatz von Conques." In *Variorum Munera Florum: Latinität als prägende Kraft mittelalterlicher Kultur: Festschrift für Hans F. Haefele zu seinem sechzigsten Geburtstag,* pp. 129–140. Edited by Adolf Reinle, Ludwig Schmugge, and Peter Stotz. Sigmaringen: 1985.

Remensnyder, Amy G. "Un problème de cultures ou de culture? La statue-reliquaire et les *joca* de sainte Foy de Conques dans le *Liber miraculorum sancte Fidis* de Bernard d'Angers." *Cahiers de Civilisation Médiévale* 33 (1990): 351–379.

Revillout, C. "Etude historique et littéraire sur l'ouvrage latin intitulé *Vie de saint Guillaume*." *Mémoires de la Société Archéologique de Montpellier* 6 (1870–1876): 495–576.

Rosenwein, Barbara. "Property, Peace, and Privacy: The Medieval Immunity." Paper presented at the annual meeting of the American Historical Association, New York, December 1990.

———. *To Be the Neighbor of Saint Peter: The Social Meaning of Cluny's Property, 909–1049.* Ithaca, N.Y.: 1989.

Rouche, Michel. *L'Aquitaine des Wisigoths aux Arabes 418–781: Naissance d'une région.* Paris: 1979.

Rupin, Ernst. *L'abbaye et les cloîtres de Moissac.* Paris: 1897.

———. "La chasse de saint Calmine à Laguenne." *Bulletin de la société scientifique, historique et archéologique de la Corrèze* 13 (1891): 353–362.

Sahlins, Marshall. *Islands of History.* Chicago: 1985.

Sahlins, Peter. *Boundaries: The Making of France and Spain in the Pyrenees.* Berkeley: 1990.

Saints and Their Cults: Studies in Religious Sociology, Folklore and History. Edited by Stephen Wilson. Cambridge: 1983.

Saint-Sever: Millénaire de l'abbaye. Colloque international 25, 26 et 27 mai 1985. Mont-de-Marsan: 1986.

Saltet, Louis. "Saint Germier: Etude critique sur sa vie." *Annales du Midi* 13 (1910): 146–175.

Sargent, Steven. "Religious Responses to Social Violence in Eleventh-Century Aquitaine." *Historical Reflections / Réflexions Historiques* 12 (1985): 219–240.

Saxer, Victor. "Le culte et la légende hagiographique de saint Guillaume à Gellone." In *La chanson de geste et le mythe carolingien*, 2:565–589.

——. "Légende épique et légende hagiographique: Problème d'origines et d'évolution des chansons de geste." *Revue des Sciences Religieuses* 33 (1959): 372–395.

Schapiro, Meyer. "The Romanesque Sculpture of Moissac I and II." In Meyer Schapiro, *Romanesque Art*, pp. 131–264. New York: 1977.

Schmid, Paul. "Die Entstehung des Marseiller Kirchenstaates." *Archiv für Urkundenforschung* 10 (1928): 176–207; 11 (1930): 138–152.

Schneidmüller, Bernd. *Karolingische Tradition und frühes französisches Königtum: Untersuchungen zur Herrschaftslegitimation der westfränkisch-französichen Monarchie im 10. Jahrhundert.* Wiesbaden: 1979.

——. *Nomen patriae: Die Entstehung Frankreichs in der politisch-geographischen Terminologie (10.–13. Jahrhundert).* Sigmaringen: 1987.

Schramm, Percy Ernst. *Herrschaftszeichen und Staatssymbolik: Beiträge zu ihrer Geschichte vom dritten bis zum sechzehnten Jahrhundert.* Schriften der MGH, 13.1–3. Stuttgart: 1954–1956.

——. *Der König von Frankreich.* 2 vols. Weimar: 1939.

Schreiber, Georg. *Kurie und Kloster im 12. Jahrhundert.* 2 vols. Kirchenrechtliche Abhandlungen, 65–66, 67–68. Amsterdam: 1965 (reprint of 1910 ed.).

Schwarz, Wilhelm. "*Jurisdicio* und *Condicio:* Eine Untersuchung zu den *Privilegia libertatis* der Klöster." *Zeitschrift der Savigny-Stiftung für Rechtsgeschichte: Kanonistische Abteilung* 45 (1959): 34–98.

Schwering-Illert, Gisela. *Die ehemalige französische Abteikirche Saint-Sauveur im Charroux (Vienne) im 11. und 12. Jh.: Ein Vorschlag zur Rekonstruktion und Deutung der romanischen Bauteile.* Düsseldorf: 1963.

Schwineköper, Berent. "Christus-Reliquien-Verehrung und Politik." *Blätter für deutsche Landesgeschichte* 117 (1981): 183–281.

Semmler, Josef. "Karl der Grosse und das fränkische Mönchtum." In *Karl der Grosse*, 2:255–289.

——. "Traditio und Königsschutz: Studien zur Geschichte der königlichen monasteria." *Zeitschrift der Savigny-Stiftung für Rechtsgeschichte: Kanonistische Abteilung* 45 (1959): 1–33.

Sivéry, Gérard. *Saint Louis et son siècle.* Paris: 1983.

Smith, Anthony D. *The Ethnic Origins of Nations.* New York: 1986; rpt. 1988.

Sohn, Andreas. *Der Abbatiat Ademars von Saint-Martial de Limoges (1063–1114): Ein Beitrag zur Geschichte des cluniacensischen Klösterverbandes.* Münster: 1989.

Spiegel, Gabrielle M. "*Pseudo-Turpin,* the Crisis of the Aristocracy and the Beginnings of Vernacular Historiography in France." *Journal of Medieval History* 12 (1986): 207–223.

——. "The *Reditus regni ad stirpem Karoli Magni:* A New Look." *French Historical Studies* 7 (1971): 145–174.

——. *Romancing the Past: The Rise of Vernacular Prose Historiography in Thirteenth-Century France.* Berkeley: 1993.

Stock, Brian. *The Implications of Literacy: Written Language and Models of Interpretation in the Eleventh and Twelfth Centuries.* Princeton: 1983.

Stoddard, Whitney. *The Façade of Saint-Gilles: Its Influence on French Sculpture.* Middletown, Conn.: 1973.

Swiechowski, Zygmut. *Sculpture romane d'Auvergne*. Clermont-Ferrand: 1973.

Szabó-Bechstein, Brigitte. "Libertas Ecclesiae:" Ein Schlüsselbegriff des Investiturstreits und seine Vorgeschichte, 4.–11. Jahrhundert. Studi Gregoriani, 12. Rome: 1985.

Taralon, Dominique. "'Le reliquaire de Pepin' du trésor de Conques." Maitrîse, Paris IV, 1988/89.

Terpak, Frances. "Local Politics: The Charlemagne Legend in Medieval Narbonne." *Res* 25 (1994): 96–110.

——. "The Romanesque Architecture and Sculpture of Saint Caprais in Agen." Ph.D. diss., Yale University, 1982.

Thurston, Herbert. "The Alphabet and the Consecration of Churches." *The Month* 115 (1910): 621–631.

Tisset, Pierre. *L'abbaye de Gellone au diocèse de Lodève des origines au XIIIe siècle*. Paris: 1933.

Tock, Benoît-Michel. "Les textes non diplomatiques dans les cartulaires de la province de Reims." In *Les cartulaires*, pp. 45–58.

Les trésors des églises de France: Musée des Arts Décoratifs, Paris, 1965. Paris: 1965.

Valeri, Valerio. "Constitutive History: Genealogy and Narrative in the Legitimation of Hawaiian Kingship." In *Culture through Time*, pp. 154–192.

Werner, Karl Ferdinand. "Die Legitimität der Kapetinger und die Entstehung des *Reditus regni francorum ad stirpem Karoli*." *Die Welt als Geschichte* 12 (1952): 203–225.

Winzer, Ulrich. *S. Gilles: Studien zum Rechtsstatus und Beziehungsnetz einer Abtei im Spiegel ihrer Memorialüberlieferung*. Münstersche Mittelalter-Schriften, 59. Munich: 1988.

Wolff, Philippe. "Note sur le faux diplôme de 755 pour le monastère de Figeac." In Philippe Wolff, *Regards sur le Midi médiéval*, pp. 293–331. Toulouse: 1978.

Wolfram, Herwig. *History of the Goths*. Translated by Thomas J. Dunlap. Berkeley: 1988.

Wollasch, Joachim. *Mönchtum des Mittelalters zwischen Kirche und Welt*. Münstersche Mittelalter-Schriften, 7. Munich: 1973.

——. "Questions-clé du monachisme européen avant l'an mil." In *Saint-Sever*, pp. 13–26.

Zaal, J. W. B. *"A lei francesca" (Sainte Foy, v. 20): Etude sur les chansons de saints galloromanes du XIe siècle*. Leiden: 1962.

Zimmermann, Michel. "La datation des documents catalans du IXe au XIIe siècle: Un itinéraire politique." *Annales du Midi* 93 (1981): 345–375.

Index

Aachen, 151, 154, 155–156, 158, 172, 175, 182n.124

Abraham, 52–53, 124

Ademar of Chabannes, 34, 36, 139, 141, 171n.87; and legends, 52n.31, 109–110, 118n.35, 137, 143–144, 164n.52, 166, 273n.256, 295, 312, 324

Agaune, 30

Agen, 77, 78; Saint-Caprais of, 152n.14

Aláo, monastery of, 26

Alaric II, king of the Visigoths, 123–124, 128, 148

Albigensian Crusade, 12, 250–251, 284–285, 287, 293

Alboynus (Albodenus). *See* Clairvaux-d'Aveyron

Alcuin, 74, 279n.284

Alet, legend of, 78, 79, 81, 169–170, 309

Alexander II, Pope, 190, 254–255, 258n.189, 270n.243, 277, 278

Alexander III, Pope, 91n.5, 235n.91, 277

Alexander the Great, 59n.65

Alfonse-Jourdain, count of Toulouse, 231, 234–235, 248

Almodis (mother of Raymond IV, count of Toulouse), 231, 236

Almodis (wife of Stephen, viscount of Gévaudan), 52, 78, 94

Amandus, Saint, 129

Amator, Saint. *See* Rocamadour, legend of

Amelius, bishop of Uzès, 224

Anastasius IV, Pope, 256, 270, 304

angels, 44, 52–53, 65, 80, 90, 96, 121, 177, 184, 189

Angevin kings, 7, 93n.11, 106n.75, 208. *See also* Henry II

Aniane, 23, 56, 189n.158, 261, 264n.212; conflict with bishops of Maguelone, 254–257; conflict with Gellone, 68, 70–71, 75, 276–284, 295; legend of, 74–75, 80, 169, 186, 291, 304, 309–311

animals, in legends, 42, 57–58, 62–63, 92; deer, 57, 60–65, 75; dragons, 66–67, 100, 131; griffins, 59, 65, 129; horses, 60, 82–83; lions, 75; oxen, 59; snakes, 61

anointing, royal, 135–137

Ansbertus, abbot of Moissac, 102, 127

apostles, 34, 40; in legends, 95–99, 107, 143, 266, 294

Aquitaine, 7–11, 131, 138, 145, 148, 152, 208; dukes of, 26, 105, 109–110, 114, 120, 144; kings of, 116, 146, 153, 273. *See also specific dukes and kings*

Arians, 123–124, 131

aristocracy, 3n.10, 40; power limited in legends, 64–65, 111, 230, 251; relations with monasteries, 5–6, 39, 243–251, 264–265; role in foundation, 22, 24–25, 28, 29; role in legends, 77–78, 93–95, 103–106, 109–112. *See also* kings: relations with aristocracy; lordship: secular

Auch, legend of archbishopric, 119, 123–126, 216, 291, 297, 311

Aurillac, 21, 27, 165n.53

Austremonius, Saint. *See* Issoire: legend of; Mozac: legend of

347